Multi-Objective and Multi-Attribute Optimisation for Sustainable Development Decision Aiding

Multi-Objective and Multi-Attribute Optimisation for Sustainable Development Decision Aiding

Special Issue Editors

Edmundas Kazimieras Zavadskas
Jurgita Antuchevičienė
Samarjit Kar

MDPI • Basel • Beijing • Wuhan • Barcelona • Belgrade

Special Issue Editors
Edmundas Kazimieras Zavadskas
Vilnius Gediminas Technical University
Lithuania

Jurgita Antuchevičienė
Vilnius Gediminas Technical University
Lithuania

Samarjit Kar
National Institute of Technology Durgapur
India

Editorial Office
MDPI
St. Alban-Anlage 66
4052 Basel, Switzerland

This is a reprint of articles from the Special Issue published online in the open access journal *Sustainability* (ISSN 2071-1050) from 2018 to 2019 (available at: https://www.mdpi.com/journal/sustainability/special_issues/Multi-Objective_Multi-Attribute_Optimisation_Sustainable_Development_Decision_Aiding)

For citation purposes, cite each article independently as indicated on the article page online and as indicated below:

LastName, A.A.; LastName, B.B.; LastName, C.C. Article Title. *Journal Name* **Year**, *Article Number*, Page Range.

ISBN 978-3-03921-142-5 (Pbk)
ISBN 978-3-03921-143-2 (PDF)

© 2019 by the authors. Articles in this book are Open Access and distributed under the Creative Commons Attribution (CC BY) license, which allows users to download, copy and build upon published articles, as long as the author and publisher are properly credited, which ensures maximum dissemination and a wider impact of our publications.

The book as a whole is distributed by MDPI under the terms and conditions of the Creative Commons license CC BY-NC-ND.

Contents

About the Special Issue Editors vii

Edmundas Kazimieras Zavadskas, Jurgita Antucheviciene and Samarjit Kar
Multi-Objective and Multi-Attribute Optimization for Sustainable Development Decision Aiding
Reprinted from: *Sustainability* **2019**, *11*, 3069, doi:10.3390/su11113069 1

Aijun Liu, Haiyang Liu, Sang-Bing Tsai, Hui Lu, Xiao Zhang and Jiangtao Wang
Using a Hybrid Model on Joint Scheduling of Berths and Quay Cranes—From a Sustainable Perspective
Reprinted from: *Sustainability* **2018**, *10*, 1959, doi:10.3390/su10061959 7

Suwin Sleesongsom and Sujin Bureerat
Vibration Suppression of a Single-Cylinder Engine by Means of Multi-objective Evolutionary Optimisation
Reprinted from: *Sustainability* **2018**, *10*, 2067, doi:10.3390/su10062067 22

Wojciech Drozd and Agnieszka Leśniak
Ecological Wall Systems as an Element of Sustainable Development—Cost Issues
Reprinted from: *Sustainability* **2018**, *10*, 2234, doi:10.3390/su10072234 41

R. Krishankumar, K. S. Ravichandran, J. Premaladha, Samarjit Kar, Edmundas Kazimieras Zavadskas and Jurgita Antucheviciene
A Decision Framework under a Linguistic Hesitant Fuzzy Set for Solving Multi-Criteria Group Decision Making Problems
Reprinted from: *Sustainability* **2018**, *10*, 2608, doi:10.3390/su10082608 56

Hongbo Li, Zhe Xu and Wenchao Wei
Bi-Objective Scheduling Optimization for Discrete Time/Cost Trade-Off in Projects
Reprinted from: *Sustainability* **2018**, *10*, 2802, doi:10.3390/su10082802 77

Željko Stević, Dragan Pamučar, Marko Subotić, Jurgita Antuchevičiene and Edmundas Kazimieras Zavadskas
The Location Selection for Roundabout Construction Using Rough BWM-Rough WASPAS Approach Based on a New Rough Hamy Aggregator
Reprinted from: *Sustainability* **2018**, *10*, 2817, doi:10.3390/su10082817 92

Radosław Winiczenko, Krzysztof Górnicki, Agnieszka Kaleta, Monika Janaszek-Mańkowska, Aneta Choińska and Jedrzej Trajer
Apple Cubes Drying and Rehydration. Multiobjective Optimization of the Processes
Reprinted from: *Sustainability* **2018**, *10*, 4126, doi:10.3390/su10114126 119

Abteen Ijadi Maghsoodi, Arta Ijadi Maghsoodi, Amir Mosavi, Timon Rabczuk and Edmundas Kazimieras Zavadskas
Renewable Energy Technology Selection Problem Using Integrated H-SWARA-MULTIMOORA Approach
Reprinted from: *Sustainability* **2018**, *10*, 4481, doi:10.3390/su10124481 131

Li Wang, Huan Shi and Lu Gan
Healthcare Facility Location-Allocation Optimization for China's Developing Cities Utilizing a Multi-Objective Decision Support Approach
Reprinted from: *Sustainability* **2018**, *10*, 4580, doi:10.3390/su10124580 149

Weizhang Liang, Suizhi Luo and Guoyan Zhao
Evaluation of Cleaner Production for Gold Mines Employing a Hybrid Multi-Criteria Decision Making Approach
Reprinted from: *Sustainability* **2019**, *11*, 146, doi:10.3390/su11010146 171

Aarti Singh, Sushil, Samarjit Kar and Dragan Pamucar
Stakeholder Role for Developing a Conceptual Framework of Sustainability in Organization
Reprinted from: *Sustainability* **2019**, *11*, 208, doi:10.3390/su11010208 191

Miroslaw Smieszek, Magdalena Dobrzanska and Pawel Dobrzanski
Rzeszow as a City Taking Steps Towards Developing Sustainable Public Transport
Reprinted from: *Sustainability* **2019**, *11*, 402, doi:10.3390/su11020402 207

Zenonas Turskis, Nikolaj Goranin, Assel Nurusheva and Seilkhan Boranbayev
A Fuzzy WASPAS-Based Approach to Determine Critical Information Infrastructures of EU Sustainable Development
Reprinted from: *Sustainability* **2019**, *11*, 424, doi:10.3390/su11020424 225

Alireza Chalekaee, Zenonas Turskis, Mostafa Khanzadi, Gholamreza Ghodrati Amiri and Violeta Keršulienė
A New Hybrid MCDM Model with Grey Numbers for the Construction Delay Change Response Problem
Reprinted from: *Sustainability* **2019**, *11*, 776, doi:10.3390/su11030776 250

Małgorzata Fedorczak-Cisak, Alicja Kowalska-Koczwara, Krzysztof Nering, Filip Pachla, Elżbieta Radziszewska-Zielina, Grzegorz Śladowski, Tadeusz Tatara and Bartłomiej Ziarko
Evaluation of the Criteria for Selecting Proposed Variants of Utility Functions in the Adaptation of Historic Regional Architecture
Reprinted from: *Sustainability* **2019**, *11*, 1094, doi:10.3390/su11041094 266

Katarzyna Nosal Hoy, Katarzyna Solecka and Andrzej Szarata
The Application of the Multiple Criteria Decision Aid to Assess Transport Policy Measures Focusing on Innovation
Reprinted from: *Sustainability* **2019**, *11*, 1472, doi:10.3390/su11051472 295

Zaher Mundher Yaseen, Mohammad Ehteram, Md. Shabbir Hossain, Chow Ming Fai, Suhana Binti Koting, Nuruol Syuhadaa Mohd, Wan Zurina Binti Jaafar, Haitham Abdulmohsin Afan, Lai Sai Hin, Nuratiah Zaini, Ali Najah Ahmed and Ahmed El-Shafie
A Novel Hybrid Evolutionary Data-Intelligence Algorithm for Irrigation and Power Production Management: Application to Multi-Purpose Reservoir Systems
Reprinted from: *Sustainability* **2019**, *11*, 1953, doi:10.3390/su11071953 318

Seyit Ali Erdogan, Jonas Šaparauskas and Zenonas Turskis
A Multi-Criteria Decision-Making Model to Choose the Best Option for Sustainable Construction Management
Reprinted from: *Sustainability* **2019**, *11*, 2239, doi:10.3390/su11082239 346

Galina Shevchenko, Leonas Ustinovichius and Dariusz Walasek
The Evaluation of the Contractor's Risk in Implementing the Investment Projects in Construction by Using the Verbal Analysis Methods
Reprinted from: *Sustainability* **2019**, *11*, 2660, doi:10.3390/su11092660 365

About the Special Issue Editors

Edmundas Kazimieras Zavadskas, PhD, DSc, is Professor at the Department of Construction Management and Real Estate, Chief Research Fellow at the Laboratory of Operational Research, Research Institute of Sustainable Construction, Vilnius Gediminas Technical University, Lithuania. He received his PhD in Building Structures (1973) and Dr Sc. (1987) in Building Technology and Management. He is a member of the Lithuanian and several foreign Academies of Sciences, Doctore Honoris Causa from Poznan, Saint Petersburg, and Kiev Universities, the Honorary International Chair Professor in the National Taipei University of Technology. Awarded by the International Association of Grey System and Uncertain Analysis (GSUA) for his huge input in Grey System field, Zavadskas has been elected to Honorary Fellowship of International Association of Grey System and Uncertain Analysis, a part of IEEE (2016), awarded by "Neutrosophic Science—International Association" for distinguished achievements in neutrosophics, and has been conferred an honorary membership (2016), and awarded the Thomson Reuters certificate for as a most highly cited scientist (2014). A highly cited researcher in the field of Cross-Field (2018), Zavadskas is recognized for exceptional research performance demonstrated by the production of multiple highly cited papers that rank in the top 1% by citations for field and year in the Web of Science. Zavadskas' main research interests include multi-criteria decision-making, operations research, decision support systems, multiple-criteria optimization in construction technology and management. With over 470 publications in Clarivate Analytics Web of Science, h-index = 55, a number of monographs in Lithuanian, English, German, and Russian, Zavadskas is also Editor-in-Chief of the journals Technological and Economic Development of Economy and Journal of Civil Engineering and Management, as well as Guest Editor of over 10 Special Issues related to decision making in engineering and management.

Jurgita Antuchevičienė, PhD, is Professor at the Department of Construction Management and Real Estate at Vilnius Gediminas Technical University, Lithuania. She received her PhD in Civil Engineering in 2005. Her research interests include multiple-criteria decision-making theory and applications, sustainable development, construction technology and management. With over 90 publications in Clarivate Analytics Web of Science, h-index = 23, Antucheviciene is a member of IEEE SMC, Systems Science and Engineering Technical Committee—Grey Systems, and of two EURO Working Groups: Multicriteria Decision Aiding (EWG—MCDA) and Operations Research in Sustainable Development and Civil Engineering (EWG—ORSDCE). She is also Deputy Editor-in-Chief of Journal of Civil Engineering and Management and an Editorial Board member of Applied Soft Computing and Sustainability journals. Antucheviciene has served as Guest Editor of several Special Issues: "Decision Making Methods and Applications in Civil Engineering" (2015) and "Mathematical Models for Dealing with Risk in Engineering" (2016) in Mathematical Problems in Engineering, "Managing Information Uncertainty and Complexity in Decision-Making" (2017) in Complexity, "Civil Engineering and Symmetry" and "Solution Models based on Symmetric and Asymmetric Information" (2018) in Symmetry, "Sustainability in Construction Engineering" (2018) in Sustainability, as well as "Multiple-Criteria Decision-Making (MCDM) Techniques for Business Processes Information Management" (2018) in Information.

Samarjit Kar, PhD, is Professor and HOD in the Department of Mathematics, National Institute of Technology Durgapur, India. He received his PhD degree in Inventory Management in Uncertain Environment from Vidyasagar University, India, in 2001. His current research interests include operations research and optimization, soft computing, uncertainty theory, and financial modeling. He has published over 120 referred articles in international journals and authored five edited book volumes in Springer. His articles have been cited more than 2900 times on Google Scholar and have appeared in prestigious journals including European Journal of Operational Research, Interface, Computers and Operations Research, Annals of Operations Research, International Journal of Production Economics, IEEE Transactions on Fuzzy Systems, IEEE Transactions on Circuits and Systems for Video Technology, Information Sciences, Expert Systems with Applications, Applied Soft Computing, Applied Mathematical Modeling, Computers and Operations Research, Computers and Industrial Engineering, Applied Mathematics and Computation, Computers and Mathematics with Applications, and Soft Computing. Kar is serving as Guest Editor of IEEE Transaction on Fuzzy Systems and Sustainability (MDPI).

Editorial

Multi-Objective and Multi-Attribute Optimization for Sustainable Development Decision Aiding

Edmundas Kazimieras Zavadskas [1,2], Jurgita Antucheviciene [1,*] and Samarjit Kar [3]

[1] Department of Construction Management and Real Estate, Vilnius Gediminas Technical University, Sauletekio al. 11, Vilnius LT-10223, Lithuania; edmundas.zavadskas@vgtu.lt
[2] Institute of Sustainable Construction, Vilnius Gediminas Technical University, Sauletekio al. 11, Vilnius LT-10223, Lithuania
[3] Department of Mathematics, National Institute of Technology Durgapur, Durgapur 713209, West Bengal, India; dr.samarjitkar@gmail.com
* Correspondence: jurgita.antucheviciene@vgtu.lt; Tel.: +370-5-274-5233

Received: 23 May 2019; Accepted: 27 May 2019; Published: 31 May 2019

Abstract: Optimization is considered as a decision-making process to get the most out of available resources for the best attainable results. Many real-world problems are multi-objective or multi-attribute problems that naturally involve several competing objectives that are required to be optimized simultaneously, while respecting some constraints or selecting among feasible discrete alternatives. In this Special Issue, 19 research papers co-authored by 88 researchers from 14 different countries explore aspects of multi-objective or multi-attribute modelling and optimization in crisp or uncertain environments by suggesting multiple-attribute decision-making (MADM) and multi-objective decision-making (MODM) approaches. The papers elaborate the approaches on the state-of-the-art case studies in selected areas of applications related to sustainable development decision aiding in engineering and management, including construction, transportation, infrastructure development, production, and organization management.

Keywords: multiple-attribute decision-making (MADM); multi-objective decision-making (MODM); optimization; engineering; management; sustainable development

1. Introduction

Sustainable decision-making has a direct impact on the economy, the environment, and society. Researchers are continuously trying to adopt it in their research domain, mainly in the field of financial modeling, supply chain, healthcare system, transport system, construction management, business intelligence, etc. However, most of the real-life problems that we encountered in these domains were not limited to single criterion decision-making problems. Therefore, many researchers are motivated to develop some new models in these areas under a multi-criteria/multi-objective decision-making framework.

Some authors (Zimmermann [1]; Chen and Hwang [2]) have divided multi-criteria decision making (MCDM) into two categories: (1) multi-attribute decision making (MADM), which concentrates on problems with discrete decision spaces; and (2) multi-objective decision making (MODM) problems, which naturally involve several competing objectives that are required to be optimized simultaneously. From a practical viewpoint, MADM is associated with problems where the number of alternatives are predetermined. The decision maker (DM) is to select/prioritize/rank a finite number of courses of action. Alternatively, MODM is associated with problems in which the alternatives have been non-predetermined.

It is often said that the only certain thing about the data involved in real world decision-making problems is uncertainty. This uncertainty is caused by many reasons, as the available data are not always exact or precise, there is insufficient data and linguistic information, there is a lack of evidence, decision makers' judgments are subjective and vague, statistical analysis is imperfect, etc.

Over past few decades, many researchers developed a number of theories/tools/techniques to deal with real-life uncertainty problems. Fuzzy set (Zadeh [3]), Dempster Shafer theory (Shafer [4]), rough set (Pawlak [5]), intuitionistic fuzzy sets (Atanassov [6]), grey set (Deng [7]), and hybrid sets (Liu [8]) are among the most successful approaches that efficiently handle uncertainty in decision-making problems. These techniques have been successfully applied by many researchers in the context of uncertain environments addressing mathematical, theoretical, and behavioral aspects of real-life applications.

Yet, the literature is still promising in the above-mentioned domains, and many research gaps remain. Consequently, we have introduced this Special Issue to identify the underlying research themes and suggest directions for future research. Thus, the purpose of this Special Issue is to propose a research agenda for multiple-attribute decision-making (MADM) and multi-objective decision-making (MODM) approaches for sustainable engineering and management decisions in crisp or uncertain environments.

2. Contributions

The Special Issue collects 19 original research papers. The papers contribute to multi-objective and multi-attribute optimization by offering multiple-attribute decision-making (MADM) and multi-objective decision-making (MODM) approaches for sustainable engineering and management decisions in crisp or uncertain environments.

The topics of the Special Issue attracted attention of a wide scientific community: 88 scientists from 14 countries contributed to the Issue. Distribution of papers according to countries is presented in Figure 1.

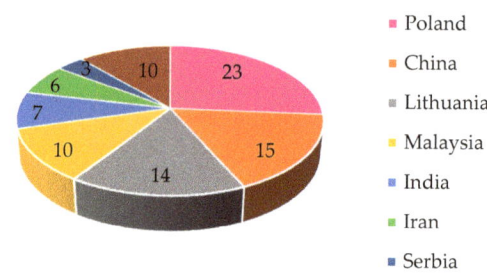

Figure 1. Number of publications from different countries.

The largest number of Authors were from Poland (23 authors). China and Lithuania contributed almost equally, with 15 and 14 authors, respectively. Next came Malaysia, with 10 authors. Seven contributors were from India, six from Iran, and three from Serbia. Authors from the following seven countries contributed from 1 to 2 papers: Vietnam, Kazakhstan, Germany, Saudi Arabia, Hungary, Bosnia and Herzegovina, and Thailand.

As international collectives prepared almost a half of papers, the distribution of papers according to authors' affiliations is presented in Table 1.

Authors and co-authors from Lithuania contributed seven papers, mostly in international collectives in collaboration with Iran, Kazakhstan, Poland, India, Serbia, Bosnia and Herzegovina, Germany, Hungary, and Saudi Arabia. Authors from Poland contributed six papers, but only to a single international publication with Lithuanian co-authors. Authors from China prepared four papers without international collaboration. Two papers involve cooperation of authors from three countries: Serbia, Bosnia and Herzegovina, and Lithuania, as well as Vietnam, Iran, and Malaysia. A single paper united researchers from five countries from Europa and Asia: Germany, Hungary, Lithuania, Iran, and Saudi Arabia.

Table 1. Publications by countries.

Countries	Number of Papers
Poland	5
China	4
Thailand	1
Lithuania	1
Iran–Lithuania	1
Kazakhstan–Lithuania	1
Poland–Lithuania	1
India–Lithuania	1
Serbia–Bosnia and Herzegovina–Lithuania	1
Germany–Hungary–Saudi Arabia–Iran–Lithuania	1
Vietnam–Iran–Malaysia	1

Distribution of papers according to research areas is presented in Figure 2.

The publications explore aspects of multi-objective or multi-attribute modelling and optimization in crisp or uncertain environments by suggesting multiple-attribute decision-making (MADM) and multi-objective decision-making (MODM) approaches, or several other optimization tools. MADM optimization area attracted slightly more attention; 10 papers contributed to the area, while MODM optimization was explored in six papers.

The papers elaborate usual or extended optimization approaches on the state-of-the-art case studies related to sustainable development decision aiding in engineering and management, including construction, transportation, infrastructure development, production, and organization management. All the mentioned application areas gained almost some attention; from two to six papers contributed to each area.

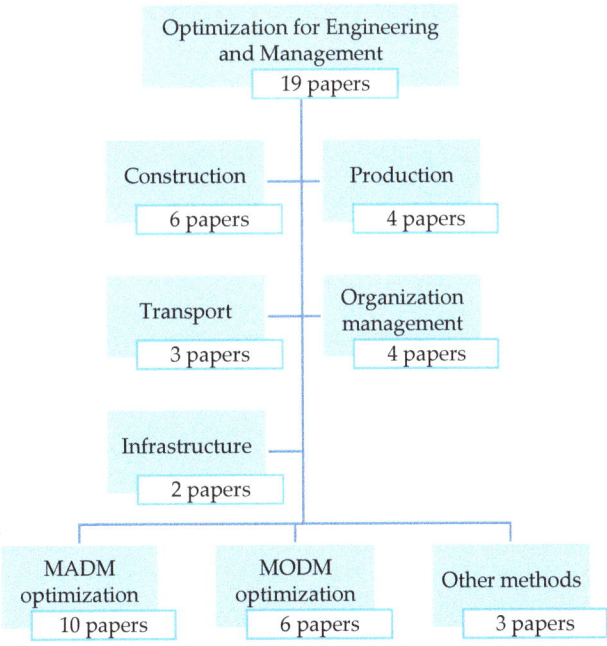

Figure 2. Research areas of publications.

The most numerous application areas can be considered construction engineering (five papers). MADM and MODM approaches to support sustainable decisions can be applied in the area.

Two papers analyze construction project management. One paper suggests sustainable construction project management model aimed at practical use; therefore, a rather well known analytic hierarchy process (AHP) method is applied. A comprehensive set of criteria is developed, and a Turkish case study is presented. The other paper is aimed at evaluating contractors risk of investment project in construction. The originality of the paper is based on a fact that a special case of MADM–verbal analysis is suggested, while usual risk valuation methods are more often applied in the literature [9,10].

Energy efficiency and comfort of use of buildings is another topical issue in the literature [11,12]. Adaption of historic regional architecture in terms of energy efficiency and comfort of use of buildings is analyzed in one paper of the current Issue. A set of assessment criteria is proposed, and the new utility functions considered. The example of historic building located in Zakopane, Poland is presented.

Ecological wall systems as a significant component of sustainable construction are analyzed. Three variants of ecological walls made from local materials are suggested, and their cost calculation is provided. You can find similar topics in other publications, related to design of sustainable facades [13], roofs [14], or floors [15].

Construction delay problems considering sustainable environment requirements are analyzed. The authors develop a new model that combines several different MCDM methods under uncertainty: a Step-wise Weight Assessment Ratio Analysis (SWARA), the Technique for Order Preference by Similarity to Ideal Solution with Grey numbers in Minkowski Space (TOPSIS-GM), Additive Ratio ASsessment with Grey numbers (ARAS-G) techniques, and Geometric Mean. A case study of the housing industry is a market of Mashad, Iran.

A topical problem of location selection in construction is solved in [16,17]. The authors of one paper prepare a hierarchical programming model and design a bi-level multi-objective particle swarm optimization (BLMOPSO) algorithm to deal with the healthcare facility location decisions. The suggested approach can be applied for various facilities location decisions. The next paper related to location selection analyzes traffic infrastructure and an optimal roundabout location. MADM problem is solved in an uncertain environment; therefore, application of rough set theory is suggested. Rough Best–Worst Method (Rough BWM) and Rough-Weighted Aggregated Sum Product Assessment (Rough WASPAS) methods are applied. The input to methodological novelty of the approach lays in developing a Rough Hamy aggregator.

The other paper related to transportation suggests applying MADM methods for assessing transport policy in terms of innovation. The authors of the paper demonstrate the application of a simple additive weighting (SAW) method to evaluate policy measures in surface transportation.

Public transport problems and development of sustainable public transport are discussed. Development of the city increases transport problems related to emission of pollutant, travel time, etc. The paper analysis actions and measures taken for development of sustainable transportation in Rzeszow, Poland.

Several papers analyze infrastructure problems as water or energy supply. A hybrid MODM method for water resource management is presented. The researchers implement hybrid novel meta-heuristic algorithms: the bat algorithm (BA) and particle swarm optimization (PSO). They are applied for power production and irrigation supply problems.

In another paper, renewable energy technology selection is solved by applying hybrid optimization: Step-Wise Weight Assessment Ratio Analysis approach with a hierarchical arrangement (H-SWARA) and Multi-Objective Optimization on the basis of Ratio Analysis plus the full MULTIplicative form (MULTIMOORA). An Iranian case study is presented.

A hybrid MADM approach is also applied for assessing cleaner production in gold mine. At first, crisp numbers and probabilistic linguistic term sets (PLTSs) are simultaneously applied to evaluate quantitative and qualitative information, and expert method based on PLTSs is used to calculate criteria relative significance. Next, an extended Tomada de Decisão Interativa Multicritério (TODIM) method with hybrid values is suggested to rank the alternatives.

A hybrid MODM model is developed for optimization of the traffic path in port scheduling. The model is built and solved by an improved non-dominated sorting genetic algorithm II (NSGA-II). A case study of scheduling of berths and quay cranes is presented.

Multi-objective evolutionary optimization for the passive vibration suppression of a single-cylindrical engine is presented. A hybrid of multi-objective population-based incremental learning, and differential evolution (RPBIL-DE) is adapted.

Multi-objective optimization of processes of apple cubes drying and rehydration are analyzed. To simulate and optimize parameters of drying and rehydration processes, hybrid methods of artificial neural network (ANN) and multi-objective genetic algorithm (MOGA) are developed.

One more hybrid approach for scheduling optimization in projects is developed. Two algorithms are suggested: the first one is based on the non-dominated sorting genetic algorithm II (NSGA-II) with a special critical path-based crossover operator, and the second algorithm is a steepest descent heuristic that solves the discrete time/cost trade-off problem with different deadlines.

Sustainable organizations are analyzed [18–21]. Total interpretive structural modeling (TISM) has been applied for identifying the links among the sustainability factors in organizations. The paper, submitted to the Special Issue, presents the fourth dimension of sustainability involving stakeholders besides three usual dimensions of economy, natural environment, and social environment.

Hospital evaluation problem is analyzed. As decision-makers are faced with qualitative criteria, a linguistic hesitant fuzzy set (LHFS) is adopted. A new aggregation operator—simple linguistic hesitant fuzzy weighted geometry (SLHFWG)—is proposed under the LHFS context. Criteria relative significances are estimated using a newly proposed linguistic hesitant fuzzy statistical variance (LHFSV) method, and alternatives are ranked using the new linguistic hesitant fuzzy VIKOR (visekriterijumska optimizacijai kompromisno resenje) under the LHFS context (LHFVIKOR) method.

A topical question of critical information infrastructures of European Union sustainable development is discussed. Integrated MADM techniques under uncertainty involving fuzzy Weighted Aggregated Sum Product ASsessment (WASPAS-F) and analytic hierarchy process (AHP) methods are suggested to be applied.

3. Conclusions

The scope of the Special Issue raised the interest of numerous researchers; papers involving 88 researchers from 14 countries were published.

Papers contribute to sustainable development by offering crisp or uncertain multiple-attribute decision-making (MADM) and multi-objective decision-making (MODM) approaches.

The main topics of papers published in the Special Issue mainly cover five research areas in engineering and management, including construction, transportation, infrastructure development, production, and organization management.

Author Contributions: All authors contributed equally to this work.

Acknowledgments: Authors express their gratitude to the journal *Sustainability* for offering an academic platform for researchers to contribute and exchange their recent findings in sustainable construction.

Conflicts of Interest: The authors declare no conflict of interest.

References

1. Zimmermann, H. *Fuzzy Set Theory and Its Applications*, 2nd ed.; Kluwer Academic Publishers: Boston, MA, USA, 1991.
2. Chen, S.-J.; Hwang, C.-L. Fuzzy multiple attribute decision making methods. In *Fuzzy Multiple Attribute Decision Making*; Springer: Berlin/Heidelberg, Germany, 1992; pp. 289–486.
3. Zadeh, L. Fuzzy sets. *Inf. Control* **1965**, *8*, 338–353. [CrossRef]

4. Shafer, G. *A Mathematical Theory of Evidence*; Princeton University Press: Princeton, NJ, USA, 1976.
5. Pawlak, Z. Rough sets. *Int. J. Comput. Inf. Sci.* **1982**, *11*, 341–354. [CrossRef]
6. Atanassov, K. Intuitionistic fuzzy sets. *Fuzzy Sets Syst.* **1986**, *20*, 87–96. [CrossRef]
7. Deng, J.L. Introduction to Grey system theory. *J. Grey Syst.* **1989**, *1*, 1–24.
8. Liu, B. *Uncertainty Theory: An Introduction to Its Axiomatic Foundations*; Springer: Berlin, Germany, 2004.
9. Khanzadi, M.; Turskis, Z.; Ghodrati Amiri, G.; Chalekaee, A. A model of discrete zero-sum two-person matrix games with grey numbers to solve dispute resolution problems in construction. *J. Civ. Eng. Manag.* **2017**, *23*, 824–835. [CrossRef]
10. Asadi, P.; Rezaeian Zeidi, J.; Mojibi, T.; Yazdani-Chamzini, A.; Tamošaitienė, J. Project risk evaluation by using a new fuzzy model based on Elena Guideline. *J. Civ. Eng. Manag.* **2018**, *24*, 284–300. [CrossRef]
11. Zavadskas, E.K.; Antucheviciene, J.; Kalibatas, D.; Kalibatiene, D. Achieving Nearly Zero-Energy Buildings by applying multi-attribute assessment. *Energy Build.* **2017**, *143*, 162–172. [CrossRef]
12. Harkouss, F.; Fardoun, F.; Biwole, P.H. Passive design optimization of low energy buildings in different climates. *Energy* **2018**, *165*, 591–613. [CrossRef]
13. Moghtadernejad, S.; Chouinard, L.E.; Mirza, M.S. Multi-criteria decision-making methods for preliminary design of sustainable facades. *J. Build. Eng.* **2018**, *19*, 181–190. [CrossRef]
14. Kalibatas, D.; Kovaitis, V. Selecting the most effective alternative of waterproofing membranes for multifunctional inverted flat roofs. *J. Civ. Eng. Manag.* **2017**, *23*, 650–660. [CrossRef]
15. Ilce, A.C.; Ozkaya, K. An integrated intelligent system for construction industry: A case study of raised floor material. *Technol. Econ. Dev. Econ.* **2018**, *24*, 1866–1884. [CrossRef]
16. Bausys, R.; Juodagalviene, B. Garage location selection for residential house by WASPAS-SVNS method. *J. Civ. Eng. Manag.* **2017**, *23*, 421–429. [CrossRef]
17. Barauskas, A.; Jakovlevas-Mateckis, K.; Palevicius, V.; Antucheviciene, J. Ranking conceptual locations for a park-and-ride parking lot using EDAS method. *Gradevinar* **2018**, *70*, 975–983.
18. Ibrahim, Y.; Ahmed, I.; Minai, M.S. The influence of institutional characteristics of financial performance of microfinance institutions in the OIC countries. *Econ. Sociol.* **2018**, *11*, 19–35. [CrossRef] [PubMed]
19. Tabatabaei, S.A.N.; Omran, E.S.; Hashemi, S.; Sedaghat, M. Presenting sustainable HRM model based on balances scorecard in knowledge based ICT companies (the case of Iran). *Econ. Sociol.* **2017**, *10*, 107–124. [CrossRef]
20. Mikusova, M. To be or not to be a business responsible for sustainable development? Survey from small Czech businesses. *Econ. Res.* **2017**, *30*, 1318–1338.
21. Mohammadi, M.A.D.; Mardani, A.; Khan, M.N.A.A.; Streimikiene, D. Corporate sustainability disclosure and market valuation in a Middle Eastern Nation: Evidence from listed firms on the Tehran Stock Exchange: Sensitive industries versus non-sensitive industries. *Econ. Res.* **2018**, *31*, 1488–1511. [CrossRef]

© 2019 by the authors. Licensee MDPI, Basel, Switzerland. This article is an open access article distributed under the terms and conditions of the Creative Commons Attribution (CC BY) license (http://creativecommons.org/licenses/by/4.0/).

Article

Using a Hybrid Model on Joint Scheduling of Berths and Quay Cranes—From a Sustainable Perspective

Aijun Liu [1,2], **Haiyang Liu** [1], **Sang-Bing Tsai** [3,4,*], **Hui Lu** [5], **Xiao Zhang** [1] **and Jiangtao Wang** [4]

1. Department of Management Engineering, School of Economics & Management, Xidian University, Xi'an 710071, China; ajliu@xidian.edu.cn (A.L.); ocean@stu.xidian.edu.cn (H.L.); zhangxiao.neu@163.com (X.Z.)
2. Guangdong Provincial Key Laboratory of Computer Integrated Manufacturing, Guangdong University of Technology, Guangzhou 510006, China
3. College of Business Administration, Capital University of Economics and Business, Beijing 100070, China
4. Zhongshan Institute, University of Electronic Science and Technology, Zhongshan 528400, China; jiangtao-w@foxmail.com
5. Tianhua College, Shanghai Normal University, Shanghai 201815, China; janetluck@126.com
* Correspondence: sangbing@hotmail.com

Received: 15 May 2018; Accepted: 5 June 2018; Published: 11 June 2018

Abstract: In response to the problem of the unfair distribution of berths and quay cranes, as well as the optimization of the traffic path in port scheduling, a berth-crane joint scheduling model is proposed. Firstly, a ship is coded according to its geographical location and its arrival time in the form 0, 1. Then, the shortest port time, the minimum system cost, and the minimum unfairness are taken into account with the status quo of the port. Thus, a multi-objective joint scheduling model is established and solved by an improved NSGA-II algorithm. Finally, a practical example is given to verify the validity of the proposed method, the stable and the convergent of the proposed method are proved by many times computer simulations. The novelty of this paper is that we have taken psychological factors of fairness as well as social factors of sustainable development into consideration, and proposed an improved NSGA-II algorithm with random repair operator and self-adaptive operator to solve the multi-objective decision problem on joint scheduling of berths and quay crane.

Keywords: port scheduling; berth-quay crane joint scheduling; optimization study; hybrid mathematical model; multi-objective decision-making (MODM); sustainability

1. Introduction

With the acceleration of economic globalization, the marine transport industry is growing rapidly. In the current doldrums of the international shipping market, the prices for ship repairs are not picking up, so the ship repair business should consider how to reduce costs and to improve corporate profits. Due to the limited resources of berths in a harbor, it is the key to maximizing the efficiency of the allocation of resources and efficiently allocating resources when undertaking multiple ships. The optimal allocation of port resources is an important guarantee for the sustainable development of marine transportation industry, involves the optimal operation of berths, and the rational allocation of quay cranes.

The optimization of ship berth scheduling is of much significance and practical value to improving the efficiency of a shipyard. At present, the theoretical research on the optimal dispatching of berths at a shipyard has become a hot spot. Many scholars have studied the port-scheduling problem from the sustainable perspective. Kang et al. [1] constructed environmental technology, process quality improvement, monitoring and upgrading, communication cooperation, and actively participates in the five factor analysis model, which was committed to the sustainability of port operation as a descriptive and diagnostic management tool. Han et al. [2] considered the rational utilization of resources and the sustainable development of port operation and management, and then proposed a multi-objective optimization model to minimize the consumption of resources and the minimum moving distance of the shore bridge. From the perspective of environmental sustainability, Hu et al. [3] established a nonlinear multi-objective mixed integer programming model, which considered the fuel consumption and the emission of ships, and analyzed the effects of the wharf cranes number on the port operation cost, the fuel consumption of ships, and the emission of pollution gas. Di et al. [4] systematically reviewed the literature on environmental sustainability of green ports; the Balanced Scorecard and Tableau de Bord are identified and proposed as managerial accounting instruments for assessing, monitoring, measuring, controlling, and reporting the organizational processes. In addition, some scholars have discussed the comprehensive evaluation of green port [5–7] and the sustainable development of the port from the perspective of supply chain sustainability [8–12].

Generally, ship berth scheduling is proved to be an NP (Non-deterministic Polynomial) problem with multiple objectives and multi-faceted factors that affect each other [13], thus it is also a multi-objective decision-making (MODM) problem and the MODM method can be applied to solve specific sustainability problems [14–18]. The research on berth scheduling can be summarized by the following three aspects (Figure 1): (1) Terminal berth scheduling optimization model and algorithm research. Golias et al. [19] established a two-objective optimization mathematical model to minimize the average time and range of a ship's total service and proposed a heuristic algorithm to solve the problem of robust berth scheduling. To solve the problem of berth and yard allocation, Robenek et al. [20] proposed an exact algorithm that was based on the branch and price framework to solve the integration problem, and used the mixed integer programming method; (2) Study of the theory and method of berth disturbance recovery. Xu et al. [21] studied the location and time costs of berth deviations based on the theory of interference management and established the interference management model. The multi-objective genetic algorithm was used to solve the model and to obtain a more efficient berth allocation plan; (3) Simulations of terminal berth dispatching systems. Taking into account the randomness of the discharge/loading operations, Legato et al. [22] constructed a strategy-based mathematical programming model and an operational-level simulation model using an event-based Monte Carlo simulator to study the Berth Allocation Decision Problem (BAP). To minimize ship loading and unloading times, Al-Dhaheri et al. [23] considered the transit times between the terminals and the yards during the entire container loading and unloading process, then proposed a stochastic mixed integer programming model for the Quay Cranes Scheduling Problem (QCSP), and established a container scheduling simulation model that was based on a genetic algorithm to reveal the dynamics and uncertainty. In general, research on scheduling optimization models and algorithms is the basis of the study of the problem of berth scheduling, which has stimulated the interest of many scholars.

The remainder of this paper is organized as follows. Section 2 is the review of the literature about berth scheduling. Section 3 describes the problem and offers several hypotheses. Section 4 explains the berth and the quay crane joint dispatching model. Section 5 demonstrates a numerical example and compares the results of different algorithms. Finally, Section 6 presents the conclusions.

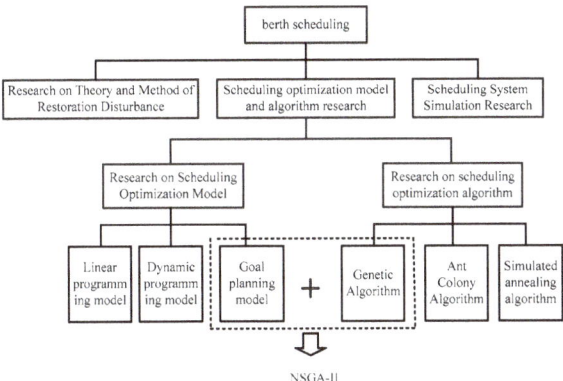

Figure 1. The main research topics of berth optimization scheduling.

2. Literature Review

A growing consensus recognizes the need to shift society products and services towards more sustainable models [24–27]. In recent years, green ports have become the mainstream of sustainable development of the global ports. The competition among container terminals becomes more and more fierce, and almost all of the container terminals bear the pressure to attract more customers. How to rationally scheduling port resources to improve the service level of container terminals and improve customer satisfaction has aroused wide attention of scholars at home and abroad. This review of the literature about port scheduling covers the scheduling models first, and then the optimization algorithms.

To maximize the berth throughput and reliability of berth scheduling, Robenek et al. [20] proposed a mixed integer programming model based on branch and price framework to solve the two key optimization problems of berth distribution and distribution of cargo ports in bulk cargo ports. Xu et al. [28] proposed an expression for solving the berth scheduling problem by introducing a delayed buffer concept to simulate the ship's delay and the uncertainty of the processing time. However, this expression is assumed under the continuous berth space hypothesis, but not for discrete berths. When considering the uncertainties of ship arrival and running times, Zhen et al. [29] explored the uncertainty in the port scheduling problem and constructed a two-stage decision model. Then, he conducted some computational analysis of the performance of the berth allocation process in an uncertain environment. The author used the rescheduling strategy to deal with the initial plan, but the reality of the environment did not match because the proposed model was too complex. Monaco et al. [30] transformed the discrete berth problem into a dynamic scheduling problem and obtained the best scheme by using an improved Lagrangian heuristic algorithm. Lee et al. [31] formally described the discrete berth and the quay crane scheduling problem by mixing the integer programming model. To solve the berth allocation problem of a multi-user container terminal, Imai et al. [32] introduced the Lagrangian slack variable when solving the minimum waiting time of a ship and turned the static berth scheduling problem into a dynamic berth scheduling problem. Han et al. [33] used the probability density function to represent the uncertainty of the arrival and the processing time of a ship. This method does not require the probability distribution of the arrival and processing times of a ship, but it does not comprehensively consider the optimization objectives, while only a few people take the impact of unfair psychological factors into account.

Regarding optimization algorithms, Kim et al. [34] proposed a simulated annealing method for solving the problem of additional costs incurred when a ship is at an inappropriate location and resolved the problem of port fines that were incurred when detained ships depart later than scheduled. Hsu [35] when combined with improved particle swarm optimization and event based heuristic algorithm, a hybrid particle swarm optimization (HPSO) algorithm is proposed to solve the problem of discrete and dynamic berth and wharf crane distribution. To solve the problem of berth allocation, Oliveira et al. [36] proposed a hybrid clustering search method that was based on a simulated annealing algorithm to improve the terminal space distribution logistics by reducing the total service time of each ship. To solve the problem of discrete and dynamic berth allocation, more specifically, to allocate the discrete berth positions of ships while minimizing both the total waiting and processing times of all ships, Ting et al. [37] proposed a particle swarm optimization solution that effectively improves the efficiency of the solution and reduces the computational time. To make berths more flexible, Imai et al. [38] proposed a dynamic scheduling problem of jagged berths, studied the problem of berth scheduling with realistic constraints, and introduced a heuristic algorithm to solve the problem of continuous berth allocation. Finally, a large number of experiments have shown this heuristic algorithm to be superior and proven the feasibility of using a genetic algorithm to solve berth scheduling in a dynamic environment. Umang et al. [39] used precise and heuristic algorithms for berth allocation in discrete ports. Lee et al. [31] proposed an improved genetic algorithm in order to obtain an approximate optimal solution.

The problem of port scheduling is already complex and uncertain, and there has been little research on unfair psychological factors, proposed models are very different from how ports actually work. Therefore, based on the actual work processes of ports, this paper constructs a multi-objective mathematical model with five objective functions, and proposes a port berth-shore bridge joint dispatching method to deal with the problem of berth scheduling and the rational distribution of berths. Then, the model is solved by using a fast and unpredictable improved genetic algorithm (NSGA-II), which was based on Pareto optimality.

3. Problem Description and Assumptions

The joint scheduling of berths and shore bridges can be described as follows. Assume that A is a collection of ships at a port, M is the port berth collection, a is the ship number, and i is the berth number, where $a \in A, a = 1, 2, \ldots, k$ and $i \in M, i = 1, 2, \ldots, m$. A ship arrives at a port, then moves to the best working berth (each vessel has one or more best working berths to enable the system to achieve a multi-objective Pareto optimality), discharges, and finally leaves the port. If there is no free berth when the ship arrives, then there will be a certain waiting time. After the ship has been unloaded, there must be a certain staying time for the loading of goods. For loading or unloading a ship, there needs to be a reasonable distribution of shore bridges, because it is necessary to have the equitable allocation and the highest utilization of shore bridge resources [32,33].

The main content of this paper is about the joint optimization of the berth-shore bridges of a port. The diagram of the joint operation of berths-store bridges is shown in Figure 2. Suppose that Berths 1, 2, 3, and 4 are available to Ship 3, which enters the port as Ship 2 is loading/unloading in Berth 1. Ship 3 has two options, one of which is to enter Berth 1 for loading/unloading after Ship 2 has left, while the other option is to find the best available working berth.

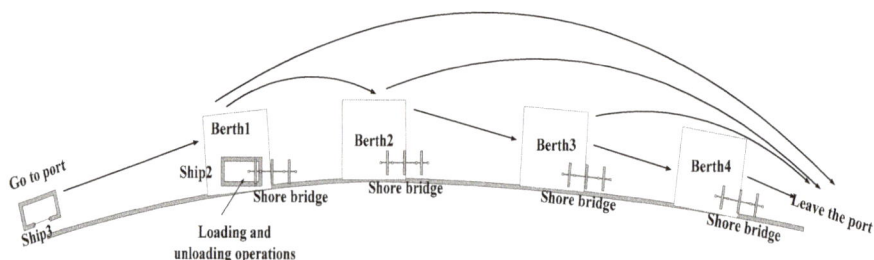

Figure 2. Schematic diagram of the joint operation of berths.

As shown in Figure 3, the time during which a ship is parked at the port is mainly composed of waiting for a particular berth to become available (waiting time), moving to the best working berth (moving time), and time for loading/unloading of the ship.

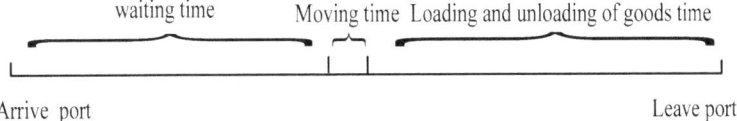

Figure 3. Composition of the time that ships spend in port.

Since the distances among the berths are short, the shift and waiting times can be ignored. It is:

$$t_1 = t_2 + t_3 \tag{1}$$

$$t_2 = \frac{R_a}{v} \tag{2}$$

$$t'_2 = \frac{R_{a0}}{v} \tag{3}$$

$$t_4 = t'_2 + t_3 \tag{4}$$

$$t_0 = t_1 + t_4 \tag{5}$$

t_0 is the actual time in port for ship a, t_1 is the waiting time, t_2 is the remaining unloading time of the previous vessel before ship a, t'_2 is the unloading time, t_3 is the stay time mainly for loading, and t_4 is the total loading and unloading time of the system. Formula (1) represents the required time for ship a to wait for the loading/unloading of the previous ship (remaining unloading and stay time). Formulas (2) and (3) are the unloading times of the ship. Formula (4) represents the required time to load and unload cargo (unloading and stay time) of ship a. Formula (5) is the actual formula for the calculation of ship a in port.

The problem of berth allocation that is discussed in this chapter is based on the following assumptions: (1) Each ship has an ideal berth for unloading and loading; (2) Each berth formulate a minimum and maximum number of distributable shore bridges; (3) Due to the short distances among berths, the moving time is negligible compared to the waiting time; (4) The subsequent migration distance of the ship can be obtained directly (the distances among the berths is approximated instead); (5) The costs of use and labor service of the same berth's shore bridge are the same, but those for different berths are not necessarily the same; (6) The water depth of each berth can meet the requirements of any ship's docking; (7) Each berth serves only one ship at a time; and, (8) The stay time of each ship is the same.

4. Construction of Joint Scheduling Model of the Port and Quay Cranes

According to the actual production characteristics of shipyard terminals, this paper creatively considers the influencing factors of customer unfairness and establishes a multi-objective mathematical model with the objective of shortest time in port, minimum system cost, and minimum unfairness. The parameters and meanings that are associated with the model are shown in Table 1.

Table 1. Model-related parameters and meaning.

Symbol	Meaning
i	Berth number
j	The jth ship is served at a berth
m	Number of berths
f_a	The ath ship's departure time
s_a	The ath ship's arrivals time
L_a	The length of ath ship (m)
l_a	The migration distance of ath ship
c_1	The cost coefficient of ship migration (yuan/m)
c_2	Berth labor service cost coefficient (yuan/one)
c_3	Cost coefficient of each berth bridge used (yuan/one)
Q_i	Service cost of the ith berth (yuan/day)
u_{ai}	Decision variables: if the ship at berth i, the value is 1, or 0
$v_{\alpha\beta}$	Decision variables: only when berth α and berth β are selected at the same time, the value is 1; otherwise, 0.
α, β	Indicates any two berths
p_i	The cost of the ith berth bridge (yuan/one)
r_i	The number of shore bridges required by each ship at the ith berth (one)
L	Total length of port (m)
n_i	The total number of berths allocated by the ith berth (one)
w_i	The total amount of ship loading and unloading at the ith berth (t)
$\bar{u}$	The maximum number of quarries allowed for each berth
u	The minimum number of quarries to be allocated to each berth
LB_i	The length of the ith berth (m)
v	The loading and unloading speed of shore bridge (t/min)

4.1. Model Building

(1) Minimum stay time in port: f_1.

The optimized time in port for a ship is the difference between the departure and arrival times.

$$f_1 = \min \sum_{a=1}^{k} (f_a - s_a) \qquad (6)$$

(2) Minimum system cost: f_2

The total cost, including shifting process cost (mainly related to the shifting distance), artificial services costs, such as berth maintenance and use of quay crane (including the manufacture, operation, and maintenance), of the system is incurred while a ship is in port.

$$f_2 = c_1 \min \sum_{a=1}^{k} l_a + c_2 \min \sum_{i=1}^{m} Q_i u_{ai} + c_3 \min \sum_{i=1}^{m} p_i r_i u_{ai} \qquad (7)$$

(3) Minimum unfairness: f_3

According to the theory of justice in management, only when the ratio of pay and effort is equal to the proportion of the pay and effort of others will fairness be produced. Similarly, we believe that it is necessary to consider the ratio of the loading and unloading quantity and the number of the matched quay crane in the distribution, so as to minimize the sense of the unfairness of the customers. Therefore:

$$f_3 = \min \sqrt{\sum_{1 \leq \alpha < \beta \leq m} \left[\frac{w_\beta}{n_\beta} - \frac{w_\alpha}{n_\alpha} \right]^2 v_{\alpha\beta}} \qquad (8)$$

where $\alpha = 1, 2, \ldots, m-1; \beta = 2, 3, \ldots, m$.

Based on the above analysis, a multi-objective optimization model is constructed, as follows:

$$\begin{cases} f_1 = \min \sum_{a=1}^{k} (f_a - s_a) \\ f_2 = c_1 \min \sum_{a=1}^{k} l_a + c_2 \min \sum_{i=1}^{m} Q_i u_{ai} + c_3 \min \sum_{i=1}^{m} p_i r_i u_{ai} \\ f_3 = \min \sqrt{\sum_{1 \leq \alpha < \beta \leq m} \left[\frac{w_\beta}{n_\beta} - \frac{w_\alpha}{n_\alpha}\right]^2 v_{\alpha\beta}} \end{cases} \quad (9)$$

Constraint conditions:

$$f_a - s_a > 0 \quad (10)$$

$$l_a < L_i \quad (11)$$

$$\sum_{i=1}^{m} L_i < L \quad (12)$$

$$\underline{u} \leq n_i \leq \overline{u} \quad (13)$$

$$r_{ij} \leq n_i \quad (14)$$

$$i = 1, 2, \ldots, m, \quad j = 1, 2, \ldots, N_i \quad (15)$$

Formula (10) means that the arrival time of ship a is less than its departure time. Formula (11) means that the length of ship a is less than the length of the berth where it parks. Formula (12) means that the total length of the berth is less than the total length of the quay. Formula (13) signifies the quantity constraint of the quay bridge that is allocated by each berth. Formula (14) means that the number of quay cranes used by every ship on berth i cannot exceed the total number of cranes allocated to the berth.

4.2. Algorithm Flow and Steps for Problem-Solving

The algorithm flow of the improved NSGA-II algorithm is based on random repair and self-adaptive operators, as shown in Figure 4.

The steps for the solution are as follows:

(1) According to the objective function and constraints, the initial population is generated randomly. The population size is set as P, then the individual ships are coded with the three-tier coding form as 0, 1. The first tier represents the berth. The corresponding code is 1 if the ship stays in the berth; otherwise, the code is 0. The second tier is the number of berths that is matched to the berth. The third is the service sequence, which indicates how many vessels are served at the berth. As shown in Figure 5, the order indicates the first ship to be served by the third on Berth 1, on which Bridges 2, 3, and 5 are selected.

(2) Improvement strategy.

① Random repair operator. To prevent the duplication of individuals in the genetic process, gene repair was performed on individuals that did not meet the principle of mutual exclusion in the population.

② Self-adaptive operator

$$P_m = P_{mmin} + (P_{mmax} - P_{mmin}) \times \frac{(G_{max} - G)}{G_{max}} \quad (16)$$

$$P_c = P_{cmin} + (P_{cmax} - P_{cmin}) \times \frac{(G_{max} - G)}{G_{max}} \quad (17)$$

(3) According to Equation (9), calculate target fitness.

(4) Use fast non-dominated sorting and crowding comparison operators (Formula (18)). To evaluate the fitness of the parent, the first filial generation is generated by genetic manipulation, such as selection, crossover, and mutation, while genetic repair is performed with the random repair operator.

$$d_a = \sum_{t=1}^{T} \left(\left| f_t^{\lambda+1} - f_t^{\lambda-1} \right| \right) \tag{18}$$

where $f_t^{\lambda+1}$ represents the $(\lambda + 1)$th objective function value of the tth individual. Similarly, $f_t^{\lambda-1}$ represents the tth objective function value of the $(\lambda - 1)$th individual.

(5) The termination condition judgment. If the maximum evolution generation is reached, then the evolutionary is terminated. Otherwise, the evolution generation increases one.

(6) The parent and progeny populations are combined to form a new combined population with a scale of 2P. The fast, non-dominated sorting algorithm and the crowding comparison operator are used to evaluate all of the individuals in the merged population. The best individuals are chosen as the parent population of the iteration to achieve elite protection.

(7) Return to Step (3).

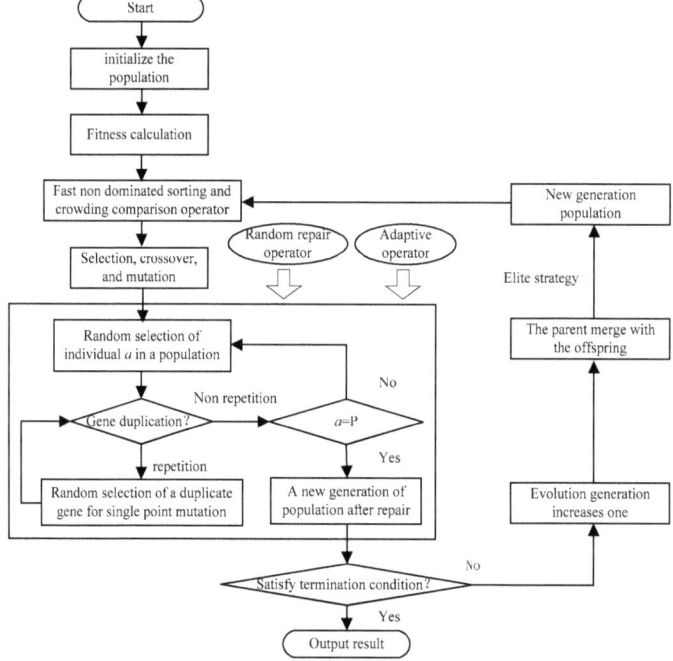

Figure 4. The algorithm flow of the improved NSGA-II.

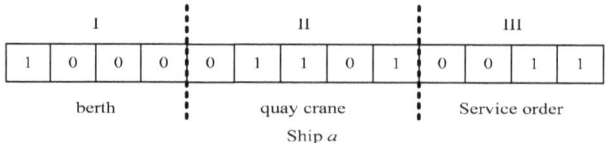

Figure 5. Coding pattern.

5. Case Study

In the container freight port in city Z of China, there are only four discrete berths and 15 quay cranes. The efficiency of the quay crane is 30 t/min, and the ship's stay time (mainly loading) is 30 min. The port is busy, the waiting times are long, there is an unreasonable number of quay cranes under different berths causing a serious waste of resources, and unfairness occurs regarding berth-shore bridges, causing customer and employee dissatisfaction. To better solve the above problems, the data recorded from the ship to the port in the day of the port (as shown in Tables 2–5) are simulated. By using the method that is given in this paper, the population size of the improved NSGA-II algorithm is set to 200 individuals and the maximum iteration number is set to 200 times, $p_{mmin} = 0.1$, $p_{mmax} = 0.5$, $p_{cmin} = 0.3$, $p_{cmax} = 0.8$. The simulation was run on Windows 2007 MATLAB 2016b software and compared to GA and standard (original) NSGA-II. The results are shown in Figures 6–10. In GA and standard NSGA-II, the cross-probability is set to 0.8 and the mutation probability is set to 0.1.

Table 2. Relevant data of an international container port in city Z.

Ship Number	Arrival Time	Departure Time	Hull Length/m	Freight Capacity/t
1	00:19	05:30	100	11,531
2	02:17	04:30	62	17,390
3	02:43	03:30	45	18,158
4	03:10	04:30	46	7650
5	06:39	09:00	72	8500
6	07:45	11:15	83	20,400
7	08:05	11:00	99	29,172
8	08:37	11:30	100	25,616
9	09:10	10:30	53	11,320
10	10:26	18:00	164	16,092
11	10:41	12:30	81	17,843
12	11:07	12:00	57	13,015
13	11:31	16:00	97	19,800
14	12:06	16:00	130	21,825
15	13:13	19:00	125	26,338

Table 3. Berth-related data.

	Berth Length/m	Minimum Number of Quay Crane	Maximum Number of Quay Crane
1	200	2	5
2	200	2	5
3	300	1	5
4	260	2	5

Table 4. Shifting distances among different berths.

Berth	1	2	3	4
1	-	700	970	1350
2	700	-	270	650
3	970	270	-	380
4	1350	650	380	-

Table 5. Related parameters.

Parameters	Related Data
c_1	0.3
c_2	0.55
c_3	0.65
L	1500 m
Q_1	270 yuan/day
Q_2	220 yuan/day
Q_3	260 yuan/day
Q_4	210 yuan/day
P_1	200 yuan/one
P_2	240 yuan/one
P_3	197 yuan/one
P_4	230 yuan/one

Using the improved NSGA-II and standard NSGA-II algorithms for the simulation, the shortest arrival time of the ship is obtained, as shown in Figures 6 and 7. As the number of iterations increases, the shortest time converges to a constant minimum value in port time.

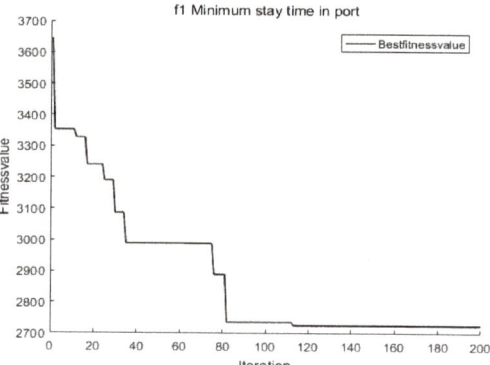

Figure 6. The improved NSGA-II in port time convergence curve.

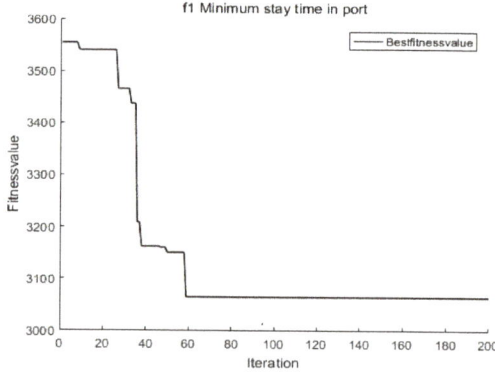

Figure 7. The original NSGA-II in port time convergence curve.

At the same time, in the GA algorithm, we let the fitness function $f = f_1 + f_2 + f_3$. The result is shown in Figure 8.

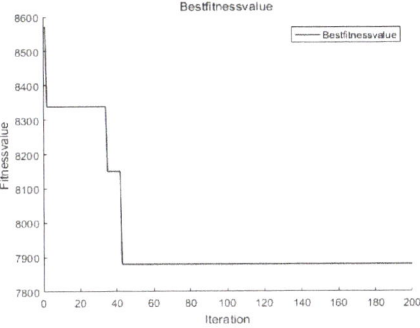

Figure 8. GA algorithm output convergence curve.

The comparative diagrams of the outputs of the proposed adaptive improved NSGA-II method and the original NSGA-II are shown in Figures 9–11.

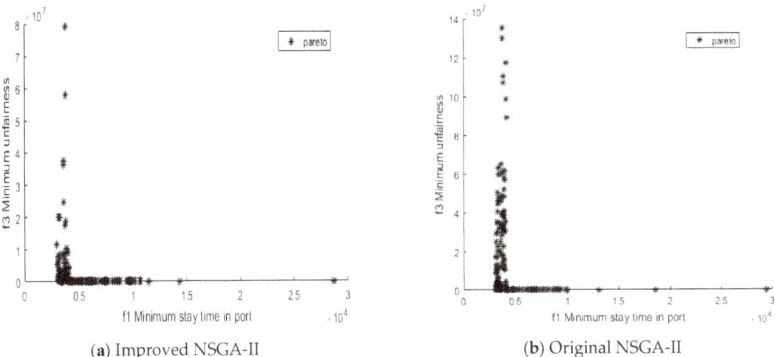

(**a**) Improved NSGA-II   (**b**) Original NSGA-II

Figure 9. Relationship between f_1 and f_3.

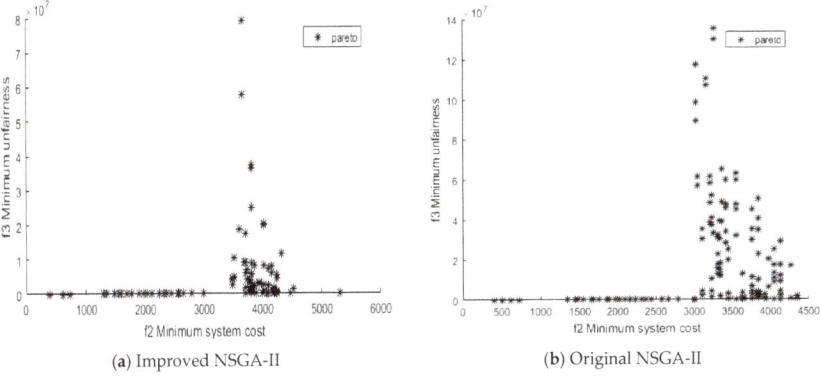

(**a**) Improved NSGA-II   (**b**) Original NSGA-II

Figure 10. Relationship between f_2 and f_3.

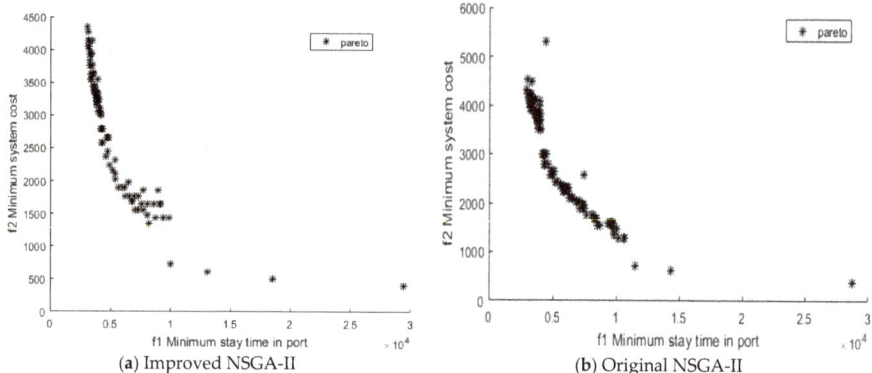

Figure 11. Relationship between f_1 and f_2.

As can be seen from Figures 6–8, the improved NSGA-II method, though declining in convergence rate, has been greatly improved in terms of optimization objectives. For example, for the shortest time in port, the proposed method converges at 2720 and the calculation result of the general (Original) NSGA-II is 3060. In order to illustrate the solution performance of our proposed method is stable, 20 times simulations on Windows 2007 MATLAB 2016b software were run. As far as the objective function f_1 is concerned, the statistical data and results show that there are 17 times of the improved NSGA-II method converge to 2720 ± 20, and the other three times are in the range of 2720 ± 50, which proves that the solution performance of our method is stable.

As can be seen from the comparison of Figures 9–11, the non-inferior solution set obtained by the proposed method is more likely to fall into the local optimum and the quality of the solution has also been greatly improved. When considering that the berths should be maximized and utilized, only the five groups of non-inferior solutions that were obtained by this method are listed below. The results of the joint allocation of berth-shore quays by GA are shown in Table 6.

Table 6. Five sets of non-inferior solutions.

Ship	Parking Berth (Matching Number of Quayside)				
1	1(5)	2(5)	2(5)	3(4)	1(5)
2	1(5)	2(5)	2(5)	3(4)	1(5)
3	2(5)	1(5)	1(5)	3(4)	2(4)
4	1(5)	2(5)	3(4)	1(5)	1(5)
5	1(5)	1(5)	3(4)	1(5)	1(5)
6	2(5)	2(5)	2(5)	1(5)	1(5)
7	3(4)	3(4)	1(5)	2(5)	3(4)
8	3(4)	2(5)	2(5)	2(5)	2(4)
9	1(5)	1(5)	3(4)	1(5)	1(5)
10	2(5)	1(5)	1(5)	1(5)	1(5)
11	1(5)	2(5)	3(4)	3(4)	2(4)
12	1(5)	3(4)	1(5)	1(5)	1(5)
13	1(5)	1(5)	1(5)	1(5)	1(5)
14	2(5)	3(4)	2(5)	1(5)	3(4)
15	2(5)	1(5)	3(4)	2(5)	1(5)

From Tables 6 and 7, we can see that the method proposed in this paper can make the berths more effective (this paper considers three berths but only two berths are obtained by GA), while considering the comprehensive optimization of each objective. The shore bridge distribution is more balanced and reasonable.

Table 7. Joint-distribution of various ships obtained by GA.

Ship	Parking Berth (Matching Number of Quayside)	Ship	Parking Berth (Matching Number of Quayside)
1	1(5)	9	1(5)
2	1(5)	10	2(5)
3	1(5)	11	1(5)
4	2(5)	12	2(5)
5	1(5)	13	2(5)
6	2(5)	14	1(5)
7	2(5)	15	1(5)
8	2(5)		

6. Conclusions

To solve the problem of long waiting times for ships, the serious waste of resources that are caused by the unreasonable matching of the quayside and the unfair allocation of wharfs to berths, this paper discusses the joint scheduling problem of berthing and shore quays, and makes the following main contributions.

(1) A multi-objective mathematical model with the shortest time in port, minimum system total cost, and minimum inequity is constructed to provide a multi-objective optimization solution to the port problem.

(2) The introduction of random repair and adaptive operators to improve NSGA-II can effectively avoid falling into the local optimal and premature convergence problems, while improving the understanding of the search performance to ensure the diversity of the population.

(3) By comparing the results with the original NSGA-II and the GA algorithms with the actual example of a port terminal, the feasibility and effectiveness of the proposed method have been verified.

This paper proposes a joint berth-shore quay scheduling model to solve the problem of matching dock berths and shore quaysides by adopting the improved NSGA-II with random repair and adaptive operators. A Pareto frontier was obtained. Five sets of representative Pareto non-inferior solutions were selected in order to provide decision-making support to shipyard managers.

Author Contributions: Writing: A.L., H.L.(Haiyang Liu), S.-B.T.; Providing case and idea: A.L., H.L.(Haiyang Liu); Providing revised advice: S.-B.T., H.L.(Hui Lu), X.Z., J.W.

Funding: The study was supported by "Central University Science Research Foundation of China" (JB170609), "Research Fund from Key Laboratory of computer integrated manufacturing in Guangdong Province" (CIMSOF2016002), "State Key Laboratory for Manufacturing Systems Engineering (Xi'an Jiaotong University)" (sklms2017005), "China Postdoctoral Science Foundation funded project"(2016M590929), and "Shaanxi Natural Science Foundation Project" (2017JM7004) and Zhongshan City Science and Technology Bureau Project (No. 2017B1015).

Conflicts of Interest: The authors declare no conflict of interest.

References

1. Kang, D.; Kim, S. Conceptual model development of sustainability practices: The case of port operations for collaboration and governance. *Sustainability* **2017**, *9*, 2333. [CrossRef]
2. Han, X.L.; Gong, X.; Jo, J. A new continuous berth allocation and quay crane assignment model in container terminal. *Comput. Ind. Eng.* **2015**, *89*, 15–22. [CrossRef]
3. Hu, Q.M.; Hu, Z.H.; Du, Y. Berth and quay-crane allocation problem considering fuel consumption and emissions from vessels. *Comput. Ind. Eng.* **2014**, *70*, 1–10. [CrossRef]
4. Di Vaio, A.; Varriale, L. Management innovation for environmental sustainability in seaports: Managerial accounting instruments and training for competitive green ports beyond the regulations. *Sustainability* **2018**, *10*, 783. [CrossRef]
5. Papaefthimiou, S.; Maragkogianni, A.; Andriosopoulos, K. Evaluation of cruise ships emissions in the Mediterranean basin: The case of Greek ports. *Int. J. Sustain. Transp.* **2016**, *10*, 985–994. [CrossRef]
6. Chen, Z.; Pak, M. A Delphi analysis on green performance evaluation indices for ports in China. *Marit. Policy Manag.* **2017**, *44*, 537–550. [CrossRef]

7. Schipper, C.A.; Vreugdenhil, H.; de Jong, M.P.C. A sustainability assessment of ports and port-city plans: Comparing ambitions with achievements. *Transp. Res. Part D-Transp. Environ.* **2017**, *57*, 84–111. [CrossRef]
8. Asgari, N.; Hassani, A.; Jones, D.; Nguye, H.H. Sustainability ranking of the UK major ports: Methodology and case study. *Transp. Res. Part E-Logist. Transp. Rev.* **2015**, *78*, 19–39. [CrossRef]
9. Frojan, P.; Correcher, J.F.; Alvarez-Valdes, R.; Koulouris, G.; Tamarit, J.M. The continuous berth allocation problem in a container terminal with multiple quays. *Expert Syst. Appl.* **2015**, *42*, 7356–7366. [CrossRef]
10. Lun, Y.V.; Lai, K.H.; Wong, C.W.; Cheng, T.C. Environmental governance mechanisms in shipping firms and their environmental performance. *Transp. Res. Part E-Logist. Transp. Rev.* **2015**, *78*, 82–92.
11. Rodrigues, V.S.; Pettit, S.; Harris, I.; Beresford, A.; Piecyk, M.; Yang, Z.; Ng, A. UK supply chain carbon mitigation strategies using alternative ports and multimodal freight transport operations. *Transp. Res. Part E-Logist. Transp. Rev.* **2015**, *78*, 40–56. [CrossRef]
12. Yang, L.; Cai, Y.; Zhong, X.; Shi, Y.; Zhang, Z. A carbon emission evaluation for an integrated logistics system—A case study of the port of Shenzhen. *Sustainability* **2017**, *9*, 462. [CrossRef]
13. Tang, M.; Gong, D.; Liu, S.; Zhang, H. Applying multi-phase particle swarm optimization to solve bulk cargo port scheduling problem. *Adv. Prod. Eng. Manag.* **2016**, *11*, 299. [CrossRef]
14. Li, Q.; Huang, J.; Wang, C.; Lin, H.; Zhang, J.; Jiang, J.; Wang, B. Land development suitability evaluation of Pingtan island based on scenario analysis and landscape ecological quality evaluation. *Sustainability* **2017**, *9*, 1292. [CrossRef]
15. Baiocchi, V.; Lelo, K.; Polettini, A.; Pomi, R. Land suitability for waste disposal in metropolitan areas. *Waste Manag. Res.* **2014**, *32*, 707–716. [CrossRef] [PubMed]
16. Hamzeh, S.; Mokarram, M.; Haratian, A.; Bartholomeus, H.; Ligtenberg, A.; Bregt, A.K. Feature selection as a time and cost-saving approach for land suitability classification (case study of Shavur Plain, Iran). *Agriculture* **2016**, *6*, 52. [CrossRef]
17. Azadnia, A.H.; Saman, M.Z.M.; Wong, K.Y. Sustainable supplier selection and order lot-sizing: An integrated multi-objective decision-making process. *Int. J. Prod. Res.* **2015**, *53*, 383–408. [CrossRef]
18. Bai, C.; Fahimnia, B.; Sarkis, J. Sustainable transport fleet appraisal using a hybrid multi-objective decision making approach. *Ann. Oper. Res.* **2017**, *250*, 309–340. [CrossRef]
19. Golias, M.; Portal, I.; Konur, D.; Kaisar, E.; Kolomvos, G. Robust berth scheduling at marine container terminals via hierarchical optimization. *Comput. Oper. Res.* **2014**, *41*, 412–422. [CrossRef]
20. Robenek, T.; Umang, N.; Bierlaire, M.; Ropke, S. A branch-and-price algorithm to solve the integrated berth allocation and yard assignment problem in bulk ports. *Eur. J. Oper. Res.* **2014**, *235*, 399–411. [CrossRef]
21. Xu, R.; Wu, W. Study on disruption management models of continuous berth allocation at Shipyard Jetties. *J. Residuals Sci. Technol.* **2016**, *13*. [CrossRef]
22. Legato, P.; Mazza, R.M.; Gullì, D. Integrating tactical and operational berth allocation decisions via Simulation–Optimization. *Comput. Ind. Eng.* **2014**, *78*, 84–94. [CrossRef]
23. Al-Dhaheri, N.; Jebali, A.; Diabat, A. A simulation-based Genetic Algorithm approach for the quay crane scheduling under uncertainty. *Simul. Model. Pract. Theory* **2016**, *66*, 122–138. [CrossRef]
24. Tsai, S.B.; Yu, J.; Ma, L.; Luo, F.; Zhou, J.; Chen, Q.; Xu, L. A study on solving the production process problems of the photovoltaic cell industry. *Renew. Sustain. Energy Rev.* **2018**, *82*, 3546–3553. [CrossRef]
25. Tsai, S.B.; Zhou, J.; Gao, Y.; Wang, J.; Li, G.; Zheng, Y.; Ren, P.; Xu, W. Combining FMEA with DEMATEL models to solve production process problems. *PLoS ONE* **2017**. [CrossRef] [PubMed]
26. Liu, W.; Wei, Q.; Huang, S.Q.; Tsai, S.B. Doing good again? A multilevel institutional perspective on corporate environmental responsibility and philanthropic strategy. *Int. J. Environ. Res. Public Health* **2017**, *14*, 1283. [CrossRef] [PubMed]
27. Du, P.; Xu, L.; Chen, Q.; Tsai, S.B. Pricing competition on innovative product between innovator and entrant imitator facing strategic customers. *Int. J. Prod. Res.* **2016**. [CrossRef]
28. Xu, Y.; Chen, Q.; Quan, X. Robust berth scheduling with uncertain vessel delay and handling time. *Ann. Oper. Res.* **2012**, *192*, 123–140. [CrossRef]
29. Zhen, L.; Lee, L.H.; Chew, E.P. A decision model for berth allocation under uncertainty. *Eur. J. Oper. Res.* **2011**, *212*, 54–68. [CrossRef]
30. Monaco, M.F.; Sammarra, M. The berth allocation problem: A strong formulation solved by a lagrangean approach. *Trans. Sci.* **2007**, *41*, 265–280. [CrossRef]

31. Lee, D.H.; Qiu Wang, H. Integrated discrete berth allocation and quay crane scheduling in port container terminals. *Eng. Optim.* **2010**, *42*, 747–761. [CrossRef]
32. Imai, A.; Nishimura, E.; Papadimitriou, S. The dynamic berth allocation problem for a container port. *Transp. Res. Part B* **2005**, *39*, 401–417. [CrossRef]
33. Han, X.; Lu, Z.; Xi, L. A proactive approach for simultaneous berth and quay crane scheduling problem with stochastic arrival and handling time. *Eur. J. Oper. Res.* **2010**, *207*, 1327–1340. [CrossRef]
34. Kim, K.H.; Moon, K.C. Berth scheduling by simulated annealing. *Transp. Res. Part B* **2003**, *37*, 541–560. [CrossRef]
35. Hsu, H.P. A HPSO for solving dynamic and discrete berth allocation problem and dynamic quay crane assignment problem simultaneously. *Swarm Evol. Comput.* **2016**, *27*, 156–168. [CrossRef]
36. Oliveira, R.D. Clustering search for the berth allocation problem. *Expert Syst. Appl.* **2012**, *39*, 5499–5505. [CrossRef]
37. Ting, C.J.; Wu, K.C.; Chou, H. Particle swarm optimization algorithm for the berth allocation problem. *Expert Syst. Appl.* **2014**, *41*, 1543–1550. [CrossRef]
38. Imai, A.; Sun, X.; Nishimura, E.; Papadimitriou, S. Berth allocation in a container port: Using a continuous location space approach. *Transp. Res. Part B* **2008**, *39*, 199–221. [CrossRef]
39. Umang, N.; Bierlaire, M.; Vacca, I. Exact and heuristic methods to solve the berth allocation problem in bulk ports. *Transp. Res. Part E-Logist. Transp. Rev.* **2013**, *54*, 14–31. [CrossRef]

© 2018 by the authors. Licensee MDPI, Basel, Switzerland. This article is an open access article distributed under the terms and conditions of the Creative Commons Attribution (CC BY) license (http://creativecommons.org/licenses/by/4.0/).

Article

Vibration Suppression of a Single-Cylinder Engine by Means of Multi-objective Evolutionary Optimisation

Suwin Sleesongsom [1,*] and Sujin Bureerat [2]

[1] Department of Aeronautical Engineering and Commercial Pilot, International Academy of Aviation Industry, King Mongkut's Institute of Technology Ladkrabang, Bangkok 10520, Thailand

[2] Sustainable and Infrastructure Development Center, Department of Mechanical Engineering, Faculty of Engineering, KhonKaen University, KhonKaen City 40002, Thailand; sujbur@kku.ac.th

* Correspondence: suwins2000@yahoo.com; Tel.: +66-02-329-800

Received: 31 May 2018; Accepted: 15 June 2018; Published: 18 June 2018

Abstract: This paper presents a new design strategy for the passive vibration suppression of a single-cylindrical engine (SCE) through multi-objective evolutionary optimisation. The vibration causes machine damages and human pain, which are unsustainable problems that need to be alleviated. Mathematical forced vibration analyses of a single-cylinder engine, including dynamic pressure force due to ignition combustion, are presented. A multi-objective design problem is set to find the shape and size variables of the crank and connecting rod of the engine. The objective functions consist of the minimisation of the crank and connecting rod mass, and the minimisation of vibration response while the SCE is subject to inertial force and pressure force. Moreover, design constraints include crank and rod safety. The design problem is tackled by using an adaptation of a hybrid of multi-objective population-based incremental learning and differential evolution (RPBIL-DE). The optimum results found that the proposed design strategy is a powerful tool for the vibration suppression of SCE.

Keywords: vibration suppression; single-cylinder engine; multi-objective evolutionary algorithms; dynamic analysis; crank–slider

1. Introduction

A single-cylinder engine (SCE) is one of the most widely used engines, especially in motorcycles, which are the most popular two-wheel automotive in this world. It is also included in a variety of applications particularly for agricultural proposes such as the driving pump, walking tractor, lawnmower, etc. In contrast with the applications, the vibration of this engine is the main problem at present. Two causes of vibration are from moving links in a crank–slider mechanism and ignition pressure due to combustion process. These can be a cause of machine damages, human discomfort, and user-accumulated fatigue and pain. SCE vibration can be alleviated in two ways i.e., balancing and isolation.

Balancing a SCE can be classified as active and passive balancing [1]. Active balancing is a method for reducing shaking force and moment by introducing dummy pistons and geared revolving counter weights, etc. Passive balancing, on the other hand, is a method used to reduce shaking force and moment by the addition or removal of mass from various portions of the moving links.

Research work toward this area has been continually made. Lowen et al. [2] summarised the techniques for the force and moment balancing of linkages. Zhang and Chen [3] have applied vibration suppression of a four-bar linkage by using the weighted sum method, which is a means to convert multi-objective optimisation to become a problem with one design objective. The counterweights' mass parameters were set as design variables in this passive balancing. Snyman et al. [4] have applied an unconstrained optimisation problem to minimise the transmission of engine vibration due to inertial forces to the supporting structure where the case study is a mounted four-cylinder V-engine rotating at idling speed by an active balancing method. The individual balancing masses and associated phase angles of counter rotating balancing masses were chosen as design variables. Chiou et al. [5] proposed an optimum design in which disk counterweights were added to reduce shaking force and moment of the drag-link drive of mechanical presses. Sleesongsom [6] proposed applying multi-objective optimisation to reduce the engine mount translation and rotation displacements of SCE where the normalised normal constraint method [7], in combination with sequential quadratic programming, is an optimiser. The use of finite element analysis and optimisation codes for connecting rod [8], crankshaft [9], and piston design [10] has been conducted. In addition, the finite element technique has been used to optimise the crankshaft parameters of a single-cylinder motorcycle engine to reduce vibration without considering the gas pressure force inside the combustion chamber [11].

The second vibration suppression technique for the engine is vibration isolation. The challenge for designers and engineers is how to properly select vibration isolators in order to minimise the force transmission to the engine base [11–13] and the powertrain mounting system [14,15]. Further work focuses on optimisation of engine mounting systems and blocks can be found in References [16–23], while the literature of using meta-heuristic algorithms (MHs) or evolutionary algorithms (EAs) for engine mounting and engine part design can be seen further in Reference [24].

Both methods has been studied and used in industry, but the new design technique still lacks development. Recent works of automotive technology have focused on designing the motor of an electric vehicle (EV) to increase its efficiency and reduce vibration [25]. This kind of automotive uses an electric motor as a power or hybrid with the traditional engine. This research focuses on optimising the flux-weakening performance and reducing the vibration of an Interior permanent magnet (IPM) motor for EVs using the evolutionary algorithm (EA), which focuses on the source of vibration similar to our present research. Furthermore, this kind of designing problem is multi-objective optimisation, but the authors compromise it to be a single objective. So, in the present research, we focus on using a multi-objective evolutionary algorithm (MOEA) to alleviate the vibration of a single-cylinder engine.

This research proposes a new design strategy for the vibration suppression of a single-cylinder engine using a multi-objective evolutionary algorithm (MOEA). In this design, design variables including the shape and sizing parameters of the engine are proposed to suppress the inertia force and pressure force, which are the main vibration causes of this kind of engine. The MOEA optimiser is the hybrid of multi-objective population-based incremental learning and differential evolution (RPBIL-DE). The new design technique can reduce the vibrations that cause machine damages, human discomfort, and user-accumulated fatigue and pain, which can lead to sustainable development.

2. Single-Cylinder Engine Model

Herein, vibration analysis of a single-cylinder engine system is simplified for ease in the computation of an optimisation process. The kinematic and dynamic force analyses of a crank–slider with external ignition forces are carried out, while the obtained reactions will be used as external forces for the engine box and mounting system.

2.1. Kinematic and Kinetic Analyses

Figure 1 shows a crank–slider with the crank radius R and connecting rod L. The parameters θ_2 and θ_3 are the angular positions of links 2 and 3, respectively, while x is the position vector of the piston. Given that θ_2, $\dot{\theta}_2$, and $\ddot{\theta}_2$ are known input variables, we can have the relation:

$$R \sin(\theta_2) = L \sin(\theta_3) \tag{1}$$

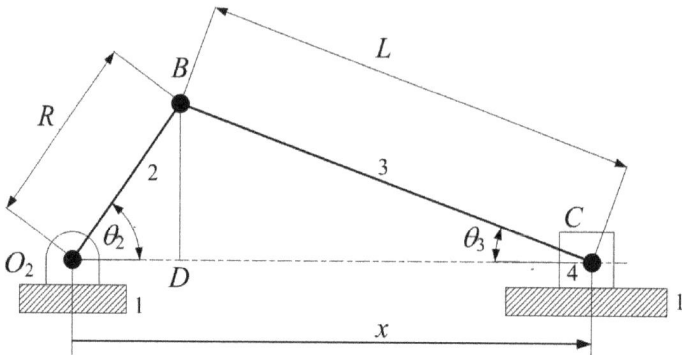

Figure 1. Single-cylinder engine model.

Having determined the first and second-order derivatives of Equation (1) with respect to time t and rearranged the derivative equations, the parameters $\dot{\theta}_3$ and $\ddot{\theta}_3$ can be obtained as:

$$\begin{aligned} \theta_3 &= \arcsin(R\sin(\theta_2)/L) \\ \dot{\theta}_3 &= [R\dot{\theta}_2\cos(\theta_2)]/[L\cos(\theta_3)] \\ \ddot{\theta}_3 &= \left\{ L\dot{\theta}_3^2\sin(\theta_3) + R[\ddot{\theta}_2\cos(\theta_2) - \dot{\theta}_2^2\sin(\theta_2)] \right\}/[L\cos(\theta_3)] \end{aligned} \quad (2)$$

The position of the piston can be written as:

$$x = R\cos\theta_2 + L\cos(\theta_3) \quad (3)$$

The velocity and acceleration of the piston can then be determined by differentiating Equation (3):

$$\begin{aligned} \dot{x} &= -R\dot{\theta}_2\sin\theta_2 - L\dot{\theta}_3\sin(\theta_3) \\ \ddot{x} &= -R[\dot{\theta}_2^2\cos\theta_2 + \ddot{\theta}_2\sin\theta_2] - L[\dot{\theta}_3^2\cos(\theta_3) + \ddot{\theta}_3\sin(\theta_3)] \end{aligned} \quad (4)$$

For the kinematic analysis of a crank–slider, if we have the input values of θ_2, $\dot{\theta}_2$, and $\ddot{\theta}_2$, the angular position, velocity, and acceleration of link 3, as well as the position, velocity, and acceleration of piston 4, can be computed using Equations (1)–(4).

For dynamic force analysis in this paper, the crank–slider system is thought of as being kinematically driven by input angular velocity and acceleration at the input link 2. The kinematic analysis can be accomplished as previously detailed. A free-body diagram of a crank–slider at a particular motion phase is shown in Figure 2. The piston is subject to external forces due to gas pressure P, while the moment M_2 is applied at link 2, so as to meet its prescribed motion. The force analysis can be computed using the following system of equations:

$$[A]\{F\} = \{RHS\} \quad (5)$$

Where:

$$A = \begin{bmatrix} I_{2\times 2} & I_{2\times 2} & 0_{2\times 2} & 0_{2\times 1} & 0_{2\times 1} \\ [-r_{O_2/G_2,y} \quad r_{O_2/G_2,x}] & [-r_{B/G_2,y} \quad r_{B/G_2,x}] & 0_{1\times 2} & 0 & 1 \\ 0_{2\times 2} & -I_{2\times 2} & I_{2\times 1} & 0_{2\times 1} & 0_{2\times 1} \\ 0_{1\times 2} & [r_{B/G_3,y} \quad r_{B/G_3,x}] & [-r_{C/G_3,y} \quad r_{C/G_3,x}] & 0 & 0 \\ 0_{2\times 2} & 0_{2\times 2} & -I_{2\times 2} & \begin{bmatrix} 0 \\ 1 \end{bmatrix} & 0_{2\times 1} \end{bmatrix}$$

$$F = \{F_{12,x}F_{12,y}F_{32,x}F_{32,y}F_{43,x}F_{43,y}F_{14,y}M_2\}^T$$

and: $\mathbf{RHS} = \begin{Bmatrix} m_2 a_{G_2} \\ I_{G_2}\alpha_2 \\ m_3 a_{G_3} \\ I_{G_3}\alpha_3 \\ m_4 a_C - F_P \end{Bmatrix}$.

F_{ij} is the constrained force acting at body i by body j, m_i is the mass of body i, I_{Gi} is the moment of inertia with respect to the axis at the centroid of body i, $r_{i/j}$ is the relative position vector of point i with respect to point j, and a_C and a_{G2} are the acceleration vector of link 4 (piston) and the centre of gravity i in the x–y coordinates, respectively. The gas pressure P (kPa) in one cycle for some engine has been proposed by Asadi et al. [8] as follows:

$$P = \begin{cases} 101.3 & 0 \leq \theta_2 \leq \pi \\ 7.53x^{-1.21} & \pi \leq \theta_2 \leq 2\pi \\ 2950 & 2\pi \leq \theta_2 \leq 13/6\pi \\ 29.8x^{-1.21} & 9/4\pi \leq \theta_2 \leq 3\pi \\ 101.3 & 3\pi \leq \theta_2 \leq 4\pi \end{cases} \text{(kPa)} \qquad (6)$$

Where x in above equation is in Equation (3).

The external force F_P due to gas pressure can be computed by:

$$F_P = (P - P_{atm})A_p \qquad (7)$$

Where P_{atm} is atmosphere pressure (kPa) and A_p is the piston area (m²).

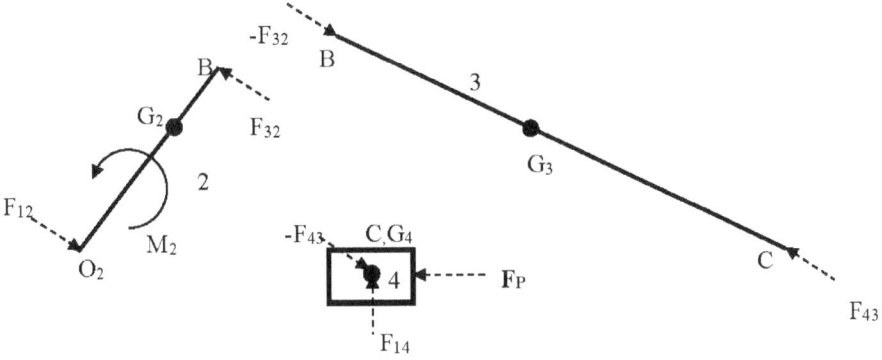

Figure 2. Free-body diagram of a crank–slider.

2.2. Engine Vibration System

A mounted engine system will be modeled as a simple spring-mass system with the rigid mass having six degrees of freedom. Linear spring behavior is assumed as shown in Figure 3, while force and displacement relation can be written as:

$$\mathbf{F} = k(\mathbf{r} - \mathbf{r}_0) = k\delta\mathbf{r} \tag{8}$$

Where k is spring stiffness, $\mathbf{r}_0$ is the position of the unstretched spring, $\mathbf{r}$ is the position vector of the spring under the force $\mathbf{F}$, and $\delta\mathbf{r}$ is a spring translational vector.

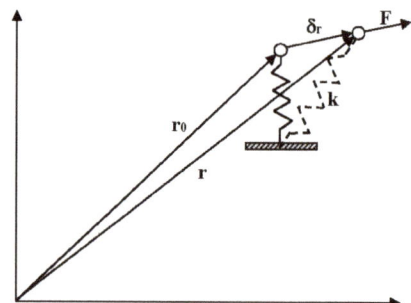

Figure 3. Spring displacement vector in three-dimensional spaces.

A rigid body attached with a number of linear springs is given in Figure 4. From the figure, the position vector of the i-th spring can be expressed with respect to the centroid position as:

$$\mathbf{r}_i = \mathbf{r}_c + \mathbf{r}_{ci} \tag{9}$$

Where $\mathbf{r}_i$ is the position vector of spring I, $\mathbf{r}_c$ is the position vector of the mass centre, and $\mathbf{r}_{ci}$ is the potion vector of spring i with respect to the centroid.

When the body is in motion, the derivation of the vectors in Equation (9) can be written as:

$$\delta\mathbf{r}_i = \delta\mathbf{r}_c + \delta\mathbf{r}_{ci} \tag{10}$$

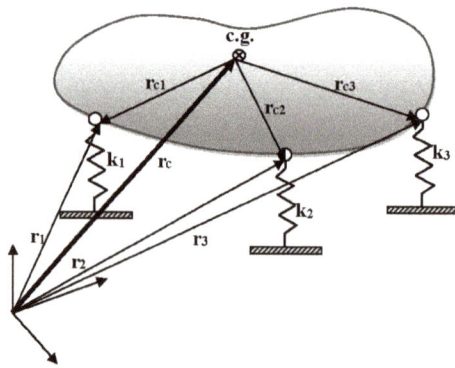

Figure 4. Vector position of spring position relative to the center of mass.

As the centroid and the *i*-th point are at the same body, we can have:

$$\delta r_i = \delta r_c + \delta\theta \times r_{ci} \tag{11}$$

Where $\delta\theta$ is the vector of rotation displacements of the body. The translation and rotation vectors can be defined as:

$$\delta r_c = \begin{bmatrix} u_x \\ u_y \\ u_z \end{bmatrix}, \delta\theta = \begin{bmatrix} \theta_x \\ \theta_y \\ \theta_z \end{bmatrix} \tag{12}$$

Where u_i is the translation in *i*-th direction and θ_i is the angular displacement in the *i*-th axis. The rigid body has six degrees of freedom, as shown in Figure 5. By substituting Equation (12) into Equation (11), we have:

$$\delta r_i = \begin{bmatrix} u_x + \theta_y r_{ci,z} - \theta_z r_{ci,y} \\ u_y + \theta_z r_{ci,x} - \theta_x r_{ci,z} \\ u_z + \theta_x r_{ci,y} - \theta_y r_{ci,x} \end{bmatrix} = \begin{bmatrix} 1 & 0 & 0 & 0 & r_{ci,z} & -r_{ci,y} \\ 0 & 1 & 0 & -r_{ci,z} & 0 & r_{ci,x} \\ 0 & 0 & 1 & r_{ci,y} & -r_{ci,x} & 0 \end{bmatrix} \begin{bmatrix} u_x \\ u_y \\ u_z \\ \theta_x \\ \theta_y \\ \theta_z \end{bmatrix} = T_i d \tag{13}$$

Where T_i is called a transformation matrix for the *i*-th spring and d is the displacement vector of the body. As a result, elastic potential energy of the *i*-th spring is:

$$U_i = \frac{1}{2} k_i \delta r_i^T \delta r = \frac{1}{2} d^T (k_i T_i^T T_i) d = \frac{1}{2} d^T K_i d \tag{14}$$

If the spring-mass system has *n* linear springs, the total elastic potential energy can be computed as:

$$U = \frac{1}{2} d^T \left(\sum_{i=1}^{n} K_i \right) d = \frac{1}{2} d^T K d \tag{15}$$

Where K is the stiffness matrix of the system. The kinetic energy or the work due to inertial forces can be computed as:

$$T = \frac{1}{2} m \dot{\delta r}_c^T \dot{\delta r}_c + \frac{1}{2} \dot{\delta\theta}^T I \dot{\delta\theta} = \frac{1}{2} \dot{d}^T M \dot{d} \tag{16}$$

Where:

$$M = \begin{bmatrix} m & 0 \\ 0 & I \end{bmatrix} = \begin{bmatrix} m & 0 & 0 & 0 & 0 & 0 \\ 0 & m & 0 & 0 & 0 & 0 \\ 0 & 0 & m & 0 & 0 & 0 \\ 0 & 0 & 0 & I_{xx} & -I_{xy} & -I_{xz} \\ 0 & 0 & 0 & -I_{yx} & I_{yy} & -I_{yz} \\ 0 & 0 & 0 & -I_{zx} & -I_{zy} & I_{zz} \end{bmatrix} \tag{17}$$

m is body mass, and I is the matrix of moments of inertia. Adding the work done by external forces to the system, a vibration model of a three-dimensional (3D) spring-mass system can be expressed as:

$$M\ddot{d} + Kd = F \tag{18}$$

Damping can be added to the model using a proportional damping matrix or a Reylize damping i.e.,

$$C = \alpha M + \beta K \tag{19}$$

Where α and β are the proportional damping constants to be specified. The dynamic model then becomes:

$$\mathbf{M}\ddot{\mathbf{d}} + \mathbf{C}\dot{\mathbf{d}} + \mathbf{K}\mathbf{d} = \mathbf{F}(t) \qquad (20)$$

In this work, numerical solutions of the system of differential equations in Equation (20) can be carried out by using Newmark's integration technique [26].

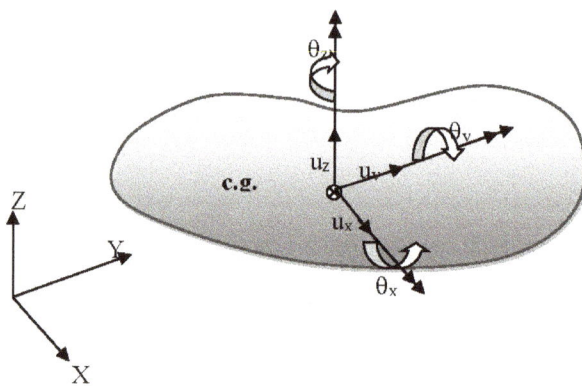

Figure 5. Degree of freedom of rigid body in three-dimensional spaces.

3. Hybrid RPBIL-DE for Multi-Objective Optimisation

The multi-objective design problems of trusses [27,28] and mechanisms [29,30] have been solved with the hybridisation of real-code population-based incremental learning and differential evolution (RPBIL-DE). This optimizer is found to be one of the high-performance multi-objective optimisers, and is therefore selected to solve our problem in this study. The algorithm is extended from References [31,32] by integrating into it the differential evolution (DE) operators in the main procedure of real-code population-based incremental learning (RPBIL), leading to a hybrid algorithm [27]. This technique is developed to avoid a premature convergence searching of RPBIL due to the probability of matrix updating relying on the current best solution. The mutation and crossover of DE are incorporated into a RPBIL procedure. This hybridisation has been proved that it can increase the population diversity for multi-objective optimisation. Additionally, the non-dominated solutions can be chosen using a clustering technique that is detailed in Reference [33]. The RPBIL-DE and DE operator partsare shown in Algorithm 1, where F is a scaling factor, p_c is a crossover probability, and CR is the probability of selecting an element of an offspring c in binomial crossover.

Algorithm 1. Multi-objective RPBIL-DE [27].

Input: N_G(number of generation), N_P (population size), n_I(number of subinterval), N_T(number of trays), objective function name (*fun*), Pareto archive size (N_A)
Output: $\mathbf{x}^{best}$, $\mathbf{f}^{best}$
Initialisation: $P_{ij} = 1/n_I$ for each tray, where P_{ij} is a probability matrix
Main steps
: Generate a real-code population **X** from the probability trays and find $\mathbf{f} = fun(\mathbf{X})$
: Find a Pareto archive **A**
1: For i = 1 to N_G
2: Separate the non-dominated solutions into N_T groups using a clustering technique, and find the centroid $\mathbf{r}_G$ of each group
3: Update each tray P_{ij} based on $\mathbf{r}_G$
4: Generate a real-code population **X** from the probability trays
5: For j = 1 to N_P recombine **X** and **A** using DE operators
5.1: Select **p** from **A** randomly
5.2: Select **q** and **r** from **X** randomly, $\mathbf{q} \neq \mathbf{r}$
5.3: Calculate $\mathbf{c} = \mathbf{p} + F(\mathbf{q} - \mathbf{r})$ (DE/best/1/bin)
5.4: Set c_i into its bound constraints.
5.5: If *rand* < p_c, perform crossover
5.5.1: For k = 1 to n
5.5.2: If *rand* < CR, $y_k = c_k$
5.5.3: Otherwise, $y_{j,k} = p_k$
5.5.4: End
6: End
7: New real-code population is $Y = \{\mathbf{y}_1, \ldots, \mathbf{y}_j, \ldots, \mathbf{y}_{NP}\}$ and find $\mathbf{f} = fun(\mathbf{Y})$
8: Find non-dominated solutions from $\mathbf{Y} \cup \mathbf{A}$ and replace the members in **A** with these solutions
9: If the number of archive members is larger than N_A, remove some of the members using a clustering technique
10: End

For more details of RPBIL-DE, see Reference [27].

4. Design Problems

A simplified forced vibration model is used in this study instead of the more complicated model as presented in Reference [34]. Figure 6 displays the vibration model of a mounted single-cylinder engine where the mass matrix (including mass and moments of inertia) and the mass centre of the engine system are set to be constant. The engine box is attached to the ground by using four liner springs as shown. The origin of the reference rectangular coordinates is located at the engine box mass centre. For a computational procedure, forces and moments due to the moving links of a crank–slider are computed separately. Then, the dynamic force vector is obtained as:

$$\mathbf{F}(t) = \begin{Bmatrix} F_x \\ F_y \\ F_z \\ M_x \\ M_y \\ M_z \end{Bmatrix} = \begin{Bmatrix} F_{21,x} \\ F_{21,y} + F_{41,y} \\ 0 \\ \mathbf{R}_{O/G} \times \mathbf{F}_{21} + \mathbf{R}_{C/G} \times \mathbf{F}_{41} \end{Bmatrix} \quad (21)$$

Where $\mathbf{R}_{C/G} = \mathbf{R}_{O/G} + \begin{Bmatrix} x \\ 0 \\ 0 \end{Bmatrix}$.

The parameters according to the kinematic, force, and vibration analyses are given in Table 1. The external force due to pressure inside the cylinder followed Equation (6). The fidelity of the optimisation result in the next section is affected by the pressure force and inertia force, which will be studied in the next section. International System of Units (SI) are used unless otherwise specified. Figure 7 displays the top and front views of the crank. The parameters used to define the crank dimensions and shape are t_C, l_P, R_{C1}, R_{C2}, R_2, r_C, and ψ. If the values of those parameters are known, the mass centre and moment of inertia of the crank can be calculated. Figure 8 shows the connecting rod where nine design parameters are used to define the shape and dimensions of the rod as l_1, l_2, b_1, b_2, R_1, R_2, t, r_{p1}, and r_{p2}. It should be noted that the crank and rod are created for design demonstration in this paper. For practical applications, their shapes may be defined differently. From Figures 7 and 8, $l_P = l_1$, and $R_2 = R_{C2}$, so 14 parameters are assigned as elements of a design vector as $\mathbf{x} = \{R_{C1}, R_{C2}, r_C, R_2, \psi, l_P, t_C, R_1, r_{p1}, r_{p2}, l_2, t, b_1, \text{and } b_2\}^T$.

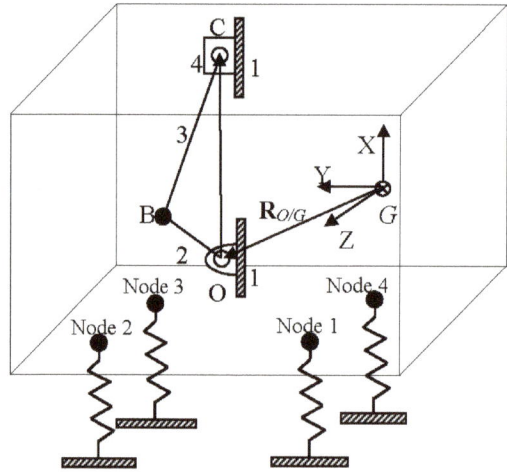

Figure 6. A single-cylinder engine and its engine box.

Table 1. System parameters.

Parameters	Symbols	Quantities
Total engine mass	m	14.528 kg
Piston mass	m_4	0.2 kg
Moment of inertia	$I_{xx}, I_{yy}, I_{zz}, I_{xy}, I_{xz}, I_{yz}$	0.0768, 0.0640, 0.0812, 0, 0, 0 kg-m^2
Centre of gravity	$\mathbf{R}_G$	$[0,0,0]^T$ m
Crank shaft centre	$\mathbf{R}_{O/G}$	$[-0.760, -0.0232, 0.0100]^T$ m
Mount stiffness	k	4×10^6 N/m
Crank length	R	0.1 m
Connecting rod length	L	0.3 m
Material density	ρ	7850 kg/m^3
Piston diameter	d	100 mm

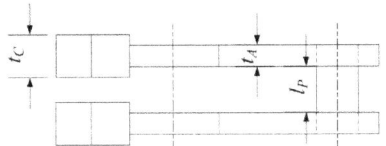

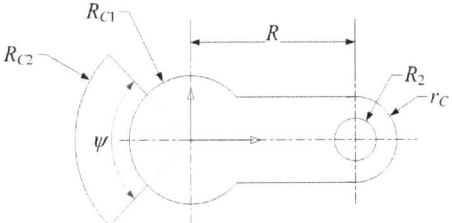

Figure 7. Model of crank and design parameters.

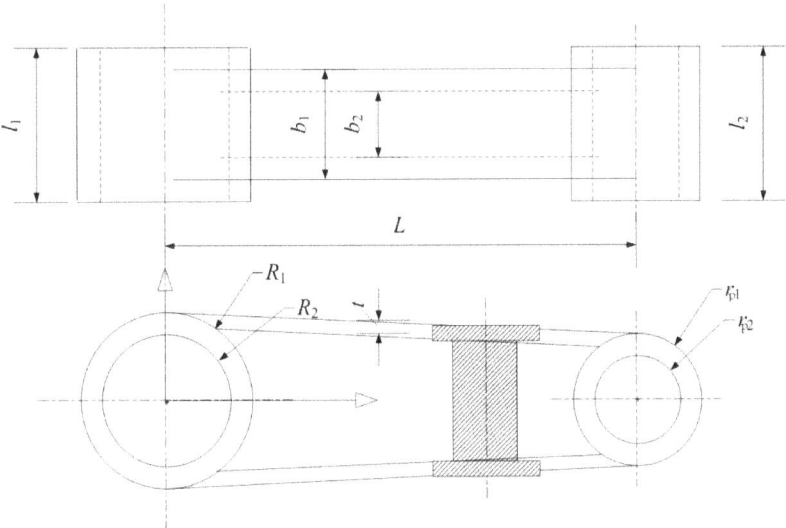

Figure 8. Model of the connecting rod and design parameters.

The multi-objective design problem for this work is posed to find a design variable vector **x** such that:

$$\text{Min: } \mathbf{f} = \{f_1(\mathbf{x}), f_2(\mathbf{x})\}^T \quad (22)$$

Subject to:

$$\sigma_{\text{Crank}} \leq \sigma_{\text{all}}$$

$$\sigma_{\text{Rod}} \leq \sigma_{\text{all}}$$

$$\lambda_{\text{Rod}} \geq 1$$

$$r_{p1} \geq r_{p2} + 0.005 \text{ m}$$

$$l_2 \geq b_1 + 0.005 \text{ m}$$
$$b_1 \geq b_2 + 0.02 \text{ m}$$
$$r_{p1} \geq r_{p2} + 0.005 \text{ m}$$
$$l_1 \geq l_2$$
$$R_1 \geq r_{p1} + 0.002 \text{ m}$$
$$r_{C1} \geq R_2 + 0.002 \text{ m}$$
$$R_{C1} \geq r_{c1} + 0.002 \text{ m}$$
$$R_1 \geq R_2 + 0.002 \text{ m}$$
$$\mathbf{x}^l \leq \mathbf{x} \leq \mathbf{x}^u$$

Where σ_{Crank} is the maximum stress on the crank, σ_{all} is an allowable stress, and σ_{Rod} is the maximum stress on the connecting rod. The bound constraints are set as $\mathbf{x}^l$ = {0.03, 0.05, 0.015, 0.01, $\pi/6$, 0.03, 0.01, 0.03, 0.02, 0.01, 0.02, 0.002, 0.02, and 0.01}^{T}, and $\mathbf{x}^u$ = {0.045, 0.09, 0.04, 0.03, π, 0.05, 0.03, 0.05, 0.03, 0.03, 0.04, 0.005, 0.04, and 0.03}^{T}. The buckling factor for the rod λ_{Rod} is defined as the ratio of critical load to applied load. The first three design constraints are set for structural safety, while the other constraints are assigned for manufacturing tolerances and practicality. The objective functions used in this study are set as $\mathbf{f} = \{u_{rms} + \theta_{rms}, mass\}^T$. The root mean squares (RMS) of the vibration translations (u_{rms}) and rotations (θ_{rms}) over the period $t \in [0, t_{max}]$ can be computed as:

$$u_{rms} = \sqrt{\frac{1}{T}\int (u_{\dot{x}}^2 + u_{\dot{y}}^2 + u_{\dot{z}}^2) dt} \tag{23}$$

and:

$$\theta_{rms} = \sqrt{\frac{1}{T}\int (\theta_{\dot{x}}^2 + \theta_{\dot{y}}^2 + \theta_{\dot{z}}^2) dt} \tag{24}$$

In the function evaluation process, with the given input design vector $\mathbf{x}$ being decoded, the shape and sizing parameters are repaired to meet constraints 4–12, and the inertial properties of the crank and rod can then be computed (the rest of constraints will be handled by using the non-dominated sorting scheme [35]. Then kinematic and dynamic force analyses are carried out as detailed in Section 2. A simple finite element model using a three-dimensional (3D) beam element is applied to determine the maximum stresses on the crank and rod. A buckling factor is also calculated in the cases of the rod. Also, the obtained dynamic forces are used as external excitation for the vibration model of the engine. Having obtained a dynamic response, the objective functions can then be computed.

Three multi-objective optimisation problems with the same design objectives and constraints but different engine rotational speeds are posed as:

OPT1: min $\{u_{rms} + \theta_{rms}, mass\}$, constant crank angular speed 1000 rpm
OPT2: min $\{u_{rms} + \theta_{rms}, mass\}$, constant crank angular speed 1500 rpm
OPT3: min $\{u_{rms} + \theta_{rms}, mass\}$, constant crank angular speed 2000 rpm

The RPBIL-DE is used to tackle each design problem, with 10 runs starting with the same initial population. The population size is set to be 100, while the total number of iterations is 150. The crank and connecting rod are made of alloy steel AISI 4140H with a Young's modulus of 211.65 GPa, σ_{yt} = 417.1 MPa, and density of 7850 kg/m^3. For each finite element analysis, the maximum compressive force over the period of time [0, t_{max}] will be used for buckling calculation.

5. Pressure Force and Inertia Force Validation

The gas pressure force and inertia force exert on the engine box similar to an external force. The fidelity of the both forces is very important in the vibration analysis of the single-cylinder engine, which we will do by considering the forces versus the crank angle. The gas pressure force, inertia force, and total force in one cycle is coded by using MATLAB commercial software over the interval $[0, t_{max}]$, as shown in Figures 9–11 at 1000 rpm. The maximum gas pressure force exerted on the piston head occurred at the maximum torque, but the maximum tensile force occurred during the maximum revolution speed [8]. Figure 9 shows that the maximum gas pressure force is 22,374 N, which occurs in the combustion process. The inertial force due to the slider–crank mechanism in the x direction is show in Figure 10; meanwhile, the maximum inertia in positive direction is 1141N, while the negative inertia force is 2286 N. Figure 11 shows the total force due to the gas pressure force and inertia force that give the maximum gas pressure force as 20,364 N, while the maximum tensile force is 2867 N. All of the diagrams indicate similar trends to the work by Reference [8], while the magnitude of all of the forces are different, as a result of the differences in the system parameters.

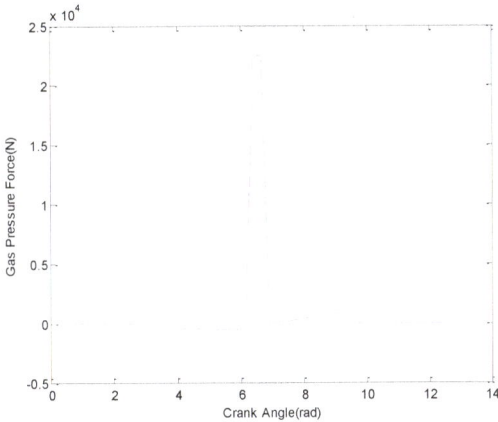

Figure 9. Gas pressure force versus crank angle at 1000 rpm.

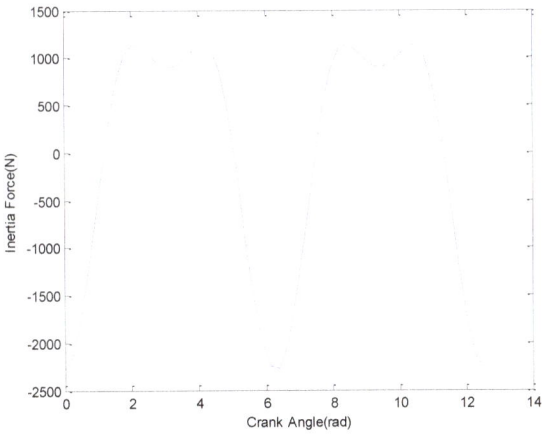

Figure 10. Inertia force due to crank slider versus crank angle at 1000 rpm.

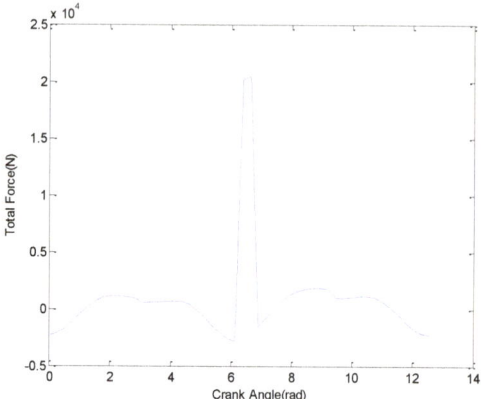

Figure 11. Total force due to gas pressure force and inertia force versus crank angle at 1000 rpm.

6. Design Results

We implemented the RPBIL-DE for solving the design problems, ran 10 OPT1-3 runs, and chose the best front based on the hypervolume indicator of each design problem. According to its definition, the larger the hypervolume, the better the Pareto front. Figures 12–14 show the best front at each engine speed. The results from minimising vibrations (RMS) and the mass of the single cylinder engine (kg) at the engine speed of 1000 rpm are in the ranges of [0.06402 0.06402] and [2.688 4.998] kg, respectively. The vibration and engine mass at the engine speed of 1500 rpm are in the ranges of [0.06252 0.06252] and [2.688 4.986] kg. At the engine speed of 2000 rpm, the results are in the ranges of [0.06012 0.06012] and [2.688 4.957] kg for vibration magnitude and engine mass, respectively. Some selected design solutions of each design problem in Figures 12–14 and the corresponding crank–sliders of each front are illustrated in Figures 15–17.

Dynamic analyses of the crank–sliders in Figures 15–17 are carried out, and the results are shown in Figures 18–23. Figures 18, 20 and 22 display the components of the translational displacements of the six engines, while Figures 19, 21 and 23 display the components of the rotational displacements of the six engines. From our design results, when focusing on vibration amplitude, it is found that our technique can control the vibration amplitude to oscillate in a small strip throughout the Pareto front, while the changing of mass is in accordance with the shape design parameters of the moving parts of a single cylinder.

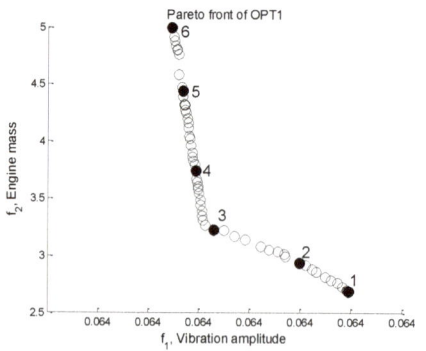

Figure 12. The best Pareto front of OPT1.

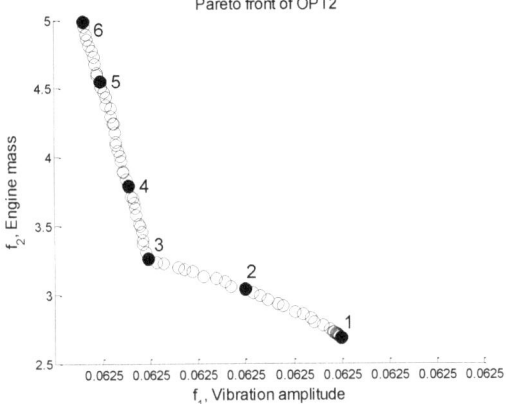

Figure 13. The best Pareto front of OPT2.

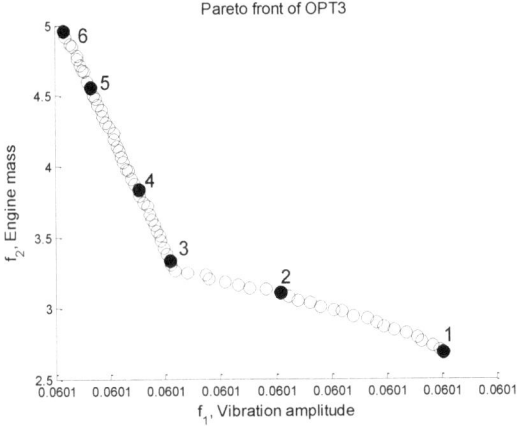

Figure 14. The best Pareto front of OPT3.

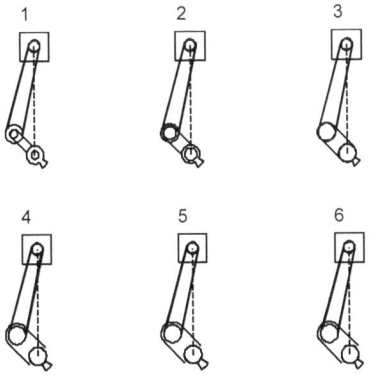

Figure 15. Some selected design solutions of OPT1.

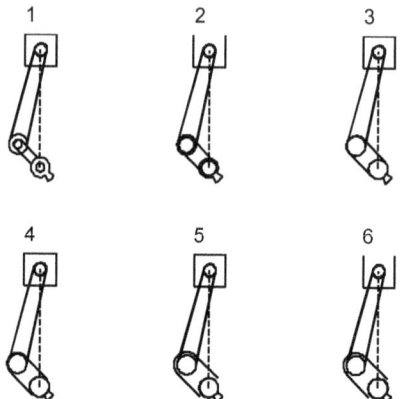

Figure 16. Some selected design solutions of OPT2.

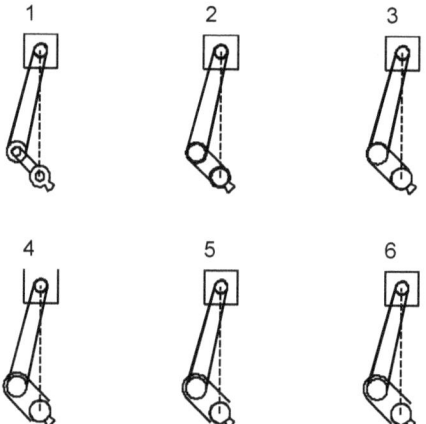

Figure 17. Some selected design solutions of OPT3.

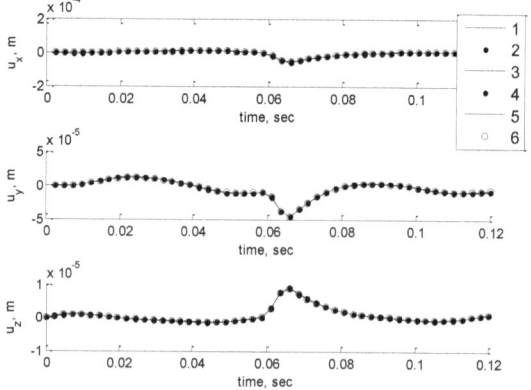

Figure 18. The components of the translational displacements of the six engines in Figure 15.

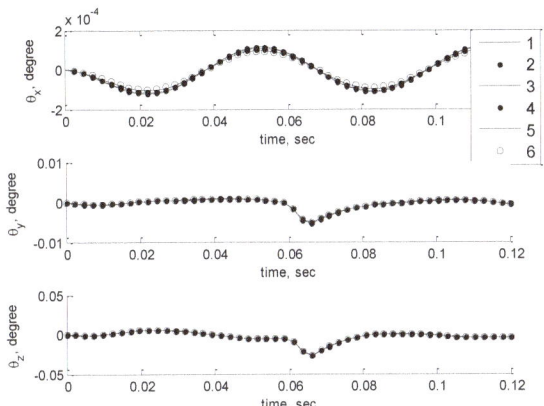

Figure 19. The components of the rotational displacements of the six engines in Figure 15.

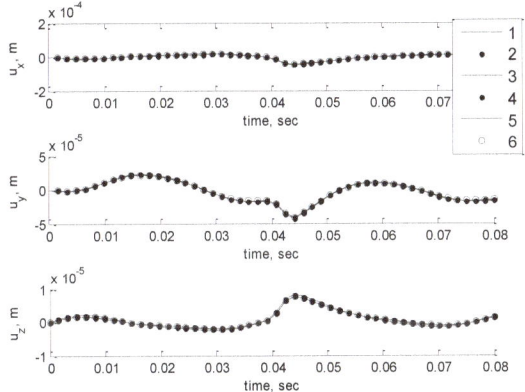

Figure 20. The components of the translational displacements of the six engines in Figure 16.

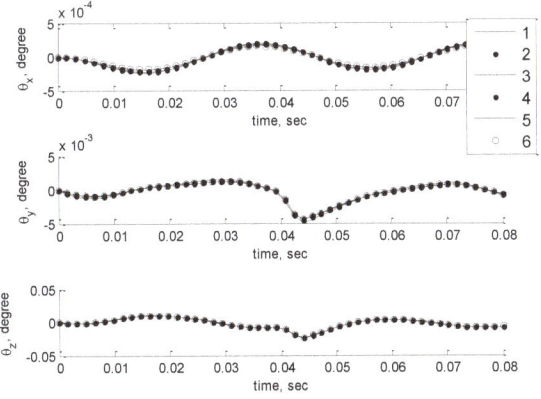

Figure 21. The components of the rotational displacements of the six engines in Figure 16.

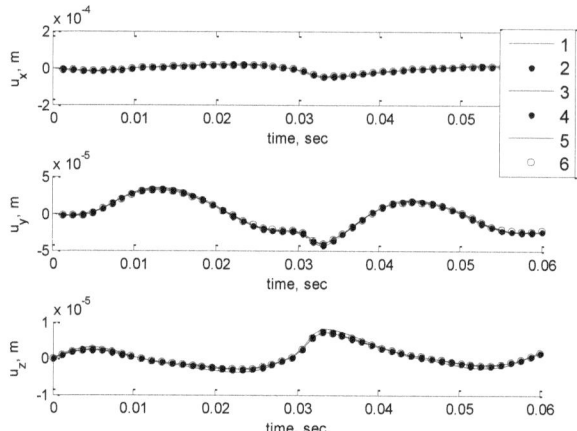

Figure 22. The components of the translational displacements of the six engines in Figure 17.

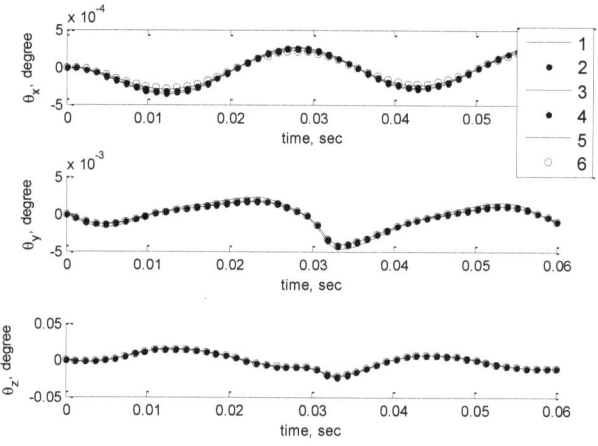

Figure 23. The components of the rotational displacements of the six engines in Figure 17.

7. Conclusions

The vibration suppression of a single-cylinder engine by means of multi-objective evolutionary optimisation is proposed. Simple kinematic and dynamic force analyses of a single cylinder are presented. The multi-objective design problems are posed to minimise the mass of the engine mechanism and vibration amplitudes of the engine system. We implemented RPBIL-DE to solve the design problems. The obtained design solutions are illustrated and analysed. The computation results reveal that the proposed design process for forming the moving parts of a single-cylinder engine is practical. Our technique can control the vibration amplitude to oscillate in a small strip throughout the Pareto front by optimisation of the moving parts of a single-cylinder engine. With the use of RPBIL-DE, multiple solutions for decision-making can be obtained within one optimisation run. Future work will be the use of three-dimensional finite element analysis for calculating the design constraints. This could be a time-consuming process, which may require a surrogate-assisted MOEA. Also, different shapes of the crank and connecting rod should be studied.

Author Contributions: Suwin Sleesongsom and Sujin Bureerat conceived and designed the numerical experiments; Suwin Sleesongsom performed the numerical experiments; Suwin Sleesongsom and Sujin Bureerat analyzed the data; Suwin Sleesongsom wrote the paper.

Acknowledgments: The authors are grateful for the financial support provided by the Thailand Research Fund, and King Mongkut's Institute of Technology Ladkrabang.

Conflicts of Interest: The authors declare no conflict of interest.

References

1. Paul, B. *Kinematics and Dynamics of Planar Machinery*; Pretice-Hall: New Jersey, NJ, USA, 1979.
2. Lowen, G.G.; Tapper, F.R.; Berkof, R.S. Balancing of linkages-an update. *Mech. Mach. Theory* **1983**, *18*, 213–220. [CrossRef]
3. Zhang, S.M.; Chen, J.H. The Optimum balance of shaking force and shaking moment of linkage. *Mech. Mach. Theory* **1994**, *30*, 589–597.
4. Snyman, J.A.; Heyns, P.S.; Vermeulen, P.J. Vibration isolation of a mounted engine through optimization. *Mech. Mach. Theory* **1995**, *30*, 109–118. [CrossRef]
5. Chiou, S.T.; Bai, G.J.; Chang, W.K. Optimum balancing designs of drag-link drive of mechanical presses for precision cutting. *Int. J. Mach. Tools Manuf.* **1998**, *38*, 131–141. [CrossRef]
6. Sleesongsom, S. Vibration suppression of a single cylinder engine by using normalized normal constraint. In Proceedings of the TISD2006, Khon Kaen, Thailand, 25–27 January 2006; pp. 342–349.
7. Messac, A.; Ismail-Yahaya, A.; Mattson, C.A. The normalized normal constraint method for generating the Pareto frontier. *Struct. Multidiscip. Optim.* **2002**, *25*, 86–98. [CrossRef]
8. Asadi, M.R.; Rasekh, M.; Golmohammadi, A.; Jafari, A.; Kheiralipour, K.; Borghei, A.M. Optimization of connecting rod of MF-285 tractor. *J. Agric. Technol.* **2010**, *6*, 649–662.
9. Cevik, M.; Kanpolat, E.; Rebbert, M. *Shape Optimization of a Single Cylinder Engine Crankshaft*; SAE Technical Paper 2011-01-1077; SAE: Detroit, MI, USA, 2011. [CrossRef]
10. Lydia Mahanthi, D.; Venkata Siva Murali, C.; Mohan, R. Design Analysis and Optimization of a Four Stroke Single Cylinder Diesel Engine Piston. *Imp. J. Interdiscip. Res.* **2017**, *3*, 719–725.
11. Ganguly, A.; Bhatia, N.; Agarwal, V.; Mohite, U. *Balancing Optimization of a Motorcycle Engine Crankshaft for Vibration Reduction*; SAE Technical Paper 2016-01-1060; SAE: Detroit, MI, USA, 2016.
12. Spiekerman, C.E.; Radcliffe, C.J.; Goodman, E.D. Optimal design and simulation of vibration isolation system. *J. Mech. Trans. Autom. Des.* **1985**, *107*, 271–276. [CrossRef]
13. Swanson, D.A.; Wu, H.T.; Ashrafiuon, H. Optimization of aircraft engine suspension systems. *J. Aircr.* **1993**, *30*, 978–984. [CrossRef]
14. Liette, J.; Dreyer, J.T.; Singh, R. Critical examination of isolation system design paradigms for a coupled powertrain and frame: Partial torque roll axis decoupling methods given practical constraints. *J. Sound Vib.* **2014**, *333*, 7089–7108. [CrossRef]
15. Qin, W.; Shangguan, W.Q.; Luo, G.; Luo, G.; Xie, Z. A method for estimating mount isolations of powertrain mounting systems. *J. Sound Vib.* **2018**, *426*, 278–295. [CrossRef]
16. Tao, J.S.; Lui, G.R.; Lam, K.Y. Design optimization of marine engine-mount system. *J. Sound Vib.* **2000**, *235*, 477–494. [CrossRef]
17. Kaul, S.; Dhingra, A.K. Kriging modeling for engine mount optimization in motorcycles. In Proceedings of the IMECE2009, Lake Buena Vista, FL, USA, 13–19 November 2009; pp. 1–12.
18. Fan, R.L.; Wang, J.Z.; Lu, Z.H. Vibration isolation optimization for automotive engine mounting system. *Trans. Chin. Soc. Intern. Combust. Eng.* **2010**, *28*, 269–274.
19. Li, Q.; Zhao, J.C.; Zhao, B.; Zhu, X.S. Parameter optimization of a hydraulic engine mount based on a genetic neural network. *Proc. Inst. Mech. Eng. Part D J. Automob. Eng.* **2009**, *223*, 1109–1117. [CrossRef]
20. Lee, D.H.; Hwang, W.S.; Kim, C.M. Design sensitivity analysis and optimization of an engine mount system using an FRF-based substructuring method. *J. Sound Vib.* **2002**, *255*, 383–397. [CrossRef]
21. Ohadi, A.R.; Maghsoodi, G. Simulation of engine vibration on nonlinear hydraulic engine mounts. *J. Vib. Acoust.* **2007**, *129*, 417–424. [CrossRef]
22. Bi, F.R.; Du, X.F.; Shao, K.; Zhang, J.H. Block design of diesel engine for low vibration based on topography optimization. *Trans. Chin. Soc. Intern. Combust. Eng.* **2010**, *28*, 459–463.

23. Jia, W.X.; Hao, Z.Y.; Xu, H.M. Light-weight design of single cylinder engine block based on structure optimization. *J. Zhejiang Univ.* **2008**, *2*, 224.
24. Ayarani-N, M.H.; Yao, X.; Xu, H. Meta-heuristic algorithms in car engine design: A literature survey. *IEEE Trans. Evol. Comput.* **2015**, *19*, 609–629. [CrossRef]
25. Ma, F.; Yin, H.; Wei, L.; Tian, G.; Gao, H. Design and optimization of IPM motor considering flux weakening capability and vibration for electric vehicle application. *Sustainability* **2018**, *10*, 1533. [CrossRef]
26. Newmark's Method of Direct Integration. Available online: http://www.softeng.rl.ac.uk/st/projects/felib3/Docs/html/Intro/intro-node52.html (accessed on 25 May 2018).
27. Pholdee, N.; Bureerat, S. Hybridisation of real-code population-based incremental learning and differential evolution for multiobjective design of trusses. *Inf. Sci.* **2013**, *223*, 136–152. [CrossRef]
28. Pholdee, N.; Bureerat, S. Hybrid real-code population-based incremental learning and approximate gradients for multi-objective truss design. *Eng. Optim.* **2014**, *46*, 1032–1051. [CrossRef]
29. Sleesongsom, S.; Bureerat, S. Multiobjective optimization of a steering linkage. *J. Mech. Sci. Technol.* **2016**, *30*, 3681–3691. [CrossRef]
30. Sleesongsom, S.; Bureerat, S. Optimization of Steering Linkage Including the Effect of McPherson Strut Front Suspension. *Lect. Notes Comput. Sci.* **2018**, *10941*, 612–623.
31. Bureerat, S. Hybrid population-based incremental learning using real codes. *Lect. Notes Comput. Sci.* **2011**, *6683*, 379–391.
32. Das, S.; Suganthan, P.N. Differential evolution: A survey of the state-of-the-art. *IEEE Trans. Evolut. Comput.* **2011**, *15*, 4–31. [CrossRef]
33. Bandyopadhyay, S.; Saha, S.; Maulik, U.; Deb, K. A simulated annealing-based multiobjective optimization algorithm: AMOSA. *IEEE Trans. Evolut. Comput.* **2008**, *12*, 269–283. [CrossRef]
34. Muravyov, A.; Hutton, S.G. Analysis of an engine-mount system with time-dependent mass and velocity matrix. *J. Sound Vib.* **1998**, *209*, 143–162. [CrossRef]
35. Deb, K.; Pratap, A.; Meyarivan, T. Constrained test problems for multi-objective evolutionary optimization. *Lect. Notes Comput. Sci.* **2001**, *1993/2001*, 284–298.

© 2018 by the authors. Licensee MDPI, Basel, Switzerland. This article is an open access article distributed under the terms and conditions of the Creative Commons Attribution (CC BY) license (http://creativecommons.org/licenses/by/4.0/).

Article

Ecological Wall Systems as an Element of Sustainable Development—Cost Issues

Wojciech Drozd * and Agnieszka Leśniak

Institute of Construction Management, Tadeusz Kościuszko Cracow University of Technology, Warszawska 24 St., 31-155 Kraków, Poland; alesniak@izwbit.pk.edu.pl
* Correspondence: wdrozd@ztob.pk.edu.pl

Received: 31 May 2018; Accepted: 26 June 2018; Published: 28 June 2018

Abstract: Building construction based on ecological, locally available, and slightly processed materials have a positive effect on the environment and local economy. Due to its simplicity, and thus possibility to erect a building on one's own and using inexpensive materials, it may potentially become a solution to satisfy the continuously growing demand for residential buildings. In the paper, three variants of ecological external walls were proposed: a wall made of clay blocks insulated with mineral wool boards; a wall made of clay compacted in formwork insulated with mineral wool boards; and a wooden frame structure filled with straw bales and cladded with fiberboards. The layers of the walls were chosen in such a manner that the heat transfer coefficient values for the studied variants are as equal as possible (0.2 W/m^{2}K), thus allowing for a reliable comparative study. The cost calculation of each variant of walls construction was made. The obtained results allow selection of a more advantageous solution.

Keywords: ecological building; clay blocks; compacted clay; straw bales; cost calculation

1. Introduction

The basic need of all people is to have their own shelter—a home in which they can feel safe and well. For thousands of years, men have been using raw materials available in their close vicinity for construction purposes. Until today, we admire ancient structures that have endured and continue to delight us with their beauty. At present, buildings should be designed, constructed, operated, and demolished in accordance with the requirements of sustainable development [1]. This can be achieved by a responsible choice of the construction site, building materials, and the means of project implementation, and then by building maintenance and demolition, so as to avoid degradation of the environment [2]. The construction industry has an important role in the creation of the construction environment and its impact has to be measured with relation to the way it contributes to air pollution, land use and contamination, usage of resources, water and materials depletion, water pollution, impact on human health, and climate change [3,4]. In reference [5], the authors proved that the results of developing sustainable architecture are based on changing the function of a building from a linear approach to a closed circulation plan, where a building can evolve from a consumer of energy and other resources into a virtually self-sufficient unit. Investors include green aspects in their construction projects more frequently [5–7]. They increasingly desire natural buildings where special attention is paid to the use of ecological materials (such as straw, wood, and clay), energy saving during the building process, and the health of residents. These can become an alternative for traditional buildings [8].

This study concerns building structures made of local and only slightly processed materials, including straw and clay. The technologies providing for the use of these construction materials are poorly known and not much popularised. Wall materials used in Poland include: cellular concrete produced from aerated cement-lime, lime or cement mortar, ceramic materials including bricks and hollow blocks, and light expanded clay aggregate concrete blocks. One of the most popular solutions are ceramic blocks due to their relatively low price, low thermal conductivity, and a relatively short time of wall masonry. However, in comparison to the materials that are used in natural building, ceramic hollow bricks are characterized by a higher degree of processing, and thus also lower environmental compatibility. Buildings based on natural materials are available for everyone, and they meets the criteria of sustainable development—development in which the environment and people are put first. This sort of building makes it possible to engage occupants, friends, and other people—who do not have to possess specialist qualifications—in the construction process. It allows for an aware response to the demands of sustainable development, including social integration. The simple building construction technique of straw bales or light clay allows for employing excluded persons, who are able to build homes for their own needs by themselves.

2. Literature Review

Research in the field of natural building technologies is limited. Among them: in [9], a comparison of the mechanical performance of structural elements built in three basic techniques—earth block (adobe) masonry, rammed earth, and cob—is presented. Up to present, few studies are available concerning the mechanical behavior of straw bales in buildings. Such a study is presented in reference [10], which aims at investigating the behavior of straw bales and leads to recommendations for the required bales densities. In reference [11], the viability of straw bale construction has recently been investigated, in particular, its resistance to moisture. Similarly in reference [12], two options for the use of straw to fill envelop walls were investigated in the Andean Patagonian region: the direct use of straw bales, whether in whole or in halves, and the manufacturing of straw–clay blocks. All the straw options analyzed result in significantly better thermal performance than current choices of fired bricks or concrete blocks that are commonly used in the region. In turn, in reference [13] a straw bale house located in Bavaria, Germany was evaluated. The experimental work included compression tests, moisture content, thermal stability of the bales, and pH. In article [14], authors examined the use and accuracy of a moisture probe used in the walls of a straw-bale building. This study has confirmed the use of wood-disc sensors as a robust technique for monitoring moisture content of straw-bale walls. The measurements from a number of moisture probes placed in the walls of a case study straw-bale building over a two-year period are presented. Similarly, in article [15], the results were drawn from a study on moisture monitoring in straw bale construction, including the development of an empirical equation which relates straw moisture content to surrounding microclimate relative humidity and temperature. Article [16] mentioned results from a study on the thermal conductivity of some natural plaster materials that could be used for straw bale buildings.

When analyzing the cost aspects of natural building, please pay attention to a few studies. In reference [17], the authors present green buildings that provide such financial benefits such as lower energy, waste, and water costs; lower environmental and emissions costs; lower operational and maintenance costs; as well as the increased productivity and health that conventional buildings do not possess. The comparison of traditional and modern buildings in relation to environmentally-efficient parameters can be found in reference [8,18]. In reference [2], the authors have compared walls form natural materials (straw-bale technology) with walls constructed in the traditional technology: made of cellular concrete blocks and of a ceramic air-brick insulated with Styrofoam. The evaluation criteria were the following: the cost, workload, thermal insulation, and environmental performance of the variants. The analysis revealed that the best solution for the weights assumed in the criteria was the brick wall. This solution received the highest global evaluation resulting from the comparison of the variants in relation to the chosen four criteria. It has to be mentioned that the most important criterion was the price. The natural variant of walls was the most advantageous from the insulation and environmental perspective; however, it had the worst parameters concerning cost and workload. In [19], the authors pay attention to the whole life cost and environmental impact of buildings to encourage key stakeholders to make more sustainable choices. In their opinion, a perception that more energy efficient and environmentally-friendly buildings cost more to build from the outset should be questioned.

This paper contains an analysis of three types of exterior walls made using natural building technologies: clay block wall with insulation layer consisting of mineral wool boards; a wall made of clay compacted in formwork with thermal insulation of mineral wool boards; and a wooden structure/framework filled with straw bales and covered with fiberboard. Wall layers have been selected so as to ensure that the values of heat transfer 'U' are close to each other, reaching 0.2 W/m²K. This selection of layers allowed for making a reliable comparison of wall construction costs. The article is a continuation of a research study carried out by its authors in this subject matter. In reference [7], they have presented a comparative study of these walls regarding construction time. In this article the intended purpose has been to show a comparative study for the same walls regarding their construction costs. As a matter of fact, studies on low-impact building do not show any schemes to calculate implementation costs.

3. Selection of an Object for Analysis

The design of a two-storey detached house has been used as an object for carrying out the calculations and comparative analysis. The number of exterior and interior load-bearing walls, as well as window openings and door-ways, will be used as an example for comparing construction costs. Depending on the applied materials, the wall or its individual components will be measured in m³ or m².

Due to different wall thickness values (depending on the material and technology), the external dimensions for a non-plastered structure according to the draft model have been used in the calculations. It means that the dimensions of the analyzed building are the same for each of the technologies. Therefore, the building is sized 8.20 × 8.60 m.

4. Cost Calculation Method

The detailed cost calculation method was used for building walls cost estimating. This type of calculation involves determining an estimated price of the construction works, as products of the volume of unit works, material expenditures and their prices, and the added direct costs and profit, respectively, including tax on goods and services, according to the formula [20]

$$C_k = \sum L \cdot (n \cdot c + K_{pj} + Z_j) + P_v \qquad (1)$$

where:
C_k—estimated price of the construction works,
L—volume of specified work quantity units,
$n \cdot c$—direct costs per work quantity unit,
K_{pj}—indirect costs per work quantity unit,
Z_j—calculated profit per work quantity unit,
P_v—tax on goods and services.

The indirect costs, profit, and tax on goods and services are excluded in cost calculations carried out for the purposes of comparative analysis of selected wall execution variants. It is because they are usually calculated in percentages from a given basis so they will not affect the results of the comparison.

The direct costs per work quantity unit are calculated according to the formula

$$n \cdot c = n_r \cdot c_r + \sum n_m \cdot c_{mn} + M_{pj} + \sum n_s \cdot c_s \qquad (2)$$

where:
n—unit expenditures: labor—n_r, materials—n_m, work, equipment and technological transport facilities–n_s,

c—unit costs of production factors, including: estimated labor rate per hour—c_r, unit material purchase prices—c_{mn}, unit prices of machine-hours for equipment and means of technological transport—c_s, M_{pj}—cost of supplementary materials per work quantity unit.

The direct costs of the analyzed works are calculated according to the following guidelines:

- Unit costs/expenditures of labor, materials, and equipment (*n*) are taken from the National Contractors Estimator (KNR) or derived by analogy.
- For those natural building works where no adequate catalogues exist, the costs/expenditures are derived on the basis of the available literature [21,22].
- Average prices from 'Sekocenbud' pricelist for the fourth quarter of 2017 will be applied as unit prices of production factors (materials with purchase costs and equipment). The Sekocenbud is a Polish newsletter which includes quarterly information about the prices of construction production factors in the Polish construction market. There are material prices, labor prices and prices of construction equipment lease.
- The estimated man-hour rate is 4.00 EUR/m-h.
- No cost of rent or providing additional scaffoldings is calculated for the analyzed works.
- It is assumed that the clay is obtained from the foundation trenches, thus its cost is EUR 0.00.
- It is assumed that the price of chopped straw, which is a thinning addition to the clay mass, is EUR 0.00.
- The cost of straw bales 31 × 41 × 70 cm is assumed to be 0.48 EUR per unit [23].

5. Bill of Quantities of Exterior Load-Bearing Walls of the Analyzed Building

The bill of quantities of exterior walls in the building has been developed taking into account adequate National Contractors Estimators (KNR). The names of the direct works contain the numbers of the catalogues being used or the references to items in the literature, if there is no adequate catalogue item for a given work.

5.1. Walls of Clay Blocks

The first studied structure a wall variant was made of 10 × 25 × 38 cm clay blocks insulated with mineral wool boards. The structural layer of the wall is 38-cm thick (Figure 1). On the outside, the wall is insulated with 16 cm-thick mineral wool boards and covered with lime plaster. On the inside, the wall is covered with a two-layer clay plaster.

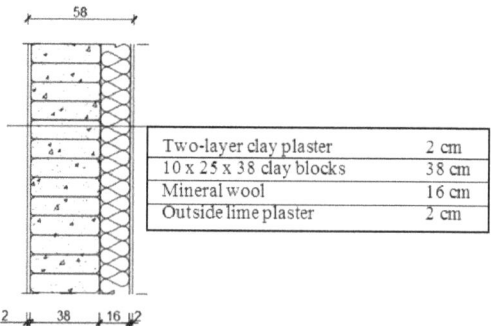

Figure 1. Cross-section of clay block wall. Source: own study.

Table 1 presents the calculations for the exterior walls made using the clay block technology.

Table 1. Bill of quantities of exterior walls in the clay block technology.

Outside Walls (Own Study. Basis [11])				
Level	Spec.	Qty. [m²]	Qty. [m²]	Qty. [m³]
Ground floor	Walls	83.01	70.22	26.68
	Openings	−12.79		
Attic	Walls	49.986	43.39	16.49
	Openings	−6.6		
		SUM	113.60	43.17
Various Works (Own Study. Basis [11])				
Level		Qty. [m]		
Ground floor		14.00		
Attic		56.80		
Prefabricated Heads (KNR 202/126/5)				
Level		Qty. [m]		
Ground floor		8.60		
Attic		3.00		
		SUM	11.60	
Thermal Insulation of Mineral Wool (KNR 33/2/4(1))				
Level	Spec.	Qty. [m²]	Qty. [m²]	
Ground floor	Walls	97.07	82.84	
	Openings	−14.23		
Attic	Walls	54.27	47.67	
	Openings	−6.6		
		SUM	130.51	
Outside Lime Plaster (KNR 202/906/2)				
Level	Spec.	Qty. [m²]	Qty. [m²]	
Ground floor	Walls	98.95	84.72	
	Openings	−14.23		
Attic	Walls	55.858	49.26	
	Openings	−6.6		
		SUM	133.98	
Double-Layer Inside Clay Plaster—1 Layer (Own Study. Basis [11])				
Level	Spec.	Qty. [m²]	Qty. [m²]	
Ground floor	Walls	78.91	67.56	
	Openings	−11.35		
Attic	Walls	48.76	42.16	
	Openings	−6.6		
		SUM	109.72	

Source: own study.

5.2. Walls of Compacted Clay

The second variant solution is the wall made of clay compacted in the formwork whose structural thickness is 30 cm (Figure 2). The formwork is demountable panels. The remaining wall layers are the same as in the clay block wall.

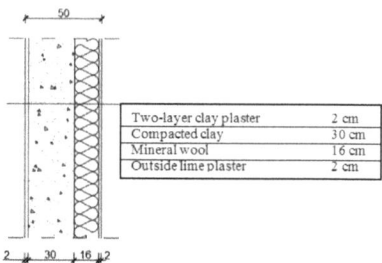

Figure 2. Cross-section of the wall made of clay compacted in formwork. Source: own.

Table 2 presents the calculations for the exterior walls made using the technology of clay rammed in formwork.

Table 2. Bill of quantities of exterior walls in the technology of clay compacted in formwork.

Outside Walls (Own Study, Basis [11])				
Level	Spec.	Qty. [m²]	Qty. [m²]	Qty. [m³]
Ground floor	Walls	83.87	71.08	21.32
	Openings	−12.79		
Attic	Walls	50.78	44.18	13.25
	Openings	−6.6		
		SUM	115.26	34.58
Various Works (Own Study, Basis [12])				
Component		Qty. [m]		
Shuttering		32.32		
Levelling layer under floor beams		46.88		
Prefabricated Heads (KNR 202/126/5)				
Level		Qty. [m]		
Ground floor		8.60		
Attic		3.00		
SUM		11.60		
Thermal Insulation of Mineral Wool (KNR 33/2/4 (1))				
Level	Spec.	Qty. [m²]	Qty. [m²]	
Ground floor	Walls	97.07	82.84	
	Openings	−14.23		
Attic	Walls	54.27	47.67	
	Openings	−6.6		
		SUM	130.51	
Outside Lime Plaster (KNR 202/906/2)				
Level	Spec.	Qty. [m²]	Qty. [m²]	
Ground floor	Walls	98.95	84.72	
	Openings	−14.23		
Attic	Walls	55.86	49.26	
	Openings	−6.6		
		SUM	133.98	
Double-Layer Inside Clay Plaster—1 Layer (Own Study, Basis [12])				
Level	Spec.	Qty. [m²]	Qty. [m²]	
Ground floor	Walls	80.63	69.28	
	Openings	−11.35		
Attic	Walls	49.81	43.21	
	Openings	−6.6		
		SUM	112.50	

Source: own study.

5.3. Walls Made Using the 'Straw-Bale' Technology

The third variant is the wall made of small 31 × 41 × 70 cm straw bales placed in a wooden frame structure (Figure 3). The frame structure will be erected in the timber-frame house technology where the posts are made as frames—so-called ladders. The wooden frame skeleton will be clad on both sides with 12-mm fiberboard for good adhesion and improved thermal insulation. The wall will have a lime plaster on the outside and a two-layer clay plaster on the inside.

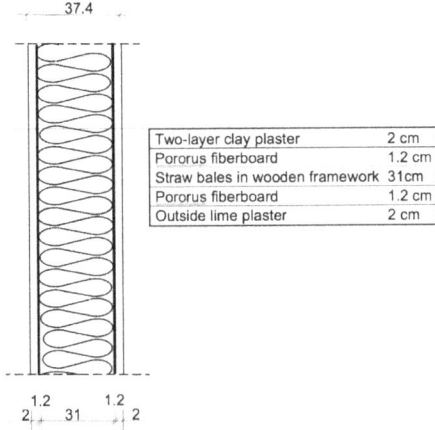

Figure 3. Cross-section of the wall made using the straw-bale technology. Source: own study.

Table 3 presents the calculations for the exterior walls made using the 'straw-bale' technology.

Table 3. Bill of quantities of the exterior walls using the 'straw-bale' technology.

Framework Structure—Columns of Outside Walls (KNR 21/4001/1)			
Level	Spec.	Qty. [m²]	Qty. [m²]
Ground floor	Walls	86.95	74.16
	Openings	−12.79	
Attic	Walls	52.63	46.03
	Openings	−6.6	
		SUM	120.19
Framework Structure—Girts and Ground Beams (KNR 21/4002/1) (KNR 21/4002/17 (1))			
Component		Qty. [m]	
Ground beams		67.01	
Girts		67.01	
Framework Structure—Heads (KNR 21/4003/8)			
Level		Qty. [m]	
Ground floor		60.00	
Attic		3.00	
SUM		11.60	
Thermal Insulation of Straw Bales (Analogy to KNR 202/613/6)			
Level	Spec.	Qty. [m²]	Qty. [m²]
Ground floor	Walls	86.95	72.72
	Openings	−14.23	
Attic	Walls	52.63	46.03
	Openings	−6.6	
		SUM	118.75

Table 3. Cont.

Framework Structure—Columns of Outside Walls (KNR 21/4001/1)			
Level	Spec.	Qty. [m²]	Qty. [m²]
Covering Framework Structure with Fibreboard Inside and Outside (KNR 21/4004/4 (1))			
Level	Spec.	Qty. [m²]	Qty. [m²]
Ground floor	Walls	182.42	153.96
	Openings	−28.46	
Attic	Walls	107.37	94.17
	Openings	−13.20	
		SUM	248.13
Outside Lime Plaster (KNR 202/906/2)			
Level	Spec.	Qty. [m²]	Qty. [m²]
Ground floor	Walls	98.95	84.72
	Openings	−14.23	
Attic	Walls	55.86	49.26
	Openings	−6.6	
		SUM	133.98
Double-Layer Inside Clay Plaster—1 Layer			
Level	Spec.	Qty. [m²]	Qty. [m²]
Ground floor	Walls	83.61	72.26
	Openings	−11.35	
Attic	Walls	51.63	45.03
	Openings	−6.6	
		SUM	117.29

Source: own study based on [14].

6. Cost Calculation for the Construction of the Walls in the Analyzed Variants

6.1. Cost Calculation for the Construction of the Clay Block Walls

Own calculation items have been set in order to determine the direct costs for the works involved in the clay preparation and incorporation, based on the subject literature content [22,23].

The calculation of the costs involved in erecting a division wall made of clay blocks includes the construction of external load-bearing walls, the making of openings in the walls, the placing of prefabricated heads, insulation of the walls with mineral wool boards, and applying external and internal plasterwork (Tables 4–7).

Table 4 presents the calculation of labor cost for the clay block walls.

Table 4. Labor cost for clay block wall.

Meas.	Total qty.	Price [EUR/m-h]	Value [EUR]
m-h	159.00	3.85	614.07
m-h	1.28	3.85	4.93
m-h	322.50	3.85	1241.63
m-h	251.25	3.85	967.31
m-h	124.63	3.85	479.83
m-h	142.06	3.85	546.90
		SUM	3854.70

Source: own study.

Table 5 presents the calculation of the material cost for the clay block walls.

Table 5. Cost of materials for clay block wall.

Item	Name	Meas.	Total qty.	Price [EUR]	Value [EUR]
1	Reinforced concrete head beam L19N/150 length 149 cm	pcs.	7.89	7.33	57.83
2	Clay blocks 10 × 25 × 38 cm	m³	43.17	0.00	0.00
3	Raw building clay	m³	38.9	0.00	0.00
4	Natural sand	m³	9.71	4.96	48.16
5	Mineral wool board Isover PT80 thickness 60 mm	m²	140.95	5.57	785.09
6	Mineral wool board Isover PT80 thickness 100 mm	m²	140.95	9.55	1346.07
7	Chopped straw	kg	272.19	0.00	0.00
8	Regular lime mortar for building	m³	0.42	35.41	14.87
9	Cement-lime mortar M2 (m.15)	m³	3.31	34.21	113.24
10	Cement-lime mortar M7 (m.50)	m³	0.09	42.28	3.81
11	Clay mortar	m³	2.19	0.00	0.00
12	Dry adhesive mortar for mineral wool boards, for light insulation—Atlas Rocker W-20	kg	522.04	0.26	135.73
	Supplementary outlays		1.00	2.80	2.80
				SUM	2507.60

Source: own study.

Table 6 presents the calculation of the equipment cost for the clay block walls.

Table 6. Equipment cost for clay block wall.

Item	Name	Meas.	Total qty.	Price [EUR/m-h]	Value [EUR]
1	Mixing pump 1.1–3.3 m³/h (1)	m-h	13.57	6.68	90.65
2	Dropside truck up to 5 t (1)	m-h	4.18	13.75	57.48
3	Electric central mast-type hoist 0.5 t	m-h	14.50	1.92	27.84
				SUM	175.97

Source: own study.

Table 7 presents the total cost of erecting the clay block walls for the analyzed building.

Table 7. Total cost of erecting clay block wall.

The Type of Cost	Cost [EUR]	Participation [%]
The labour	3854.70	60.00
The materials	2507.60	37.00
The equipment	175.97	3.00
SUM	6538.27	100.00

Source: own study.

In order to obtain the average cost of making 1 m² of a division wall of clay blocks, it is required to divide the total cost by the total area of the walls

$$C_{av} = \frac{6538.27 \text{ EUR}}{113.60 \text{ m}^2} = 57.56 \frac{\text{EUR}}{\text{m}^2} \qquad (3)$$

where:
C_{av}–the average cost of making 1 m² of wall.

6.2. Cost Calculation for the Construction of Compacted Clay Walls

Own calculation items have been set in order to determine the direct costs for the work involved in clay preparation and incorporation, based on the subject literature content.

Calculation of cost involved in erecting a division wall made of clay compacted in formwork includes the construction of outside load-bearing walls, the making of openings in the walls, the placing of prefabricated heads, insulation of the walls with mineral wool boards and applying external and internal plasterwork (Tables 8–11).

Table 8 presents the calculation of the labor cost for the walls made of clay compacted in formwork.

Table 8. Labor cost for wall made of clay compacted in formwork.

Item	Name	Meas.	Total qty.	Price [EUR/m-h]	Value [EUR]
1	Carpenters group I	m-h	116.38	3.85	448.06
2	Masons group III	m-h	1.28	3.85	4.93
3	Workers group I	m-h	235.81	3.85	907.87
4	Workers group II	m-h	75.77	3.85	291.71
5	Workers group III	m-h	14.87	3.85	57.25
6	Plasterers group II	m-h	126.21	3.85	485.91
7	Plasterers group III	m-h	142.06	3.85	546.93
				SUM	2.739.66

Source: own study.

Table 9 presents the calculation of the cost of materials for the wall made of clay compacted in formwork.

Table 9. Cost of materials for wall made of clay compacted in formwork.

Item	Name	Meas.	Total qty.	Price [EUR]	Value [EUR]
1	Reinforced concrete head beam L19N/150 length 149 cm	pcs.	7.89	7.33	57.83
2	Edged softwood boards class III, thickness 25 mm	m^3	4.49	140.33	630.08
3	Clay	m^3	42.88	0.00	0.00
4	Round nails, bare	kg	16.16	1.30	21.01
5	Sand, graining 0–4 mm	m^3	10.72	9.04	96.91
6	Mineral wool board Isover PT80 thickness 60 mm	m^2	140.95	5.57	785.09
7	Mineral wood board Isover PT80 thickness 100 mm	m^2	140.95	8.55	1205.12
8	Flat washers Uls6	pcs.	129.28	0.19	24.56
9	Threaded rod for fastening for heavy loads, cl. 4.8 M16-M20	pcs.	67.23	2.76	185.55
10	Chopped straw	kg	31.81	0.00	0.00
11	Regular lime mortar for building	m^3	0.42	35.41	14.87
12	Cement-lime mortar M2 (m.15)	m^3	3.31	34.21	113.24
13	Cement-lime mortar M7 (m.50)	m^3	0.09	42.28	3.81
14	Clay mortar	m^3	2.25	0.00	0.00
15	Dry adhesive mortar for mineral wool boards, for light insulation—Atlas Rocker W-20	kg	522.04	0.26	135.73
	Supplementary outlays		1.00	45.95	45.95
				SUM	3319.75

Source: own study.

Table 10 presents the calculation of the equipment cost for walls made of clay compacted in formwork.

Table 10. Equipment cost for wall made of clay compacted in formwork.

Name	Qty.	Total qty.	Price [EUR/m-h]	Value [EUR]
Mixing pump 1.1–3.3 m³/h (1)	m-h	13.57	6.68	90.65
Dragged soil cutter (set)	m-h	2.77	1.95	5.40
Dropside truck up to 5 t (1)	m-h	4.18	13.75	57.48
Vibratory foot rammer 66–78 kg	m-h	32.84	2.53	83.09
Passenger-cargo hoist 1.0 t	m-h	100.32	3.73	374.19
Portable window crane 0.15 t	m-h	5.64	1.12	6.31
			SUM	617.12

Source: own study.

Table 11 presents the total cost of erecting walls of clay compacted in formwork for the analyzed building.

Table 11. Total cost of erecting wall of clay compacted in formwork.

The type of cost	Cost [EUR]	Participation [%]
The labour	2709.66	41.00
The materials	0.75	50.00
The equipment	617.12	9.00
SUM	6646.53	100.00

Source: own study.

In order to obtain the average cost of making 1 m² of a division wall of clay blocks, it is required to divide the total cost by the total area of the walls

$$C_{av} = \frac{6646.53 \text{ EUR}}{115.26 \text{ m}^2} = 57.67 \frac{\text{EUR}}{\text{m}^2} \qquad (4)$$

where:
C_{av}–the average cost of making 1 m² of a wall.

6.3. Cost Calculation for the Construction of Walls Using the 'Straw-Bale' System

The calculation of direct costs involved in erection of a division wall in the 'straw-bale' system includes building a wooden framework in the 'Canadian house' system, filling the framework with straw bales, covering it on both sides with fibreboard, and applying external and internal plasterwork (Tables 12–15).

Table 12 presents the calculation of the labor cost for the walls using the 'straw-bale' technology.

Table 12. Labor cost for a wall in the 'straw-bale' technology.

Name	Measure	Total qty.	Price [EUR/m-h]	Value [EUR]
Masons group II	m-h	501.64	3.85	1931.31
Masons group III	m-h	444.33	3.85	1710.67
Workers group I	m-h	16.59	3.85	63.87
Workers group II	m-h	47.36	3.85	182.34
Plasterers group II	m-h	66.62	3.85	256.49
Plasterers group III	m-h	79.76	3.85	307.08
			SUM	4451.76

Source: own study.

Table 13 presents calculation of the material costs for the walls made using the 'straw-bale' technology.

Table 13. Cost of materials for a wall in the 'straw-bale' technology.

Item	Name	Meas.	Total qty.	Price [EUR]	Value [EUR]
1	Softwood boards planed on both sides, class II, thickness 28–45 mm	m^3	3.40	244.43	831.06
2	Round nails, zinc-coated	kg	37.73	1.54	58.10
3	Straw bales 31 × 41 × 70	pcs.	413.25	0.48	198.36
4	Plain fibreboard, porous, thickness 125 mm	m^2	272.94	1.55	423.0
5	Regular lime mortar for building	m^3	0.42	35.41	14.87
6	Cement-lime mortar M2 (m.15)	m^3	3.31	34.21	113.24
7	Cement-lime mortar M7 (m.50)	m^3	0.09	42.28	3.81
8	Clay mortar	m^3	2.35	0.00	0.00
	Supplementary outlays		1.00	24.90	24.90
				SUM	1667.40

Source: own study.

Table 14 presents calculation of equipment costs for a wall made using the 'straw-bale' technology.

Table 14. Cost of equipment for a wall in the 'straw-bale' technology.

Item	Name	Meas.	Total qty.	Price [EUR/m-h]	Value [EUR]
1	Mixing pump 1.1–3.3 m^3/h (1)	m-h	13.57	6.68	90.65
2	Dropside truck up to 5 t (1)	m-h	8.74	13.75	120.18
3	Electric central mast-type hoist 0.5 t	m-h	8.38	1.92	16.09
				SUM	226.92

Source: own study.

Table 15 presents the total cost of erecting the walls of the analyzed building using the 'straw-bale' technology.

Table 15. Total cost of erecting a wall in the 'straw-bale' technology.

The Type of Cost	Cost [EUR]	Participation [%]
The labour	451.76	70.00
The materials	1667.40	26.00
The equipment	226.92	4.00
SUM	6346.08	100.00

Source: own study.

In order to obtain the average cost of making 1 m^2 of a division wall in the 'straw-bale' technology, it is required to divide the total cost by the total area of the walls

$$C_{av} = \frac{6346.08 \text{ EUR}}{120.19 \text{ m}^2} = 52.80 \frac{\text{EUR}}{\text{m}^2} \quad (5)$$

where:
C_{av}–the average cost of making 1 m^2 of wall.

7. Comparison of the Wall Erection Costs in the Analyzed Variants

7.1. Cost of Making 1 m^2 of Wall

The cost of building 1 m^2 of wall depends directly on the construction time through labor costs. Moreover, in the simplest case, the cost is also affected by the type and volume of materials and construction equipment being used [23]. In general, the cost of erecting 1 m^2 of wall is one of the most important factors determining which technology will be chosen to make the division wall.

The wall made using the 'straw-bale' technology proved to be the cheapest solution (Figure 4); as such, the division wall made of clay blocks and clay compacted in framework turned out to be a less economic solution. The poor result obtained for a clay division wall has been primarily due to factors including the considerable amount of labor and the more expensive thermal insulation type. In the case of clay compacted in framework, shuttering makes for an additional cost.

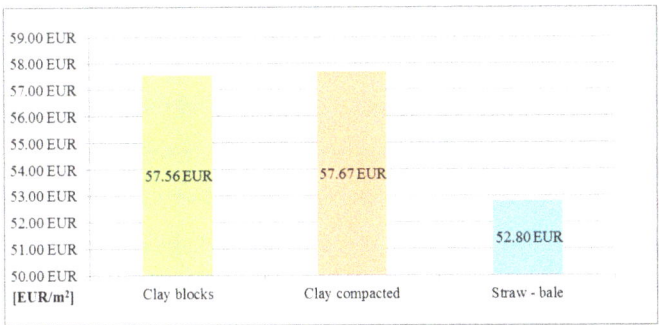

Figure 4. Cost of making 1 m² of wall depending on the chosen technology. Source: own study.

7.2. Share of Individual Components in the Wall Erection Costs

It is worth showing the cost analysis divided into labor, materials, and equipment (Figure 5). This analysis indicates which component most affects the total cost of the project, and this information may become an indication for choosing the optimal external wall. For example, when people have inexpensive manpower or time, thus being able to get involved in works by themselves, a more optimal solution for them will be to choose a wall type where the labor is the most expensive component. On the other hand, when they can get discounts or allowances from building materials wholesalers, it will be more optimal to choose the division wall for which material price is the most decisive factor in the total construction cost.

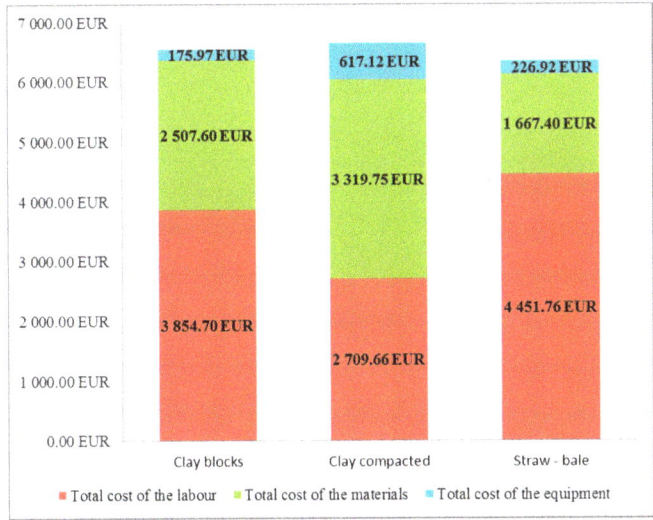

Figure 5. Division of the total wall construction cost into the costs of work/labor, material, and equipment. Source: own study.

Among the analyzed exterior wall types, the walls made of compacted clay shows the lowest labor cost. In case of a clay block division walls, the higher labor cost is primarily generated by the prolonged process of clay preparation and block formation. The walls made of straw bales in a wooden framework turned out to be the most expensive solution as regards the labor cost. More precisely, the whole framework construction determines this high labor cost.

Walls made using the 'straw-bale' technology proved to be the least expensive divisions as regards material expenditure. This is chiefly due to the very low purchase cost of the straw bales. In second place in the category of used materials cost are the walls made of clay blocks. This results from the assumption that materials including clay and chopped straw are obtained for free. The material cost is highest in the case of a compacted clay walls, which is connected with the high costs of shuttering made by the carpenter on site. This cost could be reduced if the shuttering is used at several construction sites.

The equipment cost for the analyzed division walls is comparable, differing only in the case of the compacted clay wall, where power rammers and a cargo-passenger lift are additionally used. The system formwork would increase equipment expenditures, but it would also reduce material costs.

8. Conclusions

The paper contains a comparison of construction costs for the exterior walls of a building, erected using three different technologies. The incurred costs have been estimated in detail despite a lack of up-to-date studies on the labor input required for individual works, occurring in the case of natural building technologies.

The purpose of the paper has been to provide a comparative analysis of the costs involved in erecting the exterior walls of a building based on locally available materials that may be qualified as natural building materials. This goal has been achieved.

The analyses demonstrated in the paper allow for drawing the following conclusions:

- The variant of walls made using the 'straw-bale' technology has been found to be the most advantageous among the analyzed natural building solutions. In spite of having the highest labor cost, this solution has proven to be the least expensive among all the natural building wall-making technologies.
- The high cost of clay wall variants is mostly generated by the expensive thermo-insulating layer in the form of mineral wool boards.
- When considering the lowest general cost of labor, the variant of walls made of clay compacted in formwork has proven to be the best. However, this variant has generated the highest cost of building equipment.
- The high cost of the variant of wall made of clay compacted in formwork is primarily generated by the cost of the formwork. If its cost could be spread among several buildings, or if another, more economic shuttering type could be used, the result obtained by this technology would be much better and would compete with the variant of wall made of straw in a wooden framework.
- Among the main reasons in favor of natural buildings are the free—or very inexpensive—building materials.
- The double-layer clay plaster may form an alternative for other types of wall facing used today inside a building. The cost of such plaster made manually does not exceed the cost of cement-lime plaster prepared by mechanical means.

Author Contributions: Conceptualization and Methodology, A.L.; Performed the calculation, W.D.; Writing—Original Draft Preparation, A.L., W.D.; All the authors have read and approved the final manuscript.

Funding: This research received no external funding.

Conflicts of Interest: The authors declare no conflict of interest.

References

1. Leśniak, A.; Zima, K. Cost Calculation of Construction Projects Including Sustainability Factors Using the Case Based Reasoning (CBR) Method. *Sustainability* **2018**, *10*, 1608. [CrossRef]
2. Leśniak, A.; Zima, K. Comparison of Traditional and Ecological Wall Systems Using the AHP Method. In Proceedings of the 15th International Multidisciplinary Scientific Geo Conference Surveying Geology and Mining Ecology Management (SGEM 2015), Albena, Bulgaria, 18–24 June 2015; Volume 3, pp. 157–164.
3. Zavadskas, E.K.; Vilutienė, T.; Tamošaitienė, J. Harmonization of cyclical construction processes: A systematic review. *Procedia Eng.* **2017**, *208*, 190–202. [CrossRef]
4. Zavadskas, E.K.; Antucheviciene, J.; Kalibatas, D.; Kalibatiene, D. Achieving Nearly Zero-Energy Buildings by applying multi-attribute assessment. *Energy Build.* **2017**, *143*, 162–172. [CrossRef]
5. Bonenberg, W.; Kapliński, O. The Arcithect and the Paradigms of Sustainable Development: A Review of Dilemmas. *Sustainability* **2018**, *10*, 100. [CrossRef]
6. Švajlenka, J.; Kozlovská, M. Houses Based on Wood as an Ecological and Sustainable Housing Alternative—Case Study. *Sustainability* **2018**, *10*, 1502. [CrossRef]
7. Drozd, W.; Leśniak, A.; Zaworski, S. Construction Time of Three Wall Types Made of Locally Sourced Materials: A Comparative Study. *Adv. Mater. Sci. Eng.* **2018**, *2018*, 2172575. [CrossRef]
8. Garas, G.; Allam, M.; El Dessuky, R. Straw bale construction as an economic environmental building alternative—A case study. *ARPN J. Eng. Appl. Sci.* **2009**, *4*, 54–59.
9. Miccoli, L.; Müller, U.; Fontana, P. Mechanical behaviour of earthen materials: A comparison between earth block masonry, rammed earth and cob. *Construct. Build. Mater.* **2014**, *61*, 327–339. [CrossRef]
10. Lecompte, T.; Le Duigou, A. Mechanics of straw bales for building applications. *J. Build. Eng.* **2017**, *9*, 84–90. [CrossRef]
11. Robinson, J.; Aoun, H.K.; Davison, M. Determining Moisture Levels in Straw Bale Construction. *Procedia Eng.* **2017**, *171*, 1526–1534. [CrossRef]
12. González, A.D. Energy and carbon embodied in straw and clay wall blocks produced locally in the Andean Patagonia. *Energy Build.* **2014**, *70*, 15–22. [CrossRef]
13. Ashour, T.; Georg, H.; Wu, W. Performance of straw bale wall: A case of study. *Energy Build.* **2011**, *43*, 1960–1967. [CrossRef]
14. Goodhew, S.; Grffiths, R.; Woolley, T. An investigation of the moisture content in the walls of a straw-bale building. *Build. Environ.* **2004**, *39*, 1443–1451. [CrossRef]
15. Lawrence, M.; Heath, A.; Walker, P. Determining moisture levels in straw bale construction. *Constr. Build. Mater.* **2009**, *23*, 2763–2768. [CrossRef]
16. Ashour, T.; Wieland, H.; Georg, H.; Bockisch, F.J.; Wu, W. The influence of natural reinforcement fibres on insulation values of earth plaster for straw bale buildings. *Mater. Des.* **2010**, *31*, 4676–4685. [CrossRef]
17. Kats, G. *Green Building Costs and Financial Benefits*; Massachusetts Technology Collaborative: Boston, MA, USA, 2003.
18. Brojan, L.; Petric, A.; Clouston, P.L. A comparative study of brick and Straw Bale wall systems from environmental, economical and energy perspectives. *ARPN J. Eng. Appl. Sci.* **2013**, *8*, 920–926.
19. Bartlett, E.; Howard, N. Informing the decision makers on the cost and value of green building. *Build. Res. Inf.* **2000**, *28*, 315–324. [CrossRef]
20. Plebankiewicz, E. *Fundamentals of Cost Estimation of Construction Works*; Cracow University of Technology: Krakow, Poland, 2007.
21. Institute of Housing Construction. *Temporary Principles of Erecting Clay Buildings*; Institute of Housing Construction: Warsaw, Poland, 1955.
22. Kaczyński, S. *Outline of Clay Construction*; Construction and Architecture: Warsaw Poland, 1954.
23. Drozd, W. Light clay straw bale solutions in the contemporary housing as an element of sustainable development. Selected issues. In *E3S Web of Conferences*; EDP Sciences: Les Ulis, France, 18–21 July 2016; Volume 10.

© 2018 by the authors. Licensee MDPI, Basel, Switzerland. This article is an open access article distributed under the terms and conditions of the Creative Commons Attribution (CC BY) license (http://creativecommons.org/licenses/by/4.0/).

Article

A Decision Framework under a Linguistic Hesitant Fuzzy Set for Solving Multi-Criteria Group Decision Making Problems

R. Krishankumar [1], K. S. Ravichandran [1], J. Premaladha [1], Samarjit Kar [2,*], Edmundas Kazimieras Zavadskas [3] and Jurgita Antucheviciene [4]

[1] School of computing, SASTRA University, Thanjavur 613401, India; krishankumar@sastra.ac.in (R.K.); raviks@sastra.edu (K.S.R.); premaladha@ict.sastra.edu (J.P.)
[2] Department of Mathematics, National Institute of Technology Durgapur, West Bengal 713209, India
[3] Department of Construction Technology and Management, Vilnius Gediminas Technical University, Sauletekio al. 11, Vilnius LT-10223, Lithuania; edmundas.zavadskas@vgtu.lt
[4] Laboratory of Operational Research, Research Institute of Sustainable Construction, Vilnius Gediminas Technical University, Sauletekio al. 11, Vilnius LT-10223, Lithuania; jurgita.antucheviciene@vgtu.lt
* Correspondence: samarjit.kar@maths.nitdgp.ac.in; Tel.: +91-943-478-8032

Received: 23 June 2018; Accepted: 20 July 2018; Published: 25 July 2018

Abstract: With fast-growing interest in sustainable healthcare management, proper selection and evaluation of hospitals become highly essential. Generally, experts/decision-makers (DMs) prefer qualitative information for rating objects. Motivated by this idea, in this paper, a linguistic hesitant fuzzy set (LHFS) is adopted for elicitation of preference information. The LHFS provides qualitative preferences of DMs as well as reflects their hesitancy, inconsistency, and vagueness. Motivated by the power of LHFS, in this paper we present a new decision framework that initially presents some operational laws and properties. Further, a new aggregation operator called simple linguistic hesitant fuzzy weighted geometry (SLHFWG) is proposed under the LHFS context that uses the strength of power operators. Some properties of SLHFWG are also investigated. Criteria weights are estimated using a newly proposed linguistic hesitant fuzzy statistical variance (LHFSV) method, and objects are ranked using the newly proposed linguistic hesitant fuzzy VIKOR (visekriterijumska optimizacijai kompromisno resenje) (LHFVIKOR) method, which is an extension of VIKOR under the LHFS context. The practicality and usefulness of the proposal are demonstrated by using a hospital evaluation example for sustainable healthcare management. Finally, the strengths and weaknesses of the proposal are realized by comparison with other methods.

Keywords: group decision making; hesitant fuzzy set; hospital evaluation; linguistic hesitant fuzzy set and Standard variance

1. Introduction

The WHO (World Health Organization) conducted a survey recently and predicted that by 2050, seven out of ten people would live in cities [1]. Along with such high demand for city lives, the risks and hazards also grow. To better circumvent the issue, there is an urgent need for proper and sustainable healthcare management. The AIMA (All India Management Association) [2] claimed that among various stages in sustainable healthcare management, the suitable selection of a hospital is highly substantial. Motivated by this claim, many scholars came up with different methods [3–5] for the proper evaluation and selection of hospitals. Based on the analysis, it is clear that decision maker(s)(DMs) prefer qualitative preference information for rating objects and the research on linguistic decision making is an attractive and hot topic for exploration in the present scenario. Due to factors such as lack of experience, time pressure, nature of objects, etc., DMs are unable to express their preferences quantitatively. To better circumvent this issue, Zadeh [6] introduced the idea of qualitative decision-making, where the preferences are given as linguistic terms. After the advent of the linguistic term set (LTS) [7], many scholars put forward different theories and concepts [8–10]. However, in many practical applications, expressing the viewpoints using the single linguistic term is unreasonable and impractical.

With a view of alleviating such an issue, Rodriguez et al. [11] put forward the concept of a hesitant fuzzy linguistic term set (HFLTS), which combines a hesitant fuzzy set (HFS) [12] with an LTS, where multiple terms are used by the DMs for expressing their viewpoints. Later, Rodriguez et al. [13] presented a study on different fuzzy linguistic models and claimed that HFLTS is a powerful concept for modeling uncertainty in preference elicitation. Further, motivated by the ability of HFLTS (as discussed in Reference [13]) in modeling complex linguistic terms, many scholars [14–23] presented new theories and concepts under the HFLTS context. Though the HFLTS circumvents the issue of LTS, it is not able to properly reflect the hesitancy and vagueness of the DM. Rodriguez et al. [24] conducted a survey on HFS along with some of its variants and claimed that HFS is a powerful tool for reflecting the hesitation of the DM and presented some future directions. Recently, Liao et al. [25] conducted a deep analysis on HFLTS and presented some challenges and future scope of HFLTS. Attracted by these surveys, and with a view of alleviating the challenge (discussed above), Meng et al. [26] proposed a new concept called a linguistic hesitant fuzzy set (LHFS), which addresses the qualitative preferences of DMs and also reflects the hesitancy and vagueness of the DMs. Inspired by the power of LHFS, Yu et al. [27] extended the Heronian arithmetic and geometric mean operators for LHFS and applied the same for the decision-making process. Zhou et al. [28] extended the Hamming distance and proposed new order relations under an LHFS environment. They also applied the genetic algorithm for a criteria weight calculation and used evidential reasoning for aggregation. Liu et al. [29] extended the linear programming technique for the multi-dimensional analysis of preferences (LINMAP) method for LHFS and used it for solving multi-criteria group decision-making (MCGDM) problems. Further, Zhu et al. [30] developed a new concept called a comprehensive cloud for unifying LHFSs of different lengths. They also extended power operators under an LHFS and applied the same for decision-making. Guan et al. [31] extended different distance and correlation measures under an LHFS environment for the decision-making process. Recently, Dong et al. [32] extended the popular VIKOR method to an LHFS environment and applied the same for intelligent transport system selection. Yuan et al. [33] extended the Choquet integral for LHFS and applied the same for the selection of renewable energy sources. Meng et al. [34] extended the idea of an LHFS by using interval numbers for membership values and put forward a new similarity measure for solving decision-making problems.

Based on the review conducted above, it is clear that the LHFS is an attractive concept for decision-making and the exploration of this concept has just begun. Also from the review, we identify some potential challenges, which are listed below:

1. The primary challenge encountered is that there is an urgent need for a scientific decision-making framework under an LHFS to utilize the potential power of an LHFS.
2. Following this, the idea of aggregation of LHFS-based preference information has just begun and there is a good scope for exploration. The claim by Xu and Liao [35] to produce consistent aggregated preference information is an interesting challenge to be addressed.
3. Another challenge is the calculation of criteria weights using the systematic procedure for obtaining sensible weight values.
4. Further, ranking of objects by using LHFS-based preference information is another interesting challenge to address for better decision-making under uncertain situations. Though Dong et al. [32] extended the popular VIKOR method to an LHFS, the challenge of using the method for MCGDM still needs to be addressed.
5. Finally, comprehensive comparison of the proposed framework with other methods for realizing the strength and weakness of the proposal is an attractive challenge for exploration.

Motivated by these challenges, some genuine contributions of the proposal are presented in a nutshell below:

(1) With a view of alleviating the primary challenge, a new decision framework is proposed under an LHFS context to utilize the potential power of an LHFS.
(2) Following this, a new aggregation operator called simple linguistic hesitant fuzzy weighted geometry (SLHFWG) is presented with the view of producing consistent aggregated preference information by extending the operator discussed in Reference [35] under an LHFS context. This operator also uses the idea of a power geometry operator for sensible aggregation. He et al. [36] claimed that *"whenever the relationship between the objects and criteria are to be aggregated, some unduly high and low information may have some bad impact on the aggregation process. In order to mitigate the effect, support measures are to be used which assign weights to information. This showcases the urge need for power operators during aggregation"*. Motivated by this claim, we set our focus in this direction.
(3) Further, a new method for criteria weight estimation is presented which is an extension to standard variance (SV) under an LHFS context. Previous studies on weight estimation have predominantly used entropy measures [37], optimization models [38–40], analytic hierarchy process (AHP) [41] method, and decision making trial and evaluation laboratory (DEMATEL) [42], etc., which often yields unreasonable and irrational weight values. Motivated by this challenge, we set our proposal towards this direction.
(4) Also, the popular linguistic hesitant fuzzy visekriterijumska optimizacijai kompromisno resenje (LHFVIKOR) method is adopted for selecting a suitable hospital from a set of hospitals. This example is an MCGDM problem that clarifies the practicality and usefulness of the proposed decision framework and addresses the challenge mentioned by Dong et al. [32].
(5) Finally, the strengths and weaknesses of the proposed framework is realized by comparison with other methods.

The remainder of the paper is organized as Section 2 for preliminaries, Section 3 for the LHFS and its basic concepts, where some operational laws and properties are presented, along with a new aggregation operator, criteria weight estimation method, and ranking method. Following this, in Section 4, a numerical example for hospital evaluation is demonstrated to realize the practicality and usefulness of the proposal, Section 5 presents a comparative study of the proposal with other methods, and finally, Section 6 gives the concluding remarks.

2. Preliminaries

Let us review some basics of LTS, PLTS, and HFS.

Definition 1 [7]: *Let S be a linguistic term set that is of the form $S = \{s_\alpha | \alpha = 0, 1, \ldots, n\}$, where n is a positive integer, and s_0 and s_n are the lower and upper bounds of the term set. The linguistic term s_α has the following properties:*

- s_u and s_v are two linguistic term sets, and the relation $s_u > s_v$ holds true, if $u > v$.
- Negation of s_u is given by $neg(s_u) = s_v$, such that $u + v = n$.

Definition 2 [12]: *Let Y be a reference set, and HFS on Y is a function that maps every element of Y to a subset [0,1]. Mathematically, it is given by:*

$$E = (y, h_E(y) | y \in Y) \qquad (1)$$

where $h_E(y)$ is a set of values in the range [0,1] that represent the membership values of the element $y \in Y$ to the set E.

Definition 3 [12]: *Let h, h_1, and h_2 be three hesitant fuzzy elements, where some basic operational laws are given by,*

$$h_1 \oplus h_2 = \bigcup_{\gamma_1 \in h_1, \gamma_2 \in h_2} (\gamma_1 + \gamma_2 - \gamma_1 \gamma_2) \tag{2}$$

$$h_1 \otimes h_2 = \bigcup_{\gamma_1 \in h_1, \gamma_2 \in h_2} (\gamma_1 \gamma_2) \tag{3}$$

$$\lambda h = \bigcup_{\gamma \in h} \left(1 - (1-\gamma)^\lambda \right) \tag{4}$$

$$h^\lambda = \bigcup_{\gamma \in h} \left(\gamma^\lambda \right), \lambda > 0 \tag{5}$$

$$s(h) = \bigcup_{\gamma_i \in h} \left(\frac{\sum_{i=1}^m \gamma_i}{m} \right) \text{ and } v(h) = \frac{\sqrt{\sum_{\gamma_i, \gamma_j \in h} (\gamma_i - \gamma_j)^2}}{m} \text{ where } s(h) \text{ is a score function,} \tag{6}$$

$v(h)$ is the variance function, and m is the length of the hesitant fuzzy element.

Definition 4 [26]: *Consider an LTS S of the form $S = \{s_\alpha | \alpha = 0, 1, \ldots, n\}$, then, the LHFS is a set that when applied to the linguistic terms of S yields a subset with many values in [0,1] and is mathematically defined by:*

$$L(h) = \left\{ L^k \left(h_i^k \right) \middle| L^k \in S, 0 \leq h_i^k \leq 1, k = 0, 1, \ldots, \#L(h), i = 0, 1, \ldots, m \right\} \tag{7}$$

where $L^k \left(h_i^k \right)$ is the kth linguistic term with its corresponding possible membership degrees, $\#L(h)$ is the number of linguistic term(s), and m is the number of possible membership degrees for each linguistic term.

Remark 1: *For ease of representation, we represent the linguistic hesitant fuzzy element (LHFE) as $\left(r^k, \left(h_i^k \right) \right)$, where r^k is the kth subscript of the linguistic term and $\left(h_i^k \right)$ is the possible membership degrees of $s_{r^k} \in S$.*

3. Proposed Decision Framework under LHFS Context

3.1. Some Operational Laws and Properties of LHFS

Let us now present some properties and basic operational laws.

Definition 5: *Consider an LTSS that is of the form $S = \{s_\alpha | \alpha = 0, 1, \ldots, n\}$, then the empty LHFS and full LHFS is given by:*

- *Empty LHFS $L(h) = \{\emptyset\}$;*
- *Full LHFS $L(h) = S|$with possible membership degrees;*

Definition 6: *Consider an LHFS $L(h)$ that is of the form $L(h) = \left\{ L^k \left(h_i^k \right) \middle| L^k \in S, 0 \leq h_i^k \leq 1, k = 0, 1, \ldots, \#L(h), i = 0, 1, \ldots, m \right\}$, then the complement of LHFS $L^c(h)$ is given by $L^c(h) = S - L^k$ with $h_i^{kc} = 1 - h_i^k$.*

Proposition 1: *The complement of a LHFS is involutive.*

Proof: If $L^c(h) = S - L^k$, then complement of $L^c(h)$ is given by $(L^c(h))^c = S - \left(S - L^k \right)$ with $\left(h_i^{kc} \right)^c = 1 - \left(1 - h_i^k \right) = h_i^k = L(h)$. □

Definition 7: *Consider an LTS S that is of the form $S = \{s_\alpha | \alpha = 0, 1, \ldots, n\}$, then the lower and upper bounds of LHFS are given by:*

$$\text{Upper bound of LHFS } L^+(h) = \max \left(r^k \times s \left(h^k \right) \right) \tag{8}$$

$$\text{Lower bound of LHFS } L^-(h) = \min \left(r^k \times s \left(h^k \right) \right) \tag{9}$$

where $s \left(h^k \right)$ is the score measure for the kth instance preference values.

Definition 8: Consider two LHFS $L_1(h)$ and $L_2(h)$ of the form $\left(r_1^k, h_{1i}^k\right)$ and $\left(r_2^k, h_{2i}^k\right)$, then:

$$L_1(h) \oplus L_2(h) = \left\{ \left(r_1^k + r_2^k\right) \left(h_{i1}^k + h_{i2}^k - h_{i1}^k h_{i2}^k\right) \right\} = L_3(h) \tag{10}$$

$$L_1(h) \otimes L_2(h) = \left\{ \left(r_1^k r_2^k\right) \left(h_{i1}^k h_{i2}^k\right) \right\} = L_3(h) \tag{11}$$

$$\lambda L_1(h) = \left\{ \lambda \times r_1^k, 1 - \left(1 - h_{i1}^k\right)^\lambda \right\}, \lambda > 0 \tag{12}$$

Whenever the result from Definition 8 goes out of bounds, the procedure suggested in Remark 2 is followed.

Remark 2: From Definition 8, it is clear that sometimes the linguistic part becomes out of bounds and to transform these terms within the bounds, the procedure discussed in Reference [43] is adapted.

$$r_i^k = \begin{cases} n & \text{when } r_i^k > n \\ -n & \text{when } r_i^k < -n \\ r_i^k & \text{otherwise} \end{cases}$$

Since the LTS defined in this paper follows Definition 1, the conditions 1 and 3 will hold true. On the other hand, when LTS $S = \{s_\alpha | \alpha = -n, \ldots, -1, 0, 1, \ldots, n\}$, then all three conditions mentioned above will hold true.

Property 1: *Commutative*

$$L_1(h) \oplus L_2(h) = L_2(h) \oplus L_1(h)$$

$$L_1(h) \otimes L_2(h) = L_2(h) \otimes L_1(h)$$

Property 2: *Associative*

$$(L_1(h) \oplus L_2(h)) \oplus L_3(h) = L_1(h) \oplus (L_2(h) \oplus L_3(h))$$

$$(L_1(h) \otimes L_2(h)) \otimes L_3(h) = L_1(h) \otimes (L_2(h) \otimes L_3(h))$$

Property 3: *Boundary*

$$L_1(h) \oplus L_0(h) = L_1(h)$$

$$L_1(h) \otimes L_0(h) = L_0(h)$$

$$L_1(h) \otimes L_{0^*}(h) = L_1(h)$$

Here, $L_0(h)$ is of the form $\{0, (0)\}$ and $L_{0^*}(h)$ is of the form $\{1, (1)\}$.

Example 1: Let S be a LTS given by $S = \{s_0 = none, s_1 = very\ low, s_2 = low, s_3 = mediumm, s_4 = high, s_5 = very\ high, s_6 = perfect\}$. Consider two LHFEs $L_1(h)$ and $L_2(h)$ of the form (discussed in Remark 1) $L_1(h) = \{2, (0.2, 0.3), 3, (0.25, 0.32)\}$ and $L_2(h) = \{3, (0.33, 0.42), 4, (0.3, 0.4)\}$ defined over an LTS $S = \{s_\alpha | \alpha = 0, 1, \ldots, 6\}$. Then, $L_1^+(h)$, $L_1^-(h)$, $L_1(h) \oplus L_2(h)$, $L_1(h) \otimes L_2(h)$, and $\lambda L_1(h)$ (at $\lambda = 0.4$) are given by:

$L_1^+(h) = \max(0.5, 0.855) = 0.855 = \{3, (0.25, 0.32)\};$
$L_1^-(h) = \min(0.5, 0.855) = 0.5 = \{2, (0.2, 0.3)\};$
$L_1(h) \oplus L_2(h) = \{5, (0.46, 0.59), 7, (0.48, 0.59)\} \approx \{5, (0.5, 0.6), 6, (0.5, 0.6)\};$
$L_1(h) \otimes L_2(h) = \{6, (0.066, 0.13), 12, (0.075, 0.13)\} \approx \{6, (0.066, 0.13), 6, (0.075, 0.13)\};$

$\lambda L_2(h) = \{0.4 \times 3, (0.15, 0.2), 0.4 \times 4, (0.13, 0.18)\} = \{1, (0.15, 0.2), 2, (0.13, 0.18)\}$.

Theorem 1: *Consider two LHFSs $L_1(h)$ and $L_2(h)$ that are of the form $\left(r_1^k, \left(h_{1i}^k\right)\right)$ and $\left(r_2^k, \left(h_{2i}^k\right)\right)$, then:*

(1) $\lambda(L_1(h) \bigcup L_2(h)) = \lambda L_1(h) \bigcup \lambda L_2(h) \lambda > 0$;
(2) $(\lambda_1 + \lambda_2) L_1(h) = \lambda_1 L_1(h) \bigcup \lambda_2 L_1(h) \lambda_1, \lambda_2 > 0$.

Proof: The proof of this theorem is direct and straightforward and hence we present only the theorem. □

Before getting into further discussion of the proposed concepts, it is essential that we present a flowchart representation of the proposed framework. This enhances the understanding of the framework and gives a clear idea of the decision-making process. Figure 1 depicts the flowchart of the proposed decision-making framework under an LHFS context.

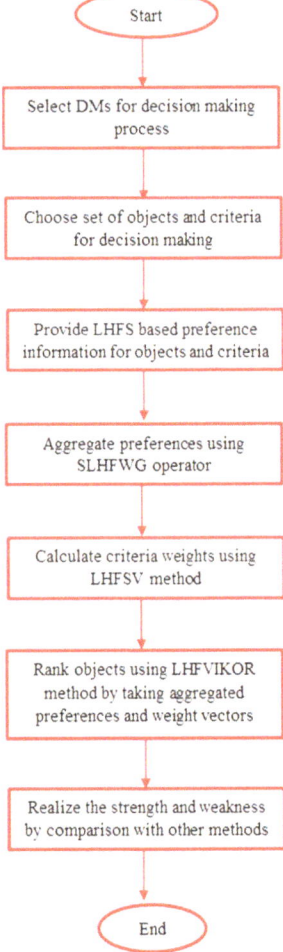

Figure 1. Flowchart of the proposed decision-framework.

3.2. Proposed SLHFWG Aggregation Operator

In this section, we present a new aggregation operator called SLHFWG that aggregates the DMs viewpoints under an LHFS context. The aggregation is carried out in two phases viz. (a) aggregation of linguistic term, and (b) aggregation of possible membership degrees. We now formally present the definition of an SLHFWG operator.

Definition 9: Consider an LHFS $L_q(h)$ that is of the form $a_q = \left(r^k_{a_q}, h^k_{ia_q}\right)$ with k linguistic terms and i possible membership degrees, then the aggregation is a mapping $X^n \to X$ defined by:

$$SLHFWG(\alpha_1, \alpha_2, \ldots, \alpha_l) = \otimes_{j=1}^{l}\left(\left(r^{*k}_{a_j}, h^{*k}_{ia_j}\right)\right) \quad (13)$$

$$SLHFWG\left(r^{*k}_{ia_j}\right) = \begin{cases} \text{Scheme 1 when all instances are unique} \\ \text{Scheme 2} \quad \text{otherwise} \end{cases} \quad (14)$$

$$SLHFWG\left(h^{*k}_{ia_j}\right) = \prod_{t=1}^{m}\left(h^k_{ia_j}\right)^{\lambda^t} \quad (15)$$

where λ^t is the weight of the tth DM and m is the total number of DMs.

Scheme 1: When the linguistic term from each DM is unique for a specific instance (i.e., frequency of occurrence is 1), average of the subscript is calculated.

Scheme 2: When linguistic terms are not unique, the term with the highest frequency is chosen as an aggregated value.

$$\lambda^t = \frac{\omega_t\left(1 + T\left(h^k_i\right)\right)}{\sum_{i=1}^{m}\omega_t\left(1 + T\left(h^k_i\right)\right)} \quad (16)$$

$$T\left(h^k_i\right) = \sum_{\substack{m,n \in DM \\ m \neq n}} S\left(h^k_m, h^k_n\right) \quad (17)$$

$$S\left(h^k_m, h^k_n\right) = \left(1 - d\left(h^k_m, h^k_n\right)\right) \quad (18)$$

$$d\left(h^k_m, h^k_n\right) = \frac{\left|h^k_m - h^k_n\right|}{\#l} \quad (19)$$

where $d\left(h^k_m, h^k_n\right)$ is the distance between the possible membership degrees of two DMs m and n, $S_t\left(h^k_i\right)$ is the support measure, and $T\left(h^k_i\right)$ is the total support measure.

Some advantages of the proposed aggregation operator are presented here:

(1) The aggregation of linguistic terms using an SLHFWG operator yields a much more sensible term with no virtual set. This can be easily realized from the formulation given in Equation (14). This ensures that the aggregation of the linguistic term is consistent and rational.

(2) Similarly, for the aggregation of the membership degrees, the motivation is gained from the power operator [44,45] and from the work of Xu and Liao [35]. As mentioned earlier by He et al. [34], the unduly high and low values cause bad effects in the aggregation process and the support measure (in formulation of power operator) is used to mitigate the same. Also, they claimed that the relationship between objects and criteria can be realized with the help of a support measure. Further, Xu and Liao [33] proposed a variant of the weighted geometry operator and claimed that the aggregation of preferences by this operator yields consistent values. The second phase of the aggregation applies the idea of a power operator to determine the relative importance of each

DM, and these values are further used for aggregating the membership degrees (motivated by the operator proposed in [33]).

(3) Finally, the proposed SLHFWG operator produces consistent non-virtual aggregated values of LHFS preferences and also helps DMs to better understand the relationship between objects and criteria.

Property 4: (Idempotency) If all values of LHFS $L_j(h) \forall j = 1, 2, \ldots, l$ are equal, then:

$$SLHFWG_\lambda(L_1(h), L_2(h), \ldots, L_l(h)) = L(h).$$

Property 5: (Boundedness) For all values of λ, the aggregation operator yields values that are of the form:

$$L^-(h) \leq SLHFWG_\lambda(L_1(h), L_2(h), \ldots, L_l(h)) \leq L^+(h).$$

Property 6: (Monotonicity) Let $L_j^*(h)$ be an LHFS ($\forall j = 1, 2, \ldots, l$) of the form $L_j^k(h) \leq L_j^{k*}(h)$ and $h_{ji}^k \leq h_{ji}^{k*}$, then:

$$SLHFWG_\lambda(L_1(h), L_2(h), \ldots, L_l(h)) \leq SLHFWG_\lambda(L_1^*(h), L_2^*(h), \ldots, L_l^*(h))$$

Property 7: (Commutative) Consider $L_j'(h)$ as any permutation of $L_j(h)(\forall j = 1, 2, \ldots, l)$, then:

$$SLHFWG_\lambda(L_1(h), L_2(h), \ldots, L_l(h)) = SLHFWG_\lambda(L_1'(h), L_2'(h), \ldots, L_l'(h))$$

Proof: The proof for these properties is straightforward and hence we confine our discussion with the elicitation of properties. □

Theorem 2: *The aggregation of LHFSs by using the proposed SLHFWG operator is also an LHFS.*

Proof: The proof for the theorem is considered in two-fold viz. linguistic aggregation and possible membership aggregation. In linguistic aggregation, the linguistic information is collected from each DM for a particular instance and SLHFWG operator is applied to aggregate the information. Clearly, the operator yields no virtual set, and hence, the aggregation of linguistic terms also forms a linguistic term which is within the defined LTS. Thus, the first fold of the theorem is proved. Following this, in the next fold, possible membership degrees are aggregated using an SLHFWG operator that gains motivation from Reference [35] and power operators. Here, we need to show that the aggregation of hesitant fuzzy values is also hesitant fuzzy in nature. For this, we consider the lemma discussed in Reference [46] that states that, for any λ with $\sum_{i=1}^{n} \lambda_i = 1$, $\prod_{i=1}^{n} x^{\lambda_i} \leq \sum_{i=1}^{n} \lambda_i x$. Motivated by this lemma, we focus the proof in this direction. $h_i^k = 0 \leq \prod_{t=1}^{n} \left(h_i^k\right)^{\lambda_t} \leq \sum_{t=1}^{n} \lambda_t h_i^k \leq \sum_{t=1}^{n} \lambda_t = 1 \forall k = 1, 2, \ldots, \#L(h)$. Since the possible membership degrees are within the range [0,1] and $\sum_{t=1}^{n} \lambda_t = 1$, we clearly show that the aggregation of possible membership degrees by using an SLHFWG operator also yields a membership degree. Thus, the aggregation of LHFS information by using the proposed SLHFWG operator is also an LHFS in nature. □

Example 2: Consider a LTS of the form $S = \{s_0 = very\ low, s_1 = low, s_2 = moderate, s_3 = high, s_4 = very\ high\}$. The snippet of LHFS information is given by $D_1 = \{3, (0.6, 0.6)\}$, $D_2 = \{1, (0.5, 0.6)\}$, and $D_3 = \{3, (0.5, 0.5)\}$. When an SLHFWG operator is applied, the aggregated LHFS information is calculated with DMs' weight values as $(0.3, 0.4, 0.3)$. The distance values between D_1, D_2 and D_1, D_3 as $d(D_1, D_2) = 0.05$, $d(D_1, D_3) = 0.1$. Similarly, $d(D_2, D_3) = 0.05$, $d(D_2, D_1) = 0.05$, $d(D_3, D_1) = 0.1$, and $d(D_3, D_2) = 0.05$. Thus, $T_1 = 1.85$, $T_2 = 1.9$, and $T_3 = 1.85$. We apply these values to Equation (16) and we get $(\lambda^1, \lambda^2, \lambda^3) = $

$(0.3, 0.4, 0.3)$. Finally, these estimated values are applied to Equation (15) and the aggregated values are given by $D_{123} = \{3, (0.53, 0.56)\}$.

3.3. Proposed LHFSV Method

In this section, criteria weights are estimated using the newly proposed LHFSV method, which is an extension to the standard variance (SV) method under an LHFS context. Motivated by the idea of Liu et al. [47], we set our focus in this direction. Further, the SV method enjoys the following advantages:

(1) Unlike previous studies on criteria weight estimation (for example analytical hierarchy process (AHP) [41], decision making trial and evaluation laboratory (DEMATEL) [42], entropy based method [37], optimization model [36–38], etc.), the proposed method does not produce unrealistic and unreasonable weight values.
(2) Also, the proposed method is simple and straightforward, and pays significant attention to those data points (criteria) that are highly conflicting. This property of SV further motivated our focus in this direction.
(3) Rao et al. [48] pointed out that unlike other statistical methods that concentrate only on the boundary points, the SV method concentrates on every data point for determining the distribution. This property of SV helps DMs to estimate criteria weights in a rational manner.
(4) Generally, relative importance is interpreted as the importance of a criterion relative to the hesitation that exists among DMs during preference elicitation. Thus, DMs' personal characteristics and stimuli play a significant role in the interpretation of relative importance [49]. Thus, criteria with a high variation in preferences are given high importance and the SV method captures and reflects this idea in a better way. Further, Kao [50] presented a geometric proof for the same claim by using the idea of frontiers and projection. This work provides sufficient mathematical justification for realizing the strength of the SV method.

Motivated and attracted by these advantages, we put forward an extension of SV method under an LHFS context. The procedure of the proposal is given below:

Step 1: Construct a weight evaluation matrix of order $(m \times n)$ with m DMs and n criteria. The LHFS information is used for evaluation.

Step 2: Calculate the score of the preference values using Equation (6) and convert the LHFS information into a single term by using Equation (20).

$$\alpha_{ij} = \sum_{k=1}^{\#instance} \left(r^k \times s\left(h^k\right) \right) \tag{20}$$

where r^k is the subscript of the kth linguistic term and $s\left(h^k\right)$ is the score of the kth probability instance.

Step 3: Calculate the variance by using Equation (21) which considers the values from Step 2.

$$var_{ij} = \frac{\sum_{i=1}^{m} \left(a_{ij} - \overline{a_{ij}}\right)^2}{m - 1} \tag{21}$$

Step 4: Normalize these variance values to calculate the relative importance of each criterion by using Equation (22).

$$\omega_j = \frac{var_{ij}}{\sum_{j=1}^{n} var_{ij}} \tag{22}$$

where ω_j is the weight of the jth criterion with $\sum_{j=1}^{n} \omega_j = 1$.

Example 3: *Consider the process of evaluation of two criteria by two DMs using LHFS information. The values are given by $D_1 = \{2, (0.2, 0.3); 3, (0.24, 0.32)\}$, $D_1 = \{3, (0.2, 0.25); 2, (0.2, 0.1)\}$ and $D_2 = \{3, (0.3, 0.4); 1, (0.33, 0.36)\}$, $D_2 = \{2, (0.2, 0.36); 3, (0.2, 0.1)\}$. By applying Equation (20), we get $D_1 = 0.5 + 0.84 = 1.34$, $D_1 = 0.67 + 0.3 = 0.97$ and $D_2 = 1.05 + 0.345 = 1.40$, $D_2 = 0.56 + 0.45 = 1.01$. Now, from Equation (21), variance is calculated and is given by $var_1 = 0.0018$ and $var_2 = 0.0008$. Finally, criteria weight is calculated using Equation (22) and it is given by $w_2 = 0.69$ and $w_2 = 0.31$.*

3.4. Procedure for LHFVIKOR Method

In this section, a new ranking method is presented which is an extension of the classical VIKOR over an LHFS context. VIKOR [51] is a compromise ranking method that is based on the principle of an L_p metric. Further, the VIKOR method finds a suitable alternative based on the closeness to an ideal solution and considers conflicting and non-commensurable criteria for evaluation. Some reasons for considering an extension of the popular VIKOR under an LHFS context are presented below:

(1) Based on the work of Opricovic and Tzeng [51], it can be clearly observed that both VIKOR and TOPSIS (technique for order preference by similarity to ideal solution) are compromise ranking methods. However, VIKOR performs better than TOPSIS in the following ways: (i) The VIKOR method considers a relative distance measure that is much more rational than the rank index of the TOPSIS method. (ii) The VIKOR method considers the attitude of the DM as a key parameter in its formulation, which is missing in TOPSIS.

(2) Further, from the work of Opricovic and Tzeng [52], it can be observed that the ranking order from PROMETHEE (preference ranking organization method for enrichment evaluation) and ELECTRE (ELimination Et Choix Traduisant la REalité) can be easily realized from the S and R parameters of the VIKOR method respectively.

(3) The VIKOR method also selects the compromise solution based on two conditions viz. acceptable stability and acceptable advantage. Also, along with the ranking order, the VIKOR method provides a rank value set (advantage rate) for backup management during uncertain situations.

Motivated by the power of the VIKOR method, in this paper efforts are made to extend the VIKOR method under an LHFS context.

The systematic procedure for the proposed LHFS-based VIKOR is presented below:

Step 1: Calculate the positive ideal solution and negative ideal solution (PIS, NIS) using Equations (23,24).

$$L^*(h) = max_{benefit}\left(\sum_{k=1}^{\#L(h)} r^k \times s\left(h^k\right)\right) (or) \, min_{cost}\left(\sum_{k=1}^{\#L(h)} r^k \times s\left(h^k\right)\right) \quad (23)$$

$$L^-(h) = max_{cost}\left(\sum_{k=1}^{\#L(h)} r^k \times s\left(h^k\right)\right) (or) \, min_{benefit}\left(\sum_{k=1}^{\#L(h)} r^k \times s\left(h^k\right)\right) \quad (24)$$

where L^* is PIS, L^- is NIS, r^k is the subscript of the kth linguistic term, and $s\left(h^k\right)$ is the score of the possible membership degrees for the kth linguistic term.

Step 2: Calculate the parameters group utility (S) and individual regret (R) using Equations (25,26).

$$S_i = \sum_{j=1}^{n} w_j \left(\frac{d(L_{ij}(h), L^*(h))}{d(L^*(h), L^-(h))}\right) \quad (25)$$

$$R_i = max_{j \in n} w_j \left(\frac{d(L_{ij}(h), L^*(h))}{d(L^*(h), L^-(h))}\right) \quad (26)$$

where ω_j the weight of the jth criterion, $d(a,b)$ is the distance between two LHFEs a and b and is given by Equation (27).

$$d(a,b) = \frac{\sqrt{\sum_{t=1}^{\#L(h)} \sum_{i=1}^{n} (r_a^t h_{ai}^t - r_b^t h_{bi}^t)^2}}{\#L(h)} \qquad (27)$$

Step 3: Calculate the merit function (Q) using Equation (28) to determine the final ranking order of the alternatives. Choose a suitable compromise solution to form the obtained ranking order. The parameters obtained from step 2 are used for the estimation of the merit function.

$$Q_i = v\left(\frac{S_i - S^*}{S^- - S^*}\right) + (1-v)\left(\frac{R_i - R^*}{R^- - R^*}\right) \qquad (28)$$

where $S^* = \min(S_i)$, $R^* = \min(R_i)$, $S^- = \max(S_i)$, $R^- = \max(R_i)$, and v is the strategy of the DM, which ranges from [0,1].

Step 4: The final ranking order is obtained by arranging the merit function (Q) in the ascending order. The alternative that has the smaller Q value is preferred more. Also, a compromise solution is selected based on the two conditions viz. acceptable advantage and acceptable stability [44].

Before demonstrating the practicality and usefulness of the proposal, it is worth discussing some intricacies of the proposal.

(1) The proposed LHFS concept extends the HFLTS concept by reflecting the hesitancy and vagueness of the DM by using possible membership degrees. This concept allows DMs to associate possible membership degrees for each linguistic term, which motivates sensible and rational decision making. Moreover, the concept circumvents the drawback of HFLTS by handling uncertainty and vagueness to a reasonable extent.
(2) Following this, a new decision framework is put forward under an LHFS context that uses LHFS information for rating objects. Initially, a new aggregation operator called SLHFWG is proposed that sensibly aggregated DMs' viewpoints without producing virtual sets.
(3) Further, a new criteria weight estimation method is proposed which is an extension to the SV method under an LHFS context. The LHSV method produces reasonable criteria weights by focusing on every data point rather than only the extreme values.
(4) Finally, a new ranking method is presented, which is an extension to the VIKOR method under an LHFS context. The method does the following: (a) PIS and NIS are calculated by using Equations (23) and (24), which identify a suitable LHFS value for each criterion and hence, the PIS and NIS is a vector of order $(1 \times n)$, where n is the number of criteria. (b) The parameters S_i, R_i, and Q_i are estimated using Equations (25)–(28), which is of order $(m \times 1)$ where m is the number of alternatives. (c) The stability of the ranking method is realized by performing a sensitivity analysis by varying the strategy parameter (v).

4. Numerical Example

This section put forwards a numerical example to demonstrate the practicality and usefulness of the proposal. Motivated by the work of Liao et al. [53] and Roy et al. [54] in the systematic evaluation of hospitals, in this paper, efforts are made to evaluate hospitals in India in a systematic manner. A survey report by IBEF (Indian Brand Equity Foundation) in August 2015 showed that India is expected to be ranked third in the global healthcare sectors with respect to incremental growth by 2020. Also, the report suggested that Indian healthcare is expected to reach USD$280 billion by 2020. With a high attraction and focus on healthcare, it becomes substantial to adopt a systematic scientific method for the rational evaluation of hospitals in India. This not only helps patients to understand hospitals better, but also helps management to improve hospitals' performance.

With this backdrop, a multi-criteria decision-making problem for hospital evaluation in India is presented which considers four hospitals rated with respect to four criteria by three DMs. The four criteria taken for evaluation were quality of doctors (C_1), reputation of the hospital (C_2), cost (C_3), and environmental risk (C_4). Among these, criteria C_1, C_2 were benefits, and C_3, C_4 were costs. The three DMs adopted LHFS information for ratings, and were advised to use the LTS $S = \{s_0 = extremely\ bad, s_1 = bad, s_2 = ordinary, s_3 = good, s_4 = very\ good\}$ as mentioned by Reference [53]. Let us now put forward the procedure for evaluation: **Step 1**: Construct three decision matrices of order (4×4) with LHFS information. This is shown in Table 1.

Table 1. Decision matrix with LHFS information.

DMs	Hospitals	Criteria Evaluation			
		C_1	C_2	C_3	C_4
D_1	H_1	3, (0.33, 0.42, 0.45) 2, (0.4, 0.3, 0.33) 4, (0.4, 0.35, 0.3)	2, (0.35, 0.44, 0.48) 0, (0.42, 0.4, 0.5) 3, (0.44, 0.48, 0.54)	0, (0.34, 0.4, 0.46) 1, (0.25, 0.45, 0.36) 3, (0.44.0.4, 0.5)	1, (0.42, 0.46, 0.5) 0, (0.33, 0.35, 0.44) 3, (0.4, 0.35, 0.44)
	H_2	2, (0.33, 0.42, 0.27) 3, (0.25, 0.44, 0.5) 1, (0.35, 0.45, 0.4)	1, (0.25, 0.35, 0.42) 2, (0.33, 0.44, 0.5) 0, (0.45, 0.52, 0.37)	2, (0.34, 0.43, 0.46) 1.(0.42, 0.44, 0.52) 0, (0.4, 0.3, 0.36)	4, (0.45, 0.52, 0.54) 2, (0.44, 0.4, 0.36) 0, (0.24, 0.4, 0.35)
	H_3	1, (0.35, 0.42, 0.5) 0, (0.42, 0.48, 0.54) 2, (0.44, 0.36, 0.4)	4, (0.44, 0.36, 0.4) 2, (0.35, 0.42, 0.4) 3, (0.4, 0.5, 0.44)	3, (0.42, 0.35, 0.5) 2, (0.44, 0.4, 0.36) 4, (0.34, 0.5, 0.48)	3, (0.4, 0.35, 0.42) 4, (0.4, 0.5, 0.45) 2, (0.35, 0.45, 0.4)
	H_4	3, (0.35, 0.44, 0.5) 4, (0.42, 0.46, 0.35) 2, (0.3, 0.4, 0.5)	3, (0.3, 0.4, 0.44) 2, (0.3, 0.42, 0.35) 1, (0.4, 0, 33, 0.5)	4, (0.3, 0.4, 0.35) 3, (0.35, 0.42, 0.44) 1, (0.22, 0.33, 0.42)	2, (0.34, 0.4, 0.45) 3, (0.33, 0.35, 0.44) 0, (0.42, 0.4, 0.3)
D_2	H_1	2, (0.3, 0.35, 0.4) 3, (0.4, 0.44, 0.5) 0, (0.4, 0.35, 0.3)	3, (0.4, 0.35, 0.42) 2, (0.44, 0.33, 0.3) 0, (0.3, 0.5, 0.38)	1, (0.44, 0.4, 0.35) 2, (0.35, 0.3, 0.4) 4, (0.4, 0.44, 0.5)	4, (0.35, 0.44, 0.4) 3, (0.35, 0.3, 0.44) 2, (0.28, 0.34, 0.45)
	H_2	1, (0.34, 0.44, 0.5) 2, (0.5, 0.42, 0.38) 3, (0.4, 0.35, 0.3)	4, (0.4, 0.35, 0.42) 0, (0.34, 0.22, 0.25) 2, (0.33.0.44.0.36)	3, (0.33, 0.35, 0.42) 4, (0.45, 0.5, 0.4) 1, (0.4, 0.3, 0.36)	3, (0.45, 0.54, 0.4) 0, (0.38, 0.42, 0.44) 2, (0.35, 0.3, 0.45)
	H_3	3, (0.4, 0.38, 0.5) 2, (0.35, 0.4, 0.3) 0, (0.3, 0.4, 0.42)	2, (0.3, 0.35, 0.38) 3, (0.35, 0.4, 0.38) 1, (0.33, 0.4, 0.5)	4, (0.3, 0.42, 0.45) 3, (0.4, 0.35, 0.38) 1, (0.42, 0.4, 0.35)	2, (0.33, 0.44, 0.48) 1, (0.4, 0.5, 0.45) 0, (0.4, 0.35, 0.3)
	H_4	1, (0.4, 0.3, 0.5) 0, (0.35, 0.44, 0.4) 2, (0.3, 0.5, 0.44)	3, (0.45, 0.5, 0.4) 2, (0.4, 0.42, 0.46) 1, (0.35, 0.4, 0.5)	2, (0.44, 0.3, 0.35) 4, (0.44, 0.35, 0.3) 1, (0.33, 0.38, 0.42)	4, (0.4, 0.33, 0.35) 3, (0.4, 0.5, 0.45) 0, (0.33, 0.43, 0.25)
D_3	H_1	4, (0.33, 0.4, 0.5) 2, (0.4, 0.3, 0.2) 1, (0.2, 0.24, 0.3)	4, (0.4, 0.44, 0.5) 3, (0.35, 0.4, 0.42) 1.(0.3, 0.4, 0.44)	2, (0.33, 0.4, 0.42) 1, (0.34, 0.4, 0.3) 0, (0.3, 0.4, 0.42)	2, (0.42, 0.4, 0.38) 1, (0.44, 0.33, 0.25) 3, (0.5, 0.43, 0.4)
	H_2	3, (0.3, 0.4, 0.35) 2, (0.45, 0.5, 0.48) 0, (0.35, 0.4, 0.44)	3, (0.4, 0.3, 0.35) 2, (0.44, 0.35, 0.5) 0, (0.35, 0.4, 0.42)	3, (0.44, 0.3, 0.4) 2, (0.35, 0.5, 0.4) 0, (0.15, 0.24, 0.3)	2, (0.44, 0.33, 0.36) 3, (0.4, 0.45, 0.35) 0, (0.3, 0.25, 0.33)
	H_3	3, (0.44, 0.4, 0.35) 2, (0.33, 0.38, 0.42) 1, (0.35, 0.4, 0.44)	1, (0.32, 0.35, 0.45) 2, (0.4, 0.35, 0.3) 4, (0.3, 0.5, 0.44)	4, (0.42, 0.35, 0.4) 3, (0.44, 0.5, 0.4) 1, (0.3, 0.25, 0.35)	3, (0.4, 0.3, 0.28) 4, (0.35, 0.4, 0.45) 1, (0.3, 0.4, 0.44)
	H_4	4, (0.4, 0.5, 0.45) 2, (0.44, 0.33, 0.22) 0, (0.4, 0.2, 0.32)	3, (0.44, 0.3, 0.4) 2, (0.33, 0.35, 0.4) 1, (0.35, 0.42, 0.33)	2, (0.33, 0.3, 0.4) 4, (0.44, 0.52, 0.38) 3, (0.35, 0.45, 0.54	2, (0.4, 0.33, 0.35) 3, (0.4, 0.42, 0.44) 0, (0.32, 0.24, 0.28)

Note: The representation of LHFE follows Remark 1. The subscript of the kth linguistic term along with their associated membership degrees is represented in this table and the same representation is followed in other places as well.

Step 2: Aggregate these matrices into a single matrix of order (4×4) by using the SLHFWG operator (refer to Section 3).

The relative importance of the DM was calculated separately for each linguistic term and this is given by Table 2. The reason for calculating the different relative importance of DM for each term is evident from the varying cognition/hesitation that the DM might have while providing the preference information. Motivated by this reason, support was calculated for each instance.

Based on the support value obtained from Table 2, the aggregated decision matrix was constructed with the LHFS information by using the SLHFWG operator and is presented in Table 3.

Table 2. Calculation of weights instance-wise for different DMs.

DMs	Hospitals	Criteria Evaluation			
		C_1	C_2	C_3	C_4
D_1	H_1	{0.30, 0.30, 0.31}	{0.30, 0.30, 0.30}	{0.30, 0.30, 0.30}	{0.30, 0.30, 0.30}
	H_2	{0.30, 0.30, 0.30}	{0.30, 0.30, 0.30}	{0.30, 0.30, 0.31}	{0.30, 0.30, 0.30}
	H_3	{0.30, 0.30, 0.31}	{0.31, 0.31, 0.31}	{0.30, 0.30, 0.30}	{0.31, 0.30, 0.31}
	H_4	{0.30, 0.30, 0.30}	{0.30, 0.30, 0.30}	{0.30, 0.30, 0.30}	{0.30, 0.30, 0.31}
D_2	H_1	{0.40, 0.39, 0.40}	{0.40, 0.40, 0.40}	{0.40, 0.40, 0.40}	{0.40, 0.40, 0.40}
	H_2	{0.40, 0.40, 0.40}	{0.40, 0.39, 0.40}	{0.40, 0.40, 0.40}	{0.40, 0.40, 0.40}
	H_3	{0.40, 0.40, 0.40}	{0.40, 0.40, 0.40}	{0.40, 0.40, 0.40}	{0.40, 0.40, 0.40}
	H_4	{0.40, 0.40, 0.40}	{0.40, 0.40, 0.40}	{0.40, 0.40, 0.40}	{0.40, 0.40, 0.40}
D_3	H_1	{0.30, 0.30, 0.30}	{0.30, 0.30, 0.30}	{0.30, 0.30, 0.30}	{0.3, 0.30, 0.31}
	H_2	{0.30, 0.31, 0.31}	{0.30, 0.31, 0.30}	{0.30, 0.31, 0.30}	{0.30, 0.30, 0.31}
	H_3	{0.30, 0.31, 0.31}	{0.30, 0.30, 0.30}	{0.30, 0.30, 0.31}	{0.30, 0.30, 0.30}
	H_4	{0.30, 0.30, 0.30}	{0.30, 0.30, 0.30}	{0.30, 0.31, 0.30}	{0.30, 0.30, 0.30}

Table 3. Aggregation of LHFS information using the SLHFWG operator.

Hospitals	Criteria Evaluation			
	C_1	C_2	C_3	C_4
H_1	3, (0.32, 0.39, 0.44), 2, (0.4, 0.35, 0.33), 2, (0.33, 0.31, 0.3)	3, (0.39, 0.40, 0.46), 2, (0.40, 0.37, 0.39), 1, (0.34, 0.46, 0.44)	1, (0.38, 0.4, 0.40), 1, (0.31, 0.37, 0.36), 2, (0.38, 0.42, 0.47)	2, (0.39, 0.43, 0.41), 1, (0.37, 0.32, 0.37), 3, (0.37, 0.37, 0.43)
H_2	2, (0.32, 0.42, 0.37), 2, (0.39, 0.45, 0.44), 1, (0.37, 0.39, 0.37)	3, (0.35, 0.33, 0.4), 2, (0.37, 0.31, 0.38), 0, (0.37, 0.45, 0.38)	3, (0.36, 0.36, 0.43), 2, (0.41, 0.48, 0.43), 0, (0.3, 0.28, 0.34)	3, (0.45, 0.46, 0.42), 2, (0.40, 0.42, 0.39), 0, (0.3, 0.31, 0.38)
H_3	3, (0.4, 0.4, 0.45), 2, (0.36, 0.42, 0.4), 1, (0.35, 0.39, 0.42)	2, (0.34, 0.35, 0.41), 2, (0.37, 0.39, 0.36), 3, (0.34, 0.46, 0.46)	4, (0.37, 0.38, 0.45), 3, (0.42, 0.41, 0.38), 1, (0.36, 0.37, 0.38)	3, (0.37, 0.37, 0.39), 4, (0.38, 0.47, 0.45), 1, (0.35, 0.39, 0.37)
H_4	3, (0.38, 0.39, 0.48), 2, (0.4, 0.40, 0.32), 1, (0.33, 0.35, 0.42)	3, (0.4, 0.4, 0.41), 2, (0.35, 0.4, 0.41), 1, (0.36, 0.38, 0.44)	2, (0.36, 0.33, 0.37), 2, (0.41, 0.42, 0.36), 1, (0.3, 0.38, 0.45)	2, (0.38, 0.35, 0.38), 3, (0.38, 0.43, 0.44), 0, (0.35, 0.35, 0.27)

Step 3: Construct criteria weight evaluation matrix and apply the LHFSV method (refer Section 3) to determine the weights of the criteria.

The LHFS information (from Table 4) was converted into single value by using the procedure from the LHFSV method. Also, from these single-valued terms, the variance was calculated and it was given by (0.49, 0.19, 0.45, 0.50) and the weight value was further calculated and it was given by $\omega_i = (0.3, 0.12, 0.28, 0.3)$.

Table 4. Evaluation of criteria weights.

DMs	Criteria Evaluation			
	C_1	C_2	C_3	C_4
D_1	2, (0.2, 0.3, 0.35) 3, (0.25, 0.33, 0.4)	2, (0.3, 0.33, 0.36) 1, (0.3, 0.4, 0.44)	1, (0.35, 0.42, 0.44) 3, (0.33, 0.4, 0.42)	1, (0.3, 0.4, 0.45) 2, (0.25, 0.35, 0.4)
D_2	2, (0.3, 0.35, 0.4) 4, (0.25, 0.35, 0.42)	1, (0.33, 0.35, 0.4) 3, (0.35, 0.4, 0.42)	3, (0.35, 0.4, 0.45) 4, (0.3, 0.4, 0.42)	2, (0.35, 0.4, 0.44) 3, (0.33, 0.4, 0.45)
D_3	3, (0.4, 0.44, 0.5) 4, (0.35, 0.4, 0.44)	2, (0.35, 0.4, 0.44) 3, (0.33, 0.36, 0.42)	1, (0.24, 0.35, 0.45) 3, (0.35, 0.4, 0.44)	2, (0.3, 0.32, 0.34) 4, (0.4, 0.45, 0.5)

Step 4: Finally rank the hospitals by using the proposed LHFS-based VIKOR method and choose a suitable hospital as a compromise solution from the set of hospitals.

Table 5 shows the PIS and NIS values for each criterion, which is calculated using Equations (23,24). The LHFS information corresponding to the determined value were chosen as PIS and NIS. Table 6 shows the values for the parameters S and R, which were calculated by using Equations (25,26). From these values, we observed that the order was given by $H_4 \succ H_3 \succ H_2 \succ H_1$ for both S and R under biased and unbiased weighting conditions.

Table 5. Ideal solution.

IS	Evaluation Criteria			
	C_1	C_2	C_3	C_4
PIS	3, (0.32, 0.39, 0.44) 2, (0.4, 0.35, 0.33) 2, (0.32, 0.31, 0.3)	2, (0.34, 0.35, 0.41) 2, (0.36, 0.39, 0.36) 2, (0.34, 0.46, 0.46)	1, (0.37, 0.4, 0.4) 1, (0.31, 0.37, 0.35) 2, (0.37, 0.42, 0.47)	2, (0.38, 0.35, 0.38) 3, (0.38, 0.43, 0.44) 0, (0.35, 0.35, 0.27)
NIS	2, (0.32, 0.42, 0.37) 2, (0.39, 0.45, 0.44) 1, (0.37, 0.4, 0.37)	3, (0.35, 0.33, 0.4) 2, (0.36, 0.31, 0.38) 0, (0.37, 0.45, 0.38)	4, (0.37, 0.38, 0.45) 3, (0.42, 0.41, 0.38) 1, (0.35, 0.37, 0.38)	3, (0.37, 0.37, 0.39) 4, (0.38, 0.47, 0.45) 1, (0.35, 0.39, 0.37)

Table 6. Group utility and individual regret.

Hospitals	Parameter(s)			
	S		R	
	b	ub	B	ub
H_1	1.2984	1.1679	1.2297	1.0248
H_2	0.9162	0.9243	0.3141	0.2618
H_3	0.6821	0.5851	0.3	0.25
H_4	0.2341	0.2844	0.1058	0.1429

Note: b is biased and ub is unbiased. The unbiased weight is given by $(1/n)$ and biased weight is calculated using the procedure in Section 3.

Further, we estimated the Q values under biased and unbiased weighting conditions by using Equations (28). The stability of the proposal was also realized by sensitivity analysis and it is shown in Table 7. From Table 7, we observe that the ranking order was $H_4 \succ H_3 \succ H_2 \succ H_1$ and the suitable hospital was H_4 (compromise solution determined using acceptable advantage and acceptable stability conditions [44]). We also inferred that the proposed framework was unaffected and stable against uncertainty and vagueness.

Table 7. Sensitivity analysis of merit function.

v Values	Hospitals	Q		Ranking Order	
		B	ub	B	ub
0.1	H_1	1	0.8743	$H_4 \succ H_3 \succ H_2 \succ H_1$	
	H_2	0.2213	0.1768		
	H_3	0.1887	0.1281		
	H_4	0	0		
0.2	H_1	1	0.8883	$H_4 \succ H_3 \succ H_2 \succ H_1$	
	H_2	0.2679	0.2376		
	H_3	0.2145	0.1516		
	H_4	0	0		

Table 7. Cont.

v Values	Hospitals	Q		Ranking Order	
		B	ub	B	ub
0.3	H_1	1	0.9023	$H_4 \succ H_3 \succ H_2 \succ H_1$	
	H_2	0.3145	0.2985		
	H_3	0.2403	0.1752		
	H_4	0	0		
0.4	H_1	1	0.9162	$H_4 \succ H_3 \succ H_2 \succ H_1$	
	H_2	0.3612	0.3593		
	H_3	0.2661	0.1988		
	H_4	0	0		
0.5	H_1	1	0.9302	$H_4 \succ H_3 \succ H_2 \succ H_1$	
	H_2	0.4078	0.4201		
	H_3	0.2919	0.2224		
	H_4	0	0		
0.6	H_1	1	0.9442	$H_4 \succ H_3 \succ H_2 \succ H_1$	
	H_2	0.4544	0.481		
	H_3	0.3177	0.246		
	H_4	0	0		
0.7	H_1	1	0.9581	$H_4 \succ H_3 \succ H_2 \succ H_1$	
	H_2	0.501	0.5418		
	H_3	0.3435	0.2696		
	H_4	0	0		
0.8	H_1	1	0.9721	$H_4 \succ H_3 \succ H_2 \succ H_1$	
	H_2	0.5476	0.6026		
	H_3	0.3693	0.2932		
	H_4	0	0		
0.9	H_1	1	0.986	$H_4 \succ H_3 \succ H_2 \succ H_1$	
	H_2	0.5942	0.6635		
	H_3	0.3951	0.3168		
	H_4	0	0		

Step 5: Compare the strengths and weaknesses of the proposal with other methods (refer Section 5).

5. Comparative Analysis: Proposed Versus others

In this section, we make efforts to realize the strengths and weaknesses of the proposal under the realm of both theoretical and numerical aspects. The factors considered for theoretic investigation were obtained from intuition and factors considered for numerical analysis were taken from Reference [55]. With a view of maintaining homogeneity in the comparison process, we considered state of the art methods like LHFS-based aggregation [30], HFLTS-based TOPSIS [16], and HFLTS-based VIKOR [21]. The same aggregated matrix was given as input to these methods, and the ranking order was investigated. Table 8 shows the ranking order obtained by different methods. From Figure 2, it can be observed that the proposed method was highly consistent with other state-of-the-art methods. Also, the HFLTS-based TOPSIS and VIKOR methods produced negative correlation values, which signify the fact that these methods used a different data structure for preference information. The LHFS information was informative and reflected the hesitation and vagueness of the DM in a better way. We further investigated the theoretic and numeric aspects of the proposal with other methods (see Table 9).

Table 8. Different ranking order from different methods.

Method(s)	Hospital(s)				Ranking Order
	H_1	H_2	H_3	H_4	
Proposed	4	3	2	1	$H_4 \succ H_3 \succ H_2 \succ H_1$
LHFS-aggregate [30]	2	1	4	3	$H_2 \succ H_1 \succ H_4 \succ H_3$
HFLTS-TOPSIS [16]	1	2	4	3	$H_1 \succ H_2 \succ H_4 \succ H_3$
HFLTS-VIKOR [21]	1	2	4	3	$H_1 \succ H_2 \succ H_4 \succ H_3$

Note: Sensitivity analysis was conducted for the VIKOR method and for the HFLTS environment; the linguistic term only was considered.

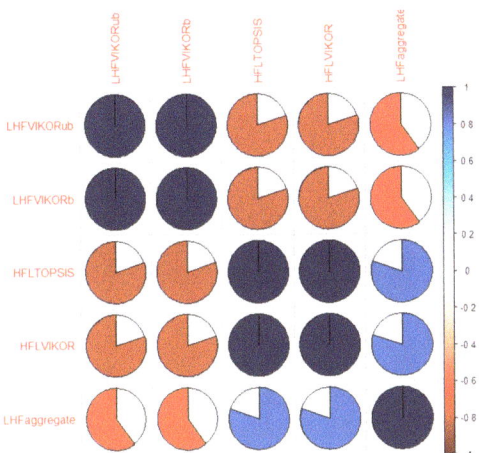

Figure 2. Spearman correlation plot.

From Table 8, we clearly observe that the proposed method produced a unique ranking order with a broad and sensible rank value set that is much more sensible and reasonable as it considered both the linguistic terms and its corresponding membership degrees to properly reflect the hesitancy in the process. In contrary, the HFLTS-based methods (discussed in Table 8) failed to properly reflect the hesitation of the DM. Further, the consistency of the proposal was realized by using the Spearman correlation method [56]. From Figure 2, it can be clearly observed that the proposed LHFS-based VIKOR method produced a correlation value of $(1, -0.8, -0.8, -0.6)$ with respect to the LHFS-based VIKOR (unbiased), HFLTS-based TOPSIS, HFLTS-based VIKOR, and LHFS-based aggregation methods. This showed that the proposed method was not relatively consistent (negative relation) with other methods and it produced a unique ranking order. Though, readers question this aspect, the reason for such values can be easily realized from the loss of information that was incurred during the process of evaluation. The methods discussed in References [16,21] miss the membership values that are highly important to reflect the hesitation of the DM. Also, method [30] loses a certain amount of information during the process of aggregation.

Table 9. Investigation of different features.

Context(s)	Method(s)			
	Proposed	LHFS-Aggregate	HFLTS-TOPSIS	HFLTS-VIKOR
Input	HFLTS + possible membership degrees	HFLTS + possible membership degrees	HFLTS only	HFLTS only
Association information	Membership degrees	Membership degrees	No	No
Weight calculation	Proposed LHFSV method	Only DM defined	Only DM defined	Only DM defined
Aggregation	Proposed SLHFWG operator	Ordered weighted arithmetic/geometry	yes	N/A
Rank value set	Broad and sensible	Narrow	Narrow	Broad in nature
Backup	Possible	Not possible	Not possible	Possible
Complexity	$O(nmt(\beta i))$ where n is number of objects, m is number of criteria, t is number of terms and βi is number of probability instances	$O(nmt(\beta i))$	$O(nmt)$	$O(nmt)$
Stability	Highly stable	Moderately stable	Moderately stable	Highly stable
Consistency	Highly consistent	Moderately consistent	Inconsistent	Inconsistent
Adequacy test	Satisfies the test	Satisfies the test when objects are repeated	Only partial adequacy test is satisfied	Satisfies the test with respect to criteria
Scalability	yes, up to max. 9 items [57]	yes, up to max.9 items	yes, up to max.9 items	yes, up to max. 9 items
Strengths	• The proposal extends HFLTS by associating possible membership degrees. • Reflects hesitation, uncertainty and vagueness in a much better manner. • Generalizes the concept of HFLTS by offering DMs freedom to give multiple possible membership degrees. • Partial ignorance is accepted • New and sensible aggregation method is presented for sensible fusion of information. • Sensible criteria weight estimation method is also presented. • Suitable objects are also selected in a rational and reasonable manner with LHFS VIKOR method.	• Generalizes the concept of HFLTS. • Partial ignorance is tolerable	• Generalizes the idea of LTS. • Partial ignorance is allowed.	
Weaknesses	• Proposal is computationally complex. • Multiple membership degrees must be collected. • Though, the proposal is effective in reflecting hesitation and gains high attraction under theoretic context, the practical sense of the proposal is still tough for DMs to adopt.	• Somewhat complex in nature. • Collection of multiple membership degrees is tough	• Hesitation, inconsistency, and vagueness of the DMs are not reflected properly. • Balancing of ignorance causes problem when done without the aid of association entities.	

To enrich our clarity further on the proposal, we make the following discussion:

1. The proposal presented a new concept (structure) to the decision-making context by extending HFLTS with possible membership degrees to better reflect hesitation and vagueness. We also investigated some attractive properties of LHFS.
2. A two-phase scientific decision-making framework was further presented under an LHFS context for rational decision-making. The framework put forward a new aggregation operator that was motivated from the work in Reference [35] and power operators for the sensible aggregation of DMs' preference information. Following this, a new criteria weight estimation method was presented for the reasonable estimation of criteria weights, which is an extension of SV method under an LHFS environment. Finally, the framework presented an extension to the popular VIKOR ranking method for MCGDM problems to select a suitable object from the set of objects.
3. As mentioned earlier, the superiority of the proposal was realized from theoretic and numerical perspectives. Clearly, Table 9 brought out the superiority of the proposal and showed that the proposed framework was a powerful aid for critical and rational decision-making.
4. Certain key factors discussed in Table 9 are: stability, which is ensured by sensitivity analysis on parameters (like weights, strategy etc.); consistency, which is ensured from Spearman correlation; robustness, which is realized from an adequacy test motivated by Reference [55]; and scalability, which is motivated by Reference [57].
5. In order to demonstrate the practicality and usefulness of the proposal, an interesting hospital evaluation problem was presented. From Table 8, we observed that the ranking order obtained from the proposal was consistent with its close counterpart. The compromise solution selected by the proposal and its close counterpart were the same and was given by H_4. Though the order coincides, the proposed LHFS-based decision framework was much superior in various factors discussed in Table 9 and also, the proposal handled the weakness of HFLTS in a much better manner.

6. Concluding Remarks

In this paper, efforts were made to present a flexible and reasonable data structure for properly reflecting DMs' hesitation and vagueness. Motivated by the power of HFLTS and possible membership degrees, we set our research focus in this direction. Some attractive operational laws, properties, etc., were also investigated. Further, a new decision framework was put forward that consisted of a new aggregation method for aggregating DMs' preference information. Some properties of the operator were also admired in this paper. A new method for the criteria weight estimation was also presented under the LHFS context for the effective and reasonable calculation of weights. Finally, the proposed framework presented an extension to the popular VIKOR method under an LHFS context for an MCGDM problem. With a view of giving a proper realization of the practicality, strength, and weakness of the proposal, a hospital evaluation problem was illustrated and a comparative study (from both a theoretic and numerical perspective) was put forward with other methods.

As a part of the future scope, weaknesses discussed in Table 9 for the proposal will be addressed; also new structures for proper and flexible representation of preference information will be presented by extending HFLTS with soft sets. Also, plans are made to automate the membership degrees for each linguistic term to better reflect the hesitation of DMs. We have also planned to combine hot concepts like machine learning, artificial intelligence, granular computing, etc., with these structures for effective decision-making in uncertain and critical situations.

Author Contributions: The individual contribution and responsibilities of the authors were as follows: Author(s) R.K., K.S.R., and J.P. designed the model for research, collected, pre-processed, and analyzed the data and the obtained inferences, and worked on the development of the paper. Author(s) S.K., E.K.Z. and J.A. provided good advice throughout the research by giving suggestions on model design, methodology, and inferences, and refined the manuscript. All the authors have read and approved the final manuscript.

Acknowledgments: The authors thank the editor and the anonymous reviewer(s) for their insights that helped improve the quality of the research. The authors also thank the funding agencies University Grants Commission (grant no. F./2015-17/RGNF-2015-17-TAM-83) and Department of Science and Technology, Ministry of Science and Technology (grant no. SR/FST/ETI-349/2013) for their financial aid.

Conflicts of Interest: The authors declare no conflicts of interest.

References

1. Kim, J.L.; Senaratna, D.M.; Ruza, J.; Kam, C.; Ng, S. Feasibility study on an evidence-based decision-support system for hospital site selection for an aging population. *Sustainability* **2015**, *7*, 2730–2744. [CrossRef]
2. Charu, S.; Priya, C.; Sowmya, R. *Innovative and Sustainable Healthcare Management: Strategies for Growth*, 2nd ed.; Deloitte: India, 2012; pp. 1–20.
3. Wang, J.; Chen, X. Method for hospital selection considering patients' expectations. In Proceedings of the 7th International Joint Conference on Computational Sciences and Optimization, CSO 2014, Beijing, China, 4–6 July 2014; pp. 361–365. [CrossRef]
4. Arasteh, M.A.; Shamshirband, S.; Yee, P.L. Using multi-attribute decision-making approaches in the selection of a hospital management system. *Technol. Health Care* **2017**, *1*, 1–17. [CrossRef] [PubMed]
5. Chen, L.; Chan, C.M.; Lee, H.C.; Chung, Y.; Lai, F. Development of a decision support engine to assist patients with hospital selection topical collection on patient facing systems. *J. Med. Syst.* **2014**, *38*, 1–8. [CrossRef] [PubMed]
6. Zadeh, L.A. The concept of a linguistic variable and its application to approximate reasoning-I. *Inf. Sci.* **1975**, *8*, 199–249. [CrossRef]
7. Herrera, F.; Herrera-Viedma, E.; Verdegay, J.L. A sequential selection process in group decision making with a linguistic assessment approach. *Inf. Sci.* **1995**, *85*, 223–239. [CrossRef]
8. Herrera, F.; Herrera-Viedma, E.; Verdegay, J.L. Linguistic measures based on fuzzy coincidence for reaching consensus in group decision making. *Int. J. Approx. Reason.* **1997**, *16*, 309–334. [CrossRef]
9. Herrera, F.; Herrera-Viedma, E.; Verdegay, J.L. A model of consensus in group decision making under linguistic assessments. *Fuzzy Sets Syst.* **1996**, *78*, 73–87. [CrossRef]
10. Xu, Z. An approach based on the uncertain LOWG and induced uncertain LOWG operators to group decision making with uncertain multiplicative linguistic preference relations. *Decis. Support Syst.* **2006**, *41*, 488–499. [CrossRef]
11. Rodriguez, R.M.; Martinez, L.; Herrera, F. Hesitant fuzzy linguistic term sets for decision making. *IEEE Trans. Fuzzy Syst.* **2012**, *20*, 109–119. [CrossRef]
12. Torra, V.; Narukawa, Y. On hesitant fuzzy sets and decision. In Proceedings of the 2009 IEEE International Conference on Fuzzy System, Jeju Island, Korea, 20–24 August 2009; pp. 1378–1382. [CrossRef]
13. Rodríguez, R.M.; Labella, A.; Martínez, L. An overview on fuzzy modelling of complex linguistic preferences in decision making. *Int. J. Comput. Intell. Syst.* **2016**, *9*, 81–94. [CrossRef]
14. Chang, K.H. Enhanced assessment of a supplier selection problem by integration of soft sets and hesitant fuzzy linguistic term set. *Proc. Inst. Mech. Eng. Part B J. Eng. Manuf.* **2015**, *229*, 1635–1644. [CrossRef]
15. Wei, C.; Zhao, N.; Tang, X. Operators and comparisons of hesitant fuzzy linguistic term sets. *IEEE Trans. Fuzzy Syst.* **2014**, *22*, 575–585. [CrossRef]
16. Beg, I.; Rashid, T. TOPSIS for hesitant fuzzy linguistic term sets. *Int. J. Intell. Syst.* **2014**, *29*, 495–524. [CrossRef]
17. Zhu, B.; Xu, Z. Consistency measures for hesitant fuzzy linguistic preference relations. *IEEE Trans. Fuzzy Syst.* **2014**, *22*, 35–45. [CrossRef]
18. Liao, H.; Xu, Z.; Zeng, X.J.; Merigo, J.M. Qualitative decision making with correlation coefficients of hesitant fuzzy linguistic term sets. *Knowl.-Based Syst.* **2015**, *76*, 127–138. [CrossRef]
19. Wu, Z.; Xu, J. Possibility distribution-based approach for MAGDM with hesitant fuzzy linguistic information. *IEEE Trans. Cybern.* **2016**, *46*, 694–705. [CrossRef] [PubMed]
20. Liao, H.; Xu, Z.; Zeng, X.J. Distance and similarity measures for hesitant fuzzy linguistic term sets and their application in multi-criteria decision making. *Inf. Sci.* **2014**, *271*, 125–142. [CrossRef]
21. Liao, H.; Xu, Z.; Zeng, X.J. Hesitant fuzzy linguistic VIKOR method and its application in qualitative multiple criteria decision making. *IEEE Trans. Fuzzy Syst.* **2014**, *23*, 1–14. [CrossRef]

22. Wu, Z. A consensus process for hesitant fuzzy linguistic preference relations. In Proceedings of the 2015 IEEE International. Conference on Fuzzy System, Istanbul, Turkey, 2–5 August 2015; pp. 1–7. [CrossRef]
23. Liao, H.; Wu, D.; Huang, Y.; Ren, P.; Xu, Z.; Verma, M. Green logistic provider selection with a hesitant fuzzy linguistic thermodynamic method integrating cumulative prospect theory and PROMETHEE. *Sustainability* **2018**, *10*, 1291. [CrossRef]
24. Rodríguez, R.M.; Martínez, L.; Torra, V.; Xu, Z.S.; Herrera, F. Hesitant Fuzzy Sets: State of the Art and Future Directions. *Int. J. Intell. Syst.* **2014**, *29*, 495–524. [CrossRef]
25. Liao, H.; Xu, Z.; Herrera-Viedma, E.; Herrera, F. Hesitant Fuzzy Linguistic Term Set and Its Application in Decision Making: A State-of-the-Art Survey. *Int. J. Fuzzy Syst.* **2017**, 1–27. [CrossRef]
26. Meng, F.; Chen, X.; Zhang, Q. Multi-attribute decision analysis under a linguistic hesitant fuzzy environment. *Inf. Sci.* **2014**, *267*, 287–305. [CrossRef]
27. Yu, S.M.; Zhou, H.; Chen, X.H.; Wang, J.Q. A multi-criteria decision-making method based on heronian mean operators under a linguistic hesitant fuzzy environment. *Asia Pac. J. Oper. Res.* **2015**, *32*, 1–35. [CrossRef]
28. Zhou, H.; Wang, J.; Zhang, H.; Chen, X. Linguistic hesitant fuzzy multi-criteria decision-making method based on evidential reasoning. *Int. J. Syst. Sci.* **2016**, *47*, 314–327. [CrossRef]
29. Liu, Y.Z.; Fan, Z.P.; Gao, G.X. An extended LINMAP method for MAGDM under linguistic hesitant fuzzy environment. *J. Intell. Fuzzy Syst.* **2016**, *30*, 2689–2703. [CrossRef]
30. Zhu, C.; Zhu, L.; Zhang, X. Linguistic hesitant fuzzy power aggregation operators and their applications in multiple attribute decision-making. *Inf. Sci.* **2016**, *367*, 809–826. [CrossRef]
31. Guan, J.; Zhou, D.; Meng, F. Distance measure and correlation coefficient for linguistic hesitant fuzzy sets and their application. *Informatica* **2017**, *28*, 237–268. [CrossRef]
32. Dong, J.Y.; Yuan, F.F.; Wan, S.P. Extended VIKOR method for multiple criteria decision-making with linguistic hesitant fuzzy information. *Comput. Ind. Eng.* **2017**, *112*, 305–319. [CrossRef]
33. Yuan, J.; Li, C.; Li, W.; Liu, D.; Li, X. Linguistic hesitant fuzzy multi-criterion decision-making for renewable energy: A case study in Jilin. *J. Clean. Prod.* **2018**, *172*, 3201–3214. [CrossRef]
34. Meng, F.; Tang, J.; Li, C. Uncertain linguistic hesitant fuzzy sets and their application in multi-attribute decision making. *Int. J. Intell. Syst.* **2018**, *33*, 586–614. [CrossRef]
35. Liao, H.; Xu, Z. Consistency of the fused intuitionistic fuzzy preference relation in group intuitionistic fuzzy analytic hierarchy process. *Appl. Soft Comput. J.* **2015**, *35*, 812–826. [CrossRef]
36. He, Y.; He, Z. Hesitant fuzzy power bonferroni means and their application to multiple attribute decision making. *IEEE Trans. Fuzzy Syst.* **2015**, *23*, 1655–1668. [CrossRef]
37. Hashemi, H.; Mousavi, S.M.; Zavadskas, E.K.; Chalekaee, A.; Turskis, Z. A new group decision model based on grey-intuitionistic fuzzy-ELECTRE and VIKOR for contractor assessment problem. *Sustainability* **2018**, *10*, 1635. [CrossRef]
38. Wan, S.; Xu, G.; Dong, J. A novel method for group decision making with interval-valued Atanassov intuitionistic fuzzy preference relations. *Inf. Sci.* **2016**, *372*, 53–71. [CrossRef]
39. Xu, Y.; Da, Q. A method for multiple attribute decision making with incomplete weight information under uncertain linguistic environment. *Knowl.-Based Syst.* **2008**, *21*, 837–841. [CrossRef]
40. Xu, Z.; Zhang, X. Hesitant fuzzy multi-attribute decision making based on TOPSIS with incomplete weight information. *Knowl.-Based Syst.* **2013**, *52*, 53–64. [CrossRef]
41. Sharma, H.K.; Roy, J.; Kar, S.; Prentkovskis, O. Multi criteria evaluation framework for prioritizing Indian railway stations using modified rough AHP-MABAC method. *Transp. Telecommun.* **2018**, *19*, 113–127. [CrossRef]
42. Debnath, A.; Roy, J.; Kar, S.; Zavadskas, E.K.; Antucheviciene, J. A hybrid MCDM approach for strategic project portfolio selection of agro by-products. *Sustainability* **2017**, *9*, 1302. [CrossRef]
43. Zhang, Y.; Xu, Z.; Liao, H. A consensus process for group decision making with probabilistic linguistic preference relations. *Inf. Sci.* **2017**, *414*, 260–275. [CrossRef]
44. Yager, R.R. The power average operator. *IEEE Trans. Syst. Cybernatics-Part A Syst. Hum.* **2001**, *31*, 724–731. [CrossRef]
45. Xu, Z.; Yager, R.R. Power-geometric operators and their use in group decision making. *IEEE Trans. Fuzzy Syst.* **2010**, *18*, 94–105.
46. Xia, M.; Xu, Z. Entropy/cross entropy-based group decision making under intuitionistic fuzzy environment. *Inf. Fusion.* **2012**, *13*, 31–47. [CrossRef]

47. Liu, S.; Chan, F.T.S.; Ran, W. Decision making for the selection of cloud vendor: An improved approach under group decision-making with integrated weights and objective/subjective attributes. *Expert Syst. Appl.* **2016**, *55*, 37–47. [CrossRef]
48. Rao, R.V.; Patel, B.K.; Parnichkun, M. Industrial robot selection using a novel decision making method considering objective and subjective preferences. *Rob. Auton. Syst.* **2011**, *59*, 367–375. [CrossRef]
49. Goldstein, W.M.; Beattie, J. *Judgments of Relative Importance in Decision Making: The Importance of Interpretation and the Interpretation of Importance*, 1st ed.; Springer: New York, NY, USA, 1991; pp. 110–137.
50. Kao, C. Weight determination for consistently ranking alternatives in multiple criteria decision analysis. *Appl. Math. Model.* **2010**, *34*, 1779–1787. [CrossRef]
51. Opricovic, S.; Tzeng, G.H. Compromise solution by MCDM methods: A comparative analysis of VIKOR and TOPSIS. *Eur. J. Oper. Res.* **2004**, *156*, 445–455. [CrossRef]
52. Opricovic, S.; Tzeng, G.H. Extended VIKOR method in comparison with outranking methods. *Eur. J. Oper. Res.* **2007**, *178*, 514–529. [CrossRef]
53. Liao, H.; Jiang, L.; Xu, Z.; Xu, J.; Herrera, F. A probabilistic linguistic linear programming method in hesitant qualitative multiple criteria decision making. *Inf. Sci.* **2017**, *416*, 341–355. [CrossRef]
54. Roy, J.; Adhikary, K.; Kar, S. A rough strength relational DEMATEL model for analysing the key success factors of hospital service quality. *Decis. Mak. Appl. Manag. Eng.* **2018**, *1*, 121–142. [CrossRef]
55. Lima Junior, F.R.; Osiro, L.; Carpinetti, L.C.R. A comparison between fuzzy AHP and fuzzy TOPSIS methods to supplier selection. *Appl. Soft Comput. J.* **2014**, *21*, 194–209. [CrossRef]
56. Spearman, C. The proof and measurement of association between two things. *Am. J. Psychol.* **1904**, *15*, 72–101. [CrossRef]
57. Saaty, T.L.; Ozdemir, M.S. Why the magic number seven plus or minus two. *Math. Comput. Model.* **2003**, *38*, 233–244. [CrossRef]

© 2018 by the authors. Licensee MDPI, Basel, Switzerland. This article is an open access article distributed under the terms and conditions of the Creative Commons Attribution (CC BY) license (http://creativecommons.org/licenses/by/4.0/).

Article

Bi-Objective Scheduling Optimization for Discrete Time/Cost Trade-Off in Projects

Hongbo Li [1], Zhe Xu [2] and Wenchao Wei [3],*

1. School of Management, Shanghai University, Shanghai 200444, China; ishongboli@gmail.com
2. School of Economics and Management, Beihang University, Beijing 100191, China; xuzhebuaa@163.com
3. School of Economics and Management, Beijing Jiaotong University, Beijing 100044, China
* Correspondence: weiwenchao@bjtu.edu.cn; Tel.: +86-10-5168-7187

Received: 5 July 2018; Accepted: 5 August 2018; Published: 7 August 2018

Abstract: In sustainable project management, time and cost are two critical factors affecting the success of a project. Time/cost trade-offs in projects accelerate the execution of some activities by increasing the amount of non-renewable resources committed to them and therefore shorten the project duration. The discrete time/cost trade-off problem (DTCTP) has been extensively studied during the past 20 years. However, due to its complexity, the DTCTP—especially the DTCTP curve problem (DTCTP-C)—has only been solved for relatively small instances. To the best of our knowledge, there is no computational performance analysis for solving the DTCTP-C on large project instances with up to 500 activities. This paper aims to fill this gap. We present two bi-objective heuristic algorithms for the DTCTP-C where both project duration and cost are minimized. The objective is to obtain a good appropriate efficient set for the large-scale instances. The first algorithm is based on the non-dominated sorting genetic algorithm II (NSGA-II) and uses a specially designed critical path-based crossover operator. The second algorithm is a steepest descent heuristic which generates efficient solutions by iteratively solving the DTCTP with different deadlines. Computational experiments are conducted to validate the proposed algorithms on a large set of randomly generated problem instances.

Keywords: bi-objective optimization; heuristics; discrete time/cost trade-off; project scheduling

1. Introduction

The importance of time/cost trade-offs in projects have been recognized since the development of the critical path method (CPM) in the late 1950s [1]. Sustainable project management requires the resources to be used in an economical and sustainable way [2–4]. In project management, it is desirable that shorter project duration is achieved at a lower total cost. The project duration can usually be shortened by accelerating the execution of activities. Most often expediting the activity durations needs to allocate more resources to these activities. In many real-life cases, such as construction projects, the resources (e.g., human resources or heavy equipment) tend to be discrete and measured by a single non-renewable one (capital or cost). Therefore, the duration of project activities can be treated as discrete non-increasing functions of the cost. This results in the discrete time/cost trade-off problem (DTCTP) [1]. Harvey and Patterson [5] and Hindelang and Muth [6] first proposed the DTCTP, which is a special case of the multi-mode resource-constrained project scheduling problem [7].

In the DTCTP, each activity has multiple execution modes which are characterized by specific time and cost combinations. In terms of the objective function, the DTCTP can be divided into three versions: the deadline problem (DTCTP-D), the budget problem (DTCTP-B) and the time/cost trade-off curve problem (DTCTP-C). In the DTCTP-D, given a set of modes and a project deadline, the objective is to minimize the total project cost by specifying an execution mode for each activity. In the DTCTP-B, a project budget is given and the objective is to determine the modes that minimize the project makespan. In the DTCTP-C, the objective is to determine the Pareto curve that minimizes the project makespan and cost simultaneously. In the remainder of this paper, we focus on the DTCTP-C.

Numerous exact and heuristic methods have been proposed for solving the DTCTP. Because the DTCTP is strongly NP-hard [8], exact algorithms—such as a branch and bound procedure and dynamic programming—can only solve relatively small instances [9–12]. Heuristic or meta-heuristic methods are more practical for solving large instances within a reasonable time [13–15]. For more detailed excellent literature reviews on the DTCTP, we refer to De et al. [9] and Demeulemeester and Herroelen [1].

Despite the vast majority of the research efforts in the DTCTP, there are few studies that have considered solving the DTCTP with more than 200 activities. Sonmez and Bettemir [16] developed a hybrid genetic algorithm for the DTCTP-D and tested it on problem instances with up to 630 activities. However, they only use ten instances to evaluate their algorithm which limits the generalizability of the algorithm. To the best of our knowledge, there are no heuristic algorithms for the DTCTP-C that solves representative instances with up to 500 activities in the existing literature. However, in practice, it is common that a project will most likely consist of hundreds of activities [17]. This motivates us to study efficient heuristic algorithms. Moreover, the lack of computational performance analysis is another common drawback for the past research in the DTCTP. Some papers only used simple examples to test their algorithms [18,19], which usually cannot fully prove the effectiveness and adaptability of the algorithms.

The purpose of this paper is to develop and verify two heuristics and to obtain a good appropriate efficient set for the large-scale DTCTP-C. The contributions of this paper are three-fold:

(1) We propose a bi-objective hybrid genetic algorithm (BHGA) for the DTCTP-C by introducing a critical path based crossover operator in the non-dominated sorting genetic algorithm II (NSGA-II) [20]. As an effective multi-objective optimization meta-heuristic algorithm, NSGA-II has been widely used to solve the DTCTP [21,22]. Our BHGA further exploits the knowledge of the DTCTP-C and enhances the searching efficiency of the NSGA-II for the DTCTP-C.

(2) We propose a steepest descent heuristic for the DTCTP-C to obtain efficient solutions by iteratively solving the DTCTP with different deadlines. We design a special neighborhood search procedure based on the inherent characteristics of the DTCTP-C. Our experimental results show that the proposed steepest descent heuristic outperforms the NSGA-II based BHGA.

(3) We conduct extensive computational performance analysis for the proposed heuristics. We use factorial experimental design to randomly generate a large number of instances (with up to 500 activities) in order to validate and compare our heuristic approaches.

This paper is organized as follows. In the next section, we give the description and the model formulation of the DTCTP-C. Section 3 provides a bi-objective hybrid genetic algorithm for the DTCTP-C. In Section 4, we propose a steepest descent heuristic for the DTCTP-C. In Section 5, we present the computational results. Finally, Section 6 concludes the paper with future research directions.

2. Problem Statement and Model Formulation

2.1. DTCTP-C

The DTCTP-C under study is described as follows. A project network $G = (N, A)$ is represented in activity-on-node format, where the set of nodes N denotes the activities $N = \{1, \ldots, n\}$, and the set of directed arcs A represents the finish–start, zero-lag precedence relations $A \subseteq N \times N$. The nodes are topologically numbered from the single start node 1 to the single terminal node n, $n = |N|$, where nodes 1 and n are dummy activities. Each activity i ($i = 1, \ldots, n$) has $|M_i|$ modes, characterized by a duration–cost pair (d_{ij}, c_{ij}), $j = 1, \ldots, |M_i|$, where M_i is the set of modes of activity i, $M_i = \{1, 2, \ldots, m\}$. The duration d_{ij} of an activity $i \in N$ is a discrete, non-increasing function of the amount of a single non-renewable resources (c_{ij}) committed to it, i.e., if $k < l$ ($k, l \in M_i$), then $d_{ik} < d_{il}$ and $c_{ik} > c_{il}$. The dummy activities 1 and n have only one execution mode with zero duration/cost. For the remainder of the paper, we need to assume the reader be familiar with CPM [1].

A sequence of distinct activities is called a *path*. The *length* of a path is calculated as the sum of the durations of all activities belonging to this path. A *critical path* is the longest path from activity 1 to activity n. There may exist more than one critical path. Each delay caused to a critical (path) activity incurs a delay in the global project. For a more detailed discussion on the CPM, we refer to Demeulemeester and Herroelen [1].

In the DTCTP, given a mode $m_i = (d_{ij}, c_{ij})$ ($j = 1, \ldots, M_i$) for each activity i, the start time of activity i can be computed as the maximum of the earliest finish times of all the predecessors of activity i in accordance with the CPM.

The solution of the DTCTP-C can be represented by a baseline schedule or a selected set of modes, i.e., a mode assignment vector $m = (m_1, m_2, \ldots, m_n)$, $m_i \in M_i$, $i \in N$. Given a mode assignment vector m, the corresponding project makespan $t(m)$ is the critical path length and the project cost $c(m)$ is the sum of the cost for all the activities. Then, the baseline schedule, i.e., a vector $S^B = (s_1, s_2, \ldots, s_n)$ of start times ($s_i \geq 0$, $i \in N$), can be obtained by calculating the earliest start time of each activity based on the CPM.

2.2. Model Formulation of the DTCTP-C

The DTCTP-C involves the determination of a set of efficient project baseline schedules (or a set of efficient mode assignment vectors), while satisfying the precedence relations constraints with the objective of minimizing both the project makespan and the project cost. The bi-objective mixed integer linear programming formulation for the DTCTP-C is written as follows:

$$\text{minimize } s_n \tag{1}$$

$$\text{minimize } \sum_{i \in N} \sum_{m \in M_i} c_{im} x_{im} \tag{2}$$

subject to:

$$\sum_{m \in M_i} x_{im} = 1 \; \forall (i,j) \in A \tag{3}$$

$$s_i + \sum_{m \in M_i} d_{im} x_{im} \leq s_j \; \forall (i,j) \in A \tag{4}$$

$$s_i \geq 0 \; \forall i \in N \tag{5}$$

$$x_{im} \in \{0,1\} \; \forall m \in M_i, \forall i \in N \tag{6}$$

where s_i and x_{im} are decision variables. x_{im} is a 0–1 variable which is 1 if mode m is selected for executing activity i and 0 otherwise. The first objective (1) minimizes the project makespan $t(m)$ which is equal to the start time s_n of the dummy end activity n. The second objective (2) minimizes the total project cost $c(m)$. The constraints in (3) ensure that exactly one execution mode is assigned to each activity. The constraints in (4) represent the precedence relations. The constraints in (5) ensure that the activity's start times are non-negative. The constraints in (6) guarantee that x_{im} is a binary variable.

A mode assignment vector $m = (m_1, m_2, \ldots, m_n)$ is called *efficient* if there does not exist any other mode assignment vector m' such that the project makespan $t(m') \leq t(m)$ and the total project cost $c(m') \leq c(m)$, with at least one strict inequality. The corresponding objective function value vector $(t(m), c(m))$ is called non-dominated. The set of non-dominated objective function value vectors ND is also referred to as the Pareto frontier or the time/cost trade-off curve. The objective of the DTCTP-C boils down to find a set of efficient solutions (mode assignment vectors or modes): the efficient (non-dominated or Pareto-optimal) set E.

2.3. Example

We use an example to illustrate the problem under consideration. Figure 1 shows a project network, in which each node has a corresponding activity number placed inside the node. For each activity, its modes are shown next to the node. The activities 1 and 5 are two dummy activities and have only one mode with zero duration/cost. Activity 2/3/4 has 2/1/3 mode(s), respectively.

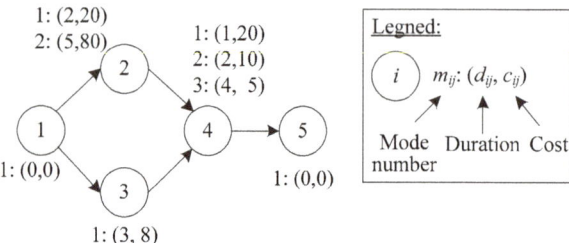

Figure 1. The example project network.

There are six mode combinations for the example project. In other words, there are six solutions (mode assignment vectors) in total for this DTCTP-C instance. In Figure 2, the six solutions are represented in a two-dimensional objective space. The number besides each point shows the corresponding project makespan, cost, and mode assignment vector, respectively. The DTCTP-C aims to find the Pareto-optimal solutions which have been associated to the points P_1, P_2, P_3, P_5 and P_6 in Figure 2. Figure 2 also shows the Pareto frontier.

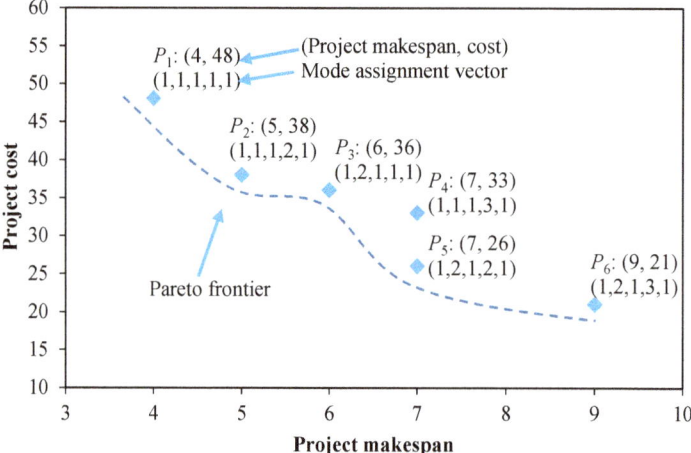

Figure 2. The Pareto frontier of the example project.

3. Bi-Objective Hybrid Genetic Algorithm

NSGA-II is a fast and elitist multi-objective algorithm that aims at obtaining good approximations of the non-dominated set of solutions [20,23–25]. In order to exploit the knowledge of the DTCTP-C, we introduce a critical path based crossover operator into the NSGA-II. The resulting algorithm is a bi-objective hybrid genetic algorithm (BHGA). Unlike the standard crossover operators which tend to randomly choose parts of the good solutions without any guarantee, our critical path based crossover operator can guarantee the offspring inherit the parts of the good solutions that contribute most to the objectives.

3.1. Schedule Encoding and Decoding

As mentioned in Section 2.1, a schedule can be determined by a mode assignment vector. Therefore, in the BHGA, a mode assignment vector $m = (m_1, m_2, \ldots, m_n)$ is used as a chromosome. The length of each chromosome is $n = |N|$. Each gene $m_i \in M_i$ ($i \in N$) in the chromosome corresponds to a mode of activity i. Note that since the dummy start and end activities have zero duration/cost, their modes are always unchanged in the BHGA.

Once a mode assignment vector (chromosome) is given, the baseline schedule $S^B = (s_1, s_2, \ldots, s_n)$ can be obtained by calculating the earliest start time of each activity in accordance with the CPM. In this way, a chromosome is decoded into a schedule.

With the above-mentioned schedule encoding and decoding mechanisms, given a chromosome, the corresponding objective function values (project duration and cost) can be calculated according to Equations (1) and (2). The fitness of a chromosome is represented by their non-domination rank (see next section).

Consider the example project in Figure 1, a possible chromosome for this project is shown in Figure 3. The length of this chromosome is equal to the number of activities, i.e., 5. Each gene corresponds to a mode number. For example, the mode number of activities 3 and 4 are 1 and 3, respectively. We can get the baseline schedule (0, 0, 0, 5, 9) by decoding this chromosome. The resulting project duration and cost are 9 and 21, respectively.

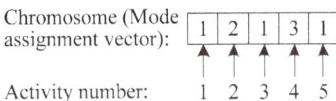

Figure 3. A possible chromosome corresponding to the example project of Figure 1.

3.2. Selection Operator

The binary tournament selection operator is used for selecting parent chromosomes. Two chromosomes are randomly chosen and the one with a lower non-domination rank is added to the matting pool. However, if both chromosomes have the same rank, the one with a greater crowding distance value will be chosen.

In NSGA-II, the non-domination rank of each chromosome is obtained by the fast non-dominated sorting approach [20]. Assume that the current population size is P, we find out all the non-dominated chromosomes and put them into the non-dominated set F_1 with rank 1. Then, we find out the non-dominated chromosomes from the remaining population and put them into the non-dominated set F_2 with rank 2. Repeat the process until all chromosomes are put into the corresponding non-dominated set F_p with rank p. By doing so, the population is divided into p ($p \leq P$) disjoint sub-populations (non-dominated sets) and satisfies the condition that the non-dominated set with a smaller index dominates the non-dominated set with a larger index (i.e., F_i dominates F_j, if $i < j$).

For chromosomes with either the smallest or the largest function values, their crowding distances are infinite. For other chromosomes, crowding distance is defined as the absolute normalized difference between the objective function values of two adjacent chromosomes. Therefore, the chromosomes with greater crowding distance value have more opportunities to be involved in the evolution process, which can maintain the population diversity.

3.3. Critical Path Crossover Operator

The crossover operator ensures that the good characteristics of the parent chromosomes can be inherited by the offspring. Given a chromosome, the corresponding project duration is determined by the critical path length. In the DTCTP-C, a short critical path length and a low total cost are desirable characteristics in a chromosome. However, shorter project duration is usually accompanied by higher project cost. Therefore, it is not always reasonable to transmit all activities on the critical path to the offspring. Instead, we set a threshold τ that determines the number of critical path activities transmitted to the offspring. In doing so, we might generate offspring with satisfying performance in both project duration and cost.

Based on the above observations, we develop a critical path crossover operator and the procedure is shown in Algorithm 1. In the critical path crossover operator, we first define the critical path ratio (CPR) as the proportion of the critical activities in a chromosome i, i.e., $CPR_i = N_c/N$, where N_c is the number of critical activities in the corresponding schedule after decoding chromosome i. Each chromosome is chosen for crossover with probability P_c according to tournament selection. Given two chromosomes to be crossed, we select the one with shorter (longer) makespan as the father (mother) chromosome. The son chromosome is generated in the following way: the value of the threshold τ for the CPR is randomly selected from the interval $[l, u]$ ($0 < l < u < 1$, l and u are parameters and need to be determined by users). If the CPR of the father chromosome is less than τ, then the son inherits all critical activities of the father, and the mother determines the remaining positions. Otherwise, the son only inherits $100 \times \tau\%$ of critical activities of the father, and the mother determines the remaining positions. In order to ensure the diversity of the offspring, the daughter is generated in such a way that the daughter inherits the non-critical path activities of the mother chromosome and the father determines the remaining positions.

Algorithm 1. The Critical Path Based Crossover Operator.

Step 1: Given two chromosomes, select the one with shorter (longer) makespan as the father (mother) chromosome.

Step 2: Compute the critical path ratio (CPR) for the father chromosome CPR_f.

Step 3: Generate the son chromosome.

- Choose τ randomly from the interval $[l, u]$.
- If $CPR_f < \tau$

    Put the genes that lie on the critical path of the father chromosome to the corresponding positions of the son chromosome.

- Else

    Select $100 \times \tau\%$ of critical activities randomly from the father chromosome and put them to the corresponding positions of the son chromosome.
- End if
- The remaining positions of the son are determined by the corresponding genes of the mother chromosome.

Step 4: Generate the daughter chromosome

- Put the genes that lie on the non-critical path of the mother chromosome to the corresponding positions of the daughter chromosome.
- The remaining positions of the daughter chromosome are inherited from the corresponding genes of the father chromosome.

3.4. Mutation Operator

In our algorithm, one-point mutation is used. Each chromosome has a probability P_m to be selected to mutate. For the chosen chromosome, one of its genes is randomly selected and its value is randomly changed to a different mode.

3.5. Algorithm Framework

In the BHGA, initial populations are generated randomly. In each iteration of the BHGA, the genetic operators (i.e., selection, crossover, and mutation operators) are applied to the chromosomes. The chromosomes with better fitness values have a higher chance to survive and enter next iteration. After a given number of iterations, the remaining populations will belong to or be close to the Pareto optimal set. The framework of the BHGA is described in Algorithm 2.

Algorithm 2. The Framework of the BHGA.
Step 1: Initialization. Generate the initial population P with size N randomly. Compute the objective function value for each chromosome of P.
Step 2: Fast non-dominated sorting. Perform fast non-dominated sorting on the initial population P. Compute the rank and the crowding distance for each chromosome of P.
Step 3: Genetic operation.   Select N/2 chromosomes from P using binary tournament, resulting in the population Q.   Generate offspring population R by performing the *critical path crossover* and mutation operator on Q. $P' \leftarrow P \cup Q$.   Perform fast non-dominated sorting on population P'.   Update P by selecting N best chromosomes from P' based on the rank and the crowding distance.
Step 4: If the maximum number of generations is not reached, then go to *Step 3*; else: return P.

4. Steepest Descent Heuristic

The basic idea of our steepest descent heuristic is as follows. The solution space of the DTCTP-C could be divided into different parts in terms of the project deadline. For a given project deadline, we are able to find a solution with minimum project cost (this corresponds to solving a DTCTP-D). For a well-chosen project deadline, the resulting project duration and cost are most likely non-dominated. Hence, in this section, we obtain efficient solutions for the DTCTP-C by iteratively solving the DTCTP with different deadlines (i.e., DTCTP-D). In each iteration, given a project deadline, the solution that minimizes the total project cost is determined with the steepest descent search procedure presented in this section. Then the resulting solution is used as a start point for the next iteration. The solution returned by each iteration is (appropriately) Pareto-optimal.

4.1. Algorithm Framework

The steepest descent heuristic mainly consists of two stages: an initialization stage and a steepest descent search stage. Algorithm 3 gives the framework of our steepest descent heuristic. In Algorithm 3, a solution is also represented by a mode assignment vector $m = (m_1, m_2, \ldots, m_n)$ which specifies the execution mode m_i for each activity i.

In the initialization stage, the modes of each activity are sorted in the non-decreasing order of durations and labeled from 1 to $|M_i|$. The initial solution (mode assignment) m is generated by setting the mode of each activity at their crash mode $m^{crash} = (1, 1, \ldots, 1)_n$. In the crash mode, all activities are set to their shortest duration. The normal mode m^{normal} in which all activities are set to their normal modes (longest duration) and the crash mode m^{crash} are obviously two efficient solutions. Therefore, they are added to the efficient set E. ITER is a predefined number used to control the number of repetitions of the steepest descent search in stage 2.

Algorithm 3. The Framework of the Steepest Descent Heuristic.

Stage 1: Initialization.
    For each activity i, sort its modes in the order of nondecreasing duration and label the resulting modes from 1 to $|M_i|$.
    $m \leftarrow m^{crash}$.
    $E \leftarrow \{m^{crash}, m^{normal}\}$.
    $ND \leftarrow \{(t(m^{crash}), c(m^{crash})), (t(m^{normal}), c(m^{normal}))\}$.
    $step \leftarrow \lfloor (t(m^{normal}) - t(m^{crash}))/ITER \rfloor$.
    $\delta \leftarrow t(m^{crash}) + step$.
Stage 2: Iterative steepest descent.
    For $i = 1$ to ITER
        $m' \leftarrow $ **sd_search**(m, δ).
        $\delta \leftarrow t(m') + step$.
        if $c(m') \leq c(m)$ then $E \leftarrow E \cup \{m'\}$.
        $m \leftarrow m'$.
    End for
    For each $m \in E$
        calculate $t(m), c(m)$.
        $ND \leftarrow ND \cup \{(t(m), c(m))\}$.
    End for
    Return efficient set E and non-dominated set ND.

In the second stage, the steepest descent search is repeated for ITER times to iteratively solve the DTCTP-D(δ) with different deadline δ. These deadlines are determined as follows. In the DTCTP, we can obtain the longest $(t(m^{normal}))$ and shortest project makespan $(t(m^{crash}))$ by choosing the normal and crash mode, respectively. Let the time increment $step = \lfloor (t(m^{normal}) - t(m^{crash}))/ITER \rfloor$. Then, in each iteration, the project deadline δ will be updated by adding $step$ to the current deadline δ which is calculated according to the current mode assignment.

In each iteration of Stage 2, the specific DTCTP-D(δ) is solved by the steepest decent search procedure 'sd_search( )'. 'sd_search( )' returns a mode assignment with minimum total project cost. After completing all iterations, we obtain the set of efficient solutions E and the corresponding non-dominated set ND. It can be observed that ITER (or $step$) determines the value of different project deadlines and hence it has an influence on the quality and quantity of the solutions in E.

4.2. Neighborhood and the Steepest Decent Search Procedure 'sd_search( )'

We construct the neighborhood of a specific mode assignment vector $m = (m_1, m_2, \ldots, m_n)$ by changing the mode m_i of each activity i to its right adjacent one m_i', $i \in N$ ($m_i' = m_i + 1$). We call this operation *right* move. Because the modes of each activity are already sorted in the non-decreasing order of durations (this also leads to a decreasing order of cost), the right move guarantees that the resulting total project cost satisfies $c(m') \leq c(m')$. The maximum number of possible moves equals n.

Given a mode assignment m, all of its neighbors are evaluated and then the one that yields the biggest reduction in cost without violating the project deadline constrains is chosen as the updated starting solution. In order to avoid calculating critical path for every move, we determine whether the project deadline constraint is violated in the following way. For an activity on the critical path, it is allowed to move to its neighbor mode, only when the difference between the activity's neighbor duration and current duration is less than the difference between the project deadline and critical path length. For an activity that is not on the critical path, it is allowed to move to its neighbor mode, only when the difference between the activity's neighbor duration and current duration is less than the difference between the project deadline and critical path length plus the activity's total float. In doing so, certain computational time can be reduced.

If the neighborhood is examined entirely without any improvement, we have found a local optimum and terminate the search procedure.

In Algorithm 4, we give the pseudo-code for the steepest decent search procedure 'sd_search( )'. $CPL(m)$ is the critical path length that is calculated based on the mode assignment m. $CA(m)$ is the set of activities that lie on the critical path(s) given the mode assignment m. *Best_activity* represents the activity that leads to the best improvement in the total project cost if a right move is performed on this activity. CB is the current best improvement value of the total cost. $TF(i)$ represents the total float of activity i.

Algorithm 4. The Steepest Decent Search Procedure.

---

procedure sd_search(m, δ)
best_activity $\leftarrow 0$.
Repeat
    $CB \leftarrow 0$.
    $\Delta d \leftarrow \delta - CPL(m)$.
    For each activity i and its current mode number m_i
        If $i \in CA(m)$ and $m_i \neq 1$ and $d_{i(m_i+1)} - d_{im_i} < \Delta d$
            If $c_{im_i} - c_{i(m_i+1)} > CB$
                $CB \leftarrow c_{im_i} - c_{i(m_i+1)}$.
                best_activity $\leftarrow i$.
            End if
        End if
        If $i \notin CA(m)$ and $m_i \neq 1$ and $d_{i(m_i+1)} - d_{im_i} < \Delta d + TF(i)$
            If $c_{im_i} - c_{i(m_i+1)} > CB$
                $CB \leftarrow c_{im_i} - c_{i(m_i+1)}$
                best_activity $\leftarrow i$.
            End if
        End if
    End for
    If best_activity $\neq 0$ then $m_{best\_activity} \leftarrow m_{best\_activity} + 1$.
Until $CB == 0$
$m \leftarrow (m_1, m_2, \ldots, m_n)$.
Return m.

4.3. Example

In this section, we use the example of Figure 1 to illustrate our steepest descent heuristic. We will let the steepest descent heuristic iterates three times (i.e., ITER = 3). The three iterations correspond to three rectangles (labeled with "Iteration 1/2/3") that are shown in Figure 4. Figure 4 is created by adding the three rectangles to Figure 2. Each rectangle is associated with a project deadline and hence resulting in a DTCTP-D. In each iteration, a mode assignment vector will be used as the input, and all of its neighbors (associated with each rectangle) will be evaluated without violating the project deadline constraints. In other words, we need to find a mode assignment that minimizes the project cost given the project deadline specified by each rectangle.

As shown in Figure 4, points P_1 and P_6 correspond to crash mode and normal mode, respectively. Therefore, P_1 (corresponds to the mode (1, 1, 1, 1, 1)) and P_6 (corresponds to the mode (1, 2, 1, 3, 1)) are selected as two efficient solutions and added to the non-dominated set in the initialization stage.

Then the second stage which consists of three iterations begins. In Iteration 1, the project deadline is set to 6. The crash mode P_1 (1, 1, 1, 1, 1) is used as the initial solution. According to the definition of the right move given in Section 4.2, P_2 and P_3 are two neighbors of P_1. Since selecting P_3 will yield the biggest reduction in cost (48 − 36 = 12) and the total cost of P_3 (which is 36) is lower than that of P_1 (which is 48), we add P_3 to the non-dominated set, and P_3 will be the input of the second iteration.

In Iteration 2, the project deadline is 8. P_3 has only one neighbor P_5 and the total cost of P_5 (which is 26) is lower than that of P_3 (which is 36). Hence P_5 is added to the non-dominated set and will be the input of the next iteration. In the last iteration, there is only one solution P_6. Because P_6 corresponds to the normal mode and has been added to the non-dominated set in the initialization stage, there are no other solutions to evaluate and the steepest descent heuristic terminates.

In this example, the steepest descent heuristic found four efficient solutions (P_1, P_3, P_5, and P_6) and only P_2 is missed.

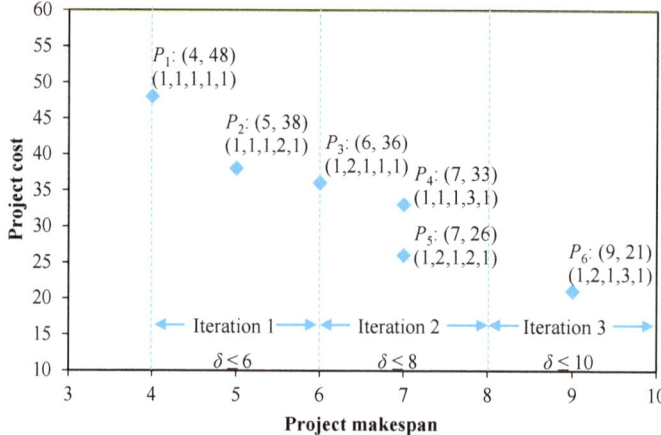

Figure 4. The DTCTP-C instance can be seen as three DTCTP-D instances.

5. Computational Experiments

We have randomly generated a large number of problem instances to compare the performance of our algorithms. All of our algorithms are implemented in Matlab version R2010b and run on an Intel Core i5 2.40 GHz portable computer equipped with Windows 7. It is necessary to note that there is no research that has reported computational results for the large-scale DTCTP-C. Therefore, we only compare the performance of our two algorithms and our results can be served as the benchmark for future research.

5.1. Problem Instances Generation

In order to evaluate our algorithms, *RanGen2* [26,27], which can generate strongly random networks in activity-on-the-node format, is used to construct 600 test instances using the parameter settings in Table 1. RanGen2 uses the serial/parallel indicator (I2) to measure the topological structure of a network. I2 measures the closeness of a network to a parallel or serial graph, ranging from 0 (indicating completely parallel) to 1 (indicating completely serial). For more information about the I2 indicator, we refer to Valadares Tavares et al. [28]. Specifying 5 settings for the number of activities, 4 settings for the number of execution modes, and 3 settings for the I2, we generated 10 problem instances for each of the 5 × 4 × 3 parameter settings, resulting in 600 instances in total.

Table 1. The parameter settings of the problem instances.

Number of activities	100; 200; 300; 400; 500
Number of modes	Fixed at 4; 8; or randomly chosen from the interval [4, 20]; [8, 30]
I2	0.3; 0.5; 0.7
Activity durations	Randomly selected from the interval [1, 50]
Activity normal costs	Randomly selected from the interval [1, 10]
Slope	Randomly selected from the interval [1, 8]

In DTCTP, the types of cost functions could be linear, convex, concave, or random. We focus on the random one which is more general [26]. Following Demeulemeester et al. [26], the modes of an activity are generated in the following way: Firstly, the number of modes $|M_i|$ is determined according to the modes parameter shown in Table 1. Then, $|M_i|$ different values are randomly chosen from the discrete uniform distribution [1, 50] as the durations and are sorted in ascending order $(d_{i|M_i|}, d_{i(|M_i|-1)}, \cdots, d_{i1})$. In order to generate activity cost, starting with the normal duration mode $d_{i|M_i|}$, its corresponding cost $c_{i|M_i|}$ is randomly chosen from the discrete uniform distribution [1,10]. By randomly choosing a slope s from the discrete uniform distribution [1, 8], we can calculate the cost of the next mode as $c_{i(|M_i|-1)} = c_{i|M_i|} + s \times (d_{i|M_i|} - d_{i(|M_i|-1)})$, and we repeat this stepwise procedure until the mode corresponding to the maximum cost is reached.

5.2. Parameter Settings of the Algorithms

There are multiple settings of the parameters of our algorithms. For the BHGA, the parameters include: the threshold τ in the critical path crossover, crossover probability, mutation probability, population size, and the maximum number of generations. In our preliminary experiments, we found that fixing the first three parameters as the following values is decent enough to produce good results:

- Threshold τ is randomly chosen from the interval [0.3, 0.9].
- Crossover probability = 0.8.
- Mutation probability = 0.2.

For the remaining parameters of the BHGA, assigning two settings for the population size, and two settings for the maximum number of generations (as shown in Table 2), we therefore obtain four variants of the BHGA: BHGA1, BHGA2, BHGA3, and BHGA4. For the steepest decent heuristic, the maximum number of iterations (ITER) is the only parameter and is assigned two settings (as shown in Table 2). Hence, we obtain two variants: SD1 and SD2.

Table 2. The parameter settings of the algorithms.

BHGA1	
Population size	50
Number of generations	50
BHGA2	
Population size	50
Number of generations	100
BHGA3	
Population size	100
Number of generations	50
BHGA4	
Population size	100
Number of generations	100
SD1	
Number of iterations	50
SD2	
Number of iterations	100

5.3. Experimental Results

In order to evaluate the performance of our six algorithms, we calculate the following metrics for each algorithm over all instances: the CPU time and the coverage metric e. In our experiment, the exact Pareto-optimal solutions are hardly known since the scale of the test instances is large. In this case, the coverage metric e which measures the percentage of efficient solutions in the obtained efficient set E that is produced by a specific algorithm is a suitable alternative. For a given algorithm ALG ($ALG \in \{BHGA1, BHGA2, BHGA3, BHGA4, SD1, SD2\}$), the corresponding coverage metric $e(ALG)$ is calculated as [29]

$$e(ALG) = \frac{|E(ALG) \cap E|}{|E|} \tag{7}$$

where E(ALG) is the efficient set obtained by algorithm ALG. Efficient set E is obtained by removing the dominated modes from the union set E(BHGA1) ∪ E(BHGA2) ∪ E(BHGA3) ∪ E(BHGA4) ∪ E(SD1) ∪ E(SD2). Obviously, the coverage metric value ranges from 0 to 1. For a specific algorithm, the more efficient solutions it contributes, the closer its coverage metric value will be to 1.

Table 3 presents the average CPU time over all problem instances solved by each of the six algorithms. Table 4 has a similar format to Table 3 and shows the mean, median, and interquartile range (IQR) of the coverage metric e for different algorithms. As shown in the row labeled 'All instances' in Tables 3 and 4, the proposed steepest decent heuristic (SD2) outperforms the BHGA (1–4) over all 600 problem instances in terms of computational time and coverage metric. For the steepest decent method, better results are obtained with a large number of iterations (SD2) and the required computational expense does not increase significantly. For the BHGA, a large population size and generation lead to better results (BHGA4) at the expense of more computational time.

Table 3. The average CPU time of different algorithms (in seconds).

	BHGA1	BHGA2	BHGA3	BHGA4	SD1	SD2
All instances	5.29	10.19	14.32	28.98	4.19	4.49
Number of activities						
100	2.93	5.98	8.07	17.07	0.65	0.73
200	4.01	8.09	10.11	22.22	1.89	2.01
300	5.31	10.28	14.38	27.54	3.63	4.00
400	6.33	12.03	17.54	34.26	5.87	6.24
500	7.87	14.56	21.51	43.83	8.90	9.45
Number of modes						
4	5.27	10.20	14.31	28.99	1.42	1.63
8	5.23	10.20	14.42	28.84	3.05	3.30
[4,20]	5.36	10.18	14.33	29.11	4.68	5.04
[8,30]	5.32	10.17	14.23	28.99	7.61	7.97
I2						
0.3	4.68	9.30	13.34	27.03	4.01	4.33
0.5	5.26	9.84	14.12	28.20	4.14	4.40
0.7	5.94	11.42	15.51	31.72	4.42	4.73

Table 4. The mean, median, and IQR of the coverage metric e for different algorithms.

		BHGA1	BHGA2	BHGA3	BHGA4	SD1	SD2
	Mean	0.04	0.05	0.13	0.23	0.12	0.46
All instances	Median	0.03	0.04	0.12	0.22	0.10	0.46
	IQR	0.03	0.04	0.13	0.20	0.12	0.30
Number of activities							
	Mean	0.03	0.05	0.15	0.33	0.13	0.35
100	Median	0.03	0.04	0.13	0.29	0.11	0.37
	IQR	0.02	0.03	0.10	0.32	0.14	0.31
	Mean	0.03	0.04	0.13	0.22	0.13	0.48
200	Median	0.03	0.04	0.10	0.21	0.11	0.51
	IQR	0.02	0.02	0.11	0.19	0.09	0.27
	Mean	0.03	0.05	0.14	0.22	0.12	0.47
300	Median	0.03	0.05	0.13	0.26	0.10	0.44
	IQR	0.03	0.04	0.16	0.25	0.13	0.34
	Mean	0.03	0.04	0.12	0.18	0.12	0.53
400	Median	0.03	0.04	0.11	0.16	0.11	0.53
	IQR	0.02	0.03	0.10	0.14	0.11	0.20

Table 4. Cont.

		BHGA1	BHGA2	BHGA3	BHGA4	SD1	SD2
	Mean	0.04	0.05	0.14	0.22	0.11	0.46
500	Median	0.04	0.05	0.14	0.25	0.09	0.41
	IQR	0.03	0.04	0.15	0.25	0.10	0.38
Number of modes							
	Mean	0.02	0.04	0.08	0.21	0.14	0.55
4	Median	0.02	0.03	0.07	0.17	0.10	0.59
	IQR	0.02	0.03	0.08	0.21	0.16	0.28
	Mean	0.03	0.05	0.13	0.23	0.13	0.47
8	Median	0.03	0.04	0.12	0.20	0.11	0.46
	IQR	0.03	0.04	0.13	0.21	0.10	0.29
	Mean	0.04	0.05	0.16	0.27	0.11	0.40
[4,20]	Median	0.04	0.05	0.16	0.25	0.09	0.39
	IQR	0.02	0.04	0.14	0.21	0.11	0.31
	Mean	0.04	0.06	0.16	0.24	0.11	0.42
[8,30]	Median	0.04	0.05	0.16	0.24	0.10	0.41
	IQR	0.03	0.03	0.10	0.20	0.10	0.25
I2							
	Mean	0.03	0.04	0.07	0.11	0.18	0.60
0.3	Median	0.02	0.03	0.16	0.10	0.18	0.62
	IQR	0.02	0.02	0.07	0.09	0.12	0.17
	Mean	0.04	0.05	0.14	0.22	0.11	0.47
0.5	Median	0.04	0.05	0.14	0.23	0.10	0.45
	IQR	0.03	0.03	0.10	0.11	0.09	0.20
	Mean	0.04	0.06	0.19	0.37	0.07	0.30
0.7	Median	0.04	0.05	0.20	0.35	0.06	0.28
	IQR	0.03	0.04	0.12	0.16	0.06	0.16

According to the rows labeled 'Number of activities', 'Number of modes', and 'I2' in Table 3, we observe that the three factors have a negative impact on CPU time: the more complex the test instance, the more the average CPU time is required.

It can be seen from Table 4 that the number of activities has a weak impact on the coverage metric, and the impact is especially slight for the BHGA. However, the impact of the number of activities does not show a regular pattern for the SD2, which probably means that we need to adjust the number of iterations according to the number of activities. For both the BHGA and the SD, the impacts of both the number of modes and the I2 on the coverage metric are opposite. For the BHGA, the higher both the number of modes and the I2, the greater the number of efficient solutions obtained. However, the SD shows an opposite behavior. This is because the performance of the SD is affected by the parameter *step* which determines the project duration increment in each iteration. For a more complex instance, it is necessary to use a relatively small value for *step*. While in our experiments, the value of *step* is fixed for each instance.

Overall, the steepest descent heuristic SD2 obtains more efficient solutions than other algorithms in promising computational time. Specifically, our SD2 outperforms the BHGA in both solution quality and computation efficiency. Compared with the SD1, our SD2 produces much better solutions and the required CPU time has only slightly increased.

6. Conclusions and Future Research

Time/cost trade-offs in projects are concerned with building baseline schedules that minimize project duration and cost simultaneously. In this paper, we presented two bi-objective heuristic algorithms for solving large-scale DTCTP-C with the aim of obtaining a good appropriate efficient solution set. The first algorithm BHGA is based on the NSGA-II. We devise a critical path based crossover operator to further exploits the knowledge of the DTCTP-C and improve the searching efficiency of the NSGA-II. The second algorithm is a steepest descent heuristic which generates efficient solutions by iteratively solving the DTCTP with different deadlines. We design a specified neighborhood search procedure based on the steepest descent search logic. Computational experience on the randomly generated problem data set validated both algorithms. Computational results reveal that our steepest descent heuristic algorithm outperforms the BHGA in terms of both the computational time and the coverage metric.

For future research, it will be a promising topic to devise more efficient and effective meta-heuristics for the DTCTP. It will also make our algorithms more practical by integrating them into project management decision support systems.

Author Contributions: H.L. conceived and designed the entire study; H.L., Z.X., and W.W. analyzed the data; H.L. and W.W. wrote the paper.

Funding: This research was funded by the Humanities and Social Sciences Foundation of the Ministry of Education of China (grant number 15YJCZH077), the National Science Foundation of China (grant numbers 71602106, 71271019, 7161101015, 71702097), the Fundamental Funds for Humanities and Social Sciences of Beijing Jiaotong University (grant number 2017jbwy004), and the College Young Teachers Training Program of Shanghai Municipal Education Commission (grant number ZZSD16025).

Acknowledgments: The authors thank the editor and reviewers for providing valuable suggestions that have improved the quality of this paper.

Conflicts of Interest: The authors declare no conflict of interest.

References

1. Demeulemeester, E.L.; Herroelen, W.S. *Project Scheduling: A Research Handbook*; Kluwer Academic Pub: Dordrecht, The Netherlands, 2002.
2. Dobrovolskienė, N.; Tamošiūnienė, R. Sustainability-oriented financial resource allocation in a project portfolio through multi-criteria decision-making. *Sustainability* **2016**, *8*, 485. [CrossRef]
3. Li, H.; Dong, X. Multi-mode resource leveling in projects with mode-dependent generalized precedence relations. *Expert Syst. Appl.* **2018**, *97*, 193–204. [CrossRef]
4. Li, H.; Xiong, L.; Liu, Y.; Li, H. An effective genetic algorithm for the resource levelling problem with generalised precedence relations. *Int. J. Prod. Res.* **2018**, *56*, 2054–2075. [CrossRef]
5. Harvey, R.T.; Patterson, J.H. An implicit enumeration algorithm for the time/cost tradeoff problem in project network analysis. *Found. Control Eng.* **1979**, *4*, 107–117.
6. Hindelang, T.J.; Muth, J.F. A dynamic programming algorithm for decision CPM networks. *Oper. Res.* **1979**, *27*, 225–241. [CrossRef]
7. Brucker, P.; Drexl, A.; Möhring, R.; Neumann, K.; Pesch, E. Resource-constrained project scheduling: Notation, classification, models, and methods. *Eur. J. Oper. Res.* **1999**, *112*, 3–41. [CrossRef]
8. De, P.; Dunne, E.J.; Ghosh, J.B.; Wells, C.E. Complexity of the discrete time-cost tradeoff problem for project networks. *Oper. Res.* **1997**, *45*, 302–306. [CrossRef]
9. De, P.; James Dunne, E.; Ghosh, J.B.; Wells, C.E. The discrete time-cost tradeoff problem revisited. *Eur. J. Oper. Res.* **1995**, *81*, 225–238. [CrossRef]
10. Demeulemeester, E.; Herroelen, W.; Elmaghraby, S.E. Optimal procedures for the discrete time/cost trade-off problem in project networks. *Eur. J. Oper. Res.* **1996**, *88*, 50–68. [CrossRef]
11. Moussourakis, J.; Haksever, C. Flexible model for time/cost tradeoff problem. *J. Constr. Eng. Manag.* **2004**, *130*, 307–314. [CrossRef]
12. Hazır, Ö.; Haouari, M.; Erel, E. Discrete time/cost trade-off problem: A decomposition-based solution algorithm for the budget version. *Comput. Oper. Res.* **2010**, *37*, 649–655. [CrossRef]
13. Akkan, C.; Drexl, A.; Kimms, A. Network decomposition-based benchmark results for the discrete time-cost tradeoff problem. *Eur. J. Oper. Res.* **2005**, *165*, 339–358. [CrossRef]
14. Vanhoucke, M.; Debels, D. The discrete time/cost trade-off problem: Extensions and heuristic procedures. *J. Sched.* **2007**, *10*, 311–326. [CrossRef]

15. Afruzi, E.N.; Najafi, A.A.; Roghanian, E.; Mazinani, M. A multi-objective imperialist competitive algorithm for solving discrete time, cost and quality trade-off problems with mode-identity and resource-constrained situations. *Comput. Oper. Res.* **2014**, *50*, 80–96. [CrossRef]
16. Sonmez, R.; Bettemir, Ö.H. A hybrid genetic algorithm for the discrete time-cost trade-off problem. *Expert Syst. Appl.* **2012**, *39*, 11428–11434. [CrossRef]
17. Wiest, J.D. A heuristic model for scheduling large projects with limited resources. *Manag. Sci.* **1967**, *13*, B-359. [CrossRef]
18. Feng, C.W.; Liu, L.; Burns, S.A. Using genetic algorithms to solve construction time-cost trade-off problems. *J. Comput. Civ. Eng.* **1997**, *11*, 184–189. [CrossRef]
19. Zheng, D.X.; Ng, S.T.; Kumaraswamy, M.M. Applying Pareto ranking and niche formation to genetic algorithm-based multiobjective time-cost optimization. *J. Constr. Eng. Manag.* **2005**, *131*, 81–91. [CrossRef]
20. Deb, K.; Pratap, A.; Agarwal, S.; Meyarivan, T.A.M.T. A fast and elitist multiobjective genetic algorithm: NSGA-II. *IEEE Trans. Evol. Comput.* **2002**, *6*, 182–197. [CrossRef]
21. Afruzi, E.N.; Roghanian, E.; Najafi, A.A.; Mazinani, M. A multi-mode resource-constrained discrete time–cost tradeoff problem solving using an adjusted fuzzy dominance genetic algorithm. *Sci. Iran.* **2013**, *20*, 931–944.
22. Fallah-Mehdipour, E.; Haddad, O.B.; Tabari, M.M.R.; Mariño, M.A. Extraction of decision alternatives in construction management projects: Application and adaptation of NSGA-II and MOPSO. *Expert Syst. Appl.* **2012**, *39*, 2794–2803. [CrossRef]
23. Kar, M.B.; Kar, S.; Guo, S.; Li, X.; Majumder, S. A new bi-objective fuzzy portfolio selection model and its solution through evolutionary algorithms. *Soft Comput.* **2018**, 1–15. [CrossRef]
24. Majumder, S.; Kar, S. Multi-criteria shortest path for rough graph. *J. Ambient Intell. Hum. Comput.* **2017**, 1–25. [CrossRef]
25. Kar, M.B.; Majumder, S.; Kar, S.; Pal, T. Cross-entropy based multi-objective uncertain portfolio selection problem. *J. Intell. Fuzzy Syst.* **2017**, *32*, 4467–4483. [CrossRef]
26. Demeulemeester, E.; Vanhoucke, M.; Herroelen, W. RanGen: A random network generator for activity-on-the-node networks. *J. Sched.* **2003**, *6*, 17–38. [CrossRef]
27. Vanhoucke, M.; Coelho, J.; Debels, D.; Maenhout, B.; Tavares, L.V. An evaluation of the adequacy of project network generators with systematically sampled networks. *Eur. J. Oper. Res.* **2008**, *187*, 511–524. [CrossRef]
28. Valadares Tavares, L.; Antunes Ferreira, J.; Silva Coelho, J. The risk of delay of a project in terms of the morphology of its network. *Eur. J. Oper. Res.* **1999**, *119*, 510–537. [CrossRef]
29. Al-Fawzan, M.A.; Haouari, M. A bi-objective model for robust resource-constrained project scheduling. *Int. J. Prod. Econ.* **2005**, *96*, 175–187. [CrossRef]

© 2018 by the authors. Licensee MDPI, Basel, Switzerland. This article is an open access article distributed under the terms and conditions of the Creative Commons Attribution (CC BY) license (http://creativecommons.org/licenses/by/4.0/).

Article

The Location Selection for Roundabout Construction Using Rough BWM-Rough WASPAS Approach Based on a New Rough Hamy Aggregator

Željko Stević [1,*], Dragan Pamučar [2], Marko Subotić [1], Jurgita Antuchevičiene [3] and Edmundas Kazimieras Zavadskas [4]

1. Faculty of Transport and Traffic Engineering Doboj, University of East Sarajevo, Vojvode Mišića 52, 74000 Doboj, Bosnia and Herzegovina; msubota@gmail.com
2. Department of Logistics, University of Defence in Belgrade, Pavla Jurisica Sturma 33, 11000 Belgrade, Serbia; dpamucar@gmail.com
3. Department of Construction Management and Real Estate, Vilnius Gediminas Technical University, LT-10223 Vilnius, Lithuania; jurgita.antucheviciene@vgtu.lt
4. Institute of Sustainable Construction, Faculty of Civil Engineering, Vilnius Gediminas Technical University, Sauletekio al. 11, LT-10223 Vilnius, Lithuania; edmundas.zavadskas@vgtu.lt
* Correspondence: zeljkostevic88@yahoo.com or zeljko.stevic@sf.ues.rs.ba

Received: 2 July 2018; Accepted: 6 August 2018; Published: 8 August 2018

Abstract: An adequately functionally located traffic infrastructure is an important factor in the mobility of people because it affects the quality of traffic, safety and efficiency of carrying out transportation activities. Locating a roundabout on an urban network is an imperative for road engineering to address traffic problems such as reduction of traffic congestion, enhancement of security and sustainability, etc. Therefore, this paper evaluates potential locations for roundabout construction using Rough BWM (Best Worst Method) and Rough WASPAS (Weighted Aggregated Sum Product Assessment) models. Determination of relative criterion weights on the basis of which the potential locations were evaluated was carried out using the Rough BWM method. In this paper, in order to enable the most precise consensus for group decision-making, a Rough Hamy aggregator has been developed. The main advantage of the Hamy mean (HM) operator is that it can capture the interrelationships among multi-input arguments and can provide DMs more options. Until now, there is no research based on HM operator for aggregating imprecise and uncertain information. The obtained indicators are described through eight alternatives. The results show that the fifth and sixth alternatives are the locations that should have a priority in the construction of roundabouts from the perspective of sustainable development, which is confirmed throughout changes of parameter k and with comparing to other methods in the sensitivity analysis.

Keywords: Rough Hamy aggregator; sustainable traffic; Rough BWM; Rough WASPAS; construction; roundabout

1. Introduction

Increase in a number of traffic accidents and the development of modern traffic signaling have affected realistic traffic solutions at intersections aimed at constructing roundabouts, which has improved the capacity and safety of traffic participants. Roundabouts have become very attractive for implementation since the last decades of the 20th century [1]. Some states in the USA (Maryland and Florida) introduce contemporary roundabouts into permanent practical application, where for their use and construction, the US Department of Transportation issued a manual in 2000 [2]. In European countries, experts believe that roundabouts reduce a number of accidents and affect capacity increase, resulting in high utilization attractiveness since the 1980s. In the Netherlands, France, Norway,

Denmark and other European countries, the number of roundabouts progressively increases. In the Netherlands [3], turbo-roundabouts with 20 to 30% higher speeds of movement in them and with greater safety are introduced. These roundabouts possess a specific central circle (called a cutting tool). This phenomenon requires the introduction of modern circle intersections (MCI), which characterize the smaller diameter of the central island in relation to standard roundabouts [4]. The specificity of MCI installation in the research is conditioned by the appearance of various installations and free urban space, and often the specific requirements of urban environment. At the intersections regulated by light signals, there is a problem of the junction of the flows of pedestrians and vehicles, which adversely affects pedestrians, as a "vulnerable" category. This case is especially striking at Russian light signaling intersections, where drivers often drive under the influence of alcohol or go through a red light [3]. According to the studies [5], the performance of roundabouts was considered based on the criteria of road properties, the capacity and the location. Their study consists of the observation of two types of roundabouts with and without pedestrian crossings and cycling paths. The purpose of their discussion was to analyze the roundabouts with and without cycling paths, according to the given criteria. The trend of roundabout construction has also been transferred to less urban areas, and observing the territory of Bosnia and Herzegovina (B&H) it is possible to notice their constant growth in urban areas. An example of that are the urban areas of Bijeljina, Derventa, Trebinje, Prnjavor, Brčko, Tuzla and others. For the purpose of solving traffic congestion and increasing safety on main roads, the trend is the construction of roundabouts. In the Doboj region of the central part of Bosnia and Herzegovina, a rural network with first-order main roads is notable, with intersections that are not regulated by roundabouts. Considering that the position of the town of Doboj is defined as the intersection zone of primary routes, it is assumed that a number of circle intersections are required in the zone, from the aspect of safety-manageable sustainability. This paper has several aims. The first aim of the paper is to create a new methodology for evaluating potential locations for the construction of roundabouts. The second aim of the paper is the development of a novel Rough Hamy aggregator to achieve a consensus for group decision-making and enhance this field. The main advantage of the Hamy mean (HM) operator is that it can capture the interrelationships among multi-input arguments and can provide DMs more options. Until now, there is no research based on HM operator for aggregating imprecise and uncertain information. So it is necessary to propose some HM operators for rough numbers. In some practical situations, there are interrelationships among attributes and we need to capture the interrelationships among the attribute values to deal with complex decision-making problems. The third aim of the paper is to develop a model for the construction of a roundabout in Doboj applying the integrated Rough Best Worst Method (BWM) and Rough Weighted Aggregated Sum Product Assessment (WASPAS) approach.

Until now, there is no research based on integration Rough BWM and Rough WASPAS methods. This Integrated model based on new Rough Hamy aggregator has significance on academic front because can be used in different areas for solving the various problem. His contribution is related with developing new aggregator which is more precise from other. This is explained in detail in section Materials and methods. Beside that this integrated model has significance on the practical front because was used for solving an important problem which is one of the main prerequisites for sustainability and efficiency development of road engineering.

After introductory considerations describing the importance of the topic and the reasons for its selection, the paper is structured through five other sections. In Section 2, a review of the literature on the application of multi-criteria decision-making for the construction of traffic infrastructure is given. Section 3 presents the methods divided into three parts. In the first part, the Rough BWM algorithm is presented, in the second part, the Rough WASPAS method, and in the third part, the development of a novel Rough Hamy aggregator is shown. Section 4 of the paper is solving a specific case study in the town of Doboj. Subsequently, in Section 5, the sensitivity analysis is performed, and in Section 6, conclusions with guidelines for future research are given.

2. Literature Review

2.1. Review of MCDM Methods in Traffic Engineering

Increasing the capacity of road engineering according to Li et al. [6] has become an important way of solving traffic problems, and roundabouts in addition to a large number of benefits also affect the increase of traffic capacity [7] and greater traffic flow [8]. A roundabout properly constructed according to Prateli et al. [9] can significantly influence the increase in traffic safety, as confirmed by Antov et al. [10] who determine that the construction of roundabouts is an effective way of increasing safety. In order to determine certain parameters on the basis of which certain decisions can be made and analyzes performed, it is necessary to use optimization techniques of operational research. Multi-criteria decision-making can be used as an adequate tool for making valid decisions. Sohn [11] carried out a study in which it was necessary to eliminate unnecessary overpasses that had lost their positive function in the traffic flow and became a burden for the environment. He used the Analytic Hierarchy Process (AHP) to assess the most important criteria for eliminating the overpasses. Podvezko and Sivilevičius [12] applied the same method to determine the influence of traffic factor interaction on the rate of traffic accidents. In order to optimize geometry, traffic efficiency and traffic safety, Pilko et al. [13] created a new multi-criteria and simultaneous multi-objective optimization (MOO) model using the AHP method for evaluating and ranking traffic and geometric elements. Its applicability in the field of traffic engineering, the AHP method also confirms in the paper [14] where it is used for the evaluation of road section design in an urban environment. The TOPSIS (Technique for Order of Preference by Similarity to Ideal Solution) method was used to evaluate locations with roundabouts and noise analysis in them [15]. The multi-criteria approach was also applied in [16] for the identification of priority black spots in order to increase the safety in traffic. It is important to note that the most important criterion in this research is the criterion of a specific location whose integral part is a roundabout. Four types of intersections, among which one alternative is a roundabout, have been evaluated using the AHP method in [17] based on five criteria. The usefulness of applying multi-criteria decision-making methods is also reflected in the analysis of traffic capacity, i.e., evaluation of the variants for the reconstruction of circle intersection. In [18], six variants were evaluated based on eight criteria for roundabout reconstruction in Zagreb. In research in [19], a multi-criteria model was used, which implied the integration of Fuzzy AHP method with WSM (Weighted Sum Method), ELECTRE (ELimination Et Choix Traduisant la REalité) and TOPSIS methods to evaluate alternatives for noise reduction in traffic, i.e., increase traffic sustainability. The Fuzzy AHP method was also applied in [20] in action plans for noise. The research in [21] uses a multi-criteria model that includes the AHP method to evaluate the effectiveness of traffic calming measures. A hybrid multi-criteria model that combines Fuzzy AHP, TOPSIS and gray correlation techniques is presented in [22] for the evaluation of traffic congestion rates. The hybrid fuzzy multi-criteria model is also used in [23] to mitigate congestion at the Ninoy Aquino airport. The model integrates the fuzzy set theory, ANP (Analytic Network Process), DEMATEL (DEcision-MAking Trial and Evaluation Laboratory) and TOPSIS methods. The hybrid model created by the combination of SWARA (Step-wise Weight Assessment Ratio Analysis) and VIKOR (VIseKriterijumska Optimizacija I Kompromisno Resenje) methods in [24] was used for the selection of the optimal alternative of mechanical longitudinal ventilation of tunnel pollutants during automobile accidents. PROMETHEE (Preference Ranking Organization METHod for Enrichment of Evaluations) method was applied in the Spanish provinces to determine urban road safety [25], while in [26] the authors used different normalization methods for selection of road alignment variants. The AHP method was applied in [27], for ranking various on-road emission mitigation strategies including reduce, avoid, and replace.

2.2. Review of Methods for Location Selection Problems

According to Drezner [28] the study of location selection has a long and extensive history spanning many general research fields including operations research (or management science), industrial engineering, geography, economics, computer science, mathematics, marketing, electrical engineering, urban planning. According to Kahraman et al. [29] evaluation of specific sites in the selected community is commonly termed microanalysis.

The conventional approaches to location selection include heuristics [30], integer programming [31], nonlinear programming [32], multi-objective goal programming [33], analog approach [34], Analytic Hierarchy Process [35], multi-attribute utility method [36], multiple regression analysis [37] and other. According to [29] these approaches can only provide a set of systematic steps for problem solving without considering the relationships between the decisions factors globally. Moreover, the ability and experience of the analyst(s) may also influence significantly the final outcome. In addition, artificial intelligence (AI) techniques, such as expert systems, artificial neural networks (ANNs), and fuzzy set theory are used in location selection.

Depending on the type of location problems, different methods are applied as already shown. In the last decade, MCDM (Multi-criteria Decision Making) methods are widely used to solve location problems [38–42]. Zhao et al. [41] use a combination of AHP and TOPSIS method for construction of a metro-integrated logistics system. Using TOPSIS method they performed the evaluation of the importance of each metro station. Nazari et al. [42] are performed research with the aim to select a suitable site for photovoltaic installation in Iran. Four different locations are evaluated based on TOPSIS method. Samanlioglu and Ayağ, [40] use combination of fuzzy AHP and fuzzy PROMETHEE II for selection the best location for a solar power plant. The integration of single-valued neutrosophic sets and the WASPAS method was used to determine the location problem of a garage for a residential house in [43]. WASPAS was extended in [39] with interval neutrosophic sets for the solar-wind power station location selection problem.

2.3. Summarized Overview of Used MCDM Approaches and a Brief Overview of the Advantages of the Proposed Model

Table 1 gives an overview of the most commonly used MCDM methods with the main topic, approach and results.

Table 1. Overview of the used Multi-criteria Decision Making (MCDM) methods in road engineering and location selection.

Ref.	Approach	Purpose of Application
[11]	AHP	elimination of unnecessary overpasses that had lost their positive function in the traffic flow
[12]	AHP	determination of the influence of traffic factor interaction on the rate of traffic accidents
[13]	MOO and AHP	evaluation and ranking traffic and geometric elements
[14]	AHP	evaluation of road section design in an urban environment
[15]	TOPSIS	evaluation of locations with roundabouts and noise analysis in them
[16]	Delphi and TOPSIS	identification of priority black spots in order to increase the safety in traffic
[17]	AHP	evaluation of four types of intersections
[18]	AHP	evaluation of variants for roundabout reconstruction
[19]	Fuzzy AHP, WSM ELECTRE and TOPSIS	evaluation of the alternatives for noise reduction in traffic
[20]	Fuzzy AHP	prioritizing road stretches included in a noise action plans
[21]	AHP	evaluation of the effectiveness of traffic calming measures
[22]	Fuzzy AHP and TOPSIS	evaluation of traffic congestion rates
[23]	ANP, DEMATEL, fuzzy set theory and TOPSIS	mitigation of congestion at the Ninoy Aquino airport

Table 1. Cont.

Ref.	Approach	Purpose of Application
[24]	SWARA and VIKOR	selection of the optimal alternative of mechanical longitudinal ventilation of tunnel pollutants during automobile accidents
[25]	PROMETHEE	determination of urban road safety
[27]	AHP	ranking various on-road emission mitigation strategies
[39]	WASPAS with interval neutrosophic sets	the solar-wind power station location selection
[40]	Fuzzy AHP and Fuzzy PROMETHEE II	selection the best location for a solar power plant
[41]	AHP and TOPSIS	construction of a metro-integrated logistics system
[42]	TOPSIS	selection of suitable site for photovoltaic installation
[43]	WASPAS with single-valued neutrosophic sets	determination of the location problem of a garage for a residential house

The nature of the problem in this study is different in relation to the above-mentioned research. In relation to research by Zhao et al. [41], we have fewer variables that have influence on problem solving. In the integrated logistic system created in the mentioned paper, the P-median model is also used, because the distribution of goods is considered in which it is necessary to determine the distributions hub. In this paper, the existing traffic infrastructure is a limitation for the formation of a different model. When it comes to the applied methods, the possibility of using the P-median model due to the above is excluded. The application of the proposed Rough BWM-WASPAS model based on rough Hamy aggregator is better option than the application of conventional and exploited MCDM methods such as AHP and TOPSIS.

Fuzzy set theory has serious difficulties in producing valid answers in decision making by fuzzifying judgments. No theorems are available about its workability when it is applied indiscriminately as a number crunching approach to numerical measurements that represent judgment [44]. When judgments are allowed to vary in choice over the values of a fundamental scale, as in the AHP, these judgments are themselves already fuzzy [45]. In addition to increasing the complexity of manipulations, the fuzzification of numbers complicates the computational process and often leads to less desirable instead of more desirable results [46]. In some situations, the fuzzy AHP method can also result in the wrong decision and the choice of the worst criterion (alternative) as the best [45,46]. Compared with research [40] where the authors use a combination of fuzzy AHP and fuzzy PROMETHEE II, our proposed model is better from the reasons which are previously mentioned. The advantage of the proposed model comparing with fuzzy theory is that the integration of rough numbers into the MCDM methods according to Stević et al. [47] exploits the subjectivity and unclear assessment of the experts and avoids assumptions, which is not the case when applying fuzzy theory.

Advantage of the proposed model based on rough Hamy aggregator as follow. As a result, some traditional aggregation operators, such as the Bonferroni mean (BM) [48], Rough Number Averaging (RNA) operator or Rough Number Geometric (RNG), can be applied to reflect interactions among input arguments. However, compared with the ordinary BM, the HM can consider the interrelationship among multi-input arguments whereas the ordinary BM can only capture the interrelationship between two input arguments. On the other hand, the HM is more general than the RNA and RNG, and the RNA and RNG are a special cases of HM operator. Therefore, the HM is more suitable to model interactions among input arguments than the BM, RNA and RNG.

3. Materials and Methods

3.1. Proposed Methodology

Figure 1 shows the methodology for the location selection for roundabout construction; it consists of three phases. Each of these phases and steps are explained in detail.

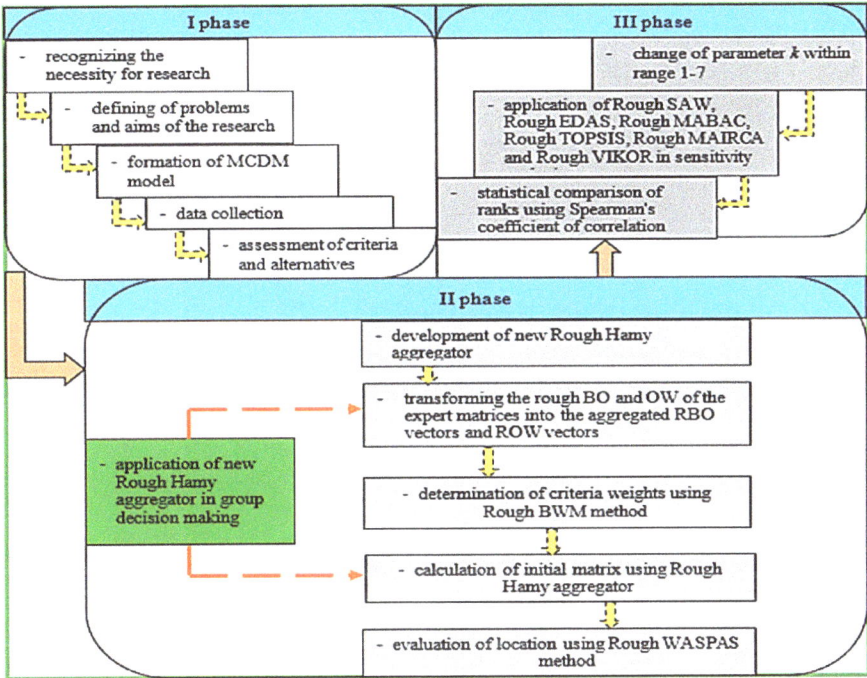

Figure 1. Proposed model for location selection for roundabout construction.

The proposed model for location selection for roundabout construction in Doboj consists of three phases and 13 steps. The first phase consists of five steps, from which the first step recognizing of the necessity for research. In the Doboj region of the central part of Bosnia and Herzegovina, a rural network with first-order main roads is notable, with intersections that are not regulated by roundabouts. The second step represents defining the problems and objectives of the research related to the need for the construction roundabout. In addition, the research objectives also relate to the identification of priority locations and the construction of the roundabout on that locations. In the third step of the first phase, a multi-criteria model was formed which consist of eight criteria, six alternatives, and seven decision-makers (DMs). The next step is collecting data that implies empirical research on the measurement of traffic parameters and the collection of other data from other sources. After the data collection was completed, the evaluation of criteria and alternatives by seven experts was carried out. The second phase involves the development of a new Rough Hamy aggregator, processing, and analysis of the collected data. The first step at this phase is the development of a new Rough Hamy aggregator used to transform rough Best to Other (BO) and Other to Worst (OW) into aggregated vectors in the second step and to calculate the initial decision matrix in the fourth step. The third step is a determination of the criteria weights using Rough BWM, while the fifth step of this phase represents the evaluation of locations using the Rough WASPAS method. The third phase of the proposed model is a sensitivity analysis which consists of three steps. First, a change in the k parameter has been made and a check on its influence on the ranking of the alternative. After that, a comparison was made with six different methods in the second step, while in the third calculated Spearman's coefficient of correlation showing a high level of correlation of ranks.

Advantages of the proposed model are as follow. The main advantage of the Hamy mean (HM) operator is that it can capture the interrelationships among multi-input arguments and can provide DMs more options. Until now, there is no research based on HM operator for aggregating imprecise and uncertain information. So it is necessary to propose some HM operators for rough numbers. In some practical situations, there are interrelationships among attributes and we need to capture the interrelationships among the attribute values to deal with complex decision-making problems. As a result, some traditional aggregation operators, such as the Bonferroni mean (BM) [48], Rough Number Averaging (RNA) operator or Rough Number Geometric (RNG), can be applied to reflect interactions among input arguments. However, compared with the ordinary BM, the HM can consider the interrelationship among multi-input arguments whereas the ordinary BM can only capture the interrelationship between two input arguments. On the other hand, the HM is more general than the RNA and RNG, and the RNA and RNG are a special cases of HM operator. Therefore, the HM is more suitable to model interactions among input arguments than the BM, RNA and RNG.

Determining the significance of criteria is one of the most important stages in the decision-making process [49–51]. Practically doesn't exist the problem of multi-criteria decision-making in which criteria have the equal importance. Taking into account previously said, the methods for determining the weight values are an important factor for making valid decisions. The BWM [52] is one of more recent methods. Some of the advantages of using BWM are as follows: (1) in comparison with the AHP method, which until the establishment of this method was in comparable and most commonly used to determine weight coefficients, it requires a smaller number of pairwise comparisons (in the AHP method, the number of comparisons is $n(n-1)/2$, while, for the BWM, the number of comparisons is $2n-3$; (2) weight coefficients determined using the BWM are more reliable, since comparisons in this method are made with a higher degree of consistency compared with the AHP method; (3) with most MCDM models (e.g., AHP), the degree of consistency checks whether the comparison of criteria is consistent or not, while, in BWM, the degree of consistency is used to determine the level of consistency because the outputs from BWM are always consistent; and (4) the BWM for pairwise comparison of the criteria requires only integer values, which is not the case with other MCDM methods (e.g., AHP) which also require fractional numbers [52]. Additionally, the Rough BWM makes it possible to bridge the existing gap that exists in the BWM methodology by applying a new approach in treating imprecision that is based on RN. This approach has been used in several studies in a very short time [53–55], therefore its complete algorithm has not been shown in this paper. The Rough BWM model in [53] is used to determine weight coefficients of the criteria for location selection for wind farms, while in [54], it is used to determine the importance of the criteria for selecting wagons for a logistics company. Interval Rough fuzzy BWM has been applied in [55] to a study of the optimal selection of firefighting helicopters. The Rough BWM is expected to be increasingly used in the future, which is one of the reasons for its application in this paper.

Bearing in mind all the advantages of using rough theory [56,57] in the MCDM to represent ambiguity, vagueness and uncertainty, the authors in the paper [58] made modification of the WASPAS algorithm using rough numbers. According to Stojić et al. [58] in comparison with other concepts, a novel rough WASPAS approach has some advantages that can be described as follows. The first reason is its advantage in comparison with grey theory. Grey relation analysis provides a well-structured analytical framework for a multi-criteria decision-making process, but it lacks the capability to characterize the subjective perceptions of designers in the evaluation process. Rough set theory may help here, because rough sets can facilitate effective representation of vague information or imprecise data. Also, a very important advantage of using rough set theory to handle vagueness and uncertainty is that it expresses vagueness by means of the boundary region of a set instead of membership function. In addition, the integration of rough numbers in MCDM methods gives the possibility to explore subjective and unclear evaluation of the experts and to avoid assumptions, which is not the case when applying fuzzy theory. According to Hashemkhani Zolfani et al. [59], the main advantage of the WASPAS method is its high degree of reliability. Different aggregation parameter and the proportion adjustment parameter facilitate the whole procedures of a dynamic selection. In the paper [39] aggregation parameter setting is based on the requirement of the real application and subjective preference of DMs, which makes the extended WASPAS technique feasible in dealing with the reality which is the case in this research also.

Integration of rough numbers and the WASPAS method with advantages of both concepts presents a very important support in decision-making in everyday conflicting situations. It is important to note that until now, there is no research based on integration Rough BWM and Rough WASPAS methods. This is also one of the advantages of the proposed methodology.

3.2. Novel Rough Hamy Mean Operators and Their Operations

To adequately solve decision-making problems with vague or imprecise information according to Mardani et al. [60], the fuzzy set theory [61] and aggregation operator theory have become powerful tools. In addition to fuzzy logic, the rough set theory [62,63] also adequately fulfills these advantages, so in this paper, a new Rough Hamy aggregator for group decision-making has been developed.

The Hamy mean (HM) [64] is used for aggregation of values while simultaneously including mutual correlations among multiple arguments and is defined in the following way:

Definition 1. [64]. *Assume that x_i ($i = 1, 2, \ldots, n$) represent a set of non-negative real numbers and a parameter $k = 1, 2, \ldots, n$, then HM is defined as:*

$$HM^{(k)}(x_1, x_2, \ldots, x_n) = \frac{\sum_{1 \leq i_1 < \ldots < i_k \leq n} \left(\prod_{j=1}^{k} x_{i_j} \right)^{1/k}}{\binom{n}{k}}, \quad (1)$$

where $(i_1, i_2, \ldots, i_k)$ includes all k-tuple combinations of $(1, 2, \ldots, n)$ and $\binom{n}{k}$ represents a binomial coefficient calculated as:

$$\binom{n}{k} = \frac{n!}{k!(n-k)!}, \quad (2)$$

Based on the predefined operations on rough numbers (RNs), the next part shows HM operator for averaging RNs. In the forthcoming section, besides performing the RNHM operator, some specific cases of this new operator for RNs are shown.

Definition 2. *Assume that $RN(\varphi_1) = [\underline{Lim}(\varphi_1), \overline{Lim}(\varphi_1)]$ and $RN(\varphi_2) = [\underline{Lim}(\varphi_2), \overline{Lim}(\varphi_2)]$ are two RNs, then RNHM operator is defined as follows:*

$$RNHM^{(k)}\{RN(\varphi_1), RN(\varphi_2), \ldots, RN(\varphi_n)\} = \frac{\sum_{1 \leq i_1 < \ldots < i_k \leq n} \left(\prod_{j=1}^{k} RN(\varphi_{i_j}) \right)^{1/k}}{\binom{n}{k}}, \quad (3)$$

where $(i_1, i_2, \ldots, i_k)$ includes all k-tuple combinations of $(1, 2, \ldots, n)$ and $\binom{n}{k}$ represents a binomial coefficient and $\binom{n}{k} = \frac{n!}{k!(n-k)!}$.

Theorem 1. Let $RN(\varphi_j) = [\underline{Lim}(\varphi_j), \overline{Lim}(\varphi_j)]$; $(j = 1, 2, \ldots, n)$ represent a set of RNs in R. The aggregated values of rough numbers from a set R can be determined using the expression (3) and then the next expression:

$$RNHM^{(k)}\{RN(\varphi_1), RN(\varphi_2), \ldots, RN(\varphi_n)\} = [\underline{Lim}(\varphi_{RNHM}), \overline{Lim}(\varphi_{RNHM}))] =$$

$$= \left[\left(\frac{\sum_{1 \leq i_1 < \ldots < i_k \leq n} \left(\prod_{j=1}^{k} \underline{Lim}(\varphi_{i_j}) \right)^{1/k}}{\binom{n}{k}} \right), \left(\frac{\sum_{1 \leq i_1 < \ldots < i_k \leq n} \left(\prod_{j=1}^{k} \overline{Lim}(\varphi_{i_j}) \right)^{1/k}}{\binom{n}{k}} \right) \right], \quad (4)$$

Example 1. Let $RN(\varphi_1) = [2, 3]$, $RN(\varphi_2) = [3, 5]$, $RN(\varphi_3) = [1, 3]$ and $RN(\varphi_3) = [5, 8]$ be four RNs, then the shown RNHM operator (assume that $k = 2$) can be used for their aggregation obtaining the aggregated value $RNHM^{(k)}\{RN(\varphi_1), RN(\varphi_2), RN(\varphi_3), RN(\varphi_4)\} = [\underline{Lim}(\varphi_\alpha), \overline{Lim}(\varphi_\alpha)]$.

(i). $\frac{1}{\binom{n}{k}} = \frac{k!(n-k)!}{n!} = \frac{2!(4-2)!}{2!} = \frac{1}{6}$

(ii). $\underline{Lim}(\varphi_\alpha) = \frac{\sum_{1 \leq i_1 < \ldots < i_k \leq 4} \left(\prod_{j=1}^{2} \underline{Lim}(\varphi_{i_j}) \right)^{1/2}}{\binom{4}{2}} = \frac{(2 \times 3)^{1/2} + (2 \times 1)^{1/2} + (2 \times 5)^{1/2} + (3 \times 1)^{1/2} + (3 \times 5)^{1/2} + (1 \times 5)^{1/2}}{6} = 2.478$

(iii). $\underline{Lim}(\varphi_\alpha) = \frac{\sum_{1 \leq i_1 < \ldots < i_k \leq 4} \left(\prod_{j=1}^{2} \overline{Lim}(\varphi_{i_j}) \right)^{1/2}}{\binom{4}{2}} = \frac{(3 \times 5)^{1/2} + (3 \times 3)^{1/2} + (3 \times 8)^{1/2} + (5 \times 3)^{1/2} + (5 \times 8)^{1/2} + (3 \times 8)^{1/2}}{6} = 4.478$

In this way, the aggregated value $RNHM^{(2)}\{RN(\varphi_1), RN(\varphi_2), RN(\varphi_3), RN(\varphi_4)\} = [2.478, 4.478]$ is obtained.

Theorem 2. (Idempotency). If $RN(\varphi_j) = RN(\varphi) = [\underline{Lim}(\varphi), \overline{Lim}(\varphi)]$ for all $(j = 1, 2, \ldots, n)$, then $RNHM\{RN(\varphi), RN(\varphi), \ldots, RN(\varphi)\} = RN(\varphi) = [\underline{Lim}(\varphi), \overline{Lim}(\varphi)]$.

Theorem 3. (Commutativity). Let RN rough set $(RN(\varphi'_1), RN(\varphi'_2), \ldots, RN(\varphi'_n))$ be any permutation of $(RN(\varphi_1), RN(\varphi_2), \ldots, RN(\varphi_n))$.

Then $RNHM\{RN(\varphi_1), RN(\varphi_2), \ldots, RN(\varphi_n)\} = RNHM\{RN(\varphi'_1), RN(\varphi'_2), \ldots, RN(\varphi'_n)\}$.

Theorem 4. (Boundedness). Let $RN(\varphi_j) = [\underline{Lim}(\varphi_j), \overline{Lim}(\varphi_j)]$; $(j = 1, 2, \ldots, n)$, be a collection of RNs in R, let $RN(\varphi_j^-) = [\min\{\underline{Lim}(\varphi_j)\}, \min\{\overline{Lim}(\varphi_j)\}]$ and $RN(\varphi_j^+) = [\max\{\underline{Lim}(\varphi_j)\}, \max\{\overline{Lim}(\varphi_j)\}]$, then we have $RN(\varphi_j^-) \leq RNHM\{RN(\varphi_1), RN(\varphi_2), \ldots, RN(\varphi_n)\} \leq RN(\varphi_j^+)$.

Theorem 5. (Monotonicity). Let $RN(\varphi_j) = [\underline{Lim}(\varphi_j), \overline{Lim}(\varphi_j)]$, $RN(\phi_j) = [\underline{Lim}(\phi_j), \overline{Lim}(\phi_j)]$; $(j = 1, 2, \ldots, n)$, be two collections of RNs, if $\underline{Lim}(\varphi_j) \leq \underline{Lim}(\phi_j)$, $\overline{Lim}(\varphi_j) \leq \overline{Lim}(\phi_j)$ for all j, then $RNHM\{RN(\varphi_1), RN(\varphi_2), \ldots, RN(\varphi_n)\} \leq RNHM\{RN(\phi_1), RN(\phi_2), \ldots, RN(\phi_n)\}$.

All proofs of theorems are shown in Appendix A. In the next section, a discussion in which some specific cases of RNHM operator depending on the change of parameter k has been presented.

Case 1. When $k = 1$, then the RNHM operator (4) can be reduced into the RNA (Rough Number Averaging) operator

$$RNHM^{(1)}\{RN(\varphi_1), RN(\varphi_2), \ldots, RN(\varphi_n)\} = \left[\frac{\sum_{1 \leq i_1 \leq n} \left(\prod_{j=1}^{1} Lim(\varphi_{i_j}) \right)^{1/1}}{\binom{n}{1}}, \frac{\sum_{1 \leq i_1 \leq n} \left(\prod_{j=1}^{1} \overline{Lim}(\varphi_{i_j}) \right)^{1/1}}{\binom{n}{1}} \right]$$

$$= \left[\frac{1}{n} \sum_{1 \leq i_1 \leq n} \left(Lim(\varphi_{i_j}) \right), \frac{1}{n} \sum_{1 \leq i_1 \leq n} \left(\overline{Lim}(\varphi_{i_j}) \right) \right]; (let\ i_1 = i)$$

$$= \left[\frac{1}{n} \sum_{i=1}^{n} \left(Lim(\varphi_{i_j}) \right), \frac{1}{n} \sum_{i=1}^{n} \left(\overline{Lim}(\varphi_{i_j}) \right) \right] = RNA\{RN(\varphi_1), RN(\varphi_2), \ldots, RN(\varphi_n)\}$$

Case 2. When $k = n$, then the RNHM operator (4) can be reduced into the RNG (Rough Number Geometric) operator:

$$RNHM^{(n)}\{RN(\varphi_1), RN(\varphi_2), \ldots, RN(\varphi_n)\} = \frac{\sum_{1 \leq i_1 < \cdots < i_k \leq n} \left(\prod_{j=1}^{n} RN(\varphi_{i_j}) \right)^{1/n}}{\binom{n}{n}}$$

$$= \left[\frac{\sum_{1 \leq i_1 < \cdots < i_k \leq n} \left(\prod_{j=1}^{n} Lim(\varphi_{i_j}) \right)^{1/n}}{\binom{n}{n}}, \frac{\sum_{1 \leq i_1 < \cdots < i_k \leq n} \left(\prod_{j=1}^{n} \overline{Lim}(\varphi_{i_j}) \right)^{1/n}}{\binom{n}{n}} \right]$$

$$= \left[\left(\prod_{j=1}^{n} Lim(\varphi_{i_j}) \right)^{1/n}, \left(\prod_{j=1}^{n} \overline{Lim}(\varphi_{i_j}) \right)^{1/n} \right]; (let\ i_j = j) = \left[\left(\prod_{j=1}^{n} Lim(\varphi_i) \right)^{1/n}, \left(\prod_{j=1}^{n} \overline{Lim}(\varphi_i) \right)^{1/n} \right] = \prod_{j=1}^{n} RN(\varphi_i)^{1/n}$$

4. The Location Selection for Roundabout Construction in Doboj

The location selection for the construction of a roundabout consists of several stages that are described in detail below. The first stage implies the formation of a multi-criteria model based on the real needs of traffic infrastructure in Doboj. The second stage implies collecting data based on performed measurements of traffic indicators and based on other sources such as the Interior Ministry where data on the number of traffic accidents at the locations for roundabout construction were obtained. The third stage refers to the expert evaluation of the importance of criteria as the first step and the determination of the weights of the criteria using the Rough BWM method as the second step. The fourth stage is an interpretation of the application of the developed Rough Hamy aggregator for obtaining the initial decision-making matrix, while the fifth stage represents the evaluation of locations based on the Rough WASPAS method.

4.1. Forming a Multi-Criteria Model

Six locations (Figure 2) of which one is located in the very center of the town, four locations which represent the connection between the streets for the entrance into/exit from the town and the first-order main road, and one location where the first-order main roads intersect are evaluated based on a total of eight criteria presented in Table 2.

Figure 2. Potential locations for roundabout construction.

Table 2. Criteria in a multi-criteria model and their interpretation.

Ord. No.	Criterion	Criterion Description
1	Flow of vehicles	The number of vehicles passing through the observed road intersection in a unit of time in both directions.
2	Flow of pedestrians	The number of pedestrians crossing the observed intersection at the point for pedestrian movement (pedestrian crossing, zebra, etc.) at a given time interval.
3	Traffic safety indicator	The number of traffic accidents on the observed section of the road
4	Costs of construction and exploitation	Cost estimation (construction, exploitation and maintenance)
5	Type of intersection	Three-way or four-way intersections
6	Average vehicle intensity per access arm	The limit intensity is the intensity at the entry arm into the intersection of 360 PA/h
7	Functional criterion of spatial fitting	What is the primary role of the intersection observed? This section analyzes what type of intersection is the most acceptable due to its role in traffic.
8	Public opinion	It implies a survey of local population that have chosen one of the offered locations as a priority for the construction of a roundabout.

Table 2 shows the criteria and a detailed interpretation of their meaning. The criteria are selected according to current needs of the city Doboj and relevant literature which considered the similar researches [65–68]. In all mentioned researches criteria are organized in few categories: traffic criteria, safety, functionality, performance, cost et. The criteria used in this study are the most commonly used criteria in Croatia: functional criterion, spatially-urbanistic criterion, traffic flow criterion, design and technical criterion, traffic safety criterion, capacity criterion, environmental criterion economic criterion, Serbia and Slovenia: functional criterion, capacity criterion, spatial criterion, design and technical criterion, traffic safety criterion and economic criterion [69]. Results that provided in research [70] indicate that public support continued to increase with time, presumably because traffic participants became more informed and comfortable with this form of traffic control. According to that the application of the last criterion in this research have justification.

The second (traffic flows of pedestrians) and the fourth criterion (costs of construction and exploitation) belong to the cost criteria, i.e., they need to be minimized. The fourth (costs of construction and exploitation) and seventh criterion (functionality or criterion of spatial fitting) are qualitative criteria that are not easily measurable and they are evaluated on the basis of experts' forecasts who are familiar with potential locations, current infrastructure, and current intersections. After empirical research where the data for each location was determined, the group of seven experts carried out an assessment of all the criteria and alternatives.

Figure 2 shows potential locations for the construction of roundabouts in Doboj. The first location is the exit from the town onto the M17 main road towards Modriča (left), and towards Sarajevo (right). The second location represents a three-way intersection that is a junction of the M17 and M14 main roads, while the third location is after 300 m and connects the exit from the town with the M17 main road. The fourth location represents a four-way intersection that connects the main street with the M17 main road and the railway station, while the fifth location represents the last exit from the town towards Sarajevo and it is a four-way intersection with an additional side road access. The sixth location is a location in the center of the town.

4.2. Data Collection

Flow measurement was performed at the sampling level in the period September–November 2017. The data collected for each location based on the established criteria are presented in Table 3.

Table 3. Values of alternatives according to criteria.

	C_1	C_2	C_3	C_4	C_5	C_6	C_7	C_8
A_1	1256	8	2	3	3	419	7	85
A_2	2194	4	2	9	3	731	5	89
A_3	1037	5	4	7	3	346	3	45
A_4	2878	32	3	7	4	720	5	8
A_5	1052	2	4	5	4	263	5	27
A_6	4197	124	1	3	4	1050	7	74

Table 3 shows the values for all the locations according to established criteria. It can be noticed that the highest intensity of traffic flows of vehicles and pedestrians belongs to the sixth location with 4197 vehicles and 124 pedestrians in one hour. Locations 4 and 2 have slightly less intensity regarding vehicle flows, while the intensity of pedestrians is 32 for the fourth, and only four for the second location. The remaining locations have double less intensity than the two previously mentioned locations, and almost four times less than the sixth location. If the sixth and fourth location are excluded, the flows of pedestrians are very small. The reason is that the sixth location is in the town center, and the fourth location represents the connection between entering the town and the railway station. Regarding the number of traffic accidents, the largest number of accidents occurred at locations 3 and 5, four accidents per each, while the lowest number of accidents occurred at the sixth location. The average vehicle intensity per an arm (Table 4) is the largest at the sixth location, 1050, while for the second and fourth location it is almost identical, 731 and 720, respectively. The minimum intensity per an arm is at the fifth location because this location has four arms and an additional arm that is not represented in the paper as an arm, as it represents a side road that is not frequent. Based on the public opinion survey for potential locations, the largest number of citizens have characterized the first two locations as a priority for the construction of a roundabout, and as the third one, they designated the sixth location. The fourth and seventh criterion fall into the qualitative group, so their evaluation is carried out by seven experts, while the other criteria are of quantitative nature.

Table 4. Average intensity of vehicles per the arms at all locations.

				Location 1—Exit from the Old Town onto the M17 Main Road					
Direction		Bare-Maglaj		Bare-Old Town		Maglaj-Bare		Maglaj-Old Town		Old Town-Bare		Old Town-Maglaj		Σ
Trucks		64		12		64		12		12		24		176
Passenger vehicles		268		84		388		108		160		72		1080

	Location 2—The Bridge, So-Called "Japanac", Which Represents the Entrance into the Town from Tuzla					
Direction	"Japanac"-Maglaj	"Japanac"-Bare	Maglaj-"Japanac"	Maglaj-Bare	Bare-Maglaj	Bare-"Japanac"	Σ
Trucks	60	52	72	84	112	80	462
Passenger vehicles	200	240	360	380	272	280	1732

	Location 3—The Intersection on the M17 Main Road at Flea Market				
Direction	Bare-Maglaj	Bare-Town Entrance	Maglaj-Bare	Maglaj-Town Entrance	Town Exit-Bare	Town Exit-Maglaj	Σ
Trucks	76	0	80	0	0	0	156
Passenger vehicles	244	108	384	24	100	24	884

	Location 4—Traffic-Light Intersection on the M17 Main Road						
Direction	Town-Railwaystation	Town-Maglaj	Town-Bare	Bare-Maglaj	Bare-Town	Bare-r. Stat.	Maglaj-Bare	Mag.-Town	Mag.-r. Station	R. stat.-Bare	R. Stat.-Maglaj	R. Stat.-Town	Σ
Trucks	9	15	24	90	15	27	96	27	24	30	25	15	397
Passenger vehicles	153	225	240	270	105	135	300	270	120	132	246	285	2481

	Location 5—Intersection at the Entrance into/Exit from the Town via Usora				
Direction	Bare-Maglaj	Bare-Usora	Maglaj-Bare	Maglaj-Usora	Usora-Bare	Usora-Maglaj	Σ
Trucks	68	0	100	4	0	4	176
Passenger vehicles	232	140	288	152	24	40	876

	Location 6—Intersection in the Town at the Junction of Jug Bogdana and Cara Dušana Street							
Direction	Church-Vladimirka	Church-Center	Church-Bingo	Vlad.-Church	Vlad.-Center	Vlad.-Bingo	Center-Church	Center-Vlad.	Center-Bingo	Bingo-Center	Bingo-Church	Bingo-Vlad.	Σ
Trucks	9	15	24	90	15	27	96	27	24	30	25	15	397
Passenger vehicles	569	292	478	507	139	234	222	129	374	403	365	88	3800

4.3. Criteria Weight Calculation Using Rough BWM

Evaluation of the criteria has been carried out using the scale, where 1 signifies insignificant domination, while 9 signifies exceptional domination. Expert comparisons through Best to Other and Other to Worst vectors are shown in Table 5.

Table 5. Best to Other (BO) and Other to Worst (OW) vectors of expert judgment.

	BO							OW						
Criteria	E_1	E_2	E_3	E_4	E_5	E_6	E_7	E_1	E_2	E_3	E_4	E_5	E_6	E_7
C_1	1	1	2	1	1	1	1	6	6	4	6	8	7	7
C_2	2	3	3	4	4	1	2	5	4	3	3	3	6	5
C_3	1	2	1	2	2	1	1	6	5	5	5	5	6	6
C_4	3	4	4	3	3	4	5	3	3	2	4	4	3	2
C_5	2	3	3	3	5	2	2	4	4	3	4	2	5	5
C_6	4	5	4	4	6	1	5	2	2	2	3	1	6	2
C_7	3	4	4	5	7	5	2	3	3	2	2	1	2	5
C_8	6	6	5	6	8	7	7	1	1	1	1	1	1	1

Using the expressions (1)–(6) in [71], the crisp expert evaluations shown in BO and OW vectors are transformed into RNs (Table 6).

Table 6. Rough Best to Other (BO) and Other to Worst (OW) vectors of expert judgment.

	BO						
Criteria	E_1	E_2	E_3	E_4	E_5	E_6	E_7
C_1	[1, 1.14]	[1, 1.16]	[1.16, 2]	[1, 1.02]	[1, 1.04]	[1, 1.04]	[1, 1.04]
C_2	[1.67, 2.96]	[2.34, 3.5]	[2.08, 3.67]	[2.53, 4]	[2.26, 4]	[1, 2.05]	[1.84, 2.32]
C_3	[1, 1.43]	[1.49, 2]	[1, 1.35]	[1.42, 2]	[1.27, 2]	[1, 1.19]	[1, 1.23]
C_4	[3, 3.71]	[3.62, 4.25]	[3.45, 4.33]	[3, 3.62]	[3, 3.68]	[3.46, 4.5]	[3.54, 5]
C_5	[2, 2.86]	[2.64, 3.5]	[2.48, 3.67]	[2.42, 4]	[2.71, 5]	[2, 2.34]	[2, 2.44]
C_6	[3.25, 4.59]	[3.86, 5.33]	[3.06, 4.63]	[3.03, 4.79]	[3.76, 6]	[1, 3.33]	[3.73, 5]
C_7	[2.5, 4.61]	[3.33, 4.88]	[2.83, 5.06]	[3.69, 5.67]	[3.85, 7]	[3.38, 5]	[2, 3.21]
C_8	[5.75, 6.63]	[5.67, 6.74]	[5, 6.45]	[5.81, 6.89]	[6.41, 8]	[6.09, 7]	[6.01, 7]

	OW						
Criteria	E_1	E_2	E_3	E_4	E_5	E_6	E_7
C_1	[5.5, 6.61]	[5.33, 6.71]	[4, 6.26]	[5.61, 6.86]	[6.16, 8]	[5.82, 7]	[5.7, 7]
C_2	[3.88, 5.33]	[3.25, 4.79]	[3, 4]	[3, 4.04]	[3, 4.04]	[4.04, 6]	[3.61, 5]
C_3	[5.43, 6]	[5, 5.35]	[5, 5.41]	[5, 5.41]	[5, 5.41]	[5.41, 6]	[5.27, 6]
C_4	[2.67, 3.33]	[2.6, 3.4]	[2, 2.95]	[3.04, 4]	[2.75, 4]	[2.55, 3.01]	[2, 2.58]
C_5	[3.48, 4.4]	[3.37, 4,5]	[2.5, 4.06]	[3.34, 4.67]	[2, 3.6]	[3.79, 5]	[3.36, 5]
C_6	[1.8, 2.8]	[1.75, 2.93]	[1.7, 3.11]	[2.02, 4.5]	[1, 2.4]	[2.55, 6]	[1.65, 2.2]
C_7	[2.22, 3.67]	[2.1, 4]	[1.75, 2.63]	[1.67, 2.65]	[1, 2.38]	[1.81, 2.78]	[2.33, 5]
C_8	[1, 1]	[1, 1]	[1, 1]	[1, 1]	[1, 1]	[1, 1]	[1, 1]

After the transformation of the crisp value into RN, the rough BO and OW of the expert matrices are transformed into the aggregated rough BO vectors and rough OW vectors using rough Hamy aggregator, Table 7.

Table 7. Aggregated Rough BO and Rough OW vectors.

Best: C_1	RN	Worst: C_8	RN
C_1	[1.02, 1.18]	C_1	[5.42, 6.91]
C_2	[2.10, 3.16]	C_2	[3.38, 4.71]
C_3	[1.41, 1.58]	C_3	[5.16, 5.65]
C_4	[3.33, 4.14]	C_4	[2.50, 3.30]
C_5	[2.78, 3.34]	C_5	[3.08, 4.45]
C_6	[3.10, 4.77]	C_6	[1.75, 3.30]
C_7	[3.58, 5.00]	C_7	[1.81, 3.24]
C_8	[6.13, 6.95]	C_8	[1.00, 1.00]

On the basis of rough BO and rough OW vectors, the calculation of optimal values of rough weight coefficients of the criteria is performed. Based on the data in Table 4, a nonlinearly constrained optimization problem is introduced, which is represented by concrete numbers.

$$\min \zeta$$
s.t.
$$\begin{cases} \left|\frac{w_1^L}{w_1^U} - 1.18\right| \leq \zeta; \left|\frac{w_1^L}{w_2^U} - 3.16\right| \leq \zeta; \left|\frac{w_1^L}{w_3^U} - 1.58\right| \leq \zeta; \left|\frac{w_1^L}{w_4^U} - 4.14\right| \leq \zeta; \left|\frac{w_1^L}{w_5^U} - 3.34\right| \leq \zeta; \left|\frac{w_1^L}{w_6^U} - 4.77\right| \leq \zeta; \left|\frac{w_1^L}{w_7^U} - 5.00\right| \leq \zeta; \left|\frac{w_1^L}{w_8^U} - 6.95\right| \leq \zeta; \\ \left|\frac{w_1^U}{w_1^L} - 1.02\right| \leq \zeta; \left|\frac{w_1^U}{w_2^L} - 2.10\right| \leq \zeta; \left|\frac{w_1^U}{w_3^L} - 1.41\right| \leq \zeta; \left|\frac{w_1^U}{w_4^L} - 3.33\right| \leq \zeta; \left|\frac{w_1^U}{w_5^L} - 2.78\right| \leq \zeta; \left|\frac{w_1^U}{w_6^L} - 3.10\right| \leq \zeta; \left|\frac{w_1^U}{w_7^L} - 3.58\right| \leq \zeta; \left|\frac{w_1^U}{w_8^L} - 6.13\right| \leq \zeta; \\ \left|\frac{w_1^L}{w_8^U} - 6.91\right| \leq \zeta; \left|\frac{w_2^L}{w_8^U} - 4.71\right| \leq \zeta; \left|\frac{w_3^L}{w_8^U} - 5.65\right| \leq \zeta; \left|\frac{w_4^L}{w_8^U} - 3.30\right| \leq \zeta; \left|\frac{w_5^L}{w_8^U} - 4.45\right| \leq \zeta; \left|\frac{w_6^L}{w_8^U} - 3.30\right| \leq \zeta; \left|\frac{w_7^L}{w_8^U} - 3.24\right| \leq \zeta; \left|\frac{w_8^L}{w_8^U} - 1.00\right| \leq \zeta; \\ \left|\frac{w_1^U}{w_8^L} - 5.42\right| \leq \zeta; \left|\frac{w_2^U}{w_8^L} - 3.38\right| \leq \zeta; \left|\frac{w_3^U}{w_8^L} - 5.16\right| \leq \zeta; \left|\frac{w_4^U}{w_8^L} - 2.50\right| \leq \zeta; \left|\frac{w_5^U}{w_8^L} - 3.08\right| \leq \zeta; \left|\frac{w_6^U}{w_8^L} - 1.75\right| \leq \zeta; \left|\frac{w_7^U}{w_8^L} - 1.81\right| \leq \zeta; \left|\frac{w_8^U}{w_8^L} - 1.00\right| \leq \zeta; \\ \sum_{j=1}^{8} w_j^L \leq 1; \sum_{j=1}^{8} w_j^U \geq 1; \\ w_j^L \leq w_j^U, \forall j = 1, 2, \ldots, 8; w_j^L, w_j^U \geq 0, \forall j = 1, 2, \ldots, 8 \end{cases}$$

By solving the presented model, the optimal values of rough weight coefficients of the criteria were obtained.

$$RN(w_1) = [0.240,\ 0.295],$$
$$RN(w_2) = [0.131,\ 0.131],$$
$$RN(w_3) = [0.165,\ 0.165],$$
$$RN(w_4) = [0.055,\ 0.098],$$
$$RN(w_5) = [0.121,\ 0.121],$$
$$RN(w_6) = [0.057,\ 0.079],$$
$$RN(w_7) = [0.051,\ 0.076],$$
$$RN(w_8) = [0.037,\ 0.037].$$

By analyzing the rough weight coefficients of the criteria of optimality, we observe that the conditions are satisfied that $\sum_{j=1}^{n} w_j^L \leq 1$ and $\sum_{j=1}^{n} w_j^U \geq 1$, since $\sum_{j=1}^{8} w_j^L = 0.854 \leq 1$ and $\sum_{j=1}^{8} w_j^U = 1.000 \geq 1$. In addition, the requirement is that $0 \leq w_j^L \leq w_j^U \leq 1$, that is, the general condition that applies to the values of the weight coefficients of the criteria being in the interval $w_j \in [0, 1], (j = 1, 2, \ldots, 8)$.

By solving the model, the value ζ^*, which amounts to $\zeta^* = 1.148$, was obtained. The value ζ^* was used to determine the consistency ratio. Since we obtain the value $\bar{a}_{BW}$, i.e., a_{BW}^U on the basis of aggregated experts' decisions, it is not possible to define in advance the values of the consistency index ζ. Reference [52] defined the values of the consistency index (ζ) for crisp BWM. Because this relates to RBWM, for the value $a_{BW}^U = 6.95$, the value $CI(\max \zeta) = 3.595$ is defined and the value $CR = 0.319$ is obtained. Based on [52], the obtained CR value was assessed as satisfactory.

4.4. Aggregation of an Initial Matrix on the Basis of the Developed Rough Hamy Aggregator

Table 8 shows the evaluation of locations according to all criteria based on the evaluation of seven experts in the field of traffic. The evaluation was performed in the period November 2017–February 2018.

Table 8. Evaluation of locations according to criteria by seven experts.

	A_1							A_2							A_3						
C_1	3	3	5	3	3	3	1	5	5	7	5	5	5	3	1	1	3	3	3	3	1
C_2	5	3	3	3	3	3	1	3	1	3	1	3	1	1	3	1	3	3	3	1	1
C_3	5	3	1	5	3	3	3	5	3	1	5	3	3	3	9	7	5	9	7	5	7
C_4	5	3	5	3	1	3	3	7	1	7	5	5	7	9	5	1	5	3	3	7	7
C_5	7	5	7	7	5	7	5	7	5	7	5	7	5	7	5	7	7	5	7	5	
C_6	5	5	3	5	3	5	3	7	7	5	7	5	7	5	3	5	1	5	3	3	1
C_7	7	7	9	7	9	7	7	9	9	7	7	7	7	5	5	7	5	5	7	7	3
C_8	9	7	9	7	9	7	9	9	7	9	7	9	7	9	5	5	5	5	5	5	5
	A_4							A_5							A_6						
C_1	7	5	7	5	5	5	5	1	1	3	3	3	3	1	9	7	9	7	9	7	7
C_2	7	7	5	5	7	5	5	1	1	1	1	1	1	1	9	9	7	9	9	9	9
C_3	7	5	3	7	5	3	5	9	7	5	9	7	5	7	1	1	1	3	1	1	1
C_4	5	3	7	5	3	3	7	3	1	3	5	3	3	5	5	1	3	3	3	1	3
C_5	9	7	9	9	7	9	7	9	7	9	9	7	9	7	9	7	9	9	7	9	7
C_6	7	7	5	7	5	7	5	1	3	1	3	3	1	1	9	9	7	9	9	9	7
C_7	5	7	5	3	3	7	5	7	7	7	5	5	9	5	5	9	5	7	7	7	7
C_8	1	3	1	1	1	1	1	3	3	3	5	3	5	3	7	7	7	5	7	5	7

After the transformation of experts' evaluations into rough numbers, seven rough matrices are obtained that are aggregated into the aggregated rough matrix using the RNHM operator (3). Using the expression (3), the transformation of experts' individual rough matrices into RGM is performed. Thus, for example, in position A_1–C_1, we obtain the following values in expert correspondent matrices: $RN(x_{11}^{E1}) = [2.67, 3.33]$, $RN(x_{11}^{E2}) = [2.67, 3.33]$, $RN(x_{11}^{E3}) = [3.00, 5.00]$, $RN(x_{11}^{E4}) = [2.67, 3.33]$, $RN(x_{11}^{E5}) = [2.67, 3.33]$, $RN(x_{11}^{E6}) = [2.67, 3.33]$ and $RN(x_{11}^{E7}) = [1.00, 3.00]$. Based on the proposed values, the expression (3) and taking that $k = 2$, in position A_1-C_1, the aggregation of values is performed:

(a) $\dfrac{1}{\binom{n}{k}} = \dfrac{k!(n-k)!}{n!} = \dfrac{2!(7-2)!}{7!} = \dfrac{1}{21}$

(b) $Lim(x_{11}) = \dfrac{\sum_{1\leq i_1 < \ldots < i_k \leq 7} \left(\prod_{j=1}^{2} Lim(x_{i_j})\right)^{1/2}}{\binom{7}{2}} =$

$= \dfrac{(2.67\times2.67)^{1/2}+(2.67\times3)^{1/2}+(2.67\times3)^{1/2}+(2.67\times2.67)^{1/2}+\ldots+(2.67\times1)^{1/2}+(2.67\times1)^{1/2}}{21} = 2.417$

(c) $\overline{Lim}(x_{11}) = \dfrac{\sum_{1\leq i_1 < \ldots < i_k \leq 7} \left(\prod_{j=1}^{2} \overline{Lim}(\varphi_{i_j})\right)^{1/2}}{\binom{7}{2}} =$

$= \dfrac{(3.33\times3.33)^{1/2}+(3.33\times5)^{1/2}+(2\times5)^{1/2}+(3.33\times3.33)^{1/2}+\ldots+(3.33\times3)^{1/2}+(3.33\times3)^{1/2}}{21} = 3.494$

In this way, we obtain the aggregated value $RNHM^{(2)}\{RN(x_{11}^1), RN(x_{11}^2), RN(x_{11}^3), \ldots, RN(x_{11}^7)\} = [2.417, 3.494]$. As for the $k = 2$ values used in this paper, it was selected for a better display of the value aggregation using the Hamy aggregator and since it is a recommendation to use $k = 2$ for the initial aggregation in the papers [72,73]. An additional analysis of the change in the value of the parameter k showed that there were no changes in the ranks, and hence the decision to select the values k = 2 was confirmed. Similarly, we obtain the remaining elements of RGM, Table 9.

Table 9. Group rough matrix obtained using the Rough Hamy aggregator.

	C_1	C_2	C_3	C_4	C_5	C_6	C_7	C_8
A_1	[2.42, 3.49]	[2.42, 3.49]	[2.49, 3.97]	[2.49, 3.97]	[5.63, 6.62]	[3.63, 4.62]	[7.16, 7.96]	[7.64, 8.63]
A_2	[4.45, 5.5]	[1.33, 2.31]	[2.49, 3.97]	[4.07, 7.21]	[5.63, 6.62]	[5.63, 6.62]	[6.54, 7.98]	[7.64, 8.63]
A_3	[1.59, 2.61]	[1.59, 2.61]	[6.06, 7.89]	[2.89, 5.73]	[5.63, 6.62]	[1.99, 3.87]	[4.69, 6.35]	[5, 5]
A_4	[5.16, 5.96]	[5.36, 6.33]	[4.04, 5.89]	[3.68, 5.69]	[7.64, 8.63]	[5.63, 6.62]	[4.04, 5.89]	[1.04, 1.48]
A_5	[1.59, 2.61]	[1, 1]	[6.06, 7.89]	[2.49, 3.97]	[7.64, 8.63]	[1.33, 2.31]	[5.62, 7.23]	[3.16, 3.95]
A_6	[7.36, 8.34]	[8.45, 8.96]	[1.04, 1.48]	[1.93, 3.39]	[7.64, 8.63]	[8.01, 8.83]	[5.98, 7.41]	[6, 6.83]

4.5. Evaluation of Locations Using Rough WASPAS Methods

After all previous calculations and obtaining the averaging Rough Hamy initial matrix, it is necessary to apply the Equations (8) and (9) from [58] o normalize the initial matrix. An example of normalization for the criteria belonging to the benefit group is:

$$n_{21} = \left[\frac{x_{ij}^L}{x_{ij}^{+U}}; \frac{x_{ij}^U}{x_{ij}^{+L}} \right] = \left[\frac{x_{21}^L}{x_{61}^{+U}}; \frac{x_{21}^U}{x_{61}^{+L}} \right] = \left[\frac{4.45}{8.34}; \frac{5.50}{7.36} \right] = [0.53, 0.75],$$

and for the criteria belonging to the cost group:

$$n_{12} = \left[\frac{x_{ij}^{-L}}{x_{ij}^{U}}; \frac{x_{ij}^{-U}}{x_{ij}^{L}} \right] = \left[\frac{x_{15}^L}{x_{12}^{U}}; \frac{x_{15}^U}{x_{12}^{L}} \right] = \left[\frac{1.00}{3.49}; \frac{1.00}{2.42} \right] = [0.29, 0.41],$$

In the same way, all the elements of the normalized matrix should be calculated, Table 10:

Table 10. Normalized matrix.

	C_1	C_2	C_3	C_4	C_5	C_6	C_7	C_8
A_1	[0.29, 0.47]	[0.29, 0.41]	[0.32, 0.65]	[0.49, 1.36]	[0.65, 0.87]	[0.41, 0.58]	[0.9, 1.11]	[0.89, 1.13]
A_2	[0.53, 0.75]	[0.43, 0.75]	[0.32, 0.65]	[0.27, 0.83]	[0.65, 0.87]	[0.64, 0.83]	[0.82, 1.11]	[0.89, 1.13]
A_3	[0.19, 0.35]	[0.38, 0.63]	[0.77, 1.3]	[0.34, 1.17]	[0.65, 0.87]	[0.23, 0.48]	[0.59, 0.89]	[0.58, 0.65]
A_4	[0.62, 0.81]	[0.16, 0.19]	[0.51, 0.97]	[0.34, 0.92]	[0.89, 1.13]	[0.64, 0.83]	[0.51, 0.82]	[0.12, 0.19]
A_5	[0.19, 0.35]	[1, 1]	[0.77, 1.3]	[0.49, 1.36]	[0.89, 1.13]	[0.15, 0.29]	[0.7, 1.01]	[0.37, 0.52]
A_6	[0.88, 1.13]	[0.11, 0.12]	[0.13, 0.24]	[0.57, 1.76]	[0.89, 1.13]	[0.91, 1.1]	[0.75, 1.04]	[0.7, 0.89]

The next step is weighting the normalized matrix with the weights of criteria obtained by using the Rough BWM method. In order to obtain the weighted normalized matrix shown in Table 11, the Equation (11) from [58] should be applied.

Table 11. Weighted normalized matrix.

	C_1	C_2	C_3	C_4	C_5	C_6	C_7	C_8
A_1	[0.07, 0.14]	[0.04, 0.05]	[0.05, 0.11]	[0.03, 0.13]	[0.08, 0.10]	[0.02, 0.05]	[0.05, 0.08]	[0.03, 0.04]
A_2	[0.13, 0.22]	[0.06, 0.10]	[0.05, 0.11]	[0.01, 0.08]	[0.08, 0.10]	[0.04, 0.07]	[0.04, 0.09]	[0.03, 0.04]
A_3	[0.05, 0.10]	[0.05, 0.08]	[0.13, 0.21]	[0.02, 0.02]	[0.08, 0.10]	[0.01, 0.04]	[0.03, 0.07]	[0.02, 0.02]
A_4	[0.15, 0.24]	[0.02, 0.02]	[0.08, 0.16]	[0.02, 0.09]	[0.11, 0.14]	[0.04, 0.07]	[0.03, 0.06]	[0, 0.01]
A_5	[0.05, 0.10]	[0.13, 0.13]	[0.13, 0.21]	[0.03, 0.13]	[0.11, 0.14]	[0.01, 0.02]	[0.04, 0.08]	[0.01, 0.02]
A_6	[0.21, 0.33]	[0.01, 0.02]	[0.02, 0.04]	[0.03, 0.17]	[0.11, 0.14]	[0.05, 0.09]	[0.04, 0.08]	[0.03, 0.03]

The seventh step summarizes the values by the rows and the matrix Q_i. is obtained. Applying the Equation (13) from step 8 from [58], the following matrix is obtained:

$$Q_i \begin{bmatrix} [0.366, 0.712] \\ [0.440, 0.804] \\ [0.383, 0.751] \\ [0.445, 0.785] \\ [0.493, 0.838] \\ [0.501, 0.987] \end{bmatrix} \quad P_i \begin{bmatrix} [0.449, 0.656] \\ [0.542, 0.795] \\ [0.446, 0.667] \\ [0.508, 0.692] \\ [0.518, 0.713] \\ [0.483, 0.673] \end{bmatrix}$$

The relative values of the alternatives (Table 12) are calculated in the ninth step by applying the Equation (14), while λ is obtained by applying the Equation (15) [58] and it is:

$$\lambda = [0.828, 1.253]$$

Table 12. Determining relative value alternatives and ranking.

	$\lambda \times Q_i$	$(1 - \lambda) \times P_i$	A_i	Rank
A_1	[0.303, 0.891]	[−0.113, 0.113]	[0.189, 1.004]	6
A_2	[0.364, 1.007]	[−0.137, 0.137]	[0.227, 1.144]	3
A_3	[0.317, 0.940]	[−0.113, 0.115]	[0.205, 1.055]	5
A_4	[0.369, 0.983]	[−0.128, 0.119]	[0.240, 1.102]	4
A_5	[0.409, 1.050]	[−0.131, 0.123]	[0.278, 1.172]	2
A_6	[0.415, 1.124]	[−0.122, 0.116]	[0.293, 1.240]	1

Based on the presented calculation it can be noticed that the location under the rank number 6 is the best and is a priority for the construction of a roundabout. Since it is the location that has the largest traffic flow of pedestrians, the alternative solution for this location is the installation of a traffic light at this intersection, as it is well-known that if there is a high rate of pedestrians for the roundabout, alternative solutions are used. The intensity of pedestrians at this location for the period of one hour is 124 and, according to the authors' opinion, it is not a limitation for the roundabout construction. Location 6 represents the location in the town center. The second location for the construction of a roundabout is location 5 representing the last exit from the town towards Sarajevo and which is a four-way intersection with an additional side road. There is often traffic congestion at this intersection with town streets being its arms, so there is often a situation where drivers carelessly merge onto a main road, as evidenced by a number of accidents. Considering the above, the priority for the construction of a roundabout at this location is justified. Table 12 shows the results for all the locations and their ranks.

5. Sensitivity Analysis

In order to discuss the influence of the parameter k, we can adopt different values of parameter k in our proposed method to rank the alternatives, and the results are listed in Table 13. As we can see from Table 13 and Figure 3, the ranking orders are same with the parameter k changes in this example.

Table 13. Ranking results by utilizing the different k.

Alte.	k = 1	k = 2	k = 3	k = 4	k = 5	k = 6	k = 7
A1	0.595	0.597	0.599	0.669	0.679	0.681	0.682
A2	0.702	0.686	0.685	0.739	0.746	0.747	0.748
A3	0.638	0.630	0.631	0.694	0.703	0.704	0.705
A4	0.684	0.671	0.669	0.718	0.726	0.727	0.728
A5	0.734	0.725	0.726	0.749	0.754	0.755	0.756
A6	0.767	0.766	0.768	0.774	0.778	0.778	0.779
Ranking	A6 > A5 > A2 > A4 > A3 > A1	A6 > A5 > A2 > A4 > A3 > A1	A6 > A5 > A2 > A4 > A3 > A1	A6 > A5 > A2 > A4 > A3 > A1	A6 > A5 > A2 > A4 > A3 > A1	A6 > A5 > A2 > A4 > A3 > A1	A6 > A5 > A2 > A4 > A3 > A1

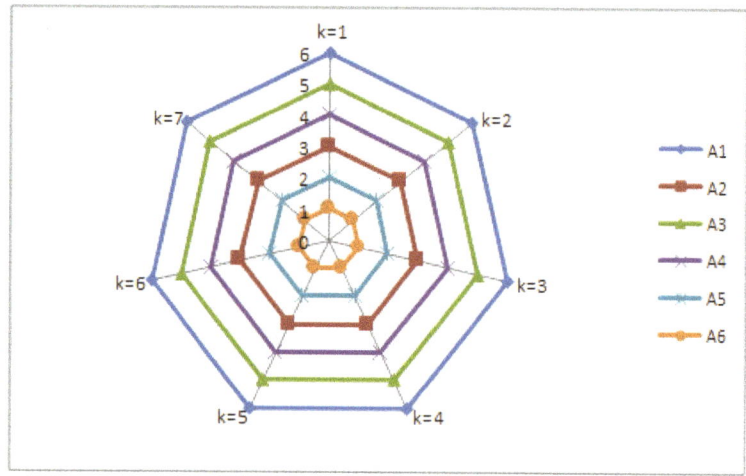

Figure 3. Results of sensitivity analysis.

For all changes of parameter k the ranking results are same, i.e., A6 > A5 > A2 > A4 > A3 > A1. This verifies that the proposed method based on the RNHM can provide more flexibility and adaptability in information aggregation and take full advantage of parameter change to solve MCDM problems in which there are interrelationships between the attributes. In real-world decision-making situations, DMs can choose the appropriate value in accordance with their risk preferences. That is, it is more effective for DMs to select adaptive value of the parameter k according to their risk attitude. If the DM favors risk, he/she can take the parameter as small as possible; if the DM dislikes risk, he can take the parameter as large as possible. Therefore, the proposed method provides a general and flexible way to express the DMs' preference and/or real requirements by utilizing the different parameter k in the decision process.

In the sensitivity analysis, a multi-criteria problem was calculated by applying other rough methods to verify the validity of the model, i.e., the results obtained. For this purpose, the following methods were used: Rough SAW (Simple Additive Weighting) [54], Rough EDAS (Evaluation based on Distance from Average Solution) [47], Rough MABAC (Multi-Attributive Border Approximation Area Comparison) [74] and Rough TOPSIS (Technique for Order of Preference by Similarity to Ideal Solution) [75], Rough MAIRCA (Multi-Attributive Ideal-Real Comparative Analysis) [76] and Rough VIKOR (VIseKriterijumska Optimizacija I Kompromisno Resenje) [77].

From Figure 4 it can be seen that the sixth location is the best solution in all formed scenarios, i.e., by applying all other methods mentioned above. Location 5 is in the second position three times, using Rough WASPAS, Rough EDAS and Rough SAW, while by applying Rough VIKOR and Rough TOPSIS it is in the fourth place, which is a consequence of similarity in the methodology of these two methods. The fourth location is in the second position four times, while in other scenarios it is twice in the third and twice in the fourth position. The alternative 2 is in the third or fourth place in all scenarios, while the third and the first alternative exchange their ranks in the fifth, i.e., sixth place. Since there is a change in the ranking of alternatives, it is necessary to perform a statistical comparison of ranks, i.e., to determine their correlation. Table 14 shows Spearman's coefficient of correlation.

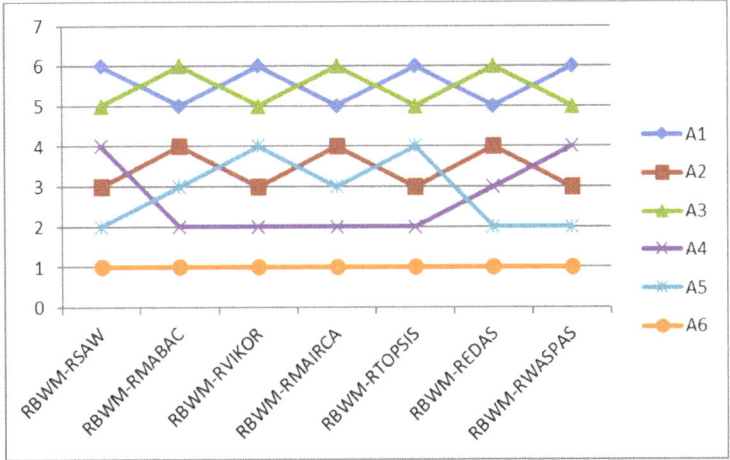

Figure 4. Ranking alternatives using different methods.

Table 14. Spearman's coefficient of correlation for rank location using different methods.

Methods	RBWM-RWASPAS	RBWM-RSAW	RBWM-RMABAC	RBWM-RVIKOR	RBWM-RMAIRCA	RBWM-RTOPSIS	RBWM-REDAS	Average
RBWM-RWASPAS	1.000	1.000	0.771	0.771	0.771	0.771	0.886	0.853
RBWM-RSAW	-	1.000	0.771	0.771	0.771	0.771	0.886	0.828
RBWM-RMABAC	-	-	1.000	0.886	1.000	0.886	0.943	0.943
RBWM-RVIKOR	-	-	-	1.000	0.886	1.000	0.771	0.914
RBWM-RMAIRCA	-	-	-	-	1.000	0.886	0.943	0.943
RBWM-RTOPSIS	-	-	-	-	-	1.000	0.771	0.886
RBWM-REDAS	-	-	-	-	-	-	1.000	1.000
Overall average								0.910

Based on the total calculated statistical correlation coefficient (0.910) it can be concluded that the ranks are in high correlation in all the created scenarios. Regarding rank correlation of Rough WASPAS with other methods, the highest correlation is with Rough SAW where the ranks are in total correlation, i.e., SCC is 1.00. It has a slightly lower correlation with Rough EDAS (0.886), while with others, it has a correlation of 0.771. As it has already been said, Rough SAW and Rough WASPAS have total correlation, hence the Rough SAW has the same correlation with other approaches as Rough WASPAS. Rough MABAC and Rough MAIRCA also have total correlation of ranks, as well as Rough VIKOR and Rough TOPSIS. The correlation coefficient of Rough MABAC, i.e., Rough MAIRCA with Rough EDAS is high and is 0.943, while the correlation coefficient of Rough VIKOR and Rough TOPSIS with Rough EDAS is 0.771. Considering the overall ranks and correlation coefficients, it can be concluded that the model obtained is very stable and the ranks are in high correlation, since all values higher than 0.80 according to Keshavarz Ghorabaee et al. [78] represent a very high correlation of ranks.

6. Conclusions

In this paper, a novel Rough Hamy aggregator has been developed to achieve a more favorable consensus for group decision-making, which is one of the key contributions of the paper.

The development of a new aggregator and the formation of an integrated Rough BWM-Rough WASPAS model further enrich the area of multi-criteria decision-making. Observing the advantages of the complete model, it is possible to make decisions that are more precise because an initial matrix has more accurate values, eliminates subjectivity and reduces uncertainty in a decision-making process.

The developed model was applied to a case study of the location selection for the construction of roundabout in the town of Doboj, which is one of the essential factors for increasing the mobility and functional sustainability of the town. Taking into account the geographic position of Doboj, there is an imperative for the construction of a roundabout on the territory covered by this urban area. The position itself causes significant share of transit flows, increasing negative externalities to the sustainability of traffic. The solution is certainly the construction of roundabouts that significantly eliminate or reduce the current negative effects. In the paper, six potential locations evaluated by using the Rough BWM-Rough WASPAS model are considered.

Based on the obtained results it can be concluded that the sixth location is the best from the aspect of the defined optimization criterion and is a priority for the construction of a roundabout. Location 6 represents the location that is in the town center. The second location priority for the construction of a roundabout is the location 5 representing the last exit from the town towards Sarajevo and a four-way intersection with an additional side road. There is very often traffic congestion at this intersection with town streets being its arms. Taking into account the above, the priority for the construction of a roundabout at the mentioned locations is considered as justified. Through the sensitivity analysis, in which the scenarios were created by applying different approaches, the model stability was verified.

Future research with respect to this paper are in relation to the development of a model that will enable the measurement of parameters that enhance traffic sustainability and the possibility of developing new approaches in the area of multi-criteria decision-making.

Author Contributions: Each author has participated and contributed sufficiently to take public responsibility for appropriate portions of the content.

Funding: This research received no external funding.

Conflicts of Interest: The authors declare no conflict of interest.

Appendix A

Proof of the Theorem 1. Based on the operations with RN:

(1) $\prod_{j=1}^{k} RN(\varphi_{i_j}) = \left[\prod_{j=1}^{k} \underline{Lim}(\varphi_{i_j}), \prod_{j=1}^{k} \overline{Lim}(\varphi_{i_j}) \right],$

(2) $\left(\prod_{j=1}^{k} RN(\varphi_{i_j}) \right)^{1/k} = \left[\left(\prod_{j=1}^{k} \underline{Lim}(\varphi_{i_j}) \right)^{1/k}, \left(\prod_{j=1}^{k} \overline{Lim}(\varphi_{i_j}) \right)^{1/k} \right],$

(3) $\sum_{1 \leq i_1 < \ldots < i_k \leq n} \left(\prod_{j=1}^{k} RN(\varphi_{i_j}) \right)^{1/k} = \left[\sum_{1 \leq i_1 < \ldots < i_k \leq n} \left(\prod_{j=1}^{k} \underline{Lim}(\varphi_{i_j}) \right)^{1/k}, \sum_{1 \leq i_1 < \ldots < i_k \leq n} \left(\prod_{j=1}^{k} \overline{Lim}(\varphi_{i_j}) \right)^{1/k} \right],$

(4) $\dfrac{1}{\binom{n}{k}} \sum_{1 \leq i_1 < \ldots < i_k \leq n} \left(\prod_{j=1}^{k} RN(\varphi_{i_j}) \right)^{1/k} = \left[\dfrac{1}{\binom{n}{k}} \sum_{1 \leq i_1 < \ldots < i_k \leq n} \left(\prod_{j=1}^{k} \underline{Lim}(\varphi_{i_j}) \right)^{1/k}, \dfrac{1}{\binom{n}{k}} \sum_{1 \leq i_1 < \ldots < i_k \leq n} \left(\prod_{j=1}^{k} \overline{Lim}(\varphi_{i_j}) \right)^{1/k} \right].$

Besides, since

$$0 \leq \frac{1}{\binom{n}{k}} \sum_{1 \leq i_1 < \ldots < i_k \leq n} \left(\prod_{j=1}^{k} \underline{Lim}(\varphi_{i_j}) \right)^{1/k} \leq \underline{Lim}(\varphi_{RNHM}),$$

$$\underline{Lim}(\varphi_{RNHM}) \leq \frac{1}{\binom{n}{k}} \sum_{1 \leq i_1 < \ldots < i_k \leq n} \left(\prod_{j=1}^{k} \overline{Lim}(\varphi_{i_j}) \right)^{1/k} \leq \overline{Lim}(\varphi_{RNHM})$$

then
$$\left[\frac{1}{\binom{n}{k}} \sum_{1 \leq i_1 < \ldots < i_k \leq n} \left(\prod_{j=1}^{k} \underline{Lim}(\varphi_{i_j}) \right)^{1/k}, \frac{1}{\binom{n}{k}} \sum_{1 \leq i_1 < \ldots < i_k \leq n} \left(\prod_{j=1}^{k} \overline{Lim}(\varphi_{i_j}) \right)^{1/k} \right]$$
represents RN, so that Theorem 1 has been proved. □

Proof of the Theorem 2. Since $RN(\varphi_j) = [\underline{Lim}(\varphi_j), \overline{Lim}(\varphi_j)] = RN(\varphi); (j = 1, 2, \ldots, n)$, then using Theorem 1, the following calculations are obtained:

$$RNHM^{(k)}\{RN(\varphi), RN(\varphi), \ldots, RN(\varphi)\} = [\underline{Lim}(\varphi), \overline{Lim}(\varphi)] =$$

$$= \left[\frac{1}{\binom{n}{k}} \sum_{1 \leq i_1 < \ldots < i_k \leq n} \left(\prod_{j=1}^{k} \underline{Lim}(\varphi_{i_j}) \right)^{1/k}, \frac{1}{\binom{n}{k}} \sum_{1 \leq i_1 < \ldots < i_k \leq n} \left(\prod_{j=1}^{k} \overline{Lim}(\varphi_{i_j}) \right)^{1/k} \right]$$

$$= \left[\frac{1}{\binom{n}{k}} \left(\underline{Lim}(\varphi_{i_j}) \right), \frac{1}{\binom{n}{k}} \left(\overline{Lim}(\varphi_{i_j}) \right) \right] = [\underline{Lim}(\varphi), \overline{Lim}(\varphi)] = RN(\varphi)$$

□

Proof of the Theorem 3. Based on Definition 2, the conclusion is obvious:

$$RNHM^{(k)}\{RN(\varphi'_1), RN(\varphi'_2), \ldots, RN(\varphi'_n)\} = \left[\frac{1}{\binom{n}{k}} \sum_{1 \leq i_1 < \ldots < i_k \leq n} \left(\prod_{j=1}^{k} \underline{Lim}(\varphi'_{i_j}) \right)^{1/k}, \frac{1}{\binom{n}{k}} \sum_{1 \leq i_1 < \ldots < i_k \leq n} \left(\prod_{j=1}^{k} \overline{Lim}(\varphi'_{i_j}) \right)^{1/k} \right] =$$

$$= \left[\frac{1}{\binom{n}{k}} \sum_{1 \leq i_1 < \ldots < i_k \leq n} \left(\prod_{j=1}^{k} \underline{Lim}(\varphi_{i_j}) \right)^{1/k}, \frac{1}{\binom{n}{k}} \sum_{1 \leq i_1 < \ldots < i_k \leq n} \left(\prod_{j=1}^{k} \overline{Lim}(\varphi_{i_j}) \right)^{1/k} \right] = RNHM^{(k)}\{RN(\varphi_{i_j}), RN(\varphi_{i_j}), \ldots, RN(\varphi_{i_j})\}$$

□

Proof of the Theorem 4. Let $RN(\varphi_j^-) = \min\{RN(\varphi_1), RN(\varphi_2), \ldots, RN(\varphi_n)\} = [\underline{Lim}(\varphi_j^-), \overline{Lim}(\varphi_j^-)]$ and $RN(\varphi_j^+) = \max\{RN(\varphi_1), RN(\varphi_2), \ldots, RN(\varphi_n)\} = [\underline{Lim}(\varphi_j^+), \overline{Lim}(\varphi_j^+)]$. Then we have $\underline{Lim}(\varphi_j^-) = \min_j\{\underline{Lim}(\varphi_j)\}, \overline{Lim}(\varphi_j^-) = \min_j\{\overline{Lim}(\varphi_j)\}, \underline{Lim}(\varphi_j^+) = \max_j\{\underline{Lim}(\varphi_j)\}$ and $\overline{Lim}(\varphi_j^+) = \max_j\{\overline{Lim}(\varphi_j)\}$. Based on that, we have that

$$\frac{1}{\binom{n}{k}} \sum_{1 \leq i_1 < \ldots < i_k \leq n} \left(\prod_{j=1}^{k} \underline{Lim}(\varphi_{i_j}^-) \right)^{1/k} \leq \frac{1}{\binom{n}{k}} \sum_{1 \leq i_1 < \ldots < i_k \leq n} \left(\prod_{j=1}^{k} \underline{Lim}(\varphi_{i_j}) \right)^{1/k} \leq \frac{1}{\binom{n}{k}} \sum_{1 \leq i_1 < \ldots < i_k \leq n} \left(\prod_{j=1}^{k} \underline{Lim}(\varphi_{i_j}^+) \right)^{1/k}$$

$$\frac{1}{\binom{n}{k}} \sum_{1\leq i_1<\ldots<i_k\leq n} \left(\prod_{j=1}^{k} \underline{Lim}(\varphi_{i_j}^-)\right)^{1/k} \leq \frac{1}{\binom{n}{k}} \sum_{1\leq i_1<\ldots<i_k\leq n} \left(\prod_{j=1}^{k} \underline{Lim}(\varphi_{i_j})\right)^{1/k} \leq \frac{1}{\binom{n}{k}} \sum_{1\leq i_1<\ldots<i_k\leq n} \left(\prod_{j=1}^{k} \underline{Lim}(\varphi_{i_j}^+)\right)^{1/k}$$

According to the inequalities shown above, we can conclude that $RN(\varphi_j^-) \leq RNHM\{RN(\varphi_1), RN(\varphi_2), \ldots, RN(\varphi_n)\} \leq RN(\varphi_j^+)$. □

Proof of the Theorem 5. Since $0 \leq \underline{Lim}(\varphi_j) \leq \underline{Lim}(\phi_j)$, $0 \leq \overline{Lim}(\varphi_j) \leq \overline{Lim}(\phi_j)$, then based on Theorem 1 it is obtained that

$$\frac{1}{\binom{n}{k}} \sum_{1\leq i_1<\ldots<i_k\leq n} \left(\prod_{j=1}^{k} \underline{Lim}(\varphi_{i_j})\right)^{1/k} \leq \frac{1}{\binom{n}{k}} \sum_{1\leq i_1<\ldots<i_k\leq n} \left(\prod_{j=1}^{k} \underline{Lim}(\phi_{i_j})\right)^{1/k}$$

$$\frac{1}{\binom{n}{k}} \sum_{1\leq i_1<\ldots<i_k\leq n} \left(\prod_{j=1}^{k} \overline{Lim}(\varphi_{i_j})\right)^{1/k} \leq \frac{1}{\binom{n}{k}} \sum_{1\leq i_1<\ldots<i_k\leq n} \left(\prod_{j=1}^{k} \overline{Lim}(\phi_{i_j})\right)^{1/k}$$

Let $RN(\varphi) = RNHM\{RN(\varphi_1), RN(\varphi_2), \ldots, RN(\varphi_n)\}$ and $RN(\phi) = RNHM\{RN(\phi_1), RN(\phi_2), \ldots, RN(\phi_n)\}$ be two RNs, then:

(1) If $\underline{Lim}(\varphi) \leq \underline{Lim}(\phi)$ and $\overline{Lim}(\varphi) \leq \overline{Lim}(\phi)$, then it is obtained that $RNHM\{RN(\varphi_1), RN(\varphi_2), \ldots, RN(\varphi_n)\} \leq RNHM\{RN(\phi_1), RN(\phi_2), \ldots, RN(\phi_n)\}$;

(2) If $\underline{Lim}(\varphi) = \underline{Lim}(\phi)$ and $\overline{Lim}(\varphi) = \overline{Lim}(\phi)$, then it can be concluded that there are the following equalities:

$$\frac{1}{\binom{n}{k}} \sum_{1\leq i_1<\ldots<i_k\leq n} \left(\prod_{j=1}^{k} \underline{Lim}(\varphi_{i_j})\right)^{1/k} = \frac{1}{\binom{n}{k}} \sum_{1\leq i_1<\ldots<i_k\leq n} \left(\prod_{j=1}^{k} \underline{Lim}(\phi_{i_j})\right)^{1/k}$$

$$\frac{1}{\binom{n}{k}} \sum_{1\leq i_1<\ldots<i_k\leq n} \left(\prod_{j=1}^{k} \overline{Lim}(\varphi_{i_j})\right)^{1/k} = \frac{1}{\binom{n}{k}} \sum_{1\leq i_1<\ldots<i_k\leq n} \left(\prod_{j=1}^{k} \overline{Lim}(\phi_{i_j})\right)^{1/k}$$

Finally, it can be concluded that there is the following inequality: $RNHM\{RN(\varphi_1), RN(\varphi_2), \ldots, RN(\varphi_n)\} \leq RNHM\{RN(\phi_1), RN(\phi_2), \ldots, RN(\phi_n)\}$. □

References

1. Brown, M. *The Design of Roundabouts*; TRL State of the Art Review; Her Majesty Stationary Office: London, UK, 1995.
2. Hels, T.; Orozova-Bekkevold, I. The effect of roundabout design features on cyclist accident rate. *Accid. Anal. Prev.* **2007**, *39*, 300–307. [CrossRef] [PubMed]
3. Vasilyeva, E.; Sazonova, T. Justification of the Expediency of Creating Circular Intersections in Modern Cities. *Earth Environ. Sci.* **2017**, *90*, 012116. [CrossRef]
4. Mottaeva, A. Innovative Aspects of Ecological and Economic Management of Investment and Construction Activities for the Sustainable Development of the Region. *MATEC Web Conf.* **2016**, *73*, 07020. [CrossRef]
5. Møller, M.; Hels, T. Cyclists' perception of risk in roundabouts. *Accid. Anal. Prev.* **2008**, *40*, 1055–1062. [CrossRef] [PubMed]
6. Li, Y.; Zhao, L.; Suo, J. Comprehensive assessment on sustainable development of highway transportation capacity based on entropy weight and TOPSIS. *Sustainability* **2014**, *6*, 4685–4693. [CrossRef]

7. Pratelli, A. Design of modern roundabouts in urban traffic systems. *WIT Trans. Built Environ.* **2006**, *89*, 11.
8. Retting, R.A.; Mandavilli, S.; McCartt, A.T.; Russell, E.R. Roundabouts, traffic flow and public opinion. *Traffic Eng. Control* **2006**, *47*, 268–272.
9. Pratelli, A.; Sechi, P.; Roy Souleyrette, R. Upgrading Traffic Circles to Modern Roundabouts to Improve Safety and Efficiency–Case Studies from Italy. *Promet-Traffic Transp.* **2018**, *30*, 217–229. [CrossRef]
10. Antov, D.; Abel, K.; Sürje, P.; Rouk, H.; Roivas, T. Speed reduction effects of urban roundabouts. *Balt. J. Road Bridge Eng.* **2009**, *4*. [CrossRef]
11. Sohn, K. A systematic decision criterion for the elimination of useless overpasses. *Transp. Res. Part A Policy Pract.* **2008**, *42*, 1043–1055. [CrossRef]
12. Podvezko, V.; Sivilevičius, H. The use of AHP and rank correlation methods for determining the significance of the interaction between the elements of a transport system having a strong influence on traffic safety. *Transport* **2013**, *28*, 389–403. [CrossRef]
13. Pilko, H.; Mandžuka, S.; Barić, D. Urban single-lane roundabouts: A new analytical approach using multi-criteria and simultaneous multi-objective optimization of geometry design, efficiency and safety. *Transp. Res. Part C Emerg. Technol.* **2017**, *80*, 257–271. [CrossRef]
14. Barić, D.; Pilko, H.; Strujić, J. An analytic hierarchy process model to evaluate road section design. *Transport* **2016**, *31*, 312–321. [CrossRef]
15. Singh, T.P.; Nigam, S.P.; Singh, D.G.; Agrawal, V.P. Analysis and Validation of Traffic Noise under Dynamic Condition Near Roundabout Using Madm Approach. Ph.D. Thesis, LM Thapar School of Management, Behra, India, 2013.
16. Pirdavani, A.; Brijs, T.; Wets, G. A Multiple Criteria Decision-Making Approach for Prioritizing Accident Hotspots in the Absence of Crash Data. *Transp. Rev.* **2010**, *30*, 97–113. [CrossRef]
17. Murat, Y.S.; Arslan, T.; Cakici, Z.; Akçam, C. Analytical Hierarchy Process (AHP) based Decision Support System for Urban Intersections in Transportation Planning. In *Using Decision Support Systems for Transportation Planning Efficiency*; IGI Global: Hershey, PA, USA, 2016; pp. 203–222.
18. Legac, I.; Pilko, H.; Brcic, D. Analysis of traffic capacity and design for the reconstruction of a large roundabout in the city of Zagreb. *Intersec. Control Saf.* **2013**, *66*, 17.
19. Ruiz-Padillo, A.; Ruiz, D.P.; Torija, A.J.; Ramos-Ridao, Á. Selection of suitable alternatives to reduce the environmental impact of road traffic noise using a fuzzy multi-criteria decision model. *Environ. Impact Assess. Rev.* **2016**, *61*, 8–18. [CrossRef]
20. Ruiz-Padillo, A.; Torija, A.J.; Ramos-Ridao, A.F.; Ruiz, D.P. Application of the fuzzy analytic hierarchy process in multi-criteria decision in noise action plans: Prioritizing road stretches. *Environ. Model. Softw.* **2016**, *81*, 45–55. [CrossRef]
21. Joo, S.; Lee, G.; Oh, C. A multi-criteria analysis framework including environmental and health impacts for evaluating traffic calming measures at the road network level. *Int. J. Sustain. Transp.* **2017**, 1–9. [CrossRef]
22. Hao, N.; Feng, Y.; Zhang, K.; Tian, G.; Zhang, L.; Jia, H. Evaluation of traffic congestion degree: An integrated approach. *Int. J. Distrib. Sens. Netw.* **2017**, *13*. [CrossRef]
23. Bongo, M.F.; Ocampo, L.A. A hybrid fuzzy MCDM approach for mitigating airport congestion: A case in Ninoy Aquino International Airport. *J. Air Transp. Manag.* **2017**, *63*, 1–16. [CrossRef]
24. Hashemkhani Zolfani, S.; Esfahani, M.H.; Bitarafan, M.; Zavadskas, E.K.; Arefi, S.L. Developing a new hybrid MCDM method for selection of the optimal alternative of mechanical longitudinal ventilation of tunnel pollutants during automobile accidents. *Transport* **2013**, *28*, 89–96. [CrossRef]
25. Castro-Nuño, M.; Arévalo-Quijada, M.T. Assessing urban road safety through multidimensional indexes: Application of multicriteria decision making analysis to rank the Spanish provinces. *Transp. Policy* **2018**, *68*, 118–129. [CrossRef]
26. Gardziejczyk, W.; Zabicki, P. Normalization and variant assessment methods in selection of road alignment variants–case study. *J. Civ. Eng. Manag.* **2017**, *23*, 510–523. [CrossRef]
27. Javid, R.J.; Nejat, A.; Hayhoe, K. Selection of CO_2 mitigation strategies for road transportation in the United States using a multi-criteria approach. *Renew. Sustain. Energy Rev.* **2014**, *38*, 960–972. [CrossRef]
28. Drezner, Z. *Facility Location: A Survey of Applications and Methods*; Springer: New York, NY, USA, 1995.
29. Kahraman, C.; Ruan, D.; Doğan, I. Fuzzy group decision-making for facility location selection. *Inf. Sci.* **2003**, *157*, 135–153. [CrossRef]

30. Berman, O.; Drezner, Z.; Wesolowsky, G.O. Location of facilities on a network with groups of demand points. *IIE Trans.* **2001**, *33*, 637–648. [CrossRef]
31. Melkote, S.; Daskin, M.S. Capacitated facility location/network design problems. *Eur. J. Oper. Res.* **2001**, *129*, 481–495. [CrossRef]
32. Nanthavanij, S.; Yenradee, P. Predicting the optimum number, location, and signal sound level of auditory warning devices for manufacturing facilities. *Int. J. Ind. Ergon.* **1999**, *24*, 569–578. [CrossRef]
33. Badri, M.A. Combining the analytic hierarchy process and goal programming for global facility location-allocation problem. *Int. J. Prod. Econ.* **1999**, *62*, 237–248. [CrossRef]
34. Applebaum, W. The analog method for estimating potential store sales. *Guid. Stor. Locat. Res.* **1968**, *3*, 127–144.
35. Stević, Ž.; Vesković, S.; Vasiljević, M.; Tepić, G. The selection of the logistics center location using AHP method. In Proceedings of the 2nd Logistics International Conference, Belgrade, Serbia, 21–23 May 2015; pp. 86–91.
36. Benjamin, C.O.; Chi, S.C.; Gaber, T.; Riordan, C.A. Comparing BP and ART II neural network classifiers for facility location. *Comput. Ind. Eng.* **1995**, *28*, 43–50. [CrossRef]
37. Satani, N.; Uchida, A.; Deguchi, A.; Ohgai, A.; Sato, S.; Hagishima, S. Commercial facility location model using multiple regression analysis. *Comput. Environ. Urban Syst.* **1998**, *22*, 219–240. [CrossRef]
38. Chauhan, A.; Singh, A. A hybrid multi-criteria decision making method approach for selecting a sustainable location of healthcare waste disposal facility. *J. Clean. Prod.* **2016**, *139*, 1001–1010. [CrossRef]
39. Nie, R.X.; Wang, J.Q.; Zhang, H.Y. Solving solar-wind power station location problem using an extended weighted aggregated sum product assessment (WASPAS) technique with interval neutrosophic sets. *Symmetry* **2017**, *9*, 106. [CrossRef]
40. Samanlioglu, F.; Ayağ, Z. A fuzzy AHP-PROMETHEE II approach for evaluation of solar power plant location alternatives in Turkey. *J. Intell. Fuzzy Syst.* **2017**, *33*, 859–871. [CrossRef]
41. Zhao, L.; Li, H.; Li, M.; Sun, Y.; Hu, Q.; Mao, S.; Li, J.; Xue, J. Location selection of intra-city distribution hubs in the metro-integrated logistics system. *Tunn. Undergr. Space Technol.* **2018**, *80*, 246–256. [CrossRef]
42. Nazari, M.A.; Aslani, A.; Ghasempour, R. Analysis of solar farm site selection based on TOPSIS approach. *Int. J. Soc. Ecol. Sustain. Dev.* **2018**, *9*, 12–25. [CrossRef]
43. Baušys, R.; Juodagalvienė, B. Garage location selection for residential house by WASPAS-SVNS method. *J. Civ. Eng. Manag.* **2017**, *23*, 421–429. [CrossRef]
44. Pamučar, D.; Stević, Ž.; Zavadskas, E.K. Integration of interval rough AHP and interval rough MABAC methods for evaluating university web pages. *Appl. Soft Comput.* **2018**, *67*, 141–163. [CrossRef]
45. Saaty, T.L.; Tran, L.T. On the invalidity of fuzzifying numerical judgments in the Analytic Hierarchy Process. *Math. Comput. Model.* **2007**, *46*, 962–975. [CrossRef]
46. Wang, Y.M.; Luo, Y.; Hua, Z. On the extent analysis method for fuzzy AHP and its applications. *Eur. J. Oper. Res.* **2008**, *186*, 735–747. [CrossRef]
47. Stević, Ž.; Pamučar, D.; Vasiljević, M.; Stojić, G.; Korica, S. Novel Integrated Multi-Criteria Model for Supplier Selection: Case Study Construction Company. *Symmetry* **2017**, *9*, 279. [CrossRef]
48. Yager, R.R. On generalized Bonferroni mean operators for multi-criteria aggregation. *Int. J. Approx. Reason.* **2009**, *50*, 1279–1286. [CrossRef]
49. Petrović, G.S.; Madić, M.; Antucheviciene, J. An approach for robust decision making rule generation: Solving transport and logistics decision making problems. *Expert Syst. Appl.* **2018**, *106*, 263–276. [CrossRef]
50. Stefanovic-Marinovic, J.; Troha, S.; Milovančevic, M. An Application of Multicriteria Optimization to the Two-Carrier Two-Speed Planetary Gear Trains. *Facta Univ. Ser. Mech. Eng.* **2017**, *15*, 85–95. [CrossRef]
51. Chatterjee, P.; Mondal, S.; Boral, S.; Banerjee, A.; Chakraborty, S. A novel hybrid method for non-traditional machining process selection using factor relationship and multi-attributive border approximation method. *Facta Univ. Ser. Mech. Eng.* **2017**, *15*, 439–456. [CrossRef]
52. Rezaei, J. Best-worst multi-criteria decision-making method. *Omega* **2015**, *53*, 49–57. [CrossRef]
53. Pamučar, D.; Gigović, L.; Bajić, Z.; Janošević, M. Location selection for wind farms using GIS multi-criteria hybrid model: An approach based on fuzzy and rough numbers. *Sustainability* **2017**, *9*, 1315. [CrossRef]
54. Stević, Ž.; Pamučar, D.; Zavadskas, E.K.; Ćirović, G.; Prentkovskis, O. The Selection of Wagons for the Internal Transport of a Logistics Company: A Novel Approach Based on Rough BWM and Rough SAW Methods. *Symmetry* **2017**, *9*, 264. [CrossRef]

55. Pamučar, D.; Petrović, I.; Ćirović, G. Modification of the Best–Worst and MABAC methods: A novel approach based on interval-valued fuzzy-rough numbers. *Expert Syst. Appl.* **2018**, *91*, 89–106. [CrossRef]
56. Pawlak, Z. *Rough Sets: Theoretical Aspects of Reasoning about Data*; Springer: Berlin, Germany, 1991.
57. Pawlak, Z. Anatomy of conflicts. *Bull. Eur. Assoc. Theor. Comput. Sci.* **1993**, *50*, 234–247.
58. Stojić, G.; Stević, Ž.; Antuchevičienė, J.; Pamučar, D.; Vasiljević, M. A Novel Rough WASPAS Approach for Supplier Selection in a Company Manufacturing PVC Carpentry Products. *Information* **2018**, *9*, 121. [CrossRef]
59. Hashemkhani Zolfani, S.; Aghdaie, M.H.; Derakhti, A.; Zavadskas, E.K.; Varzandeh, M.H.M. Decision making on business issues with foresight perspective; an application of new hybrid MCDM model in shopping mall locating. *Expert Syst. Appl.* **2013**, *40*, 7111–7121. [CrossRef]
60. Mardani, A.; Nilashi, M.; Zavadskas, E.K.; Awang, S.R.; Zare, H.; Jamal, N.M. Decision making methods based on fuzzy aggregation operators: Three decades review from 1986 to 2017. *Int. J. Inf. Technol. Decis. Mak.* **2018**, *17*, 391–466. [CrossRef]
61. Božanić, D.; Tešić, D.; Milićević, J. A hybrid fuzzy AHP-MABAC model: Application in the Serbian Army—The selection of the location for deep wading as a technique of crossing the river by tanks. *Decis. Mak. Appl. Manag. Eng.* **2018**, *1*, 143–164. [CrossRef]
62. Roy, J.; Adhikary, K.; Kar, S.; Pamučar, D. A rough strength relational DEMATEL model for analysing the key success factors of hospital service quality. *Decis. Mak. Appl. Manag. Eng.* **2018**, *1*, 121–142. [CrossRef]
63. Vasiljevic, M.; Fazlollahtabar, H.; Stevic, Z.; Veskovic, S. A rough multicriteria approach for evaluation of the supplier criteria in automotive industry. *Decis. Mak. Appl. Manag. Eng.* **2018**, *1*, 82–96. [CrossRef]
64. Hara, T.; Uchiyama, M.; Takahasi, S.E. A refinement of various mean inequalities. *J. Inequal. Appl.* **1998**, *2*, 387–395. [CrossRef]
65. Day, C.M.; Hainen, A.M.; Bullock, D.M. *Best Practices for Roundabouts on State Highways*; Publication Joint Transportation Research Program, Indiana Department of Transportation and Purdue University: West Lafayette, Indiana, 2013.
66. Benekohal, R.F.; Atluri, V. *Roundabout Evaluation and Design: A Site Selection Procedure*; Illinois Center for Transportation (ICT): Rantoul, IL, USA, 2009.
67. Deluka-Tibljaš, A.; Babić, S.; Cuculić, M.; Šurdonja, S. Possible reconstructions of intersections in urban areas by using roundabouts. In Proceedings of the The First International Conference on Road and Rail Infrastructure (CETRA 2010), Road and Rail Infrastructure, Opatija, Croatia, 17–18 May 2010; pp. 171–178.
68. Steiner, R.L.; Washburn, S.; Elefteriadou, L.; Gan, A.; Alluri, P.; Michalaka, D.; Xu, R.; Rachmat, S.; Lytle, B.; Cavaretta, A. *Roundabouts and Access Management*; State of Florida Department of Transportation: Florida, FL, USA, 2014.
69. Kozić, M.; Šurdonja, S.; Deluka-Tibljaš, A.; Karleuša, B.; Cuculić, M. Criteria for urban traffic infrastructure analyses–case study of implementation of Croatian Guidelines for Rounabouts on State Roads. In Proceedings of the 4th International Conference on Road and Rail Infrastructure, Šibenik, Croatia, 23–25 May 2016.
70. Retting, R.; Kyrychenko, S.; McCartt, A. Long-term trends in public opinion following construction of roundabouts. *Transp. Res. Rec. J. Transp. Res. Board* **2007**, *2019*, 219–224. [CrossRef]
71. Zavadskas, E.K.; Stević, Ž.; Tanackov, I.; Prentkovskis, O. A Novel Multicriteria Approach–Rough Step-Wise Weight Assessment Ratio Analysis Method (R-SWARA) and Its Application in Logistics. *Stud. Inf. Control* **2018**, *27*, 97–106. [CrossRef]
72. Qin, J. Interval type-2 fuzzy Hamy mean operators and their application in multiple criteria decision making. *Granul. Comput.* **2017**, *2*, 249–269. [CrossRef]
73. Liu, P.; You, X. Some linguistic neutrosophic Hamy mean operators and their application to multi-attribute group decision making. *PLoS ONE* **2018**, *13*, e0193027. [CrossRef] [PubMed]
74. Roy, J.; Chatterjee, K.; Bandhopadhyay, A.; Kar, S. Evaluation and selection of Medical Tourism sites: A rough AHP based MABAC approach. *arXiv*, 2016.
75. Song, W.; Ming, X.; Wu, Z.; Zhu, B. A rough TOPSIS approach for failure mode and effects analysis in uncertain environments. *Qual. Reliab. Eng. Int.* **2014**, *30*, 473–486. [CrossRef]
76. Pamučar, D.; Mihajlović, M.; Obradović, R.; Atanasković, P. Novel approach to group multi-criteria decision making based on interval rough numbers: Hybrid DEMATEL-ANP-MAIRCA model. *Expert Syst. Appl.* **2017**, *88*, 58–80. [CrossRef]

77. Zhu, G.N.; Hu, J.; Qi, J.; Gu, C.C.; Peng, Y.H. An integrated AHP and VIKOR for design concept evaluation based on rough number. *Adv. Eng. Inf.* **2015**, *29*, 408–418. [CrossRef]
78. Keshavarz Ghorabaee, M.; Zavadskas, E.K.; Turskis, Z.; Antucheviciene, J. A new combinative distance-based assessment (CODAS) method for multi-criteria decision-making. *Econ. Comput. Econ. Cybern. Stud. Res.* **2016**, *50*, 25–44.

© 2018 by the authors. Licensee MDPI, Basel, Switzerland. This article is an open access article distributed under the terms and conditions of the Creative Commons Attribution (CC BY) license (http://creativecommons.org/licenses/by/4.0/).

Article

Apple Cubes Drying and Rehydration. Multiobjective Optimization of the Processes

Radosław Winiczenko, Krzysztof Górnicki *, Agnieszka Kaleta, Monika Janaszek-Mańkowska, Aneta Choińska and Jędrzej Trajer

Department of Fundamental Engineering, Warsaw University of Life Sciences, Nowoursynowska 164 St., 02-787 Warsaw, Poland; radoslaw_winiczenko@sggw.pl (R.W.); agnieszka_kaleta@sggw.pl (A.K.); monika_janaszek@sggw.pl (M.J.-M.); aneta_choinska@sggw.pl (A.C.); jedrzej_trajer@sggw.pl (J.T.)
* Correspondence: krzysztof_gornicki@sggw.pl; Tel.: +48-22-593-46-18

Received: 17 October 2018; Accepted: 5 November 2018; Published: 9 November 2018

Abstract: The effect of convective drying temperature (T_d), air velocity (v), rehydration temperature (T_r), and kind of rehydrating medium (pH) was studied on the following apple quality parameters: water absorption capacity (WAC), volume ratio (VR) color difference (CD). To model, simulate, and optimize parameters of the drying and rehydration processes hybrid methods artificial neural network and multiobjective genetic algorithm (MOGA) were developed. MOGA was adapted to the apple tissue, where the simultaneous minimization of CD and VR and the maximization of WAC were considered. The following parameters range were applied, $50 \leq T_d \leq 70\,°C$ and $0.01 \leq v \leq 6\,m/s$ for drying and $20 \leq T_r \leq 95\,°C$ for rehydration. Distilled water (pH = 5.45), 0.5% solution of citric acid (pH = 2.12), and apple juice (pH = 3.20) were used as rehydrating media. For determining the rehydrated apple quality parameters the mathematical formulas were developed. The following best result was found. T_d = 50.1 °C, v = 4.0 m/s, T_r = 20.1 °C, and pH = 2.1. The values of WAC, VR, and CD were determined as 4.93, 0.44, and 0.46, respectively. Experimental verification was done, the maximum error of modeling was lower than 5.6%.

Keywords: optimization; genetic algorithm; artificial neural network; apple; drying; rehydration

1. Introduction

Drying is one of the most common and the oldest methods of biological materials (fruits and vegetables) preservation. It consumes between 7 and 15% of total industrial energy production [1].

Dehydration is a complex process involving moisture removal. Two processes occur simultaneously during drying, namely energy transfer (mostly of heat) from the surrounding environment to the wet solid and mass transfer (moisture transfer) from inside of the solid to the surface and then its evaporation to the surrounding environment [2].

The objective in drying of biological materials is the reduction of the amount of free-water in the solids to such a level, at which deteriorative processes caused mainly by microbiological growth, chemical reactions, and enzymatic activity are greatly minimized. Due to the initial moisture content of approximately 74–90% w.b., vegetables and fruits are particularly susceptible to deteriorative processes [3].

During drying, however, disadvantageous changes in the material quality occur, among others: color changes due to nonenzymatic and enzymatic browning reactions, shape and size changes, shrinking, changes in texture, aromas loss, changes of the crystalline structure, hindered rehydration, lipids oxidation, protein denaturation, and loss and degradation of nutritional compounds e.g., vitamins, phenolic compounds, carotenoids, and ascorbic acid [4,5]. Therefore, the proper choice of drying parameters, not only due to energy consumption, but above all for the quality of the final product is so important.

Rehydration is very important quality property for died products. It is a complex process intended to restore the properties of the fresh product by contacting dried products with a liquid [6,7]. The following physical mechanisms occur during the rehydration, water imbibition, internal diffusion, and convection through large open pores and at the surface. Two cross-current mass fluxes take part in the previously discussed process: a water flux from the rehydrating medium to the product and solutes flux (acids, sugars, vitamins, and minerals) from the product to the medium [8–10]. Powder–water interactions during rehydration are divided into steps: wetting, sinking, dispersing and, when the product is soluble, dissolution [11].

The process of rehydration is influenced by the following intrinsic factors, product chemical composition, its microstructure [12], predrying treatment [13,14], dehydration methods [15,16], extrinsic conditions [17,18] such as the composition of rehydrating medium [19,20], temperature [21,22], and hydrodynamic conditions [23].

Genetic algorithms (GA) are optimization methods useful in irregular experimental regions. This optimization tool is applied in such ranges as computer programming, forecasting, image recognition, control, optimization of mechanical and electronic systems, data analysis, and production management and engineering [24]. The computation efficiency of genetic algorithms could be significantly improved by their interoperating with artificial neural networks (ANN), data exploration, and fuzzy systems. ANN and GA were used for fruit storage process optimization [25]. It was found that such an intelligent approach gave better results than traditional computational techniques.

Most optimization studies not only in food industry consider to single-objective optimization, whereas multiobjective optimization (MOO), due to its mathematical complexity, has been rarely used [26,27]. An effective hybrid multiobjective evolutionary algorithm for the energy-efficient scheduling problem [28,29] and for the the passive vibration suppression of an engine [30] were proposed.

MOO is used in food industry for optimization of pre-fry microwave drying of French fries [31], convective drying of apple cubes [32], and in the process of thermal sterilization [33]. Thakur et al. [34] used MOO to balance cost and traceability in bulk grain handing, whereas Hadiyanto et al. [35] applied MOO to improve the product range of a baking system. Multiobjective optimization has been proposed for the roasting processes of beef [36] and turkey breast [37].

The aims of the study were to apply the MOO method to optimize the quality of rehydrated apples parameters by determining factors of the drying and rehydration processes. The effect of drying air temperature, drying air velocity, and the kind and temperature of the rehydrating medium on the following quality parameters of rehydrated apples was evaluated, color, volume, and water absorption capacity index.

2. Materials and Methods

2.1. Material

Apples (var. Ligol) were purchased at a Warsaw market. Fresh and high-quality lots were chosen (initial moisture content ca. 85% w.b.). Just before drying, washed and peeled apples were cut into 10 ± 1 mm cubes thickness.

2.2. Drying Process

The methods used for drying of raw apples were follows: natural convection (the drying air velocity $v = 0.01$ m/s), forced convection ($v = 0.5$ and $v = 2$ m/s), and fluidized bed drying ($v = 6$ m/s).

The drying experiments were carried at following drying air temperatures (T_d): 50, 60, and 70 °C. The final moisture content of dried material was ca. 9% w.b. Drying equipment and way of conducting the experiments were described in the papers [38–40].

The dried apples obtained at the same drying conditions from the three independent experiments were mixed and stored for further analysis in a sealed container for one week at the temperature 20 °C.

2.3. Rehydration Process

The rehydration process of dehydrated apple cubes was carried out at temperatures (T_r): 20, 45, 70, and 95 °C in the following media, distilled water (pH = 5.45), 0.5% solution of citric acid (pH = 2.12), and apple juice (pH = 3.20). The rehydration of samples lasted from 6 h (T_r = 20 °C) to 2 h (T_r = 95 °C) and was carried out in triplicate. The temperature of rehydrating liquids was constant. The initial mass of each dried sample used in rehydration amounted to ca. 10 g. Mass of dehydrated apple cubes to rehydrating medium mass ratio at the beginning of the rehydration amounted to 1:20. The values of rehydrating media pH were measured using a pH-meter, BW 10 (Trotec GmbH & Co. KG, Heinsberg, Germany) with 0.02 resolution.

2.4. Mass and Volume Measurements

Samples mass was measured using WPE 300 scales (RADWAG, Radom, Poland) with 0.001 g accuracy; the dry matter of solid was measured before, during, and after rehydration in accordance with AOAC standards [41]. Measurements were made in three replicates.

Volume of samples (dried and rehydrated) was calculated from buoyancy in petroleum benzine [42]. Measurements were carried out in triplicate (maximum relative error lower than 5%).

2.5. Color Determination

The color of the food product is one of the most important quality factors and plays a significant role in its appearance and consumer acceptability. The color of fresh and rehydrated apples was determined by scanner (Canon CanoScan 5600F). Obtained color images were then loaded into the sRGB color space. Mean brightness of pixels in each RGB channel of the image was used to express color parameters. Mean RGB values were linearly transformed to CIE XYZ color space and next XYZ color parameters were nonlinearly converted to CIE Lab coordinates. Reference values for XYZ (standard observer of 10°, illuminant D50) were 96.72, 100, and 81.43, respectively [43]. Chroma (C) and hue angle (h) specific for CIELCh color space were determined [44].

2.6. Quality Parameters

The following parameters were used for description of the quality of rehydrated apple cubes,

- Water absorption capacity index (WAC) calculated from the formula [45]:

$$\text{WAC} = \frac{M_r(100 - s_r) - M_d(100 - s_d)}{M_0(100 - s_0) - M_d(100 - s_d)} \qquad (1)$$

where, M—the mass (g), s—the dry matter content, and subscripts 0, d, and r refer to before drying, dry, and rehydrated, respectively. Discussed index WAC gives information on the ability of the material to absorb water.

- The volume ratio (VR) is formulated as

$$\text{VR} = \frac{V_d}{V_r} \qquad (2)$$

where, V_d—volume of dried apple cube (after drying) and V_r—volume after rehydration in m^3.

- Color difference (CD) between the fresh and rehydrated samples determined as [46]

$$CD = \sqrt{\left(\frac{\Delta L}{K_L S_L}\right)^2 + \left(\frac{\Delta C}{K_C S_C}\right)^2 + \left(\frac{\Delta H}{K_H S_H}\right)^2} \qquad (3)$$

where: S_L, S_C, and S_H are the weight functions adjusting internal non-uniform structure of CIELab and $S_L = 1$, $S_C = 1 + 0.045C$, and $S_H = 1 + 0.015C$, whereas K_L, K_C, and K_H (equal to 1) describe the variation from the reference conditions, ΔH, ΔL, and ΔC describe the difference between tested ($_T$) and standard ($_S$) samples in hue, luminance, and chroma, respectively. $\Delta H = 2\sqrt{C_T \cdot C_S} \cdot \sin\left(\frac{\Delta h}{2}\right)$, $\Delta L = L_T - L_S$ and $\Delta C = C_T - C_S$.

2.7. Quality Parameters Modeling Using ANN

Each of the ANN layers (input, output, and hidden) is built from neurons (nodes) and is fully connected to the next layer [47]. Input layer produces linear function which is a weighted sum of input variables. The hidden layer processes data with a nonlinear transfer function. The output layer processes data with a linear or nonlinear transfer function [48]. A backpropagation (BP) algorithm has been employed. The ANN has four neurons in the input layer (parameters of the drying and rehydration processes: T_d, v, T_r, and pH) and three neurons in the output layer (quality parameters: CD, VR, and WAC). Values of these parameters have been normalized in the range of 0–1.

In order to gain the optimal ANN architecture different number of neurons and activation functions were tried. Details of choice the best of ANN structure are described in a previous work [49]. Mean Squared Error (MSE) was calculated by

$$MSE = \frac{\sum_{i=1}^{N}\left(x_{exp,i} - x_{pred,i}\right)^2}{N} \quad (4)$$

where, N—the test cases number, x—the output value, subscripts exp and pred refer to experiment and prediction, respectively, and correlation coefficients (R) were used to check the performance of each ANN.

Chosen cases (114) were randomly divided into training—77 samples (70%), validation—17 samples (15%), and testing—17 samples (15%) sets. ANNs were implemented in MATLAB and the Levenberg–Marquardt algorithm was used for training [50].

To identify the critical parameters and their degree of impact on the ANN outputs, sensitivity analysis was performed. The backward stepwise method was used. This method consists of step by step rejecting one input variable, and testing the effect on the output results. The largest value of MSE due to one input omission shows the most important input [51].

2.8. Multiobjective Optimization (MOO) Problem

The following MOO task was taken: the determination of set of optimal conditions of drying and rehydration processes. The WAC function was maximized, whereas CD and VR functions were minimized subject to constraints on the drying and rehydration parameters. Equation (5) presents the MOO problem.

$$\text{Min}(x) = \begin{cases} \text{Max WAC}(T_d, v, T_r, pH) \\ \text{Min VR}(T_d, v, T_r, pH) \\ \text{Min CD}(T_d, v, T_r, pH) \\ 50\,°C \leq T_d \leq 70\,°C \\ 0.01\,m/s \leq v \leq 6\,m/s \\ 2.12 \leq pH \leq 5.45 \\ 20\,°C \leq T_r \leq 95\,°C \end{cases} \quad (5)$$

The Pareto front for discussed MOO problem was generated using an elitist nondominated sorting genetic algorithm (NSGA II) and was implemented in MATLAB (Figure 1).

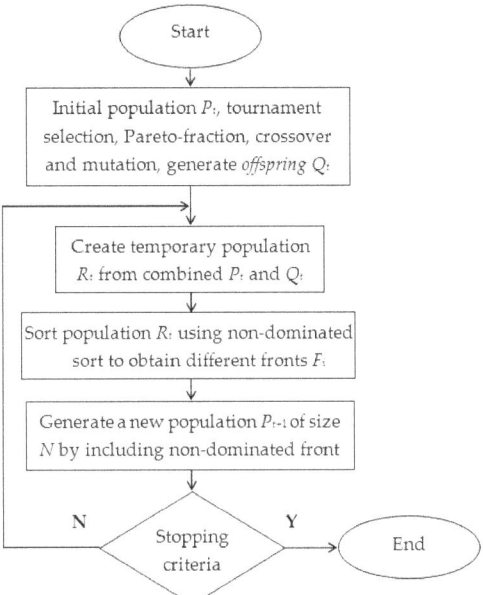

Figure 1. Flowchart of the elitist nondominated sorting genetic algorithm used (NSGA II).

The optimization procedure stopped at function tolerance equal to 10^{-6}.

3. Results and Discussion

3.1. ANN

In order to approximate functional relations between drying and rehydration processes variables (T_d, v, pH, and T_r) and apple quality parameters (WAC, VR, and CD), different ANN structures with various transfer functions were tested. Considering the highest R and the lowest MSE the best result (MSE = 0.0019) were obtained for ANN presented in Figure 2. The hidden and output layers of the ANN processed data with a log-sigmoid transfer functions.

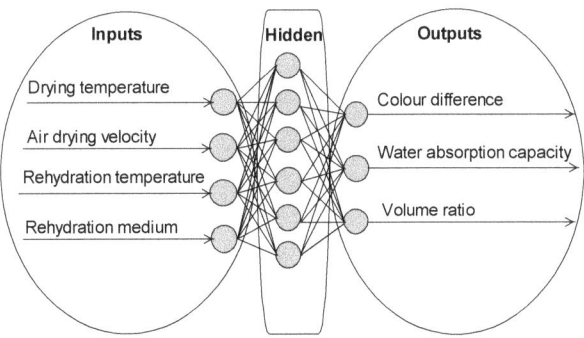

Figure 2. The best of artificial neural network (ANN) structure.

Figure 3 shows the ANN best validation performance. MSE = 0.0019 at the 16th iteration with changes of MSE at training, validation, and testing phase. Mean squared error determined for test and validation sets had similar characteristics. Insignificant overfitting was observed. Final MSE values for training, validation and test sets were 0.0014, 0.0019, and 0.0017, respectively.

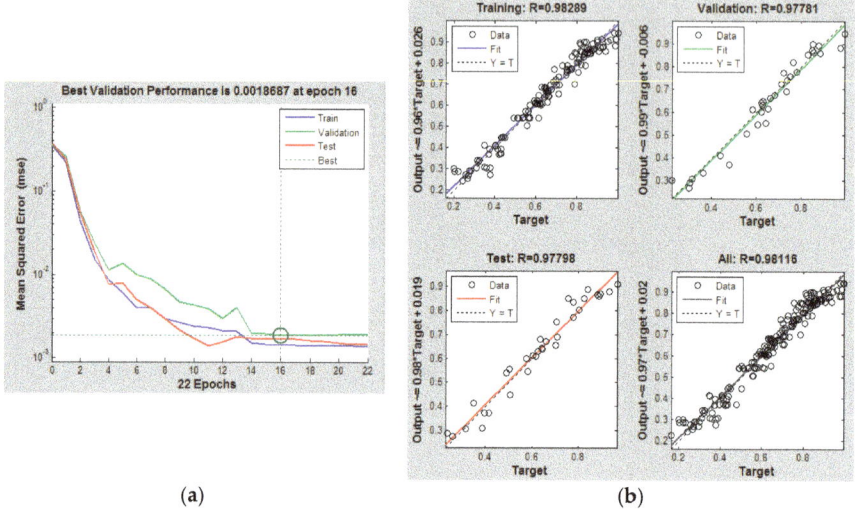

(a) (b)

Figure 3. ANN best validation performance (**a**) and ANN goodness of fit (**b**).

Additionally, high R-values between predicted and experimental data (0.9778–0.9829) mean good agreement between data predicted by ANN and experimental results (Figure 3).

3.2. Mathematical Formulations

Quality parameters WAC, VR, and CD were determined with the following formulas (from ANN).

$$\text{WAC} = \frac{1}{1 + \exp^{-(1.9043F_1 - 1.8376F_2 + 2.0638F_3 + 0.6350*F_4 - 1.0502F_5 + 1.3317F_6 - 2.1991)}} \tag{6}$$

$$\text{VR} = \frac{1}{1 + \exp^{-(-0.7714F_1 + 0.8390F_2 + 4.3547F_3 - 2.2097F_4 - 2.0998F_5 - 0.4509F_6 - 1.0072)}} \tag{7}$$

$$\text{CD} = \frac{1}{1 + \exp^{-(-3.5956F_1 + 0.6489F_2 - 0.3165F_3 - 3.0398F_4 + 4.5572F_5 - 1.1678F_6 + 5.8421)}} \tag{8}$$

where $F_{(i=1 \div 6)}$

$$F_i = \frac{1}{1 + \exp^{-W_i}} \tag{9}$$

and W_1–W_5 can be determined as follows

$$W_i = D_{1i}T_d + D_{2i}v + D_{3i}\text{pH} + D_{4i}T_r + D_{5i} \tag{10}$$

where constants D_{ji} in Equation (10) are shown in Table 1.

Table 1. Weights and biases in Equation (10).

i	D_{1i}	D_{2i}	D_{3i}	D_{4i}	D_{5i}
1	−11.1588	−7.7592	−0.6697	1.5380	18.4940
2	−1.0835	−0.1818	−9.6281	−3.8191	10.5589
3	−15.0529	−4.9146	8.6942	−2.8797	17.9134
4	−8.7055	−0.6294	4.3391	−14.9923	17.1001
5	−11.8990	−18.2054	−1.8929	2.3569	9.2392
6	−3.6760	1.6062	−17.8052	−5.5386	11.8517

The normalization of the T_d, v, pH, and T_r values were conducted dividing them by 70, 6, 5.5, and 95, respectively, whereas the values of quality parameters (WAC, VR, and CD) were normalized by dividing them by 0.54, 0.64, and 27 respectively. Equations (6)–(10) were used for MOO (Equation (5)).

The sensitivity analysis showed that T_d has the greatest impact on all the quality parameters obtained from the ANN. V, pH, and T_r occupied the 2nd, 3rd, and 4th position, respectively. In the case of testing the sensitivity analysis of ANN only for CD, T_d has the greatest impact on this quality parameter and next positions occupied the T_r, v, and pH. However, when the ANN is used to designate only VR, the greatest impact on VR is in the following sequence: pH, T_r, v, and T_d. Taking into account only the WAC, the order is as follows pH, v, T_r, and T_d.

3.3. MOO

The MOO problem (Equation (5)) was solved with GA. The size of population was assumed as 30. The controlled parameters of NSGA II were as follows. The mutation function was Adaptive feasible and the crossover function was Heuristic with default ratio of 1.2. Number of generations was 300 and Pareto front population fraction was 0.8.

Table 2 and Figure 4 show 24 design points of the Pareto set and the nondominated points of Pareto front, respectively.

Table 2. Pareto optimal set given in random order.

Pareto ID	WAC (−)	VR (−)	CD (−)	T_d (°C)	v (m/s)	pH (−)	T_r (°C)
1 *	0.4610	0.4406	4.9339	50.0726	4.0269	2.1231	20.0787
2	0.2496	0.5829	26.3198	59.1482	0.3961	2.1268	84.6113
3	0.3505	0.5290	14.8788	56.8466	1.4085	2.5738	67.7296
4	0.2987	0.6130	24.6705	60.4821	2.1437	2.3132	91.4555
5	0.3560	0.5128	13.2246	56.9539	1.3443	2.4292	63.7404
6	0.3490	0.5876	21.8093	57.4686	1.5863	2.9835	81.2848
7	0.4427	0.2771	20.9616	53.2569	0.1899	4.6265	72.0360
8	0.4767	0.3696	12.1261	52.1816	0.7663	4.9951	75.2174
9	0.3854	0.4775	8.8345	53.1772	3.4738	2.8495	33.9584
10	0.4395	0.3129	19.4062	53.5391	0.2951	4.4393	71.1104
11	0.4607	0.2376	20.2743	50.6788	0.1718	5.4014	66.2427
12	0.4494	0.1935	23.0974	50.0522	0.0151	5.3859	66.7517
13	0.4884	0.3929	7.2222	61.1844	1.9569	5.4500	59.5787
14	0.4310	0.2173	23.7054	52.1683	0.0145	4.7001	71.9461
15*	0.4459	0.4501	5.7222	51.7956	3.3349	2.2060	31.0002
16	0.4519	0.3629	16.3099	55.2706	0.4085	4.4603	72.3659
17	0.3722	0.4924	10.4412	55.9213	1.7468	2.3832	57.1886
18	0.3659	0.4950	10.9728	56.3231	1.6107	2.4896	58.2014
19	0.4725	0.4049	8.1156	55.7922	1.1456	4.8176	57.8621
20	0.4665	0.3310	14.7560	53.9473	0.4089	4.8891	69.1178
21	0.3001	0.6125	24.6999	60.7488	2.4932	2.3504	92.8243
22	0.2810	0.5220	26.1803	57.1793	0.2308	2.8994	81.7101
23	0.2053	0.5559	26.8543	60.0454	0.0122	2.1271	91.4352
24	0.4432	0.3274	18.2983	53.5391	0.3576	4.4393	71.1104

* Best solution.

Conflicting relations between all the objective functions of drying and rehydration processes quality have been observed, therefore finding a solution that simultaneously optimizes all taken quality parameters is not possible. Figure 4 shows that the increase in CD causes both increase and decrease in VR (clearly larger). The WAC index increases slightly or decreases (especially for large CD) as the CD increases. The WAC index increases slightly, then drops sharply with the increase in VR.

As far as the CD is concerned the best solution is for ID 1 (CD = 4.93), however for WAC and VR the best solution can be assumed at ID 13 (WAC = 0.49) and ID 4 (VR = 0.61), respectively.

In case of the smallest value of CD (ID 1) where VR = 0.44 and WAC = 0.46, the optimum values of drying and rehydration processes variables were T_d = 50.1 °C, v = 4.0 m/s, rehydrating medium: solution of citric acid (pH = 2.12), rehydrating temperature 20.1 °C. At these conditions the value of VR was 28.1% smaller than the greatest VR (ID 4) and the value of WAC was 5.6% smaller than the greatest WAC (ID 13). A slightly worse result of optimal solution was obtained for ID 15. The values of WAC, VR, and CD were 0.45, 0.46, and 5.7, respectively. It can be stated that at ID 15 the value of CD was 16.0% greater than the smallest CD (ID 1), VR was 26.6% smaller than the greatest VR (ID 4), and WAC was 8.7% smaller than the greatest value of WAC (ID 13).

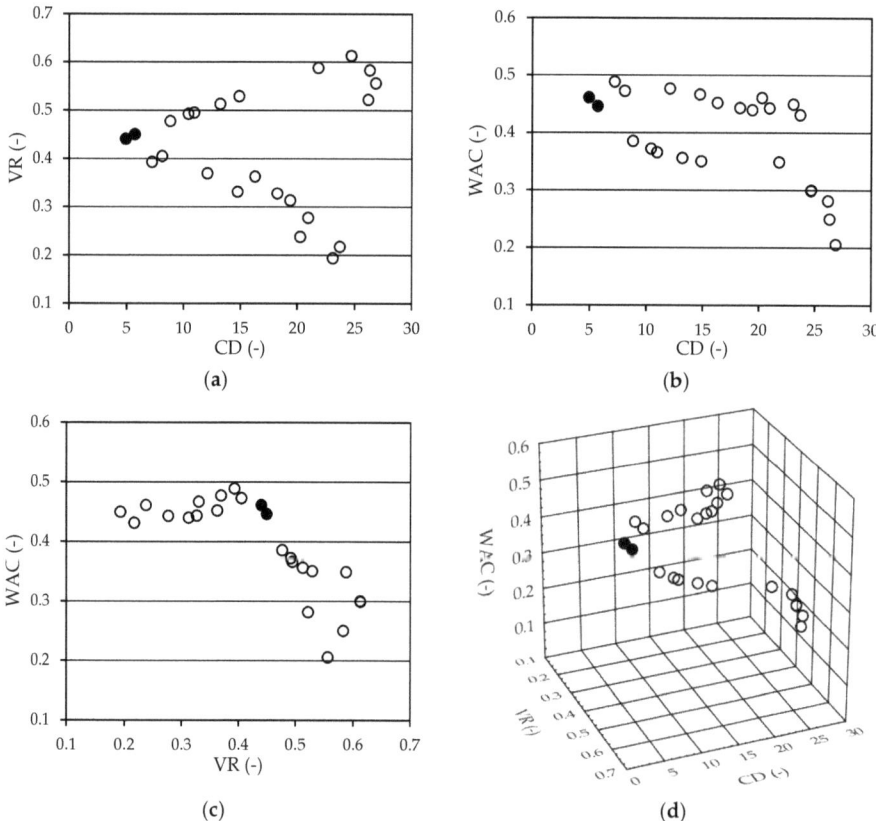

Figure 4. Two-dimensional (a–c) and three-dimensional (d) views of Pareto front; (●)—the best solutions.

However, taking into account the greatest value of VR (ID 4) for which CD = 24.67 and WAC = 0.30 the optimum values of the process variables were T_d = 60.5 °C, v = 2.1 m/s, pH = 2.21, and T_r = 31.0 °C. It can be noticed that at these conditions the value of CD was 400% greater than the smallest CD (ID 1) and WAC was 38.9% smaller than the greatest value of WAC (ID 13).

Again, taking into account the greatest value of WAC (ID 13, CD = 7.22, VR = 0.39) the optimum values of the process variables were T_d = 61.2 °C, v = 2.0 m/s, pH = 5.45, T_r = 59.6 °C, and CD was 46.4% greater than the smallest CD (ID 1), VR was 35.9% smaller than the greatest value of VR (ID 4).

It can be seen from Table 2 that point for which all taken functions (maximum WAC and VR, minimum CD) achieved simultaneously their optimum values cannot be find. Then the solution is formulated by set of nondominated solutions in Pareto sense. It can be stated therefore that the choice of one solution depends on the individual requirements.

Taking into account the differences in the obtained values for various strategies (ID 1, ID 4, and ID 13), we recommend Pareto solution as ID 1 (minimum CD).

Results of the model validation follow. The validation was done using the same values of process parameters (T_d = 50.1 °C, v = 4.0 m/s, T_r = 20.1 °C, and pH = 2.12) to demonstrate the reliability of predicted quality parameters values. The dehydration process was carried out in a fluidized bed dryer, whereas the rehydration process was carried out in a solution of citric acid. The values of WAC, VR, and CD were 0.45, 0.45, and 5.21, respectively, and they were very close to the values predicted by ANN (0.46, 0.44, and 4.93). The maximum error of modeling was lower than 5.60%.

In our work and in the literature [32,52] various processes parameters (drying and rehydration) and various quality criteria were considered. Winiczenko et al. [52] carried out optimization of the drying and rehydration (in distilled water) processes of apple using MOGA algorithm. They obtained the following recommended processes parameters. T_d = 50.1 °C, v = 0.03 m/s, and T_r = 67.5 °C. Moreover, Winiczenko et al. [32] conducted optimization of the drying process of apple using a NSGA II algorithm. It turned out that the following drying process parameters can be recommended, T_d = 65 °C, v = 1.0 m/s.

It should be stressed, however, that it turned out from the present work and from the literature that finding the conditions of the drying and rehydration processes that simultaneously optimized different quality parameters of rehydrated apple seems to be impossible. Therefore, as far as the optimization of the drying and rehydration processes is concerned, it should be determined which quality parameter of rehydrated apple is considered most important or decisive in the given situation.

4. Conclusions

The drying process brings about the undesirable changes in the quality of dehydrated product. The application of convenient food requires its hydration. It is important to search for methods of drying and rehydration processes optimizing to ensure good quality of dried food.

The paper used a novel MOO method (based on ANN, GA, and Pareto optimization) for optimizing of processes of apple drying and rehydration. A novel MOO GA method with consideration of the simultaneous maximization of WAC and minimization of CD and VR, as rehydrated apple quality parameters, was successfully applied.

The back-propagation algorithm for ANN training was sufficient to predict the rehydrated apple quality. The mathematical formulas (from the ANN) for determining WAC, VR, and CD were obtained. It was found that relationships between drying and rehydration processes variables and quality characteristics of rehydrated apple are nonlinear. The ANN with sigmoidal transfer function may be used for predicting the quality of rehydrated apple.

The optimum values of processes variables, gained by the MOO GA, were T_d = 50.1 °C, v = 4.0 m/s, pH 2.1, and T_r = 20.1 °C. WAC, VR, and CD for dehydrated and next rehydrated apple at these terms: 0.46, 0.44, and 4.9, respectively. Experimental verification gave the value of the maximum error of modeling lower than 5.6%. The investigations proved that finding the conditions of the considered processes that simultaneously optimize three discussed quality parameters (WAC, VR, and CD) of rehydrated apples is impossible.

Author Contributions: R.W.: Formal analysis, methodology, and software, K.G.: Conceptualization, formal analysis, investigation, methodology, software, and writing of the manuscript, A.K.: Conceptualization, project administration, supervision, and writing of the manuscript, M.J.-M.: Supervision and investigation, A.C.: Investigation, J.T.: Critical review of manuscript.

Funding: Polish National Science Centre, N N 313 780940.

Conflicts of Interest: The authors declare no conflict of interest.

References

1. Dincer, I.; Dost, S. A modelling study for moisture diffusivities and moisture transfer coefficients in drying of solid objects. *Int. J. Energy Res.* **1996**, *20*, 531–539. [CrossRef]
2. Raponi, F.; Moscetti, R.; Monarca, D.; Colantoni, A.; Massantini, R. Monitoring and optimization of the process of drying fruits and vegetables using computer vision: A Review. *Sustainability* **2017**, *9*, 2009. [CrossRef]
3. Koszela, K.; Otrzasek, J.; Zaborowicz, M.; Boniecki, P.; Mueller, W.; Raba, B.; Lewicki, A.; Przybyl, K. Quality assessment of microwave-vacuum dried material with the use of computer image analysis and neural model. In *Proc. SPIE 9159, Sixth International Conference on Digital Image Processing (ICDIP 2014), Athens, Greece, April 5-6, 2014*; Falco, C.M., Chang, C.-C., Jiang, X., Eds.; SPIE: Bellingham, WA, USA, 2014; Volume 915913, pp. 1–9.
4. Nindo, C.I.; Sun, T.; Wang, S.W.; Tang, J.; Powers, J.R. Evaluation of drying technologies for retention of physical quality and antioxidants in asparagus (Asparagus officinalis, L.). *LWT—Food Sci. Technol.* **2003**, *36*, 507–516. [CrossRef]
5. Sacilik, K.; Elicin, A.K. The thin layer drying characteristics of organic apple slices. *J. Food Eng.* **2006**, *73*, 281–289. [CrossRef]
6. Deng, Y.; Luo, Y.; Wang, Y.; Yue, J.; Liu, Z.; Zhong, Y.; Zhao, Y.; Yang, H. Drying-induced protein and microstructure damages of squid fillets affected moisture distribution and rehydration ability during rehydration. *J. Food Eng.* **2014**, *123*, 23–31. [CrossRef]
7. Maldonado, S.; Arnau, E.; Bertuzzi, M.A. Effect of temperature and pretreatment on water diffusion during rehydration of dehydrated mangoes. *J. Food Eng.* **2010**, *96*, 333–341. [CrossRef]
8. Giraldo, G.; Vázquez, R.; Martín-Esparza, M.E.; Chiralt, A. Rehydration kinetics and soluble solids lixiviation of candied mango fruit as affected by sucrose concentration. *J. Food Eng.* **2006**, *77*, 825–834. [CrossRef]
9. Marabi, A.; Livings, S.; Jacobson, M.; Saguy, I.S. Normalized Weibull distribution for modeling rehydration of food particulates. *Eur. Food Res. Technol.* **2003**, *217*, 311–318. [CrossRef]
10. Nayak, C.A.; Suguna, K.; Rastogi, N.K. Combined effect of gamma-irradiation and osmotic treatment on mass transfer during rehydration of carrots. *J. Food Eng.* **2006**, *74*, 134–142. [CrossRef]
11. Wangler, J.; Kohlus, R. Development and validation of methods to characterize rehydration behavior of food hydrocolloids. *Food Hydrocoll.* **2018**, *82*, 500–509. [CrossRef]
12. Rojas, M.L.; Augusto, P.E.D. Microstructure elements affect the mass transfer in foods: The case of convective drying and rehydration of pumpkin. *LWT—Food Sci. Technol.* **2018**, *93*, 102–108. [CrossRef]
13. Ricce, C.; Rojas, M.L.; Miano, A.C.; Siche, R.; Augusto, P.E.D. Ultrasound pre-treatment enhances the carrot drying and rehydration. *Food Res. Int.* **2016**, *89*, 701–708. [CrossRef] [PubMed]
14. Rojas, M.L.; Augusto, P.E.D. Ethanol pre-treatment improves vegetable drying and rehydration: Kinetics, mechanisms and impact on viscoelastic properties. *J. Food Eng.* **2018**, *233*, 17–27. [CrossRef]
15. Benseddik, A.; Azzi, A.; Zidoune, M.N.; Khanniche, R.; Besombes, C. Empirical and diffusion models of rehydration process of differently dried pumpkin slices. *J. Saudi Soc. Agric. Sci.* **2018**. [CrossRef]
16. Link, J.V.; Tribuzi, G.; Laurindo, J.B. Improving quality of dried fruits: A comparison between conductive multi-flash and traditional drying methods. *LWT—Food Sci. Technol.* **2017**, *84*, 717–725. [CrossRef]
17. Doymaz, İ.; Sahin, M. Effect of temperature and pre-treatment on drying and rehydration characteristics of broccoli slices. *J. Food Meas. Charact.* **2016**, *10*, 364–373. [CrossRef]
18. Giri, S.K.; Prasad, S. Drying kinetics and rehydration characteristics of microwave-vacuum and convective hot-air dried mushrooms. *J. Food Eng.* **2007**, *78*, 512–521. [CrossRef]
19. Atarés, L.; Chiralt, A.; González-Martínez, C. Effect of solute on osmotic dehydration and rehydration of vacuum impregnated apple cylinders (cv. Granny Smith). *J. Food Eng.* **2008**, *89*, 49–56. [CrossRef]

20. Saguy, I.S.; Marabi, A.; Wallach, R. Liquid imbibition during rehydration of dry porous foods. *Innov. Food Sci. Emerg. Technol.* **2005**, *6*, 37–43. [CrossRef]
21. Aral, S.; Beşe, A.V. Convective drying of hawthorn fruit (*Crataegus* spp.): Effect of experimental parameters on drying kinetics, color, shrinkage, and rehydration capacity. *Food Chem.* **2016**, *210*, 577–584. [CrossRef] [PubMed]
22. Markowski, M.; Zielińska, M. Kinetics of water absorption and soluble-solid loss of hot-air-dried carrots during rehydration: Rehydration kinetics and soluble-solid loss of carrots. *Int. J. Food Sci. Technol.* **2011**, *46*, 1122–1128. [CrossRef]
23. Ergün, K.; Çalışkan, G.; Dirim, S.N. Determination of the drying and rehydration kinetics of freeze dried kiwi (*Actinidia deliciosa*) slices. *Heat Mass Transf.* **2016**, *52*, 2697–2705. [CrossRef]
24. Cagnoni, S.; Lutton, R.; Olague, G. *Genetic and Evolutionary Computation for Image Processing and Analysis*; EURASIP Book Series on Signal Processing and Communications; Hindawi Publishing Corporation: New York, NY, USA, 2007; ISBN 978-977-454-001-1.
25. Morimoto, T.; De Baerdemaeker, J.; Hashimoto, Y. An intelligent approach for optimal control of fruit-storage process using neural networks and genetic algorithms. *Comput. Electron. Agric.* **1997**, *18*, 205–224. [CrossRef]
26. Abakarov, A.; Sushkov, Y.; Almonacid, S.; Simpson, R. Multiobjective optimization approach: Thermal food processing. *J. Food Sci.* **2009**, *74*, E471–E487. [CrossRef] [PubMed]
27. Ma, F.; Yin, H.; Wei, L.; Tian, G.; Gao, H. Design and optimization of IPM motor considering flux weakening capability and vibration for electric vehicle applications. *Sustainability* **2018**, *10*, 1533. [CrossRef]
28. Yin, L.; Li, X.; Lu, C.; Gao, L. Energy-efficient scheduling problem using an effective hybrid multi-objective evolutionary algorithm. *Sustainability* **2016**, *8*, 1268. [CrossRef]
29. Han, Y.; Yu, H.; Sun, C. Simulation-based multiobjective optimization of timber-glass residential buildings in severe cold regions. *Sustainability* **2017**, *9*, 2353. [CrossRef]
30. Sleesongsom, S.; Bureerat, S. Vibration suppression of a single-cylinder engine by means of multi-objective evolutionary optimisation. *Sustainability* **2018**, *10*, 2067. [CrossRef]
31. Shahraki, M.H.; Ziaiifar, A.M.; Kashaninejad, S.M.; Ghorbani, M. Optimization of pre-fry microwave drying of french fries using response surface methodology and genetic algorithms. *J. Food Process. Preserv.* **2014**, *38*, 535–550. [CrossRef]
32. Winiczenko, R.; Górnicki, K.; Kaleta, A.; Martynenko, A.; Janaszek-Mańkowska, M.; Trajer, J. Multi-objective optimization of convective drying of apple cubes. *Comput. Electron. Agric.* **2018**, *145*, 341–348. [CrossRef]
33. Sendín, J.O.H.; Alonso, A.A.; Banga, J.R. Efficient and robust multi-objective optimization of food processing: A novel approach with application to thermal sterilization. *J. Food Eng.* **2010**, *98*, 317–324. [CrossRef]
34. Thakur, M.; Wang, L.; Hurburgh, C.R. A multi-objective optimization approach to balancing cost and traceability in bulk grain handling. *J. Food Eng.* **2010**, *101*, 193–200. [CrossRef]
35. Hadiyanto, H.; Boom, R.M.; Van Straten, G.; Van Boxtel, A.J.B.; Esveld, D.C. Multi-objective optimization to improve the product range of baking systems. *J. Food Process. Eng.* **2009**, *32*, 709–729. [CrossRef]
36. Goñi, S.M.; Salvadori, V.O. Model-based multi-objective optimization of beef roasting. *J. Food Eng.* **2012**, *111*, 92–101. [CrossRef]
37. Białobrzewski, I.; Danowska-Oziewicz, M.; Karpińska-Tymoszczyk, M.; Nalepa, B.; Markowski, M.; Myhan, R. Turkey breast roasting—Process optimization. *J. Food Eng.* **2010**, *96*, 394–400. [CrossRef]
38. Górnicki, K.; Kaleta, A. Drying curve modelling of blanched carrot cubes under natural convection condition. *J. Food Eng.* **2007**, *82*, 160–170. [CrossRef]
39. Kaleta, A.; Górnicki, K. Evaluation of drying models of apple (var. McIntosh) dried in a convective dryer. *Int. J. Food Sci. Technol.* **2010**, *45*, 891–898. [CrossRef]
40. Kaleta, A.; Górnicki, K.; Winiczenko, R.; Chojnacka, A. Evaluation of drying models of apple (var. Ligol) dried in a fluidized bed dryer. *Energy Convers. Manag.* **2013**, *67*, 179–185. [CrossRef]
41. Horwitz, W. *Official Methods of Analysis of the Association of Official's Analytical Chemists*; Association of Official Analytical Chemists (AOAC): Arlington, VA, USA, 2003.
42. Mazza, G. Dehydration of carrots. Effects of pre-drying treatments on moisture transport and product quality. *Int. J. Food Sci. Technol.* **1983**, *18*, 113–123. [CrossRef]
43. *Colorimetry*, 3rd ed.; International Commission on Illumination; Technical Report CIE15:2004; CIE Central Bureau: Vienna, Austria, 2004. Available online: https://archive.org/details/gov.law.cie.15.2004 (accessed on 2 June 2017).

44. Schanda, J. CIE Colorimetry. In *Colorimetry: Understanding the CIE System*; Schanda, J., Ed.; John Wiley & Sons, Inc.: Hoboken, NJ, USA, 2007; pp. 25–78, ISBN 978-0-470-17563-7.
45. Lewicki, P.P. Some remarks on rehydration of dried foods. *J. Food Eng.* **1998**, *36*, 81–87. [CrossRef]
46. Witt, K. CIE Color Difference Metrics. In *Colorimetry: Understanding the CIE System*; Schanda, J., Ed.; John Wiley & Sons, Inc.: Hoboken, NJ, USA, 2007; pp. 79–100, ISBN 978-0-470-17563-7.
47. Okuyucu, H.; Kurt, A.; Arcaklioglu, E. Artificial neural network application to the friction stir welding of aluminum plates. *Mater. Des.* **2007**, *28*, 78–84. [CrossRef]
48. Shojaeefard, M.H.; Behnagh, R.A.; Akbari, M.; Givi, M.K.B.; Farhani, F. Modelling and Pareto optimization of mechanical properties of friction stir welded AA7075/AA5083 butt joints using neural network and particle swarm algorithm. *Mater. Des.* **2013**, *44*, 190–198. [CrossRef]
49. Rutkowski, L. *Computational Intelligence*; Springer: Berlin/Heidelberg, Germany, 2008; ISBN 978-3-540-76287-4.
50. Winiczenko, R.; Górnicki, K.; Kaleta, A.; Janaszek-Mańkowska, M. Optimisation of ANN topology for predicting the rehydrated apple cubes colour change using RSM and GA. *Neural Comput. Appl.* **2018**, *30*, 1795–1809. [CrossRef] [PubMed]
51. Gevrey, M.; Dimopoulos, I.; Lek, S. Review and comparison of methods to study the contribution of variables in artificial neural network models. *Ecol. Model.* **2003**, *160*, 249–264. [CrossRef]
52. Winiczenko, R.; Górnicki, K.; Kaleta, A.; Janaszek-Mańkowska, M.; Trajer, J. Multi-objective optimization of the apple drying and rehydration processes parameters. *Emir. J. Food Agric.* **2018**, *30*, 1–9. [CrossRef]

© 2018 by the authors. Licensee MDPI, Basel, Switzerland. This article is an open access article distributed under the terms and conditions of the Creative Commons Attribution (CC BY) license (http://creativecommons.org/licenses/by/4.0/).

Article

Renewable Energy Technology Selection Problem Using Integrated H-SWARA-MULTIMOORA Approach

Abteen Ijadi Maghsoodi [1,*], Arta Ijadi Maghsoodi [2], Amir Mosavi [3,4,6], Timon Rabczuk [5,6] and Edmundas Kazimieras Zavadskas [7]

1. Department of Industrial Engineering, Science and Research Branch, Islamic Azad University, Tehran 1477893855, Iran
2. Department of Chemical and Petroleum Engineering, Science and Research Branch, Islamic Azad University, Tehran 1477893855, Iran; arta.ijadimaghsoodi@srbiau.ac.ir
3. Institute of Automation, Kando Kalman Faculty of Electrical Engineering, Obuda University, 1034 Budapest, Hungary; amir.mosavi@kvk.uni-obuda.hu
4. Institute of Advanced Studies Koszeg, iASK, 9730 Koszeg, Hungary
5. Department of Computer Engineering, College of Computer and Information Sciences, King Saud University, Riyadh 11362, Saudi Arabia
6. Institute of Structural Mechanics, Bauhaus Universität-Weimar, D-99423 Weimar, Germany; timon.rabczuk@uni-weimar.de
7. Institute of Sustainable Construction, Vilnius Gediminas Technical University, LT-10223 Vilnius, Lithuania; edmundas.zavadskas@vgtu.lt
* Correspondence: aimaghsoodi@srbiau.ac.ir; Tel.: +98-912-643-3448

Received: 28 October 2018; Accepted: 25 November 2018; Published: 28 November 2018

Abstract: Due to the adaptation of recent pollution mitigation and justification policies there has been a growing trend for electricity generation from various renewable resources. The selection of the optimal renewable energy technology could be measured as a complex problem due to the complication of forthcoming circumstances in any country. Consequently, the proposed similar complex assessment problem can be tackled with the support of Multiple Attribute Decision Making (MADM) methods. The current research study investigates a technology selection problem by proposing a hybrid MADM approach based on the Step-Wise Weight Assessment Ratio Analysis (SWARA) approach with a hierarchical arrangement combined with the Multi-Objective Optimization on the basis of Ratio Analysis plus the full MULTIplicative form (MULTIMOORA). Ultimately, a conceptual case study regarding the selection of the optimal renewable energy technology based on a conceptual development project in Iran has been examined by the proposed combinative MADM methodology.

Keywords: renewable energy; technology selection problem; sustainable energy evaluation; sustainable energy developments; sustainable developments; hierarchical SWARA; MULTIMOORA; multiple criteria decision making (MCDM); Multiple Attribute Decision Making (MADM); ranking

1. Introduction

In a century that technological advancements and continuous developments are at the cutting edge, it is unreasonable to only be dependent on unsecure and limited sources such as fossil fuels. It is clear that this dependence is not a secure preference due to the energy demand and population growth all around the world. Renewable energy sources count as a key alternative to fossil fuels, which plays a crucial part in supplementing energy via clean alternative energy sources. In the past few years, many research studies have found that these environmentally friendly energy sources are capable of replacing limited and conservative energy sources [1]. There are quite a few renewable energy technologies that have been developed vastly in past few years such as wind energy, hydropower, solar radiation, and geothermal energy. One of the most challenging practical issues in order to use renewable energy sources is to select which technology will provide the optimal solution based on various factors and attributes. This means while multiple renewable energy technologies are available, there are also various socio-economic criteria that have to be considered. Hence, this problem counts as a decision-making problem.

It is just a fact that almost every time there is a similar complex problem regarding the selection and assessment of the best alternative, one of the optimal ways to resolve it is multiple attribute decision-making (MADM) approaches. Therefore, in the case of the current study, due to the availability of multi-dimensional criteria along with multiple alternatives, the decision-making process can be measured as an MADM problem [2]. In the past few years, many energy planning systems have utilized MADM approaches to obtain elevated productivity and efficiency in development and execution of renewable energy technologies [1,3–5]. The main reason for attracting substantial attention to this approach is because these methods can be aimed at complex problems that are considered a mixture of multiple criteria. Moreover, despite the fact that there are few papers available in the literature of energy planning systems, none of the previous studies tackled a renewable technology selection problem in Iran. This is unexpected, because Iran is a country of four seasons, which has a huge potential to grow in green and sustainable developments in regards to renewable energy technologies.

The primary motivation of the current study is to tackle a renewable energy technology selection problem presenting a hybrid MADM approach including a Multi-Objective Optimization on the basis of Ratio Analysis plus the full MULTIplicative form (MULTIMOORA) method combined with a hierarchical Step-Wise Weight Assessment Ratio Analysis (SWARA) approach. In this regard, the present study considered multiple criteria along with multiple renewable energy technologies as alternatives to form the main decision matrix. Various quantitative and qualitative criteria were identified and evaluated in order to find and select the optimal renewable energy source. The mentioned criteria were defined based on their associated sub-criteria obtained from literature review and expert comments. Moreover, the experts were requested to evaluate the criteria and sub-criteria in view of their significance in renewable energy technologies. Eventually, the hierarchical SWARA method was combined with the MULTIMOORA approach to assess and evaluate the renewable energy technologies.

The remainder of the current study is organized as follows. Section 2 provide a comprehensive literature overview of the applications and developments of the MCDM approaches in renewable energy technology selection along with reviews on the MULTIMOORA and SWARA methods. In Section 3, the hybrid MADM approach incorporating the H-SWARA method along with the MULTIMOORA technique is provided to clarify the research methodology of the present study. Moreover, Section 4 presents the applications of the suggested approach in a real-world case study for a renewable energy technology selection problem directed by a cross-industrial multi-national company in Iran based on a conceptual development program, whereas Section 5 offers a conclusion of the current research study along with guidelines for forthcoming and future studies.

2. Literature Review

2.1. Survey on Applications of MCDM Methods in Renewable Energy Technology Selection

The necessity of using renewable energies has been discussed all over the world for many years. It is a clear fact that the evaluation process of the renewable energy technology projects counts as a multi-attribute decision making (MADM) problem. In the past few years, many research studies have tackled the renewable energy technology selection problem with various MADM methods.

Kaya and Kahraman [6] applied a hybrid MADM approach based on integrated fuzzy VlseKriterijumska Optimizacija I Kompromisno Resenje (VIKOR) and analytic hierarchy process (AHP) methodology in a renewable energy development planning problem in Turkey. Yazdani-Chamzini et al. [1] suggested an application of the COPRAS (COmplex PRoportional ASsessment) method combined with an Analytic Hierarchy Process (AHP) approach to tackle a problem in regard to the best renewable energy project for the Spanish Government. Ahmad and Tahar [7] presented an application of AHP in an assessment of renewable energy sources aimed at sustainable expansion of electricity generation systems in Malaysia.

Şengül et al. [8] presented an application of the fuzzy TOPSIS (techniques for order performance by similarity to ideal solution) method consolidated with the interval Shannon's entropy to evaluate renewable energy sources in Turkey. Ignatius et al. [9] suggested multiple renewable energy planning schemes utilizing a hybrid method utilizing fuzzy VIKOR and AHP approaches selecting the optimal and suitable renewable energy option in Istanbul. Büyüközkan and Güleryüz [10] proposed a hybrid MCDM methodology based on the combination of Decision Making Trial and Evaluation Laboratory Model (DEMATEL) technique with Analytic Network Process (ANP) for renewable energy resources selection in Turkey. Kumar et al. [11] presented a comprehensive review of MCDM methods applied in sustainable renewable energy developments. Haddad et al. [12] suggested a hybrid approach combining the AHP method and experts' feedback to evaluate various renewable energy preferences for the Algerian electricity system. Büyüközkan and Güleryüz [13] proposed a hybrid method integrating linguistic interval fuzzy sets with DEMATEL, ANP, TOPSIS techniques to present an assessment of renewable energy resources in Turkey.

Çolak and Kaya [4] presented an application of the hybrid AHP method established on interval type-2 fuzzy sets and hesitant fuzzy TOPSIS approach to prioritize the renewable energy options in Turkey. van de Kaa et al. [14] suggested an application of the best-worst method (BWM) in a selection process in regard to biomass thermochemical conversion technology in the Netherlands. Yazdani et al. [2] applied a combinative MADM method utilizing DEMATEL-ANP approach for the evaluation and selection of renewable electricity generation technologies in the EU. Büyüközkan et al. [5] proposed a novel renewable energy selection model for United Nations' sustainable development goals based on a combination of AHP method with COPRAS technique using hesitant fuzzy linguistic (HFL) term set arrangements. Wu et al. [15] suggested an assessment of the renewable power sources utilizing a fuzzy MCDM based on cumulative prospect theory in China. Karunathilake et al. [16] proposed an application of a fuzzy MCDM methodology under uncertainty in renewable energy selection for net-zero energy communities.

2.2. Survey on Applications and Developments of the MULTIMOORA Method

One of the most effective and straightforward MADM methods that have been suggested in recent years is the multi-objective optimization on the basis of ratio analysis (MOORA) plus the full multiplicative form (MULTIMOORA) which were established by Brauers and Zavadskas [17]. The MULTIMOORA method incorporates three subordinate ranks including the ratio system (RS), the reference point (RP), and the full multiplicative form (FMF), by utilizing the theory of dominance to obtain the ultimate rank of the method. There have been many applications and developments of the MULTIMOORA method in recent years in various fields [18–23].

Few examples of developments and propositions of the mentioned approach are demonstrated in this section. Hafezalkotob et al. [24] recommended an extension of the MULTIMOORA approach with interval-valued numbers to tackle a material selection problem regarding the optimal material for power gears. Deliktas and Ustun [25] applied a combination of the fuzzy MULTIMOORA and multi-choice conic goal programming in a student assessment problem. Ijadi Maghsoodi et al. [26] proposed an application of the MULTIMOORA method integrated Shannon's entropy in a similar complex selection problem considering the optimal organizational performance appraisal method in Iran. Brauers et al. [27] applied the MULTIMOORA approach in a comparison of the effectiveness factor of the firms offering facilities management along with a comprehensive facilities management sector analysis and future forecast in Lithuania. Wu et al. [28] proposed an extension of the MULTIMOORA approach by combining the technique with the probabilistic linguistic distance measures and the Borda rule applied in a selection problem consisting of the joint karaoke television brands.

Ijadi Maghsoodi et al. [29] suggested a novel and hybrid framework based on cluster analysis and the MULTIMOORA approach in a big data supplier selection problem in an information and communications technology (ICT) organization in Iran. Peng and Wang [30] suggested a group MCDM method based on the MULTIMOORA approach combined with the normal cloud model and Z-numbers. Hafezalkotob et al. [31] presented a combinative decision support system consolidating target-based WASPAS and MULTIMOORA methods with the BWM in an olive harvester machine selection problem. Tian et al. [32] suggested an improved version of the MULTIMOORA technique in regard to interdependent inputs of simplified neutrosophic linguistic term sets and information. Eghbali-Zarch et al. [33] presented an application of the SWARA consolidated with MULTIMOORA method in a fuzzy environment in a medication selection problem and pharmacological therapy selection for Type 2 Diabetes (T2D).

2.3. Survey on Applications and Developments of the SWARA Method

The Step-Wise Weight Assessment Ratio Analysis (SWARA) method is a newly-proposed method which is applied in order to weight the criteria suggested by Kersuliene et al. [34]. The proposed method is applied on experts' knowledge, information, and experiences of the criteria in order to calculate the significance of coefficients. Few examples of propositions and applications of the SWARA method in various fields are demonstrated in the current section.

Hashemkhani Zolfani et al. [35] proposed a hybrid method combining the SWARA and Weighted Aggregated Sum-Product Assessment (WASPAS) approaches which have been applied on a selection of a suitable locations for a new shopping mall in Tehran, Iran. Keršulienė and Turskis [36] suggested a hybrid method based on additive ratio assessment (ARAS) method using the principles of fusion of fuzzy information combined with the SWARA approach which applied to an architect selection problem. Hashemkhani Zolfani et al. [37] recommended a hybrid methodology based on the SWARA and VIKOR methods used in a problem considering the selection of the optimal mechanical longitudinal ventilation of tunnel pollutants during automobile accidents. Similarly, Hashemkhani Zolfani et al. [38] investigated the success factors of online games based on explorer with the SWARA method. Hashemkhani Zolfani et al. [39] suggested an application of the SWARA method combined with Yin-Yang balance (YYB) theory in producing and designing products with new perspectives consisting of both international and local views. Hashemkhani Zolfani and Bahrami [40] had investigated high tech industries in Iran to prioritize them based on investments consisting of the SWARA-COPRAS approach. Vafaeipour et al. [41] applied the SWARA-WASPAS technique in an assessment of 25 scattered cities all around regions of Iran to prioritize the implementation of solar projects.

Karabasevic et al. [42] offered a combination of the SWARA-ARAS method in order to present an assessment of companies according to the indicators of corporate social responsibility. Hashemkhani Zolfani et al. [43] applied the SWARA-COPRAS method in an assessment considering construction projects of hotels based on environmental sustainability. Hashemkhani Zolfani et al. [44] suggested an application of the SWARA method in a project selection consisting of technology foresight about research and development projects. Yazdani et al. [45] applied a combination of SWARA, WASPAS methods with the quality function deployment (QFD) framework in a green supplier selection problem. Nakhaei et al. [46] presented an application of the Simple Multi-Attribute Ranking Technique (SMART) combined with SWARA method for rapid evaluation of the vulnerability of office buildings to blast in the Swiss Re Tower. Karabasevic et al. [47] proposed an application of the SWARA-ARAS approach in a personnel selection problem. Nakhaei et al. [48] suggested the SWARA-COPRAS method in an evaluation of light supply in the public underground safe spaces. Tayyar and Durmuş [49] compared three type of weighting method including Max100, SWARA and Pairwise Weight Elicitation Methods (WEM) in MCDM problems to select the optimal car to buy. Mavi et al. [50] applied a hybrid SWARA-MOORA technique based on fuzzy set input data in order to select the optimal sustainable third-party reverse logistics provider in the plastic industry. Dahooie et al. [51] applied a novel approach considering SWARA-ARAS method using interval-valued fuzzy sets for evaluation of oil and gas well drilling projects. Dahooie et al. [52] applied the SWARA-ARAS-G approach in a competency-based IT personnel selection problem.

2.4. Research Gaps and Contributions of the Current Study

While there were a number of research studies in the field of renewable energy technology selection in recent years, there are only a few studies that have covered the applications of MADM approaches in this area of research. In this regard, in the current study, a hybrid proposition was made based on an MADM approach to aid the evaluation of the renewable energy selection problem. To the best of authors' knowledge, not a single study proposed and developed an application of the hybrid integrated H-SWARA-MULTIMOORA approach in a renewable energy technology selection. Moreover, in this study, a hierarchical structure of the SWARA weighting technique was demonstrated, that is an innovative approach to consider criteria along with their related attributes as sub-criteria in a similar complex problem in regard to a renewable energy technology selection problem.

Moreover, there is not a single study that analyzed renewable energy technology selection in Iran. Although there have been many studies that analyzed different aspects of renewable energy sources in Iran, none of the research studies have investigated multiple choices of renewable energies for the recent development programs in Iran. Based on expert comments, in more than 80% of the renewable energy development programs, the final decision of the final renewable source selection has been imposed by governments and policymakers without paying enough attention to the aspects of associated circumstances of multiple renewable energy sources. The reason for this problem is that still, in many third world countries, sustainability of renewable energies counts as a vanity project for governments. In this study, a conceptual renewable energy technology selection was analyzed in order to elucidate the best renewable energy source in a specific area supported by a multi-cultural cross-industrial organization targeting green developments in Iran. After identifying multiple criteria from the literature of renewable energy technologies, various attributes and their related criteria were selected by experts, along with multiple options as alternatives of the renewable energy sources. Furthermore, in this study, an integrated MADM method based on the H-SWARA-MULTIMOORA approach was applied in order to consider the hierarchical structure of the criteria along with giving an optimal solution to the renewable energy selection problem in the suggested case-study. Therefore, the novelties of the current study are both in practical and theoretical aspects. To summarize, the aims of the current study is twofold. First, the problem modeling of a conceptual renewable energy technology selection based on a conceptual development program in a specific part of Iran with a hybrid novel MADM method. Second, the development of a hybrid MADM method based on a hierarchical structure with a combination of the SWARA and MULTIMOORA methods.

3. Materials and Methods

3.1. Hierarchical Step-Wise Weight Assessment Ratio Analysis (H-SWARA)

As overviewed in Section 2.3. Kersuliene et al. [34] suggested the SWARA method in order to achieve the weights of the criteria in an MADM problem. The SWARA technique is recognized as an expert-oriented method where all of the analyzed criteria are ranked from the first to the last one based on experts' explanations. The SWARA method assigns the weight of the most significant criterion as the first ranked objects, and evidently, the lowest precedence is set to the least significant criterion. Accordingly, based on the average value of ranks, overall ranks are computed. Due to the straightforwardness of the SWARA method, the decision-makers can easily conduct a teamwork. Accordingly, based on the average value of ranks, overall ranks are achieved. The foundation and initial procedure for the determination of the criteria weights employing SWARA method can be initiated by arranging each and every criterion based on expert interpretations and remarks [1]. Then, after the primary assortment, the comparative significance of the average value s_j should be obtained from the second criterion.

Computation of this value is based on a simple procedure; the relative importance of the criterion j in relation to the previous criterion $j-1$, employing a number between 1 and 9. The next step is to calculate the coefficient k_j as determined in Equation (1) [34]:

$$k_j = \begin{cases} 1 & j = 1 \\ s_j + 1 & j > 1 \end{cases}, \qquad (1)$$

Consequently, the computation of the recalculated weight w_j can be obtained as demonstrated in Equation (2) [35]:

$$w_j = \begin{cases} 1 & j = 1 \\ \frac{x_j - 1}{k_j} & j > 1 \end{cases}, \qquad (2)$$

The final step in the calculation of the criteria weights is to obtain the results of the Equation (3) as the final weight of the criteria calculated from the SWARA approach. In which, q_j signifies the relative weight of the criterion j [34,35].

$$q_j = \frac{w_j}{\sum_{k=1}^{n} w_j}. \qquad (3)$$

To include sub-criteria evaluations of the SWARA approach, a hierarchical form influenced by the AHP method has been consolidated with the suggested technique. The AHP method apprehensions a hierarchical structure based on the pairwise comparison [53,54]. Accordingly, in order to apply the mentioned hierarchical form to the SWARA technique, weights of criteria and sub-criteria need to be obtained to calculate the final weights of decision-making attributes. In order to present a clarification on the hierarchical structure of the SWARA method, Figure 1 illustrates the hierarchical structure of the proposed renewable energy technology selection problem based on the conceptual development of the current research study. Eventually, in Section 4, the mathematical calculation of the process is demonstrated extensively based on a real-world case-study.

3.2. Multi-Objective Optimization on the Basis of Ratio Analysis Plus the Full Multiplicative Form (MULTIMOORA)

Brauers and Zavadskas [17] extended the multi-objective optimization by ratio analysis (MOORA) adding the full multiplicative form to the MOORA method which resulted in the MULTIMOORA method. This robust technique is established based on three parts including the ratio system, the reference point, and the full multiplicative form [27]. Similar to any other MADM approach, the first stage of the MULTIMOORA technique is to form the decision matrix X based on the performance index x_{ij} of ith alternative respecting jth attribute $i = 1, 2, \ldots m$ and $j = 1, 2, \ldots n$ [29]. It is also worth mentioning that w_j signifies the significance coefficients of jth attribute $j = 1, 2, \ldots n$. In this study the significance coefficients or weights of criteria have been obtained from the SWARA method.

$$X = [x_{ij}]_{m \times n}, \qquad (4)$$

$$w_j^s = [w_j]_n, \ w_j^s = [w_j]_n. \qquad (5)$$

Moreover, to make performance indices related to each alternative and criterion comparable in the MULTIMOORA method, the decision matrix parameters should be dimensionless. The primary reason that the decision matrix should be dimensionless is that different criteria have different measurement scales, for example cost and time might be two criteria in a similar complex problem. In order to consider both in the computation procedure these attributes should be normalized [26].

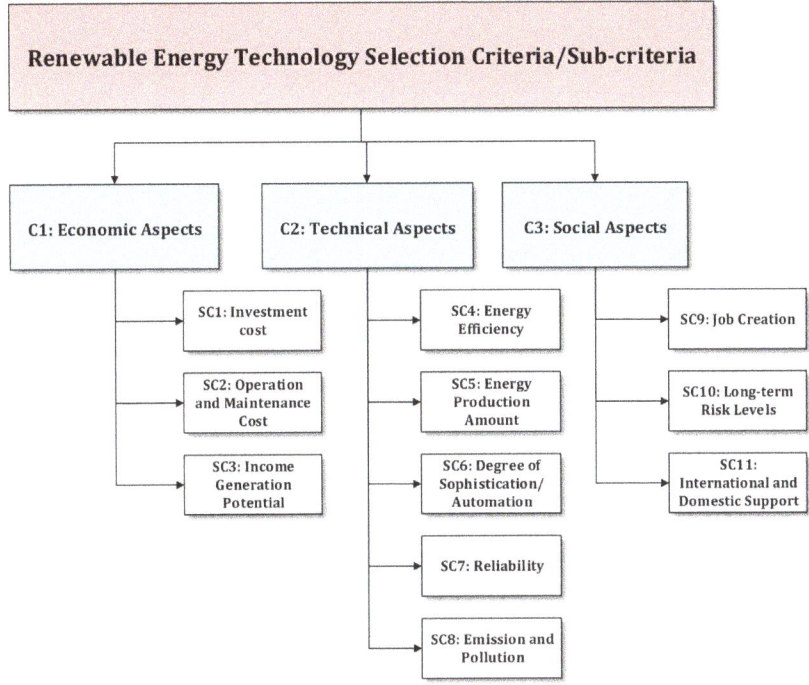

Figure 1. The hierarchical structure of the proposed renewable energy technology selection problem criteria and sub-criteria.

For that reason, the decision matrix is a normalization ratio of comparison amongst individual responses of each alternative associated with each criterion as a numerator, and a denominator that is a demonstrative for all alternative performances on that criterion [26]. The dimension dominator is computed based on the square root of the sum of squares of performance indices per attribute, as presented in Equation (6) [29]. In which, X_{ij}^* signifies the normalized performance index of ith alternative regarding jth attribute $i = 1, 2, \ldots m$ and $j = 1, 2, \ldots n$ and x_{ij} displays the performance index of ith alternative with respect to jth attribute $i = 1, 2, \ldots m$ and $j = 1, 2, \ldots n$ [17].

$$X_{ij}^* = \frac{x_{ij}}{\sqrt[2]{\sum_{i=1}^{m} x_{ij}^2}}. \tag{6}$$

3.2.1. The Ratio System Approach

The foundations of the ratio system are based on the normalization of the decision matrix utilizing Equation (6), in which the normalized performance indices are added for beneficial attributes or subtracted for non-beneficial attributes which means that these responses are added in case of maximization and subtracted in case of minimization.

The total assessment values y_i^* of alternative j along with the weights of criteria calculated from the SWARA method w_j can be positive or negative based on the totals of calculations using Equation (7) [26]. In which, g specifies the objectives in order to be maximized and $(n - g)$ designates the objectives being minimized. Consequently, the optimal alternative of the ratio system A_{RS}^* is an ordinal ranking of its associated assessment value y_i^* which has the highest total calculated based on Equation (8) [17].

$$y_i^* = \sum_{j=1}^{g} w_j X_{ij}^* - \sum_{j=g+1}^{n} w_j X_{ij}^*, \qquad (7)$$

$$A_{RS}^* = \{A_i | max_i y_i^*\}. \qquad (8)$$

3.2.2. The Reference Point Approach

Similar to the ratio system, the second stage of the MULTIMOORA method starts based on the normalization calculations of Equation (6). A maximal objective reference point is also determined in the technique which is acquired by Equation (9) [27]. In which, r_j symbolises the ith co-ordinate of the maximal objective reference point vector [24].

$$r_j = \begin{cases} max_i X_{ij}^* & \text{in case of maximization} \\ min_i X_{ij}^* & \text{in case of minimization} \end{cases} \qquad (9)$$

Subsequently, the maximum value of the deviation of a performance index from the reference point r_j which could be obtained as $(r_j - X_{ij}^*)$ for each alternative z_i^* respecting weights of all criteria calculated from the SWARA method w_j can be calculated as Equation (10) [24]. Eventually, computation of the ideal alternative A_{RP}^* is obtained by calculating the minimum value of the assessment value z_i^* obtained from Equation (11) [55].

$$z_i^* = max_j \left| (w_j r_j - w_j X_{ij}^*) \right|, \qquad (10)$$

$$A_{RP}^* = \{A_i | min_i z_i^*\}. \qquad (11)$$

3.2.3. The Full Multiplicative Form

The third phase of the MULTIMOORA method has been developed based on a concept in economic mathematics by Brauers and Zavadskas entitled the full multiplicative form [55].

Equation (12) provides the calculation of the full multiplicative form, in which g denotes as the objectives to be maximized and $(n - g)$ specifies as the objectives to be minimized [55]. The numerator of Equation (12) indicates the product of performance indices of ith alternative relating to beneficial attributes. The denominator of Equation (12) i.e., U_i' characterizes the product of performance indices of ith alternative relating to non-beneficial criteria respecting weights of each criterion obtained from the SWARA approach w_j.

Moreover, by using normalized measurements of the decision matrix which have obtained from Equation (6), similar equation to U_i' can be established as Equation (13). It is worth mentioning that, in order to preserve a harmony among all parts of calculations in the current study the normalized form of the full multiplicative form has been used in order to calculate the assessment values of the full multiplicative form U_i^*.

$$U_i' = \frac{\prod_{j=1}^{g}(x_{ij})^{w_j}}{\prod_{j=g+1}^{n}(x_{ij})^{w_j}}, \qquad (12)$$

$$U_i^* = \frac{\prod_{j=1}^{g}(X_{ij}^*)^{w_j}}{\prod_{j=g+1}^{n}(X_{ij}^*)^{w_j}}. \qquad (13)$$

Consequently, the ideal alternative A_{MF}^* is achieved regarding the maximum assessment value A_i between all assessment values of U_i^* presented in Equation (14) [26].

$$A_{MF}^* = \{A_i | max_i U_i^*\}. \qquad (14)$$

3.2.4. The Dominance Theory

The final stage of the MULTIMOORA method is the utilization of the dominance theory for integrating and ranking subordinate alternatives [26,56–59]. In this method after calculating of the subordinate ranks, they can be integrated into a final ranking, which is the final step of the MULTIMOORA method. In dominance theory, a summary of the arrangement of the three MULTIMOORA methods is made based on cardinal and ordinal scales [57]. For a more detailed explanation of the dominance theory, readers can refer to the studies of Brauers and Zavadskas [58].

Eventually, the flow diagram of the MULTIMOORA method combined with H-SWARA technique for selecting the optimal renewable energy source is illustrated in Figure 2. Furthermore, in order to develop a better understanding of the current methodology a real-world case study in regards to a renewable energy source technology selection process is presented in Section 4.

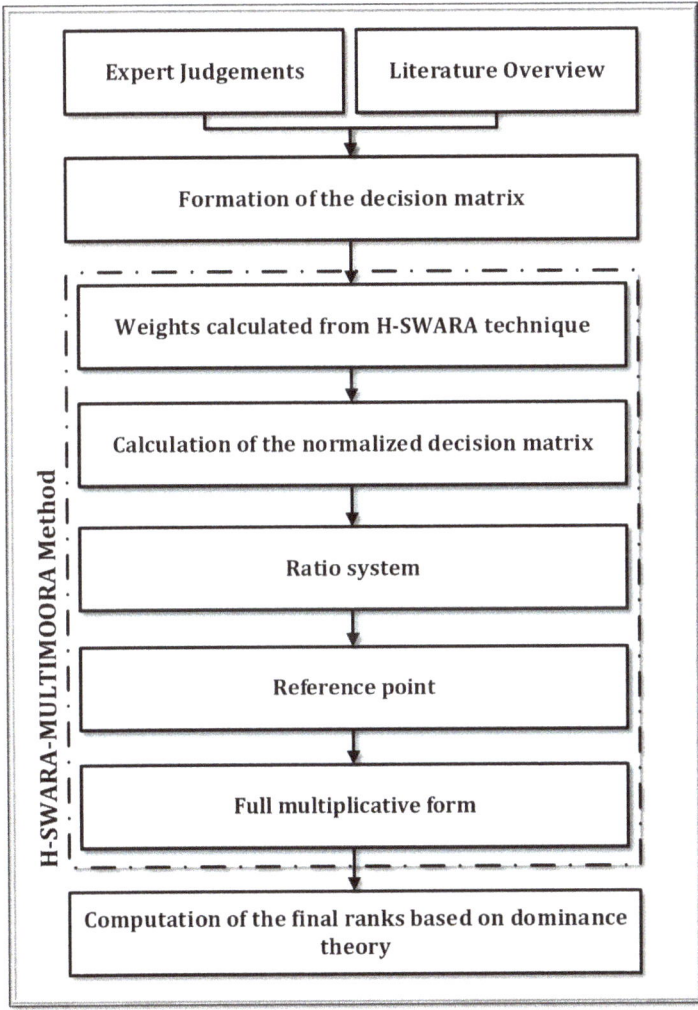

Figure 2. Flow diagram of selecting the optimal renewable energy source technology utilizing the H-SWARA-MULTIMOORA approach.

4. Findings and Results

The current study is a practical implementation of the H-SWARA-MULTIMOORA approach in order to clarify a conceptual development program in regards to a renewable energy technology selection problem. One of the main purposes of the current study, after identifying the accurate selection criteria and alternatives for the proposed problem, is to present a hybrid technique based on the combination of the hierarchical SWARA method with the MULTIMOORA method. Moreover, the data collection procedure of the current study is based on a conceptual development program in Iran. The case study of this conceptual development program was analyzed in order to choose an optimal renewable energy technology in a large desert lying in the middle of the Iranian plateau called the Dasht e Kavir or Great Salt Desert.

The primary climate structure in Dasht e Kavir is dry, which receives little rainfall or snow. The mountains that surround Dasht e Kavir deliver adequate amount of runoff which is enough to create massive seasonal lakes, marshlands and playas. In regard to the temperature it can reach 50 °C (122 °F) in summer, and the average temperature in December to January is 22 °C (72 °F). Temperatures of day and night can fluctuate as much as 70 °C (158 °F) over various times of the year. It is also worth mentioning that rainfall usually occurs in winter. There are also occasional sandstorms happening between January and March along with marshes, seasonal lakes and seasonal river beds.

The proposed project is maintained by a multi-cultural cross-industrial organization targeting green developments in Iran. The reason that this area has been selected for future renewable energy development is a sustainability program that the government suggested in order to increase the green developments of the Dasht e Kavir area.

The mentioned sustainability program was established based on a core research program, in which both sensible and rational technologies along with drastic measures and developments have been considered in order to modify an extensive overview of all the available technologies.

Furthermore, the renewable energy technologies by means of alternatives are based on the conceptual development case-study selected by experts, including; (A1) Wind energy (Wind turbine), (A2) Photovoltaic system, (A3) Solar thermal energy (STE), (A4) Geothermal energy/power, (A5) Hydropower energy, (A6) Biogas and Biofuel. Nevertheless, alternatives and the selection criteria of the current study were selected based on expert comments along with the influence of previous literature, but mostly these considerations are based on the case-study that was provided from the green development program in Iran.

It is clear that, from the short description that was mentioned about the Dasht e Kavir area, some of the considered alternatives may count as far-reaching and drastic measures. This attention is only because of the nature of a conceptual development program, which is conceptual to the core. Figure 3 illustrates the selected area in regard to establishing a renewable energy technology based on a conceptual development program in the Dasht e Kavir area.

A set of criteria for applying the proposed hybrid approach were collected and identified based on previous literature on renewable energies and sustainable evaluation, along with the considerations of the real-world conceptual development program case-study that is proposed in the current study, which have been categorized in Table 1 including the description of each criterion and their related sub-criteria.

Additionally, the population of the current study includes specialists, policymakers, and academics who took part in the location selection problem of the case-study, who are also responsible and directly dealing with the final decision of the renewable energy selection problem. Furthermore, the essential research data used in the current case-study has been collected through interview, based on a question and answer (Q&A) approach. The linguistic terms of the Q&A along with the numerical values of has been demonstrated in Table 2.

Table 1. Selection criteria and sub-criteria for renewable energy technology assessment (References [1,2,10,11,13,60,61]).

Criteria ID	Criteria	Sub-Criteria ID	Sub-Criteria (Functional Requirement)	Description/Definition
C1	Economic Aspects	SC1	Investment cost (Minimum)	One of the significant attributes of selecting the optimal renewable energy source is the primary investment cost that has to be funded in order to start the project.
		SC2	Operation and Maintenance Cost (Minimum)	It is clear that only with intensive care and maintenance high-tech equipment, such as renewable energy sources, will stay operational. Therefore, there might be many costs imposed on the operational procedures.
		SC3	Income Generation Potential (Maximum)	Although the main purpose of the renewable energies is to replace limited sources of energy such as fossil fuels in regard to their limitations, it is still important for policymakers to comprehend renewables as sources for additional revenue.
C2	Technical Aspects	SC4	Energy Efficiency (Maximum)	One of the essential elements in selecting the optimal renewable energy is the conversion and efficiency rate of the specified technologies in order to select the most appropriate and ideal technology.
		SC5	Energy Production Amount (Maximum)	One of the important characteristics of optimal renewable energy technology is the amount of energy production. Obviously, the higher the amount a technology produces, it is superior to other technologies.
		SC6	The Degree of Sophistication (Minimum)	One of the critical factors in selecting any kind of technology is the level of sophistication because it is important to make sure that the efficiency of energy production will not decrease due to complication and lack of appropriate knowledge.
		SC7	Reliability (Maximum)	Compatibility with the environmental properties along with the reliability over a long period with the environmental settings of the establishment are important attributes for selecting the optimal technology.
		SC8	Emission and Pollution (Minimum)	While one of the primary purposes of replacing limited sources of energy with renewable energies is the environmental aspects and reduction of pollution factors, utilizing such technologies might also have minor environmental damages which should be considered in the selection process.
C3	Social Concerns	SC9	Job Creation (Maximum)	One of the considerable aspects of any new technology in the perspective of social concern is job creation. Therefore, it is important to select a technology which could provide such social context that could support societies to improve the perspective of the cultural concerns towards such technological advancements.
		SC10	Long-Term Risk Levels (Minimum)	The cost of devaluation and depreciation over a long period might be the reason that policymakers negate to agree to establish specific technologies. As such technologies and the related knowledge is novel to many countries, they consider the long-term risk factors with higher attention in order to choose a technology which contains the minimum amount of risk levels in regard to socio-economic aspects.
		SC11	International and Domestic Support (Maximum)	It is a clear fact that without the support of international and governmental policy-makers, it is close to impossible to facilitate and establish a renewable energy in a practical way. As these projects still count as vanity projects in many third world countries, it is problematic and difficult to gain the attention of government policy makers in regard to renewable technologies.

Figure 3. The geographical area of the sustainable/green development project.

Table 2. Linguistic indicator and the corresponding numbers.

Linguistic Indicator	Alphabetic Values of Verbal Comments	Numerical Value of Verbal Comments
Very Poor	VP	1
Poor	P	2
Moderate	M	3
Good	G	4
Very Good	VG	5

The definitive target of the Q&A was to complete the decision matrix shown in Table 3 based on the linguistic definitions and the corresponding numbers.

It is important to mention that the suggested case-study in this research was not chosen randomly. This particular case was targeted in order to analyze a specific area in Iran, in regard to selecting an optimal renewable energy source based on several criteria obtaining detailed understandings that other case studies would not be able to offer due to the specific structure of the conceptual development program in the area of Dasht e Kavir, which is also changeable in case of modification in the environment and projects.

Table 3. Decision matrix for selecting the optimal renewable energy technology.

Renewable Energy Technology	Criteria and Sub-Criteria										
	C1			C2					C3		
	SC1	SC2	SC3	SC4	SC5	SC6	SC7	SC8	SC9	SC10	SC11
Wind energy (Wind turbine) [A1]	3	3	3	3	3	2	3	1	4	3	3
Photovoltaic system [A2]	2	2	3	3	4	2	4	1	2	2	3
Solar thermal energy (STE) [A3]	3	2	3	3	3	3	3	1	2	2	3
Geothermal energy/power [A4]	3	3	2	3	3	3	3	2	2	3	2
Hydropower energy [A5]	4	4	4	4	4	3	2	2	3	4	1
Biogas and Biofuel [A6]	3	3	3	2	3	3	3	2	3	2	2

As comprehensively mentioned in Section 3, in the current study, after identification of criteria and alternatives which forms the main decision matrix, the first step is to calculate the optimal weights of criteria and sub-criteria based on the H-SWARA technique. In order to calculate the weight of criteria and sub-criteria of the renewable energy selection problem, this study used a hierarchical form based on the calculation procedure of the AHP methodology.

In this regard, weights of sub-criteria related to each criterion should be calculated, after calculating criteria and sub-criteria weights, the final weight of each sub-criteria will be obtained based on a simple multiplication of sub-criteria to the associated criteria. As mentioned in the previous sections, the first step of using the H-SWARA method is to obtain the order of criteria based on preferences of decision-makers in order to calculate the final weights of the SWARA approach.

Accordingly, Table 4 demonstrates the final results of the criteria and sub-criteria weights utilizing the H-SWARA method including managerial aspects and technical specification.

Table 4. Final results of the H-SWARA method to weight the selection criteria.

Sub-Criterion	Order Based on Significance	The Comparative Importance of Average Value s_j	Coefficient k_j	Recalculated Weight w_j	Final Weight q_j	H-SWARA Weights
SC1	1	-	1	1	0.468	0.240
SC2	2	4	1.444	0.692	0.324	0.166
SC3	3	5	1.556	0.445	0.208	0.107
SC4	3	4	1.444	0.519	0.171	0.034
SC5	1	1	-	1	0.329	0.066
SC6	5	2	1.222	0.348	0.114	0.023
SC7	2	3	1.333	0.750	0.247	0.049
SC8	4	2	1.222	0.425	0.140	0.028
SC9	2	4	1.444	0.692	0.328	0.095
SC10	3	6	1.667	0.415	0.197	0.057
SC11	1	1	-	1	0.474	0.137

Criterion	Order Based on Significance	The Comparative Importance of Average Value s_j	Coefficient k_j	Recalculated Weight w_j	Final Weight q_j
C1	1	-	1	1	0.512
C2	3	4	1.444	0.389	0.288
C3	2	7	1.778	0.563	0.200

It is just a clear fact that, based on the result of the H-SWARA method investment cost, operation and maintenance cost, and international and domestic support counts as the most important factors in the process of the proposed technology selection problem, respectively. Clearly, due to the novelty and complexity of such technologies, a substantial financial plan regarding investment along with operational and maintenance cost is needed [62]. Moreover, because these sustainability development projects are considered mega projects without major sponsorships of international and domestic organizations along with governmental support, it is near to impossible to promote and assemble such projects.

Consequently, based on the calculated weights of the criteria and the preliminary decision matrix formed based on expert comments and previous literature, the final decision matrix of the current study is presented in Table 5, which includes the comments along with weights of criteria calculated from the H-SWARA method.

Moreover, as aforementioned in previous sections, in order to utilize the MULTIMOORA method, the decision matrix has to transform into dimensionless numbers based on a normalization technique in order to form a dimensionless decision matrix. Therefore, in the current study in order to compare normalized numbers to each other and form a normalized matrix, Equation (6) was used. The normalized decision matrix is shown in Table 6.

Table 5. Decision matrix for selecting the optimal renewable energy technology with final criteria weights.

Renewable Energy Technology	Criteria and Sub-Criteria										
	C1				C2				C3		
	SC1	SC2	SC3	SC4	SC5	SC6	SC7	SC8	SC9	SC10	SC11
A1	3	3	3	3	3	2	3	1	4	3	3
A2	2	2	3	3	4	2	4	1	2	2	3
A3	3	2	3	3	3	3	3	1	2	2	3
A4	3	3	2	3	3	3	3	2	2	3	2
A5	4	4	4	4	4	3	2	2	3	4	1
A6	3	3	3	2	3	3	3	2	3	2	2
H-SWARA weights	0.240	0.166	0.107	0.034	0.066	0.023	0.049	0.028	0.095	0.057	0.137

Table 6. Normalized decision matrix for selecting the optimal renewable energy technology.

Renewable Energy Technology	Criteria and Sub-Criteria										
	C1				C2				C3		
	SC1	SC2	SC3	SC4	SC5	SC6	SC7	SC8	SC9	SC10	SC11
A1	0.400	0.420	0.400	0.400	0.363	0.301	0.400	0.258	0.589	0.442	0.500
A2	0.267	0.280	0.400	0.400	0.485	0.301	0.534	0.258	0.294	0.294	0.500
A3	0.400	0.280	0.400	0.400	0.363	0.452	0.400	0.258	0.294	0.294	0.500
A4	0.400	0.420	0.267	0.400	0.363	0.452	0.400	0.516	0.294	0.442	0.333
A5	0.534	0.560	0.534	0.534	0.485	0.452	0.267	0.516	0.442	0.589	0.166
A6	0.400	0.420	0.400	0.267	0.363	0.452	0.400	0.516	0.442	0.294	0.332
H-SWARA weights	0.240	0.166	0.107	0.034	0.066	0.023	0.049	0.028	0.095	0.057	0.137

Accordingly, based on the weights calculated from the H-SWARA approach along with the normalized decision matrix, the assessment values and final ranks of the integrated H-SWARA-MULTIMOORA method can be calculated based on Equations (7), (10) and (13) for the ratio system y_i^*, the reference point approach z_i^*, and the full multiplicative form u_i^*, respectively. Table 7 determines the final results of the proposed approach in the suggested renewable energy technology selection. Furthermore, the ranking of the H-SWARA-MULTIMOORA approach is acquired by the assessment values and the final rank of the method regarding dominance theory.

Table 7. Assessment values and rankings of the H-SWARA-MULTIMOORA approach for the renewable energy technology selection problem.

Renewable Energy Technology	Assessment Values			Ranks			Final Rank
	y_i^*	z_i^*	u_i^*	y_i^*	z_i^*	u_i^*	
A1	0.019	0.032	1.093	3	3	3	3
A2	0.69	0.028	1.277	1	1	1	1
A3	0.019	0.032	1.110	2	2	2	2
A4	−0.056	0.032	0.901	5	4	5	5
A5	−0.094	0.064	0.810	6	6	6	6
A6	−0.024	0.032	0.987	4	5	4	4

Consequently, it is clear that based on the H-SAWARA-MULTIMOORA approach, the best renewable energy solution for the area of Dasht e Kavir is the Photovoltaic system. While Iran is one of the richest countries in regard to multiple energy sources with an extensive amount of fossil fuels, such as petroleum and natural gas, it is unfortunate that with a high potential of renewable energy establishments, there is only a little attention to renewable energies. The results of the current study showed that the suggested area of Dasht e Kavir is a possible establishment target to find renewable energy sources such as Photovoltaic systems. In addition, it is worth mentioning that the solar thermal energy and wind energy obtained second and third place, respectively, because of the specified geographical properties of the Dasht e Kavir.

One of the main reasons that wind energy is also considered in this area is due to the light and heavy sand storms during different seasons. Ultimately, although based on the findings of the current study and expert comments the Photovoltaic system is the most appropriate renewable energy technology for the area of Dasht e Kavir, it is worth mentioning that a hybrid approach in such areas is also recommended in this study. In other words, due to a vast amount of winds along with the astral nature of the desert, and because in this study it has been shown that the Photovoltaic system, solar thermal energy and wind energy are the best solutions, one of the solutions in the development program could be a combination establishment of these technologies in order to obtain the optimal energy output.

5. Conclusions

It is clear that the rapid progression of energy appeals due to the increase in population and production companies, along with the escalation of air pollutants and greenhouse gas emissions, causing substantial developments on renewable energies and their associated technologies. Outstanding expansions and developments of interdisciplinary research studies produced various alternatives in the case of renewable energies based on multiple considerations, such as socio-economic and environmental issues. This only means renewable energy technology selection problems are a similar complex problem based on multiple criteria and alternatives, due to the complication of evaluating different technologies and renewable energy sources with multiple attributes.

The current study proposed a hybrid MADM evaluation for selecting the optimal renewable energy technology in a conceptual development project in Iran. After a comprehensive identification of the assessment criteria based on previous literature, candidate technology alternatives for the renewable energy sources were provided based on expert judgments, in order to establish a primary decision matrix. Moreover, the MULTIMOORA approach integrated with the hierarchical SWARA technique was utilized to provide an assessment of the optimal renewable energy technologies applied to a conceptual case-study, in a multi-cultural cross-industrial organization targeting green developments in Iran. Consequently, based on the final assessment of the decision-making problem, it was shown that the best renewable energy solutions for the area of Dasht e Kavir are the Photovoltaic system, thermal energy and wind energy, respectively. The findings of the current study conclude that although Iran is one of the richest countries in regard to specific sources, such as petroleum and natural gas, there is a huge potential in order to enrich and revise the possible policies on sustainable development programs and renewable energy sources.

Suggestions for forthcoming developments of the proposed study may be as the following. First, the input data of the MADM approach can be integrated with certain mathematical structures such as fuzzy sets in order to comprehend uncertainty in the methodology. Second, it is suggested to implement such methodology in other geographical locations within the analyzed country and outside that area, and to compare the results of such analyses with the outcomes of the current study. Third, although the current study selected a specific renewable energy technology, it is clear that different criteria will have different effects on the decision process. Therefore, it is strongly recommended to analyze the same problem in the same geographical location based on different criteria and assessment models, and to compare the result to this study in order to obtain a comparison of different views and perspectives for the proposed, similar complex problem.

Author Contributions: Conceptualization, A.I.M. (Abteen Ijadi Maghsoodi) and A.I.M. (Arta Ijadi Maghsoodi); methodology, A.I.M. (Abteen Ijadi Maghsoodi); validation, A.M., E.K.Z. and T.R.; investigation, A.I.M. (Abteen Ijadi Maghsoodi); resources, A.I.M. (Arta Ijadi Maghsoodi); data curation, A.I.M. (Abteen Ijadi Maghsoodi); writing—original draft preparation, A.I.M. (Abteen Ijadi Maghsoodi), A.I.M. (Arta Ijadi Maghsoodi) and A.M.; writing—review and editing, A.I.M. (Abteen Ijadi Maghsoodi), A.M., E.K.Z., T.R.; supervision, E.K.Z., T.R., A.M.; project administration, A.I.M. (Abteen Ijadi Maghsoodi).

Funding: This research received no external funding.

Acknowledgments: The authors would like to thank the anonymous reviewers for their insightful comments and constructive suggestions. Additionally, the authors wish to appreciatively acknowledge Arsalan Rokhnejad who helped us with the data resources in our research study.

Conflicts of Interest: The authors declare no conflict of interest.

References

1. Yazdani-Chamzini, A.; Fouladgar, M.M.; Zavadskas, E.K.; Moini, S.H.H. Selecting the optimal renewable energy using multi criteria decision making. *J. Bus. Econ. Manag.* **2013**, *14*, 957–978. [CrossRef]
2. Yazdani, M.; Chatterjee, P.; Zavadskas, E.K.; Streimikiene, D. A novel integrated decision-making approach for the evaluation and selection of renewable energy technologies. *Clean Technol. Environ. Policy* **2018**, *20*, 403–420. [CrossRef]
3. Mardani, A.; Zavadskas, E.K.; Streimikiene, D.; Jusoh, A.; Nor, K.M.D.; Khoshnoudi, M. Using fuzzy multiple criteria decision making approaches for evaluating energy saving technologies and solutions in five star hotels: A new hierarchical framework. *Energy* **2016**, *117*, 131–148. [CrossRef]
4. Çolak, M.; Kaya, İ. Prioritization of renewable energy alternatives by using an integrated fuzzy MCDM model: A real case application for Turkey. *Renew. Sustain. Energy Rev.* **2017**, *80*, 840–853. [CrossRef]
5. Büyüközkan, G.; Karabulut, Y.; Mukul, E. A novel renewable energy selection model for United Nations' sustainable development goals. *Energy* **2018**, *165*, 290–302. [CrossRef]
6. Kaya, T.; Kahraman, C. Multicriteria renewable energy planning using an integrated fuzzy VIKOR & AHP methodology: The case of Istanbul. *Energy* **2010**, *35*, 2517–2527.
7. Ahmad, S.; Tahar, R.M. Selection of renewable energy sources for sustainable development of electricity generation system using analytic hierarchy process: A case of Malaysia. *Renew. Energy* **2014**, *63*, 458–466. [CrossRef]
8. Şengül, Ü.; Eren, M.; Shiraz, S.E.; Gezder, V.; Şengül, A.B.; Shiraz, S.E.; Gezder, V. Fuzzy TOPSIS method for ranking renewable energy supply systems in Turkey. *Renew. Energy* **2015**, *75*, 617–625. [CrossRef]
9. Ignatius, J.; Rahman, A.; Yazdani, M.; Šaparauskas, J.; Haron, S.H. An integrated fuzzy ANP–QFD approach for green building assessment. *J. Civ. Eng. Manag.* **2016**, *22*, 551–563. [CrossRef]
10. Büyüközkan, G.; Güleryüz, S. An integrated DEMATEL-ANP approach for renewable energy resources selection in Turkey. *Int. J. Prod. Econ.* **2016**, *182*, 435–448. [CrossRef]
11. Kumar, A.; Sah, B.; Singh, A.R.; Deng, Y.; He, X.; Kumar, P.; Bansal, R.C. A review of multi criteria decision making (MCDM) towards sustainable renewable energy development. *Renew. Sustain. Energy Rev.* **2017**, *69*, 596–609. [CrossRef]
12. Haddad, B.; Liazid, A.; Ferreira, P. A multi-criteria approach to rank renewables for the Algerian electricity system. *Renew. Energy* **2017**, *107*, 462–472. [CrossRef]
13. Büyüközkan, G.; Güleryüz, S. Evaluation of Renewable Energy Resources in Turkey using an integrated MCDM approach with linguistic interval fuzzy preference relations. *Energy* **2017**, *123*, 149–163. [CrossRef]
14. Van de Kaa, G.; Kamp, L.; Rezaei, J. Selection of biomass thermochemical conversion technology in the Netherlands: A best worst method approach. *J. Clean. Prod.* **2017**, *166*, 32–39. [CrossRef]
15. Wu, Y.; Xu, C.; Zhang, T. Evaluation of renewable power sources using a fuzzy MCDM based on cumulative prospect theory: A case in China. *Energy* **2018**, *147*, 1227–1239. [CrossRef]
16. Karunathilake, H.; Hewage, K.; Mérida, W.; Sadiq, R. Renewable energy selection for net-zero energy communities: Life cycle based decision making under uncertainty. *Renew. Energy* **2019**, *130*, 558–573. [CrossRef]
17. Brauers, W.K.M.; Zavadskas, E.K. The MOORA method and its application to privatization in a transition economy by A new method: The MOORA method. *Control Cybern.* **2006**, *35*, 445–469.
18. Akkaya, G.; Turanoğlu, B.; Öztaş, S. An integrated fuzzy AHP and fuzzy MOORA approach to the problem of industrial engineering sector choosing. *Expert Syst. Appl.* **2015**, *42*, 9565–9573. [CrossRef]
19. Çebi, F.; Otay, İ. A two-stage fuzzy approach for supplier evaluation and order allocation problem with quantity discounts and lead time. *Inf. Sci. (Ny)* **2016**, *339*, 143–157. [CrossRef]
20. Mishra, S.; Sahu, A.K.; Datta, S.; Mahapatra, S.S. Application of fuzzy integrated MULTIMOORA method towards supplier/partner selection in agile supply chain. *Int. J. Oper. Res.* **2015**, *22*, 466–514. [CrossRef]

21. Hafezalkotob, A.; Hafezalkotob, A. Interval target-based VIKOR method supported on interval distance and preference degree for machine selection. *Eng. Appl. Artif. Intell.* **2017**, *57*, 184–196. [CrossRef]
22. Altuntas, S.; Dereli, T.; Yilmaz, M.K. Evaluation of excavator technologies: Application of data fusion based MULTIMOORA methods. *J. Civ. Eng. Manag.* **2015**, *21*, 977–997. [CrossRef]
23. Liu, H.C.; Fan, X.J.; Li, P.; Chen, Y.Z. Evaluating the risk of failure modes with extended MULTIMOORA method under fuzzy environment. *Eng. Appl. Artif. Intell.* **2014**, *34*, 168–177. [CrossRef]
24. Hafezalkotob, A.; Hafezalkotob, A.; Sayadi, M.K. Extension of MULTIMOORA method with interval numbers: An application in materials selection. *Appl. Math. Model.* **2016**, *40*, 1372–1386. [CrossRef]
25. Deliktas, D.; Ustun, O. Student selection and assignment methodology based on fuzzy MULTIMOORA and multichoice goal programming. *Int. Trans. Oper. Res.* **2017**, *24*, 1173–1195. [CrossRef]
26. Maghsoodi, A.I.; Abouhamzeh, G.; Khalilzadeh, M.; Zavadskas, E.K. Ranking and selecting the best performance appraisal method using the MULTIMOORA approach integrated Shannon's entropy. *Front. Bus. Res. China* **2018**, *12*, 2. [CrossRef]
27. Brauers, W.K.M.; Zavadskas, E.K.; Lepkova, N. The future of facilities management in Lithuania. *Rom. J. Econ. Forecast.* **2017**, *20*, 98–115.
28. Wu, X.; Liao, H.; Xu, Z.; Hafezalkotob, A.; Herrera, F. Probabilistic Linguistic MULTIMOORA: A Multi-Criteria Decision Making Method Based on the Probabilistic Linguistic Expectation Function and the Improved Borda Rule. *IEEE Trans. Fuzzy Syst.* **2018**, *6706*, 1. [CrossRef]
29. Maghsoodi, A.I.; Kavian, A.; Khalilzadeh, M.; Brauers, W.K.M. CLUS-MCDA: A Novel Framework based on Cluster Analysis and Multiple Criteria Decision Theory in a Supplier Selection Problem. *Comput. Ind. Eng.* **2018**, *118*, 409–422. [CrossRef]
30. Peng, H.; Wang, J. A Multicriteria Group Decision-Making Method Based on the Normal Cloud Model with Zadeh's Z-numbers. *IEEE Trans. Fuzzy Syst.* **2018**. [CrossRef]
31. Hafezalkotob, A.; Hami-Dindar, A.; Rabie, N.; Hafezalkotob, A. A decision support system for agricultural machines and equipment selection: A case study on olive harvester machines. *Comput. Electron. Agric.* **2018**, *148*, 207–216. [CrossRef]
32. Tian, Z.-P.; Wang, J.; Wang, J.-Q.; Zhang, H.-Y. An improved MULTIMOORA approach for multi-criteria decision-making based on interdependent inputs of simplified neutrosophic linguistic information. *Neural Comput. Appl.* **2017**, *28*, 585–597. [CrossRef]
33. Eghbali-Zarch, M.; Tavakkoli-Moghaddam, R.; Esfahanian, F.; Sepehri, M.M.; Azaron, A. Pharmacological therapy selection of type 2 diabetes based on the SWARA and modified MULTIMOORA methods under a fuzzy environment. *Artif. Intell. Med.* **2018**, *87*, 20–33. [CrossRef] [PubMed]
34. Keršuliene, V.; Zavadskas, E.K.; Turskis, Z. Selection of Rational Dispute Resolution Method by Applying New Step-Wise Weight Assessment Ratio Analysis (Swara). *J. Bus. Econ. Manag.* **2010**, *11*, 243–258. [CrossRef]
35. Hashemkhani Zolfani, S.; Aghdaie, M.H.; Derakhti, A.; Zavadskas, E.K.; Varzandeh, M.H.M. Decision making on business issues with foresight perspective; An application of new hybrid MCDM model in shopping mall locating. *Expert Syst. Appl.* **2013**, *40*, 7111–7121. [CrossRef]
36. Keršulienė, V.; Turskis, Z. Integrated fuzzy multiple criteria decision making model for architect selection. *Technol. Econ. Dev. Econ.* **2011**, *17*, 645–666. [CrossRef]
37. Zolfani, S.H.; Esfahani, M.H.; Bitarafan, M.; Zavadskas, E.K.; Arefi, S.L. Developing a new hybrid MCDM method for selection of the optimal alternative of mechanical longitudinal ventilation of tunnel pollutants during automobile accidents. *Transport* **2013**, *28*, 89–96. [CrossRef]
38. Zolfani, S.H.; Farrokhzad, M.; Turskis, Z. Investigating on successful factors of online games based on explorer. *E+M Ekon. Manag.* **2013**, *16*, 161–169.
39. Zolfani, S.H.; Zavadskas, E.K.; Turskis, Z. Design of Products with Both International and Local Perspectives based on Yin-Yang Balance Theory and Swara Method. *Econ. Res. Istraživanja* **2013**, *26*, 153–166. [CrossRef]
40. Zolfani, S.H.; Bahrami, M. Investment prioritizing in high tech industries based on SWARA-COPRAS approach. *Technol. Econ. Dev. Econ.* **2014**, *20*, 534–553. [CrossRef]
41. Vafaeipour, M.; Zolfani, S.H.; Varzandeh, M.H.M.; Derakhti, A.; Eshkalag, M.K. Assessment of regions priority for implementation of solar projects in Iran: New application of a hybrid multi-criteria decision making approach. *Energy Convers. Manag.* **2014**, *86*, 653–663. [CrossRef]
42. Karabasevic, D.; Paunkovic, J.; Stanujkic, D. Ranking of companies according to the indicators of corporate social responsibility based on SWARA and ARAS methods. *Serbian J. Manag.* **2015**, *11*, 43–53. [CrossRef]

43. Zolfani, S.H.; Pourhossein, M.; Yazdani, M.; Zavadskas, E.K. Evaluating construction projects of hotels based on environmental sustainability with MCDM framework. *Alexandria Eng. J.* **2015**, *57*, 357–365. [CrossRef]
44. Zolfani, S.H.; Salimi, J.; Maknoon, R.; Kildiene, S. Technology foresight about R&D projects selection; application of SWARA method at the policy making level. *Eng. Econ.* **2015**, *26*, 571–580.
45. Yazdani, M.; Zolfani, S.H.; Zavadskas, E.K. New integration of MCDM methods and QFD in the selection of green suppliers. *J. Bus. Econ. Manag.* **2016**, *1699*, 1–17. [CrossRef]
46. Nakhaei, J.; Bitarafan, M.; Arefi, S.L.; Kapliński, O. Model for rapid assessment of vulnerability of office buildings to blast using SWARA and SMART methods (a case study of swiss re tower). *J. Civ. Eng. Manag.* **2016**, *22*, 831–843. [CrossRef]
47. Karabasevic, D.; Zavadskas, E.K.; Turskis, Z.; Stanujkic, D. The Framework for the Selection of Personnel Based on the SWARA and ARAS Methods Under Uncertainties. *Informatica* **2016**, *27*, 49–65. [CrossRef]
48. Nakhaei, J.; Arefi, S.L.; Bitarafan, M.; Kildienė, S. Evaluation of light supply in the public underground safe spaces by using of COPRAS-SWARA methods. *Int. J. Strateg. Prop. Manag.* **2016**, *20*, 198–206. [CrossRef]
49. Tayyar, N.; Durmuş, M. Comparison of Max100, SWARA and Pairwise Weight Elicitation Methods. *Int. J. Eng. Res. Appl.* **2017**, *7*, 67–78. [CrossRef]
50. Mavi, R.K.; Goh, M.; Zarbakhshnia, N. Sustainable third-party reverse logistic provider selection with fuzzy SWARA and fuzzy MOORA in plastic industry. *Int. J. Adv. Manuf. Technol.* **2017**, *91*, 2401–2418. [CrossRef]
51. Dahooie, J.H.; Zavadskas, E.K.; Abolhasani, M.; Vanaki, A.; Turskis, Z. A novel approach for evaluation of projects using an interval-valued fuzzy additive ratio assessment (ARAS) method: A case study of oil and gas well drilling projects. *Symmetry* **2018**, *10*, 45. [CrossRef]
52. Dahooie, J.H.; Abadi, E.B.J.; Vanaki, A.S.; Firoozfar, H.R. Competency-based IT personnel selection using a hybrid SWARA and ARAS-G methodology. *Hum. Factors Ergon. Manuf.* **2018**, *28*, 5–16. [CrossRef]
53. Saaty, T.L. How to make a decision: The analytic hierarchy process. *Eur. J. Oper. Res.* **1990**, *48*, 9–26. [CrossRef]
54. Saaty, T.L. Decision making with the analytic hierarchy process. *Int. J. Serv. Sci.* **2008**, *1*, 83. [CrossRef]
55. Brauers, W.K.M.; Zavadskas, E.K. Project management by multimoora as an instrument for transition economies. *Technol. Econ. Dev. Econ.* **2010**, *16*, 5–24. [CrossRef]
56. Brauers, W.K.M.; Baležentis, A.; Baležentis, T. Multimoora for the EU member states updated with fuzzy number theory. *Technol. Econ. Dev. Econ.* **2011**, *17*, 259–290. [CrossRef]
57. Brauers, W.K.M.; Zavadskas, E.K. Robustness of MULTIMOORA: A method for multi-objective optimization. *Informatica* **2012**, *23*, 1–25.
58. Brauers, W.K.M.; Zavadskas, E.K. Multimoora Optimization Used to Decide on a Bank Loan to Buy Property. *Technol. Econ. Dev. Econ.* **2011**, *17*, 174–188. [CrossRef]
59. Hafezalkotob, A.; Hafezalkotob, A. Comprehensive MULTIMOORA method with target-based attributes and integrated significant coefficients for materials selection in biomedical applications. *Mater. Des.* **2015**, *87*, 949–959. [CrossRef]
60. Bahrami, M.; Abbaszadeh, P. An overview of renewable energies in Iran. *Renew. Sustain. Energy Rev.* **2013**, *24*, 198–208. [CrossRef]
61. Mollahosseini, A.; Hosseini, S.A.; Jabbari, M.; Figoli, A.; Rahimpour, A. Renewable energy management and market in Iran: A holistic review on current state and future demands. *Renew. Sustain. Energy Rev.* **2017**, *80*, 774–788. [CrossRef]
62. Maghsoodi, A.I.; Hafezalkotob, A.; Ari, I.A.; Maghsoodi, S.I.; Hafezalkotob, A. Selection of Waste Lubricant Oil Regenerative Technology Using Entropy-Weighted Risk-Based Fuzzy Axiomatic Design Approach. *Informatica* **2018**, *29*, 41–74. [CrossRef]

© 2018 by the authors. Licensee MDPI, Basel, Switzerland. This article is an open access article distributed under the terms and conditions of the Creative Commons Attribution (CC BY) license (http://creativecommons.org/licenses/by/4.0/).

Article

Healthcare Facility Location-Allocation Optimization for China's Developing Cities Utilizing a Multi-Objective Decision Support Approach

Li Wang, Huan Shi and Lu Gan *

College of Architecture and Urban-Rural Planning, Sichuan Agricultural University, Dujiangyan 611830, China; wangli5451@stu.sicau.edu.cn (L.W.), shihuan@stu.sicau.edu.cn (H.S.)
* Correspondence: ganlu_soarpb@sicau.edu.cn; Tel.: +86-138-8042-0832

Received: 1 November 2018; Accepted: 26 November 2018; Published: 4 December 2018

Abstract: With rapid development of the healthcare network, the location-allocation problems of public facilities under increased integration and aggregation needs have been widely researched in China's developing cites. Since strategic formulation involves multiple conflicting objectives and stakeholders, this paper presents a practicable hierarchical location-allocation model from the perspective of supply and demand to characterize the trade-off between social, economical and environmental factors. Due to the difficulties of rationally describing and the efficient calculation of location-allocation problems as a typical Non-deterministic Polynomial-Hard (NP-hard) problem with uncertainty, there are three crucial challenges for this study: (1) combining continuous location model with discrete potential positions; (2) introducing reasonable multiple conflicting objectives; (3) adapting and modifying appropriate meta-heuristic algorithms. First, we set up a hierarchical programming model, which incorporates four objective functions based on the actual backgrounds. Second, a bi-level multi-objective particle swarm optimization (BLMOPSO) algorithm is designed to deal with the binary location decision and capacity adjustment simultaneously. Finally, a realistic case study contains sixteen patient points with maximum of six open treatment units is tested to validate the availability and applicability of the whole approach. The results demonstrate that the proposed model is suitable to be applied as an extensive planning tool for decision makers (DMs) to generate policies and strategies in healthcare and design other facility projects.

Keywords: healthcare facility; location-allocation problem; multiple objective optimization; bi-level programming; particle swarm optimization (PSO)

1. Introduction

Sustainable urbanization has been raising living standards and enhancing household income tremendously. China's government makes efforts to invest abundant funds to ensure healthcare insurance, and require health cost reductions to 30% by the end of 2018 [1]. On the basis of rural revitalization policy in China, the demand for rational and available healthcare facility planning has attracted widespread attention. One of the most crucial issues is to achieve high healthcare service quality in developing cities or rural areas, which contributes to a comprehensive understanding of the development process overall within the whole healthcare system. With the worldwide trend of tremendous population growth, diseases increasing and environmental degradation, healthcare facility location problems (HCFLPs) have become increasingly noticeable in human society [2,3]. Unreasonable and unconsidered healthcare facility (HCF) location will impede economic growth, as well as increase morbidity and mortality. In some developing cities, the treatment technology and medical equipment of most hospitals may not satisfy the rigid demand due to the lagging economy. Therefore, completing the basic healthcare services in rural and remote regions should be prioritized. As a vital element in strategic management, optimizing HCF location plays a significant role in decision making for private and public organizations such as schools, warehouses and retail stores [2]. Selecting appropriate positions is not only able to improve the service accessibility for patients, but also simultaneously enhance the service quality [4].

Furthermore, most scholars have been focusing on location assignment for health system but ignoring the significance of improving capacity. It is obvious that different stakeholders (i.e., suppliers and customers) have their preferential objectives in facility location problems (FLPs) [5]. Local governments generally expect to expand the scope of services to acquire higher social benefits, while the patients pursue greater capacity of each facility to obtain a better treatment environment. Thus, keeping the capacity in balance becomes a novel tendency in FLPs, which promotes availability gradually. Moreover, when generating healthcare planning strategy, decision-makers (DMs) will take numerous factors into account, such as travel distance, construction and management cost, transportation convenience, and capacity constraints [6–9]. Since these objectives often conflict with each other, a multiple objective decision making (MODM) approach is introduced to solve such a complex planning problem.

As the strategy horizon moves forward constantly, an uncertain environment needs to be taken into account for long-range planning [8]. In a realistic world, the decision making process in a medical system involves a degree of uncertainty [10]. For instance, there is probability between medical demand and cost, which leads to distinct optimal solutions. Combined with the aforementioned objectives, the computational procedure of this Non-deterministic Polynomial-Hard (NP-hard) problem becomes extraordinary sophisticated and diverse. To solve this problem, particle swarm optimization (PSO) algorithm is introduced to find optimal solutions due to its fast convergence and effective search ability [11]. The PSO algorithm has been proved to successfully find optimal solutions under complex continuous search spaces. Although it does not guarantee optimality, it is appropriate for the current application [12].

In general, this study aims to find applicable location-allocation solutions in uncertain environment, which plays a critical role to ensure access to public facilities and personal demands. Bi-level multiple objective programming is introduced to determine location and capacity distribution concurrently. In addition, a modified PSO algorithm is utilized to equilibrate the trade-off between complicated and multidimensional objectives. The eventual optimal results are reflected as two aspects: introduce new facilities and upgrade existing capacities.

The remainder of this paper is organized as follows: Section 2 analyzes the current researches and Section 3 describes the main problems in healthcare system. In Section 4, the modeling process and algorithm application are introduced in detail. Following this, Section 5 provides a numerical example to validate the availability and applicability of our approach. Finally, Section 6 gives the conclusions and future research directions.

2. Literature Review

Research in healthcare strategic planning involves various aspects like location and capacity allocation. Plenty of scholars make efforts to do independent but complementary research on healthcare systems. The literature we have reviewed can be classified in four parts: (1) healthcare facility location problems; (2) MODM methods; (3) uncertainty analysis; (4) meta-heuristic algorithms.

2.1. Healthcare Facility Location Problems

In the field of healthcare, illogical HCF location decisions have multiple negative effects on society rather than one single effect [2]. An inaccessible HCF is more likely to increase the risk of morbidity and mortality, as well as provoke public discontent. Therefore, facility location-allocation modeling has become crucial. The hierarchical components of healthcare facilities in urban and rural regions are organized quite different. The delivery system of developing cities is relatively independent and have informal institutions compared with the national standard. According to the National Bureau of Statistics, the local Sanitary Bureau in China, and a literature summary, the healthcare system in developing cities is composed of three hierarchies: primary, middle and high [13,14]. The primary healthcare is a village-based management that cures the basic minor ailments in village regions, including Village Clinics, Healthy Centre and District Clinics. The Community Health Care Centre, Maternity and Child Care Centre, and Sanitation Station set up in townships provide middle healthcare to satisfy most residents in a township. Furthermore, the high-level system is able to conduct more comprehensive treatment for patients with serious illness. These facilities can be defined as General Hospitals, Chinese Medicine Hospitals and Specialized Hospitals. The three levels of public healthcare system in rural areas are summarized in Figure 1.

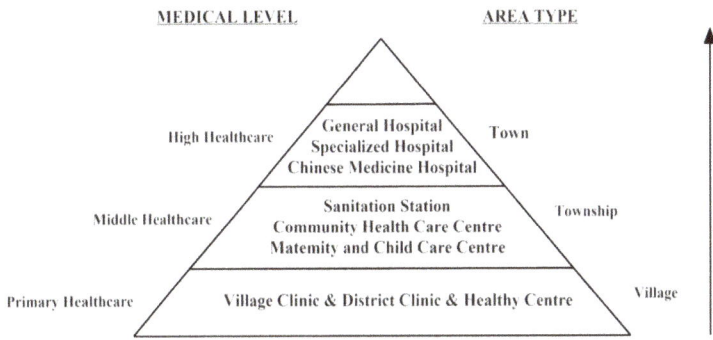

Figure 1. Healthcare facility hierarchy in rural areas.

Previous research discovered that the poor location, inadequate supply or excessive capacity can aggravate the cost burden [9]. Thus, four well known location-allocation models have been studied: the p-median location problem, p-center location problem, set covering location problem, and maximal covering location problem [2,15–20]. Hakimi [17] firstly proposed the concept of p-median to minimize the total transport distance and cost between the demand points and selected facilities with fixed quantity. The p-center problem, also known as the minmax problem, is raised to minimize any demand points served by the nearest facility. Toregas et al. [20] introduced the set covering problem aiming to minimize the total facility number or allocation costs to cover all of the demand points. Church and Revelle [15] presented the maximal covering problem which focused on satisfying as many demand points as possible on the premise of constant facility number. In another study, the continue facility location problem, known as multi-source Weber problems, have also been well studied in FLPs. Venkateshan et al. [21] considered the continuous Euclidean space as an essential element when addressing the trade-off between multiple stakeholders in a Weber problem. Drezner et al. [22] denoted the most common objective in a classic Weber problem is to minimize the weighted sum of Euclidean distance between facility and demand points. Uno et al [23] regarded the uncertainty and vagueness as other important factors in a Weber problem when they find an optimal facility location with weighted distance. Unlike the discrete location models, this type of optimal model can select any location within a path or area as a candidate point [18]. In summary, DMs should choose specific location model with different sources constrained.

2.2. Multiple Objective Decision Making (MODM) Methods

In reality, numerous approaches have been utilized to solve FLPs (Table 1). Multiple objective optimization as a representative branch in mathematical programming, can be adapted to all kinds of location problems. There is a tendency that a growing number of decision makers prefer to pursuing multiple objectives in a realistic world. For instance, Farahani et al. [24] determined that the location of HCFs should consider both cost minimization and service availability maximization objectives to serve the patients efficiently. Ye and Kim [25] reduced the construction cost and maximized service coverage to ensure the total demands within limited facility capability. Syam and Côté [26] regarded the treatment cost and the facility size as equally momentous targets for non-profit service organization. Schuldt et al. [27] uncovered the consumers with distinct complication rates to affect hospital choice by their preferences. Whatever the purpose they contribute to, the ultimate result is to obtain the supreme social-economical-environmental benefits. Therefore, a MODM approach is introduced to balance tradeoffs between multiple objectives effectively. This method can provide a set of pareto solutions understood as parallel scenarios (i.e., spatial distribution and capacity allocation) by comparing the value of each objective. All pareto solutions are superior to the rest of the solutions when all objectives are considered but are inferior to others in only one or more objectives [28,29]. As a result, DMs can select proper scenarios from the pareto plans based on their preference to support their further decisions. Moreover, based on practical consideration, heterogeneous participants affect the determination in HCFLPs [9]. That is to say, choosing an appropriate facility location is depended on not only governments' strategies but also patients' behavior. Consequently, it is suitable to combine MODM method with multilevel programming to undertake planning research.

Table 1. Methods in healthcare facility location problems (HCFLPs).

Authors	Major Approach	Problem Type
Karatas et al. [6], etc.	Multi-objective optimization	Facility location
Czerwiński et al. [16], etc.	Mixed-integer linear programming	Healthcare location-allocation
Ye et al. [25], etc	GIS integration	
Schuldt et al [30], etc.	Multilevel programming	Hospital network planning
Schuldt et al. [27]	Conjoint analysis	
Mestre et al. [8]	Uncertainty modelling	
Syam and Côté [26], etc.	Integer programming	

2.3. Uncertainty Analysis

The location-allocation strategy cannot ignore uncertain elements [31]. Although the traditional deterministic location model can process the statistical and empirical data sufficiently, it falls short in the handling capacity under probabilistic or probable situations. Zarrinpoor et al. [31] proved that environmental uncertainty such as economic structure upgrade, climate change and population migration, will definitely influence human behavior and lead to random demands. Mestre et al. [8] discovered that there are few stochastic location models for a healthcare system focus on uncertainty analysis, and they considered different uncertainty assumptions in real-world applications. In a healthcare system, the treatment demand is seriously impacted by resident population and incidence rate, which make requirements for doctors or sickbeds more flexible. Furthermore, some indescribable or ambiguous information such as satisfaction degree, service quality and operating cost, will also lead to distinction in allocation schemes. Accordingly, considering both fuzzy and stochastic factors has the advantage of simulating actual scenarios.

2.4. Meta-Heuristic Algorithm

Establishing HCF location model requires multiple objective and constraint functions, as well as intricate binary variables. For example, the continuous coordinate will generate numerous possible solutions due to its alterable values. HCFLP is studied as a NP-hard problem, requiring a tremendous amount of calculation as the scale of problem increase [2], especially under the strategic background of healthcare planning. The existing exact algorithms often calculate the location model beyond an acceptable time, and lose accuracy when they encounter a considerably large number of instances. In order to efficiently solve such complex problems generated from multiple objective programming and other computational issues, meta-heuristic algorithm such as a genetic algorithm [16], Lagrangian relaxation [32], simulated annealing [2], and PSO [33] have been widely studied in recent years.

3. Problems Description and Framework

3.1. Challenge Description

According to the literature review, we have summarized three main challenges to overcome: (1) selecting befitting location model; (2) searching available multiple objectives; (3) employing an effective intelligence algorithm.

Challenge 1. Location model:

Currently, the most popular facility location models can be definitely divided into two categories: discrete location model and continuous model. The discrete model ordinarily selects appropriate geographic position within limited candidate locations, while the continuous model allows the facilities constructed anywhere in the feasible areas [34]. With reference to Ahmadi-Javid et al. and Güneş et al. [2,19], the covering-based models are representatively suitable for healthcare facilities. Moreover, the location models that we studied belongs to the type of binary integer programming [35]. This kind of variable can act as a control switch determining whether the healthcare units can be set up in a potential position. In this paper, with previous status analysis, two types of models are combined to provide a universally applicable theory. It is noteworthy that if a constrained position can be shrunk to some tiny point, the continuous variables can be discretized.

Challenge 2. Multiple objectives:

The objectives in HCFLPs may often be conflicting due to external and internal factors. Table 2 summarized the most frequent factors bases on the literature we studied. Obviously, most of scholars pay more attention to travel distance and facility costs, which belong to the component of social and economic benefit. An increasing number of customers concentrate on service quality when they choose a hospital. Although most optimal goals focus on balancing the trade-off amongst the previous aspects, to the best of our knowledge, few scholars attach importance to the essentiality of environmental factors. In addition, healthcare capacity (i.e,. number of beds) has indirectly impacted on patients' consumption behavior in the service industry [36]. That is to say, the facility capacity should also be regarded as object variables rather than just constraining the condition. Consequently, this study utilizes the MODM method to establish a bi-level structural model based on the economic–social–environmental perspective. For each hierarchy, the upper-level addresses the HCF location-allocation problem while the lower-level adjusts the capacity scale.

Table 2. Impact factors of HCFLPs.

Authors	Factors Type	Factors Name	Total Cite
Güneş et al. [5], etc.	social	travel distance/time	11
Schuldt et al. [27]		service quality	4
Zhang et al. [36], etc.		expected waiting time	2
Vidyarthi and Jayaswal [3]		traffic congestion	1
Current et al. [7], etc.	economic	facility cost	7
Jia et al. [4], etc.		capacity	6
Güneş and Nickel [9], etc.		travel cost	3
Ye and Kim [25], etc.		facility amount	2
Syam at al. [26]		operate cost	1
Brimberg et al. [18]		service costs	1
Jia et al. [4], etc.	environmental	geographic accessibility	3
Zarrinpoor et al. [31]		disruption risk	1

Challenge 3. Optimization algorithm:

The MODM approach will provide decision makers with a set of non-dominated points, also known as pareto solutions [37]. For the solutions on a non-dominated frontier, none of the objective function values can be improved without degrading one or more of the other objective function values. Moreover, for any given multi-objective problem, the challenge is to find a representative subset of pareto optimal solutions. Many HCFLPs involve a set of non-dominated points that may include a very large number of feasible points. To solve this problem, the PSO algorithm is capable of searching the practical equilibrium between the conflicting objectives in an uncertain environment. This meta-heuristic algorithm can dynamically alter the HCF location and capacity, even meet the worst-case scenario [8].

3.2. Research Framework

The framework of healthcare facility location-allocation optimization for developing cities in China can be shown in Figure 2.

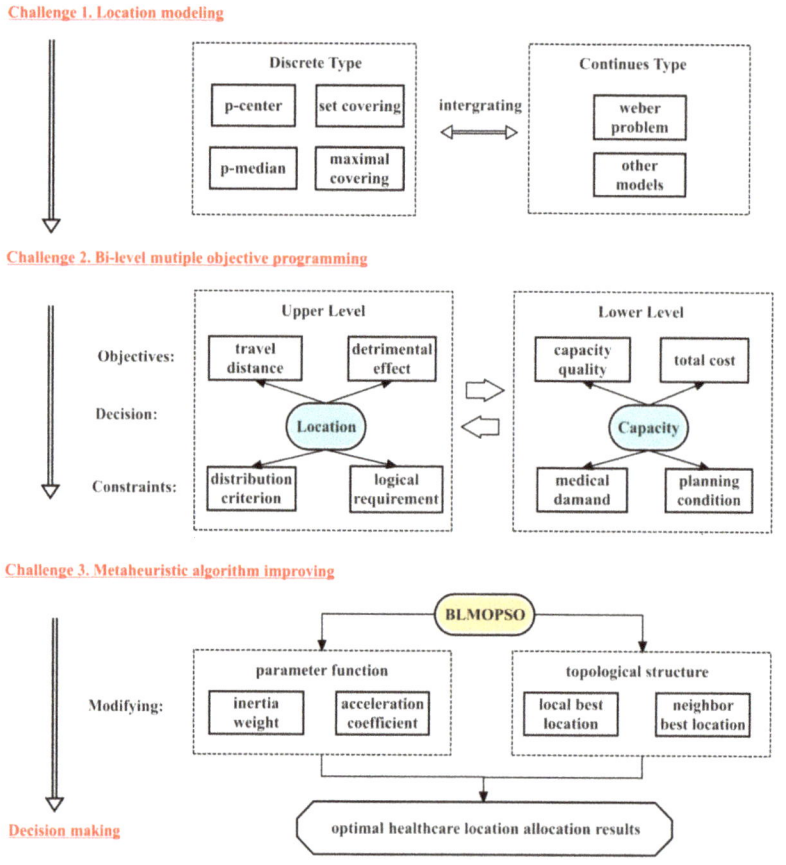

Figure 2. Framework of healthcare facility location-allocation optimization for developing cities in China. BLMOPSO, bi-level multi-objective particle swarm optimization.

4. Materials and Methods

4.1. MODM Programming

Due to the conflict relationship among the objectives, this research proposes a bi-level multiple objective programming from the perspective of suppliers and customers. On one hand, the upper-level (i.e., dominant layer) integrates continuous and discrete location models to determine the potential location of HCF, improving service quality, reducing facility costs, and promoting environmental benefits. On another hand, the lower-level (i.e., the subordinate layer) determines the capacity requirement according to the optimal locations. Equation (1) describes the integrated mathematical model.

$$\min F_1 : S = \sum_i^I \sum_j^J \left(P_{ij} \times d_{ij} \times x_{ij} \right)$$

$$\min F_2 : L = \left(\alpha_1 \times \sum_{ta}^{TA} \phi_{ta} \times \sqrt{\left(x_e - AT_e^{ta}\right)^2 + \left(x_n - AT_n^{ta}\right)^2} \right.$$

$$\left. + \alpha_2 \times \sum_{qa}^{QA} \varphi_{qa} \times \sqrt{\left(x_e - AQ_e^{qa}\right)^2 + \left(x_n - AQ_n^{qa}\right)^2} \right) \times y_j$$

$$s.t. \sum_j^J x_{ij} = 1; \forall i \in I \sum_j^J y_j = 1 x_e \in R^+ x_n \in R^+ x_{ij} \in \{0,1\}; \forall i \in I; \forall j \in J \quad (1)$$

$$y_j \in \{0,1\}; \forall j \in J \max G_1 : S = \sum_j^J \left(\frac{k_j}{\sum_i^I d_{ij}} \right) \times y_j$$

$$\min G_2 : C = \sum_{j=1}^J \left(\left(BP \times BA \times k_j + RP \times RA \times k_j \right) \times y_j \right.$$

$$\left. + \left(\left(k_j - EC_j\right) \times \left(\widetilde{\eta}_1 + SP \times AV + (1-SP) \times AV'\right) \right) \times z_j \right)$$

$$s.t. z_j \in \{0,1\}; \forall j \in J k_j \geq \sum_i^I \left(P_{ij} \times x_{ij}\right); \forall j \in J \sum_j^J k_j \geq TP k_j \in R^+$$

where the first two objectives $F_1 : S$ and $F_2 : L$ represent the social and environmental benefits, which are established from the perspective of customers. The objectives of $G_1 : S$ and $G_2 : C$ based on the suppliers' angle pursue social and economic benefits respectively. The detailed description of each function is stated below.

4.1.1. Upper-Level Programming: Objective Functions

HCFs act as public service facilities, providing an applicable and comfortable environment for patients. The medical demand expects to be assigned to the closest open facility, as well as a peaceful recovery condition [39]. Hence, this research considers two conflicting objectives on the upper-level to realize location optimization: (1) minimize the anticipant travel distance to reach HCF; (2) minimize the detrimental effect to provide a tranquil medical environment.

The most common optimization criteria are the travel distance and travel time, which are dominated by the "cost" of the patient's arrival at the hospital [40]. The patients usually expect to seek the nearest hospital with an eligible department. In the current study, the Euclidean distance has been widely used to measure social impact as it is constant over time [19]. It is a straight line between the patients' individual addresses and potential facility sites. Moreover, the patient demand and disease incidence in a practical sense are not accurate variables. They are uncertain and are probabilistically influenced by external and physiological factors. According to Jia et al. [4] and Wei et al. [41], the stochastic treatment demand is given as follows:

$$P_{ij} = R_i \times \Pr_{ij} \times \widetilde{\zeta} \quad (2)$$

$$\Pr_{ij} = \frac{\frac{k_j}{d_{ij}}}{\sum_j^J \left(\frac{k_j}{d_{ij}}\right)} \tag{3}$$

$$d_{ij} = \begin{cases} \sqrt{(x_e - F_e^i)^2 + (x_n - F_n^i)^2}, & x_{ij} = 1 \\ 0, & x_{ij} \neq 1 \end{cases} \tag{4}$$

where P_{ij} = customer demand (i.e., patient number); R_i = residents' number at site i; $\Pr_{ij}$ = probability of a patient travelling to a facility j; $\tilde{\zeta}$ = disease incidence, which is a random variable; k_j = facility capacity (i.e., number of sickbeds); d_{ij} = Euclidean distance (dominated in kilometers in this paper) between resident site i and facility j; x_e and x_e = candidate facility location, which represent the coordinate of east longitude and north latitude; F_e^i and F_n^i = coordinate of patient site; x_{ij} = 1 means demand i is assigned to facility j.

Therefore, the first objective for social benefit can be described by Equation (5), which minimizes the overall travel distance for all patients:

$$\min F_1 : S = \sum_i^I \sum_j^J (P_{ij} \times d_{ij} \times x_{ij}) \tag{5}$$

where $F_1 : S$ = service objective, considering the total travel distance in an uncertain environment. The value of $\tilde{\zeta}$ is set as uniform distribution.

In the view of the location criteria, the public HCFs are supposed to be built in a relatively quiet environment to provide favorable conditions for local patients. Tumultuous surroundings such as a vegetable market, commercial centre and construction site will no doubt impede recovery. Moreover, the location of HCFs should be adjacent to a convenient arterial road in cased of unexpected emergencies. Congested traffic cannot ensure a timely rescue, which probably increase the morbidity and mortality of the sick. Thereby, it is necessary to provide a better therapeutic environment for patients' care and incorporate it into the optimal model.

$$\min F_2 : L = \left(\alpha_1 \times \sum_{ta}^{TA} \phi_{ta} \times \sqrt{(x_e - AT_e^{ta})^2 + (x_n - AT_n^{ta})^2} + \alpha_2 \times \sum_{qa}^{QA} \varphi_{qa} \times \sqrt{(x_e - AQ_e^{qa})^2 + (x_n - AQ_n^{qa})^2} \right) \times y_j \tag{6}$$

where $F_2 : L$ = location objective, considering the environment elements; α_1 and α_2 = weight for two types of condition; ϕ_{ta} = weight for traffic advantage area; AT_e^{ta} and AT_n^{ta} = coordinate of traffic advantage area; φ_{qa} = weight for quiet area; AQ_e^{qa} and AQ_n^{qa} = coordinate of quiet area; y_j= 1 represents a new facility will be built at site j.

4.1.2. Upper-Level Programming: Constraints

First, we assume each demand point is served by just one facility in the cities with a dispersed distribution of population.

$$\sum_j^J x_{ij} = 1; \forall i \in I \tag{7}$$

$$x_{ij} \in \{0,1\}; \quad \forall i \in I; \quad \forall j \in J \tag{8}$$

Second, the binary decision variable represents whether the facility should be located at site. In order to decrease the building costs, this research assumes only one new facility will be set up.

$$\sum_j^J y_j = 1 \tag{9}$$

$$y_j \in \{0,1\}; \forall j \in J \tag{10}$$

At last, it is clear that the optimal location should be positive.

$$x_e \in R^+; x_n \in R^+ \tag{11}$$

4.1.3. Lower-Level Programming: Objective Functions

Other than the location-allocation assignment, the performance of a healthcare system likewise relies on the capacity of these facilities [25]. Decision making for capacity is promoted by perspective on resource constraints [9]. Thereby, adjusting the capacity structure (i.e., number of sickbeds) plays a significant role in providing an effective medical service. An eligible facility is supposed to have adequate capacity to satisfy medical demand as well as guarantee the fundamental requirements. On the one hand, superabundant doctors and sickbeds will result in resource waste. On the other hand, if the facility service exceed the threshold limit, the patients will feel discontented when meeting service delays, reduced diagnosis time, etc. Consequently, low-level programming modifies the facility capability involving two contradictory objectives: (1) maximize the capacity quality for patients; (2) minimize the total cost for governments.

Abundant capacity ensures a healthcare system's service quality and provides reasonable distribution of public funding [41,42]. The general criterion of measuring capacity is to estimate the number of sickbeds [9]. Furthermore, local governments expect to assign as many patients as possible to improve service quality. Thus, the service capacity is profoundly affected by the decision variables on the upper-level programming.

$$\max G_1 : S = \sum_j^J \left(\frac{k_j}{\sum_i^I d_{ij}} \right) \times y_j \tag{12}$$

where $G_1 : S$ = social objective, considering the facility capacity.

In addition, developing cites with a lagging economy and restricted healthcare resources not only need accessibility in a healthcare system, but also pursue the minimum financial budget for government. Landa-Torres et al. [43] found that constructing and managing a new public facility is linearly dependent on capacity. Güneş and Nickel [9] believed that facility capacity can be regarded as decision variables associated with building cost in an optimal model. If too many sickbeds are allocated, the maintenance charge will go up, whereas deficient capacity is unable to meet a satisfactory standard [25]. Choosing the proper quantity of sickbeds is crucial to guarantee the optimal capacity and minimize the total costs. Therefore, the second objective on the lower level is to reducing the total costs, including building costs, expansion costs and operating costs [29,42].

$$\min G_2 : C = \sum_{j=1}^{J} \left((BP \times BA \times k_j + RP \times RA \times k_j) \times y_j + \left((k_j - EC_j) \times (\tilde{\eta}_1 + SP \times AV + (1 - SP) \times AV') \right) \times z_j \right) \tag{13}$$

where $G_2 : C$ = economic objective, considering removal, expansion and operations management; BP = building price; BA = unit building area; k_j = facility capacity (i.e., number of sickbed); RP = rental price; RA = unit rental area; EC_j = existing capacity; $\tilde{\eta}_1$ = sickbed price, which is considered as fuzzy variables; SP = proportion of senior doctor to patient; AV = average wage of senior doctor; AV' = average wage of ordinary doctor; z_j = 1 represents $k_j \geq EC_j$. In addition, the unit of price used in this paper is the CNY, and the unit of acreage is square meters.

4.1.4. Lower-Level Programming: Constraints

First, the expansion costs in Equation (13) will be calculated when the prospective sickbeds exceed the existing capacity.

$$z_j \in \{0,1\}; \forall j \in J \tag{14}$$

Second, the number of sickbed for each hospital should satisfy overall patients in covered residential areas [43].

$$k_j \geq \sum_i^I (P_{ij} \times x_{ij}); \forall j \in J \quad (15)$$

Third, the total capacity should be able to accommodate all of the patients.

$$\sum_j^J k_j \geq TP \quad (16)$$

where TP = total patients.

At last, the capacitance range of each hospital should not be negative.

$$k_j \in R^+ \quad (17)$$

4.2. Particle Swarm Optimization (PSO) Algorithm for Healthcare Facility Location Problems (HCFLPs)

4.2.1. Bi-Level Multi-Objective Particle Swarm Optimization (BLMOPSO)

PSO is an evolutionary computation algorithm inspired by the food-seeking behavior of birds and social co-operation of fish, initially developed by Kennedy and Eberhart [44]. It has been resoundingly utilized to solve complicated problems with multiple objectives. Due to merits of a simple control structure and few variables, the PSO is able to produce effective results within a short time to determine appropriate locations. It can search sets of pareto solutions in a complex and stochastic environment to provide various scenarios for decision making. With reference to [45,46], many works based on PSO have been modifying this meta-heuristic algorithm. For instance, Ye et al. [47] adjusted the topologies to control the searching mechanism and maintain optimal diversity. Peng et al. [48] modified the inertia weight to balance both the exploration and exploitation ability of PSO. Wang et al. [49] revised the searching mechanism by considering the individual's neighborhood to adjust the velocity of the particles. The adjustments of these researchers can be classified into three aspects: parameters, topologies and searching strategies. For detail, the inertia weights and constriction factors enhance both global and local search, and the acceleration coefficients are able to achieve better stability. Furthermore, the topology structure leads to variants of the algorithm, which ensures the diversity of the optimal solutions. At the same time, the hybridized PSO aims to implement the target of exploration and exploitation by integrating different character of other algorithms. The conventional variants or specializations are summarized in Table 3.

Table 3. Conventional adjustments on particle swarm optimization (PSO).

Authors	Area of Modification	Detail Description
Ratnaweera et al. [50]	Linear varying inertia weight	Control the individual velocity
Naka et al. [51]	Nonlinear inertia weight	Ensure the velocity toward the lowest dynamic range
Clerc and Kennedy [52]	Constriction Factor	Adjust the updating of the whole velocity
Xing and Xiao [53]	Acceleration Coefficients	Generate stochastic influence on velocity of different groups
Wang et al. [49]	Topologies	Exchange the cooperative information amongst each particle
Li et al. [54], Niknam et al. [55], Mandloi and Bhatia [56]	Hybrid Technique	Integrate others intelligent algorithms such as Genetic Algorithm (GA), Simulated Annealing (SA) and Ant Colony Optimization (ACO)

In order to avoid premature convergence and increase the diversity of the optimal results, modifying the topology structure is an appropriate measure and has been widely used in the development of PSO. Prakash et al. [57] introduced a fitness predator optimizer to provide more optimal in multi-objective programming. Marinakis [58] developed an expanding neighborhood topology PSO algorithm to solve a discrete location routing problem. Therefore, this paper proposes the BLMOPSO, modifying two aspects (i.e., parameter function and topology structure), to increase the global searching ability based on the characteristic of a master–slave equilibrium optimization model. The particle updating mechanism is described in Figure 3, which enhances accuracy and robustness while reducing computation time. The optimal results can be divided into two sets of non-dominated solutions for heterogeneous agents (i.e., government and patient) respectively to provide diverse strategies in HCFLPs.

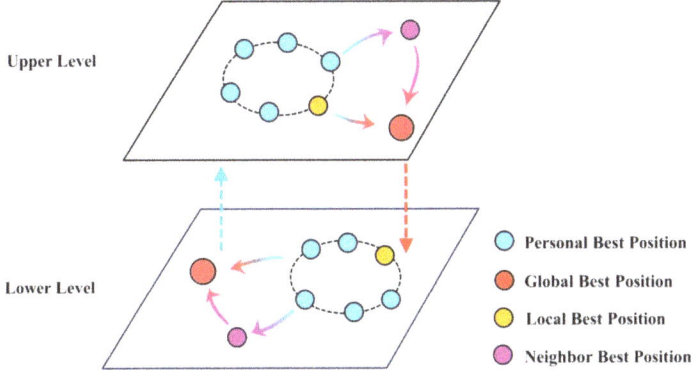

Figure 3. Bi-level-based update process.

4.2.2. Overall Procedure of the Proposed Algorithm

The procedure of the proposed algorithm is shown in Figure 4 including 10 steps.

1. Set the parameters in the upper-level programming, including swarm size, particle position and velocity, iterations, inertia weights, acceleration coefficients and random variables $\widetilde{\widetilde{\zeta}}$.
2. Update the control parameters and compute the fitness values of two upper-level objectives.
3. Estimate and replace the upper-level pareto solutions.
4. Obtain the $pbest_s$, $gbest_s$, $lbest_s$, $nbest_s$ through the aforementioned approach.
5. Set the similar type of parameters as step 1 on the lower level, and generate fuzzy variables $\widetilde{\eta}$ based on confidence levels α.
6. Renewal the correlative parameters on the lower level.
7. Compute the fitness values by incorporating solutions from upper level.
8. Obtain the $pbest_s'$, $gbest_s'$, $lbest_s'$, $nbest_s'$ on the lower level.
9. Check the lower level termination: if the algorithm acquires the best solution or met the maximum iteration, stop the lower level program. Otherwise, go back to Step 6.
10. Check the BLMOPSO termination: if the algorithm gains the appropriate Pareto solutions or met the maximum iteration, then stop the BLMOPSO procedure. Otherwise, go back to Step 2.

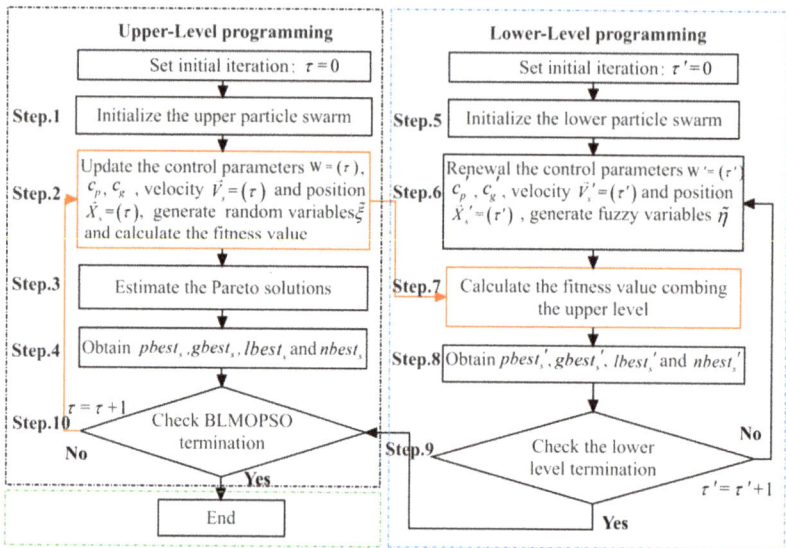

Figure 4. Flow chart of the bi-level multi-objective particle swarm optimization (BLMOPSO) algorithm.

4.2.3. Solution Representation

The particle swarm contains a range of particles with multiple dimensions, and each of them represents a potential optimal solution. Accordingly, the potential solutions on the upper level are x_e and x_n (i.e., HCF location) combining the coordinates of latitude and longitude, while $k_j = (k_1, k_2, ..., k_J)^T$ are the sickbed number on behalf of facility capacity obtained by the lower level.

4.2.4. Parameter Setting

On the basis of Kennedy and Eberhart, and Gan et al. [59], initializing the control parameters is the critical step to ensure desired algorithmic outcome. The indispensable variables are set up as follows: first, Set s ($s = 1, 2, ..., S$) particles with h ($h = 1, 2, ..., H$) dimension. Second, restrict inertia weight in $[\omega^{min}, \omega^{max}]$, personal acceleration coefficient in $[c_p^{min}, c_p^{max}]$, and global acceleration coefficient in $[c_g^{min}, c_g^{max}]$. Third, initialize the local best acceleration constant c_l, and near neighbor best acceleration constant c_n. Last, generate the velocity $\vec{v}_{sh}$ within the range of $[v^{min}, v^{max}]$, and position $\vec{x}_{sh}$ within the allowed coordinate scope. Notably, all content types of parameters in the lower level are set to the same in the upper level.

4.2.5. Particle Evaluation

The proposed technique requires the algorithm to compare and analyze the fitness value iteratively to obtain the pareto solutions. Thus, it is necessary to utilizing appropriate method to evaluated the entire particle in each iteration. According to [59], the evaluation process is depicted in detail as follows: First, putting $\vec{x}_{sh}(\tau)$ into objective functions $F_1 : S$, $F_2 : L$, $G_1 : S$ and $G_2 : E$, and calculating the fitness values $Fitness(\vec{x}_{sh})$ respectively. Second, using the pareto archived evolution strategy procedure and test procedure (refer to [59]) to obtain the $pbest_s$, which represents the effect of personal experiences. For each group, employing the same approach can select the $lbest_s$ to expand local searching ability. Third, applying the roulette to acquire the $gbest_s$, which represents the social component. Fourth, computing the local fitness value $\frac{\sum |Fitness(\vec{x}_{dh}) - Fitness(\vec{x}_{sh})|}{|\vec{x}_{dh} \vec{x}_{sh}|}$ ($|\vec{x}_{dh} \vec{x}_{sh}|$ is the Euclidean distance between particle and its dth neighbor) in each group, and regard the maximum as the $nbest_s$ to increase particle diversity. After several iteration calculations, the final results can provide DMs with a set of preferential and appropriate solutions.

4.2.6. Particle Updating

In order to improve the convergence of the algorithm, Zhang et al. [60] introduced a time-variant adjustment strategy for the major parameters, which is given as follows. The inertia weight ω affects the current velocity of a particle by controlling the influence of previous velocity. The growing value of ω assists the swarm to broaden its exploration, and the decrease value of ω motivates it to enhance its exploitation. Thus, the earlier stage of iteration should maintain a large liner weight to ensure the particle searching thoroughly. When the majority of solution spaces have been explored, the inertia weight needs to be slowed down in order to find a better result. According to this renewed mechanism, the ω for iteration τ is updated by the following:

$$\omega(\tau) = \left(\omega^{max-min} \times \frac{\tau}{\tau_{max}^{min}} \right) \tag{18}$$

where ω is restricted in range $\left[\omega^{min^{max}} \right]$, and τ_{max} is the maximum iteration.

The acceleration coefficients c_p and c_g have momentous influence on searching ability. The lager c_p facilitates emanative search while the small c_g improves partially converge. The two parameters are updated by the following:

$$c_p(\tau) = \left(c_p^{max-min} \times \frac{(\tau_{max}())}{\tau_{max} + c_p^{min}} \right) \tag{19}$$

$$c_g(\tau) = \left(c_g^{max-min} \times \frac{\tau}{\tau_{max} + p^{min}} \right) \tag{20}$$

where c_p and c_g are limited in the interval to avoid premature convergence as well.

In order to make the optimal solution become more diverse, a variant topology structure is developed by adding two novel cognitive experiences, which decrease the effect of the social collaboration process. The velocity and position are updated by the following:

$$\vec{v}_{sh}(\tau+1) = \omega(\tau)\vec{v}_{sh}(\tau) + c_p(\tau)u_r\left[\psi_{psh} - \vec{x}_{sh}(\tau)\right] + c_g(\tau)u_r\left[\psi_{gsh} - \vec{x}_{sh}(\tau)\right] + \\ c_l u_r\left[\psi_{lsh} - \vec{x}_{sh}(\tau)\right] + c_n u_n\left[\psi_{lsh} - \vec{x}_{sh}(\tau)\right] \tag{21}$$

$$\vec{x}_{sh}(\tau+1) = \vec{x}_{sh}(\tau) + \vec{v}_{sh}(\tau+1) \tag{22}$$

The velocity update function of a particle is composed of five parts. The first three parts $\omega(\tau)\vec{v}_{sh}(\tau)$, $c_p(\tau)u_r\left[\psi_{psh} - \vec{x}_{sh}(\tau)\right]$ and $c_n u_n\left[\psi_{lsh} - \vec{x}_{sh}(\tau)\right]$ are the traditional direction memories, which represent the original experience, the personal experience and mutual cooperation experience, respectively. The new part $c_l u_r\left[\psi_{lsh} - \vec{x}_{sh}(\tau)\right]$ called the local cognitive indicates a pareto solution generated by an adjacent subswarm of a particle. Moreover, the neighbor cognitive $c_n u_n\left[\psi_{lsh} - \vec{x}_{sh}(\tau)\right]$ represents the major variety comparing a particle with its neighbors.

5. Case Study

In order to verify the effectiveness of the proposed optimal model, we use computational experiments based on the depressed region of Mao County, which is located in the northwest of Sichuan province. The test aims to illustrate how the proposed model can be applied to support healthcare planners in location and allocation decisions in an uncertain environment.

5.1. Study Area

Mao County has a per capita GDP of 30046 CNY in 2017, and is a remote region with poor economic development accessibility. The detailed location of study area is shown in Figure 5. In our investigations, this developing region needs to provide sufficient healthcare facilities to the large scattered residents. What is more, there are 5 middle healthcare units and sixteen patient areas located in the township, which are presented in Figure 6A. The total sickbed number of existing hospitals is 527, which does not satisfy the total requirements for nearly 800 (i.e., $TP = 800$). Furthermore, the transportation advantage areas and environmentally tranquil areas around the existing hospitals are marked in Figure 6B.

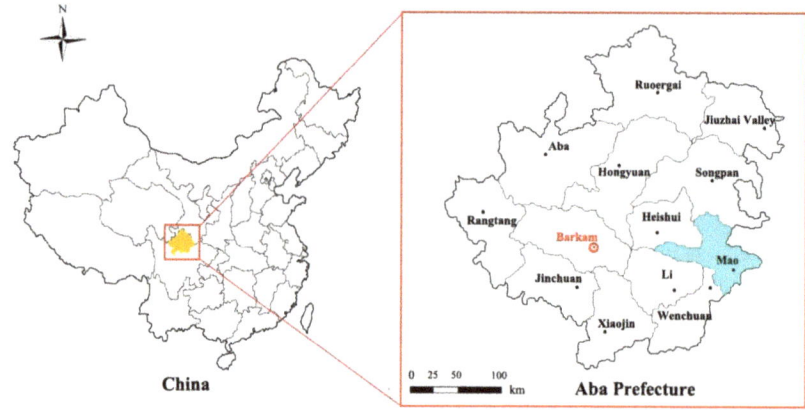

Figure 5. Location of study area.

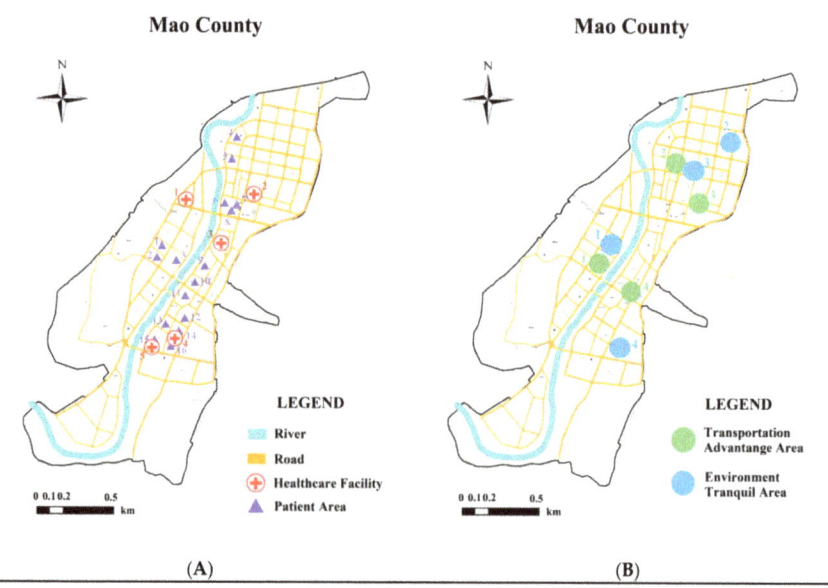

Figure 6. (A) Healthcare facility and patient areas; (B) Environmental elements in Mao County.

5.2. Date Acquisition and Processing

The numerical data about population, medical demand, healthcare information, etc., are obtained from two types of organization, i.e. governmental agencies and academic institutions. According to our field investigation in local governments, the map data referring to residential distribution and healthcare network are retrieved from Statistical Bureau, Health and Family Planning Bureau and Land Source Bureau. In order to obtain the weights for environmental elements, the authors have contacted five experienced experts from the Center for Rural Construction Integrated Management (CRCIM) in Sichuan Agriculture University. The experts selected four essential areas respectively from each environmental type (Figure 6B), and gave the comprehensive weights (Table 4) based on the method of the analytic hierarchy process (AHP) [61]. Moreover, they proposed the morbidity of patient is generated by a uniform distribution $\tilde{\xi} \sim U(0.1, 0.7)$, and the uncertain sickbed price using a triangular fuzzy number $\tilde{\eta} = (3500, 4000, 4500)$ with a confidence level of 90%.

Table 4. The weights for environmental factors.

Environmental Type			
α_1	α_2		
0.34	0.66		
Transportation Advantage Area			
ϕ_1	ϕ_2	ϕ_3	ϕ_4
0.13	0.18	0.37	0.32
Environmentally Tranquil Area			
φ_1	φ_2	φ_3	φ_4
0.11	0.31	0.36	0.22

5.3. Case Solution

The BLMOPSO algorithm was conducted on a Windows 10 personal computer with 8 GB of RAM running at 2.8 GHz on an Intel Core i7 processor. The control parameters on each level were set as follows: iteration $\tau = 30$, swarm size $s = 20$, inertia weight in [0.1,0.9], personal and global acceleration coefficient in, local and near neighbor best acceleration constant $c_l = c_n = 0.2$.

Since operating one iteration on the upper-level needs 30 iterations on the lower-level, the performance period grows exponentially. After 900 iterations in total, the pareto solutions were generated within average 7 minutes. The seven solutions on the upper level are demonstrated in Table 5, indicating the position and patient allocation scheme when constructing a new HCF. Notably, each location solution has a group of capacity scenarios on the lower level. Due to the space limitation, this research picked one of the capacity optimal solutions corresponding to an allocation scheme, which is shown in Table 6.

Table 5. The pareto solutions on the upper level.

No.	N	E	Patient Area															
			1	2	3	4	5	6	7	8	9	10	11	12	13	14	15	16
1	31°41′35.05″	103°51′28.77″	2	4	2	1	3	3	3	3	4	4	5	5	5	5	6	5
2	31°41′37.09″	103°51′23.34″	2	4	2	1	1	3	3	3	4	4	5	5	5	5	6	5
3	31°41′40.18″	103°51′33.00″	2	4	2	1	3	3	3	3	4	4	5	5	5	5	6	5
4	31°41′39.32″	103°51′37.63″	2	4	2	1	1	3	3	3	4	4	5	5	5	5	6	5
5	31°40′59.34″	103°51′26.53″	2	4	2	1	3	3	3	3	4	4	5	5	5	5	6	5
6	31°41′53.40″	103°51′44.01″	2	4	2	1	3	3	3	3	4	4	5	5	5	5	6	5
7	31°41′35.52″	103°51′35.94″	2	4	2	1	3	3	3	3	4	4	5	5	5	5	6	5

Table 6. The pareto solutions relating to No.1 on the lower level.

No.	Number of Sickbed											
	1		2		3		4		5		6	
Original	-		200		120		107		60		40	
1	289	+289	394	+194	319	+199	34	−73	102	+42	318	+278
2	133	+133	500	+300	212	+92	144	+37	402	+342	105	+65
3	433	+433	341	+141	447	+327	261	+154	417	+357	396	+356
4	309	+309	432	+232	429	+309	329	+222	384	+324	246	+206
5	174	+174	305	+105	264	+144	255	+148	214	+154	233	+193
6	377	+377	401	+201	438	+318	305	+198	393	+333	306	+266
7	56	+56	489	+289	335	+215	349	+242	242	+182	58	+18
8	190	+190	394	+194	383	+263	313	+206	302	+242	229	+189
9	32	+32	365	+165	370	+250	396	+289	69	+9	66	+26

5.4. Analytic Results

With respect to alternative decision making, Figure 7A provides all of optimal solutions for governments to choose their preferences. That is to say, looking for to high service quality may situate the location far away from arterial road or quiet districts and, vice versa, pursuing a suitable medical environment could aggravate the travel burden. Furthermore, on the basis of primary results summarized in the tables as above, the location distributions of HCFs are illustrated in Figure 7B.

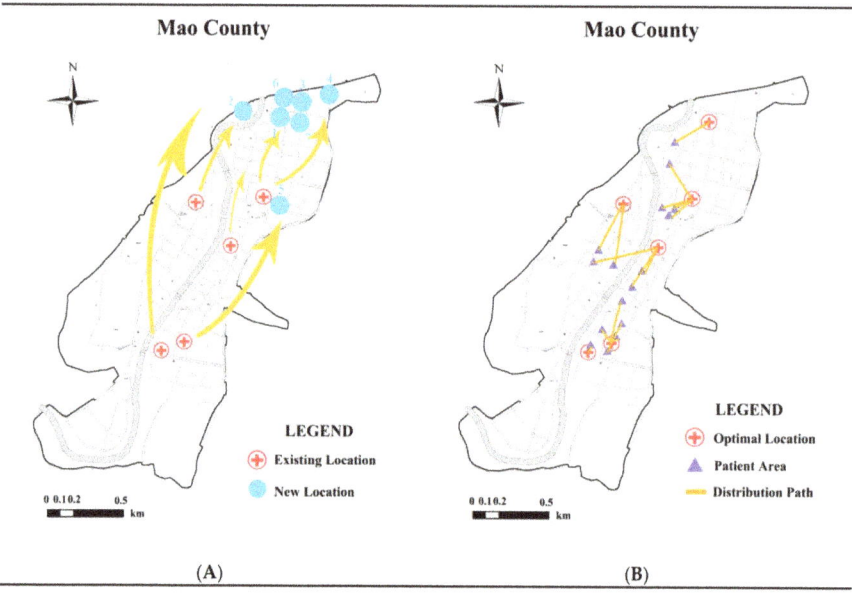

Figure 7. (A) Optimal location scheme; (B) spatial distribution.

Figure 8 displays the capacity allocation for one of the options selected in Table 6. Obviously, availability and accessibility can be promoted by adding more sickbeds, but also cause the construction costs to rise. On the contrary, controlling the facility capacity can ease the financial pressure, but it may delay the best treatment for patients as well. Within this context, DMs should find a tradeoff among such conflicting objectives under different situations.

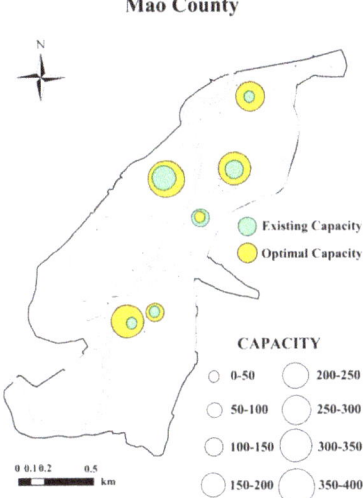

Figure 8. Capacity allocation.

5.5. Comparative Analysis

This research compares the BLMPPSO with basic PSO in HCFLPs to validate its efficiency. Due to the complexity of multiple objective optimization compared to single objective programming, we studied four metrics of performance proposed in Gan et al. [40] to further illustrate the exploration and exploitation ability of the algorithm. Table 7 describes the iterative process of the pareto solutions, which discloses the diversity of the results. Table 8 collects different types of indicator value, and shows that the proposed algorithm performs better in all directions.

Table 7. Iterative process of the pareto solutions.

Iteration	The Average Distance	The Distribution	The Extent	The Set Convergence	The Solution Amount
1	0.0568	0.3333	3.8649	0.3333	3
2	0.0547	0.6000	5.6127	0.6000	5
3	0.0547	0.6000	5.6127	1.0000	5
4	0.0409	0.5000	5.8634	0.7500	4
5	0.0409	0.5000	5.8634	1.0000	4
6	0.0762	0.6000	5.8634	0.8000	5
7	0.0762	0.6000	5.8634	1.0000	5
8	0.0762	0.6000	5.8634	1.0000	5
10	0.0762	0.6000	5.8634	1.0000	5
12	0.0762	0.6000	5.8634	1.0000	5
15	0.0762	0.6000	5.8634	1.0000	5
18	0.0762	0.6000	5.8634	1.0000	5
20	0.0762	0.6000	5.8634	1.0000	5
22	0.0922	0.6667	5.8634	0.6667	6
23	0.0922	0.6667	5.8634	1.0000	6
24	0.0922	0.6667	5.8634	1.0000	6
25	0.0922	0.6667	5.8634	1.0000	6
26	0.0425	0.7143	5.8634	0.8571	7
27	0.0425	0.7143	5.8634	1.0000	7
28	0.0425	0.7143	5.8634	1.0000	7
29	0.0425	0.7143	5.8634	1.0000	7
30	0.0425	0.7143	5.8634	1.0000	7

Table 8. Comparison of BLMOPSO and basic PSO.

Algorithm Type	Iteration	The average Distance	The Distribution	The Extent	The set Convergence	The Solution Amount
BLMOPSO	30	0.0425	0.7143	5.8634	1.0000	7
Basic PSO	30	0.1712	0.5000	5.3036	1.0000	4

5.6. Stability Analysis

The eventual optimal solutions are acquired based on 30 tests in order to avoid accidental events. Although the experience is likely to generate other potential situations, the authors select one of the results that occurred most frequently. The test statistics are recorded in Table 9. In addition, the performance metric of "the extent" can test the stability of the results as well. Thus, the authors compared and calculated the error rates amongst the pareto solutions which with the same solution amount. Table 10 shows that most of error rates are no more than 5%. According to these two tables, the solutions obtained in this study are credible and reasonable.

Table 9. Frequency of the pareto solution.

Solution Amount	Occurrence Amount	Percentage
7	12	33.33%
8	4	16.67%
6	3	16.67%
5	3	13.33%
10	2	6.67%
others	4	13.33%
total	30	100.00%

Table 10. Error rate of the pareto solution.

No.	Solution Amount	The Extent		Error Rate
Original	7	5.8634		-
1	7	5.7702	−0.0932	−1.59%
2	7	5.9289	0.0655	1.12%
3	7	5.9289	0.0655	1.12%
4	7	5.7494	−0.1140	−1.94%
5	7	5.4991	−0.3643	−6.21%
6	7	5.9435	0.0801	1.37%
7	7	6.1374	0.2740	4.67%
8	7	5.5974	−0.2660	−4.54%
9	7	−0.1889	−0.1889	−3.22%
10	7	5.6943	−0.1691	−2.88%
11	7	6.2093	0.3459	5.90%

6. Conclusions and Future Research

This study presents a location-allocation optimal model for China's healthcare system to enhance availability and accessibility by using bi-level multiple objective programming in an uncertain environment. The upper level considers the conflicts of social and environmental factors on location decision, while the lower level adjusts the facility capacity, including service quality and financial costs simultaneously. Since-facility spatial distribution is a complex and time-consuming problem, and an ameliorated BLMOPSO algorithm is designed to improve the accuracy of the results. In order to verify the applicability and versatility of the proposed model, an extensive computational experiment has been carried out by using the data obtained from a field investigation. It balances the tradeoffs among the four conflicting optimal targets, analyzes the efficiency of location decisions, and estimates the requirement for capacity increase. Moreover, the optimal pareto solutions illustrate that the

DMs' preference has a significant bearing on the spatial and capacity assignment of patient areas to healthcare units.

The characteristic contributions of this paper are: (1) the hierarchical programming carries out the location and capacity assignment to maintain a balance between supply and demand; (2) the proposed model considers uncertainty associated with medical demand and costs to simulate possible realization; (3) BLMOPSO is designed to efficiently tackle such a NP-hard problem by means of improving the global search and reducing the probability of falling into premature convergence; (4) the optimal results pave the way for the practical application in healthcare network design, and also can be popularized in other types of public facilities such as schools, warehouses and police stations.

The current research is original, and will be needed for future work in at least two aspects. On one hand, choosing an appropriate location depends on not only the external environment but also internal factors such as competition among hospitals, classes of patients and diagnostic cost. On the other hand, the optimal objectives of urban and rural areas may differ and should be adjusted according to regional conditions.

Author Contributions: Li Wang conceived the framework, designed the model, implemented the entire experiments and wrote the majority of the manuscript; Huan Shi carried out the field research, collected the data and provided constructive suggestions on mathematical theory; Lu Gan proposed novel ideas and technical scenarios, refined the manuscript and improved the use of language. All the authors have read and approved the final manuscript.

Funding: This research was funded by the Humanities Social and Sciences Research Funds of Education Ministry (Grant No. 15XJC630001), the Key Funds of Sichuan Social Science Research Institution "System Science and Enterprise Development Research" (Grant No. Xq18B06), and the Foundation of Chengdu Science and Technology (Grant No. 2017-RK00-00274-ZF).

Conflicts of Interest: The authors declare no conflict of interest.

References

1. Healthcare in China. Available online: https://en.wikipedia.org/wiki/Healthcare_in_China (accessed on 30 October 2018).
2. Ahmadi-Javid, A.; Seyedi, P.; Syam, S.S. A survey of healthcare facility location. *Comput. Oper. Res.* **2016**, *79*, 223–263. [CrossRef]
3. Vidyarthi, N.; Jayaswal, S. Efficient solution of a class of location–allocation problems with stochastic demand and congestion. *Comput. Oper. Res.* **2014**, *48*, 20–30. [CrossRef]
4. Jia, T.; Tao, H.; Qin, K.; Wang, Y.L.; Liu, C.K.; Gao, Q.L. Selecting the optimal healthcare centers with a modified P-median model: a visual analytic perspective. *Int. J. Health. Geogr.* **2014**, *13*, 1–15. [CrossRef] [PubMed]
5. Güneş, E.D.; Yaman, H.; Çekyay, B.; Verter, V. Matching patient and physician preferences in designing a primary care facility network. *J. Oper. Res. Soc.* **2014**, *65*, 483–496. [CrossRef]
6. Karatas, M.; Yakıcı, E. An iterative solution approach to a multi-objective facility location problem. *Appl Soft Comput.* **2017**, *26*, 272–287. [CrossRef]
7. Current, J.; Min, H.; Schilling, D. Multi-objective analysis of facility location decisions. *Eur. J. Oper. Res.* **1990**, *49*, 295–307. [CrossRef]
8. Mestre, A.M.; Oliveira, M.D.; Barbosa-Póvoa, A.P. Location–allocation approaches for hospital network planning under uncertainty. *Eur. J. Oper. Res.* **2015**, *240*, 791–806. [CrossRef]
9. Güneş, E.D.; Nickel, S. Location Problems in Healthcare. In *Location Science*; Laporte, G., Nickel, S., Saldanha da Gama, F., Eds.; Publisher: Springer, Cham, Germany, 2015; pp. 555–579.
10. Das, S.; Kar, S. Group decision making in medical system: An intuitionistic fuzzy soft set approach. *Appl. Soft. Comput.* **2014**, *24*, 196–211. [CrossRef]
11. Hassanien, A.E.; Grosan, C.; Tolba, M.F. Applications of Intelligent Optimization in Biology and Medicine. Springer: Cham, Germany, 2016.
12. Clerc, M.; Kennedy, J. The particle swarm - explosion, stability, and convergence in a multidimensional complex space. *IEEE. Trans. Evol. Comput.* **2002**, *6*, 58–73. [CrossRef]

13. Li, X.; Lu, J.; Hu, S.; Cheng, K.; Maeseneer, J.D.; Meng, Q.; Mossialos, E.; Xu, D.R.; Yip, W.; Zhang, H.; Krumholz, H.M.; Jiang, L.; Hu, S. The primary health-care system in China. *Lancet* **2017**, *390*, 2584–2594. [CrossRef]
14. Wang, X.; Yang, H.; Duan, Z.; Pan, J. Spatial accessibility of primary health care in China: A case study in Sichuan Province. *Soc. Sci. Med.* **2018**, *209*, 14–24. [CrossRef] [PubMed]
15. Church, R.; Velle, C.R. The maximal covering location problem. *Pap. Reg. Sci. Assoc.* **1974**, *32*, 101–118. [CrossRef]
16. Czerwiński, A.M.; Więckowska, B. Location-allocation model for external beam radiotherapy as an example of an evidence-based management tool implemented in healthcare sector in Poland. *Radiat Oncol.* **2018**, *127*, 154–160. [CrossRef] [PubMed]
17. Hakimi, S.L. Optimum locations of switching centers and the absolute centers and medians of a graph. *Oper. Res.* **1964**, *12*, 450–459. [CrossRef]
18. Brimberg, J.; Drezner, Z.; Mladenović, N.; Salhi, S. A new local search for continuous location problems ☆. *Eur. J. Oper. Res.* **2014**, *232*, 256–265. [CrossRef]
19. Farahani, R.Z.; Asgari, N.; Heidari, N.; Hosseininia, M.; Goh, M. Covering problems in facility location: A review. *Comput. Ind. Eng.* **2012**, *62*, 368–407. [CrossRef]
20. Toregas, C.; Swain, R.; Revelle, C.; Bergman, L. The location of emergency service facilities. *Oper. Res.* **1971**, *19*, 1363–1373. [CrossRef]
21. Venkateshan, P.; Ballou, R.H.; Mathur, K.; Maruthasalam, A.P.P. A Two-echelon joint continuous-discrete location model. *Eur. J. Oper. Res.* **2017**, *262*, 1028–1039. [CrossRef]
22. Drezner, T.; Drezner, Z.; Schöbel, A. The Weber obnoxious facility location model: A Big Arc Small Arc approach. *Comput. Oper. Res.* **2018**, *98*, 240–250. [CrossRef]
23. Uno, T.; Kato, K.; Katagiri, H. Fuzzy random weighted Weber problems in facility location. *Procedia Comput. Sci.* **2015**, *60*, 936–943. [CrossRef]
24. Farahani, R.Z.; Hekmatfar, M.; Fahimnia, B.; Kazemzadeh, N. Hierarchical facility location problem: Models, classifications, techniques, and applications. *Comput. Ind. Eng.* **2014**, *68*, 104–117. [CrossRef]
25. Ye, H.; Kim, H. Locating healthcare facilities using a network-based covering location problem. *Geojournal* **2016**, *81*, 1–16. [CrossRef]
26. Syam, S.S.; Côté, M.J. A comprehensive location-allocation method for specialized healthcare services. *Oper. Res. Health Care* **2012**, *1*, 73–83. [CrossRef]
27. Schuldt, J.; Doktor, A.; Lichters, M.; Vogt, B.; Robra, B.P. Insurees' preferences in hospital choice—A population-based study. *Health Policy* **2017**, *121*, 1040–1046. [CrossRef] [PubMed]
28. Srinivas, N.; Deb, K. Muiltiobjective optimization using nondominated sorting in genetic algorithms. *Evol Comput.* **2014**, *2*, 221–248. [CrossRef]
29. Zhang, W.; Cao, K.; Liu, S.; Huang, B. A multi-objective optimization approach for health-care facility location-allocation problems in highly developed cities such as Hong Kong. *Comput. Environ. Urban. Syst.* **2016**, *59*, 220–230. [CrossRef]
30. Mandloi, M.; Bhatia, V. A low-complexity hybrid algorithm based on particle swarm and ant colony optimization for large-MIMO detection. *Expert Syst. Appl.* **2016**, *50*, 66–74. [CrossRef]
31. Zarrinpoor, N.; Fallahnezhad, M.S.; Pishvaee, M.S. Design of a reliable hierarchical location-allocation model under disruptions for health service networks: A two-stage robust approach. *Comput. Ind. Eng.* **2017**, *109*, 130–150. [CrossRef]
32. Kim, D.G.; Kim, Y.D. A Lagrangian heuristic algorithm for a public healthcare facility location problem. *Ann. Oper. Res.* **2013**, *206*, 221–240. [CrossRef]
33. Elkady, S.K.; Abdelsalam, H.M. A Modified Particle Swarm Optimization Algorithm for Solving Capacitated Maximal Covering Location Problem in Healthcare Systems. In *Applications of Intelligent Optimization in Biology and Medicine*; Hassanien, A.E., Grosan, C., Fahmy, Tolba.M., Eds.; Springer: Cham, Germany, 2016; pp. 117–133. ISBN 978-3-319-21211-1.
34. Eiselt, H.A.; Marianov, V. Foundations of Location Analysis. In *International Series in Operations Research & Management Science l.*; Publisher: Springer, Boston, MA, USA, 2011.
35. Syam, S.S.; Côté, M.J. A location–allocation model for service providers with application to not-for-profit health care organizations. *Omega* **2010**, *38*, 157–166. [CrossRef]

36. Zhang, Y.; Atkins, D. Medical Facility Network Design: User-Choice and System-Optimal Models. *Eur. J. Oper. Res.* **2018**, *273*, 305–319. [CrossRef]
37. Collette, Y.; Siarry, P. *Multiobjective Optimization*; Springer: Berlin, Germany, 2003.
38. Mestre, A.M.; Oliveira, M.D.; Barbosa-Póvoa, A. Organizing hospitals into networks: a hierarchical and multiservice model to define location, supply and referrals in planned hospital systems. *Or. Spectru.* **2012**, *34*, 319–348. [CrossRef]
39. Stummer, C.; Doerner, K.; Focke, A.; Heidenberger, K. Determining Location and Size of Medical Departments in a Hospital Network: A Multiobjective Decision Support Approach. *Health. Care. Manag. Sci.* **2004**, *7*, 63–71. [CrossRef] [PubMed]
40. Wei, G.; Xin, W.; Mcgregor, S.E. Optimization of preventive health care facility locations. *Int. J. Health. Geogr.* **2010**, *9*, 17. [CrossRef] [PubMed]
41. Shariff, S.S.R.; Moin, N.H.; Omar, M. Location allocation modeling for healthcare facility planning in Malaysia. *Comput. Ind. Eng.* **2012**, *62*, 1000–1010. [CrossRef]
42. Verter, V.; Lapierre, S.D. Location of Preventive Health Care Facilities. *Ann. Oper. Res.* **2002**, *110*, 123–132. [CrossRef]
43. Landa-Torres, I.; Manjarres, D.; Salcedo-Sanz, S.; Del Ser, J.; Gil-Lopez, S. A multi-objective grouping Harmony Search algorithm for the optimal distribution of 24-hour medical emergency units. *Expert Syst. Appl.* **2013**, *40*, 2343–2349. [CrossRef]
44. Kennedy, J.; Eberhart, R. Particle swarm optimization. In Proceedings of the IEEE International Conference on Neural Networks, Perth, WA, Australia, 27 November–1 December 1995. [CrossRef]
45. Poli, R.; Kennedy, J.; Blackwell, T. Particle Swarm Optimization: An Overview. *Swarm Intell.* **2007**, *1*, 33–57. [CrossRef]
46. Sengupta, S.; Basak, S.; Peters, R.A. Particle Swarm Optimization: A Survey of Historical and Recent Developments with Hybridization Perspectives. *Mach. Learn. Knowl. Extr.* **2018**, *1*, 157–191. [CrossRef]
47. Ye, W.; Feng, W.; Fan, S. A novel multi-swarm particle swarm optimization with dynamic learning strategy. *Appl. Soft. Comput.* **2017**, *61*, 832–843. [CrossRef]
48. Peng, Z.; Manier, H.; Manier, M.A. Particle swarm optimization for capacitated location-routing problem. *IFAC-Papers. OnLine.* **2017**, *50*, 14668–14673. [CrossRef]
49. Wang, S.; Watada, J. A hybrid modified PSO approach to VaR-based facility location problems with variable capacity in fuzzy random uncertainty. *Inf. Sci.* **2012**, *192*, 3–18. [CrossRef]
50. Ratnaweera, A.; Halgamuge, S.; Watson, H. Particle Swarm Optimization with Self-Adaptive Acceleration Coefficients. In Proceedings of the First International Conference on Fuzzy Systems and Knowledge Discovery, Guilin, China, 14–17 October 2003; pp. 264–268.
51. Naka, S.; Genji, T.; Yura, T.; Fukuyama, Y. Practical Distribution State Estimation using Hybrid Particle Swarm Optimization. In Proceedings of the IEEE Power Engineering Society Winter Meeting, Columbus, OH, USA, 28 January–1 February 2001; Volume 2, pp. 815–820.
52. Clerc, M.; Kennedy, J. The Particle Swarm-Explosion, Stability and Convergence in a Multidimensional Complex Space. *IEEE Trans. Evol. Comput.* **2002**, *6*, 58–73. [CrossRef]
53. Xing, J.; Xiao, D. New Metropolis Coefficients of Particle Swarm Optimization. In Proceedings of the 2008 Chinese Control and Decision Conference, Yantai, Shandong, China, 2–4 July 2008; pp. 3518–3521.
54. Li, C.; Zhai, R.; Liu, H.; Yang, Y.; Wu, H. Optimization of a heliostat field layout using hybrid PSO-GA algorithm. *Appl. Therm. Eng.* **2018**, *128*, 33–41. [CrossRef]
55. Niknam, T.; Narimani, M.R.; Jabbari, M. Dynamic optimal power flow using hybrid particle swarm optimization and simulated annealing. *Int. Trans. Electr. Energy Syst.* **2013**, *23*, 975–1001. [CrossRef]
56. Mandloi, M.; Bhatia, V. A low-complexity hybrid algorithm based on particle swarm and ant colony optimization for large-MIMO detection. *Expert. Syst. Appl.* **2016**, *50*, 66–74. [CrossRef]
57. Prakash, J.; Singh, P.K.; Kishor, A. Integrating fitness predator optimizer with multi-objective PSO for dynamic partitional clustering. *Prog. Artif. Intell.* **2018**, *7*, 1–17. [CrossRef]
58. Marinakis, Y. An improved particle swarm optimization algorithm for the capacitated location routing problem and for the location routing problem with stochastic demands. *Appl. Soft. Comput.* **2015**, *37*, 680–701. [CrossRef]
59. Gan, L.; Wang, L.; Hu, L. Gathered Village Location Optimization for Chinese Sustainable Urbanization Using an Integrated MODM Approach under Bi-Uncertain Environment. *Sustain.* **2017**, *9*, 1907. [CrossRef]

60. Zhang, R.; Chang, P.C.; Song, S.; Wu, C. Local search enhanced multi-objective PSO algorithm for scheduling textile production processes with environmental considerations. *Appl. Soft. Comput.* **2017**, *61*, 447–467. [CrossRef]
61. Karayalcin, I.I. The analytic hierarchy process: Planning, priority setting, resource allocation. *Eur. J. Oper. Res.* **1982**, *9*, 97–98. [CrossRef]

© 2018 by the authors. Licensee MDPI, Basel, Switzerland. This article is an open access article distributed under the terms and conditions of the Creative Commons Attribution (CC BY) license (http://creativecommons.org/licenses/by/4.0/).

Article

Evaluation of Cleaner Production for Gold Mines Employing a Hybrid Multi-Criteria Decision Making Approach

Weizhang Liang [1], Suizhi Luo [2] and Guoyan Zhao [1,*]

1 School of Resources and Safety Engineering, Central South University, Changsha 410083, China; wzlian@csu.edu.cn
2 School of Systems Engineering, National University of Defense Technology, Changsha 410073, China; szlluo@csu.edu.cn
* Correspondence: gyzhao@csu.edu.cn

Received: 14 November 2018; Accepted: 22 December 2018; Published: 28 December 2018

Abstract: Implementing cleaner production (CP) is effective to resolve the contradiction between economic growth and environmental crisis. To avoid destroying the ecological environment in the exploitation process of mineral resources, CP has been developed in many gold mines to achieve the goal of sustainable development. Thus, this paper aims to propose a favorable approach to assess CP for gold mines. First, according to the specific characteristics of gold mines, an evaluation criteria system of CP is established. Meanwhile, considering the diversity of evaluation information, crisp numbers and probabilistic linguistic term sets (PLTSs) are adopted to indicate the quantitative and qualitative information, respectively. Subsequently, a modified experts grading method based on PLTSs is proposed to calculate the sub-criteria weights' values. Following this, an extended Tomada de Decisão Interativa Multicritério (TODIM) method with hybrid evaluation values is presented to obtain the ranking order. Finally, the hybrid multi-criteria decision making (MCDM) approach is applied to a case of assessing CP for gold mines to demonstrate its feasibility. Furthermore, the robustness and advantages of this approach are justified by sensitivity and comparison analyses. The results show that the proposed approach is feasible to solve such kinds of evaluation problems with hybrid decision making information and can provide some managerial suggestions for government and enterprises.

Keywords: cleaner production (CP); extended Tomada de Decisão Interativa Multicritério (TODIM); probabilistic linguistic term sets (PLTSs); hybrid multi-criteria decision making (MCDM); gold mines

1. Introduction

Gold, as an important strategic mineral, is not only a special currency for reserves and investment, but also an essential material for jewelry, electronics, communications, and other industries [1]. However, considerable environmental problems occur as a result of the large-scale mining of gold ore [2,3]. Because of the particularity of gold ore, the component of gold is very low. In general, one ton of ore only contains a few grams of gold. Thus, in comparison with other types of ores, more waste residue may be produced during the gold mine's lifetime [4–6]. As the gold ore is mined by the drilling and blasting method, quantities of waste gas [7,8], such as dust and blasting fumes, are emitted into the sky. Besides, most of the gold is extracted using fluoride, which leads to the discharge of a huge amount of waste water [9–11]. Numerous toxic and harmful substances are contained in this waste, which do great harm to the surrounding environment. In addition, as the traditional linear production model is still employed in many gold mines, the resource utilization efficiency in these mines is quite low [12].

Unlike the traditional production mode that achieves economic growth at the expense of environmental disruption, cleaner production (CP) is an innovative production approach. It applies an integrated preventative environmental strategy to processes, products, and services, so as to increase resource efficiency and reduce environmental pollution [13–15]. On account of the great issues of resources scarcity and environmental crisis, CP is essential for mines. Hilson and Nayee [16] defined CP in the mining sector as a superior level of environmental performance, which can only be achieved through improved strategy and housekeeping, sound process control, optimized plant layout, and the implementation of efficient management techniques. Song and Zhou [17] put forward a mining CP system, which is composed of a training system, lifecycle CP system, and monitoring and auditing system. Hilson [18] suggested that CP practices in the mining industry can be classified into three kinds, that is, managerial changes, policy changes, and physical changes. Rajaram et al. [19] deemed that sustainable mining is conducted in a manner that balances economic, environmental, and social considerations. The application of CP can help enterprises improve economic efficiency under the prerequisite of environmental protection [20–22]. Owing to the huge advantages of industrial pollution prevention, more and more mine enterprises prefer to adopt the novel CP pattern instead of the traditional one.

In order to assess the specific performance of CP for different enterprises, it is significant to develop appropriate and efficient evaluation methods [23]. Considering the variety of criteria, many researchers think that the evaluation of CP is a multi-criteria decision making (MCDM) problem. Tseng et al. [24] adopted the fuzzy analytic hierarchy process (AHP) method to discuss the different criteria for CP implementation in printed wire board manufacturing companies. Peng and Li [25] presented a fuzzy-soft comprehensive evaluation model to evaluate CP for aviation enterprises. Basappaji and Nagesha [26] proposed a fuzzy logic approach to assess the CP level for agro-based industries. Gong et al. [27] employed the evidential reasoning (ER) and data envelopment analysis (DEA) cross-efficiency approach to evaluate CP for iron and steel firms. Dong et al. [28] combined the AHP method and uncertainty measurement model to evaluate the CP for phosphorus chemical enterprises. Liang et al. [29] integrated the evaluation based on distance from average solution (EDAS) method with elimination and choice translating reality (ELECTRE) approach to evaluate the CP for gold mines.

Although the above methods can be well used to solve the CP evaluation problems to a certain extent, there are still some limitations:

(1) The formats of criteria values only include crisp numbers or fuzzy numbers, which cannot describe evaluation information thoroughly. In general, both quantitative and qualitative information is contained in the evaluation process of CP. Hence, they should be expressed respectively using different types of data.

(2) Likewise, these above-mentioned evaluation methods cannot handle the MCDM issues with multiple types of assessment values. As more than one type of evaluation value, like crisp numbers, triangular fuzzy numbers, or linguistic variables, may exist in the evaluation process, hybrid MCDM methods need to be proposed.

On account of the aforementioned deficiencies of existing approaches, a novel evaluation method of CP for gold mines can be proposed. In order to conquer limitation (1), hybrid types of data can be adopted to describe evaluation information. In the real world, quantitative evaluation information can be indicated by crisp numbers, and qualitative information is often described by linguistic phrases from experts, such as bad, good, and very good [30–32]. So far, numerous linguistic extensions have been developed, such as hesitant fuzzy linguistic term sets [33], linguistic intuitionistic fuzzy sets [34], and linguistic neutrosophic sets [35]. Recently, Pang et al. [36] put forward the novel concept of PLTSs (probabilistic linguistic term sets), based on extended hesitant fuzzy linguistic term sets with probability information. Evaluation information in the form of PLTSs simultaneously contains linguistic terms and probabilistic values. By using PLTSs, the original linguistic information can be comprehensively described.

For the sake of overcoming limitation (2), a MCDM method extended by crisp numbers and PLTSs can be proposed to deal with hybrid decision making problems. Up to now, numerous extended decision-making methods based on PLTSs have been proposed one after another, like the extended technique for order preference by similarity to an ideal solution (TOPSIS) [37], vlsekriterijumska optimizacija i kompromisno resenje (VIKOR) [38], the cloud model [39] and the linear programming method [40]. Nevertheless, the Tomada de Decisão Interativa Multicritério (TODIM) method has not been combined with PLTSs. As a classical decision making method, the TODIM method presented by Gomes and Lima [41] has been successfully employed to handle a variety of evaluation issues [42–44]. On the other hand, the types of data in these methods are only PLTSs, as opposed to hybrid decision making information. Accordingly, considering the diversity of criteria, an extended TODIM method based on crisp numbers and PLTSs can be proposed to assess the CP for gold mines.

Because the influence factors and conditions of different industries are various, these existing methods are not appropriate to assess CP for gold mines. To the best of our knowledge, the research on CP evaluation for gold mines is very scarce, the evaluation system of CP should be established after considering the specific features of gold mines.

Based on the motivations mentioned above, the objective of this paper is to propose a hybrid MCDM approach for assessing CP for gold mines. The main contributions of this paper are listed as follows:

(1) The evaluation criteria of CP for gold mines are identified, and the evaluation information is processed into two types of data. The precise values for quantitative criteria are expressed by crisp numbers, and the linguistic values for qualitative criteria are indicated by PLTSs, so that the evaluation information can be described more adequately.

(2) The modified experts grading method with PLTSs is proposed to obtain the criteria weights. The linguistic evaluation terms given by experts are expressed with PLTSs as opposed to scores or specific values, which can demonstrate the original linguistic information more fully and reasonably.

(3) A hybrid MCDM approach on the basis of an extended TODIM method is proposed to assess CP for gold mines, which can obtain stable and reliable evaluation results. Besides, these evaluation results can provide some managerial implications for government and enterprises.

For clarity, the rest of this paper is organized as follows. Section 2 introduces the evaluation criteria of CP for gold mines and some basic knowledge about PLTSs. In Section 3, three phases of the proposed hybrid MCDM approach are presented. In Section 4, the proposed approach is applied in assessing CP for gold mines. The sensitivity analysis, comparison analysis, and managerial implications are discussed in Section 5. Finally, some main conclusions are presented.

2. Materials and Methods

In this section, the evaluation criteria system of CP for gold mines is first established. Then, some basic concepts of PLTSs are introduced. These mentioned materials and methods will be useful in the remainder of this research.

2.1. Evaluation Criteria of Cleaner Production for Gold Mines

In this subsection, the evaluation criteria of CP for gold mines are recognized. However, there has not been an international standard for the evaluation of CP in gold mines so far. In order to select the appropriate criteria, some principles should be followed, which include the hierarchy principle, independence principle, combination of qualitative and quantitative criteria principle, and data with easy accessibility principle [45]. According to the specific characteristics of CP for gold mines and some existing literature [28,46,47], the evaluation criteria system is established with seven criteria and sixteen sub-criteria. The evaluation criteria system of CP for gold mines is shown in Figure 1, and the detailed descriptions of these criteria are indicated as follows.

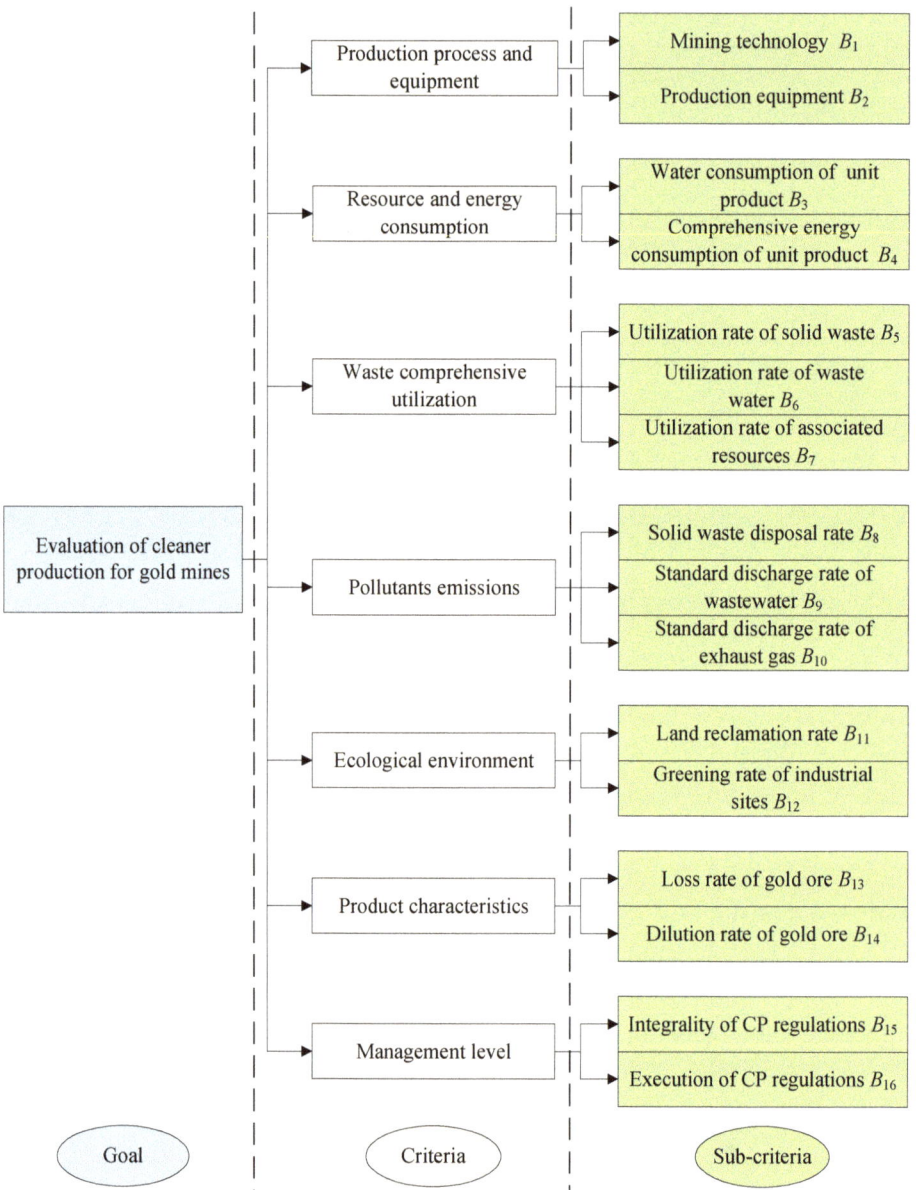

Figure 1. Evaluation criteria system of cleaner production (CP) for gold mines.

(1) Production process and equipment

Selecting the appropriate production process and equipment is a key problem for CP in gold mines. In general, the more advanced the production process and equipment, the better the performance of CP [46]. Therefore, the sub-criteria of production process and equipment contain the mining technology B_1 and production equipment B_2.

(2) Resource and energy consumption

Resource and energy are essential for the production of gold mines. During the production process, achieving the same production goals with less resources and energy is vital and encouraging. This way, the resource and energy can be utilized with higher efficiency. Besides, water, power, and fuel are main consumables in the mining process [28]. Hence, the sub-criteria of resource and energy consumption contain the water consumption of unit product B_3 and comprehensive energy consumption of unit product B_4.

(3) Waste utilization

The waste produced in gold mines is also a valuable resource, which is worth developing and utilizing. In particular, the solid waste, waste water, and associated resources are of great value, and can be utilized and recycled [48]. Accordingly, the sub-criteria of waste utilization contain the utilization rate of solid waste B_5, utilization rate of waste water B_6, and utilization rate of associated resources B_7.

(4) Pollutants emissions

Although the waste can be utilized in the whole production cycle to some extent, there is still some waste released into the environment. Among them, solid waste, waste water, and exhaust gas play important roles, which lead to environmental pollution [28]. Consequently, the sub-criteria of pollutants emissions contain the solid waste disposal rate B_8, standard discharge rate of wastewater B_9, and standard discharge rate of exhaust gas B_{10}.

(5) Ecological environment

The development of gold mines may inevitably have some adverse effects on the environment [49]. On the one hand, large tracts of land are occupied by quantities of tailings and waste stone, and the surrounding ecological environment is seriously destructed. On the other hand, the surface environment of mining area is greatly damaged because of the strata subsidence and mining disturbance. Thus, the sub-criteria of ecological environments contain the land reclamation rate B_{11} and greening rate of industrial sites B_{12}.

(6) Product characteristics

Improving product characteristics is essential for CP. The product of gold mines is mainly gold ore, and the characteristics of gold ore have great influences on the downstream productions [46]. The loss rate and dilution rate are the two important characteristics of gold ore. As a result, the sub-criteria of product characteristics contain the loss rate of gold ore B_{13} and dilution rate of gold ore B_{14}.

(7) Management level

The management level makes a dramatic impact on the performance of CP for gold mines. The establishment and implementation of corresponding regulations are important for improving CP level [16]. Thus, the sub-criteria of management level contain the integrality of CP regulations B_{15} and execution of CP regulations B_{16}.

2.2. Probabilistic Linguistic Term Sets

In this subsection, some relevant concepts of PLTSs are described as follows.

(1) The definition of linguistic term set (LTS)

Suppose there is a completely ordered and discrete LTS, denoted as $P = \{p_i | i = -m, \cdots, -1, 0, 1, \cdots, m\}$, then any element p_i in this set is a linguistic variable. For any two linguistic terms $p_a, p_b \in P$, if $a > b$, then $p_a > p_b$. Besides, the negation operator is defined as $neg(p_a) = p_{-a}$ [50].

For example, if there are the following five linguistic variables: "p_{-2} = very poor", "p_{-1} = poor", "p_0 = fair", "p_1 = good" and "p_2 = very good", then they can consist of a LTS as $P = \{p_{-2} = very\ poor, p_{-1} = poor, p_0 = fair, p_1 = good, p_2 = very\ good\}$, their preference relation is $p_2 > p_1 > p_0 > p_{-1} > p_{-2}$. Furthermore, $neg(p_{-2}) = p_2, neg(p_{-1}) = p_1, neg(p_0) = p_0, neg(p_1) = p_{-1}$, and $neg(p_2) = p_{-2}$.

(2) The definition of linguistic scale function

The linguistic scale function is defined as a mapping from a linguistic variable $p_i(i = -m, \ldots, -1, 0, 1, \ldots, m)$ to a corresponding crisp number $c_i \in [0, 1]$ [51]. Besides, the characteristic of monotonically increasing should be met. Then, the linguistic scale function can be obtained with the following equation [51]:

$$f(p_i) = c_i = \frac{i}{2m} + \frac{1}{2}. \tag{1}$$

Furthermore, the inverse function can be acquired as

$$f^{-1}(c_i) = p_{(2c_i - 1)m} \tag{2}$$

Take p_1 = good as an example, because it is in the LTS $P = \{p_{-2} = very\ poor, p_{-1} = poor, p_0 = fair, p_1 = good, p_2 = very\ good\}$, then $m = 2$. Based on Equation (1), it can map to a crisp number $c_1 = \frac{1}{2 \times 2} + \frac{1}{2} = \frac{3}{4}$. Similarly, if we know $c_i = \frac{3}{4}$, a corresponding linguistic variable $f^{-1}(c_i) = p_{(2 \times \frac{3}{4} - 1) \times 2} = p_1$ can be obtained using Equation (2).

(3) The definition of probabilistic linguistic term set (PLTS)

Given a LTS $P = \{p_i | i = -m, \ldots, -1, 0, 1, \ldots, m\}$, the probabilistic linguistic term set (PLTS) can be denoted as [36]

$$L(s) = \left\{ L^{(j)}(s^{(j)}) | L^{(j)} \in P, s^{(j)} \geq 0, j = 1, 2, \ldots, n, \sum_{j=1}^{n} s^{(j)} \leq 1 \right\} \tag{3}$$

where $L^{(j)}(s^{(j)})$ is the linguistic value $L^{(j)}$ related to the probabilistic information $s^{(j)}$, and is the number of elements in $L(s)$.

For instance, given an LTS $P = \{p_{-2} = very\ poor, p_{-1} = poor, p_0 = fair, p_1 = good, p_2 = very\ good\}$, a PLTS $L = \{p_{-1}(0.2), p_0(0.3), p_1(0.2), p_2(0.1)\}$ represents that, for an objective, the probability of getting an evaluation with "poor" is 20%, that with "fair" is 30%, that with "good" is 20%, and that with "very good" is 10%.

(4) Normalization of PLTS

Given a PLTS $L(s) = \left\{ L^{(j)}(s^{(j)}) | j = 1, 2, \ldots, n \right\}$ with $\sum_{j=1}^{n} s^{(j)} < 1$, the normalized PLTS can be calculated by [36]

$$L^N(s) = \left\{ L^{(j)}\left(\frac{s^{(j)}}{\sum_{j=1}^{n} s^{(j)}} \right) | j = 1, 2, \ldots, n \right\} \tag{4}$$

Take $L = \{p_{-1}(0.2), p_0(0.3), p_1(0.2), p_2(0.1)\}$ as an example, because $\sum_{j=1}^{n} s^{(j)} = 0.2 + 0.3 + 0.2 + 0.1 = 0.8 < 1$ using Equation (4), it can be normalized as $L^N = \left\{ p_{-1}(\frac{0.2}{0.8}), p_0(\frac{0.3}{0.8}), p_1(\frac{0.2}{0.8}), p_2(\frac{0.1}{0.8}) \right\} = \{p_{-1}(0.25), p_0(0.375), p_1(0.25), p_2(0.125)\}$

(5) The operational rules between two PLTSs

Let $L_1(s) = \left\{ L_1^{(j_1)}(s_1^{(j_1)}) | j_1 = 1, 2, \ldots, n_1 \right\}$ and $L_2(s) = \left\{ L_2^{(j_2)}(s_2^{(j_2)}) | j_2 = 1, 2, \ldots, n_2 \right\}$ be two PLTSs, and let λ be a positive real number, then the operational rules are defined as [52]

$$L_1(s) \oplus L_2(s) = f^{-1}\left(\cup_{\phi_1^{(j_1)} \in f(L_1), \phi_2^{(j_2)} \in f(L_2)} \{(\phi_1^{(j_1)} + \phi_2^{(j_2)} - \phi_1^{(j_1)} \phi_2^{(j_2)})(s_1^{(j_1)} s_2^{(j_2)})\} \right) \tag{5}$$

$$L_1(s) \otimes L_2(s) = f^{-1}\left(\cup_{\phi_1^{(j_1)} \in f(L_1), \phi_2^{(j_2)} \in f(L_2)} \{(\phi_1^{(j_1)} \phi_2^{(j_2)})(s_1^{(j_1)} s_2^{(j_2)})\} \right) \tag{6}$$

$$\lambda L_1(s) = f^{-1}\left(\cup_{\phi_1^{(j_1)} \in f(L_1)} \{(1 - (1 - \phi_1^{(j_1)})^\lambda)(s_1^{(j_1)})\} \right) \tag{7}$$

$$\overline{L}_1(s) = f^{-1}\left(\cup_{\phi_1^{(j_1)} \in f(L_1)} \{(1 - \phi_1^{(j_1)})(s_1^{(j_1)})\} \right) \tag{8}$$

$$L_1(s) \ominus L_2(s) = f^{-1}\left(\cup_{\phi_1^{(j_1)} \in f(L_1), \phi_2^{(j_2)} \in f(L_2)} \{\Pi(s_1^{(j_1)} s_2^{(j_2)})\} \right) \tag{9}$$

where $\Pi = \begin{cases} \frac{\phi_1^{(j_1)} - \phi_2^{(j_2)}}{1 - \phi_2^{(j_2)}}, & \text{if } \phi_1^{(j_1)} \geq \phi_2^{(j_2)} \text{ and } \phi_2^{(j_2)} \neq 1 \\ 0, & \text{otherwise} \end{cases}$

$$L_1(s) \oslash L_2(s) = f^{-1}\left(\cup_{\phi_1^{(j_1)} \in f(L_1), \phi_2^{(j_2)} \in f(L_2)} \{\Pi(s_1^{(j_1)} s_2^{(j_2)})\}\right) \quad (10)$$

where $\Pi = \begin{cases} \frac{\phi_1^{(j_1)}}{\phi_2^{(j_2)}}, & \text{if } \phi_1^{(j_1)} \leq \phi_2^{(j_2)} \text{ and } \phi_2^{(j_2)} \neq 0 \\ 1, & \text{otherwise} \end{cases}$.

For example, suppose $L_1(s) = \{p_{-1}(0.3), p_1(0.7)\}$, $L_2(s) = \{p_0(0.4), p_2(0.6)\}$, $\lambda = 2$, and $m = 2$, then $L_1(s) \oplus L_2(s) = \{p_{0.5}(0.12), p_{1.5}(0.28), p_2(0.6)\}$, $L_1(s) \otimes L_2(s) = \{p_{-1.5}(0.12), p_{-1}(0.18), p_{-0.5}(0.28), p_1(0.42)\}$, $\lambda L_1(s) = 2 \times L_1(s) = \{p_{0.5}(0.3), p_{1.75}(0.7)\}$, $\overline{L}_1(s) = \{p_{-1}(0.7), p_1(0.3)\}$, $L_1(s) \ominus L_2(s) = \{p_0(0.72), p_{0.5}(0.28)\}$, and $L_1(s) \oslash L_2(s) = \{p_{-1}(0.18), p_0(0.12), p_1(0.42), p_2(0.28)\}$.

(6) The distance between two PLTSs

Considering two arbitrary normalized PLTSs $L_1(s) = \{L_1^{(j)}(s_1^{(j)}) | j = 1, 2, \ldots, n_1\}$ and $L_2(s) = \{L_2^{(j)}(s_2^{(j)}) | j = 1, 2, \ldots, n_2\}$, if $n_1 = n_2$, the distance between them is defined by [36]

$$d(L_1(s), L_2(s)) = \sqrt{\sum_{j=1}^{n} \left(s_1^{(j)} r_1^{(j)} - s_2^{(j)} r_2^{(j)}\right)^2 / n_1} \quad (11)$$

where $r_1^{(j)}$ and $r_2^{(j)}$ are the subscripts of the linguistic terms $L_1^{(j)}$ and $L_2^{(j)}$, respectively.

However, if $n_1 > n_2$, $n_1 - n_2$ linguistic terms are added to $L_2(s)$, so that the numbers of linguistic terms in $L_1(s)$ and $L_2(s)$ are equal. The added linguistic terms are the smallest ones in $L_2(s)$, and the probabilities of all the linguistic terms are zero. Then, the distance between $L_1(s)$ and $L_2(s)$ can be calculated using Equation (11).

For instance, assume $L_1(s) = \{p_{-1}(0.3), p_1(0.7)\}$ and $L_2(s) = \{p_0(0.4), p_2(0.6)\}$, then $d(L_1(s), L_2(s)) \approx 0.424$.

(7) The comparison method between two PLTSs

Given a PLTS $L(s) = \{L^{(j)}(s^{(j)}) | j = 1, 2, \ldots, n\}$, the score function and deviation degree of $L(s)$ can be obtained, respectively, as [41]

$$\eta(L(s)) = \frac{1}{\sum_{j=1}^{n} s^{(j)}} \sum_{j=1}^{n} s^{(j)} L^{(j)} \quad (12)$$

$$\delta(L(s)) = \left(\sum_{j=1}^{n} (s^{(j)}(r^{(j)} - \frac{\sum_{j=1}^{n} s^{(j)} r^{(j)}}{\sum_{j=1}^{n} s^{(j)}}))^2\right)^{\frac{1}{2}} / \sum_{j=1}^{n} s^{(j)} \quad (13)$$

Then, the comparison method between two PLTSs $L_1(s) = \{L_1^{(j_1)}(s_1^{(j_1)}) | j_1 = 1, 2, \ldots, n_1\}$ and $L_2(s) = \{L_2^{(j_2)}(s_2^{(j_2)}) | j_2 = 1, 2, \ldots, n_2\}$ can be obtained by [36]

$L_1(s) \prec L_2(s)$, when $\eta(L_1(s)) < \eta(L_2(s))$ or $(\eta(L_1(s)) = \eta(L_2(s)), \delta(L_1(s)) > \delta(L_2(s)))$;
$L_1(s) \succ L_2(s)$, when $\eta(L_1(s)) > \eta(L_2(s))$ or $(\eta(L_1(s)) = \eta(L_2(s)), \delta(L_1(s)) < \delta(L_2(s)))$; and
$L_1(s) \approx L_2(s)$, when $\eta(L_1(s)) = \eta(L_2(s))$ and $\delta(L_1(s)) = \delta(L_2(s))$.

For example, given two PLTSs $L_1(s) = \{p_{-1}(0.3), p_1(0.7)\}$ and $L_2(s) = \{p_0(0.4), p_2(0.6)\}$, then $\eta(L_1(s)) = 0.4$, $\eta(L_2(s)) = 1.2$, $\delta(L_1(s)) \approx 0.917$, and $\delta(L_2(s)) \approx 0.980$. Because $\eta(L_1(s)) < \eta(L_2(s))$, then $L_1(s) \prec L_2(s)$.

3. Hybrid Multi-Criteria Decision Making Approach

A hybrid MCDM approach is proposed to evaluate the performance of CP in this section. The structure of this method is shown in Figure 2. It can be seen that this approach includes three phases: collect evaluation information, calculate the sub-criteria weights, and determine the ranking order. The specific steps are presented in the rest of this section.

Phase I: Collect hybrid evaluation information

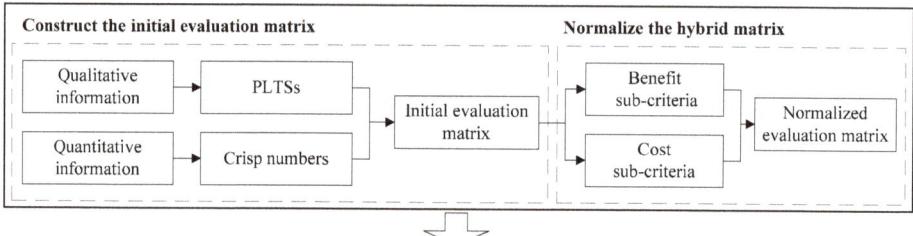

Phase II: Calculate of the criteria weights based on PLTSs

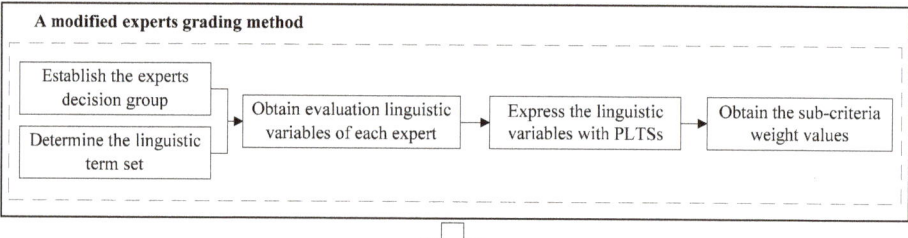

Phase III: Determine the ranking order based on extended TODIM

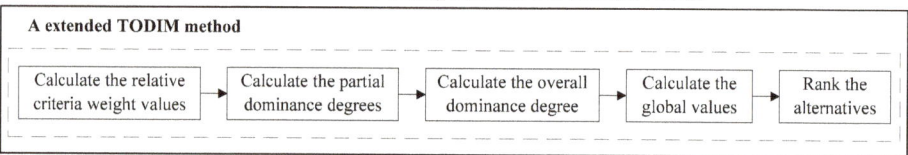

Figure 2. Structure of the proposed hybrid multi-criteria decision making (MCDM) approach. PLTS—probabilistic linguistic term set; TODIM—Tomada de Decisão Interativa Multicritério.

3.1. Phase I: Collect Hybrid Evaluation Information

In Phase I, the evaluation information is collected, and the normalized hybrid decision matrix is obtained. In this research, crisp numbers and PLTSs are adopted to indicate certain and uncertain evaluation information, respectively. Thus, the initial evaluation information can be expressed by crisp numbers and PLTSs, respectively. The calculation steps are displayed as follows.

Step 1: Construct the initial evaluation matrix

Generally, the evaluation information is composed of quantitative information expressed by crisp numbers and qualitative information denoted by linguistic variables. Considering that PLTSs can indicate the original linguistic information intuitively and comprehensively, they are employed to describe the qualitative information.

Considering that experts are accustomed to making qualitative evaluations with linguistic phrases, such as "poor", "fair", "good", and "very good" [37], the LTS can be expressed as $P_\alpha = \{p_{-3} = very\ poor, p_{-2} = poor, p_{-1} = slightly\ poor, p_0 = fair, p_1 = slightly\ good, p_2 = good, p_3 = very\ good\}$. For group decision making methods, this qualitative evaluation information from experts can be combined by PLTSs. For example, ten experts are invited to make evaluations.

If two experts consider that the value of criterion B_1 for alternative A_1 is slightly poor, three experts consider that it is fair, two experts consider that it is slightly good, one expert considers that it is good, and the remainder refuses to make a choice, then the comprehensive evaluation value of these ten experts can be expressed with a PLTS $\{p_{-1}(0.2), p_0(0.3), p_1(0.2), p_2(0.1)\}$.

Consequently, in order to express quantitative and qualitative information simultaneously, crisp numbers and PLTSs are contained in the initial evaluation matrix, which is shown as

$$Z = \begin{bmatrix} z_{11} & z_{12} & \cdots & z_{1h} & z^*_{1,h+1} & \cdots & z^*_{1,F} \\ z_{21} & z_{22} & \cdots & z_{2h} & z^*_{2,h+1} & \cdots & z^*_{2,F} \\ \vdots & \vdots & \ddots & \vdots & \vdots & \ddots & \vdots \\ z_{E1} & z_{E2} & \cdots & z_{Eh} & z^*_{E,h+1} & \cdots & z^*_{E,F} \end{bmatrix}, \quad (14)$$

where z_{ef} is a crisp number, which represents the objective evaluation value of alternative A_e ($e = 1, 2, \cdots, E$) for criterion B_f ($f = 1, 2, \cdots, h$); and $z^*_{e,f}$ is a PLTS, which demonstrates the fuzzy evaluation value of alternative A_e ($e = 1, 2, \cdots, E$) for criterion B_f ($f = h+1, h+2, \cdots, F$).

Step 2: Normalize the hybrid matrix

In general, both benefit and cost sub-criteria are included in the evaluation criteria system. In order to make the calculation convenient, the initial decision matrix should be normalized to make the type of all sub-criteria uniform.

For crisp numbers, the normalization values can be calculated by [48]

$$\bar{z}_{ef} = \begin{cases} \dfrac{z_{ef} - \min\limits_{f}(z_{ef})}{\max\limits_{f}(z_{ef}) - \min\limits_{f}(z_{ef})} & \text{for benefit criteria} \\[2ex] \dfrac{\max\limits_{f}(z_{ef}) - z_{ef}}{\max\limits_{f}(z_{ef}) - \min\limits_{f}(z_{ef})} & \text{for cost criteria} \end{cases} \quad (15)$$

For PLTSs, the normalization values can be calculated by Equation (4). Besides, for PLTSs under cost sub-criteria, the evaluation values need to be changed according to Equation (8). Afterwards, the normalized evaluation matrix can be obtained as

$$\bar{Z} = \begin{bmatrix} \bar{z}_{11} & \bar{z}_{12} & \cdots & \bar{z}_{1h} & \bar{z}^*_{1,h+1} & \cdots & \bar{z}^*_{1,F} \\ \bar{z}_{21} & \bar{z}_{22} & \cdots & \bar{z}_{2h} & \bar{z}^*_{2,h+1} & \cdots & \bar{z}^*_{2,F} \\ \vdots & \vdots & \ddots & \vdots & \vdots & \ddots & \vdots \\ \bar{z}_{E1} & \bar{z}_{E2} & \cdots & \bar{z}_{Eh} & \bar{z}^*_{E,h+1} & \cdots & \bar{z}^*_{E,F} \end{bmatrix} \quad (16)$$

3.2. Phase II: Calculate the Criteria Weights based on PLTSs

The aim of Phase II is to calculate the weight value of each criterion based on a modified experts grading method. In reality, experts are inclined to express the importance degrees of sub-criteria using linguistic phrases, such as "low", "high", and "very high". However, these linguistic phrases are all expressed by scores in the traditional experts grading method, which cannot easily describe the initial evaluation information substantially. To improve the reasonability of decision making results, a modified experts grading method with PLTSs is proposed as follows.

Step 1: Determine the LTS

Generally, the linguistic terms used by experts to express the importance of sub-criteria are very low, low, slightly low, medium, slightly high, high, and very high, respectively [42]. Then, the LTS can be expressed as $P_\alpha = \{p_{-3} = \text{very low}, p_{-2} = \text{low}, p_{-1} = \text{slightly low}, p_0 = \text{medium}, p_1 = \text{slightly high}, p_2 = \text{high}, p_3 = \text{very high}\}$.

Step 2: Express the linguistic variables with PLTSs

After the LTS is determined, experts can provide their assessments on the importance of the sub-criteria individually and anonymously. Then, the linguistic variables provided by all experts can be processed and converted to PLTSs. For example, the PLTS $\{p_1(0.3), p_2(0.2), p_3(0.5)\}$ means that 30% of experts think the importance of this criterion is slightly high, 20% of experts believe that it is high, and 50% of experts hold that it is very high.

Step 3: Obtain the sub-criteria weight values

The score function of PLTSs $\eta(L(s))_f$ for each criterion can be calculated by Equation (12). Then, the weight values can be obtained by

$$w_f = \frac{r_f}{\sum_f^F r_f} \tag{17}$$

where r_f is the subscript of linguistic term $\eta(L(s))_f$.

3.3. Phase III: Determine the Ranking Order Based on Extended TODIM

In this phase, an extended TODIM method with hybrid evaluation values is proposed to determine the rank order of alternatives. The calculation steps are as follows.

Step 1: Calculate the relative sub-criteria weight values

First, the criterion with the highest weight value could be chosen as a reference criterion, denoted as q. Then, the relative sub-criteria weight value w_{qf} of criterion B_f to the reference criterion B_q is

$$w_{qf} = w_f / w_q \tag{18}$$

Step 2: Calculate the partial dominance degrees under sub-criteria

The partial dominance matrix $\phi_f(A_e, A_g)$ indicates the degree of alternative A_e ($e = 1, 2, \cdots, E$) superior to alternative A_g ($g = 1, 2, \cdots, E$) under criterion B_f. As the evaluation matrix is composed of crisp numbers and PLTSs, the partial dominance matrix can be calculated.

For crisp numbers, the partial dominance degree is calculated by

$$\phi_f(A_e, A_g) = \begin{cases} \sqrt{\dfrac{w_{qf}}{\sum_{f=1}^{F} w_{qf}} \times d(\bar{z}_{ef}, \bar{z}_{gf})} & \bar{z}_{ef} > \bar{z}_{gf} \\ 0 & \bar{z}_{ef} = \bar{z}_{gf} \\ \dfrac{-1}{\theta}\sqrt{\dfrac{\sum_{f=1}^{F} w_{qf}}{w_{qf}} \times d(\bar{z}_{ef}, \bar{z}_{gf})} & \bar{z}_{ef} < \bar{z}_{gf} \end{cases} \tag{19}$$

where $\theta \in (0, +\infty)$ means the attenuation factor of the losses; and $d(\bar{z}_{ef}, \bar{z}_{gf})$ indicates the distance between $\bar{z}_{ef}$ and $\bar{z}_{gf}$, that is, $d(\bar{z}_{ef}, \bar{z}_{gf}) = \bar{z}_{ef} - \bar{z}_{gf}$.

For PLTSs, the partial dominance degree is obtained with

$$\phi_f(A_e, A_g) = \begin{cases} \sqrt{\dfrac{w_{qf}}{\sum_{f=1}^{F} w_{qf}} \times d(\bar{z}^*_{e,f}, \bar{z}^*_{g,f})} & \bar{z}^*_{e,f} > \bar{z}^*_{g,f} \\ 0 & \bar{z}^*_{e,f} = \bar{z}^*_{g,f} \\ \dfrac{-1}{\theta}\sqrt{\dfrac{\sum_{f=1}^{F} w_{qf}}{w_{qf}} \times d(\bar{z}^*_{e,f}, \bar{z}^*_{g,f})} & \bar{z}^*_{e,f} < \bar{z}^*_{g,f} \end{cases} \tag{20}$$

where $d(\bar{z}^*_{e,f}, \bar{z}^*_{g,f})$ indicates the distance between $\bar{z}^*_{e,f}$ and $\bar{z}^*_{g,f}$, which can be obtained by Equation (11).

Step 3: Calculate the overall dominance degree for each alternative

The dominance matrix of alternative A_e over A_g is calculated by summing up the partial dominance matrices of all sub-criteria, which can be calculated as follows:

$$\delta(A_e, A_g) = \sum_{f=1}^{F} \phi_f(A_e, A_g) \quad (21)$$

Step 4: Calculate the global values of alternatives

The global value of a certain alternative is determined by normalizing the dominance matrix, and the normalization equation is

$$V_e = \frac{\sum_{g=1}^{E} \delta(A_e, A_g) - \min \sum_{g=1}^{E} \delta(A_e, A_g)}{\max \sum_{g=1}^{E} \delta(A_e, A_g) - \min \sum_{g=1}^{E} \delta(A_e, A_g)} \quad (22)$$

Step 5: Rank the alternatives

After the value of V_e is determined, the rank of each alternative can be obtained by ordering the values of V_e. The higher the V_e value, the better the alternative.

4. Case Study

Recently, a gold production corporation in China had a plan for evaluating the performance of CP for its gold mines. After a preliminary analysis and screening, four gold mines (denoted as A_1, A_2, A_3, and A_4) were selected to be evaluated beforehand. If the evaluation results were acceptable, then the proposed method could be adopted and expanded to assess all gold mines. The development patterns of these four gold mines have a great difference, A_1 focuses on the comprehensive utilization of waste, A_2 focuses on the land reclamation, A_3 focuses on reducing the resource and energy consumption and diminishing the pollutants emission rate, and A_4 focuses on the green of industrial sites. Among them, A_3 can better enhance the utilization efficiency of gold resources and reduce environmental pollution, representing a favorable performance of CP. The specific calculation steps for assessing CP for these four gold mines are demonstrated as follows.

In Phase I, the initial sub-criteria values are obtained on the basis of on-site measurement and investigations. Particularly, as for the qualitative indicators, such as sub-criteria B_1, B_2, B_{15}, and B_{16}, a decision making team, contained by ten relevant decision makers (DMs), is invited to make evaluations under LTS P_α. These DMs need to satisfy two conditions before being selected. One is that they should have abundant work experience in the gold mining industry. Another is that they should have rich knowledge through involvement in the management of CP construction projects in mines. The concrete characteristics of the selected experts are illustrated in Table 1. Each decision maker provides their linguistic evaluations under each qualitative criterion. Thereafter, the voting results of DMs are transformed into PLTSs, as shown in Table 2.

Considering that the dimensions, types, and units of sub-criteria are various, the initial evaluation matrix must be normalized. According to Equations (8) and (15), the normalized decision making matrix is determined, as shown in Table 3.

In Phase II, the weight vector of sub-criteria is obtained based on the modified experts grading method. First, the linguistic evaluation information of sub-criteria is given by five DMs under LTS P_β, as shown in Table 4. Then, the score function value of PLTSs $\eta(L(s))_f$ for each sub-criterion is calculated based on Equation (12) (see the eighth column in Table 4). Finally, the weight vector is obtained by Equation (17), and the calculation result is demonstrated in the last column of Table 4.

Table 1. Characteristics of decision makers (DMs).

DMs	Education	Positional Titles	Employment Position	Working Years
D_1	M.S.	Senior Engineer	Mine manager	21
D_2	M.S.	Senior Engineer	Deputy mine manager	18
D_3	M.S.	Senior Engineer	Engineering technologist	19
D_4	Ph.D.	Engineer	Deputy mine manager	23
D_5	Ph.D.	Engineer	Engineering technologist	22
D_6	Ph.D.	Engineer	Senior adviser	30
D_7	Ph.D.	Senior Engineer	Mine manager	25
D_8	Ph.D.	Senior Engineer	Mine manager	33
D_9	Ph.D.	Senior Engineer	Deputy mine manager	29
D_{10}	Ph.D.	Senior Engineer	Senior adviser	35

Table 2. Initial hybrid evaluation matrix.

	A_1	A_2	A_3	A_4
B_1	$\{p_0(0.2), p_1(0.4), p_2(0.4)\}$	$\{p_1(0.4), p_2(0.4), p_3(0.2)\}$	$\{p_1(0.4), p_2(0.6)\}$	$\{p_{-1}(0.1), p_1(0.6), p_2(0.3)\}$
B_2	$\{p_1(0.7), p_2(0.3)\}$	$\{p_0(0.2), p_1(0.6), p_2(0.2)\}$	$\{p_{-1}(0.1), p_1(0.5), p_2(0.4)\}$	$\{p_1(0.5), p_2(0.5)\}$
B_3 (m³/t)	0.37	0.42	0.29	0.31
B_4 (kgce/t)	3.31	4.54	3.94	5.65
B_5 (%)	76	69	73	65
B_6 (%)	71	58	84	67
B_7 (%)	28	21	36	27
B_8 (%)	100	91	100	96
B_9 (%)	92	85	94	100
B_{10} (%)	73	93	90	80
B_{11} (%)	86	92	77	82
B_{12} (%)	74	89	86	93
B_{13} (%)	21	19	12	18
B_{14} (%)	13	19	17	15
B_{15}	$\{p_1(0.3), p_2(0.3), p_3(0.4)\}$	$\{p_1(0.6), p_2(0.4)\}$	$\{p_0(0.4), p_1(0.3), p_2(0.3)\}$	$\{p_2(0.7), p_3(0.3)\}$
B_{16}	$\{p_1(0.3), p_2(0.7)\}$	$\{p_1(0.6), p_2(0.3), p_3(0.1)\}$	$\{p_0(0.1), p_2(0.9)\}$	$\{p_{-1}(0.1), p_2(0.6), p_3(0.3)\}$

Table 3. Normalized hybrid evaluation matrix.

	A_1	A_2	A_3	A_4
B_1	$\{p_0(0.2), p_1(0.4), p_2(0.4)\}$	$\{p_1(0.4), p_2(0.4), p_3(0.2)\}$	$\{p_1(0.4), p_2(0.6), p_1(0)\}$	$\{p_{-1}(0.1), p_1(0.6), p_2(0.3)\}$
B_2	$\{p_1(0.7), p_2(0.3), p_1(0)\}$	$\{p_0(0.2), p_1(0.6), p_2(0.2)\}$	$\{p_{-1}(0.1), p_1(0.5), p_2(0.4)\}$	$\{p_1(0.5), p_2(0.5), p_1(0)\}$
B_3 (m³/t)	0.3846	0.0000	1.0000	0.8462
B_4 (kgce/t)	1.0000	0.4744	0.7308	0.0000
B_5 (%)	1.0000	0.3636	0.7273	0.0000
B_6 (%)	0.5000	0.0000	1.0000	0.3462
B_7 (%)	0.4667	0.0000	1.0000	0.4000
B_8 (%)	1.0000	0.0000	1.0000	0.5556
B_9 (%)	0.4667	0.0000	0.6000	1.0000
B_{10} (%)	0.0000	1.0000	0.8500	0.3500
B_{11} (%)	0.6000	1.0000	0.0000	0.3333
B_{12} (%)	0.0000	0.7895	0.6316	1.0000
B_{13} (%)	0.0000	0.6667	1.0000	0.7778
B_{14} (%)	1.0000	0.0000	0.3333	0.6667
B_{15}	$\{p_1(0.3), p_2(0.3), p_3(0.4)\}$	$\{p_1(0.6), p_2(0.4), p_1(0)\}$	$\{p_0(0.4), p_1(0.3), p_2(0.3)\}$	$\{p_2(0.7), p_3(0.3), p_2(0)\}$
B_{16}	$\{p_1(0.3), p_2(0.7), p_1(0)\}$	$\{p_1(0.6), p_2(0.3), p_3(0.1)\}$	$\{p_0(0.1), p_2(0.9), p_0(0)\}$	$\{p_{-1}(0.1), p_2(0.6), p_3(0.3)\}$

Table 4. Linguistic evaluation information of sub-criteria.

	D_1	D_2	D_3	D_4	D_5	$L(s)$	$\eta(L(s))_f$	w_f
B_1	Very high	High	High	High	Very high	$\{p_2(0.6), p_3(0.4)\}$	$p_{2.4}$	0.0774
B_2	High	High	Very high	Very high	Very high	$\{p_2(0.4), p_3(0.6)\}$	$p_{2.6}$	0.0839
B_3	Medium	Slightly high	High	Medium	Slightly high	$\{p_0(0.2), p_1(0.4), p_2(0.2)\}$	$p_{0.8}$	0.0258
B_4	High	Medium	Slightly high	High	Very high	$\{p_0(0.2), p_1(0.2), p_2(0.4), p_3(0.2)\}$	$p_{1.6}$	0.0516
B_5	High	Very high	Very high	High	Slightly high	$\{p_1(0.2), p_2(0.4), p_3(0.4)\}$	$p_{2.2}$	0.0710
B_6	Slightly high	Medium	High	Slightly high	Medium	$\{p_0(0.4), p_1(0.4), p_2(0.2)\}$	$p_{0.8}$	0.0258
B_7	Very high	High	Slightly high	High	Slightly high	$\{p_1(0.4), p_2(0.4), p_3(0.2)\}$	$p_{1.8}$	0.0581
B_8	High	Very high	High	Very high	high	$\{p_2(0.6), p_3(0.4)\}$	$p_{2.4}$	0.0774
B_9	Very high	Very high	high	High	Slightly high	$\{p_2(0.6), p_3(0.4)\}$	$p_{2.4}$	0.0774
B_{10}	Very high	High	Very high	High	High	$\{p_1(0.2), p_2(0.4), p_3(0.4)\}$	$p_{2.2}$	0.0710
B_{11}	Very high	Very high	High	High	Very high	$\{p_2(0.6), p_3(0.4)\}$	$p_{2.4}$	0.0774
B_{12}	High	High	High	High	High	$\{p_2(0.8), p_3(0.2)\}$	$p_{2.2}$	0.0710
B_{13}	Very high	Very high	Slightly high	High	Slightly high	$\{p_1(0.2), p_2(0.4), p_3(0.4)\}$	$p_{2.2}$	0.0710
B_{14}	High	High	Slightly high	Slightly high	High	$\{p_1(0.6), p_2(0.4)\}$	$p_{1.4}$	0.0452
B_{15}	Slightly high	Slightly high	Slightly high	Slightly high	High	$\{p_1(0.8), p_2(0.2)\}$	$p_{1.2}$	0.0387
B_{16}	High	High	Very high	Very high	High	$\{p_2(0.6), p_3(0.4)\}$	$p_{2.4}$	0.0774

In Phase III, the evaluation results of CP for gold mines are obtained with the extended TODIM method. At first, because w_2 is the largest weight value, B_2 is selected as a reference criterion. Then, based on Equation (18), the relative sub-criteria weight values are calculated as follows: $w_{12} = 0.9225$, $w_{22} = 1$, $w_{32} = 0.3075$, $w_{42} = 0.6150$, $w_{52} = 0.8462$, $w_{62} = 0.3075$, $w_{72} = 0.6925$, $w_{82} = 0.9225$, $w_{92} = 0.9225$, $w_{10,2} = 0.8462$, $w_{11,2} = 0.9225$, $w_{12,2} = 0.8462$, $w_{13,2} = 0.8462$, $w_{14,2} = 0.5387$, $w_{15,2} = 0.4613$, and $w_{16,2} = 0.9225$. Afterward, suppose $\theta = 1$, the partial dominance degrees under sub-criteria are computed based on Equations (19) and (20), and the overall dominance degree for each alternative is calculated according to Equation (21) (see Table 5).

Table 5. Dominance of each alternative over other alternatives.

	A_1	A_2	A_3	A_4
A_1	0	−11.7793	−22.1894	−14.9051
A_2	−26.9445	0	−29.9559	−25.5474
A_3	−12.7369	−7.41886	0	−9.90802
A_4	−20.3134	−12.4199	−26.099	0

Finally, based on Equation (22), the global values of alternatives are calculated as follows: $V_1 = 0.6409$, $V_2 = 0$, $V_3 = 1$, and $V_4 = 0.4508$. Becauae $V_3 > V_1 > V_4 > V_2$, the ranking order is $A_3 > A_1 > A_4 > A_2$. Therefore, the optimal alternative is A_3, and the worst alternative is A_2.

5. Discussions

5.1. Sensitivity Analysis

In this subsection, the influence of parameter θ in Equations (19) and (20) on the evaluation results is discussed. In this study, $\theta = 1$ is suggested. However, in some references [53,54], other θ values have been also employed. For the sake of confirming the stability of the decision making results, some other θ values are selected as contrasts. Generally, if $\theta > 1$, the influence of losses is weakened; and if $0 < \theta \leq 1$, the influence of losses is exacerbated. Accordingly, the θ values are divided into two categories: $0 < \theta \leq 1$ and $\theta > 1$.

The global values of alternatives under different θ values are indicated in Figure 3. It is clear that the maximum and minimum global values are always 1 and 0, respectively, whereas other global values decreased with the increasing of θ values. Besides, the ranking results with different θ values are listed in Table 6. It can be seen that the ranking orders of alternatives are always consistent (namely, $A_3 > A_1 > A_4 > A_2$). That is to say, the evaluation results are less sensitive to the θ values when the proposed method is employed. As a result, the sensitivity analysis verifies the robustness of the presented decision making framework to a certain extent.

Table 6. Ranking results with different θ values.

θ	Ranking Results	The Optimal Alternative	The Worst Alternative
$\theta = 0.2$	$A_3 > A_1 > A_4 > A_2$	A_3	A_2
$\theta = 0.4$	$A_3 > A_1 > A_4 > A_2$	A_3	A_2
$\theta = 0.6$	$A_3 > A_1 > A_4 > A_2$	A_3	A_2
$\theta = 0.8$	$A_3 > A_1 > A_4 > A_2$	A_3	A_2
$\theta = 1.0$	$A_3 > A_1 > A_4 > A_2$	A_3	A_2
$\theta = 2.0$	$A_3 > A_1 > A_4 > A_2$	A_3	A_2
$\theta = 4.0$	$A_3 > A_1 > A_4 > A_2$	A_3	A_2
$\theta = 6.0$	$A_3 > A_1 > A_4 > A_2$	A_3	A_2
$\theta = 8.0$	$A_3 > A_1 > A_4 > A_2$	A_3	A_2

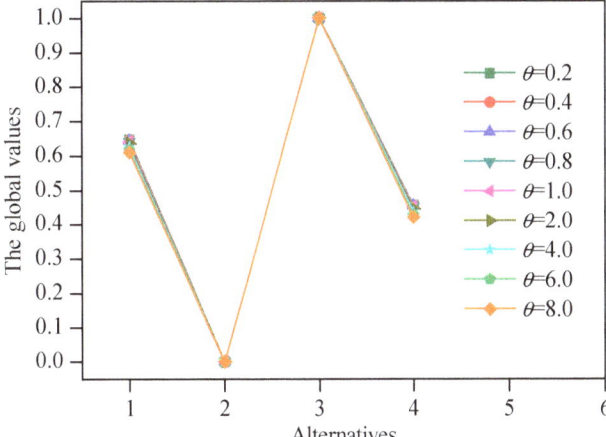

Figure 3. Global values of alternatives with different θ values.

5.2. Comparison Analysis

In this subsection, a comparison analysis with other approaches is introduced to validate the feasibility and strengths of the proposed approach.

(1) Comparison of evaluation information processing approaches

As far as we know, evaluation information in most existing studies is mainly processed to a single type of data. For example, the type of evaluation information in literature [28,55] is crisp numbers, and the information format in literature [36,38,40] is PLTSs. So far, no hybrid type of evaluation information that contains both crisp numbers and PLTSs has been put forward. In the real world, the evaluation information is usually composed of quantitative and qualitative values simultaneously. Thus, the single type of evaluation values cannot easily express evaluation information comprehensively. Although multiple types of data were adopted in some literature [56–58], this hybrid evaluation information was transformed into the same type (such as real numbers or linguistic values) in the first step of their approaches, which may lead to information loss. Considering the diversity and complexity of information in the CP evaluation for gold mines, the hybrid type of data is more suitable to indicate evaluation information. Therefore, PLTSs are employed to describe qualitative information and crisp numbers are adopted to express quantitative information. As a result, original evaluation information can be indicated more effectively.

(2) Comparison of weight determination methods

With regard to the determination methods of sub-criteria weights, the experts grading method is a typical subjective weighting approach. However, the linguistic evaluation terms given by experts are all expressed by scores or specific values in the traditional experts grading method [59]. An obvious weakness of this method is that it is difficult to indicate the original evaluation information sufficiently. In contrast, the linguistic evaluation information can be well described using PLTSs. Consequently, the traditional experts grading method is modified by introducing the idea of PLTSs in this research, so that the decision making results can be more reasonable.

(3) Comparison of ranking methods

Compared with other ranking methods, the TODIM method based on prospect theory is an available tool to deal with MCDM problems. However, the classical TODIM method is adopted to handle the MCDM issues in which sub-criteria values are in the format of crisp numbers, and cannot deal with the hybrid MCDM problems with multiple types of sub-criteria values. On account of this deficiency, Liang et al. [42] extended the TODIM method based on crisp values and triangular fuzzy numbers; Fan et al. [58] extended the TODIM method based on crisp numbers, interval numbers, and triangular fuzzy numbers; Wang and Li [60] extended the TODIM method based on crisp numbers, interval numbers, triangular fuzzy numbers, and trapezoidal fuzzy numbers. Nevertheless, the TODIM method has not been extended based on crisp numbers and PLTSs. In comparison with the existing extended TODIM method, the extended TODIM method with crisp numbers and PLTSs is more favorable for solving those kinds of MCDM problems, which include both quantitative and qualitative evaluation information. Compared with other fuzzy extensions mentioned above, PLTSs containing hesitations and probabilities can depict the qualitative information more comprehensively. As a result, the TODIM method is extended based on crisp numbers and PLTSs to assess CP for gold mines in this research.

On the basis of the above analyses, the advantages of the proposed method are summarized as follows:

(1) Two formats of data are introduced to indicate the initial evaluation information. The crisp numbers are adopted to express precise information for quantitative sub-criteria, and the PLTSs are employed to describe linguistic information for qualitative sub-criteria.

(2) The classical experts grading method is modified with PLTSs. The PLTSs, as opposed to scores or specific values, are used to express linguistic evaluation information provided by experts, so that the initial linguistic information can be described more adequately.

(3) The traditional TODIM method is extended with crisp numbers and PLTSs, which can efficiently deal with practical hybrid MCDM problems, including quantitative and qualitative evaluation information.

5.3. Managerial Implication

To evaluate CP for gold mines, this paper developed a hybrid MCDM approach. The proposed method provides suggestions for assessing CP for gold mines. In order to improve the level of CP for gold mines, some specific managerial implications are suggested as follows.

(1) For government: The government can establish an institution for regularly evaluating the performance of CP for gold mines. For the enterprises with better performance of CP, government can provide some financial subsidies or rewards, such as preferential tax and loans. However, for the enterprises with worse performance of CP, government can adopt some punitive measures, such as increasing the pollution discharge fees. Meanwhile, government can find out the weaknesses of CP in the evaluation process, so that pertinent measures can be taken. For example, if some CP technologies in most enterprises are poor, government can increase investment to research and develop these technologies.

(2) For enterprises: Enterprises can know their own problems and recognize the gap between themselves and other companies in the evaluation process. For improving the performance of CP, on the one hand, enterprises can develop a CP technology system. The key points of CP technology systems include the following: advanced mining technology, energy cascade utilization technology, resource-saving technology, waste utilization technology, 'zero emission' technology, and land greening technology. Through adopting CP technologies, the economic and environmental benefits will be greatly enhanced. On the other hand, enterprises can optimize the CP management system. First, the comprehensive CP regulations should be established and improved. Then, the CP regulations should be effectively executed. Moreover, the implementation process should be specially supervised and evaluated.

6. Conclusions

As the traditional production pattern has caused plenty of resource loss and serious environmental pollution in the development of mineral resources, implementing CP has become an effective guarantee to achieve sustainable development for mining enterprises. This paper focused on proposing a hybrid MCDM approach to evaluate CP for gold mines. Considering the specific features of gold mines, the evaluation criteria system of CP was established with twelve quantitative sub-criteria and four qualitative sub-criteria. In order to describe evaluation information more adequately, the quantitative sub-criteria were expressed by crisp numbers, and the qualitative sub-criteria were indicated by PLTSs. Considering that the experts are inclined to describe the importance degrees of sub-criteria using linguistic variables, the traditional experts grading method was modified with PLTSs to obtain the sub-criteria weights. Besides, an extended TODIM method with two types of evaluation information (crisp numbers and PLTSs) was presented to get the ranking result. Finally, the proposed hybrid MCDM approach was applied to evaluate CP for gold mines. The sensitivity analysis and comparison analysis indicated that the raised approach had strong robustness and had large advantages in solving such hybrid MCDM problems. At the same time, the evaluation results can provide some managerial implications for government and enterprises.

In the future, the proposed approach can be employed to solve hybrid MCDM issues in other fields, or more decision making methods can be developed to evaluate CP for gold mines.

Author Contributions: W.L., G.Z., and S.L. conceived and worked together to achieve this work; W.L. wrote the paper; and G.Z. made contribution to the case study. Conceptualization, G.Z.; Funding acquisition, G.Z.; Methodology, W.L.; Writing—original draft, W.L.; Writing—review & editing, G.Z. and S.L.

Funding: This research was funded by National Key Research and Development Program of China (2018YFC0604606) and National Natural Science Foundation of China (51774321).

Acknowledgments: We sincerely thank the anonymous reviewers for their helpful and constructive suggestions and the editors for their careful and patient work.

Conflicts of Interest: The authors declare no conflict of interest.

References

1. Harris, R.D.F.; Shen, J. The intrinsic value of gold: An exchange rate-free price index. *J. Int. Money Financ.* **2017**, *79*, 203–217. [CrossRef]
2. Kumah, A. Sustainability and gold mining in the developing world. *J. Clean. Prod.* **2006**, *14*, 315–323. [CrossRef]
3. Gorman, M.R.; Dzombak, D.A. A review of sustainable mining and resource management: Transitioning from the life cycle of the mine to the life cycle of the mineral. *Resour. Conserv. Recycl.* **2018**, *137*, 281–291. [CrossRef]
4. Assawincharoenkij, T.; Hauzenberger, C.; Ettinger, K.; Sutthirat, C. Mineralogical and geochemical characterization of waste rocks from a gold mine in northeastern Thailand: Application for environmental impact protection. *Environ. Sci. Pollut. Res.* **2018**, *25*, 3488–3500. [CrossRef] [PubMed]
5. Kiventerä, J.; Lancellotti, I.; Catauro, M.; Dal Poggetto, F.; Leonelli, C.; Illikainen, M. Alkali activation as new option for gold mine tailings inertization. *J. Clean. Prod.* **2018**, *187*, 76–84. [CrossRef]
6. Xiao, R.; Wang, S.; Li, R.H.; Wang, J.J.; Zhang, Z.Q. Soil heavy metal contamination and health risks associated with artisanal gold mining in Tongguan, Shaanxi, China. *Ecotoxicol. Environ. Saf.* **2017**, *141*, 17–24. [CrossRef] [PubMed]
7. Mayala, L.P.; Veiga, M.M.; Khorzoughi, M.B. Assessment of mine ventilation systems and air pollution impacts on artisanal tanzanite miners at Merelani, Tanzania. *J. Clean. Prod.* **2016**, *116*, 118–124. [CrossRef]
8. Euler, D.S. Application of ventilation management programs for improved mine safety. *Int. J. Min. Sci. Technol.* **2017**, *27*, 647–650.
9. Jordaan, M.A.; Mimba, M.E.; NguemheFils, S.C.; Edith-Etakah, B.T.; Shapi, M.; Penaye, J.; Davies, T.C. Occurrence and levels of potentially harmful elements (PHEs) in natural waters of the gold mining areas of the Kette-Batouri region of Eastern Cameroon. *Environ. Monit. Assess.* **2018**, *190*, 416. [CrossRef] [PubMed]
10. Tomiyasu, T.; Kodamatani, H.; Hamada, Y.K.; Matsuyama, A.; Imura, R.; Taniguchi, Y.; Hidayati, N.; Rahajoe, J.S. Distribution of total mercury and methylmercury around the small-scale gold mining area along the Cikaniki River, Bogor, Indonesia. *Environ. Sci. Pollut. Res.* **2017**, *24*, 2643–2652. [CrossRef] [PubMed]
11. Carvalho, P.C.S.; Neiva, A.M.R.; Silva, M.M.V.G.; Santos, A.C.T. Human health risks in an old gold mining area with circum-neutral drainage, central Portugal. *Environ. Geochem. Health* **2017**, *39*, 43–62. [CrossRef] [PubMed]

12. Drace, K.; Kiefer, A.M.; Veiga, M.M.; Williams, M.K.; Ascari, B.; Knapper, K.A.; Logan, K.M.; Breslin, V.M.; Skidmore, A.; Bolt, D.A.; et al. Mercury-free, small-scale artisanal gold mining in Mozambique: Utilization of magnets to isolate gold at clean tech mine. *J. Clean. Prod.* **2012**, *32*, 88–95. [CrossRef]
13. Gutiérrez Aguilar, C.M.; Panameño, R.; Perez Velazquez, A.; Angel Álvarez, B.E.; Kiperstok, A.; César, S.F. Cleaner production applied in a small furniture industry in Brazil: Addressing focused changes in design to reduce waste. *Sustainability* **2017**, *9*, 1867. [CrossRef]
14. Matos, L.M.; Anholon, R.; da Silva, D.; Ordoñez, R.E.C.; Quelhas, O.L.G.; Leal Filho, W.; de Santa-Eulalia, L.A. Implementation of cleaner production: A ten-year retrospective on benefits and difficulties found. *J. Clean. Prod.* **2018**, *187*, 409–420. [CrossRef]
15. Malinauskienė, M.; Kliopova, I.; Slavickaitė, M.; Staniškis, J.K. Integrating resource criticality assessment into evaluation of cleaner production possibilities for increasing resource efficiency. *Clean Technol. Environ.* **2016**, *18*, 1333–1344. [CrossRef]
16. Hilson, G.; Nayee, V. Environmental management system implementation in the mining industry: A key to achieving cleaner production. *Int. J. Miner. Process.* **2002**, *64*, 19–41. [CrossRef]
17. Song, S.Q.; Zhou, Y.Z. Demonstration research on cleaner production of mines. *China Popul. Resour. Environ.* **2003**, *13*, 106–110.
18. Hilson, G. Defining "cleaner production" and "pollution prevention" in the mining context. *Miner. Eng.* **2003**, *16*, 305–321. [CrossRef]
19. Rajaram, R.; Dutta, S.; Parameswaran, K. *Sustainable Mining Practices: A Global Perspective*; Taylor & Francis: London, UK, 2005.
20. Fan, Y.V.; Varbanov, P.S.; Klemeš, J.J.; Nemet, A. Process efficiency optimisation and integration for cleaner production. *J. Clean. Prod.* **2018**, *174*, 177–183. [CrossRef]
21. Severo, E.A.; de Guimarães, J.C.F.; Dorion, E.C.H. Cleaner production, social responsibility and eco-innovation: Generations' perception for a sustainable future. *J. Clean. Prod.* **2018**, *186*, 91–103. [CrossRef]
22. Liang, W.Z.; Zhao, G.Y.; Luo, S.Z. Linguistic neutrosophic Hamacher aggregation operators and the application in evaluating land reclamation schemes for mines. *PLoS ONE* **2018**, *13*, e0206178. [CrossRef] [PubMed]
23. Zhang, P.L.; Duan, N.; Dan, Z.G.; Shi, F.F.; Wang, H.F. An understandable and practicable cleaner production assessment model. *J. Clean. Prod.* **2018**, *187*, 1094–1102. [CrossRef]
24. Tseng, M.L.; Lin, Y.H.; Chiu, A.S. Fuzzy AHP-based study of cleaner production implementation in Taiwan PWB manufacturer. *J. Clean. Prod.* **2009**, *17*, 1249–1256. [CrossRef]
25. Peng, W.G.; Li, C.G. Fuzzy-Soft set in the field of cleaner production evaluation for aviation industry. *Commun. Inf. Sci. Manag. Eng.* **2012**, *2*, 39–43.
26. Basappaji, K.M.; Nagesha, N. Assessment of cleaner production level in agro based industries—A fuzzy logic approach. *Energy Proced.* **2014**, *54*, 127–134. [CrossRef]
27. Gong, B.G.; Guo, D.D.; Zhang, X.Q.; Cheng, J.S. An approach for evaluating cleaner production performance in iron and steel enterprises involving competitive relationships. *J. Clean. Prod.* **2017**, *142*, 739–748. [CrossRef]
28. Dong, L.J.; Shu, W.W.; Li, X.B.; Zhang, J.M. Quantitative evaluation and case studies of cleaner mining with multiple indexes considering uncertainty factors for phosphorus mines. *J. Clean. Prod.* **2018**, *183*, 319–334. [CrossRef]
29. Liang, W.Z.; Zhao, G.Y.; Luo, S.Z. An integrated EDAS-ELECTRE method with picture fuzzy information for cleaner production evaluation in gold mines. *IEEE Access* **2018**, *6*, 65747–65759. [CrossRef]
30. Liang, W.Z.; Zhao, G.Y.; Luo, S.Z. Selecting the optimal mine ventilation system via a decision making framework under hesitant linguistic environment. *Symmetry* **2018**, *10*, 283. [CrossRef]
31. Luo, S.Z.; Cheng, P.F.; Wang, J.Q.; Huang, Y.J. Selecting project delivery systems based on simplified neutrosophic linguistic preference relations. *Symmetry* **2017**, *9*, 151. [CrossRef]
32. Liang, W.Z.; Zhao, G.Y.; Wu, H. Evaluating investment risks of metallic mines using an extended TOPSIS method with linguistic neutrosophic numbers. *Symmetry* **2017**, *9*, 149. [CrossRef]
33. Rodriguez, R.M.; Martinez, L.; Herrera, F. Hesitant fuzzy linguistic term sets for decision making. *IEEE Trans. Fuzzy Syst.* **2012**, *20*, 109–119. [CrossRef]
34. Yager, R.R. Multicriteria decision making with ordinal/linguistic intuitionistic fuzzy sets for mobile apps. *IEEE Trans. Fuzzy Syst.* **2016**, *24*, 590–599. [CrossRef]

35. Liang, W.Z.; Zhao, G.Y.; Hong, C.S. Selecting the optimal mining method with extended multi-objective optimization by ratio analysis plus the full multiplicative form (MULTIMOORA) approach. *Neural Comput. Appl.* **2018**. [CrossRef]
36. Pang, Q.; Wang, H.; Xu, Z.S. Probabilistic linguistic term sets in multi-attribute group decision making. *Inf. Sci.* **2016**, *369*, 128–143. [CrossRef]
37. Wei, G.W. Grey relational analysis model for dynamic hybrid multiple attribute decision making. *Knowl. Based Syst.* **2011**, *24*, 672–679. [CrossRef]
38. Zhang, X.L.; Xing, X.M. Probabilistic linguistic VIKOR method to evaluate green supply chain initiatives. *Sustainability* **2017**, *9*, 1231. [CrossRef]
39. Peng, H.G.; Zhang, H.Y.; Wang, J.Q. Cloud decision support model for selecting hotels on TripAdvisor.com with probabilistic linguistic information. *Int. J. Hosp. Manag.* **2018**, *68*, 124–138. [CrossRef]
40. Liao, H.C.; Jiang, L.S.; Xu, Z.S.; Xu, J.P.; Herrera, F. A linear programming method for multiple criteria decision making with probabilistic linguistic information. *Inf. Sci.* **2017**, *415*, 341–355. [CrossRef]
41. Gomes, L.F.A.M.; Lima, M.M.P.P. TODIM: Basics and application to multicriteria ranking of projects with environmental impacts. *Found. Comput. Decis. Sci.* **1992**, *16*, 113–127.
42. Liang, W.Z.; Zhao, G.Y.; Wu, H.; Chen, Y. Assessing the risk degree of goafs by employing hybrid TODIM method under uncertainty. *Bull. Eng. Geol. Environ.* **2018**. [CrossRef]
43. Tosun, Ö.; Akyüz, G. A fuzzy TODIM approach for the supplier selection problem. *Int. J. Comput. Int. Syst.* **2015**, *8*, 317–329. [CrossRef]
44. Zindani, D.; Maity, S.R.; Bhowmik, S.; Chakraborty, S. A material selection approach using the TODIM (TOmada de Decisao Interativa Multicriterio) method and its analysis. *Int. J. Mater. Res.* **2017**, *108*, 345–354. [CrossRef]
45. Wu, M.Q.; An, Y.L.; Zhou, X.D.; Xiao, Y. Establishment of the index system of cleaner production assessment of phosplate minesddphosplate mines of Guiyang a case study. *Environ. Sci. Manag.* **2009**, *34*, 189–194.
46. Zhou, H.L.; Yang, S.; Chen, J.H. Research and application of cleaner production evaluation index system in gold mine. *Gold Sci. Technol.* **2017**, *25*, 93–100.
47. Liang, W.Z.; Zhao, G.Y.; Hong, C.S. Performance Assessment of Circular Economy for Phosphorus Chemical Firms Based on VIKOR-QUALIFLEX Method. *J. Clean. Prod.* **2018**, *196*, 1365–1378. [CrossRef]
48. Liang, W.Z.; Zhao, G.Y.; Wu, H.; Dai, B. Risk assessment of rockburst via an extended MABAC method under fuzzy environment. *Tunn. Undergr. Space Technol.* **2019**, *83*, 533–544. [CrossRef]
49. Basu, A.J.; van Zyl, D.J. Industrial ecology framework for achieving cleaner production in the mining and minerals industry. *J. Clean. Prod.* **2006**, *14*, 299–304. [CrossRef]
50. Xu, Z.S. Deviation measures of linguistic preference relations in group decision making. *Omega* **2005**, *33*, 249–254. [CrossRef]
51. Gou, X.J.; Xu, Z.S.; Liao, H.C. Multiple criteria decision making based on Bonferroni means with hesitant fuzzy linguistic information. *Soft Comput.* **2017**, *21*, 6515–6529. [CrossRef]
52. Gou, X.J.; Xu, Z.S. Novel basic operational laws for linguistic terms, hesitant fuzzy linguistic term sets and probabilistic linguistic term sets. *Inf. Sci.* **2016**, *372*, 407–427. [CrossRef]
53. Krohling, R.A.; de Souza, T.T. Combining prospect theory and fuzzy numbers to multi-criteria decision making. *Expert Syst. Appl.* **2012**, *39*, 11487–11493. [CrossRef]
54. Qin, Q.D.; Liang, F.Q.; Li, L.; Chen, Y.W.; Yu, G.F. A TODIM-based multi-criteria group decision making with triangular intuitionistic fuzzy numbers. *Appl. Soft Comput.* **2017**, *55*, 93–107. [CrossRef]
55. Gomes, L.F.A.M. An application of the TODIM method to the multicriteria rental evaluation of residential properties. *Eur. J. Oper. Res.* **2009**, *193*, 204–211. [CrossRef]
56. Zhao, H.R.; Zhao, H.R.; Guo, S. Evaluating the comprehensive benefit of eco-industrial parks by employing multi-criteria decision making approach for circular economy. *J. Clean. Prod.* **2017**, *142*, 2262–2276. [CrossRef]
57. Liu, P.D. A novel method for hybrid multiple attribute decision making. *Knowl.-Based Syst.* **2009**, *22*, 388–391.
58. Fan, Z.P.; Zhang, X.; Chen, F.D.; Liu, Y. Extended TODIM method for hybrid multiple attribute decision making problems. *Knowl.-Based Syst.* **2013**, *42*, 40–48. [CrossRef]

59. Hossain, M.U.; Poon, C.S.; Dong, Y.H.; Lo, I.M.; Cheng, J.C. Development of social sustainability assessment method and a comparative case study on assessing recycled construction materials. *Int. J. Life Cycle Assess.* **2018**, *23*, 1654–1674. [CrossRef]
60. Wang, F.; Li, H. Novel method for hybrid multiple attribute decision making based on TODIM method. *J. Syst. Eng. Electron.* **2015**, *26*, 1023–1031. [CrossRef]

© 2018 by the authors. Licensee MDPI, Basel, Switzerland. This article is an open access article distributed under the terms and conditions of the Creative Commons Attribution (CC BY) license (http://creativecommons.org/licenses/by/4.0/).

Article

Stakeholder Role for Developing a Conceptual Framework of Sustainability in Organization

Aarti Singh [1], Sushil [1], Samarjit Kar [2] and Dragan Pamucar [3,*]

[1] Department of Management Studies, Indian Institute of Technology Delhi, New Delhi 110 016, India; singhaartij@gmail.com (A.S.); profsushil@gmail.com (S.)
[2] Department of Mathematics, National Institute of Technology Durgapur, West Bengal 713 209, India; dr.samarjitkar@gmail.com
[3] Department of Logistics, University of Defence, Military Academy, 11000 Belgrade, Serbia
* Correspondence: dpamucar@gmail.com

Received: 9 December 2018; Accepted: 26 December 2018; Published: 3 January 2019

Abstract: The purpose of this research is to frame the hierarchical pathway treading the sustainability factors from driving to dependent elements. Hence, this study starts with a brief literature review of the sustainable organization which enables the expansion of sustainability into essential factors. Experts further verified these identified factors and used for framing the hierarchical framework of sustainability in organizations. Total Interpretive Structural Modeling (TISM) has been applied for identifying the driving factor of sustainability and delivering the crucial links among the sustainability factors in organizations. While most of the organizations focus on sustainability by considering the Triple Bottom Line (TBL) framework, this paper has presented the fourth dimension of sustainability which drives sustainability in organizations. The hierarchical relationship is vital to identify the vitality and significance of factors. This in turn provides an efficient approach to achieve sustainability in organizations. The expert's review has been calculated statistically to validate the factors and conceptual hierarchical framework. Hence, the policymakers make use of sustainability hierarchy to frame a correct and efficient policy for maintaining sustainable practices that help managers to shift their priorities of an organization at the managerial level from economic growth to sustainable development. Finally, the future research direction and the limitation of the study are discussed.

Keywords: conceptual framework; organizations; sustainability; sustainability hierarchy; Total Interpretive Structural Modeling (TISM)

1. Introduction

The sustainability concept has been evolved as an environmental need and gradually moved to the need of dynamic business environment. The turbulent nature of economy, environment, and human will force a business to adopt sustainability measures [1]. Applied to the business perspective, sustainability is defined as capturing the turbulence of business without affecting economic growth of the organization [2]. For instance, in India sustainability plays a vital role in the holistic growth of the nation as it provides a basic framework for the development of organizations. Most organizations deal with the dynamics of business through TBL; it aids the organization to deal with multidimensional view of sustainability [3]. John Elkington introduced the TBL framework in mid-1990s. Before the TBL framework, the primary concern of organizations was economic growth, but it induced environmental and social aspects as two most important aspects along with economic aspects to measure sustainable growth in organizations. It can also be termed the 3P aspect as it covers people, profit, and planet [4]. Sustainability has been observed as challenge to accomplish this goal [5–7]. Thus, sustainability seems simple to understand but difficult to conceive by organizations because it requires the collaboration of stakeholders to achieve the comprehensive coverage of its 3P aspect [8–10]. This sustainable view generates need for an underlying conceptual framework which sharply defines the hierarchy of sustainability in the organization so that returns to the shareholder can be maximized [11,12]. The objective of this paper is to find the hierarchical relationship between sustainability drivers to show how sustainability factors are related to each other. Drivers of sustainability have been studied in the past but in this research, the theory of relationship among these drivers have been studied by using the TISM methodology. This study also highlights the locus of stakeholders among other environmental, economic and societal factors of sustainability. TISM is the best-suited methodology for finding the hierarchical relationship among sustainability factors because in TISM the hierarchy has been plotted in the form of diagraph by involving experts, and connections in each level also stated in the hierarchy. Hence, total ten factors have been identified as essential factors which define sustainability in organizations.

2. Sustainability in the Organization

Sustainability regarding the environmental system can be defined as maintaining constant equilibrium with the outer environment [13,14]. The trajectory of sustainability has been initiated by sustainable societies which were reported in a Brundtland report in 1974 [15]. This basic definition of sustainability can be easily linked to the well-recognized definition of sustainability as per WCED (1987) as "Sustainability is about meeting the needs of the present without compromising the ability of future generations to meet their needs" [16]. In spite of an explicit definition of sustainability, it is difficult for the organization to understand and adapt it. Most organizations develop their strategy for adopting sustainability in their organizations, or they utilize the developed frameworks and tools for working sustainably. The interrelation of three dimensions of sustainability (namely people, planet, and profit) will provide the basis for sustainability in the organization [17,18]. Thus, sustainability in the organization has been viewed as promoting their business and gaining profit without ignoring society and the environment. Sustainable organizations provide solutions for fulfilling elementary needs to improve the lives of people, now and in the future with least possible environmental impacts and the highest possible economic and social yield [19].

A sustainable organization has a holistic concept of development that is understood as having three top pillars, namely economic vitality, social equity, and a healthy natural environment form basis of its development, which was also proposed in the TBL. These three essential pillars contribute directly or indirectly to the progress of the firm [20,21]. The sustainability of the organizations has been studied through the various models proposed by various authors. Some of the literature about the models has been summarized in Table 1.

Table 1. Models for Sustainable Organizations.

S. No.	Model	The Conclusion of Sustainability Models	References
1	Theory of the Firm Model	This model explains the conjunction of two industries for maintaining social attribute of product and CSR activity of organizations.	[22]
2	Society versus Firm Model	Sustainability implies sustainable competitive advantage not sustainable development firms.	[23]
3	Shareholder value creation model	How the business organizations maintain the dynamic, sustainable development without compromising shareholder value.	[24]
4	Triple Value Triangle Model	Sustainable development through the axes of the triangle where each axis represents the social, environmental and economic values.	[25]
5	Sustainable value creating a model	Essential actions were taken by different level of stakeholders for maintaining sustainability in organization.	[26]
6	Sustainability Sweet Spot Model	This model represents sustainability as a sweet spot.	[27]
7	Organizational Sustainability Model	This model presents the definition of a stakeholder which satisfies the demands of each level of stakeholders in the organization.	[28]
8	Integrated Management of Quality and Sustainability Model	Corporate sustainability has been discussed in this model. It has been abstracted as economic, social and environmental bottom lines.	[29]
9	Star Model	Government and customer (as a driver) are also an essential part of sustainability, along with the environment, society and economy.	[21]
10	Sustainable enterprise model innovation	A conceptual framework which helps to learn development processes, densities faced during trade-off for sustainable enterprises.	[30]
11	NINR Logic Model for Center Sustainability	Center Sustainability includes strategies to control resources for providing the long-term sustainability while planning a center.	[31]
12	The SOSTARE model	Stepwise assimilated farm sustainability valuations about technical efficiency, and its impact on environmental and economic sustainability.	[32]

It is understood from the study of the models that sustainability in the organization is associated with TBL. It is evident from the literature that profit motivates an organization, but its performance grows when it takes care of people and the planet. Along with this view, other views about sustainability have been summarized in Table 2.

Table 2. Explanation of Sustainability in Organizations.

S. No.	Authors	Sustainability Intent of the Organization
1	Byerlee [33]	The organization promotes sustainable practices at the time of crisis.
2	Shrivastava [34]	Linking the effect of populations on ecosystems.
3	Ulhoi et al. [19]	Solutions for fulfilling simple needs with minimum environmental impact and the maximum economic and social return.
4	Philips and Reichart [35]	Stakeholder status in the non-human environment.
5	Kefalas [36]	Environmentally Sustainable Organization (ESO) as a system approach.
6	Hart and Milstein [24]	Sustainable-value framework for designing shareholder value of the organization.
7	Swart et al. [37]	Sustainability science and scenario analysis are the problems of the future.
8	Figge and Hahn [38]	This research article discusses corporate contributions to sustainability.
9	Du Pisani [39]	Demand for natural resources and their effect on the environment was an endless concern all through human history.
10	Darby and Jenkins [40]	Measure social accounting procedures and tools to quantify social enterprise (SE) contribution to retaining sustainability.
11	Sen and Swierczek [41]	Societal, environmental and stakeholder dimensions for active organizational functions through case analysis of US and Asian international firms.
12	Parrish [42]	What creates a sustainable enterprise through exploration of its principle and purpose.
13	Nguyen and Slater [43]	Discussed hitting the sustainability sweet spot in the sweet spot model.
14	Kocmanova et al. [44]	Business sustainability has been studied in term of environmental, social and corporate governance performance small and medium enterprises in the Czech Republic.
15	Kiron et al. [45]	Sustainability terminology, to cover environmental, economic and societal topics. Long-term perspective has been studied in term of sustainability factors.
16	Barth and Michelsen [46]	Education is contributing to sustainability.
17	Munoz et al. [47]	The ontological framework has been developed to eases the environmental performance of an organization.
18	Jain [48]	The Concept of Triple Bottom Line Reporting in India's Perspective.
19	Rambaud and Richard [49]	Sustainability as "Triple Depreciation Line" instead of "Triple Bottom Line".

The sustainable organization study reveals that sustainability in organizations has been broadly categorized into three main factors. The categorization includes environmental factors, economic factors, and social factors and along with these three factors, stakeholders have also emerged as an essential factor for defining sustainability in the organization as shown in Figure 1 (the rhombus model below). These factors have been further fragmented for a thorough explanation.

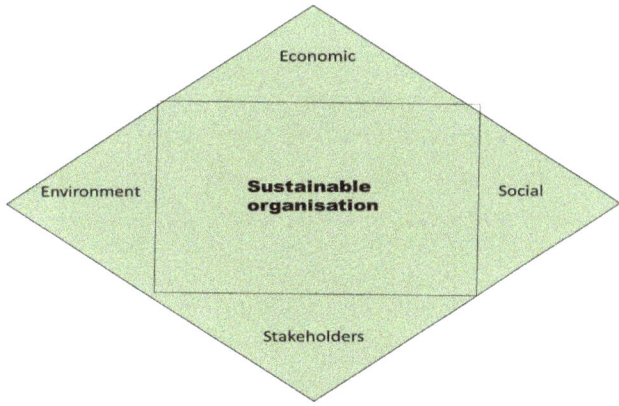

Figure 1. Factors for Defining the Sustainable Organization (rhombus model).

3. Research Methodology

The literature review can be defined as "a systematic, explicit, and reproducible design for identifying, evaluating, and interpreting the existing body of recorded documents". The literature has been analyzed to systematically summarize the existing research and to identify the essential factors which define sustainability in an organization.

The mixed method research has been used for the verifying and identifying of crucial sustainability factors from the literature [50–54]. Directed content analysis has been used for defining sustainability and identifying the sustainability factors in an organization.

The steps of methods have been explained as:

Step I: Identify and verification of factors in the organizational context through content analysis.

Step II: Develop the hierarchical relationship between the sustainability factors in the organization using TISM.

Step III: Validating the hierarchical model of sustainability in the organizational context through expert opinions.

3.1. Content Analysis for Factor Identification

Content analysis is defined as "Any technique for making inferences by objectively and systematically identifying specified characteristics of messages" [55]. Content analysis is used for both scientific and managerial research where the research problem has been explored systematically and quantitatively [56,57].

3.2. TISM Development for the Conceptualization of Sustainability in the Organization

TISM is an interpretive extension of ISM methodology [58,59]. It interprets the relationships among the factors by determining "what," "how" and "why". The hierarchical relationships have then been developed between verified sustainability factors in organizations. "What" is used to define the concept answering what types of element are present. "How" provides hierarchy between the elements and "Why" explains why the relationship is there between the elements. Thus, these three aspects of theory building provide a conceptual relationship between the sustainability factors for developing the conceptual model of sustainability in an organization [21,60].

3.3. t-Test for Data Verification

The *t*-test is a hypothesis testing technique where the identified factors have been analyzed through hypothesis. In this study, it is used for factor verification and validating TISM links, by developing hypothesis according to these links.

4. Step I: Identify and Verification of Factors in the Organizational Context through Content Analysis

4.1. Descriptive Analysis

A publication from 1993–2016 has been reviewed for analysis of the sustainability concept. The wide range of publication and models has been studied to find the sustainability factors in an organization. However, the literature on sustainability started from the Brundtland report. The year wise distribution of studies has been shown in Figure 2. The research articles from sustainability, management, environmental, organizational, business ethics, science, and technology journals have been considered in this study. This includes literature reviews, modeling, and conceptual and sustainability research articles.

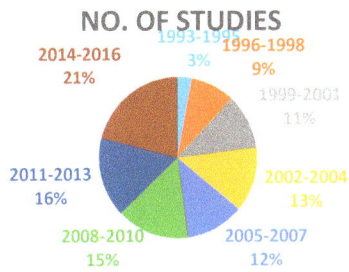

Figure 2. The Year Wise Distribution of Studies.

The sustainability research articles are divided into factors and the study has been carried out by the occurrence of factors present in the research articles, as mentioned in Figures 3 and 4. The frequency of the occurrence of factors is shown in Figure 5. The content analysis continued with the coding of identified articles. The relevant articles have been coded from the literature related to sustainability and stakeholder's involvement in an organization. The combination of directed and summative content analysis has been used manually to analyze the literature. The keyword and literature coding methodology has been used for coding the literature. During the coding of the literature, ten categorizations have occurred, which are taken as essential factors for defining sustainability aspects in the organization.

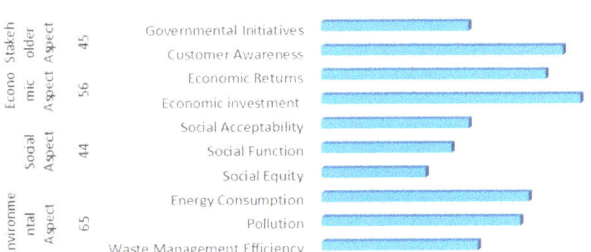

Figure 3. The Factor Wise Sustainability Research Articles Distribution.

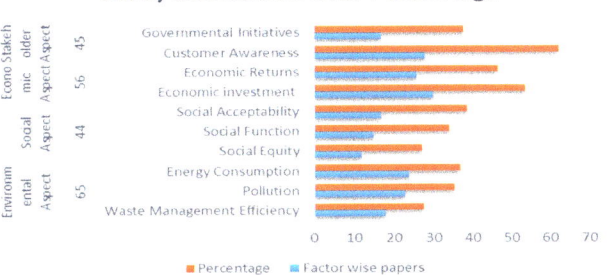

Figure 4. The Percentage-wise Study Distribution.

Figure 5. The Frequency of Occurrence of Factors.

From the content analysis, ten sustainability factors have been identified from the literature. These factors are present in literature, and keyword coding and a literature coding system have been used for identifying the factors. The factors with their coding and specifications are shown in Table 3.

Table 3. Factors with their Coding and Specifications.

Factor	Coding
Environmental Aspect	
Waste Management efficiency (SENF1)	Waste Management efficiency, waste management, waste management used for creating sustainability in the organization, eco-efficiency of the organization, eco-efficiency was used to co-relate the environment with economic growth, organization waste minimization, organizational waste, recycling, organizational waste reduction.
Pollution (SENF2)	Environmental Kuznets curve, environmental pollution, sustainable organizations are majorly concerned about pollution, environmental degradation.
Energy consumption (SENF3)	Energy consumption affects energy requirements, green energy, substitution of traditional energy sources, payback from green energy, solar energy, environmental load, greenhouse gas emission.
The social aspect of sustainability	
Social Function (SSCF4)	The functional aspect of the organization toward society, social approaches, the economic benefit to the society, employment creation, providing training and vocational education.
Social Equity (SSCF5)	Employment equity among the organization. Stakeholder participation rate, employees wage fairness, positioning and promotion of organization staffs.
Social acceptability (SSCF6)	Perception and participation of employees in the organization, societal perception, opinion of society, societies' view about the organization, understanding the needs of people and stakeholders, organizational development.
Economic Aspect	
Economic Returns (SECF7)	Profit maximization. Organizational earning, organization profit, financial returns environmental and social welfare maximization, economic capital, natural resource capital, long-term returns by making more profit as well as fulfilling responsibilities towards nature.
Economic Investment (SECF8)	Organizations utilize their core capabilities for absorbing sustainable changes without affecting growth, dynamic capability of gaining, the competitive advantages, investment over sustainability, investment over green energy, investment over social acceptability, social function, and investment over innovation.
Stakeholders Aspect	
Customer Awareness (SSHF9)	Customers demand green products, customer preference, critical selection of products, customer awareness of choosing sustainable products and organization, mindful consumption pull the organization towards responsible, social and societal marketing which promotes sustainability.
Governmental Initiatives (SSHF10)	Government policies, direct regulations, direct and indirect governmental initiatives, government forms a political ecology for nurturing sustainability, governmental incentives, rules for avoiding exploitation of human rights and empowers the society.

4.2. Verification of Identified Sustainability Factors in the Organization

Verification further strengthens these factors from experts. The groups of experts have been identified by using judgmental sampling. The expert's opinion has been captured by applying hypothesis testing through a *t*-test. The *t*-test is further verified by using a reliability test over the data. The hypothesis was developed for identified sustainability factors which were statistically calculated for verifying sustainability factors by using SPSS 20 software [61]. Here, the null hypothesis and alternate hypothesis have been developed to examine expert reviews through a *t*-test for testing these hypotheses. The developed hypotheses are:

H(0): Null Hypothesis: There is no significant difference between the observed mean and specified mean for factor Fn.

H(A): Alternate Hypothesis: There is a definite significant difference between observed mean and specified mean for factor Fn (where, N = 10).

The questionnaire has been designed using a five-point Likert scale which used for verification of sustainability factors. This exercise included Forty-Seven experts from sustainability backgrounds. Participant experts include senior managers, CEOs, and educational experts who have extensive knowledge about sustainability. In this hypothesis testing, the test value 3.5 was used for factors verification. The *t*-test statistic for hypothesis testing results is shown in Table 4.

Table 4. The *t*-Test Analysis of Sustainability Factors (N = 47).

S. No.	Factors	Mean	Std. Deviation	Test Value = 3.5		Result
				Sig.(2tailed) Mean Difference	*t* Value	
1	Waste Management Efficiency	4.26	0.846	0.000	6.120	Significant
2	Pollution	3.94	0.791	0.000	3.779	Significant
3	Energy Consumption	3.94	0.870	0.001	3.437	Significant
4	Social Equity	4.11	0.729	0.000	5.700	Significant
5	Social Function	4.09	0.830	0.000	4.835	Significant
6	Social Acceptability	4.15	0.932	0.000	4.773	Significant
7	Economic investment	4.34	0.788	0.000	7.313	Significant
8	Economic Returns	4.11	0.429	0.00	9.68	Significant
9	Customer Awareness	3.96	.806	0.000	3.889	Significant
10	Governmental Initiatives	4.26	0.736	0.000	7.033	Significant

Note: N = number of respondents. * Significant, if significance value 2-tailed < 0.05.

4.3. Reliability Analysis

According to Weber (1990), "To make valid inferences from the text, it is important that the classification procedure be reliable in the sense of being consistent: Different people should code the same text in the same way" [62]. It uses to reduce the error and to correct the factors identified through codes. The Scott (1995) pi formula has been used for checking the correctness of identified factors [63].

The formula is

$$Pi = (Po-Pe)/(1-Pe)$$

where Po = Observed percentage of agreement; Pe = Percentage of agreement expected by chance.

t-test calculates the expert's opinion used for verification of factors, and the Cronbach's Alpha of reliability is 0.783, which indicates the intercoder agreement is 78%. This shows considerable strength of agreement with the data, as shown in Table 5.

Table 5. Reliability Analysis of *t*-Test Data (N = 47).

Reliability Statistics	
Cronbach's Alpha	Number of Items
0.786	10

5. Step II: Develop the Hierarchical Relationship between the Sustainability Factors in the Organization Using TISM

Total Interpretive Structural Modeling (TISM)

The verified sustainability factors have been used to model the conceptual framework for sustainability in the organization. The TISM model of sustainability has been carried out using the following steps:

Step I. Identifying and defining elements

The factors used to define sustainability in the organization that has been defined above in the study are summarized in Table 3.

Step II. Define Contextual Relationship and Interpretation of Relationship

In this step, the contextual relationship has been identified as "Factor A influences Factor B." This contextual relationship helped to draw the relationship between the sustainability factors.

Step III. Interpretive Logic of Pairwise Comparison

The 'Interpretive Logic Knowledge Base' developed by using a footprint in the numeric form of 0 and 1 to prepare a reachability matrix of expert opinions. The pairwise comparison of identified and verified sustainability factors have been plotted regarding the reachability matrix.

Step IV: Transitivity Check

This step is an extension of the previous one. Here the transitivity of reachability has been checked for finding the transitive links among the sustainability factors in the organization. Transitivity can be explained as "the property in which if factor A is influencing factor B, and factor B are influencing factor C then, factor A should influence factor C." The outcome is known as a transitive reachability matrix (TRM) is shown in the appendix (Table A1).

Step V: Level Partition on Reachability Matrix

The interaction of antecedent and reachability set has been plotted in the level partitioning. The factor which has the same reachability sets and intersection set come at the first level in the hierarchy. The first level factor has been removed, and the same process is repeated for further leveling in the matrix. The level partitioning of sustainability factors exhibited in the appendix (Table A2).

Step VI: Digraph Development and Total Interpretive Structural Model formation

The pictographic representation of factors on the basis level partitioning is known as a digraph. The links obtained between the two nodes in the digraph are further interpreted. The complete interpretation of links forms the TISM model. In Figure 6, the interpretation links are shown in the form of a link number. The TISM model is subjected to different checks as suggested by Sushil (2016) [59].

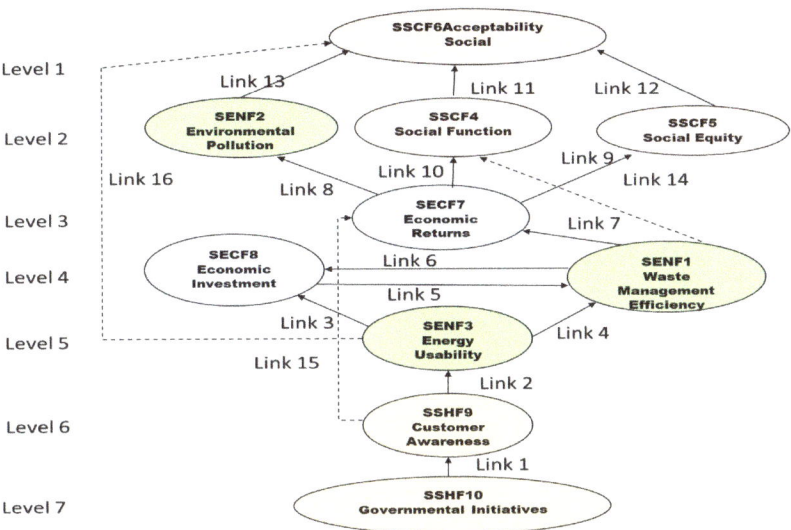

Figure 6. Initial TISM for Sustainability in the organization without Interpretation.

6. Step III: Validating the Hierarchical Model of Sustainability in the Organizational Context through Experts Opinion

Validation of TISM

Quantitative and qualitative analysis have been used together for strong validation of a concept. Here, the hypothesis testing has been used for validation of each TISM linkage through a *t*-test. There were 16 linkages, and each link was verified for validation of a complete TISM model. The survey has been conducted over thirty-five respondents; all respondents from sustainability backgrounds (having more than ten years' experience) were chosen for validation of each link developed in the TISM model. Sixteen questions were developed one for each linkage, and a questionnaire was prepared over the five-point Likert scale from strongly disagree to agree strongly.

Common null and the alternate hypotheses have been developed for analyzing 16 linkages of the TISM model. The developed hypotheses are:

Null Hypothesis: Hi (0): There is no significant difference between the observed mean and specified mean in respective factor linkages.

Alternate Hypothesis: Hi (A): There is a significant difference between the observed mean and specified mean in respective factor linkages.

The SPSS 20 software has been used for conducting a one-tailed *t*-test with 3.5 test value as shown in Table 6.

Table 6. Result of Hypothesis Testing ($N = 35$).

S. No.	Factors Link	Mean	Std. Deviation	Sig.(2tailed) Mean Difference	t-Value	Accept/Reject *
1	Link1	4.24	0.831	0.000	4.454	Accept
2	Link2	4.32	0.802	0.000	5.112	Accept
3	Link4	4.40	0.577	0.000	7.794	Accept
4	Link3	4.40	0.707	0.000	6.364	Accept
5	Link6	4.28	0.891	0.000	4.379	Accept
6	Link5	4.20	0.764	0.000	4.583	Accept
7	Link7	4.04	0.978	0.011	2.760	Accept
8	Link8	4.04	0.978	0.011	2.760	Accept
9	Link9	4.20	0.957	0.001	3.656	Accept
10	Link10	4.08	0.862	0.003	3.364	Accept
11	Link11	4.36	0.757	0.000	5.679	Accept
12	Link12	4.20	0.913	0.001	3.834	Accept
13	Link13	4.08	0.759	0.001	3.819	Accept
14	Link 14	3.92	1.213	0.106	1.683	Reject
15	Link15	4.20	0.866	0.000	4.041	Accept
16	Link16	3.96	0.676	0.002	3.404	Accept

Note: * Accept, if significance value two-tailed <0.05. N = number of respondents.

Based on the analysis, the links with a significance level less than five percent were accepted and the links above five percent were rejected. All links except link 14 are accepted in the final TISM model. The validated TISM model with accepted links is shown in Figure 7.

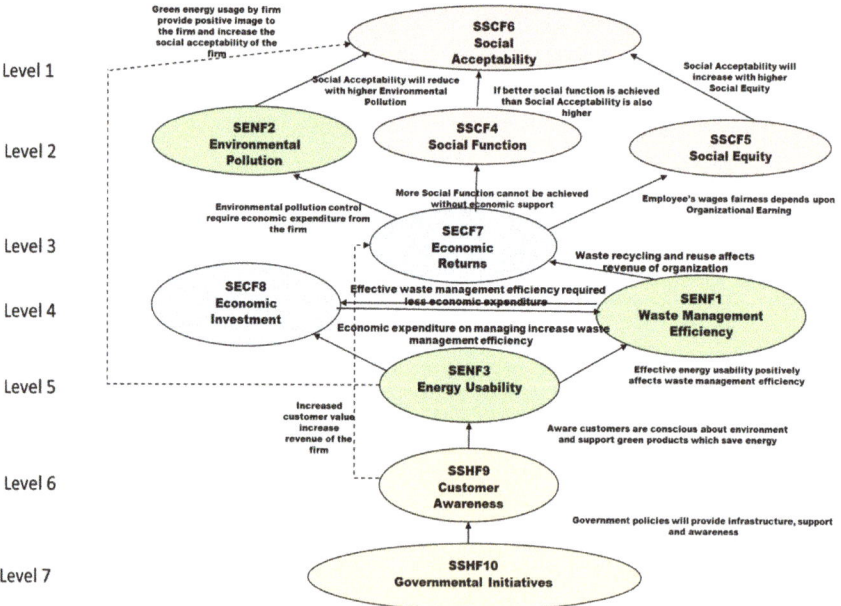

Figure 7. Final TISM model for Sustainability in the organization.

7. Results and Discussion

The final TISM model represents the path of creating sustainability in the organization with its dependent and driver factors. The final TISM model shows that social aspect is the depending aspect of sustainability and social acceptability is the dependent factor of sustainability. Meanwhile, the stakeholder aspect is the driving aspect of sustainability and government initiatives are the primary driving factor for maintaining sustainability in an organization [64]. The TISM approach has been used for framing the conceptual framework; it is differentiated from previous literature by forming the hierarchical conceptual framework of sustainability which supplements the TBL with the fourth dimension, i.e., the stakeholder. The driving factor government initiative helps in creating awareness about sustainability in the organization through its policies and actions. The driving nature of factor government initiative is easy to understand in mining industries where the role of government can be understood in term of global mining initiatives through ISO certification (ISO 14001) which helps in sustainable mining; this generates an awareness in global customers of sustainable mining [65–67]. After government, the customer plays a vital role in awakening the organization. The customer's view is the primary cause of sustainability developments in business and marketing [68]. Customer opinion is best supported as sustainably aware customers choose sustainable products and force organizations to create sustainable products or to operate sustainably [69,70]. The environmental aspect for generating sustainability in the organization is highlighted by Shrivastava (1995) in his article "Environmental technologies and competitive advantage" [71]. Thus, in an organization, energy consumption and waste management efficiency depend on economic investment for running organizations sustainably and this provides the economic returns to organizations. The economic returns act as a morale booster for organizations and motivate them to control pollution. All these aspects of social function and social equity will improve the social acceptability of an organization [72]. The final TISM model also indicates that a sustainable organization should focus on social issues by providing good social equity among their employees through wages fairness, flexibility among job for female employees, and by involving employees in social functions. The final sustainability hierarchy shows that mediating factor, i.e., economic investment has an indirect effect over sustainability, meaning the economic investment in sustainability will require some payback period. A sustainable organization needs to manage its waste through a reducing, recycling, reuse, and recovery process for improving waste management efficiency and economic returns [73–75].

7.1. Implications

This study indicates the hierarchical relationship among the sustainability factors which can be used by an authority to decide priorities and develop policies for proper implementation of sustainability in an organization.

This study also indicates that increased shareholder value will heighten shifts towards sustainability. It also shows that sustainability enhancing policies aggravate awareness which results in higher sustainable economic growth for organizations.

The study indicates that environmental factors act as an intermediary which promotes the positive social acceptance and relationship of a sustainable organization. Hence, sustainable organization should focus on environmental aspects by developing pollution control, waste management equipment, and effective energy utilization. These measures would improve the social acceptability of an organization. A positive image of a sustainable organization helps in creating new customers which in turn improves the economic gains of the organization. This study shows that CSR expenditure is not forfeited but pointedly contributes to turnover and providing a positive image to shareholder funds.

7.2. Limitations

This study tries to evaluate the hierarchy of relationships between the sustainability factors where stakeholder perspectives act as a driver for sustainability in the organization. The data is limited to customers and the government only. The actual meaning of shareholder is not limited as it can be extended to initiators of sustainability, this can also entail shareholder involvement from all aspects of the organization. It seems to be a challenging process but adds a new paradigm to achieve sustainability in organizations. A corporation can be established as an example by its accountable assurances to stakeholders.

8. Conclusions and Future Research Directions

Sustainability is the need for a dynamic business environment. It is defined as sustaining natural resources for future consumption which exposes a new arena of responsible utilization of natural resources. This explanation leads organizations to consume the natural resources responsibly in order to protect them from reaching a tipping point. This study provides a pathway which helps in achieving sustainable economic growth by increasing the social acceptability of the organization through the contribution of stakeholders. This study shows that instead of fragmenting the sustainability into drivers, there is a need for a responsible integrated path for achieving sustainability in an organization. It is also found that investing in energy efficiency, waste management, pollution control equipment and plans would provide returns directly through savings and indirectly by increasing the social value of a participating organization. This study provides a holistic approach and drivers which promote sustainability in an organization. Future research is required in standardization and developing the role of social entities to promote. The relationship can be further studied in terms of a cause-effect relationship to find the cause elements and effect elements for achieving sustainability in an organization. The polarity of relationships can be studied in future to provide positive and negative relationships among the sustainability hierarchy.

Author Contributions: The individual contribution and responsibilities of the authors were as follows: A.S. finds the factors, validate them, collect and analyzed the data, form model, and validate it for the development of paper. S., S.K. and D.P. provided good advice throughout the research, by giving suggestions on model design, methodology, inferences and refined the manuscript. All the authors have read and approved the final manuscript.

Funding: This research received no external funding.

Acknowledgments: We would like to express our gratitude to the editor and reviewers, and all experts for helping us to carry out this work. We would like to acknowledge Department of Management Studies, Indian Institute of Technology Delhi, India, for supporting the work.

Conflicts of Interest: The authors declare no conflicts of interest.

Appendix A

Table A1. Transitive Reachability Matrix.

Sustainability Factors	SENF1	SENF2	SENF3	SSCF4	SSCF5	SSCF6	SECF7	SECF8	SSHF9	SSHF10
SENF1	1	1	0	1*	1*	1	1	1	0	0
SENF2	0	1	0	0	0	1	0	0	0	0
SENF3	1	1	1	1*	1*	1*	1	1	0	0
SSCF4	0	0	0	1	0	1	0	0	0	0
SSCF5	0	0	0	0	1	1	0	0	0	0
SSCF6	0	0	0	0	0	1	0	0	0	0
SECF7	0	1	0	1	1	1	1	0	0	0
SECF8	1	1	0	1	1	1	1*	1	0	0
SSHF9	1	1	1	1**	1**	1	1*	1*	1	0
SSHF10	1	1	1	1	1	1	1	1	1	1

Note: * Transitive Relationship, ** Second Order Transitive Link.

Table A2. Partitioning the Reachability Matrix into Different Levels.

Sustainability Factors	Reachability Set	Antecedent Set	Intersection Set	Level
SENF1	1,2,4,5,6,7,8	1,3,8,9,10	1,8	
SENF2	2,6	1,2,3,7,8,9,10	2	
SENF3	1,2,3,4,5,6,7,8	3,9,10	3	
SSCF4	4,6	1,3,4,7,8,9,10	4	
SSCF5	5,6	1,3,5,7,8,9,10	5	
SSCF6	6	1,2,3,4,5,6,7,8,9,10	6	1
SECF7	2,4,5,6,7	1,3,7,8,9,10	7	
SECF8	1,2,4,5,6,7,8	1,3,8,9,10	1,8	
SSHF9	1,2,3,4,5,6,7,8,9	9,10	9	
SSHF10	1,2,3,4,5,6,7,8,9,10	10	10	
Sustainability Factors	Reachability set	Antecedent set	Intersection set	Level
SENF1	1,2,4,5,6,7,8	1,3,8,9,10	1,8	
SENF2	2	1,2,3,7,8,9,10	2	2
SENF3	1,2,3,4,5,6,7,8	3,9,10	3	
SSCF4	4	1,3,4,7,8,9,10	4	2
SSCF5	5	1,3,5,7,8,9,10	5	2
SECF7	2,4,5,6,7	1,3,7,8,9,10	7	
SECF8	1,2,4,5,6,7,8	1,3,8,9,10	1,8	
SSHF9	1,2,3,4,5,6,7,8,9	9,10	9	
SSHF10	1,2,3,4,5,6,7,8,9,10	10	10	
Sustainability Factors	Reachability set	Antecedent set	Intersection set	Level
SENF1	1,7,8	1,3,8,9,10	1,8	
SENF3	1,3, 7,8	3,9,10	3	
SECF7	7	1,3,7,8,9,10	7	3
SECF8	1,7,8	1,3,8,9,10	1,8	
SSHF9	1,3,7,8,9	9,10	9	
SSHF10	1,3,7,8,9,10	10	10	
Sustainability Factors	Reachability set	Antecedent set	Intersection set	Level
SENF1	1,8	1,3,8,9,10	1,8	4
SENF3	1,3,8	3,9,10	3	
SECF8	1,8	1,3,8,9,10	1,8	4
SSHF9	1,3,8,9	9,10	9	
SSHF10	1,3,8,9,10	10	10	
Sustainability Factors	Reachability set	Antecedent set	Intersection set	Level
SENF1	3	3,9,10	3	5
SSHF9	3,4,5,9	9,10	9	
SSHF10	3,9,10	10	10	
Sustainability Factors	Reachability set	Antecedent set	Intersection set	Level
SSHF9	9	9,10	9	6
SSHF10	9,10	10	10	
Sustainability Factors	Reachability set	Antecedent set	Intersection set	Level
SSHF10	10	10	10	7

References

1. Scheffer, M.; Carpenter, S.; Foley, J.A.; Folke, C.; Walker, B. Catastrophic shifts in ecosystems. *Nature* **2001**, *413*, 591–596. [CrossRef] [PubMed]
2. Grewatsch, S.; Kleindienst, I. When does it pay to be good? Moderators and mediators in the corporate sustainability–corporate financial performance relationship: A critical review. *J. Bus. Ethics* **2017**, *145*, 383–416. [CrossRef]
3. Lee, S.; Geum, Y.; Lee, H.; Park, Y. Dynamic and multidimensional measurement of product-service system (PSS) sustainability: A triple bottom line (TBL)-based system dynamics approach. *J. Clean. Prod.* **2012**, *32*, 173–182. [CrossRef]
4. Hall, T.J. The triple bottom line: What is it and how does it work? *Indiana Bus. Rev.* **2011**, *86*, 4.
5. Gray, R.; Milne, M. Sustainability reporting: who's kidding whom? *Chart. Account. J. N. Z.* **2002**, *81*, 66–70.

6. Gray, R. Does sustainability reporting improve corporate behaviour?: Wrong question? Right time? *Account. Bus. Res.* **2006**, *36*, 65–88. [CrossRef]
7. Walton, S.; Tregidga, H.; Milne, M.J. *The Triple-Bottom-Line: Benchmarking New Zealand's Early Reporters*; University of Otago: Dunedin, New Zealand, 2003.
8. Bebbington, J. Sustainable development: A review of the international development, business and accounting literature. In *Accounting Forum*; Blackwell Publishers Ltd.: Hoboken, NJ, USA, 2001; Volume 25, pp. 128–157.
9. Erusalimsky, A.; Gray, R.; Spence, C. Towards a more systematic study of standalone corporate social and environmental: An exploratory pilot study of UK reporting. *Soc. Environ. Account. J.* **2006**, *26*, 12–19. [CrossRef]
10. Milne, M.J.; Gray, R. W(h)ither ecology? The triple bottom line, the global reporting initiative, and corporate sustainability reporting. *J. Bus. Ethics* **2013**, *118*, 13–29. [CrossRef]
11. Epstein, M.J.; Roy, M.J. Sustainability in action: Identifying and measuring the key performance drivers. *Long Range Plan.* **2001**, *34*, 585–604. [CrossRef]
12. Kopelman, S.; Weber, J.M.; Messick, D.M. Commons dilemma management: Recent experimental results. In Proceedings of the 8th Biennial Conference of the International Society for the Study of Common Property, Bloomington, IN, USA, 31 May–4 June 2000.
13. Holling, C.S. The Resilience of Terrestrial Ecosystems; Local Surprise and Global Change. In *Sustainable Development of the Biosphere*; Clark, W.C., Munn, R.E., Eds.; Cambridge University Press: Cambridge, UK, 1986; pp. 292–317.
14. Chatterjee, K.; Pamucar, D.; Zavadskas, E.K. Evaluating the performance of suppliers based on using the R'AMATEL-MAIRCA method for green supply chain implementation in electronics industry. *J. Clean. Prod.* **2018**, *184*, 101–129. [CrossRef]
15. Lozano, R. Envisioning sustainability three-dimensionally. *J. Clean. Prod.* **2008**, *16*, 1838–1846. [CrossRef]
16. Lele, S.M. Sustainable development: A critical review. *World Dev.* **1991**, *19*, 607–621. [CrossRef]
17. Lozano, R.; Huisingh, D. Inter-linking issues and dimensions in sustainability reporting. *J. Clean. Prod.* **2011**, *19*, 99–107. [CrossRef]
18. Singla, A.; Ahuja, I.P.S.; Sethi, A.P.S. The effects of demand pull strategies on sustainable development in manufacturing industries. *Int. J. Innov. Eng. Technol.* **2017**, *8*, 27–34.
19. Ulhoi, J.P.; Madsen, H.; Kjaer, M. *Training in Environmental Management: Industry and Sustainability*; Office for Official Publications of the European Communities: Luxembourg, 1999; p. 43.
20. Stenzel, P.L. Sustainability, the triple bottom line, and the global reporting initiative. *Glob. Edge Bus. Rev.* **2010**, *4*, 1–2.
21. Sushil. Interpreting the Interpretive Structural Model. *Glob. J. Flex. Syst. Manag.* **2012**, *13*, 87–106. [CrossRef]
22. McWilliams, A.; Siegel, D. Corporate social responsibility: A theory of the firm perspective. *Acad. Manag. Rev.* **2001**, *26*, 117–127. [CrossRef]
23. Bansal, P. The corporate challenges of sustainable development. *Acad. Manag. Exec.* **2002**, *16*, 122–131. [CrossRef]
24. Hart, S.L.; Milstein, M.B. Creating sustainable value. *Acad. Manag. Exec.* **2003**, *17*, 56–67. [CrossRef]
25. Roberts, B.; Cohen, M. Enhancing sustainable development by triple value adding to the core business of government. *Econ. Dev. Q.* **2002**, *16*, 127–137. [CrossRef]
26. Jovane, F.; Yoshikawa, H.; Alting, L.; Boer, C.R.; Westkamper, E.; Williams, D.; Paci, A.M. The incoming global technological and industrial revolution towards competitive sustainable manufacturing. *CIRP Ann.-Manuf. Technol.* **2008**, *57*, 641–659. [CrossRef]
27. Nguyen, D.K.; Slater, S.F. Hitting the sustainability sweet spot: Having it all. *J. Bus. Strategy* **2010**, *31*, 5–11. [CrossRef]
28. Garvare, R.; Johansson, P. Management for sustainability–a stakeholder theory. *Total Qual. Manag.* **2010**, *21*, 737–744. [CrossRef]
29. Asif, M.; Searcy, C.; Garvare, R.; Ahmad, N. Including sustainability in business excellence models. *Total Qual. Manag. Bus. Excell.* **2011**, *22*, 773–786. [CrossRef]
30. Zollo, M.; Cennamo, C.; Neumann, K. Beyond what and why: Understanding organizational evolution towards sustainable enterprise models. *Organ. Environ.* **2013**, *26*, 241–259. [CrossRef]

31. Dorsey, S.G.; Schiffman, R.; Redeker, N.S.; Heitkemper, M.; McCloskey, D.J.; Weglicki, L.S.; Grady, P.A. NINR Centers of Excellence: A logic model for sustainability, leveraging resources and collaboration to accelerate cross-disciplinary science. *Nurs. Outlook* **2014**, *62*, 384. [CrossRef] [PubMed]
32. Paracchini, M.L.; Bulgheroni, C.; Borreani, G.; Tabacco, E.; Banterle, A.; Bertoni, D.; De Paola, C. A diagnostic system to assess sustainability at a farm level: The SOSTARE model. *Agric. Syst.* **2015**, *133*, 35–53. [CrossRef]
33. Byerlee, D. Technical change, productivity, and sustainability in irrigated cropping systems of South Asia: Emerging issues in the post-green revolution Era. *J. Int. Dev.* **1992**, *4*, 477–496. [CrossRef]
34. Shrivastava, P. Environmental technologies and competitive advantage. *Strateg. Manag. J.* **1995**, *16*, 183–200. [CrossRef]
35. Phillips, R.A.; Reichart, J. The environment as a stakeholder? A fairness-based approach. *J. Bus. Ethics* **2000**, *23*, 185–197. [CrossRef]
36. Kefalas, A.G. The environmentally sustainable organization (ESO): A systems approach. *Ethics Environ.* **2001**, *6*, 90–105.
37. Swart, R.J.; Raskin, P.; Robinson, J. The problem of the future: Sustainability science and scenario analysis. *Glob. Environ. Chang.* **2004**, *14*, 137–146. [CrossRef]
38. Figge, F.; Hahn, T. Sustainable value added—Measuring corporate contributions to sustainability beyond eco-efficiency. *Ecol. Econ.* **2004**, *48*, 173–187. [CrossRef]
39. Du Pisani, J.A. Sustainable development–historical roots of the concept. *Environ. Sci.* **2006**, *3*, 83–96. [CrossRef]
40. Darby, L.; Jenkins, H. Applying sustainability indicators to the social enterprise business model: The development and application of an indicator set for Newport Wastesavers, Wales. *Int. J. Soc. Econ.* **2006**, *33*, 411–431. [CrossRef]
41. Sen, S.K.; Swierczek, F.W. Societal, environmental and stakeholder value drivers: A case analysis of us and Asian international firms. *J. Hum. Values* **2007**, *13*, 119–134. [CrossRef]
42. Parrish, B.D. Designing the sustainable enterprise. *Futures* **2007**, *39*, 846–860. [CrossRef]
43. Badi, I.; Abdulshahed, A. Prediction of the surface roughness for the end milling process using Adaptive Neuro-Fuzzy Inference System ANFIS. *Oper. Res. Eng. Sci. Theory Appl.* **2018**, *1*, 1–12. [CrossRef]
44. Kocmanova, A.; Docekalova, M.; Nemecek, P.; Simberova, I. Sustainability: Environmental, Social and Corporate Governance Performance in Czech SMEs. In Proceedings of the 15th World Multi-Conference on Systemics, Cybernetics and Informatics, Orlando, FL, USA, 19–22 July 2011; pp. 94–99.
45. Kiron, D.; Kruschwitz, N.; Haanaes, K.; Velken, I.V.S. Sustainability nears a tipping point. *MIT Sloan Manag. Rev.* **2012**, *53*, 69. [CrossRef]
46. Barth, M.; Michelsen, G. Learning for change: An educational contribution to sustainability science. *Sustain. Sci.* **2013**, *8*, 103–119. [CrossRef]
47. Munoz, E.; Capon-Garcia, E.; Lainez, J.M.; Espuna, A.; Puigjaner, L. Considering environmental assessment in an ontological framework for enterprise sustainability. *J. Clean. Prod.* **2013**, *47*, 149–164. [CrossRef]
48. Jain, A. The Concept of Triple Bottom Line Reporting and India's Perspective. *Corp. Gov.* **2014**, *4*, 5.
49. Rambaud, A.; Richard, J. The "Triple Depreciation Line" instead of the "Triple Bottom Line": Towards a genuine integrated reporting. *Crit. Perspect. Account.* **2015**, *33*, 92–116. [CrossRef]
50. Roy, J.; Adhikary, K.; Kar, S.; Pamucar, D. A rough strength relational DEMATEL model for analysing the key success factors of hospital service quality. *Decis. Mak. Appl. Manag. Eng.* **2018**, *1*, 121–142. [CrossRef]
51. Stojčić, M. Application of ANFIS model in road traffic and transportation: A literature review from 1993 to 2018. *Oper. Res. Eng. Sci. Theory Appl.* **2018**, *1*, 40–61. [CrossRef]
52. Mukhametzyanov, I.; Pamucar, D. A sensitivity analysis in MCDM problems: A statistical approach. *Decis. Mak. Appl. Manag. Eng.* **2018**, *1*, 51–80. [CrossRef]
53. Liu, F.; Aiwu, G.; Lukovac, V.; Vukic, M. A multicriteria model for the selection of the transport service provider: A single valued neutrosophic DEMATEL multicriteria model. *Decis. Mak. Appl. Manag. Eng.* **2018**, *1*, 121–130. [CrossRef]
54. Popovic, M.; Kuzmanovic, M.; Savic, G. A comparative empirical study of Analytic Hierarchy Process and Conjoint analysis: Literature review. *Decis. Mak. Appl. Manag. Eng.* **2018**, *1*, 153–163. [CrossRef]
55. Holsti, O.R. *Content Analysis for the Social Sciences and Humanities*; Addison-Wesley Pub. Co.: Reading, MA, USA, 1969.
56. Kassarjian, H.H. Content Analysis in Consumer Research. *J. Consum. Res.* **1977**, *4*, 8–18. [CrossRef]

57. Krippendorff, K. *Content Analysis: An Introduction to its Methodology*; Sage: Thousand Oaks, CA, USA, 2004.
58. Sushil. Flexibility, Viability and Sustainability. *Glob. J. Flex. Syst. Manag.* **2012**, *12*, 1–2. [CrossRef]
59. Sushil. How to Check Correctness of Total Interpretive Structural Models? *Ann. Oper. Res.* **2016**. [CrossRef]
60. Weber, R.P. *Basic Content Analysis*, 2nd ed.; SAGE Publications Inc.: Newbury Park, CA, USA, 1990.
61. Verma, J.P. *Data Analysis in Management with SPSS Software*; Springer Science & Business Media: Berlin/Heidelberg, Germany, 2012.
62. Scott, F.E. *Promotion and protection of human health in the context of sustainable development: Canada and USA*; WEHAB Working Group UN: New York, NY, USA, 2009.
63. Bamgbade, J.A.; Kamaruddeen, A.M.; Nawi, M.N.M. Malaysian construction firms' social sustainability via organizational innovativeness and government support: The mediating role of market culture. *J. Clean. Prod.* **2017**, *154*, 114–124. [CrossRef]
64. Kanda, W.; Mejía-Dugand, S.; Hjelm, O. Governmental export promotion initiatives: Awareness, participation, and perceived effectiveness among Swedish environmental technology firms. *J. Clean. Prod.* **2015**, *98*, 222–228. [CrossRef]
65. Bell, D.V. *The Role of Government in Advancing Corporate Sustainability*; Background Paper; Final Draft; Sustainable Enterprise Academy, York University: Toronto, ON, Canada, 2002.
66. Hamann, R. Mining companies' role in sustainable development: the 'why' and 'how' of corporate social responsibility from a business perspective. *Dev. South. Afr.* **2003**, *20*, 237–254. [CrossRef]
67. Luck, D.J. Broadening the concept of marketing—Too far? *J. Market.* **1969**, *33*, 53–63. [CrossRef]
68. Holm, M.; Kumar, V.; Plenborg, T. An investigation of customer accounting systems as a source of sustainable competitive advantage. *Adv. Account.* **2016**, *32*, 18–30. [CrossRef]
69. Biju, P.L.; Shalij, P.R.; Prabhushankar, G.V. Evaluation of customer requirements and sustainability requirements through the application of fuzzy analytic hierarchy process. *J. Clean. Prod.* **2015**, *108*, 808–817. [CrossRef]
70. Pamučar, D.; Lukovac, V.; Božanić, D.; Komazec, N. Multi-criteria FUCOM-MAIRCA model for the evaluation of level crossings: case study in the Republic of Serbia. *Oper. Res. Eng. Sci. Theory Appl.* **2018**, *1*, 108–129.
71. Christmann, P. Effects of "best practices" of environmental management on cost advantage: The role of complementary assets. *Acad. Manag. J.* **2000**, *43*, 663–680.
72. Cohen, B.; Winn, M.I. Market imperfections, opportunity and sustainable entrepreneurship. *J. Bus. Ventur.* **2007**, *22*, 29–49. [CrossRef]
73. Singh, A. Developing a conceptual framework of waste management in the organizational context. *Manag. Environ. Qual. Int. J.* **2017**, *28*, 786–806. [CrossRef]
74. Singh, A. Flexible Waste Management Practices in Service Sector: A Case Study. In *Global Value Chains, Flexibility and Sustainability*; Springer: Singapore, 2018; pp. 301–318.
75. Singh, A.; Raj, P. Sustainable Recycling Model for Municipal Solid Waste in Patna. *Energy Environ.* **2018**. [CrossRef]

© 2019 by the authors. Licensee MDPI, Basel, Switzerland. This article is an open access article distributed under the terms and conditions of the Creative Commons Attribution (CC BY) license (http://creativecommons.org/licenses/by/4.0/).

Article

Rzeszow as a City Taking Steps Towards Developing Sustainable Public Transport

Miroslaw Smieszek, Magdalena Dobrzanska * and Pawel Dobrzanski

Faculty of Management, Rzeszow University of Technology, al. Powstancow Warszawy 10, 35-959 Rzeszow, Poland; msmieszk@prz.edu.pl (M.S.); pd@prz.edu.pl (P.D.)
* Correspondence: md@prz.edu.pl; Tel.: +48-17-865-1602

Received: 9 December 2018; Accepted: 10 January 2019; Published: 15 January 2019

Abstract: The paper discusses problems related to the functioning of passenger transport in Rzeszow. The dynamic development of the city and the increase in the income of its inhabitants have led to significantly increased traffic within the city, which is detrimental both to the environment and the city's inhabitants. It limits the quality of life in the city and in the end generates additional costs for businesses and people in urban areas due to the congestion. In compliance with the policies of the European Union, this harmful tendency needs to be limited. Developing sustainable transportation should largely contribute to this objective. With the city of Rzeszow as example, this article discusses selected actions and measures taken as part of the development of sustainable transportation and demonstrates changes in the functioning of public transport based on the author's own research as well as data provided by the city's authorities. The analyses show that the actions taken so far have had a positive impact.

Keywords: sustainable transport; public transport; emission of pollutants; travel times; bus pass

1. Introduction

The transportation need is understood as a need to move from a starting point to a target point, within a strictly specified period of time. Problems associated with the transport of people and their mobility are especially significant within the territory of cities.

Around 70% of the European Union's (EU) population live in cities and generate around 80% of the Union's GDP [1]. Mobility in cities is, however, becoming more difficult and less efficient, as it is still largely based on the use of conventional private vehicles. These vehicles are a source of many harmful effects that generate additional costs and losses in several fields [2–6]. The most important harmful effects include: congestion, accidents, noise, air pollution, climate change and the use and deterioration of the transport and urban infrastructure [7–9]. According to European Union guidelines, cities must intensify their efforts to reverse unfavourable tendencies in the use of fuel and the emission of toxic elements [10–12]. The goal of these efforts should be reaching a 60% reduction in the emission of greenhouse gases. Due to the high density of populations in cities and the high level of traffic, a public transport system is the preferred solution for short routes [13–18]. It gives greater opportunities with respect to reducing the total emission of toxic components in the city, as compared to traffic consisting mostly of passenger cars equipped with conventional drive systems. The EU provisions concerning air quality and the increasingly stricter emission standards for road vehicles aim to ensure that city inhabitants are not exposed to the harmful effects of air pollution and particulate matter. However, almost all cities in the EU Member States still struggle to satisfy the requirements [19]. The natural environment should be exploited in a way which ensures that future generations will be able to exploit it as well [20,21]. In accordance with the principles of sustainable development, transportation should also have as small an impact on the environment as possible. Many European cities are taking steps towards achieving that goal [22–28].

One of the main aims of this study is to present the steps taken to reverse the unfavourable traffic trends and to make public transport more significant, with Rzeszow, a Polish medium-size urban area, being one such example. All steps taken by the city's authorities are in line with the philosophy of developing sustainable transport, one of the premises of which is to minimise the human impact on the environment.

This article comprises seven sections. The first serves as an introduction to the study's subject matter. The second sets forth the threats arising from road traffic. The third presents features of the city. The fourth describes in detail the public transport system in the city and the side effects of the growing number of vehicles and increasing traffic. The fifth delineates some of the courses of action taken by the city's authorities with the aim of developing sustainable transport, the sixth shows the achieved and expected results of implementing the actions suggested and the seventh is a conclusion.

2. Research Methodology

The operation of urban transport in the city has a major impact on the comfort and quality of life, the efficiency of the operation of the urban organism and the economic management of energy sources. In many cases, striving to improve selected indicators may lead to deterioration of other important properties. Closing or very significant limitation of vehicle traffic in a given area may contribute to the depopulation and change of the nature of a given area. In the undertaken activities, it is necessary to achieve a certain compromise and the factors—parameters affecting the transport system must be contained in certain permissible areas of variation.

Due to many factors subject to change and occurrence of limitations, the solution to this problem is similar to the solution of the multicriteria optimization task, under which the objective function is optimized, taking into account such features as: quality and comfort of life, safety and efficiency of the urban organism.

All research work related to the assessment of the operation and determining the direction of changes for the considered Polish city must take into account the state and scope of operation of transport systems in cities of similar size. Comparing the operation of urban transport in small cities, for example, in the range of population 50,000–100,000 with cities larger than 1 million inhabitants, it makes no sense. In each of these groups the scale of problems differs and system solutions in the area of urban transport are different. Considering groups of cities of similar size, it is possible to determine the acceptable range of changes of selected parameters and indicate potential directions of action. The direction of these activities can be determined on the basis of analysis of solutions in the field of urban transport in cities located in countries with a high degree of economic development and a high level of ecological awareness as a role model. A group of such cities includes cities from countries such as Sweden, Norway, Germany, the Netherlands and Denmark. Due to the number of inhabitants of the city under consideration Rzeszow, a group of EU cities with a population between 150–250 thousand inhabitants was selected for analysis. On the basis of 93 EU cities specified in Reference [29], the areas of variability of parameters characterizing the shares of particular forms of urban transport were determined. In 10 cities with the highest share of public transport from 32 to 63%, only one city is in Spain, a country that is an old EU member. In terms of share of individual transport, the top 10 countries are dominated by the old EU. The share of individual transport amounts from 63 to 83% there. In this group there are no cities from the aforementioned countries with a high level of economic development and high ecological awareness. Considering the share of bicycle trips in the number of completed trips in the first 10 are cities from the Netherlands, Denmark and Germany. The share of bicycle trips is from 22 to 40%. In the latter group of cities, the share of individual transport is from 21 to 63%.

Having a specific range of variability of the parameters characterizing the transport system, it is necessary to identify the threats resulting from road transport activities. This was done for road transport and for the selected city. The improvement of the operation of urban transport can be influenced by two groups of factors. These are factors that are technical or organizational—non-technical. Organizational (non-technical) factors include organization of transport routes, frequency of courses, activities aimed at increasing the environmental awareness of inhabitants and tax policy. Technical factors include a construction and development of a traffic control system, information system for travellers, car parks, bus lanes, bicycle paths and investments in ecological and zero-emission means of transport. As part of the example considered, it was examined which of these funds were used in the analysed city and the obtained and potential benefits were determined.

During the research work, the results of own research and available data from specialist literature and the Internet will be used.

3. Threats Arising from Transport

Road transport is one of the pillars of a properly functioning economy. However, it also has a negative influence on the environment. The most important harmful effects of road transport include: congestion, accidents, noise, air pollution, climate change and the use and deterioration of the transport and urban infrastructure.

Petroleum-based fuels are currently the primary fuel for road vehicles. One of the harmful effects of using these fuels is the emission of pollutants into the atmosphere, of which the most significant are carbon monoxide, carbon oxide and NOx nitrogen oxides [30]. Particulate matter also substantially contributes to the pollution levels. Figure 1 shows CO_2 emissions from various types of road vehicle between 1990 and 2015, with 1990 as the base year. These data relate to all Member States of the EU. The maximum CO_2 emissions were observed between 2006 and 2008 [31].

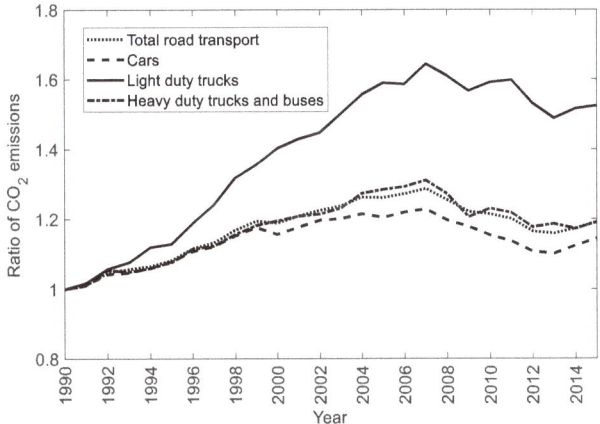

Figure 1. CO_2 emissions from various types of road vehicle in EU Member States with respect to 1990 (base year).

Total CO_2 emissions throughout the period differed with respect to individual countries. Those countries achieving high levels of economic development, such as Austria, France or Germany, saw a decrease in CO_2 emissions in relation to the maximum values reached in the 2000–2008 period (Figure 2). Countries with intensively developing and catching-up economies, such as Poland, saw a constant increase in CO_2 emissions alongside the ongoing economic development. These emissions should stabilise once the countries catch up in terms of economic development.

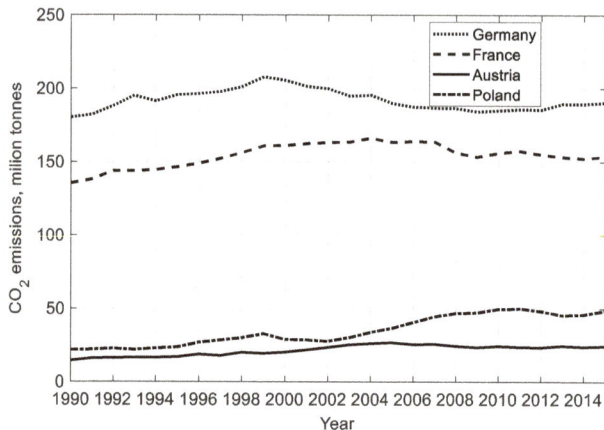

Figure 2. CO_2 emissions from road vehicles in respective EU Member States.

The harmful impact of CO_2 emissions on the environment is particularly hazardous for urban areas. According to EU data, transport contributes to 23% of CO_2 emissions within cities. Taking into account the fact that cities are relatively small in terms of their areas, the level of emissions per given unit of area is several times higher than in other areas.

Congestion can be defined as a phenomenon in which road users mutually hinder the traffic flow for their own benefit. It occurs when the capacity of the city's transport system is pushed to its limits. Congestion results in a decrease in speed or a complete lack of free movement of vehicles and pedestrians. This phenomenon does not take into account such circumstances as accidents or roadworks. Figure 3 schematically shows the traffic flow, taking vehicle saturation into account [3,32]. More detailed information about congestion can be found in works by Börjesson at all [33], Haywood at all [25], Kaddoura at all [34], Mussone at all [35], Prud'homme at all [36]. The curves illustrating vehicle speed as a function of intensity relate to two different roads. For municipal roads, a decrease in speed occurs once the traffic intensity exceeds the level of 1,500 vehicles per hour. For multilane express roads, a decrease in speed can be observed once the traffic intensity exceeds the level of 6000 vehicles per hour. In both cases, once the threshold values indicated by P1 and P2 are reached, there will be a decrease in speed and traffic. Traffic flow may be prevented in extreme cases.

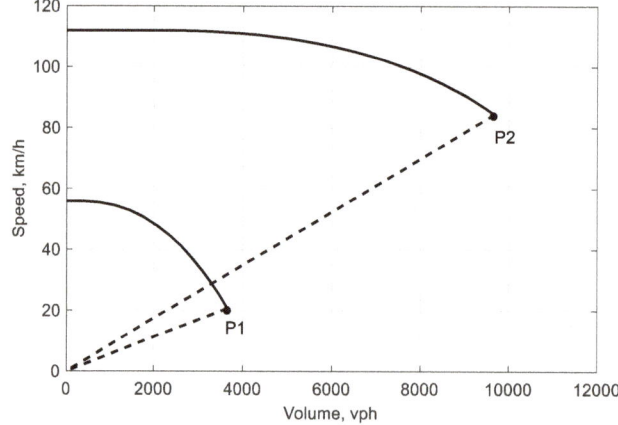

Figure 3. The effect of the number of vehicles on speed for two different types of road [3,32].

Excessive numbers of individual vehicles in a city become a cause of traffic jams, not only during peak hours but also increasingly during off peak hours. Congestion first occurs on the main transport routes and then it impacts other streets. Increasing travel times become a permanent feature of urban travel, decreasing the quality of life of the inhabitants. In many cases, congestion is described as the ratio of journey time during rush hours to journey time outside rush hours. Figure 4 shows the percentage increase in journey times arising from congestion in selected European cities [37,38].

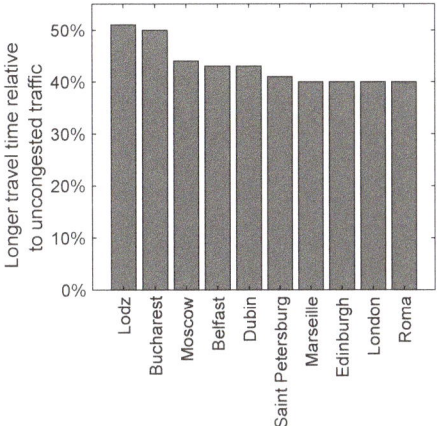

Figure 4. Percentage increase in journey times arising from congestion in selected European cities.

Congestion also generates additional external costs as well as costs related to time lost during the ever longer journeys. Engaging more public transport vehicles to transfer a given number of passengers also becomes necessary as a result of congestion. The costs incurred with relation to the negative effects of congestion are significant.

Roadway noise is defined as noise that is undesirable or detrimental to human health, caused by road vehicles. Roadway noise is of a variable nature [39]. Assessments of roadway noise use the equivalent continuous sound level (Leq), which is equivalent to the average energy emitted by the sound source over the period of time of interest. As a result, two equivalent continuous sound levels can be distinguished: a daytime and a night-time level.

The negative impact of roadway noise on the human body [40] can be considered with respect to the following categories:

- impact on human health,
- impact on human activity (taking sleep disruption into account),
- annoyance caused by the noise.

The primary processes causing noise are:

- combustion in the cylinders of an engine,
- flow of intake and exhaust gases,
- airflow around the vehicle,
- interaction between the vehicle's tyres and the road surface,
- inertia forces acting upon the vehicle's components.

When the equivalent continuous sound level of 60 dB is exceeded, a growing number of people are annoyed by the noise. People face the risk of temporary hearing loss at a Leq exceeding 70 dB and face permanent damage at a Leq exceeding 75 dB.

The increase in roadway noise-related risks in recent years is related mostly to the construction of new roads, bridges, ring roads and motorways, as well as the sudden increase in the number of vehicles in Poland. According to the latest data from 2017, there are 2,121,600 people exposed in outside urban areas with daily noise exceeding 55 dB [41]. Roadway noise is dangerous, particularly in urbanised areas. It is perceived by an increasing number of inhabitants, especially in the urban environment. In cities of over 100,000 inhabitants on the noise in the range 55–60 dB are exposed to 1,618,100 people, 1,286,900 of 60–65 dB, 65–70 dB 668,700, 203,600 70–75 dB, 75 dB over 21,200 people [41]. Public transport is the most common and the most annoying source of roadway noise. The noise emission levels for different road vehicles are as follows: passenger cars: 75–84 dB, motorcycle: 79–87 dB, lorry: 83–93 dB, bus: 86–92 dB and tram: 70–95 dB.

There is, then, a correlation between traffic intensity, vehicle speed and noise level. Figure 5 shows the relation between noise level and number of cars (for reference only), based on [42].

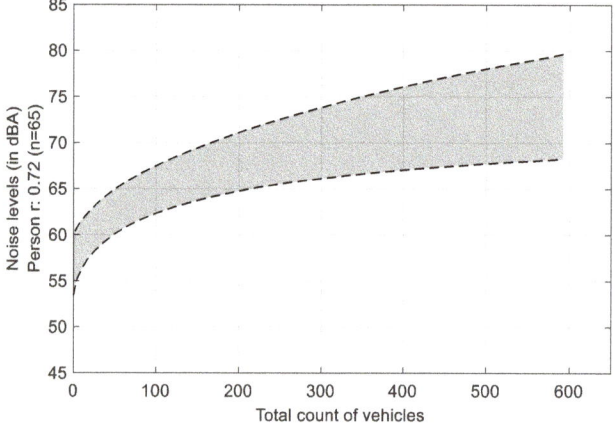

Figure 5. The influence of the number of cars in traffic on the noise generated.

This is an approximate relation. More detailed and accurate data on this matter, which take many other factors into account (such as the type of road, environment and vehicles in traffic), can be found elsewhere [32,43,44].

Road accidents are an important threat related to road transport operations. In this area, it is continuously better visible in Figure 6.

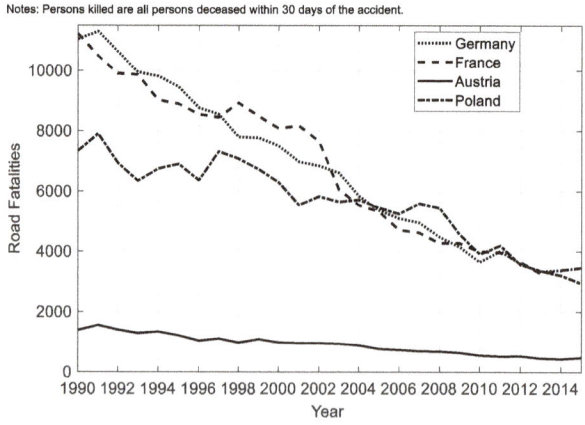

Figure 6. Road fatalities in selected countries over the years [31].

In all countries included in Figure 6, there is a decrease in the number of fatalities. However, considering the number of accidents in relation to the number of passengers and inhabitants, it can be observed that in the case of Poland, the presented results are not very favourable (Figure 7). Achieving a level of road safety such as in the old EU will require intensive action.

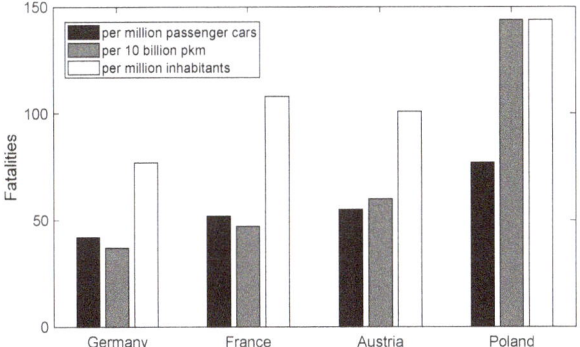

Figure 7. Road fatalities in selected countries taking into account the chosen indicators for 2015.

4. Case of the Analysed City

Rzeszow is the capital of the Subcarpathian voivodeship (a voivodeship is the area administered by a voivode in several countries of central and eastern Europe). The city forms a hub for several important road transport routes, near Poland's borders with Slovakia and Ukraine. Rzeszow is the largest city in South-East Poland, with an area of 120.4 sq. km and a population of 190,203 (30 June 2018) [45]. It is an important centre of economic, commercial, industrial, cultural and academic life. There are five higher education institutions operating in Rzeszow. The total number of students in the 2016/17 academic year was 41,787.

Rzeszow has a visibly formed zone of intercity development, with a radial-concentric layout, with the industrial and residential districts being visibly separated. The city is divided into 30 districts. The population density is one of the lowest among medium-sized cities in Poland. There are many recreational and green areas within the city. The left-bank part of Rzeszow is characterised by higher density development, including mainly residential buildings. In recent years, there has been a continuous increase of population, as shown in Figure 8a. Extending the borders of the city and expanding its area contribute greatly to increases in population, as shown in Figure 8b.

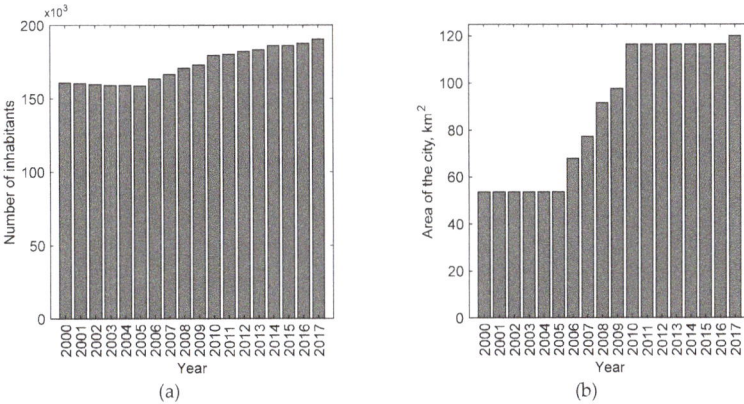

Figure 8. Development of the city in recent years: (**a**) number of inhabitants, (**b**) area of the city.

Along with the growth in the number of inhabitants (Figure 8a), there was also a growth in the number of registered passenger cars (Figure 9a).

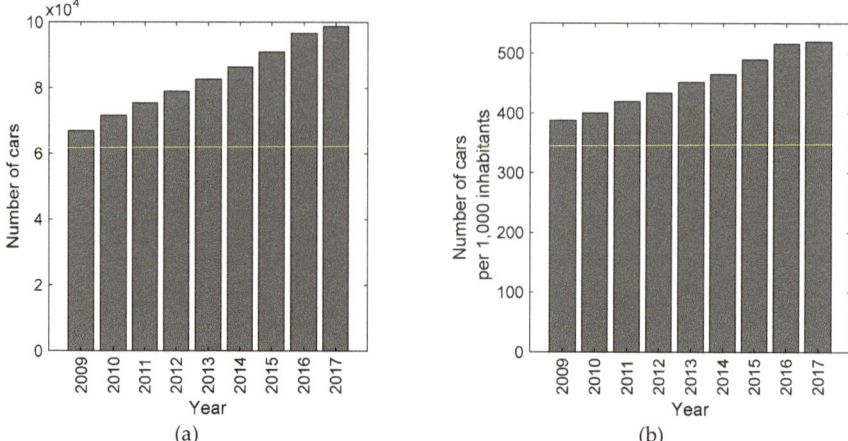

Figure 9. Number of registered passenger cars within the territory of the city: (**a**) in general, (**b**) per 1 000 inhabitants.

In the analysed years, the number of inhabitants increased by 18% and the number of registered cars increased by 47%.

The increase in the registered number of cars also caused a change in saturation rate per 1000 inhabitants as shown in the Figure 9b.

Rzeszow's road infrastructure in 2016 comprised around 274 km of hard-paved roads (Figure 10a). The period from 2010 to 2016 saw a 10% increase in the total road length. The same time period saw a 35% growth in the number of registered passenger cars. The more intense growth in passenger car numbers in relation to the growth in road length causes greater traffic density, which results, to a large degree, from the number of cars per kilometre of road. In 2016 this was 353 cars per kilometre of road, and constituted a 22% growth in relation to 2010 (Figure 10b).

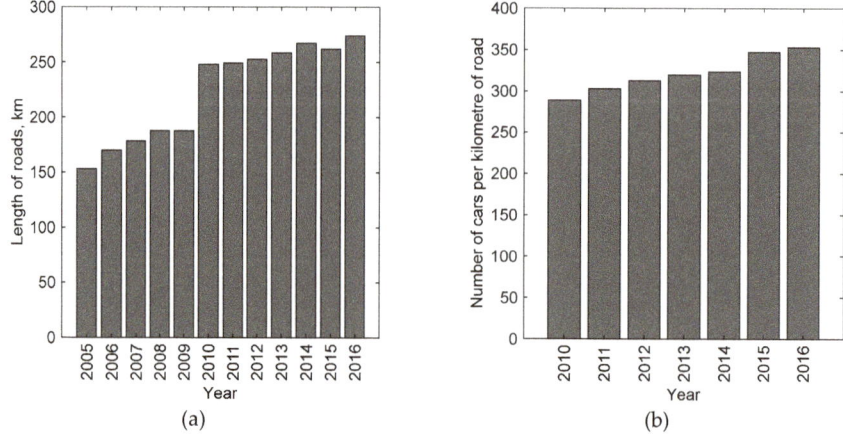

Figure 10. The total: (**a**) length of roads in Rzeszow, (**b**) number of cars per kilometre of road.

The rapid change in the total length of roads between 2009 and 2010, as shown in Figure 8a, results from neighbouring urbanised areas being incorporated into the city.

An increase in the area and population of a city generates large amounts of passengers. The transport lines of other carriers also cross the city area; however, they focus only on transporting passengers to and from Rzeszow, and it can be assumed that they do not participate in fulfilling transport needs within the territory of the city.

The public transport of Rzeszow in December 2017 [46] comprised 46 regular bus lines, 3 special lines operated by the Municipal Transport Company (MTC) and 3 night lines. These public transport lines involved the use of 179 buses. The share of low-floor and low-entry buses was 87.2% of that number. The share of buses powered by natural gas was 37.4%. Meanwhile, the average age of the fleet was 8 years.

Among these bus lines, 6 formed a group of priority lines, whose frequency during the peak period ranged between 10 and 15 minutes. Within the system of urban transport, we can additionally differentiate basic lines, with a frequency ranging between 20 and 30 minutes and supplementary lines. The urban transport of Rzeszow is characterised by two peak periods—in the morning, between 06:30 and 08:30 and in the afternoon, between 2:00 PM and 4:00 PM.

Until 2012, the transportation lines offered by MTC Rzeszow were in decline, as shown in Figure 11a. This occurred in spite of the constant increase in the number of inhabitants. The increasing transportation needs with increasing numbers of inhabitants were fulfilled mainly by individual transport. This tendency was unfavourable in terms of energy consumption and the emission of harmful substances. In 2013, the authorities of the city took decisive measures aimed at improving the functioning of urban transport in Rzeszow. Since then, a systematic growth in passengers using public transport has been observed.

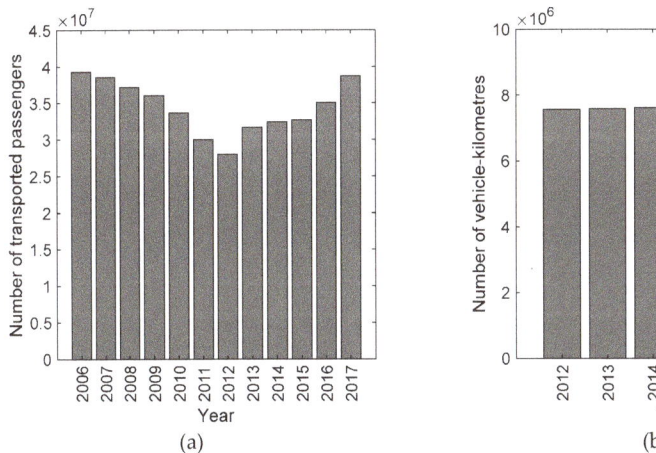

Figure 11. The number of: (**a**) transported passengers, (**b**) vehicle-kilometres.

What largely contributed to this growth was the increase in road performance, expressed in vehicle-kilometres (Figure 11b). In the period between 2012 and 2017, the number of vehicle-kilometres travelled increased by almost 20%.

The total length of the lines on which passengers were carried by MTC Rzeszow was 652 km in 2017 (Figure 12a). This was less than in 2012, when the urban transport company also provided services into the territories of neighbouring municipalities. In 2013, aside from rare cases, city buses did not leave the territory of the city.

A total of 567 bus stops form part of the infrastructure of the MTC Rzeszow transport network (Figure 12b).

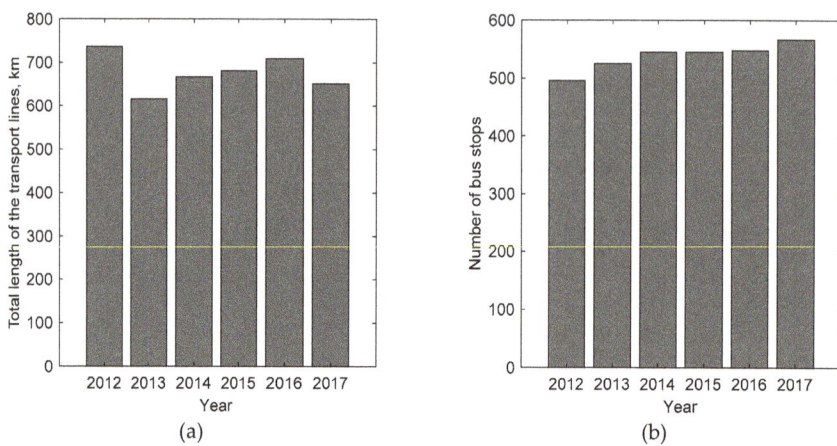

Figure 12. Transport lines in Rzeszow: (**a**) total length, (**b**) number of bus stops.

The city of Rzeszow bears witness to practically all unfavourable effects of urban development related to the functioning of transport. The increase in the number of vehicles and traffic intensity contributes to road congestion and higher journey times. The effects of congestion are clearly evident when one compares the journey times of Route 0 buses driving towards the city centre on work days and on holidays [47]. Figure 13 shows a sudden increase in the journey time throughout the afternoon rush hours, an increase of at least 40% with respect to other periods of the day. On holidays, as shown in Figure 13, the journey times between 10:00 AM and 8:00 PM did not differ much. Compared to journey times on work days, journey times on holidays were 10 to 20% shorter, afternoon rush hours notwithstanding.

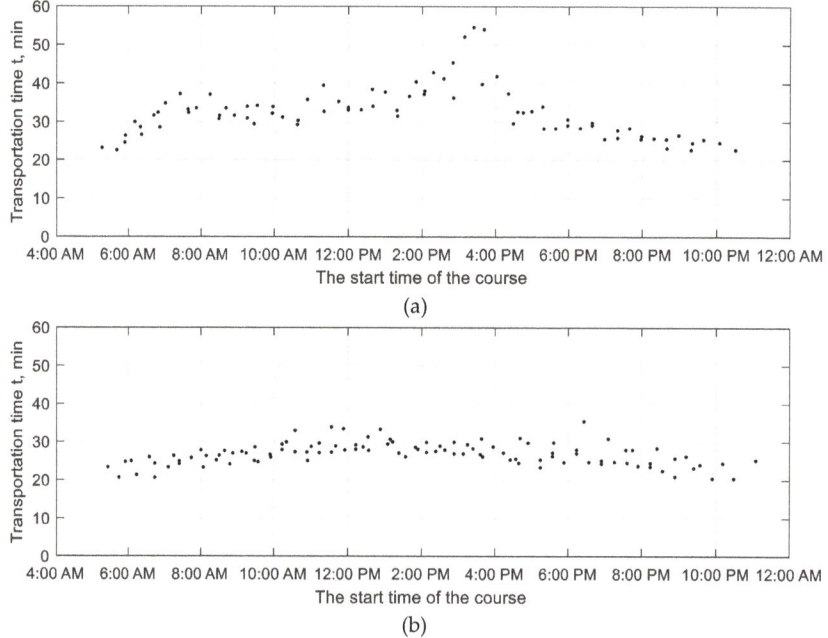

Figure 13. Journey times for Route 0 buses on: (**a**) work days (**b**) holidays.

The large number of vehicles in road traffic contributes to generating significant levels of noise. Currently, there is a large number of inhabitants and residential units exposed to roadway noise [48]. Table 1 shows relevant data concerning the number of residential units, the number of people residing in those units, and the area of Rzeszow exposed to roadway noise. The Leq coefficient was applied to assess the data in the noise column during day.

Table 1. Number of residential units, number of people residing in these units, and the area of Rzeszow exposed to roadway noise (assessed using the Leq coefficient).

Noise Level [dB]	Number of Residential Units	Number of People	City Area [km^2]
55–60	18,345	55,600	8.872
60–65	15,554	44,000	6.363
65–70	1928	4800	3.734
70–75	646	1500	1.213
>75	0	0	0.273

The highest noise levels occurred along the main city roads. Relevant data recorded on primary city roads running from the north to the south of the city are shown in Table 2.

Table 2. Comparison of roadway noise levels during the day.

Street	Equivalent Continuous Sound Level Leq [dB] Measurements	
	6:00 AM–10:00 PM	10:00 PM–6:00 AM
Gen. Jaroslawa Dabrowskiego	66.7	63.3
Leopolda Lisa-Kuli	69.1	59.1
Marszalkowska	64.2	60.8
Podkarpacka	64.0	54.6

So far, there are no data to demonstrate the direct influence of road vehicles on air pollution in Rzeszow. The station monitoring the emissions makes general measurements, which take into account various sources of pollution, including both road vehicles and local heat sources [48]. This is clearly evidenced in Figure 14. The summer months see a clear decrease in emissions of some of the substances and therefore road vehicles can be assumed to be the main source of pollution in these months. With other heat sources active in winter months, the levels of emissions rise almost fourfold.

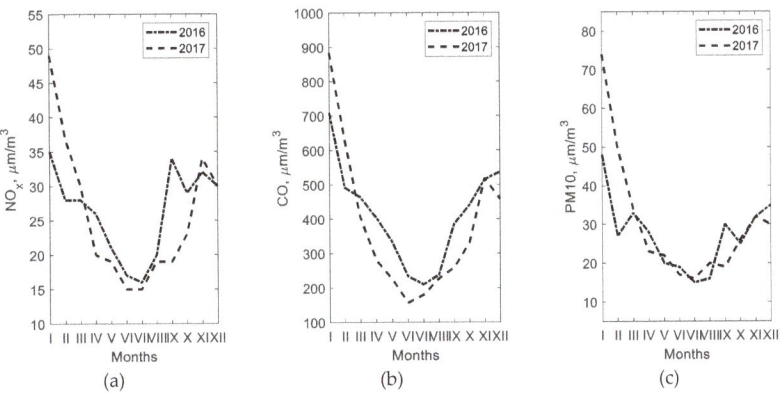

Figure 14. Emission of selected substances into the atmosphere (**a**) NOx, (**b**) CO, (**c**) PM10.

The summer months of 2017 saw a decrease in CO and NOx emissions compared to 2016.

5. Results and Planned Effects of the Actions Taken by the City's Authorities

The overall objective of the city's authorities is to change the transport preferences of its inhabitants, and thereby reduce the number of journeys by passenger cars. The actions by the authorities which aim to develop sustainable public transport can be classified into the areas in which relevant steps are taken.

The most significant areas include:

- developing the transport infrastructure (bus lanes, cycle lanes and parking lots),
- developing IT and Traffic Management systems,
- exchanging the public transport fleet.

The implementation of all these actions has been supported by relevant EU funding, under the "European Funds - for the development of Eastern Poland" programme between 2007 and 2013 [49]. As part of this programme, with respect to transport infrastructure, the local transport network was restructured and the infrastructure was modernised with public transport in mind. A total of 11.4 km of bus pass were created, ensuring more efficient functioning of public transport during the peak periods.

The differences in bus pass lengths in recent years are shown in Figure 15a, along with their routes in the city's area in Figure 15b. Furthermore, the network of cycle lanes was also developed throughout the years in which the programme was operational. This is shown in Figure 16a, while Figure 16b shows the routes of the cycle lanes throughout the city's area.

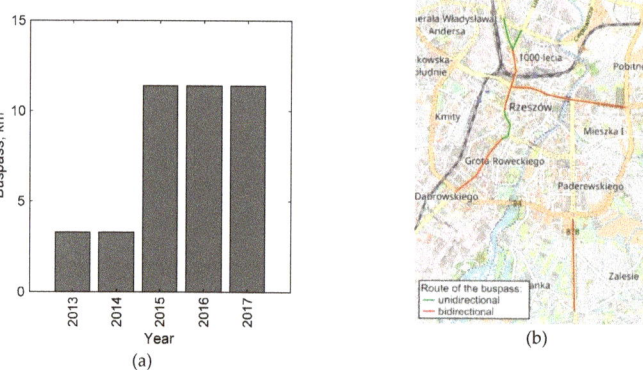

Figure 15. Length and route of the bus pass.

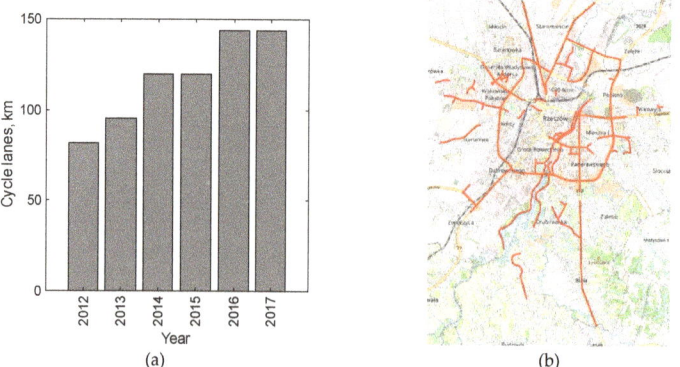

Figure 16. Length and route of the cycle lanes marked on the map of the red colour.

With respect to IT and Traffic Management systems, the Integrated Traffic and Public Transportation Management System was designed and implemented along with a dedicated ICT platform [46]. It covers:

- Area Traffic Control System, comprising:

    - a system for controlling traffic lights, to ensure fluid traffic flow and minimise waiting times at intersections,
    - a system for prioritising public transport vehicles, to give the right of way to such vehicles,
    - an information system for drivers that makes use of variable messages, to allow drivers to be quickly notified of impediments, changes in traffic organisation or recommended diversions;

- Public Transport Management System, to locate each vehicle in the city and to count the number of passengers, to give operators an opportunity to better manage service standards;
- Passenger Information System, to provide public transport passengers with information and notifications, in an efficient way. Information displays on bus stands could show the time remaining until the bus on a given route arrives, for example;
- Electronic Fare Collection System, with the aim of making public transport easier for the passengers by introducing e-tickets.

New modern buses were purchased with respect to modernising the public transport fleet. As part of the task, 80 modern ecological buses meeting the EEV emission standards were purchased, including:

- 30 12-metre buses powered by diesel fuel,
- 30 12-metre buses powered by natural gas,
- 20 10-metre buses powered by diesel fuel.

On 14 June 2017 [49] a new agreement of funding the project of the City of Rzeszow Municipality, called "The development of the public transportation system in Rzeszow" was concluded, concerning funds awarded within Operational Programme Eastern Poland 2014–2020. The project involves the purchase of 50 modern and ecological buses adjusted to the needs of disabled people. The purchase will include 10 zero-emission electric buses, to be used by the most overburdened bus lines running through the centre of the city. An appropriate system for charging batteries will be also installed in the bus depot and at the ends of the lines. As part of the programme, selected crossings, the road and pedestrian-bicycle infrastructure and bus bays will be rebuilt, along with an exchange of bus shelters. As part of the project, the Intelligent Transportation System of Rzeszow, which serves to manage the traffic and public transport within the territory of the city of Rzeszow, will be expanded with new functions. The project is to be completed on 31 December 2018.

The actions taken so far by Rzeszow's authorities to make public transport more attractive to the public have yielded some positive effects. 2012 was the last year in which there was visible decrease in the number of journeys taken by public transport. The years following saw a constant increase. The comparison of graphs illustrating Rzeszow's population growth and the increase in the number of transported passengers evidences that the increase of transported passengers was more dynamic, as shown in Figure 17a. Suitable actions by the city's authorities also contributed to greater interest in public transport with respect to journeys within the city. Taking into account the average traffic rate (determining the number of passenger journeys, according to the source [50]), an increase in the share of public transport was observed as shown in Figure 17b.

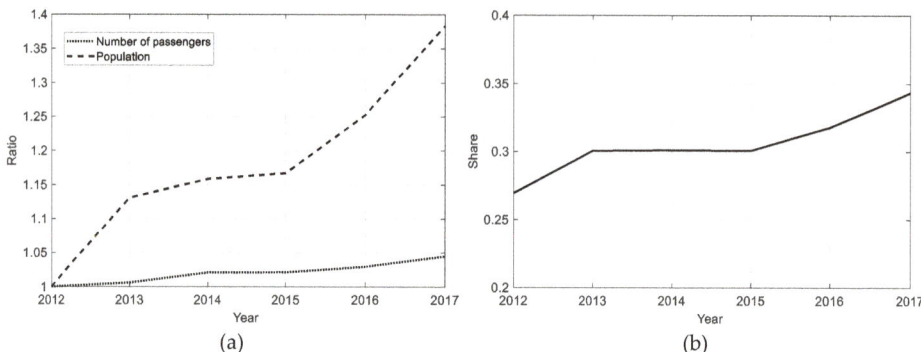

Figure 17. Indices characterising public transport in Rzeszow: (**a**) dynamics of the increase in the number of transported passengers and the city's population growth, (**b**) share of public transport in the total number of trips.

The data presented on the graphs clearly show that the steps taken by the city's authorities have been effective. In the period of interest, there was a 38% increase in number of transported passengers.

The effects visible in Figure 17a in the form of an increase in the number of passengers transported and in Figure 17b in the form of an increase share of in public transport journeys with respect to all journeys taken, result from many actions taken by the city's authorities. Certainly, one of the more significant actions was reducing the public transport journey times during rush hours by introducing bus lanes and an integrated traffic control system. Figure 18 shows the difference in journey times for Route 18 buses, which run through the heart of the city, resulting from the introduction of bus lanes and an integrated traffic control system.

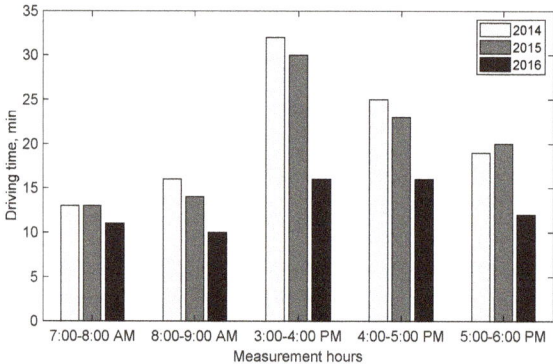

Figure 18. Journey time for Route 18 buses from Dabrowskiego to Lubelska Street—before and after the introduction of bus pass and an integrated traffic control system.

Another important course of action that the city's authorities have taken to limit the number of journeys taken using private and public means of transport are investments in cycling routes. The development of the cycling route network contributed to an increase in the interest of taking journeys by bicycle. Apart from the significant health and ecological aspects, journeys by bicycle also resulted in reducing journey time in many cases. This is evidenced by the results for just one cycling route, as shown in Figure 19.

The route is 4.1 km long. It features a cycling lane throughout the entirety of its distance. The route is mostly flat, as the total level difference amounts to 16m. The route passes along one of the most heavily trafficked roads in Rzeszow. This road constitutes one part of the ring road in the city centre and reduces journey times from the northern to the southern part of the city. Traffic jams often occur on this route.

Figure 19. The cycle route which was taken into account (red colour).

The results of the research concerning journey times for different means of transport on this route are presented in Table 3.

Table 3. An overview of journey times on the route of interest.

Time of Day/Means of Transport	Time [min]:		
	Bicycle	Car	Bus
7:30 AM	15	25	30
4:00 PM	15	35	41
8:00 PM	15	8	-

Journeys by bus take into account the time necessary for interchanges. Public transport does not operate on this route after 7:00 PM hours.

An analysis of the data included in Table 3 leads to the conclusion that only in the evening hours is it possible to complete the distance by car faster than by bicycle. Outside evening hours, the bicycle is definitely the faster means of transport, as well as being a zero-emission vehicle. The increase in the numbers of journeys taken by bicycle, and their percentage with respect to the total number of journeys taken, also contributes to reducing atmospheric pollution in the city.

The final (continuous) course of action taken by the city's authorities was investing in more ecological and convenient vehicles. The autumn of 2018 will see 10 electric zero-emission buses being put into service. The plans envisage using these buses on one of the most heavily used bus routes in Rzeszow: Route 0A and 0B. It has a circular shape and runs around the central part of the city. It begins at the main railway station and goes in both the clockwise and the counter-clockwise directions around the city, as shown in Figure 20.

Figure 20. Outline of the 0A and 0B bus routes (red color).

A total of 88 journeys in each direction are made each working day. With an average route distance of 9.5 km, the buses travel 1,672 km along this route on each working day. At an average fuel consumption of 43 dm^3 per 100 km, the buses consume 719 dm^3 of diesel fuel per working day. Taking into account the working days and holidays (when there are half the number of journeys), the total yearly consumption amounts to around 180 tonnes of fuel. The introduction of electric buses on these routes should bring a decrease in fuel consumption, and limit the emission of harmful substances into the atmosphere.

6. Conclusions

The information and results of the author's own research included in this article show that the actions taken by Rzeszow's authorities with the aim of developing sustainable transportation are consistent and durable. Technical and organizational factors were used for this. These actions are supported by appropriate EU funds [19]. They lead to an increase in the attractiveness of public transport and the development of zero-emission transport, which also includes bicycle transport. Compared to other cities, the share of cycling is very low, and in this area further decisive action by the municipal authorities is required to develop this type of transport. Investments in bicycle paths without appropriate action to change transport habits are insufficient. The increase in the number of passengers using public transport has been greater than the growth in the city's population in recent years. This positive effect has been achieved largely thanks to the steps taken by the city's authorities, which has resulted in reducing public transport journey times and allowing traffic in congested areas to become more fluid. In the immediate perspective, it is predicted that public transport will be linked with individual bicycle, pedestrian, car and railway transportation by means of transport hubs. This will create an "eco-mobility chain". Energy efficiency will further be improved with the planned and carried out purchases of modern buses (including buses with unconventional drives). With the energy efficiency of public transport improved, the negative effects on the environment can be reduced, especially concerning the emission of greenhouse gases and other toxic substances. The consistent implementation of all actions described in Section 5 on the part of the city's authorities will have a significant impact on improving the quality of life in Rzeszow and on caring for the natural environment.

Author Contributions: Conceptualization, M.S., M.D. and P.D.; Formal analysis, M.S., M.D. and P.D.; Investigation, M.S., M.D. and P.D.; Visualization, M.S., M.D. and P.D.; Writing—original draft, M.S., M.D. and P.D.

Funding: This research received no external funding.

Conflicts of Interest: The authors declare no conflict of interest.

References

1. European Commission. Report Brussels, 17.12.2013 COM (2013) 913 Final. Available online: https://ec.europa.eu (accessed on 1 September 2018).
2. Mendiluce, M.; Schipper, L. Trends in passenger transport and freight energy use in Spain. *Energy Policy* **2011**, *39*, 6466–6475. [CrossRef]
3. Pan, W.; Xue, Y.; He, H.; Lu, W. Impacts of traffic congestion on fuel rate, dissipation and particle emission in a single lane based on Nasch Model. *Phys. A* **2018**, *503*, 154–162. [CrossRef]
4. Thomas, S. How green are electric vehicles? *Int. J. Hydrog. Energy* **2012**, *37*, 6053–6062. [CrossRef]
5. Xia, T.; Nitschke, M.; Zhang, Y.; Shah, P.; Crabb, S.; Hansen, A. Traffic-related air pollution and health co-benefits of alternative transport in Adelaide, South Australia. *Environ. Int.* **2015**, *74*, 281–290. [CrossRef] [PubMed]
6. Zhang, K.; Batterman, S. Air pollution and health risks due to vehicle traffic. *Sci. Total Environ.* **2013**, *450–451*, 307–316. [CrossRef]
7. Khan, J.; Ketzel, M.; Kakosimos, K.; Sørensen, M.; Jensen, S. Road traffic air and noise pollution exposure assessment—A review of tools and techniques. *Sci. Total Environ.* **2018**, *634*, 661–676. [CrossRef]

8. Kickhöfer, B.; Kern, J. Pricing local emission exposure of road traffic: An agent-based approach. *Transp. Res. Part D* **2015**, *37*, 14–28. [CrossRef]
9. Olsson, L.; Hjalmarsson, L.; Wikström, M.; Larsson, M. Bridging the implementation gap: Combining backcasting and policy analysis to study renewable energy in urban road transport. *Transp. Policy* **2015**, *37*, 72–82. [CrossRef]
10. Jochem, P.; Babrowski, S.; Fichtner, W. Assessing CO_2 emissions of electric vehicles in Germany in 2030. *Transp. Res. Part A* **2015**, *78*, 68–83.
11. Nurhadi, L.; Borén, S.; Ny, H. A sensitivity analysis of total cost of ownership for electric public bus transport systems in Swedish medium sized cities. *Transp. Res. Procedia* **2014**, *3*, 818–827. [CrossRef]
12. Strielkowski, W. Social and Economic Implications for the Smart Grids of the Future. *Econ. Sociol.* **2017**, *10*, 310–318.
13. Chowdhury, S.; Ceder, A.; Schwalger, B. The effects of travel time and cost savings on commuters' decision to travel on public transport routes involving transfers. *J. Transp. Geogr.* **2015**, *43*, 151–159. [CrossRef]
14. Corazza, M.; Guida, U.; Musso, A.; Toz, M. A European vision for more environmentally friendly buses. *Transp. Res. Part D Transp. Environ.* **2016**, *45*, 48–63. [CrossRef]
15. Erdoğan, S.; Miller-Hooks, E. A Green Vehicle Routing Problem. *Transp. Res. Part E* **2012**, *48*, 100–114. [CrossRef]
16. Fulda, A.S.; Nimal, E. Node: Methodology for energy balance for a transportation hub and its neighbourhood. *Transp. Res. Procedia* **2014**, *4*, 25–41. [CrossRef]
17. Nosal, K.; Solecka, K. Application of AHP method for multi-criteria evaluation of variants of the integration of urban public transport. *Transp. Res. Procedia* **2014**, *3*, 269–278. [CrossRef]
18. Poliak, M.; Poliaková, A.; Mrníková, M.; Šimurková, P.; Jaśkiewicz, M.; Jurecki, R. The Competitiveness of Public Transport. *J. Compet.* **2017**, *9*, 81–97. [CrossRef]
19. Eißel, D.; Chu, C. The future of sustainable transport system for Europe. *AI Soc.* **2014**, *29*, 387–402. [CrossRef]
20. Anderson, L. Effects of using renewable fuels on vehicle emissions. *Renew. Sustain. Energy Rev.* **2015**, *47*, 162–172. [CrossRef]
21. Simionescu, M.; Albu, L.L.; Raileanu Szeles, M.; Bilan, Y. The impact of biofuels utilisation in transport on the sustainable development in the European Union. *Technol. Econ. Dev. Econ.* **2017**, *23*, 667–686. [CrossRef]
22. Androniceanu, A. The quality of the urban transport in Bucharest and how to improve it in accordance with the expectations of the citizens. *Theor. Empir. Res. Urban Manag.* **2016**, *11*, 5–18.
23. Beirao, G.; Cabral, J.A. Understanding attitudes towards public transport and private car: A qualitative study. *Transp. Policy* **2007**, *14*, 478–489. [CrossRef]
24. Fallde, M.; Eklund, M. Towards a sustainable socio-technical system of biogas for transport: The case of the city of Linkoping in Sweden. *J. Clean. Prod.* **2015**, *98*, 17–28. [CrossRef]
25. Haywood, L.; Koning, M.; Prud'homme, R. The economic cost of subway congestion: Estimates from Paris. *Econ. Transp.* **2018**, *14*, 1–8. [CrossRef]
26. Nurhadi, L.; Borén, S.; Ny, H. Advancing from efficiency to sustainability in Swedish medium-sized cities: An approach for recommending powertrains and energy carriers for public bus transport systems. *Procedia Soc. Behav. Sci.* **2014**, *111*, 1218–1225. [CrossRef]
27. Redman, L.; Friman, M.; Garling, T.; Hartig, T. Quality attributes of public transport that attract car users: A research review. *Transp. Policy* **2013**, *25*, 119–127. [CrossRef]
28. Siedler, H. Can bus rapid transit be a sustainable means of public transport in fast growing cities? Empirical evidence in the case of Oslo. *Transp. Res. Procedia* **2014**, *1*, 109–120. [CrossRef]
29. Europen Platform on Mobility Management. Available online: http://www.epomm.eu (accessed on 27 December 2018).
30. Hülsmann, F.; Regine Gerike, R.; Ketzel, M. Modelling traffic and air pollution in an integrated approach—The case of Munich. *Urban Clim.* **2014**, *10*, 732–744. [CrossRef]
31. EU Transport in Figures, Statistical Pocketbook 2017. Available online: https://ec.europa.eu (accessed on 1 September 2018).
32. Can, A.; Leclercq, L.; Lelong, J. Dynamic estimation of urban traffic noise: Influence of traffic and noise source representations. *Appl. Acoust.* **2008**, *69*, 858–867. [CrossRef]
33. Börjesson, M.; Eliasson, J.; Hugosson, M.B.; Brundell-Freij, K. The Stockholm congestion charges—5 years on. Effects, acceptability and lessons learnt. *Transp. Policy* **2012**, *20*, 1–12.

34. Kaddoura, I.; Nagel, K. Simultaneous internalization of traffic congestion and noise exposure costs. *Transportation* **2018**, *45*, 1579–1600. [CrossRef]
35. Mussone, L.; Grant-Muller, S.; Laird, J. Sensitivity analysis of traffic congestion costs in a network under a charging policy. *Case Stud. Transp. Policy* **2015**, *3*, 44–54. [CrossRef]
36. Prud'homme, R.; Koning, M.; Lenormand, L.; Fehr, A. Public transport congestion costs: The case of the Paris subway. *Transp. Policy* **2012**, *21*, 101–109. [CrossRef]
37. The Most Traffic Jam Prone Cities in Europe. Available online: https://www.statista.com (accessed on 1 October 2018).
38. TomTom Traffic Index. Available online: https://www.tomtom.com/en_gb/trafficindex/ (accessed on 1 September 2018).
39. Road Traffic Remains Biggest Source of Noise Pollution in Europe. Available online: https://www.eea.europa.eu (accessed on 1 September 2018).
40. Halonen, J.; Hansell, A.; Gulliver, J.; Morley, D.; Blangiardo, M.; Fecht, D.; Toledano, M.; Beevers, S.; Anderson, H.; Kelly, F.; et al. Road traffic noise is associated with increased cardiovascular morbidity and mortality and all-cause mortality in London. *Eur. Heart J.* **2015**, *36*, 2653–2661. [CrossRef] [PubMed]
41. European Environment Agency. Available online: https://www.eea.europa.eu (accessed on 1 September 2018).
42. Kyçyku, A.; Lajqi, S.; Hoxha, G. Analytical calculation of vehicles noise in the road traffic and graphical presentation. *IFAC-PapersOnLine* **2016**, *49*, 52–57.
43. Hamet, J.-F.; Besnard, F.; Doisy, S.; Lelong, J.; Duc, E. New vehicle noise emission for French traffic noise prediction. *Appl. Acoust.* **2010**, *71*, 861–869. [CrossRef]
44. Ramírez, A.; Domínguez, E. Modeling urban traffic noise with stochastic and deterministic traffic models. *Appl. Acoust.* **2013**, *74*, 614–621. [CrossRef]
45. Statistical Office in Rzeszów. Available online: http://rzeszow.stat.gov.pl/ (accessed on 1 September 2018).
46. Board of Urban Transport in Rzeszow. Available online: http://ztm.rzeszow.pl/ (accessed on 1 June 2018).
47. Smieszek, M.; Dobrzanska, M.; Dobrzanski, P. An Analysis of Transportation Times and the Loading of the Selected Line of Urban Communication in Rzeszow. *Adv. Mech. Eng. Transp.* **2016**, *2*, 18–23.
48. Regional Inspectorate for Environmental Protection in Rzeszow. Available online: https://stacje.wios.rzeszow.pl/ (accessed on 1 June 2018).
49. Operational Programme Eastern Poland 2014–2020. Available online: http://www.transport.rzeszow.pl (accessed on 1 June 2018).
50. Smieszek, M.; Dobrzanska, M.; Dobrzanski, P. Analysis of changes in public transport of the European Union on the example of selected cities. *Humanit. Soc. Sci.* **2016**, *21*, 137–151.

© 2019 by the authors. Licensee MDPI, Basel, Switzerland. This article is an open access article distributed under the terms and conditions of the Creative Commons Attribution (CC BY) license (http://creativecommons.org/licenses/by/4.0/).

Article

A Fuzzy WASPAS-Based Approach to Determine Critical Information Infrastructures of EU Sustainable Development

Zenonas Turskis [1], Nikolaj Goranin [2,*], Assel Nurusheva [3] and Seilkhan Boranbayev [3]

1. Institute of Sustainable Construction, Faculty of Civil Engineering, Vilnius Gediminas Technical University, Sauletekio al. 11, LT-10223 Vilnius, Lithuania; zenonas.turskis@vgtu.lt
2. Faculty of Fundamental Sciences, Vilnius Gediminas Technical University, Sauletekio al. 11, LT-10223 Vilnius, Lithuania
3. Department of Information Systems, L.N.Gumilyov Eurasian National University, Satpayev st., 2, 010008 Astana, Kazakhstan; nurusheva.assel@mail.ru (A.N.); sboranba@yandex.kz (S.B.)
* Correspondence: nikolaj.goranin@vgtu.lt

Received: 7 December 2018; Accepted: 11 January 2019; Published: 15 January 2019

Abstract: Critical information infrastructure exists in different sectors of each country. Its loss or sustainability violation will lead to a negative impact on the supply of essential services, as well as on the social or economic well-being of the population. It also may even pose a threat to people's health and lives. In the modern world, such infrastructure is more vulnerable and unstable than ever, due to rapid technological changes, and the emergence of a new type of threat—information threats. It is necessary to determine which infrastructure are of crucial importance when decision-makers aim to achieve the reliability of essential infrastructure. This article aims to solve the problem of ensuring the sustainable development of EU countries in terms of identifying critical information infrastructures. Integrated multi-criteria decision-making techniques based on fuzzy WASPAS and AHP methods are used to identify essential information infrastructures, which are related to a new type of potential threat to national security. The paper proposes a model for identifying critical information infrastructures, taking into account the sustainable development of countries.

Keywords: MCDM; critical information infrastructures; fuzzy; AHP; WSM; WASPAS

---

1. Introduction

Sustainability is one of the essential criteria of the well-being of a country's citizens [1]. Many definitions of the concept of "sustainability" exist. The meaning of most definitions comes down to "continuity through time", in context-dependent economic, environmental, and social areas [2,3]. The concept of sustainability is very old, and it represents the process itself [4–6]. It is synonymous with the concept of "sustainable development" [7]. Critical information infrastructure (CII) has a huge impact on it. CII can impact organizations or separate countries. The growing number of threats poses a real and increasing danger to the process of achieving the persistence and reliability of CII. New vulnerabilities have emerged with the development and application of information technologies in all spheres of life. Therefore, ensuring the development of vital public structures and institutions, including CII, is an essential responsibility of the government in the context of state security and sustainable development. The government must collectively prioritize, formulate clear objectives, and mitigate risks, adapting based on feedback and changing environments to achieve the stable growth of countries and core infrastructure roles. The risks are identified as "the probabilities of harm or loss". They refer to "a potentially undesirable result that may arise as a result of an incident or undesirable event". Ensuring the performance of CII at the national level aims to create protective mechanisms for managing the risks to which the country's CII may be exposed. A collaboration of various sectors within and outside the state helps to achieve these goals. CII sustainability is related to the need to maintain the viability of the environment and society, starting with administration, economic and financial institutions, those of social welfare and health, the military, and civil protection, and ending with supplies of food, water, and energy, transport, communications, etc.

The concept of "infrastructure reliability" can be understood as the ability of the infrastructure, which is in danger, to adapt to the situation and to recover from losses while preserving the functioning of critical structures and elements. Increasing the level of CII reliability is ensured through risk management. The reliability of infrastructure assets, systems, and networks means that they must be flexible and adaptable. To strengthen the reliability of CII, it is important to have accurate, timely, and valid information about threats, and the ability to analyze expected risks, identify mitigation measures, and respond to threats, and, accordingly, the ability to recover.

Thus, the sustainable development of countries can be achieved through the management of risks that are associated with possible significant threats that are aimed at CII. It is necessary to perform a set of activities to:

- identify CII;
- identify, deter, detect, and disrupt threats aimed at CII;
- reduce the vulnerability of CII, and mitigate the potential consequences of the incidents of CII;
- organize the reserves (duplicates) of CII.

The ability to overcome adverse effects is significantly affected by the availability of infrastructure. The protection of CII is based on increasing its sustainability against emergency consequences.

Countries around the world face adverse information security events in the sector of critical infrastructures [8–10]. They often lead to numerous and significant losses, the essential disruption of production, and the destruction of the environment, etc. [11–14].

The problem of CII identification is complicated by the influence on a multitude of factors. It is necessary to assess impacts on various services and areas of activity, on the environment, and on the life and health of the population, etc. CII can affect any area of activity, from government management to engineering, including sustainable development. Therefore, this problem has lots of criteria, and to solve this one, it is acceptable to use the multi-criteria decision-making (MCDM) approach. In our case, the problem is solved by using the fuzzy WASPAS method, which has not been previously used for such tasks [15–17]. The WASPAS method actually aggregates two approaches: the WSM (Weighted Sum Model) and the WPM (Weighted Product model).

There are many decision-making approaches that are applied in various fields. For example, the MCDM methods were considered in [18]. Different scientists considered the theory of decision support systems [19–21] and their practical applications in many fields of human activity [22–24]. Decision-making methods develop dynamically [25–27]. Sivilevičius et al. presented an original MADM method, which could be applied to assess different security tools [28]. MCDM has widely used decision-making techniques in science and engineering, as well as in management [29–32]. Various categories of MCDM approaches solve complicated problems [33–35].

In the last few years in the field of information technology, there has been a rise in interest in using analyses that are based on a larger number of criteria, as a decision support tool. Such criteria may include stopping the supply of electricity, natural gas, district heating, drinking water, and electronic communications to settlements and other areas.

Thus, the MCDM methodology is defined as a set of tools that supports and facilitates the decision-making process, as an approach that is based on the use of several criteria, ensuring the correct choice of CII. The use of MCDM in determining CII will ensure its objectivity and transparency in assessing the acceptability of solutions.

2. Methodology of Research and Applied Methods

2.1. Research of the Concept of CII

In the last decade, critical infrastructure study has been directed based on interdependencies from various points. The research is mainly concerned with policies in this field [36,37]. Risk analyses and comments into the existing legal framework have been described in [38,39]. The interdependent essential infrastructures are presented in [40–44]. These works are mainly focused on engineering or computer science, to design better modeling, in order to manage the infrastructure, as well as to protect the vital infrastructure [45,46].

As indicated in the Directive [47], essential infrastructure is a system, asset, or part thereof that is situated in countries, and that is very important for the control of critical societal functions and safety, etc., and the failure or breakdown of which would have a great influence on a country; as consequence of an error in keeping up those functions.

The trends and current geopolitical and geostrategic perspectives expand more and more the concept of "national security" for environmental, financial, information technology and communication, and diplomatic components. Essential infrastructures are usually sensitive to the actions of some internal or external attributes, and they are under a risk of being destroyed or made non-operational [48].

The European Union and other countries use different definitions of critical infrastructure. According to the law of the Republic of Lithuania, CII are electronic communication networks or parts of an information system or a component of a complex of information systems, or a process control system, or part of it, a cyber-incident of which can cause significant damage to national security, state economy and public interests [49]. France notes that vital infrastructure is the structure or equipment that provides critical goods and services in the formation of a society and its lifestyle [50]. The Slovenian national importance of critical infrastructure includes its necessary capabilities and services, the violation of which will have a huge influence on national security, essential social or financial operations, safety, and social security [51]. According to the Canadian National Strategy for Critical Infrastructure, critical infrastructure refers to processes, technologies, etc., that are necessary for the health, safety, or economic well-being of the population, and the impactful operation of a country [52].

Based on relevant state concepts, it can be said that each country has its own perception of critical infrastructure. Identifying critical infrastructure is not sufficient to just rely on the definition. To achieve this goal, various methods and techniques should be used. In this case, the problem of CII identification was solved by applying the MCDM approach.

2.2. Achieving the Sustainability of CII, and Potential Threats to CII

Currently, the problem of natural disasters is considered to be one of the most pressing. In recent years, there have been significant changes in views on the sustainable state and development of natural systems. This is also interrelated with the intensive development of scientific and technical (information technology (IT)) and economic potential, and the industrial development of new territories. Often the cause of environmental disasters and devastating consequences lies in the failure of a critical information resource. For example, a failure in the refining industry may cause tens or hundreds of thousands of tons of crude oil or fuel oil to be released into the marine environment. Such an accident has enormous losses, which are very difficult to estimate due to its magnitude. Accordingly, knowledge of the criticality of information infrastructures that affect natural disasters, the timely development of precautionary measures, and the restoration of destroyed territories and their socio-economic systems and ecosystems is an essential attribute for the sustainable development of systems at various levels of EU countries.

Globalization, rapid technological change, and other factors change the global security situation, and expand the list of traditional threats [53–55]. A new type of risk has appeared, such as terrorist attacks, cyber-attacks, cyber wars, etc. [56–58].

When the distributed denial-of-service (DDoS) attacks on Lithuanian websites began in 2003. Lithuania recognized that the threat of cyber-attacks is real [59]. It should be noted that by the end of 2016, a list of CII of Lithuania was approved [60]. Other countries have also previously faced cyber threats towards the critical infrastructure. In 2007, Estonia suffered greatly from politically motivated cyber-attacks (the first cyberwar) [61].

In recent years, companies of all types, including those offering critical and emergency services, have been the victims of social engineering attacks [62]. The last most infamous type of cyber threat was the WannaCry ransomware, which was one of the most impactful and propagated malware in 2017. This international wave of cyber threats is reported to have struck over 150 countries worldwide [63]. These events have increased the awareness of potential threats towards critical infrastructure that potentially endanger national security. States began to realize that new types of threats could be directed against national critical infrastructures. This infrastructure is the most sensitive and vulnerable infrastructure, which can entail a huge impact on the state and its environment.

Critical infrastructure plays the main role in countries in with regard to the importance of nationwide, socio-economic, or public security [64]. Potential threats to the critical infrastructure of its countries prompted the EU Member State to take measures to protect the essential infrastructure each country. Identifying essential infrastructure is the first step toward protect the country and the interests of people who depend on critically crucial services. Accurately defining critical infrastructure can defend them against potential threats.

The following characteristics must be considered:

- types of threats;
- threat objects;
- sources of threats.

The main types of threats directed towards sustainability include the violation of the accessibility, integrity, and confidentiality of information.

The objects, which are usually influential to CII work, can be represented as a network, an information or automated system, a process control system, etc.

The sources of key threats affecting the reliability of CII can be of two types:

- External (computer hackers (competitors), carrying out targeted destructive effects, including using computer viruses and other types of malicious codes (human-made, external), terrorists, criminal elements and structures);
- Internal (employees of an organization who are legal participants in information processing and acting outside their authority; employees of an organization who are legitimate participants in information processing and operating within their jurisdiction);
- Common acting of external and internal threats with the aim of affecting CII.

The consequences of the threats can be catastrophic, so that it is essential to take all possible actions to protect and ensure the operation of CII. Figure 1 shows one of the options that are proposed by the authors for providing the process of sustainable functioning of CII.

As can be seen from Figure 1, the identification of CII is the first phase to protect critical infrastructure. Various methods can be used to identify CII.

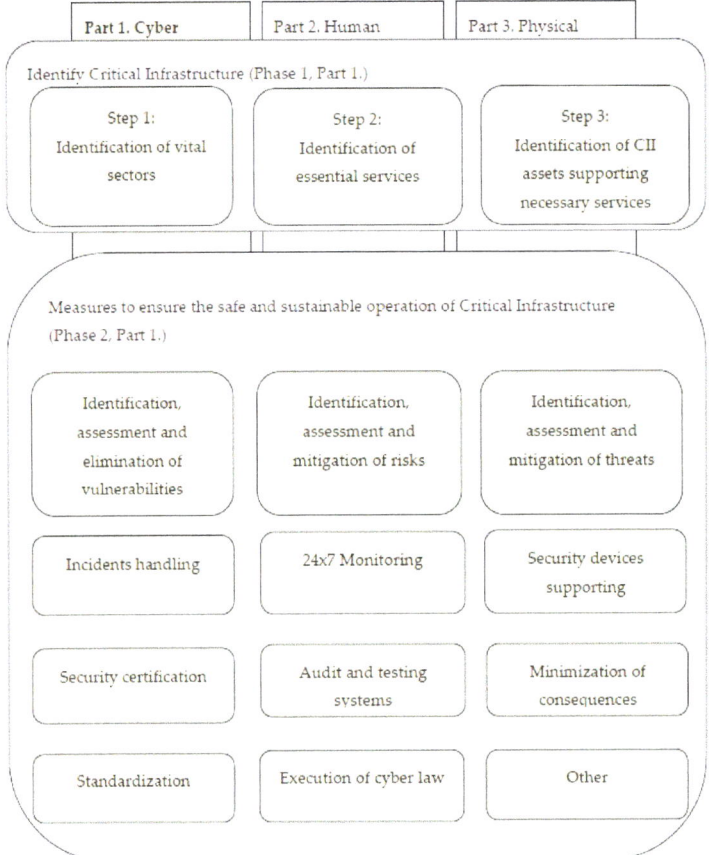

Figure 1. One of the possible variants of the critical infrastructure sustainable functioning process [65].

2.3. CII Identification Models

Various models and methodologies, which were proposed earlier by other researchers and governments, are considered in this paper.

The article by Almeida on the identification of critical infrastructure offers a multi-criteria evaluation model [66]. In the Canadian Critical Infrastructure Assessment Model, Macbeth is proposed to solve the problem, using M-MACBETH software. This method was chosen because it has a social-technical approach to development problems, and it is more convenient for decision-makers. The proposed Macbeth model is improved by the Canadian model, but this is only a theoretical model that has not been tested in practice, and the adequacy of real applicability is not evaluated [66]. Despite this, there are a large number of scientific articles that offer other methods.

Applying the AHP method for a multi-criteria task in determining the level of criticality of the water management system is proposed in [67]. This area is an important sector for all countries, and it is critical infrastructure. The goal is to identify and develop the criteria, and a list of items that will be used to identify the properties of the critical level. The AHP method is the MCDM approach that can help a decision-taker, met with the difficult issue of a multitude of criteria [68]. AHP is an effective tool that can speed up the decision-making process. It is one of the most popular methods with a comprehensive, logical and structured system. Thus, this method was useful in analyzing quantitative information in the water supply industry, and the effectiveness of water management [67].

Izuakor and White [69] continued the analysis of the methods used in relation to critical infrastructures. After research, the novel method to identify essential infrastructure was proposed, and further study in this area is suggested using several criteria of decision theory.

The countries of the European Union apply the Critical service-dependent method, which identifies the most important services. Based on these services, they are trying to identify objects or other assets that belong to the CII. This method consists of three steps, which are shown in Figure 1 [63].

The goal of most of the methods is to determine the essential resources on which governments depend, and tp guarantee that they are adequately detecting faults.

Currently, there are more than 220 identified operators of critical infrastructure. In turn, 1000 critical resources are identified [70].

The different methods to identify CII could be applied. Each of the discussed methods has its advantages and disadvantages, but the government chooses the most appropriate method, taking into account their national characteristics.

The identified critical sectors and subsectors services are shown in Table 1 [65].

Table 1. Critical sectors, sub-sectors, and services [65].

Critical Sector	Subsector	Essential Services
Energy	Electricity	Generation, transmission/distribution, and the electricity market
	Petroleum	Extraction, refinement, transport, and storage
	Natural gas	Extraction, transport/distribution, storage
Information, Communication Technologies	IT	Web services, data left/cloud, and software services
	Communications	Voice/data communication, Internet connectivity
Water	Drinking water	Water storage, distribution and quality assurance
	Wastewater	Wastewater collection and treatment
Food		Agriculture/food production, supply, distribution, quality/safety
Health		Emergency health- and hospital care, infection/epidemic control, etc.
Financial services		Banking, payment transactions, stock exchange
Public order and safety		Maintenance of public order and safety, judiciary and penal systems
Transport	Aviation	Air navigation services, airports operation
	Road transport	Bus/tram services, maintenance of the road networks
	Train transport	Management or public railway, railway transport services
	Maritime transport	Monitoring and maintenance of shipping traffic, ice-breaking functions
	Postal and Shipping	
Industry	Critical industries	Employment
	Chemical and Nuclear Industry	Storage and disposal of hazardous materials
		Safety of high-risk industrial units
Civil Administration		State functioning
Space		Protection of space-based systems
Civil protection		Emergency and rescue services
Environment		Monitoring and early warning (air and marine pollution, meteorological, groundwater)
Defense		National defense

The European Commission provides a brief of 11 essential areas: energy; information and communication technologies; water; food; health; financial public order and safety; civil administration; transport; chemical and nuclear industry; space and research [70].

To identify the objects of CII supporting critical services it is essential to determine the main factors that allow determining the degree of influence (Table 2) [65].

Table 2. The main factors that allow for the determination of the degree of influence [65,71].

Key Factors	Description
Scope or spatial distribution	The geographic zone that can be influenced by the failure or inaccessibility of a essential infrastructure (the international, national, provincial, regional level);
Severity or intensity or magnitude	The results of the interruption of a specific essential infrastructure; It can be measured as zero, minimum, moderate, or heavy. Assessment of the potential values may be used for different criteria.
Effects of time or temporal distribution	The point that the loss of a component can have a severe effect (immediately, several days, one week). The criterion defines when the loss of this part can have a significant impact. Time effects may be measured in different sizes, e.g., directly, for 24–48 hours, one week, or for a longer period.

An important criterion is an impact on the population, which indicates the number of people affected, health problems, heavy injuries, etc. Equally important is the economic impact, which reflects the impact on Gross domestic product GDP, the importance of economic losses, as well as products and the deterioration of service quality. Environmental impact testing indicates an impact on a person and the surrounding landscape and takes the main part in assessing the importance of infrastructure. Infrastructure assessment should take into account the interdependence of criteria that show a certain dependence on infrastructure with another critical infrastructure. It may also be subject to political criteria that reflect confidence in the ability of the government [72]. The European Union has, in particular, estimated the destruction of infrastructure or the severity of the consequences of its destruction, based on six criteria: impact on society, economic consequences, environmental effects, political effects, psychological effects, consequences for public health.

Some criteria for the sectoral and sub-sectoral assessment of the Lithuanian critical infrastructure are presented in Table 3. These criteria indicate the level of impact of the destruction of the particular sector, the object of the subsector, or its inability to manage critical services.

Table 3. Some criteria for the evaluation of the services of critical infrastructures in Lithuania [73].

Services	Scores			
	3	2	1	0
(K1) Environment, food, health, finance, public security and legal services, industry, government, civil protection, international relations, and security policy sectors	The service would cease to cover more than 145,000 inhabitants, or more than three municipalities, and will last more than 24 h	The service would cease to cover more than 20,000 inhabitants, which will last more than 24 h	The service would cease to cover more than 500 inhabitants, which will last more than 12 h	The service has stopped for less than 12 h
(K1) Services provided by the electricity sub-sector; Services provided by the natural gas subsector; Services provided by the district heating sector	Supply will be cut off for more than 145,000 residents or in more than three municipalities or category I consumers, which will last more than 24 h	Supply will be terminated for more than 20,000 inhabitants or a quarter of the population of the municipality, which will last more than 24 h	Supply will be terminated for more than 500 inhabitants, which will last more than 24 h	Supply will be cut off for less than 500 inhabitants
(K1) Services provided by the oil and petroleum products subsector	Supply of petroleum products will decrease by more than 25% of the average daily consumption	Supply of petroleum products will decrease by 12–25% of the average daily consumption	Supply of petroleum products will decrease by 7–12% of the average daily consumption	Supply of petroleum products will decrease, but not by more than 7% of the average daily consumption in the state

The work is not limited to the criteria for evaluating the sectoral or sub-sectoral criteria. In addition, criteria are included that indicate the significance of the impact of the destruction or damage to the object.

To apply the methodology of the Lithuanian government, the problem of CII identification was solved for three objects. Since the assessment of the critical infrastructure was not publicly available, and this data was not available, the table would be filled with random numbers in the range, from 0 to 3 points. The studied objects provided services for air transport, road transport, rail transport, sea transport, postal subsectors, so the weight of the first criterion was 1. Other results are presented in Table 4.

Table 4. An example of the matrix for assessing the critical information infrastructure (CII).

CII	Evaluation of Criteria									
	K1	K2	K3	K4	K5	K6	K7	K8	K9	K10
Criteria weights	1	1	1	1	1	3	3	1	1	1
Object 1	0	2	3	1	0	0	3	0	0	0
Object 2	0	0	1	2	2	2	1	1	0	0
Object 3	2	0	3	3	0	0	1	2	2	3

The number of objects is not limited, but in the example, there are three objects.

The weighted sum method (WSM) is used to calculate the estimates. The results obtained are: Object 1 and Object 2 have 15 scores, and Object 3 has 18 scores. Thus, object 3 has the highest priority, while object 1 and object 2 both share the second priority position. It is impossible to determine which of these objects is more significant, since the importance of the two objects is the same.

Having determined that the WSM method that is used in the above-mentioned method of identifying a CII is currently inappropriate, another MCDM method is further discussed. A methodology should be used to better define the CII, and to solve the problems of the applied WSM model. The use of points from 0 to 3 must be replaced with new ones.

Researchers have proposed different methods for define subjective or objective weights of criteria. The basic idea of assessing the significance of the criterion is that the most critical criterion gains the biggest weight.

An integrated definition of the objective significance of a criterion in the MCDM method is proposed in [74]. In practice, usually, a subjective weight is used, determined by professionals or experts. Many methods have been developed to identify the criteria weights in terms of experts' assessment of the importance (weights). The most widely used approaches include the Delphi [75], the expert judgment [76], the Analytic Hierarchy Process (AHP) [77,78], the Analytic Network Process, Step-wise weight assessment ratio analysis method (SWARA) [79], and others. For example, criteria weights are determined by applying the AHP method: the weights of the criteria are calculated based on Saaty's judgment scale and the new original scale, as presented by the authors. The ARAS (Additive Ratio Assessment) method (the MCDM approach) is applied, to solve the problem under investigation. The developed assessment method involves the Leadership in Energy and Environmental Design (LEED) system's criteria [80].

During the evaluation process, the criteria values, and the degree of domination of each criterion, i.e., the objective weight criteria, could be considered. Unlike their subjective analogues, the objective weights are rarely used in practice. The Entropy method [81–83], the LINMAP method [84], the correlation coefficient, and the standard deviation based on the objective value determination method [85], and the prediction algorithm [86] are practical methods that are often used. Combined weighing is based on the integration of both objective and subjective judgments [87,88].

In our case, according to [89], the fuzzy WASPAS method was chosen.

2.4. An MCDM Process to Identify CII

This article presents an MCDM-based model of the applicability of the MCDM method for determining CII.

One of the main stages to determine CII is the design of a mathematical model consisting of:

- a choice of essential variables;
- drawing up restrictions, which are satisfied by variables;
- a compilation of the objective function, which reflects the critical criteria for selecting the assignment of an object to a vital one.

The solution of the problem depends on the set of criteria for classifying objects as critical, as well as on their significance.

The task of classifying an information object is complicated by the presence of incomparable values of criteria, since particular criteria respectively have different units of measure, their scales are not comparable, and therefore, comparing the results that are obtained for each criterion is difficult.

Besides, the scales must be reduced and dimensionless—normalized values of criteria are used. Formally, describing the principle of optimality (the criteria of "correctness of the solution") is difficult, due to the following reasons:

- The objects considered by the theory of decision-making are so diverse that it is difficult to establish uniform principles of optimality for all classes of problems.
- The goals of the decision-making stakeholders are different and often opposite.
- The criteria for the correctness of the decision depend on the nature of the task, its goals, etc., and also on how correctly they were chosen for a particular country.
- The difficulties in selecting a solution may be hidden in the specific formulation of the problem, if unrealistic results are required.

Alternative objects are characterized by the correctness of the definition of vital criteria and their significances. They have essential meaning. This is possible, by establishing the criticality of information objects and the priority of the compared options. Using international experience and expert assessments, as well as information sources, the values of the criteria are determined [73].

In this paper, the MCDM method performs the following functions:

1. The identification of CII among the available information objects;
2. The comparison of CII, and the formation of a comparative table.

The proposed model and the stages identified for the method for the CII identification structure are shown in Figure 2.

The procedure should concentrate on an essentially imperative task: to identify the decision-taker, and to differentiate it from the issue analysis. Various variants are possible for the criteria optimization, as well as synthesizing all criteria into one criterion of defining the optimum. The criteria are exceedingly conditioned, with the priorities and critical assets being identified. The criteria for the CII evaluation should be identified with a focus on country-critical services. The main stage in forming the criteria involves choosing the basic criteria for CII identification that can be divided into sub-criteria during the procedure. This could be the criteria for the life and health of the population, the criteria for the impact on the economy of the country, the criteria for environmental damage, etc. Criteria groups have various influences on significance.

To form the steps of the MCDM method of CII, we use the model described in the article [90].

Another model, which is used for identifying CII by the MCDM method, is shown in Figure 3.

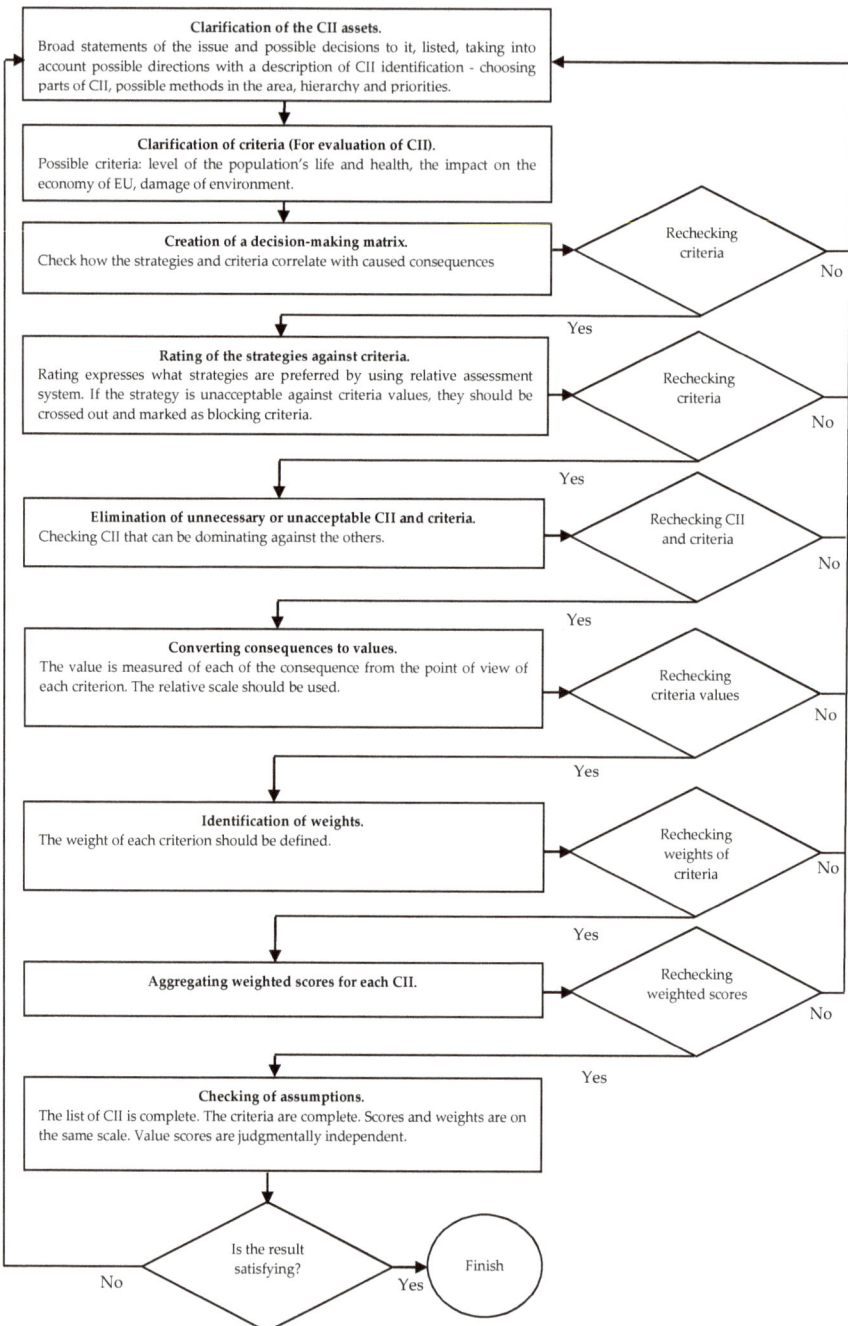

Figure 2. Steps of the multi-criteria decision-making (MCDM) approach for critical infrastructure identification [90].

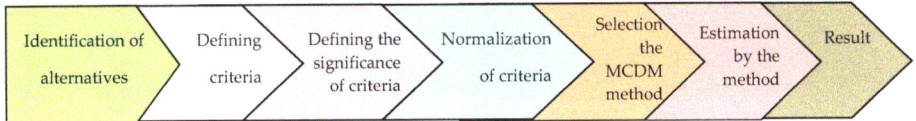

Figure 3. The MCDM model for the selection of CII.

There are several cases in which different MCDM approaches have various decisions. It might be explained because of the various mathematical artefacts that are used by different MCDM methods. However, the issue of applying a convenient MCDM approach in a specific case still exists. The choice of MCDM methods based on various parameters has already been studied by earlier researchers in [91]. When a particular MCDM method is finally recommended for a particular application, it is observed that its decision accuracy and ranking efficiency strongly depends on the value of its control parameter [92].

The most suitable solution of a problem in different areas, considering a number of criteria, such as environment, engineering, finance, etc., is the use of the MCDM method [67].

The flowchart of the proposed issue is shown in Figure 4.

Often, due to the lack of accurate data, employees spend a lot of time discussing various expert opinions. The problem-solving approach still stands.

The fuzzy set theory is a class of objects with a continuum of membership grades. Here, a fuzzy set A, presented in space X, is an ordered set of pairs. The components with 0 degrees can be unlisted:

$$A = \{(x, \mu_A(x)), x \in X\}, \forall x \in X, \text{ and } X \to [0; 1], \tag{1}$$

where A is described by its function $\mu_A : X \to [0;1]$, which associates with each component $x \in X$, a real number $\mu_A(x) \in [0;1]$. The function $\mu_A(x)$ at x identifies the grade of membership of x in A, and is accounted for by the membership degree to which x belongs to A.

An ordinary subset A of X is presented like a fuzzy set in X, with a membership function as its characteristic function:

$$\mu_A(x) = \begin{cases} 1, & x \in A; \\ 0, & x \notin A. \end{cases} \tag{2}$$

If the universe of discourse is discrete and finite with cardinality n, that is $X = \{x_1, x_1, \ldots, x_n\}$, A is calculated as:

$$A = \sum_{i=1}^{n} \frac{\mu_A(x_i)}{x_i} = \frac{\mu_A(x_1)}{x_1} + \frac{\mu_A(x_2)}{x_2} + \cdots + \frac{\mu_A(x_n)}{x_n}, \tag{3}$$

If the universe of discourse X is an interval of real numbers, the A could be shown as follows:

$$A = \int_X \frac{\mu_A(x)}{x}. \tag{4}$$

The fuzzy number A is determined to be a fuzzy triangular number, with α- lower, β-modal, and γ-upper values, if its membership function $\mu_A(x) \to [0, 1]$ is defined as:

$$\mu_A(x) = \begin{cases} \frac{1}{\beta-\alpha}x - \frac{\alpha}{\beta-\alpha}, & \text{if } x \in [\alpha, \beta], \\ \frac{1}{\beta-\gamma}x - \frac{\alpha}{\beta-\gamma}, & \text{if } x \in [\beta, \gamma], \\ 0, & \text{otherwise}, \\ \alpha \leq \beta \leq \gamma. \end{cases} \tag{5}$$

To obtain a crisp output, a defuzzification is implemented, which produces a quantifiable result in fuzzy logic, given the fuzzy sets and their corresponding membership degrees.

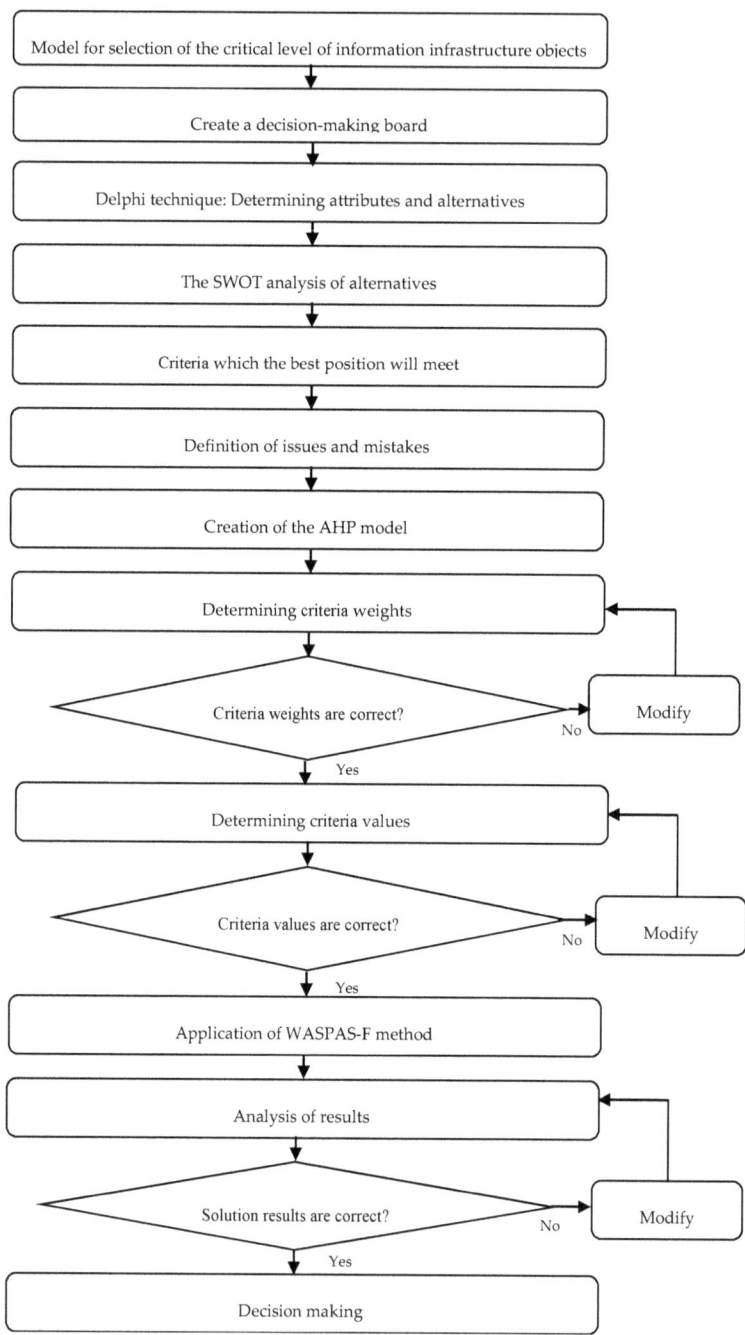

Figure 4. Flowchart of the proposed issue-solving process.

The fuzzy number is generally an expert's given subjective data. Figure 5 presents the ordinary fuzzy set membership function.

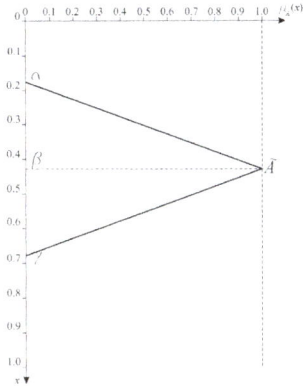

Figure 5. Triangular membership function [93].

Table 5 presents the following basic arithmetic operations for two triangular fuzzy numbers: (6) two triangular fuzzy numbers; (7) addition; (8) subtraction; (9) multiplication; (10) multiplication by constant; (11) division; (12) determining the reciprocal value; (13) the fuzzy power of raising the fuzzy numbers [94].

Table 5. Main processes on fuzzy triangular numbers [93].

Relations				
$\widetilde{x}_1 = (x_{1\alpha}, x_{1\beta}, x_{1\gamma})$, $\widetilde{x}_2 = (x_{2\alpha}, x_{2\beta}, x_{2\gamma})$	(6)	$k\widetilde{x}_1 = \begin{pmatrix} kx_{1\alpha}, \\ kx_{1\beta}, \\ kx_{1\gamma} \end{pmatrix}$	(10)
$\widetilde{x}_1 \oplus \widetilde{x}_2 = \begin{pmatrix} x_{1\alpha}+x_{2\alpha}, \\ x_{1\beta}+x_{2\beta}, \\ x_{1\gamma}+x_{2\gamma} \end{pmatrix}$	(7)	$\widetilde{x}_1(\div)\widetilde{x}_2 = \begin{pmatrix} \frac{x_{1\alpha}}{x_{2\gamma}}, \\ \frac{x_{1\beta}}{x_{2\beta}}, \\ \frac{x_{1\gamma}}{x_{2\alpha}} \end{pmatrix}$	(11)
$\widetilde{x}_1(-)\widetilde{x}_2 = \begin{pmatrix} x_{1\alpha}-x_{2\gamma}, \\ x_{1\beta}-x_{2\beta}, \\ x_{1\gamma}-x_{2\alpha} \end{pmatrix}$	(8)	$(\widetilde{x}_1)^{-1} = \begin{pmatrix} \frac{1}{x_{1\gamma}}, \\ \frac{1}{x_{1\beta}}, \\ \frac{1}{x_{1\alpha}} \end{pmatrix}$	(12)
$\widetilde{x}_1 \otimes \widetilde{x}_2 = \begin{pmatrix} x_{1\alpha}x_{2\alpha}, \\ x_{1\beta}x_{2\beta}, \\ x_{1\gamma}x_{2\gamma} \end{pmatrix}$	(9)	$(\widetilde{x}_1)^{\widetilde{x}_2} = \begin{pmatrix} x_{1\alpha}^{x_{2\gamma}}, \\ x_{1\beta}^{x_{2\beta}}, \\ x_{1\gamma}^{x_{2\alpha}} \end{pmatrix}$	(13)

A-lower, β-modal and γ-upper values of fuzzy numbers

Experts have determined the weight values $0 < \widetilde{w}_j < 1$, $\sum_{j=1}^{n} w_j = 1$. It is known that many methods are able to assess weights. Sometimes, some expert data cannot be accurately described by using numerical values. There are four main options that describe various ways of measuring the number of things in quantitative terms: nominal, ordinal, interval, or ratio scales. Likert items were proposed in [95].

Raising a fuzzy triangular number of the power of another fuzzy triangular number, if $\widetilde{x}_1 = (x_{1\alpha} \leq 1, x_{1\beta} \leq 1, x_{1\gamma} \leq 1)$, and $\widetilde{x}_2 = (x_{2\alpha} \leq 1, x_{2\beta} \leq 1, x_{2\gamma} \leq 1,)$ this is special for this situation of research.

In the analysis, an initial data matrix is created initially, in which the rows contain alternatives, and in the columns, there are selected significant indicators. Each indicator is assigned to whether it is maximized or minimized.

2.5. The WASPAS Method

The WSM approach calculates the total score of the alternative as a weighted sum of the criteria. The WPM approach was created to prevent alternatives that have poor attributes or criterion values. Zavadskas et al. used the multiplicative exponential weighting method (or WPM) to solve dynamically changing environment problems [27].

The problem solution process by applying the WASPAS-F method is shown below.

Create the fuzzy decision-making matrix by using the values $\tilde{x}_{ij}$ and the criteria weights $\tilde{w}_j$ as the decision-making matrix entries. Determine the linguistic ratings.

Usually, experts play a main role in identifying the system of criteria, the linguistic values of the qualitative criteria, and the initial criteria weights.

The initial fuzzy decision-making matrix shows the preferences for m reasonable alternatives rated on n attributes:

$$\tilde{X} = \begin{bmatrix} \tilde{x}_{11} & \cdots & \tilde{x}_{1j} & \cdots & \tilde{x}_{1n} \\ \vdots & \ddots & \vdots & \ddots & \vdots \\ \tilde{x}_{i1} & \cdots & \tilde{x}_{ij} & \cdots & \tilde{x}_{in} \\ \vdots & \ddots & \vdots & \ddots & \vdots \\ \tilde{x}_{m1} & \cdots & \tilde{x}_{mj} & \cdots & \tilde{x}_{mn} \end{bmatrix}; \quad (14)$$

$$i = \overline{1, m}; \; j = \overline{1, n},$$

where $\tilde{x}_{ij}$ is a fuzzy value that presents the performance value of the i alternative in terms of the j criteria. A tilde symbol "~" means a fuzzy set.

The process of normalization of the initial values of all criteria $\tilde{x}_{ij}$ eliminates different criteria measurement units. The values of the normalized decision-making matrix $\overline{\tilde{X}}$:

$$\overline{\tilde{X}} = \begin{bmatrix} \overline{\tilde{x}}_{11} & \cdots & \overline{\tilde{x}}_{1j} & \cdots & \overline{\tilde{x}}_{1n} \\ \vdots & \ddots & \vdots & \ddots & \vdots \\ \overline{\tilde{x}}_{i1} & \cdots & \overline{\tilde{x}}_{ij} & \cdots & \overline{\tilde{x}}_{in} \\ \vdots & \ddots & \vdots & \ddots & \vdots \\ \overline{\tilde{x}}_{m1} & \cdots & \overline{\tilde{x}}_{mj} & \cdots & \overline{\tilde{x}}_{mn} \end{bmatrix}; \quad (15)$$

are determined as follows:

$$\overline{\tilde{x}}_{ij} = \frac{\tilde{x}_{ij}}{\max_i \tilde{x}_{ij}} \; if \; \max_i \tilde{x}_{ij} \; is \; preferable;$$

$$\overline{\tilde{x}}_{ij} = \frac{\min_i \tilde{x}_{ij}}{\tilde{x}_{ij}} \; if \; \min_i \tilde{x}_{ij} \; is \; preferable; \quad (16)$$

$$i = \overline{0, m}; \; j = \overline{1, n}.$$

Determine the weighted normalized fuzzy decision-making matrix $\hat{\tilde{X}}_q$ for the WSM:

$$\hat{\tilde{X}}_q = \begin{bmatrix} \hat{\tilde{x}}_{11} & \cdots & \hat{\tilde{x}}_{1j} & \cdots & \hat{\tilde{x}}_{1n} \\ \vdots & \ddots & \vdots & \ddots & \vdots \\ \hat{\tilde{x}}_{i1} & \cdots & \hat{\tilde{x}}_{ij} & \cdots & \hat{\tilde{x}}_{in} \\ \vdots & \ddots & \vdots & \ddots & \vdots \\ \hat{\tilde{x}}_{m1} & \cdots & \hat{\tilde{x}}_{mj} & \cdots & \hat{\tilde{x}}_{mn} \end{bmatrix}; \quad (17)$$

$$\hat{\tilde{x}}_{ij} = \overline{\tilde{x}}_{ij} \tilde{w}_j; \; i = \overline{1, m}; \; j = \overline{1, n}.$$

Determine the weighted normalized fuzzy decision-making matrix $\hat{\tilde{X}}_p$ for the WPM:

$$\tilde{X}_p = \begin{bmatrix} \tilde{x}_{11} & \cdots & \tilde{x}_{1j} & \cdots & \tilde{x}_{1n} \\ \vdots & \ddots & \vdots & \ddots & \vdots \\ \tilde{x}_{i1} & \cdots & \tilde{x}_{ij} & \cdots & \tilde{x}_{in} \\ \vdots & \ddots & \vdots & \ddots & \vdots \\ \tilde{x}_{m1} & \cdots & \tilde{x}_{mj} & \cdots & \tilde{x}_{mn} \end{bmatrix}; \quad (18)$$

$$\tilde{\overline{x}}_{ij} = \tilde{x}_{ij}^{\tilde{w}_j}; \; i = \overline{1, m}; \; j = \overline{1, n}.$$

Calculate the multi-attribute utility function values:
The WSM for i alternative:

$$\tilde{Q}_i = \sum_{j=1}^{n} \tilde{\overline{x}}_{ij}; \quad i = \overline{1, m}, \quad (19)$$

The WPM for i alternative:

$$\tilde{P}_i = \prod_{j=1}^{n} \tilde{\overline{x}}_{ij}, \; i = \overline{1, m}. \quad (20)$$

The center-of-area is the most practical and easy to use for the defuzzification of the fuzzy performance measurement:

$$Q_i = \frac{1}{3}(Q_{i\alpha} + Q_{i\beta} + Q_{i\gamma}). \quad (21)$$

$$P_i = \frac{1}{3}(P_{i\alpha} + P_{i\beta} + P_{i\gamma}). \quad (22)$$

The utility function value K_i of the WASPAS-F method is calculated as follows:

$$K_i = \lambda \sum_{j=1}^{n} Q_i + (1-\lambda) \sum_{j=1}^{n} P_i; \lambda = 0, \ldots, 1, 0 \leq K_i \leq 1, \quad (23)$$

where:

$$\lambda = \frac{\sum_{i=1}^{m} P_i}{\sum_{i=1}^{m} Q_i + \sum_{i=1}^{m} P_i}. \quad (24)$$

Rank preference orders the alternatives, starting from the highest value, K_i.
A Likert-type 10-point scale was adopted to solve the problem (Figure 6).

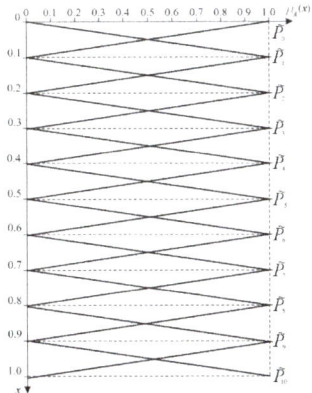

Figure 6. Membership functions of the linguistic values for criteria rating [93].

A detailed description of the problem-solving process using the AHP and WASPAS-F methods could be found in [93].

3. Results

This article analyzes the problem of identifying the CII of the country.

When solving problems of a MCDM method, first of all, a set of possible alternatives is formed, consisting of the CII. Next, the criteria are selected. A matrix of a set of alternative objects, and the criteria of their criticality are presented in Table 6.

Table 6. Matrix for CII assessment.

CII	Criteria Criticality					
	Criterion 1	Criterion 2	Criterion 3	Criterion 4	...	Criterion n
Object 1	x_{11}	x_{12}	x_{13}	x_{14}	...	x_{1n}
Object 2	x_{21}	x_{22}	x_{23}	x_{24}	...	x_{2n}
Object 3	x_{31}	x_{32}	x_{33}	x_{34}	...	x_{3n}

The criteria were identified on the basis of the sectors, which have a large EU counterpart. The list of proposed criteria is as follows:

1. The danger to life or health. This criterion is designed to assess how many people will be disturbed if the provision of a particular service stops. This criterion will cover all sub-sectoral and sectoral criteria, since the impacts considered include failure for these sectors or sub-sectors. Many sub-sectoral and sectoral criteria are estimated by the number of injured people, and by general criteria, the population health is also evaluated by their number; therefore, the unit of measure for this criterion is the population of the country.
2. The impact on the economy of the country. This criterion is widely used in the methodologies of the respective countries, and is included in the list of criteria that is recommended by the European Union. An economic impact assessment may have several expressions, but the proposed methodology deals with the number of productive working days that are lost. It is being understood as the time at which the destruction, damage, or significant damage to an infrastructure facility stops, or significantly disrupts certain activities. The number of lost production days is defined in terms of the number of lost production days multiplied by the number of employees involved in the work activity that has stopped or failed. When evaluating productive working days, it is necessary to take into account the impact of the destruction, damage, or violation of the estimated infrastructure facility on the productive working days of another infrastructure.
3. Environmental damage. The assessment of potential financial damage to the destruction of the environment or infrastructure should be carried out in accordance with the order of the Environmental Protection Law. The measure of environmental damage is the monetary value.
4. The impact of other facilities, in order to ensure the supply of basic services and continuous operation. This criterion includes the impact on the operation of another facility, which provides both the most important services, as well as other important services. Measure—the affected facilities that provide a range of important services.
5. Influence on public safety. Infrastructure damage or significant disruption can lead to widespread unrest. The impact on public safety is considered as the number of municipalities over which public safety management has been lost.
6. Damage to other European Union Member States. The destruction of the CII of one state can lead to negative consequences for other countries. This dependence is one of the important criteria for the EU countries, as its unit of measurement is the impact on the number of countries in the European Union.

Further criteria are determined by the weight, depending on their importance. More significant criteria possess higher weight values (Table 7).

Table 7. Criteria weights.

	Criterion 1	Criterion 2	Criterion 3	Criterion 4	Criterion n
Criteria weights	Weight 1	Weight 2	Weight 3	Weight 4	Weight n

The task of choosing the best alternative, in this case of the creation of a priority sequence of CII, is solved by the previously discussed MCDM methods.

In this case, seven experts were interviewed to assess the critical infrastructure alternatives. Coming both from the information security industry and academia from different European countries, they were invited to ensure the understanding of the European context and deep practical knowledge of the critical infrastructure: one from Poland (academic and industry background), one from Estonia (academic background), one from Sweden (academic background), and four from Lithuania (one of them having academic background and three from an industry background). One of the Lithuanian experts invited is one of the leading information security specialists in Lithuania, with more than 15 years of experience with key competences in critical security control development, a strong background in European knowledge (ENISA and Lithuanian Government advisor on national cybersecurity strategy), keeping CISA (Certified Information Systems Auditor), CRISC (Certified in Risk and Information Systems Control), CISSP (Certified Information Systems Security Professional), and several other security-related certifications. The majority of other experts with practical backgrounds also possessed industry-recognized security related certificates (CISA, CISM (Certified Information Security Manager), CRISC, CEH (Certified Ethical Hacker), CISSP, and others), and have experience in administering critical infrastructure, the organization of CERT (Computer emergency response teams) functions, or performing wide-scale risk assessments.

According to the results of the interview, the data obtained were summarized, and the average estimates of the seven experts were used in the article.

It should also be noted that the assessment of the criticality of the information infrastructure becomes more accurate if the number of experts is greater. Accordingly, it is preferable to take into account the opinion of several experts when assessing criticality.

Materials associated with the CII were collected and defined, and descriptions of the most significant criteria were made. The analysis was implemented. In this study, the SWOT (Strengths, Weaknesses, Opportunities, and Threats) analysis was used. Three information infrastructure alternatives, which are denoted as A_1, A_2, and A_3, were chosen as possible alternatives. The A_1 alternative is the information infrastructure of air transport, which provides both air navigation services and airport operation. A_2 is the information infrastructure of the health sector, which provides emergency and hospital healthcare services. A_3 is the financial information infrastructure, which provides banking, payment transactions, and stock exchange. The AHP approach was used to compare the criteria to each other. As mentioned above, the Likert-type ten-point scale (Figure 6) was used. In addition, a questionnaire about the experts' evaluation levels toward the CII choices was used. It consisted of 10 various levels—from "not important" ($\widetilde{P}_1$) to "extremely important" ($\widetilde{P}_6$)—on a fuzzy 10-level scale. So, the score of "not important" ($\widetilde{P}_1$) corresponded to a Triangular Fuzzy Number (TFN) of (0, 1, 1), respectively. The comparison matrix set is presented in Table 8.

The experts determined the criteria weights. Table 9 presents the integrated results of the established weights. The priority weight vector describes the significance level of the criteria in the decision matrix. After obtaining the significance levels of the criteria, the fuzzy WASPAS approach was used to assess the criticality of the information infrastructures.

Table 8. Determining the linguistic ratings.

Scale		α	γ	β
Extremely Important	EI	9	10	10
Very Important	VI	7	9	10
Important	I	5	7	9
Medium Important	MI	3	5	7
Low Important	LI	1	3	5
Not Important	NI	0	1	1

Table 9. Pairwise comparisons of the criteria weights for CII.

		x_1	x_2	x_3	x_4	x_5	x_6	w
The danger to life or health	x_1	1	3	3	5	3	3	0.38
Impact on the economy of the country	x_2	0.33	1	1	3	3	3	0.20
Damage to the environment	x_3	0.33	1.00	1	3	1	3	0.17
The influence of other facilities in ensuring the continuous operation of critical services	x_4	0.20	0.33	0.33	1	3	3	0.11
Effect on public safety	x_5	0.33	0.33	1	0.33	1	3	0.20
Damage to other European Union Member States	x_6	0.33	0.33	0.33	0.33	0.33	1	0.06

In this step of the research, fuzzy WASPAS began to establish fuzzy assessments of the alternative information infrastructures (A_1, A_2, and A_3), taking into account the criteria by applying TFNs. This is an initial decision-making matrix (DMM) for ranking alternatives, and it denotes the implementation ratings of the alternatives in accordance with the criteria. Table 10 presents a comparison of the alternatives in accordance with the criteria.

Table 10. The initial Fuzzy Multi-Criteria Decision Making (FDMM) for the CII alternatives.

	A_1			A_2			A_3			max	W
	α	γ	β	α	γ	β	α	γ	β		
x_1	7	9	10	7	9	10	1	3	5	10	0.38
x_2	7	9	10	1	3	5	5	7	9	10	0.20
x_3	1	3	5	0	1	1	1	3	5	5	0.17
x_4	1	3	5	1	3	5	3	5	7	7	0.11
x_5	7	9	10	7	9	10	1	3	5	10	0.20
x_6	5	7	9	3	5	7	3	5	7	9	0.06

The normalized decision matrix was achieved by applying relation (16) (Table 11).

Table 11. The normalized FDMM.

	A_1			A_2			A_3			W
	α	γ	β	α	γ	β	α	γ	β	
x_1	0.7	0.9	1.0	0.7	0.9	1.0	0.1	0.3	0.5	0.38
x_2	0.7	0.9	1.0	0.1	0.3	0.5	0.5	0.7	0.9	0.20
x_3	0.2	0.6	1.0	0.0	0.2	0.2	0.2	0.6	1.0	0.17
x_4	0.1	0.4	0.7	0.1	0.4	0.7	0.4	0.7	1.0	0.11
x_5	0.7	0.9	1.0	0.7	0.9	1.0	0.1	0.3	0.5	0.20
x_6	0.6	0.8	1.0	0.3	0.6	0.8	0.3	0.6	0.8	0.06

Relation (17) was applied to archive the weighted-normalized Fuzzy Multi-Criteria Decision Making (FDMM) for WSM (Table 12), and relation (18) was applied to archive the weighted-normalized FDMM for WPM (Table 13). Relations (19) and (20), respectively, were applied to determine the values of the optimality function values for WSM and WPM.

Table 12. The weighted normalized matrix for WSM.

	A$_1$			A$_2$			A$_3$		
	α	Γ	B	α	γ	β	α	γ	β
x_1	0.3	0.3	0.4	0.3	0.3	0.4	0.0	0.1	0.2
x_2	0.1	0.2	0.2	0.0	0.1	0.1	0.1	0.1	0.2
x_3	0.0	0.1	0.2	0.0	0.0	0.0	0.0	0.1	0.2
x_4	0.0	0.0	0.1	0.0	0.0	0.1	0.0	0.1	0.1
x_5	0.1	0.1	0.1	0.1	0.1	0.1	0.0	0.0	0.0
x_6	0.0	0.0	0.1	0.0	0.0	0.0	0.0	0.0	0.0
Q		0.8			0.6			0.5	
									1.83

Table 13. The weighted normalized matrix for WPM.

	A$_1$			A$_2$			A$_3$		
	α	γ	B	α	γ	β	α	γ	β
x_1	0.9	1.0	1.0	0.9	1.0	1.0	0.4	0.6	0.8
x_2	0.9	1.0	1.0	0.6	0.8	0.9	0.9	0.9	1.0
x_3	0.8	0.9	1.0	0.0	0.8	0.8	0.8	0.9	1.0
x_4	0.8	0.9	1.0	0.8	0.9	1.0	0.9	1.0	1.0
x_5	1.0	1.0	1.0	1.0	1.0	1.0	0.8	0.9	0.9
x_6	1.0	1.0	1.0	0.9	1.0	1.0	0.9	1.0	1.0
Q		5.7			5.1			5.2	
								ΣQ	16.0

The integrated utility function value of the fuzzy WASPAS technique for CII was identified by applying relation (24), as shown in Table 13. A_1 is the most critical information infrastructure in the WSM, WPM, and WASPAS approach (Table 14). A_3 is the least critical alternative among all of the CII considered. Usually, the decision-taker recommends information protection measures according to the level of the criticality of information infrastructures.

Table 14. Integrated utility function values of the fuzzy WASPAS approach.

	A_1	A_2	A_3
Q_i	0.8	0.6	0.5
P_i	5.7	5.1	5.2
λ			0.90
K_i	0.8	0.6	0.5
Rank	1	2	3

4. Discussion

There are various MCDM techniques that are widely applied. The WSM, which is now used in the different EU countries, is one of the recently developed and most widely used methods.

The results obtained according to the Lithuanian WSM-based methodology are less accurate than the results obtained by the WASPAS-F approach. The resulting value estimate was an integer. In calculations, it is often difficult to determine the priority of the object, since the results obtained may be the same and repetitive, but this is not the only drawback of this method. Given the fact that the methodology is subject to expert estimates, this limit is not appropriate. The results are subject to significant changes, and for this reason, the importance of the objects can be calculated erroneously.

In this case, CII may be incorrectly assessed, due to the problems mentioned above, as well as due to a misunderstanding of the method. The WSM method has its drawbacks associated with using the same dimensions for different criteria. The application of this approach requires that the assessments of all the criteria have the same magnitude, but the criteria of the critical infrastructure cover very broad areas. The influence is measured by the number of affected populations, the number of affected areas, and other sizes, and this method cannot be applied to solve this problem. The decision to use scores from 0 to 3 does not solve the current problem, since such a scoring system has no mathematical justification. Currently, using this method of identifying the CII, the sum of all criteria weighs from 14 to 16 scores. Such a weighting of criteria is also inappropriate, since, based on the WSM method, the weights of all the criteria must be equal to 1.

To overcome some of the shortcomings of this method, the fuzzy WASPAS method was chosen. The solved problem for identifying and ranking CII shows a more accurate result than the WSM method. The WASPAS-F method joins the advantages of the WSM and WPM approaches.

In this case, the AHP was applied to identify the importance of the criteria, while the fuzzy WASPAS was used to rank the alternative information infrastructures. The AHP method allowed for the effective determination of the weights of the criteria.

Finally, it was found that the described fuzzy WASPAS approach is practical for ranking alternatives.

Thus, the theoretical research and the practical results have demonstrated the effectiveness of using the Fuzzy WASPAS approach to identify CII. This approach can be used to identify the CII of other countries, including EU countries, as well as to solve other problems.

5. Conclusions

The socio-economic development of any country and its sustainable development, in fact, are directly dependent on the correct identification of CII, their reliability, and their safety. The achievement of the sustainable functioning of CII of countries represents for all states the essential elements in developing their strategies, the development of risk management, and the improvement of the ability to respond to information-related incidents and threats.

The stability of national security is a state of well-being of a country's citizens, because each country can exist only in a safe environment. However, each country often faces different types of threats to national security.

CII, such as the smart grid, gas and water networks, and transportation and communication networks, has a decisive impact on the quality of life and the environment development of EU.

Inaccurate identification of the list of CII may lead to the non-application of appropriate measures to protect them, which may adversely influence the environment, and the economic and political state of the country, etc.

A new model was proposed to solve the problem of identification of the criticality of information infrastructures by applying the WASPAS-F approach. Six main criteria were defined. The weights of the criteria were calculated based on the AHP method. As a result, the most important criteria were "The danger to life or health" and "Impact on the economy of the country"; the medium-important ones were "Damage to the environment" and "The influence of other facilities ensuring the continuous operation of critical services"; and the least important criteria were the "Effect on public safety" and "Damage to other European Union Member States".

This model is proposed for further use in calculating the criticality of real information infrastructures.

Author Contributions: Conceptualization, N.G.; Data curation, Z.T. and A.N.; Formal analysis, S.B.; Funding acquisition, N.G.; Investigation, A.N.; Methodology, Z.T.; Supervision, Z.T., N.G. and S.B.; Validation, Z.T.; Writing—original draft, A.N.; Writing—review & editing, Z.T., N.G. and S.B.

Funding: This research was partially funded by Ministry of Defense and Aerospace Industry of the Republic of Kazakhstan, grant number AP06851134, AP06851218.

Conflicts of Interest: The authors declare no conflict of interest.

References

1. La Greca, P.; Margani, G. Seismic and energy renovation measures for sustainable cities: A critical analysis of the Italian scenario. *Sustainability* **2018**, *10*, 254. [CrossRef]
2. Scherer, L.; Behrens, P.; de Koning, A.; Heijungs, R.; Sprecher, B.; Tukker, A. Trade-offs between social and environmental Sustainable Development Goals. *Environ. Sci. Policy* **2018**, *90*, 65–72. [CrossRef]
3. Attard, G.; Rossier, Y.; Winiarski, T.; Eisenlohr, L. Deterministic modeling of the impact of underground structures on urban groundwater temperature. *Sci. Total Environ.* **2016**, *572*, 986–994. [CrossRef] [PubMed]
4. Shearman, R. The meaning and ethics of sustainability. *Environ. Manag.* **1990**, *14*, 1–8. [CrossRef]
5. Clayton, A.M.; Radcliffe, N.J. *Sustainability: A Systems Approach*; Earthscan Publications Ltd.: London, UK, 1996.
6. Hashemkhani Zolfani, S.; Zavadskas, E.K.; Turskis, Z. Design of products with both International and Local perspectives based on Yin-Yang balance theory and SWARA method. *Econ. Res.-Ekon. Istr.* **2013**, *26*, 153–166.
7. Van de Wetering, R.; Mikalef, P.; Helms, R. Driving organizational sustainability-oriented innovation capabilities: A complex adaptive systems perspective. *Curr. Opin. Environ. Sustain.* **2017**, *28*, 71–79. [CrossRef]
8. Lim, H.S.M.; Taeihagh, A. Autonomous vehicles for smart and sustainable cities: An in-depth exploration of privacy and cybersecurity implications. *Energies* **2018**, *11*, 1062. [CrossRef]
9. Walther, T. Security supporting digitalization in the cement industry. *ZKG Int.* **2017**, *70*, 44–46.
10. John-Hopkins, M. Mapping War, Peace and Terrorism in the Global Information Environment. *J. Int. Human. Legal Stud.* **2017**, *8*, 202–233. [CrossRef]
11. Jarmakiewicz, J.; Parobczak, K.; Maslanka, K. Cybersecurity protection for power grid control infrastructures. *Int. J. Crit. Infrastruct. Prot.* **2017**, *18*, 20–33. [CrossRef]
12. Ghafir, I.; Hammoudeh, M.; Prenosil, V.; Han, L.; Hegarty, R.; Rabie, K.; Aparicio-Navarro, F.J.; Little, R.G. Detection of advanced persistent threat using machine-learning correlation analysis. *Future Gen. Comput. Syst.-Int. J. Esci.* **2018**, *89*, 349–359. [CrossRef]
13. Tuptuk, N.; Hailes, S. Security of smart manufacturing systems. *J. Manuf. Syst.* **2018**, *47*, 93–106. [CrossRef]
14. Ghafir, I.; Prenosil, V.; Hammoudeh, M.; Baker, T.; Jabbar, S.; Khalid, S.; Jaf, S. BotDet: A System for Real Time Botnet Command and Control Traffic Detection. *IEEE Access* **2018**, *6*, 38947–38958. [CrossRef]
15. Zavadskas, E.K.; Turskis, Z.; Antucheviciene, J.; Zakarevicius, A. Optimization of weighted aggregated sum product assessment. *Elektr. Elektr.* **2012**, *122*, 3–6. [CrossRef]
16. Zavadskas, E.K.; Antucheviciene, J.; Saparauskas, J.; Turskis, Z. MCDM methods WASPAS and MULTIMOORA: Verification of robustness of methods when assessing alternative solutions. *Econ. Comput. Econ. Cybern. Stud. Res.* **2013**, *47*, 5–20.
17. Zavadskas, E.K.; Turskis, Z.; Antucheviciene, J. Selecting a contractor by using a novel method for multiple attribute analysis: Weighted Aggregated Sum Product Assessment with grey values (WASPAS-G). *Stud. Inform. Control* **2015**, *24*, 141–150. [CrossRef]
18. Zavadskas, E.K; Liias, R.; Turskis, Z. Multi-attribute decision-making methods for assessment of quality in bridges and road construction: State-of-the-art surveys. *Baltic J. Road Bridge Eng.* **2008**, *3*, 152–160. [CrossRef]
19. Amott, D.; Pervan, G. Eight key issues for the decision support systems discipline. *Decis. Suppl. Syst.* **2008**, *44*, 657–672.
20. Car, N.J. Using decision models to enable better irrigation Decision Support Systems. *Comput. Electr. Agric.* **2018**, *152*, 290–301. [CrossRef]
21. Zavadskas, E.K.; Antucheviciene, J.; Vilutiene, T.; Adeli, H. Sustainable decision-making in civil engineering, construction and building technology. *Sustainability* **2018**, *10*, 14. [CrossRef]
22. Zhang, G.; Xu, Y.; Li, T. A special issue on new trends in Intelligent Decision Support Systems. *Knowl.-Based Syst.* **2012**, *32*, 1–2. [CrossRef]
23. Wen, W.; Chen, Y.H.; Chen, I.C. A knowledge-based decision support system for measuring enterprise performance. *Knowl.-Based Syst.* **2008**, *21*, 148–163. [CrossRef]
24. Ranerup, A.; Noren, L.; Sparud-Lundin, C. Decision support systems for choosing a primary health care provider in Sweden. *Patient Educ. Couns.* **2012**, *86*, 342–347. [CrossRef] [PubMed]
25. Turskis, Z. Multi-attribute contractors ranking method by applying ordering of feasible alternatives of solutions in terms of preferability technique. *Technol. Econ. Dev. Econ.* **2008**, *14*, 224–239. [CrossRef]

26. Zavadskas, E.K.; Turskis, Z.; Tamosaitiene, J. Contractor selection of construction in a competitive environment. *J. Bus. Econ. Manag.* **2008**, *9*, 181–187. [CrossRef]
27. Zavadskas, E.K.; Kaklauskas, A.; Turskis, Z.; Kalibatas, D. An approach to multi-attribute assessment of indoor environment before and after refurbishment of dwellings. *J. Environ. Eng. Landsc. Manag.* **2009**, *17*, 5–11. [CrossRef]
28. Sivilevičius, H.; Zavadskas, E.K.; Turskis, Z. Quality attributes and complex assessment methodology of the asphalt mixing plant. *Balt. J. Road Bridge Eng.* **2008**, *3*, 161–166. [CrossRef]
29. Hurley, J.S. Quantifying decision making in the critical infrastructure via the Analytic Hierarchy Process (AHP). *Int. J. Cyber Warf. Terrorism* **2017**, *7*, 23–34. [CrossRef]
30. Mardani, A.; Zavadskas, E.K.; Khalifah, Z.; Zakuan, N.; Jusoh, A.; Nor, K.M.; Khoshnoudi, M. A review of multi-criteria decision-making applications to solve energy management problems: Two decades from 1995 to 2015. *Renew. Sustain. Energy Rev.* **2017**, *71*, 216–256. [CrossRef]
31. Leśniak, A.; Kubek, D.; Plebankiewicz, E.; Zima, K.; Belniak, S. Fuzzy AHP application for supporting contractors' bidding decision. *Symmetry* **2018**, *10*, 642. [CrossRef]
32. Guarini, M.R.; Battisti, F.; Chiovitti, A. A methodology for the selection of multi-criteria decision analysis methods in real estate and land management processes. *Sustainability* **2018**, *10*, 507. [CrossRef]
33. Turskis, Z.; Zavadskas, E.K. A novel method for multiple criteria analysis: Grey additive ratio assessment (ARAS-G) method. *Informatica* **2010**, *21*, 597–610.
34. Zavadskas, E.K.; Mardani, A.; Turskis, Z.; Jusoh, A.; Nor, K.M.D. Development of TOPSIS Method to Solve Complicated Decision-Making Problems: An Overview on Developments from 2000 to 2015. *Int. J. Inf. Technol. Decis. Mak.* **2016**, *15*, 645–682. [CrossRef]
35. Strantzali, E.; Aravossis, K. Decision making in renewable energy investments: A review. *Renew. Sustain. Eng. Rev.* **2016**, *55*, 885–898. [CrossRef]
36. Kaska, K.; Trinberg, L. *Regulating Cross-Border Dependencies of Critical Information Infrastructure*; NATO Cooperative Cyber Defence Centre of Excellence (NATO CCD COE): Tallinn, Estonia, 2015.
37. Moteff, J.D. *Critical Infrastructures: Background, Policy, and Implementation*; Congressional Research Service: Washington, DC, USA, 2015. Available online: www.fas.org/sgp/crs/homesec/RL30153.pdf (accessed on 4 December 2018).
38. Van Asselt, M.B.A.; Vos, E.; Wildhaber, I. Some reflections on EU governance of critical infrastructure risks. *Eur. J. Risk Regul.* **2015**, *6*, 185–190. [CrossRef]
39. Lauta, K.C. Regulating a moving nerve: On legally defining critical infrastructure. *Eur. J. Risk Regul.* **2015**, *6*, 176–184. [CrossRef]
40. Seppanen, H.; Luokkala, P.; Zhang, Z.; Torkki, P.; Virrantaus, K. Critical infrastructure vulnerability-A method for identifying the infrastructure service failure interdependencies. *Int. J. Crit. Inf. Prot.* **2018**, *22*, 25–38. [CrossRef]
41. Zhang, P.C.; Peeta, S. A generalized modeling framework to analyze interdependencies among infrastructure systems. *Transp. Res. Part B-Methodol.* **2011**, *45*, 553–579. [CrossRef]
42. Dudenhoeffer, D.D.; Permann, M.R.; Manic, M. CIMS: A framework for infrastructure interdependency modeling and analysis. In Proceedings of the 2006 Winter Simulation Conference, Monterey, CA, USA, 3–6 December 2006; pp. 478–485.
43. Lauge, A.; Hernantes, J.; Sarriegi, J.M. Critical infrastructure dependencies: A holistic, dynamic and quantitative approach. *Int. J. Crit. Infrastruct. Prot.* **2015**, *8*, 16–23. [CrossRef]
44. Foytik, P.; Robinson, R.M. Weighting critical infrastructure dependencies to facilitate evacuations. *Int. J. Disaster Risk Reduction* **2018**, *31*, 1199–1206. [CrossRef]
45. Harasta, J. Legally critical: Defining critical infrastructure in an interconnected world. *Int. J. Crit. Infrastruct. Prot.* **2018**, *21*, 47–56. [CrossRef]
46. Kundur, D.; Contreras, J.; Srinivasan, D.; Gatsis, N.; Wang, M.; Peeta, S. Introduction to the Issue on Signal and Information Processing for Critical Infrastructures. *IEEE J. Sel. Top. Sign. Proc.* **2018**, *12*, 575–577. [CrossRef]
47. Council of the European Union. *Council Directive 2008/114/EC, on the Identification and Designation of European Critical Infrastructures and the Assessment of the Need to Improve Their Protection*; Official Journal of the European Union: Brussels, Belgium, 2008. Available online: https://eur-lex.europa.eu/eli/dir/2008/114/oj (accessed on 4 December 2018).

48. Neag, M.-M. *Critical Infrastructure Protection—The Foundation of National Security (1)*; Buletin Stiintific. "Nicolae Balcescu" Land Forces Academy: Sibiu, Romania, 2014; Volume 1, pp. 56–61. Available online: http://www.armyacademy.ro/buletin/bul1_2014/NEAG.pdf (accessed on 4 December 2018).
49. Law on Cybersecurity of the Republic of Lithuania—Lietuvos Respublikos kibernetinio saugumo įstatymas. 12.11.2014). Nr. XII-1428. Legislation register—Teisės aktų registras. Available online: https://e-seimas.lrs.lt/portal/legalAct/lt/TAD/f6958c2085dd11e495dc9901227533ee (accessed on 4 December 2018).
50. The Critical Infrastructure Protection in France. SGDSN, 2017. Available online: http://www.sgdsn.gouv.fr/uploads/2017/03/plaquette-saiv-anglais.pdf (accessed on 4 December 2018).
51. Ministry of Defence of the Republic of Slovenia. Critical Infrastructure. Available online: http://www.mo.gov.si/en/areas_of_work/critical_intrastructure/ (accessed on 4 December 2018).
52. National Strategy for Critical Infrastructure. Her Majesty the Queen in Right of Canada. 2009. Available online: https://www.publicsafety.gc.ca/cnt/rsrcs/pblctns/srtg-crtcl-nfrstrctr/srtg-crtcl-nfrstrctr-eng.pdf (accessed on 4 December 2018).
53. Nurushev, M.Z.; Diarov, M.D.; Nurusheva, A. Development of oil fields on the shelf of the Caspian Sea and the risk level of accidents. *News Nat. Acad. Sci. Rep. Kazakhstan Ser. Geol. Technol. Sci.* **2017**, *2*, 201–211.
54. Boranbayev, S.; Goranin, N.; Nurusheva, A. The methods and technologies of reliability and security of information systems and information and communication infrastructures. *J. Theor. Appl. Inf. Technol.* **2018**, *96*, 6172–6188.
55. Boranbayev, A.; Boranbayev, S.; Nurusheva, A.; Yersakhanov, K. The Modern State and the Further Development Prospects of Information Security in the Republic of Kazakhstan. In *Information Technology-New Generations*; Springer: Cham, Switzerland, 2018; pp. 33–38.
56. Boranbayev, A.; Boranbayev, S.; Yersakhanov, K.; Nurusheva, A.; Taberkhan, R. Methods of ensuring the reliability and fault tolerance of information systems. In *Information Technology-New Generations*; Springer: Cham, Switzerland, 2018; pp. 729–730.
57. Boranbayev, A.; Boranbayev, S.; Nurusheva, A. Development of a software system to ensure the reliability and fault tolerance in information systems based on expert estimates. In *Proceedings of SAI Intelligent Systems Conference*; Springer: Cham, Switzerland, 2018; pp. 924–935.
58. Boranbayev, A.; Boranbayev, S.; Nurusheva, A.; Yersakhanov, K. Development of a Software System to Ensure the Reliability and Fault Tolerance in Information Systems. *J. Eng. Appl. Sci.* **2018**, *13*, 10080–10085.
59. Strategic Research Center of the General Jonas Zemaitis Military Academy of Lithuania. Lithuanian Annual Strategic Review. 2013–2014. 2014, Volume 12. Available online: http://www.lka.lt/en/research/publications/periodical-publications/lithuanian-annual-strategic-review.html (accessed on 4 December 2018).
60. National Cyber Security Centre under the Ministry of National Defense. National Cyber Security Status Report for the Year 2017. Available online: https://www.nksc.lt/doc/en/NKSC_2017_EN.pdf (accessed on 4 December 2018).
61. Kaiser, R. The birth of cyberwar. *Political Geogr.* **2015**, *46*, 11–20. [CrossRef]
62. Ghafir, I.; Saleem, J.; Hammoudeh, M.; Faour, H.; Prenosil, V.; Jaf, S.; Jabbar, S.; Baker, T. Security threats to critical infrastructure: The human factor. *J. Supercomput.* **2018**, *74*, 4986–5002. [CrossRef]
63. Hsiao, S.C.; Kao, D.Y. The Static Analysis of WannaCry Ransomware. In Proceedings of the 20th International Conference on Advanced Communication Technology (ICACT), Chuncheon, Korea, 11–14 February 2018; pp. 153–158.
64. Yazdani, M.; Alidoosti, A.; Zavadskas, E.K. Risk analysis of critical infrastructures using fuzzy COPRAS. *Econ. Res.* **2011**, *24*, 27–40. [CrossRef]
65. European Union Agency for Network and Information Security. Methodologies for the Identification of Critical Information Infrastructure Assets and Services. 2014. Guidelines for Charting Electronic Data Communication Networks. Available online: file:///C:/Users/"%D0%90%D0%B4%D0%BC%D0%B8%D0%BD%D0%B8%D1%81%D1%82%D1%80%D0%B0%D1%82%D0%BE%D1%80/Downloads/Methodologies%20for%20the%20identification%20of%20Critical%20Information%20Infrastructure%20assets%20and%20services%20(1).pdf (accessed on 4 December 2018).
66. Almeida, A. A multi-Criteria Methodology for the Identification and Ranking of Critical Infrastructures. Lisbon, Portugal; pp. 1–10. Available online: https://fenix.tecnico.ulisboa.pt/downloadFile/395142726454/Resumo.pdf (accessed on 4 December 2018).

67. Halim, M.H.; Mohammed, A.H. Identification of critical level of assets by using Analytic Hierarchy Process for water assets management. *Int. J. Technol. Res. Appl.* **2014**, *2*, 54–58.
68. Zavadskas, E.K.; Turskis, Z.; Bagočius, V. Multi-criteria selection of a deep-water port in the Eastern Baltic Sea. *Appl. Soft Comput.* **2015**, *26*, 180–192. [CrossRef]
69. Izuakor, C.; White, R. Critical infrastructure asset identification: Policy, methodology and gap analysis. In *IFIP Advances in Information and Communication Technology*; Rice, M., Shenoi, S., Eds.; Critical Infrastructure Protection X; Springer: Cham, Switzerland, 2016; Volume 485, pp. 27–41.
70. Commission of the European Communities. Green Paper on a European Programme for Critical Infrastructure Protection, COM 576 Final. 2005. Available online: https://eur-lex.europa.eu/legal-content/GA/TXT/?uri=celex:52005DC0576 (accessed on 4 December 2018).
71. Government of Canada Position Paper on a National Strategy for Critical Infrastructure Protection. Public Safety and Emergency Preparedness Canada. 2004. Available online: http://ccpic.mai.gov.ro/docs/Canada_non_paper.pdf (accessed on 4 December 2018).
72. Communication from the Commission to the Council and the European Parliament—Protection of Critical Objects in the Fight against Terrorism. Brussels (Komisijos komunikatas Tarybai ir Europos parlamentui—Ypatingos svarbos objektų apsauga kovojant su terorizmu. Briuselis), KOM 702 galutinis. 2004. Available online: http://eur-lex.europa.eu/legal-content/LT/TXT/?uri=CELEX:52004DC0702 (accessed on 4 December 2018).
73. Resolution on the Critical Information Infrastructure Identification Methodology (Nutarimas dėl ypatingos svarbos informacinės infrastruktūros identifikavimo metodikos). 2016-07-16 Nr. 742. Register of Legal Acts. Available online: https://e-seimas.lrs.lt/portal/legalAct/lt/TAD/77d6b4914f2611e68f45bcf65e0a17ee?jfwid=q8i88m9wc (accessed on 4 December 2018).
74. Zavadskas, E.K.; Podvezko, V. Integrated determination of objective criteria weights in MCDM. *Int. J. Inf. Technol. Decis. Mak.* **2016**, *15*, 267–283. [CrossRef]
75. Hwang, C.-L.; Lin, M.-J. *Group Decision Making under Multiple Criteria: Methods and Applications*, 1st ed.; Springer: Berlin/Heidelberg, Germany, 1987; 400p.
76. Zavadskas, E.K.; Vainiunas, P.; Turskis, Z.; Tamosaitiene, J. Multiple criteria decision support system for assessment of projects managers in construction. *Int. J. Inf. Technol. Decis. Mak.* **2012**, *11*, 501–520. [CrossRef]
77. Wu, D.F.; Yang, Z.P.; Wang, N.L.; Li, C.Z.; Yang, Y.P. An Integrated Multi-Criteria Decision Making Model and AHP Weighting Uncertainty Analysis for Sustainability Assessment of Coal-Fired Power Units. *Sustainability* **2018**, *10*, 1700. [CrossRef]
78. Saaty, T.L. *The Analytic Hierarchy Process*; McGraw Hill: New York, NY, USA, 1980.
79. Keršuliene, V.; Zavadskas, E.K.; Turskis, Z. Selection of rational dispute resolution method by applying new step-wise weight assessment ratio analysis (SWARA). *J. Bus. Econ. Manag.* **2010**, *11*, 243–258. [CrossRef]
80. Medineckiene, M.; Zavadskas, E.K.; Björk, F.; Turskis, Z. Multi-criteria decision-making system for sustainable building assessment/certification. *Arch. Civil Mech. Eng.* **2015**, *15*, 11–18. [CrossRef]
81. Hwang, C.-L.; Yoon, K. Multiple Attribute Decision Making. In *Methods and Applications*, 1st ed.; A State-of-the-Art Survey; Springer: Berlin/Heidelberg, Germany, 1981; 269p.
82. Shannon, C.E. A mathematical theory of communication. *Bell Syst. Technol. J.* **1948**, *27*, 379–423, 623–656. [CrossRef]
83. Šaparauskas, J.; Zavadskas, E.K.; Turskis, Z. Selection of façade's alternatives of commercial and public buildings based on multiple criteria. *Int. J. Strateg. Prop. Manag.* **2011**, *15*, 189–203. [CrossRef]
84. Triantaphyllou, E. *Multi-Criteria Decision Making Methods: A Comparative Study*, 1st ed.; Springer: Dordrecht, The Netherlands, 2000; 290p.
85. Pekelman, D.; Sen, S.K. Mathematical programming models for the determination of attribute weights. *Manag. Sci.* **1974**, *20*, 1217–1229. [CrossRef]
86. Su, H.Z.; Qin, P.; Qin, Z.H. A method for evaluating sea dike safety. *Water Res. Manag.* **2013**, *27*, 5157–5170. [CrossRef]
87. Chatterjee, K.; Pamucar, D.; Zavadskas, E.K. Evaluating the performance of suppliers based on using the R'AMATEL-MAIRCA method for green supply chain implementation in electronics industry. *J. Clean. Prod.* **2018**, *184*, 101–129. [CrossRef]

88. Zhao, H.R.; Li, N. Optimal Siting of Charging Stations for Electric Vehicles Based on Fuzzy Delphi and Hybrid Multi-Criteria Decision Making Approaches from an Extended Sustainability Perspective. *Energy* **2016**, *9*, 270. [CrossRef]
89. Saaty, T.L.; Ergu, D. When is a decision-making method trustworthy? Criteria for evaluating multi-criteria decision-making methods. *Int. J. Inf. Technol. Decis. Mak.* **2015**, *14*, 1171–1187. [CrossRef]
90. Marozas, L.; Goranin, N.; Cenys, A.; Radvilavicius, L.; Turskis, Z. Raising effectiveness of access control systems by applying multi-criteria decision analysis: Part 1—Problem Definition. *Technol. Econ. Dev. Econ.* **2013**, *19*, 675–686. [CrossRef]
91. Li, Y.Y.; Zhang, H.Y.; Wang, J.Q. Linguistic neutrosophic sets and their application in multicriteria decision-making problems. *Int. J. Uncertain. Quant.* **2017**, *7*, 135–154. [CrossRef]
92. Chakraborty, S.; Zavadskas, E.K.; Antucheviciene, J. Applications of WASPAS method as a multi-criteria decision-making tool. *Econ. Comput. Econ. Cybern. Stud. Res.* **2015**, *49*, 5–22.
93. Turskis, Z.; Zavadskas, E.K.; Antucheviciene, J.; Kosareva, N. A hybrid model based on fuzzy AHP and fuzzy WASPAS for construction site selection. *Int. J. Comput. Commun. Control* **2015**, *10*, 873–888. [CrossRef]
94. Van Laarhoven, P.J.M.; Pedrycz, W. A Fuzzy Extension of Saaty's Priority Theory. *Fuzzy Sets Syst.* **1983**, *11*, 229–241. [CrossRef]
95. Likert, R. A technique for the measurement of attitudes. *Arch. Psychol.* **1932**, *22*, 5–55.

© 2019 by the authors. Licensee MDPI, Basel, Switzerland. This article is an open access article distributed under the terms and conditions of the Creative Commons Attribution (CC BY) license (http://creativecommons.org/licenses/by/4.0/).

Article

A New Hybrid MCDM Model with Grey Numbers for the Construction Delay Change Response Problem

Alireza Chalekaee [1,2], **Zenonas Turskis** [2], **Mostafa Khanzadi** [1], **Gholamreza Ghodrati Amiri** [3] and **Violeta Keršulienė** [4,*]

1. Construction Engineering and Management, School of Civil Engineering, Iran University of Science & Technology, Narmak, Tehran 16846, Iran; a_chalekaee@civileng.iust.ac.ir (A.C.); khanzadi@iust.ac.ir (M.K.)
2. Laboratory of Operational Research, Institute of Sustainable Construction, Faculty of Civil Engineering, Vilnius Gediminas Technical University, 10223 Vilnius, Lithuania; zenonas.turskis@vgtu.lt
3. Center of Excellence for Fundamental Studies in Structural Engineering, School of Civil Engineering, Iran University of Science & Technology, Narmak, Tehran 16846, Iran; ghodrati@iust.ac.ir
4. Department of Law, Faculty of Business Management, Vilnius Gediminas Technical University, Saulėtekio al. 11, LT-10223 Vilnius, Lithuania
* Correspondence: violeta.kersuliene@vgtu.lt; Tel.: +370-5274-5027

Received: 19 November 2018; Accepted: 28 January 2019; Published: 1 February 2019

Abstract: Stakeholders carry out construction projects under fast-changing conditions. The conditions can undermine the concept of a stable and prosperous construction plan without an appropriate permit and an active and targeted plan for environmental management. Therefore, the decision maker often faces many challenges of Multi-Criteria Decision-Making (MCDM) when it comes to solving the construction management proper response selection problem for planning delay changes when sustainable environment requirements are essential. Any addition, reduction, or modification of the original project plan is a change to the project and impacts the environment. Change occurrence is a probable issue while projects are implemented. One of the most complex tasks for the project manager is to work correctly and to find the most suitable decisions for the not precisely predetermined future expectations of a change. Therefore, the relevant criteria of values must reflect the uncertain properties of the problem model. Similar problems require fuzzy or grey MCDM methods. The paper introduces a new MCDM approach, which combines four different MCDM methods with grey numbers: the SWARA, TOPSIS-GM, Additive Ratio ASsessment with Grey Numbers (ARAS-G) techniques and Geometric Mean to cover uncertainty and improve the problem-solving model. An analysis of a case study has examined and highlighted four possible alternatives described by eight performance criteria (cost, duration, and some linguistic criteria). Stakeholders determined the best alternative, calculated the efficiency of choice, and practically implemented the best option.

Keywords: MCDM; hybrid; management; grey; SWARA; TOPSIS-GM; ARAS-G; Geomean

1. Introduction

Developing countries must promote the development of infrastructure, which has a positive effect on sustainable economic growth, to achieve a significant increase, except meeting basic needs. Residents, wealth, technology, institutions and culture are the five generic forces of change in the environment (sustainability). The design concept of a construction project may be violated without proper knowledge and sound ecological impact management, affecting the operation of projects. Stakeholders carry out construction projects in a dynamically changing environment. Therefore, they must be in line with the actual situation of a dynamic nature and may be subject to change. Change is considered to be any modification of the original scope of the project [1,2]. The time delay of project delivery with its adverse effects remains the biggest problem in the construction industry. Delay and cost overrun are an inherent part of most projects, despite the much-acquired knowledge in project management. Consequences of the construction project's time delay are multifaceted to stakeholders. Construction programs involve expensive equipment, significant overheads, substantial human resources, and modern demands on both the contractor and the client. When some of the unexpected events delay construction progress, these costs can escalate, influencing more than just the budget. Changes in project scope and properties during execution requires a review of the entire original project plan to discuss the budget, schedule, and to maintain quality. It will take more time and use of resources than the initial baseline. It can also slow down the application of effective environmental measures. A well-planned schedule is essential for planning and carrying out construction work, coordinating resources, and preparing for recovery plans. More time and resources will be needed than the initial baseline. It can also decelerate the operation of environmental protection. According to the Yin-Yang philosophy, all universal phenomena is shaped by the integration of two different cosmic energies, namely Yin and Yang. The Yin-Yang principle thus embodies duality, paradox, unity in diversity, change, and harmony, offering a holistic approach to construction and sustainable development problem-solving [3]. Environmental stressors could arise because of climate change, severe weather, or other factors would be more than adequately addressed by good engineering design, material selection, best practice, and engineering foresight. Large-scale construction projects can take 10 to 15 years from the planning to the beginning of the construction. The duration of the process leads to over expenditures, some because of inflation and some from the need to pay engineers and contractors many years in a row.

Everyone pays something for construction delays: either through direct costs, as money is spent to resolve issues, or through indirect costs. The client, on the one hand, withstands advantage loss for not putting the building to use in the scheduled time. The contractor, on the other hand, not only reports penalties of standby costs of not busy workers and tools, but also provides the spending of the destroyed material.

These changes not only affect the duration and project costs, but also have a particular impact on productivity, quality, risk, plan and project objectives, even for organizations involved in the project [4–7]. Besides, it is necessary for the project to be changed to maximize project success. Otherwise, a plan would not gain the maximum possible profit or would have some loss because of being outdated [4,8]. Therefore, it is necessary for managers to devise some responses when the project's situation is changing. For this purpose, utilizing a change management system to apply the future changes could be helpful. Hwang and Low [9], and Eshtehardian and Khodaverdi [10] mentioned that improvement in project's quantitative and qualitative performances is achieved by the companies that implement change management systems [11]. Butt et al. [12] strongly advised that all the parties involved in a project should engage during the change management process. As a Decision Support System, the change management systems determine systematic decisions for the project managers. Researchers worked on the identification of the causes and impacts of the changes that occurred to the projects. Isaac and Novan [13] devised a graph-based model for the identification of the effects of design changes in construction projects. Oyewobi et al. [14] analyzed the causes of variation orders and their impact on educational building projects. Gde Agung Yana et al. [15] examined the factors that affect the design changes in the construction of projects.

Sun and Meng [5] studied the causes and effects of changes. They categorized the reasons for changing as follows: project-related, client-related, design-related, contractor-related and external factors. The change management system should aim all possible direct and indirect factors that influence project changes. These factors, which are useful to choose the optimal changes, are some criteria like direct and indirect costs, duration, quality, productivity, and risks, usually in different dimensions. That is why we may often use Multi-Criteria Decision-Making (MCDM) to propose a change management model [5]. During recent years, different change management models for construction were introduced for different conditions [16–18]. Motawa et al. [19] showed a change simulator to evaluate the various changes and their subsequent impacts. Lee et al. [20] proposed a system dynamics framework to assess the adverse effects of errors and changes on construction performance. Zhao et al. [21] suggested a change management prediction system for the construction industry. Lee et al. [22] proposed a framework for measuring the impacts of Change Orders in construction projects and used it as a pre-risk assessment tool. Different researchers used Building Information Modelling for the management of design changes [23,24]. Isaac and Navon [25] developed a model that facilitates an automatic identification of the possible consequences of changes when they are first proposed, before their implementation in the design and planning of the project. Based on an Object-Oriented Discrete Event Simulation, Du et al. [26] presented an object-oriented DES model to investigate the change order management process. Utilizing BIM, Mejlænder-Larsen [27] devised a change control system to manage the changes in design. Francom and El Asmar [28] found positive results in applying BIM to the change performance of the projects.

Change prediction is one of the change management responses [2,21,29–32]. Isaac and Navon [33] proposed a change control tool to identify the implications of a change as soon as it is suggested.

Different studies worked on how to manage the changes in different project delivery systems, standard forms of contract [34,35]; IPD [36]; design-build [37] or comparing the delivery systems according to their function during the change process [38].

Some researchers presented the proper construction change systems for the construction condition of their countries, Oman [39], Singapore [9], Puerto Rico [40], and the United States [41]. Additionally, Gharaee Moghaddam [6] studied the availability of a change management procedure for the construction industry in Iran. He believed that a change management system tailored to the Iranian construction industry is vital.

While applying changes in the future, researchers should pay attention to the uncertainty available in the problem. Among the available methods, the grey theory is one of the tools to study the uncertainty possible in MCDM problems. Comparing with fuzzy sets theory, another tool for uncertainty study, the grey theory can be more flexible in the fuzziness situation [42].

The authors of the researches mentioned above stated that it is impossible to treat the previous models of changes when the decisions are made regarding the management projects of private investments. Consensual offers are necessary to find solutions concerning plans for private investments. Besides, the dynamic nature of the change management process needs to be considered. Moreover, a concept of uncertainty and ambiguity about a problem must be present in the problem-solving model. Therefore, some recommendations from the private investments project case study in Iran with the issue of a construction delay have been given in the article.

2. Research Methodology

The research methodology is based on the following steps:

- The literature survey about the change topic in construction management articles was presented to highlight the core idea of the study. This introduction was followed by some necessary explanations about the grey number.
- This article aims to propose some suggestions for the construction projects facing the likely change by a case study. So, in the following section, the case study is presented: a plan with the problem of construction delay, considered as an MCDM problem with grey number input.
- Possible alternatives of decision-makers mentioned.
- The governing criteria in this MCDM problem are defined and criteria weights determined.
- Criteria values are determined.
- Alternatives prioritized using grey decision-making tools.
- Discussions about the calculations and conclusions presented.

Grey Number Theory

In the subjects relating to the future, uncertainty, limited (imperfect) information or information loss are present. Grey theory is an efficient tool facing similar situations. Deng [43] introduced grey numbers as a part of the Grey System theory [44]. The numbers are categorized into three types, based on information uncertainty: white number, grey number, and black number. Let $\otimes x = [\alpha, \beta] = \{x | \alpha \leq x \leq \beta, \alpha \wedge \beta \in R\}$. Then:

If $\alpha, \beta \to \infty$, $\otimes x$ is called the black number. This number contains any meaningful information. Else, if $\alpha = \beta$, then $\otimes x$ is called the white number which means with complete information. Otherwise, $\otimes x$ is called the grey number.

The exact value of a grey number is unknown, but it represents a known interval to show the uncertainty. In practice, numerous cases in the real world are possible to rate with grey numbers. The situations where we may assess the consequences of our actions in the future is an example. Grey theory is easy to apply and flexible while dealing with ambiguity, which is its advantage over fuzzy sets theory.

Let $+$, $-$, $\times$, and $\div$ define the addition, subtraction, multiplication, and division, respectively. These operations for the grey numbers $\otimes n_1$ and $\otimes n_2$ are as follows [42,45]:

$$\text{Let } \otimes n_1 = [\alpha_1, \beta_1] = \{x | \alpha_1 \leq x \leq \beta_1, \alpha_1 \wedge \beta_1 \in R\}, \text{ and } \otimes n_2[\alpha_2, \beta_2] = \{x | \alpha_2 \leq x \leq \beta_2, \alpha_2 \wedge \beta_2 \in R\}, \quad (1)$$

Then:

$$\otimes n_1 + \otimes n_2 = (n_{1\alpha} + n_{2\beta}; n_{1\beta} + n_{2\beta}), \quad \text{Addition} \quad (2)$$

$$\otimes n_1 - \otimes n_2 = (n_{1\alpha} - n_{2\beta}; n_{1\beta} - n_{2\alpha}), \quad \text{Subtraction} \quad (3)$$

$$\otimes n_1 \times \otimes n_2 = (n_{1\alpha} \times n_{2\alpha}; n_{1\beta} \times n_{2\beta}), \quad \text{Multiplication} \quad (4)$$

$$\otimes n_1 \div \otimes n_2 = \left(\frac{n_{1\alpha}}{n_{2\beta}}; \frac{n_{1\beta}}{n_{2\alpha}}\right), \text{ only if } n_{1\alpha}, n_{2\alpha}, n_{1\beta}, \text{ and } n_{2\beta} \text{ do not contain } 0, \quad \text{Division} \quad (5)$$

$$k \times \otimes n_1 = (kn_{1\alpha}; kn_{1\beta}), \quad \text{Number product of grey numbers if } k \text{ is a positive real number} \quad (6)$$

$$(\otimes n_1)^{-1} = \left(\frac{1}{n_{1\beta}}; \frac{1}{n_{1\alpha}}\right);$$
$$(\otimes n_1)^k = \left((n_{1\alpha})^k, (n_{1\beta})^k\right), \text{ if } n_{1\alpha} \text{ and } n_{1\beta} < 1, \text{ and } k > 1;$$
$$(\otimes n_1)^k = (1, 1), \text{ if } n_{1\alpha} \text{ and } n_{1\beta} < 1, \text{ and } k = 0.$$
Exponentiation by a natural power (7)

3. Description of the Case Study

The housing industry is one the most thriving markets in Mashad, the second largest city in Iran. At the beginning of the present decade, and during construction of the first tall buildings, a construction company started to build a residential tower with the slogan: "Permanent life in a five-star hotel." After several months, another constructor launched a similar project in the vicinity of the first structure. Schedule and finish date of the projects became unbelievably significant when progressing these two projects. The target buyers of these flats were limited, so the situations for both projects were risky. Both towers had a concrete structure including shear walls and considering the climate in Mashad, they both progressed slowly. As the second project started later, it had a lag compared to its rival. With all the efforts that had been made to offset the lost time, significant changes were not probable to the project's conditions with the previous trend. Due to the first project's more favorable progress, buyers were more eager to it. Therefore, managers of the second project were confronted with a severe problem. What should they do to diminish the time lag with the first project? At that time, they intended to think about a change. After several consultation meetings, they found four possible solutions to this problem. The answers were as follows. *The first solution*: Finishing the building with two floors less. In fact, with this reduction, and without any other changes, they could offset the delay. Moreover, any additional reduction would result in some significant financial loss. *The second solution*: Increasing the personnel and acceleration in construction by 24-h daily work. *The third solution*: Structural change. This solution included shifting the concrete structure to prefabricated steel structure and modifying the specifications of the concrete used in shear walls and slabs for faster execution. *The fourth solution*: Final price reduction and quality development to increase the attraction for buyers. Therefore, the company decided to give 7% discount and to offer one-year free use of some of the facilities available, such as laundry service, playground, pool, sauna, and others. Again, the same as the first solution, this discount, and offer were the highest amount possible, without a significant loss. In the next sections, these solutions referred to as reasonable alternatives solving the MCDM problem. We name these four solutions: A_1, A_2, A_3, and A_4, respectively.

In the following section, we propose different criteria relating to the problem. As discussed in the introduction, this is a multi-dimensional MCDM problem. The requirements and their corresponding values are presented in the following sections.

3.1. Criteria Definition

After listing possible alternatives, the next step is to identify the main goals to be achieved. Seven experts with experience in the construction industry of Iran, together with the lead project authorities, were asked to form a team that defines the criteria that will affect the project's different benefits. After three consultation sessions, they indicated eight key criteria that would change the project's payout. Table 1 presents these criteria. The determination of the criteria depends on the implementation and management of the problem. Consequently, different cases have the most significant criteria, and they are defined by the decision of an appropriate group of experts.

Table 1. Criteria affecting constructor's payoff.

Criteria	Unit of Measurement	Optimal
Cost (C_1)	Million $	Min.
Duration (C_2)	Month	Min.
Uncertainty about final consequences (C_3)	Scores (1 to 5)	Min.
Related experiences in the past (C_4)	Scores (1 to 5)	Max.
The impact on the company's reputation (C_5)	Scores (1 to 5)	Max.
Side costs due to probable failure (C_6)	Scores (1 to 5)	Min.
Possible disputes in future (C_7)	Scores (1 to 5)	Min.
Safety hazards (C_8)	Scores (1 to 5)	Min.

3.2. Criteria Weights' Calculation

Criteria weight determining is a significant part of an MCDM problem with multi-dimensional criteria. It allocates a load for each dimension to make criteria comparison easier. Different criteria weight estimation methods can be used [46]. Some examples include Analytic Hierarchy Process (AHP) [47], Analytic Network Process (ANP) [48], Entropy [49], SWARA [50,51], and others. In this research, the SWARA method was applied. The approach is uncomplicated, has clear and understandable logic, and is simple to use. The SWARA method consists of the two main steps. At the first round, a group of experts acts together. The team, based on the own knowledge, ordered criteria from the most significant (given rank 1), to the least significant, the last position. At the second step, each expert acts separately. Then, a systematic comparison between each more significant criterion is made with the less significant one. Each expert makes the contrasts in the second step based on his judgement. Figure 1 shows the weight calculation procedure for the SWARA method. As the criteria weights in this MCDM problem represent the significance of each criterion, the authors asked five authorities of the constructor company to form the expert team for the SWARA method. Table 2 shows the criteria weights obtained from the SWARA method in grey numbers. Lower and upper limits of each grey number are the lowest and highest amount received from the SWARA method among for each criterion, respectively.

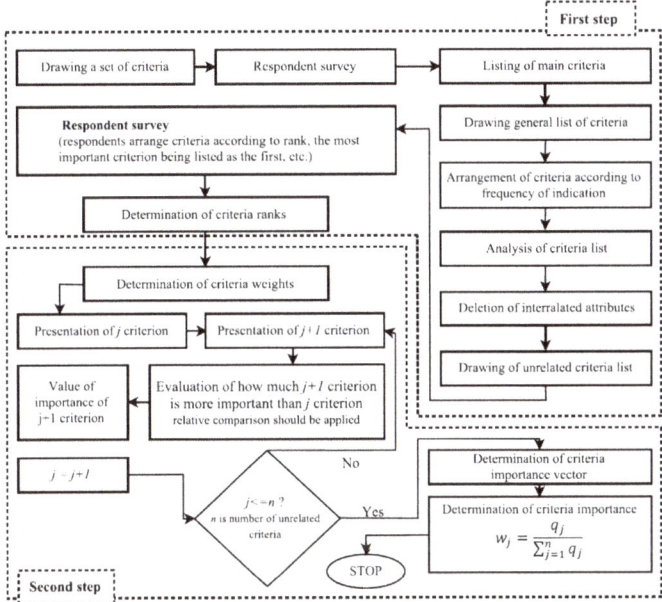

Figure 1. Weight calculation procedure for SWARA method [50].

Table 2. Criteria weights.

Criteria	Lower Limit	Upper Limit
Cost (C_1)	0.244	0.251
Duration (C_2)	0.168	0.226
Uncertainty about final consequences (C_3)	0.129	0.159
Related experiences in the past (C_4)	0.046	0.073
The impact on the company's reputation (C_5)	0.061	0.089
Side costs due to probable failure (C_6)	0.112	0.127
Possible disputes in future (C_7)	0.056	0.081
Safety hazards (C_8)	0.080	0.097

Among the eight criteria defined for this problem cost, duration and uncertainty about final consequences are the most effective ones. Table 2 shows that their cumulative weight is more than the five other criteria. In cases like ours, it is recommended to apply expert judgement to determine the values. The same as most cases in civil engineering, these values would not be precise enough with crisp numbers. Therefore, we calculated them in the shape of intervals. According to Table 2 and Figure 2, the range for some of the criteria weights like c_1, c_6, and c_8 are more close to a crisp number. It means that experts' judgements about the effect of these criteria are similar. Moreover, Equation (8) can be derived. The priority order for the five most essential criteria may also be valid for crisp values.

$$\alpha_1 \wedge \beta_1 \succ \alpha_2 \wedge \beta_2 \succ \alpha_3 \wedge \beta_3 \succ \alpha_4 \wedge \beta_4 \succ \alpha_5 \wedge \beta_5. \tag{8}$$

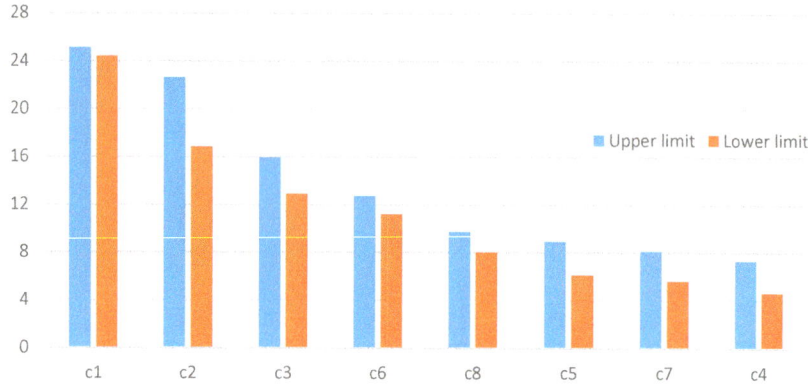

Figure 2. Criteria weights comparison.

3.3. Criteria Values Calculation

The next step to solve the proposed MCDM problem is to devise the grey decision-making matrix (GDMM). GDMM in discrete optimization problem consists of the preferences (values) of attributes (columns) for possible alternatives (rows):

$$\alpha_1 \wedge \beta_1 \succ \alpha_2 \wedge \beta_2 \succ \alpha_3 \wedge \beta_3 \succ \alpha_4 \wedge \beta_4 \succ \alpha_5 \wedge \beta_5.$$

The next step to solve the proposed MCDM problem is to devise the grey decision-making matrix (GDMM). GDMM in discrete optimization problem consists of the preferences (values) of attributes (columns) for possible alternatives (rows):

$$\otimes X = \begin{bmatrix} \otimes x_{0j} & \cdots & \otimes x_{0j} & \cdots & \otimes x_{0n} \\ \vdots & \ddots & \vdots & \ddots & \vdots \\ \otimes x_{i1} & \cdots & \otimes x_{ij} & \cdots & \otimes x_{in} \\ \vdots & \ddots & \vdots & \ddots & \vdots \\ \otimes x_{m1} & \cdots & \otimes x_{mj} & \cdots & \otimes x_{mn} \end{bmatrix}; i = \overline{1, m}; j = \overline{1, n}, \quad (9)$$

where m—the number of alternatives, n—the number of attributes describing each choice, $\otimes x_{ij} = [x_{ij\alpha}, x_{ij\beta}]$—a grey value representing the performance value of the i alternative regarding the j attribute.

The authors asked the constructor to calculate the criteria values because constructor authorities are the most familiar persons with the project. Table 3 shows their completed GDMM and the requirements weight as the first row of the table. Table 3 is the main entry for different methods in the following sections. The expert team which consisted of the project manager, site manager, and constructor authorities prepared the table. The direct cost of each solution calculated without uncertainty and the uncertainty related to C_1 is a part of the C_3 values. However, the expert team believed that crisp values for other criteria would not demonstrate a project's real situation. Therefore, each member of the expert team completed the table based on his judgment and the maximum and minimum value of the team members for each criterion value is as the upper and the lower limit of a grey number. Each member of the expert team was asked to score the criteria C_3, C_4, C_5, C_6, C_7, and C_8, based on his judgement with a value among 1 (very low), 2 (small), 3 (medium), 4 (high), and 5 (very high). The upper and lower limit of a grey number for some of the C_2 values in Table 3 is close to each other. That means that these grey numbers are almost crisp. Figure 3 shows that no one of the alternatives is optimal according to all performance criteria.

Table 3. Criteria values.

	C_1		C_2		C_3		C_4		C_5		C_6		C_7		C_8	
w	0.244	0.251	0.168	0.226	0.129	0.159	0.046	0.073	0.061	0.089	0.112	0.127	0.056	0.081	0.08	0.097
	α	β	α	β	α	β	α	β	α	β	α	β	α	β	α	β
A_0	0.24	0.24	3.82	3.82	0.46	0.46	5.00	5.00	5.00	5.00	1.15	1.15	0.46	0.46	0.46	0.46
A_1	2.05	2.05	4.97	5.03	1.5	2.5	2.6	3.4	2.6	3.4	1.5	2.5	1.5	2.5	0.6	1.4
A_2	0.65	0.65	6.9	9.1	2.6	3.4	3.5	4.4	4	5	2.6	3.4	2.6	3.4	3.5	4.4
A_3	0.31	0.31	5.75	6.32	2.6	3.4	2.6	3.4	3.5	4.4	1.5	2.5	1.5	2.5	1.5	2.5
A_4	0.82	0.82	11.97	12.04	0.6	1.4	2.6	3.4	4	5	2.6	3.4	0.6	1.4	0.6	1.4

Figure 3. Criteria weights comparison.

4. Proposed Methods for MCDM Problem Resolution

The multiple attribute utility theory (MAUT) assigns a utility value to each action. This utility is a number representing the performance of the considered response. The functions of the multiple attribute utility theory are divided into three main types: Additive (ARAS—Additive Ratio Assessment, SAW—Simple Additive Weighting, SMART—Simple Multi Attribute Rating Technique, WSM—Weighted Sum Model, and others), multiplicative (WPM—Weighted Product Model, Geomean, MEW), and reference point (TOPSIS, VICOR) methods in different spaces. Multiplicative ones are more sensitive to criteria values than additive ones. Furthermore, reference point methods are very dependent on relative differences among criteria values, are suitable only for ranking and are not resistant to reversal ranking.

Thus, a decision-maker should check the ranking of alternatives according to these three utility function forms. In the present article, we apply the TOPSIS (reference point form), the ARAS (additive), and the Geomean (multiplicative). The grey numbers used as input parameters for these methods. Here, we explain the tools used in the present article.

4.1. The TOPSIS-G Method in Minkowski Space (TOPSIS-GM)

The TOPSIS method is the second most popular method among dozens of available MCDM methods. A large number of researchers argue that it is a mathematically very sound method. Despite this, it produces a ranking of alternatives, which is one of the rankest reversal unresisting (ranking of other options is changing, when Pareto non-optimal solutions are added, or removed).

Lin et al. [52] proposed the following steps. Originally Hwang and Yoon [53] introduced three versions of the TOPSIS method using Manhattan City block, Euclidean, and Minkowski space. Later, only a few publications were published using the TOPSIS method, not in Euclidean space. According to the authors' opinion, it is better to use multidimensional space as different criteria to determine multi-criteria decision-making problems. The TOPSIS method with grey values is used to solve various issues [54–60]. Meanwhile, the authors did not find any problems when Minkowski space is used.

A problem solution by TOPSIS-GM method could be described as a systemic procedure, as is shown below.

Step 1: Normalize the $\otimes X$ matrix to obtain the normalized matrix $\otimes \overline{X}$:

$$\otimes \overline{X} = \begin{bmatrix} \overline{x}_{01} & \cdots & \overline{x}_{0j} & \cdots & \overline{x}_{0n} \\ \vdots & \ddots & \vdots & \ddots & \vdots \\ \overline{x}_{i1} & \cdots & \overline{x}_{ij} & \cdots & \overline{x}_{in} \\ \vdots & \ddots & \vdots & \ddots & \vdots \\ \overline{x}_{m1} & \cdots & \overline{x}_{mj} & \cdots & \overline{x}_{mn} \end{bmatrix}; i = \overline{1,m}; j = \overline{1,n}. \quad (10)$$

Normalized matrix is obtained through Vector normalization using Equation (11).

$$\overline{x}_{ij\alpha} = \frac{2x_{ij\alpha}}{\sqrt{\sum_{i=1}^{m} x_{ij\alpha}^2} + \sqrt{\sum_{i=1}^{m} x_{ij\beta}^2}}; \overline{x}_{ij\beta} = \frac{2x_{ij\beta}}{\sqrt{\sum_{i=1}^{m} x_{ij\alpha}^2} + \sqrt{\sum_{i=1}^{m} x_{ij\beta}^2}}; i = \overline{1,m}; j = \overline{1,n}. \quad (11)$$

Step 2: Determine the positive and negative ideal alternative, A^+ and A^-, respectively. A^+ is the optimal alternative based on optimal criteria values. A^- is the possible alternative with the lowest value for each criterion among the values presented by considered alternatives.

Step 3: Calculate the values of normalized-weighted DMM:

$$\hat{x}_{ij\alpha} = \overline{x}_{ij\alpha} \times w_{j\alpha}; \hat{x}_{ij\beta} = \overline{x}_{ij\beta} \times w_{j\beta}; i = \overline{1,m}; j = \overline{1,n}, \quad (12)$$

where w_j is the weight for the j criterion, and $\overline{x}_{ij}$ is the normalized value of the jth criterion of the ith alternative.

Step 4: Calculate separation measure from the positive and negative ideal alternatives, D_i^+ and D_i^-, respectively:

$$D_i^+ = \sqrt[8]{\frac{\sum_{j=1}^{n} (\hat{x}_{ij\alpha} - \hat{x}_{+j})^8 + \sum_{j=1}^{n} (\hat{x}_{ij\beta} - \hat{x}_{+j})^8}{2}}; i = \overline{1,m}, \quad (13)$$

$$D_i^- = \sqrt[8]{\frac{\sum_{j=1}^{n} (\hat{x}_{ij\alpha} - \hat{x}_{-j})^8 + \sum_{j=1}^{n} (\hat{x}_{ij\beta} - \hat{x}_{-j})^8}{2}}; i = \overline{1,m}, \quad (14)$$

where $\hat{x}_{+j}$ and $\hat{x}_{-j}$ are the normalized-weighted values of the jth criterion for the positive and negative ideal alternatives (A^+ and A^-), respectively.

Step 5: Calculate the relative closeness C_i^+, as follows:

$$C_i^+ = \frac{D_i^-}{D_i^+ + D_i^-}; i = \overline{1,m}. \quad (15)$$

Then, the preference order of the alternatives presented as descending order of the C_i^+ value.

4.2. Additive Ratio ASsessment with Grey Numbers (ARAS-G) Method

Turskis and Zavadskas [41] introduced the ARAS-G technique.

Step 1: The optimal alternative A_0 determination. The A_0 is the possible alternative determined by optimum criteria estimates (contrary to the TOPSIS or the COPRAS methods, where optimum values exist for selected to evaluation choices, or the best option is that which has the most significant multi-attribute utility function value).

Step 2: The normalized criteria values of matrix $\otimes \overline{X}$ calculated using the same Equation (8) as in the TOPSIS method (in ARAS method the main idea is that after criteria values are normalized, the ratio among normalized criteria values are the same as they were before normalization):

$$\overline{x}_{ij\alpha} = \frac{x_{ij\alpha}}{\sqrt{\sum_{i=1}^{m} x_{ij\alpha}^2 + x_{0\beta}^2}}; \overline{x}_{ij\beta} = \frac{x_{ij\beta}}{\sqrt{\sum_{i=1}^{m} x_{ij\alpha}^2 + x_{0\beta}^2}}; i = \overline{1,m}; j = \overline{1,n} \text{ (for benefit criteria)}. \quad (16)$$

The cost type criteria normalized through Equations (17) and (18). It is a two-stage procedure, including the calculation of the changed decision-making matrix:

$$x_{ij\alpha} = \frac{1}{x^*_{ij\alpha}}; \overline{x}_{ij\alpha} = \frac{x_{ij\alpha}}{\sqrt{\sum_{i=0}^{m} x_{ij\beta}^2 + x_{0\beta}^2}}; i = \overline{1,m}; j = \overline{1,n}. \quad (17)$$

$$x_{ij\beta} = \frac{1}{x^*_{ij\beta}}; \overline{x}_{ij\beta} = \frac{x_{ij\beta}}{\sqrt{\sum_{i=0}^{m} x_{ij\alpha}^2 + x_{0\alpha}^2}}; i = \overline{1,m}; j = \overline{1,n} \text{ (for cost criteria)}. \quad (18)$$

Step 3: Normalized-weighted DMM calculated by Equation (12).
Step 4: Transforming grey values into crisp values to obtain the utility degree of alternatives K_i:

$$S_i = \frac{\sum_{j=1}^{n} \hat{x}_{ij\alpha} + \sum_{j=1}^{n} \hat{x}_{ij\beta}}{2}; K_i = \frac{S_i}{\sum_{i=1}^{m} S_i}; i = \overline{1,m}. \quad (19)$$

Then, the options' preference order presented as descending order of the K_i: value.

4.3. The Geomean Method with Grey Numbers

The Geomean method is an MCDM utility function, and uses multiplication rather than addition to summarize criteria values. The Geomean method is an extension of the AHP multiplicative form. This approach is a useful tool when expecting the changes in relative preference order. A systemic procedure could be applied to develop it with grey number inputs:

Steps 1–3: Calculate the normalized-weighted DMM. The same normalized-weighted DMM of ARAS-G method used in this method.
Step 4: Determine the geometric mean of the alternatives GM_i, as follows:

$$GM_i = \left(\prod_{j=1}^{n} (\hat{x}_{ij\alpha} \times \hat{x}_{ij\beta}) \right)^{1/2n}; i = \overline{1,m}. \quad (20)$$

Then, the preference order of the alternatives ranked by descending order of the GM_i value.

5. Case Study Resolution

Tables 4 and 5A,B show the normalized DMM, using Equations (11), (17) and (18). Additionally, the positive and negative ideal alternatives corresponding to the TOPSIS-GM method are presented in the last two rows of Table 4, and the optimal alternative corresponding to the ARAS-G method are shown in the last row of Table 5A.

Table 4. Normalized DMM (TOPSIS-GM method).

	C_1		C_2		C_3		C_4		C_5		C_6		C_7		C_8	
w	0.244	0.251	0.168	0.226	0.129	0.159	0.046	0.073	0.061	0.089	0.112	0.127	0.056	0.081	0.08	0.097
	α	β	α	β	α	β	α	β	α	β	α	β	α	β	α	β
A_1	0.878	0.878	0.294	0.298	0.311	0.518	0.316	0.413	0.274	0.358	0.286	0.477	0.350	0.584	0.128	0.298
A_2	0.278	0.278	0.409	0.539	0.538	0.704	0.425	0.534	0.421	0.526	0.496	0.649	0.607	0.794	0.746	0.938
A_3	0.133	0.133	0.341	0.374	0.538	0.704	0.316	0.413	0.368	0.463	0.286	0.477	0.350	0.584	0.320	0.533
A_4	0.351	0.351	0.709	0.713	0.124	0.290	0.316	0.413	0.421	0.526	0.496	0.649	0.140	0.327	0.128	0.298
A^+	0.102	0.102	0.226	0.226	0.096	0.096	0.607	0.607	0.526	0.526	0.220	0.220	0.108	0.108	0.098	0.098
A^-	0.878	0.878	0.713	0.713	0.704	0.704	0.316	0.316	0.274	0.274	0.649	0.649	0.794	0.794	0.938	0.938

Table 5. (**A**) Changed decision-making matrix (Additive Ratio Assessment with Grey Numbers (ARAS-G) method); (**B**) Normalized DMM (ARAS-G method).

(A)

	C_1		C_2		C_3		C_4		C_5		C_6		C_7		C_8	
w	0.244	0.251	0.168	0.226	0.129	0.159	0.046	0.073	0.061	0.089	0.112	0.127	0.056	0.081	0.08	0.097
	α	β	α	β	α	β	α	β	α	β	α	β	α	β	α	β
A_1	0.488	0.488	0.199	0.201	0.400	0.667	3.4	2.6	3.4	2.6	0.400	0.667	0.400	0.667	0.714	1.667
A_2	1.538	1.538	0.110	0.145	0.294	0.385	4.4	3.5	5	4	0.294	0.385	0.294	0.385	0.227	0.286
A_3	3.226	3.226	0.158	0.174	0.294	0.385	3.4	2.6	4.4	3.5	0.400	0.667	0.400	0.667	0.400	0.667
A_4	1.220	1.220	0.083	0.084	0.714	1.667	3.4	2.6	5	4	0.294	0.385	0.714	1.667	0.714	1.667
A_0	4.194	4.194	0.262	0.262	2.167	2.167	5	5	5	5	0.867	0.867	2.167	2.167	2.167	2.167

(B)

	C_1		C_2		C_3		C_4		C_5		C_6		C_7		C_8	
w	0.244	0.251	0.168	0.226	0.129	0.159	0.046	0.073	0.061	0.089	0.112	0.127	0.056	0.081	0.08	0.097
	α	β	α	β	α	β	α	β	α	β	α	β	α	β	α	β
A_1	0.086	0.086	0.486	0.516	0.140	0.283	0.448	0.292	0.390	0.253	0.287	0.598	0.137	0.281	0.218	0.685
A_2	0.272	0.272	0.269	0.372	0.103	0.163	0.580	0.394	0.574	0.389	0.211	0.345	0.101	0.162	0.069	0.117
A_3	0.570	0.570	0.387	0.446	0.103	0.163	0.448	0.292	0.505	0.340	0.287	0.598	0.137	0.281	0.122	0.274
A_4	0.215	0.215	0.203	0.214	0.249	0.708	0.448	0.292	0.574	0.389	0.211	0.345	0.245	0.704	0.218	0.685
A_0	0.740	0.740	0.640	0.671	0.756	0.921	0.659	0.562	0.574	0.486	0.623	0.777	0.743	0.915	0.660	0.890

Then, normalized-weighted DMM (Tables 6 and 7) were obtained by Equation (12) for both methods.

Table 6. Normalized-weighted DMM (TOPSIS-GM method).

	C_1		C_2		C_3		C_4		C_5		C_6		C_7		C_8	
	α	β	α	β	α	β	α	β	α	β	α	β	α	β	α	β
A_1	0.214	0.220	0.049	0.067	0.040	0.082	0.015	0.030	0.017	0.032	0.032	0.061	0.020	0.047	0.010	0.029
A_2	0.068	0.070	0.069	0.122	0.069	0.112	0.020	0.039	0.026	0.047	0.056	0.082	0.034	0.064	0.060	0.091
A_3	0.032	0.033	0.057	0.085	0.069	0.112	0.015	0.030	0.022	0.041	0.032	0.061	0.020	0.047	0.026	0.052
A_4	0.086	0.088	0.119	0.161	0.016	0.046	0.015	0.030	0.026	0.047	0.056	0.082	0.008	0.026	0.010	0.029
A^+	0.025	0.026	0.038	0.051	0.012	0.015	0.028	0.044	0.032	0.047	0.025	0.028	0.006	0.009	0.008	0.010
A^-	0.214	0.220	0.120	0.161	0.091	0.112	0.015	0.023	0.017	0.024	0.073	0.082	0.044	0.064	0.075	0.091

Table 7. Normalized-weighted DMM (ARAS-G method).

	C_1		C_2		C_3		C_4		C_5		C_6		C_7		C_8	
	α	β	α	β	α	β	α	β	α	β	α	β	α	β	α	β
A_1	0.021	0.022	0.082	0.117	0.018	0.045	0.021	0.021	0.024	0.022	0.032	0.076	0.008	0.023	0.017	0.066
A_2	0.066	0.068	0.045	0.084	0.013	0.026	0.027	0.029	0.035	0.035	0.024	0.044	0.006	0.013	0.006	0.011
A_3	0.139	0.143	0.065	0.101	0.013	0.026	0.021	0.021	0.031	0.030	0.032	0.076	0.008	0.023	0.010	0.027
A_4	0.053	0.054	0.034	0.048	0.032	0.113	0.021	0.021	0.035	0.035	0.024	0.044	0.014	0.057	0.017	0.066
A_0	0.181	0.186	0.107	0.152	0.098	0.146	0.030	0.041	0.035	0.043	0.070	0.099	0.042	0.074	0.053	0.086

Using Equations (13)–(15) for TOPSIS-GM, Equation (19) for ARAS-G, and Equation (20) for the Geomean method, alternatives were prioritized. The last row of the Tables 8–10 show the preferences of alternatives in the TOPSIS-GM, ARAS-G, and Geomean methods, respectively. Presenting the results of three methods, decision-makers (the contractor's authorities) must choose the excellent alternative as the solution for the case study. Previously, Figure 3 showed that none of the options are optimal according to all criteria values.

Table 8. Separation measures and relative closeness values of alternatives for TOPSIS-GM.

	D^+	D^-	C^+
A_1	0.192	0.088	0.314
A_2	0.092	0.148	0.617
A_3	0.089	0.185	0.675
A_4	0.102	0.130	0.561
$A_3 \succ A_2 \succ A_4 \succ A_1$			

Table 9. Utility degree of alternatives for ARAS-G.

	S_i	K_i
A_1	0.307	0.307
A_2	0.266	0.266
A_3	0.382	0.382
A_4	0.334	0.334
$A_3 \succ A_4 \succ A_1 \succ A_2$		

Table 10. Geomean value of the alternatives.

	GM_i
A_1	0.0299
A_2	0.0252
A_3	0.0331
A_4	0.0361
$A_4 \succ A_3 \succ A_1 \succ A_2$	

Focusing on Figure 4, different uncertainty levels are present in the expert judgement. Upper and lower criteria values for the three most important criteria are equal (for C_1), or close to each other. However, other criteria values should be calculated using values at intervals. If the criteria are divided into four quarters, the two most important criteria are the cost (C_1) and duration (C_2) with a total weight of 45%. Possible future disputes (C_7) and related experiences in the past (C_4) with a total weight of 17% are the least important among the eight criteria under consideration. The remaining four criteria are moderate and have a total weight of 43%.

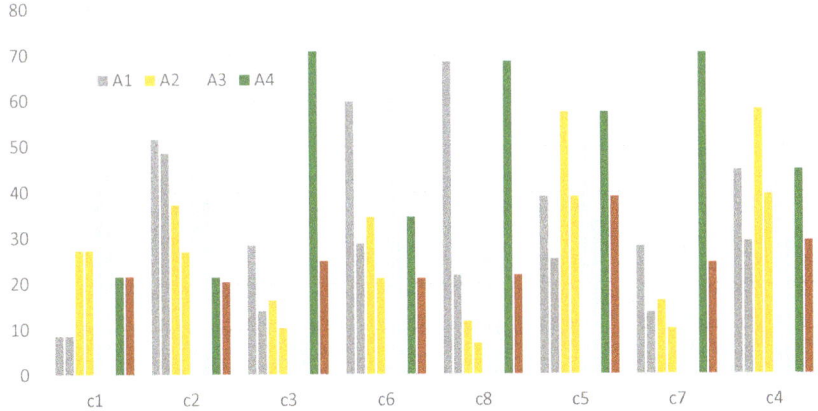

Figure 4. Criteria value comparison.

Here, grey numbers are used for their ease of use possibility. Structural change (A_3) is the best-suggested alternative by TOPSIS-GM and ARAS-G methods. Besides, the Geomean method ranked it the second with a slight difference comparing with A_4. Therefore, A_3 is the optimal solution to the proposed case study. A_3 has the lowest cost, and it is relatively fast to implement. These are the main two criteria.

The contractor implemented the result of the calculations practically. They applied the A_3 as structural changes. After the application of these changes, the structure of the tower was completed within a short term. Structure completion had a significant effect on the target buyers and amplified the hopes for the soonest possible exploit from clients' eyes. The project could even attract a remarkable number of the other tower's potential buyers. This financial boost accelerated the activities' progression more and more. At last, both contractors sold-out all of the units and immediately started the construction of their next tower in that area.

This model could be applied to a similar case when criteria are set, and weights and values updated in compliance with governing conditions.

6. Conclusions

Developing countries must promote the development of infrastructure, which has a positive effect on sustainable economic growth, to achieve a significant increase, except meeting basic needs. Sustainable construction addresses the ecological, social and economic issues of a building in the context of its community. Owner commitment, project delivery system, project team procurement, contract conditions, design integration, project team characteristics, and the construction process affect the schedule, cost, quality, and sustainable performance of green buildings and by managing these non-technical aspects, green buildings can be delivered successfully. Decision-makers must apply the appropriate change response whenever it is needed to maximize a project's success. While proposing the best change strategy, decision makers are usually confronted with a multi-dimensional MCDM problem. This problem has different aspects of ambiguity and, using the crisp numbers, push the decision-makers away from reality. Similar issues need the application of fuzzy or grey numbers. The article presents a novel, multi-criteria change management response systemic procedure when change application in projects is needed. All the input values are grey numbers in the proposed change management model. The critical criteria, which affect the problem, and their weights, are subjective. Therefore, they were defined with expert judgment method, which is a part of the SWARA method. There is no one MCDM method which is the best for all case studies. Therefore, alternatives are ranked using the TOPSIS-GM, ARAS-G and Geomean methods with grey inputs. In the case study, four possible options and eight criteria (cost, duration, and some linguistic criteria) were defined.

A_3 alternative is considered to be the best for TOPSIS-GM and ARAS-G methods. According to the Geomean method, it ranks second, and the difference from the best alternative is only 8%. It is, therefore, the most appropriate choice. The Geomean method considers A_4 as the best, while according to the ARAS-G method, it ranks second, and the difference from the best is 14%, and according to TOPSIS-GM it ranks third, and the difference is 9%. Therefore, it is the second most suitable alternative after A_3. A_2 rates as the worst by ARAS-G and TOPSIS GM. According to the GEOMEAN method, it is the third concerning a 53% difference from the best-ranked alternative. The alternative is the worst according to the TOPSIS-GM and ARAS-G methods with the variations of 30% and 31% from the worst option. It can, therefore, be considered the worst alternative. A_1 is supposed to be the worst under the TOPSIS GM method. According to the ARAS-G method, it occupies the third position, with a difference of 20%. Meanwhile, according to the Geomean G method, the worst third option has a 17% difference from the best. Therefore, it can be considered one of the worst available options.

According to the alternatives sum of ranks, the order of priorities is as follows: $A_3 \succ A_4 \succ A_1 \approx A_2$. Cost and time are the most important criteria. According to the problem solution results, the company made structural change. They shifted the concrete structure to a prefabricated steel structure and modified the specifications of the concrete used in shear walls and slabs for faster execution. The suggested alternative A_3 was implemented practically with positive results.

The model could be adopted to solve different construction delay change response problems by adding criteria, changing criteria weights, and alternatives.

Author Contributions: The following text highlights individual contribution of each coauthor of the paper. Idea: C.A. and T.Z.; Conceptualization: T.Z., C.A., and K.V.; Methodology, T.Z. and K.V.; Calculations: C.A.; Validation: C.A. and T.Z.; Formal analysis: K.M. and A.G.G.; Investigation: C.A.; Writing—original draft preparation: C.A. and T.Z., and K.V.; Review and editing: C.A., K.V., and T.Z.; Supervision: T.Z., K.M., and A.G.G.

Funding: This research received no external funding.

Conflicts of Interest: The authors declare no conflict of interest.

References

1. Zavadskas, E.K.; Kaklauskas, A.; Turskis, Z.; Kalibatas, D. An approach to multi-attribute assessment of indoor environment before and after refurbishment of dwellings. *J. Environ. Eng. Landsc. Manag.* **2009**, *17*, 5–11. [CrossRef]
2. Ibbs, C.W.; Wong, C.K.; Kwak, Y.H. Project change management system. *J. Manag. Eng.* **2001**, *17*, 159–165. [CrossRef]
3. Hashemkhani Zolfani, S.; Zavadskas, E.K.; Turskis, Z. Design of products with both International and Local perspectives based on Yin-Yang balance theory and SWARA method. *Econ. Res. Ekonomska Istraživanja* **2013**, *26*, 153–166. [CrossRef]
4. Dvir, D.; Lechler, T. Plans are nothing, changing plans is everything: The impact of changes on project success. *Res. Policy* **2004**, *33*, 1–15. [CrossRef]
5. Sun, M.; Meng, X. Taxonomy for change causes and effects in construction projects. *Int. J. Proj. Manag.* **2009**, *27*, 560–572. [CrossRef]
6. Gharaee Moghaddam, A. Change management and change process model for the Iranian construction industry. *Int. J. Manag. Bus. Res.* **2012**, *2*, 85–94.
7. Levin, P. *Construction Contract Claims, Changes, and Dispute Resolution*; American Society of Civil Engineers: Reston, VA, USA, 2016.
8. Stasis, A.; Whyte, J.; Dentten, R. A critical examination of change control processes. *Procedia CIRP* **2013**, *11*, 177–182. [CrossRef]
9. Hwang, B.; Low, L.K. Construction project change management in Singapore: Status, importance and impact. *Int. J. Proj. Manag.* **2012**, *30*, 817–826. [CrossRef]
10. Eshtehardian, E.; Khodaverdi, S. Analytical survey of construction change systems: Gaps and opportunities. *Procedia Eng.* **2016**, *161*, 944–949. [CrossRef]
11. Hornstein, H.A. The integration of project management and organizational change management is now a necessity. *Int. J. Proj. Manag.* **2015**, *33*, 291–298. [CrossRef]
12. Butt, A.; Naaranoja, M.; Savolainen, J. Project change stakeholder communication. *Int. J. Proj. Manag.* **2016**, *34*, 1579–1595. [CrossRef]
13. Isaac, S.; Navon, R. A graph-based model for the identification of the impact of design changes. *Autom. Constr.* **2013**, *31*, 31–40. [CrossRef]
14. Oyewobi, L.O.; Jimoh, R.; Ganiyu, B.O.; Shittu, A.A. Analysis of causes and impact of variation order on educational building projects. *J. Facil. Manag.* **2016**, *14*, 139–164. [CrossRef]
15. Gde Agung Yanaa, A.A.; Rusdhi, H.A.; Agung Wibowoc, M. Analysis of factors affecting design changes in construction project with Partial Least Square (PLS). *Procedia Eng.* **2015**, *125*, 40–45. [CrossRef]
16. Chen, C.; Tsui, Y.; Dzeng, R.; Wang, W. Application of project-based change management in construction: A case study. *J. Civil Eng. Manag.* **2015**, *21*, 107–118. [CrossRef]
17. Sun, M.; Fleming, A.; Senaratne, S.; Motawa, I.; Yeoh, M.L. A change management toolkit for construction projects. *Archit. Eng. Design Manag.* **2006**, *2*, 261–271. [CrossRef]
18. Al-Sedairy, S.T. A change management model for Saudi construction industry. *Int. J. Proj. Manag.* **2001**, *19*, 161–169. [CrossRef]

19. Motawa, I.A.; Anumba, C.J.; Lee, S.; Peña-Mora, F. An integrated system for change management in construction. *Autom. Constr.* **2007**, *16*, 368–377. [CrossRef]
20. Lee, S.; Peña-Mora, F.; Park, M. Quality and change management model for large scale concurrent design and construction. *J. Constr. Eng. Manag.* **2005**, *131*, 890–902. [CrossRef]
21. Zhao, Z.Y.; Lv, Q.; Zuo, J.; Zillante, G. Prediction system for change management in construction project. *J. Constr. Eng. Manag.* **2010**, *136*, 659–669. [CrossRef]
22. Lee, S.; Tae, S.; Jee, N.; Shin, S. LDA-based model for measuring impact of change orders in apartment projects and its application for prerisk assessment and postevaluation. *J. Constr. Eng. Manag.* **2015**, *141*, 04015011. [CrossRef]
23. Pilehchian, B.; Staub-French, S.; Nepal, M.P. A conceptual approach to track design changes within a multi-disciplinary building information modeling environment. *Can. J. Civ. Eng.* **2015**, *42*, 139–152. [CrossRef]
24. Medineckiene, M.; Zavadskas, E.K.; Björk, F.; Turskis, Z. Multi-criteria decision-making system for sustainable building assessment/certification. *Arch. Civ. Mech. Eng.* **2015**, *15*, 11–18. [CrossRef]
25. Isaac, S.; Navon, R. Modeling building projects as a basis for change control. *Autom. Constr.* **2009**, *18*, 656–664. [CrossRef]
26. Du, J.; El-Gafy, M.; Zhao, D. Optimization of change order management process with object-oriented discrete event simulation: Case study. *J. Constr. Eng. Manag.* **2016**, *142*, 05015018. [CrossRef]
27. Mejlænder-Larsen, O. Using a change control system and building information modelling to manage change in design. *Archit. Eng. Design Manag.* **2017**, *13*, 39–51. [CrossRef]
28. Francom, T.C.; El Asmar, M. Project quality and change performance differences associated with the use of building information modeling in design and construction projects: Univariate and multivariate analyses. *J. Constr. Eng. Manag.* **2015**, *141*, 04015028. [CrossRef]
29. Shafaat, A.; Alinizzi, M.; Mahfouz, T.; Kandil, A. Can contractors predict change orders? Investigating a historical allegation. *Constr. Res. Congr.* **2016**, 487–496. [CrossRef]
30. Heravi, G.; Charkhakan, M.H. Predicting change by evaluating the change implementation process in construction projects using event tree analysis. *J. Constr. Eng. Manag.* **2015**, *31*, 04014081. [CrossRef]
31. Ibbs, W.; Chen, C. Proactive project change-prediction tool. *J. Leg. Aff. Disput. Resolut. Eng. Constr.* **2015**, *7*, 04515003. [CrossRef]
32. Heravi, G.; Charkhakan, M.H. Predicting and tracing change-formation scenarios in construction projects using the DEMATEL technique. *J. Constr. Eng. Manag.* **2014**, *30*, 04014028. [CrossRef]
33. Isaac, S.; Navon, R. Feasibility study of an automated tool for identifying the implications of changes in construction projects. *J. Constr. Eng. Manag.* **2008**, *134*, 139–145. [CrossRef]
34. El-Adaway, I.; Fawzy, S.; Allard, T.; Runnels, A. Change order provisions under national and international standard forms of contract. *J. Leg. Aff. Disput. Resolut. Eng. Constr.* **2016**, *8*, 03716001. [CrossRef]
35. Syal, M.; Bora, M. Change order clauses in standard contract documents. *Pract. Period. Struct. Design Constr.* **2016**, *21*, 04015021. [CrossRef]
36. Ma, J.; Ma, Z.; Li, J. An IPD-based incentive mechanism to eliminate change orders in construction projects in China. *KSCE J. Civil Eng.* **2017**, *21*, 2538–2550. [CrossRef]
37. Perkins, R.A. Sources of changes in design-build contracts for a governmental owner. *J. Constr. Eng. Manag.* **2009**, *135*, 588–593. [CrossRef]
38. Hyosoo, M.; Hyun-Soo, L.; Moonseo, P.; Bogyeong, L.; Seonu, J.; Bosik, S. Cost performance comparison of project delivery methods in public sector—Focusing on mediator effect of biddropping on change orders. *Korean J. Constr. Eng. Manag.* **2015**, *16*, 86–96. [CrossRef]
39. Alnuaimi, A.S.; Taha, R.A.; Al Mohsin, M.; Al-Harthi, A.S. Causes, effects, benefits, and remedies of change orders on public construction projects in Oman. *J. Constr. Eng. Manag.* **2010**, *136*, 615–622. [CrossRef]
40. Ramos-Maldonado, D.; González-Quevedo, A.A.; Molina-Bas, O. Study of change orders in design-build-maintain projects of the XXI century schools in Puerto Rico. *Constr. Res. Congr.* **2016**. [CrossRef]
41. Serag, E.; Oloufa, A.; Malone, L.; Radwan, E. Model for quantifying the impact of change orders on project cost for U.S. roadwork construction. *J. Constr. Eng. Manag.* **2010**, *136*, 1015–1027. [CrossRef]
42. Turskis, Z.; Zavadskas, E.K. A novel method for multiple criteria analysis: Grey Additive Ratio Assessment (ARAS-G) Method. *Informatica* **2010**, *21*, 597–610.
43. Deng, J.L. Control problems of grey system. *Syst. Control Lett.* **1982**, *1*, 288–294.

44. Deng, J.L. Introduction to grey system theory. *J. Grey Theory* **1989**, *1*, 1–24.
45. Kaufmann, A.; Gupta, M.M. *Introduction to Fuzzy Arithmetic: Theory and Applications*; Van Nostrand Reinhold: New York, NY, USA, 1985.
46. Šaparauskas, J.; Zavadskas, E.K.; Turskis, Z. Selection of facade's alternatives of commercial and public buildings based on multiple criteria. *Int. J. Strateg. Prop. Manag.* **2011**, *15*, 189–203. [CrossRef]
47. Saaty, L.T. *The Analytic Hierarchy Process*; McGraw Hill Company: New York, NY, USA, 1980.
48. Saaty, L.T.; Vargas, L.G. *Models, Methods, Concepts and Applications of the Analytical Hierarchy Process*; Kluwer Academic Publishers: Boston, MA, USA, 2001.
49. Shannon, C.E. The mathematical theory of communication. *Bell Syst. Tech. J.* **1948**, *27*, 379–423. [CrossRef]
50. Keršulienė, V.; Zavadskas, E.K.; Turskis, Z. Selection of rational dispute resolution method by applying new Step-Wise Weight Assessment Ratio Analysis (SWARA). *J. Bus. Econ. Manag.* **2010**, *11*, 243–258. [CrossRef]
51. Keršulienė, V.; Turskis, Z. Integrated fuzzy multiple criteria decision making model for architect selection. *Technol. Econ. Dev. Econ.* **2011**, *17*, 645–666. [CrossRef]
52. Lin, Y.-H.; Lee, P.-C.; Chang, T.-P.; Ting, H.-I. Multi-attribute group decision making model under the condition of uncertain information. *Autom. Constr.* **2008**, *17*, 792–797. [CrossRef]
53. Hwang, C.L.; Yoon, K. *Multiple Attribute Decision Making-Methods and Applications*; Springer: Berlin, Germany, 1981.
54. Lin, Y.-H.; Lee, P.-C.; Ting, H.-I. Dynamic multi-attribute decision making model with grey number evaluations. *Exp. Syst. Appl.* **2008**, *35*, 1638–1644. [CrossRef]
55. Zavadskas, E.K.; Turskis, Z.; Tamošaitienė, J. Risk assessment of construction projects. *J. Civ. Eng. Manag.* **2010**, *16*, 33–46. [CrossRef]
56. Zavadskas, E.K.; Vilutienė, T.; Turskis, Z.; Tamošaitienė, J. Contractor selection for construction works by applying SAW-G and TOPSIS grey techniques. *J. Bus. Econ. Manag.* **2010**, *11*, 34–55. [CrossRef]
57. Hashemkhani Zolfani, S.; Sedaghat, M.; Zavadskas, E.K. Performance evaluating of rural ICT centers (telecenters), applying fuzzy AHP, SAW-G and TOPSIS Grey, a case study in Iran. *Technol. Econ. Dev. Econ.* **2012**, *18*, 364–387. [CrossRef]
58. Oztaysi, B. A decision model for information technology selection using AHP integrated TOPSIS-Grey: The case of content management systems. *Knowl. Based Syst.* **2014**, *70*, 44–54. [CrossRef]
59. Šiožinytė, E.; Antuchevičienė, J.; Kutut, V. Upgrading the old vernacular building to contemporary norms: Multiple criteria approach. *J. Civ. Eng. Manag.* **2014**, *20*, 291–298. [CrossRef]
60. Zagorskas, J.; Zavadskas, E.K.; Turskis, Z.; Burinskienė, M.; Blumberga, A.; Blumberga, D. Thermal insulation alternatives of historic brick buildings in Baltic Sea Region. *Energy Build.* **2014**, *78*, 35–42. [CrossRef]

© 2019 by the authors. Licensee MDPI, Basel, Switzerland. This article is an open access article distributed under the terms and conditions of the Creative Commons Attribution (CC BY) license (http://creativecommons.org/licenses/by/4.0/).

Article

Evaluation of the Criteria for Selecting Proposed Variants of Utility Functions in the Adaptation of Historic Regional Architecture

Małgorzata Fedorczak-Cisak [1,*], Alicja Kowalska-Koczwara [2], Krzysztof Nering [3], Filip Pachla [2], Elżbieta Radziszewska-Zielina [4], Grzegorz Śladowski [4], Tadeusz Tatara [2] and Bartłomiej Ziarko [3]

1. Malopolska Laboratory of Energy Efficient Building, Faculty of Civil Engineering, Cracow University of Technology, 31-155 Cracow, Poland
2. Institute of Structural Mechanics, Faculty of Civil Engineering, Cracow University of Technology, 31-155 Cracow, Poland; akowalska@pk.edu.pl (A.K.-K.); fpachla@pk.edu.pl (F.P.); ttatara@pk.edu.pl (T.T.)
3. Institute of Building Materials and Engineering Structures, Faculty of Civil Engineering, Cracow University of Technology, 31-155 Cracow, Poland; krzysztof.nering@pk.edu.pl (K.N.); bziarko@pk.edu.pl (B.Z.)
4. Institute of Construction Management, Faculty of Civil Engineering, Cracow University of Technology, 31-155 Cracow, Poland; eradzisz@L3.pk.edu.pl (E.R.-Z.); gsladowski@l3.pk.edu.pl (G.Ś.)
* Correspondence: mfedorczak-cisak@pk.edu.pl; Tel.: +48-696-046-050

Received: 22 January 2019; Accepted: 14 February 2019; Published: 19 February 2019

Abstract: In this article, the authors propose ways to evaluate the criteria for the considered variants of utility functions in the adaptation of historic regional architecture. The proposed set of assessment criteria (thermo-modernisation criteria, comfort of use, financial considerations, criteria of social benefits, and protection of cultural heritage) emphasises the multidimensional character of the problem of choosing a new function for a historic building. Some of the criteria are measurable while others are difficult to measure, which requires an expert approach to their assessment. The evaluation of the criteria was performed on the example of the historic building 'Stara Polana' located in Zakopane. The benchmark for the analysis was the existing condition of the 'Stara Polana' building, which is used as a hostel. The authors conducted a series of interdisciplinary studies specifying the potential of the new utility functions considered for the object in the context of the proposed criteria. The evaluation of individual criteria developed in this article is based on the multi-criteria analysis to be performed in the future and support the selection of a new function for the building in question.

Keywords: energy efficiency; comfort of use of buildings; historic buildings; sustainable development

1. Introduction

One of the tasks of modern civilisation is the protection of cultural heritage by preventing the degradation of its elements and ensuring proper conservation, development and popularisation of its values. An important resource of cultural heritage are historic buildings, which in contemporary society have a chance of survival if they are recognised by the public and have a useful function. In the literature on the subject, there is the concept of the so-called adaptability of the building, i.e., a set of various features and properties determining the simplicity of the adaptation of such a building for new utility functions [1–3]. Many factors may have an influence over the adaptive potential of historic buildings, such as the type of architectural and structural system; the type of load-bearing structure; the technical condition of the building; the quality and the physicochemical and mechanical properties of materials used to build them; and the possibility of these materials for being re-used in the adaptation process. In order to assess the adaptive capacity of the building, it is necessary to conduct a series of specialised tests of its building material as well as and evaluation of its historic value. [1]. Objects of historic regional architecture in Poland are located in Podhale in the southern part of the country (see Figure 1a) and are usually built in the traditional brick-and-wood style (Figure 1b). These buildings are a specific type of object whose adaptive capacity for new functions is restricted due to their limited ability to meet requirements such as energy efficiency and comfort of use [4].

Figure 1. (a) location of Podhale on the map of Poland; (b) example of regional architecture—constructed using brick and wood technology and functioning as a hostel.

The technology that was applied in the construction of a historic building largely influences the choice of options relating to the scope of renovations. Thermal insulation works performed on historic buildings are subject to specific formal and legal regulations. This results from construction law [5] and the Act of 23 July 2003 on the protection and care of monuments [6]. Technical and construction conditions [7] come into force on 1 January 2021 which require buildings to have an energy demand of almost zero. This applies to both new buildings and those undergoing renovation and thermo-modernisation, while historic objects are not included in the requirements. In the case of the renovation and thermo-modernisation of used historic buildings or objects covered by conservation protection, the requirements presented in Table 1 need to be met. However, it should be remembered that achieving such requirements, means operational savings on the one hand, but, on the other hand, it involves limiting the usable space due to the need to insulate the walls from the inside. Decisions regarding the level of improvement of the thermal insulation of partitions, as well as the level of comfort of use of a historic building, should depend on the current or planned function and should be taken individually for each object. The comfort of the internal environment, as well as energy efficiency, should be determined depending on the assumed function of the historic building. Other requirements apply for buildings functioning as museums or art galleries (due to the works of art), others apply for hotel buildings, and others still for conference centres and training facilities. The choice of a new function for a historic building is, therefore, difficult and complex due to the need to take into account many interdisciplinary factors [8]. This complex multidimensional decision-making process often forces decision-makers to process and evaluate information, both measurable (e.g., technical and financial data related to a historic building) and information that is harder to quantify (e.g., the cultural heritage value of a historic building and its social benefits) related to the analysed historic building [9,10]

Table 1. Heat transfer coefficient U (W/(m^2·K)) [7].

Type of Partition	Existing State	Current Requirements in Poland	Requirements for NZEB Buildings in Poland (from 2021)	Requirements for Passive Buildings	The Difference of the Existing State from the Current Requirements in Poland
External walls	0.55	0.23	0.20	0.15	239%
Roofs and floors	0.56	0.18	0.15	0.15	311%
Floor on the ground	1.75	0.30	0.30	0.15	583%
Windows	1.60	1.10	0.90	0.80	145%

In the literature many multi-criteria methods can be found for supporting the decision to select new functions for a historic building. The multi-criteria approach to the selection of a new function at historic buildings was taken into account by [11], which analysed the revitalization of historic buildings in Vilnius, Lithuania.

The authors proposed a method TOPSIS (Technique for Order Preference by Similarity to an Ideal Solution) as a tool for multi-criteria analysis of proposed utility functions in the adaptation of historic buildings. The fuzzy development of the TOPSIS method for the above purposes was continued by Zavadskas and Antucheviciene [12,13]. Another method—weighted sum—was used by Fuentes [14] when assessing the possibility of re-using four historic buildings in Spain. Wang and Zeng [15] analysed variants of utility functions for the adaptation of two historic buildings in Taipei, Taiwan. As a multi-criteria analysis tool, they used one of the structural modeling methods, the ANP (Analytic Network Process) method. Breil, Giove and Rosato [16] and Giove, Rosato and Breil [17] used the "Choquet" integral for a multi-criteria analysis of the selection of a new utility function for the Venetian Arsenal building in Italy. An interesting approach to solving the discussed decision problem was proposed by Ferretti et al. [18], who examined the possibility of using the multi-attribute value theory (MAVT) in the analysis of the preferences of historical objects in Turin to perform a specific utility function. Recently, Radziszewska-Zielina and Śladowski [19] proposed a fuzzy extension of the WINGS (Weighted Influence Non-linear Gauge System) in order to model the imprecise, incomplete and uncertain character of information that experts must process as part of the selection of a new utility function for the historic Great Armory building in Gdansk. In [20], the authors of this article proposed a multicriteria hybrid model (using the DEMATEL method (Decision Making Trial and Evaluation Laboratory) and ANP to select a utility function for the purpose of adapting the building 'Stara Polana' located in Zakopane. This article is a continuation of work on the preparation of ways to assess individual criteria for the selection of functions for the building in question, which will be the basis for the multi-criteria analysis carried out in the future based on the hybrid model proposed in the previous work [20].

In this work, the authors propose methods of assessing the criteria (measurable and difficult-to-quantify) adopted in [20] for different variants of utility functions in the adaptation of historical regional architecture in Podhale, Poland. The assessment is based on the example of the 'Stara Polana' villa in Zakopane. The criteria taken into account for the 'Stara Polana' building are shown in Figure 3.

One should pay attention to the interdependence of some proposed criteria for the selection of the utility function of a historic building. These dependencies can be linear as well as nonlinear. It is necessary to take into account interdependencies (e.g., so-called feedback) between these criteria. This leads to the adoption of the network nature of links between them. In Figure 3, network nodes symbolize the criterion data and the potential relationships between them are determined by arrows (arcs). The size (diameter) of nodes symbolizes the significance of a given criterion in the system.

2. Representative Building and Methods of Analysis

The 'Stara Polana' building is located in the centre of Zakopane. The building is owned by Cracow University of Technology; it is currently being used as a hostel. The building is located among low buildings on the main road through Zakopane: Nowotarska Street. This is a historic building, a villa in the Witkiewicz style, which was built in 1905 for the Płaza family by the builder Jan Ustupski-Kubecek. The condition of the building qualifies it for thorough renovation and thermo-modernisation. A detailed description of the building is provided in work [20]. Figure 2a shows a horizontal cross-section of the building. Figure 2b shows the vertical cross-section of the building.

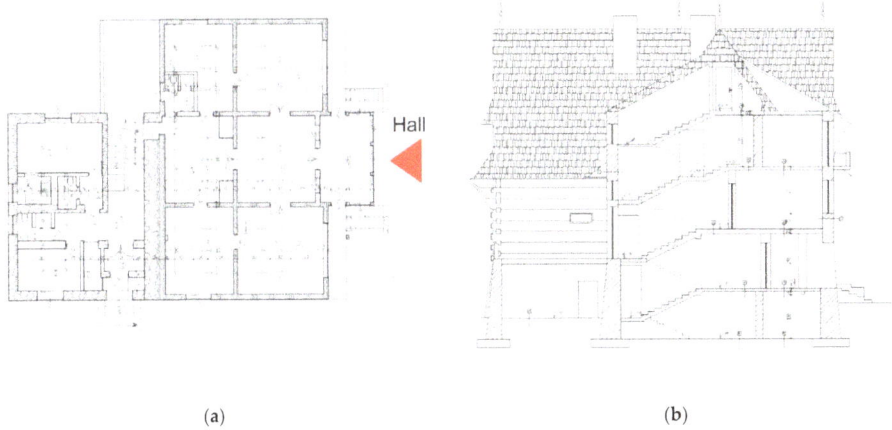

(a) (b)

Figure 2. (a) Horizontal cross section of the building; and (b) cross-section of the building.

Figure 3a shows the interior and in Figure 3b, the detail of wooden connections. The building has a basement made in brick and aboveground floors are built in wood.

(a) (b)

Figure 3. (a) Interior made from wood, with a historic stove, and (b) the detail.

The 'Stara Polana' building has not been modernized. Partitions do not meet the requirements of the regulations in force in Poland. Data regarding thermal insulation parameters of the building are presented in Table 1. Data regarding energy indicators are presented in item 3.2 and item 3.7. The building must be thermo-modernized. Mould growth is present on the basement walls.

The owner of the building has not yet decided upon the future utility function.

In agreement with the investor of the object, the authors have accepted the following possible future functions of the 'Stara Polana' villa:

1. Public building—Hostel (existing condition ('Reference variant');
2. Public building—Five-star hotel ('Variant 1');
3. Public building—Zakopane Art Gallery ('Variant 2'); and
4. Public building—Conference and training centre with accommodation option ('Variant 3')

Methods for evaluating individual criteria for the reference state and suggested variants of utility functions of the building in question are proposed later in this article.

3. Evaluation of Criteria for the Existing State and Variants of New Functions

The evaluation criteria of the reference variant and the proposed variants 1–3 are shown in Figure 4. The main criteria (Fi) are divided into sub-criteria (Fi/Pj). For the needs of the analysis, the authors propose the introduction of utility classes for each of the criteria (A–C). These classes illustrate the level of requirements for each sub-criterion (Fi/Pj). Classes for individual sub-criteria are described for each criterion.

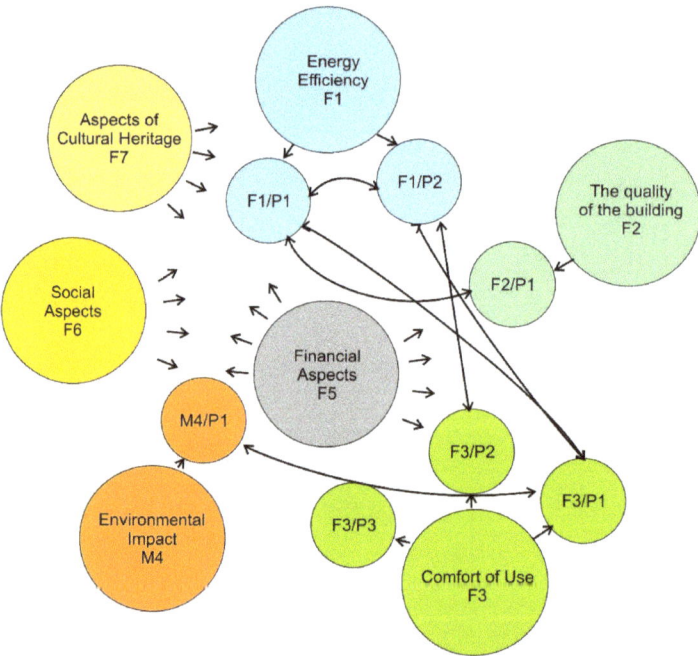

Figure 4. Proposed criteria and their mutual relationships for the purposes of choosing a new utility function for the 'Stara Polana' building; based on [20].

According to the method adopted by the authors, for each type of building function, the criteria and their values are accepted by experts. In the analysed case study, the team of experts determined the assessment criteria presented in Figure 4. As an energy efficiency criterion (F1) the following was assumed to be the subcriterion F1/P1–grade of the thermal insulation of the building's envelope. It is a criterion compatible with the standard's methodology [21,22]. Thermal insulation of the external walls is directly connected with loss of heat between the building's envelope. The second subcriterion in the energy efficiency area (F1/P2) is the final energy coefficient (EK), which is calculated according to methodology found in [23]. The EK coefficient points to the total energy consumption (heating/cooling of the building). Quality of the construction (criterion F2) is assigned by the airtightness of the building envelope. It is in accordance with the methodology found in [24]. The "in situ" tightness test is supported by thermography, according to the test method presented in [25]. With respect to criterion F3 (comfort of use of buildings), the authors have taken to evaluate the building, due to the fact that many buildings, thermo-modernized or newly designed, do not ensure the well-being of users. It should be admitted that the problem of providing the comfort in use is a topic mentioned in publications in the 1970s [26] by the Danish scientist Ole Fanger, but modern therrmomodernisation and construction systems are the reason why the concept of comfort should be treated in a multi-aspect manner. This approach to comfort design is presented in [27]. Currently is developed CEN standard 16798-1 [28] is based on the standard EN 15251 [29]. The multi-aspect comfort design is implemented by the F3/P1 sub-criterion, which specifies thermal comfort in accordance with the methodology given in [27,29,30]. The sub-criterion of the F3/P2 (vibrational comfort) is determined according to the methodology in [31], while the sub-criterion of acoustic comfort was determined in the "in situ" tests according to the methodology contained in [29,32]. The building's environmental impact criterion was determined based on the non-renewable Primary Energy index, determined in accordance with the methodology in [23]. The EP indicator is an indicator determining the use of renewable heat sources in the building use, so it directly indicates the building's environmental impact. Criteria F5, F6, and F7 are related to financial, social and cultural heritage aspects. These criteria are determined on the basis of expert knowledge and surveys of future users of the historic building in which the function will be changed.

3.1. Criterion F_1/P_1-Energy Efficiency; Improvement of Insulation of External Partitions

3.1.1. Methods

The thermal insulation of the building is determined by the heat transfer coefficient of the building envelope U (W/(m^{2}K)). This terminology is discussed in [33]. Based on the architectural and construction design as well as the technical description, the actual coefficient of external partitions for the 'Stara Polana' building was determined. The calculations were made on the basis of standards [21,22].

3.1.2. Results

Table 1 presents the results of calculations of the heat transfer coefficient U (W/(m^{2}K)) for the building envelope of the 'Stara Polana' building (reference variant). The results of calculations referring to thermal protection were made accordingly to [7]. Calculated coefficients of the external envelope of the 'Stara Polana' differ from the current requirements. As stated in the introduction, historic buildings undergoing renovation are exempt from the requirements of thermal protection due to their historic character. However, all other existing buildings that undergo thermal modernisation and renovation must meet the requirements of the technical conditions [7].

Table 2 presents adopted classes for the sub-criterion F_1/P_1 dependent upon the proposed function of the 'Stara Polana' building. As an example, the classes adopted for the requirements of the thermal insulation of external walls are presented. For variant 1 (five-star hotel), it was assumed that it will be a passive buildings corresponding to class 'A'. In variant 2 (Zakopane Art Gallery), the main focus is not on energy efficiency; therefore, class 'C' was assigned. For variant 3 (conference and training centre), the criterion of energy efficiency is important but not a priority [34].

Table 2. Classes adopted for sub-criterion F_1/P_1 heat-transfer coefficient U of external walls (W/(m²K)).

No.	Designation of the Building	Criterion F_1 F_1/P_1 (Coefficient U (W/m²rok]))
1	Reference variant—Hostel (existing state)	0.55
2	Variant 1—Five-star hotel	0–0.15—class A 0.16–0.22—class B U ≥ 0.23—class C
3	Variant 2—Zakopane Art Gallery	0–0.15—class A 0.16–0.22—class B U ≥ 0.23—class C
4	Variant 3—Conference and training centre	0–0.15—class A 0.16–0.22—class B U ≥ 0.23—class C

3.2. Criterion F_1/P_2-Energy Efficiency; Improvement of the Final Energy Index EK (kWh/(m²year))

3.2.1. Methods

Final energy is defined as thermal energy and auxiliary energy which must be delivered to the boundary of the heating system (building) with a given efficiency in order to cover the heat demand required for the heating and ventilation of the rooms. Final energy should fulfil requirements for living, and hygienic and economic needs. The value of the final energy is characterised by, inter alia, the quality of the thermal protection of rooms, thermal insulation, the tightness of the entire external envelope and the technical condition of the heating and cooling installations. The final energy value [kWh/(m²year)] was determined in accordance with the methodology stated in regulation [23] as an EK index which indicates the annual final energy demand per unit area of rooms with adjustable air temperature in a building or flat, expressed in kWh/(m²y). The EK indicator was determined in accordance with the Equation (1):

$$EK = Q_K/A_f \text{ (kWh/(m}^2 \cdot \text{year))} \tag{1}$$

where:

Qk—annual demand for final energy supplied to a building or part of a building for technical systems (kWh/year); and

Af—area of rooms with adjustable air temperature (heated or cooled surface) (m²).

Polish technical conditions [7] do not specify the minimum requirements for the EK indicator. This indicator directly refers to the energy efficiency of buildings. In German regulations regarding energy efficiency [35] on the basis of the EK indicator, energy efficiency classes of buildings are introduced. Energy demands for the heating of buildings have also been added to the energy efficiency requirements in the technical and construction regulations in Austria [36].

3.2.2. Results

The annual heat demand for heating the building (taking into account the efficiency of the heating system and heating breaks) for the reference variant of the 'Stara Polana' building is 244.79 kWh/(m²year). Improving the energy efficiency of buildings by reducing the EK indicator is associated both with improving the thermal insulation of the building envelope and modernising the installed technical equipment. The improvement classes for historic buildings are proposed in Table 3.

Table 3. Classes adopted for sub-criterion F_1/P_2 of final energy coefficient (kWh/(m²year)).

No.	Designation of the Building	Criterion F_1 F_1/P_2 (EK, kWh/m²rok)
1	Reference variant—Hostel (existing state)	244.79
2	Variant 1—Five-star hotel	EK reduction: >60%—class A >50%—class B >40%—class C
3	Variant 2—Zakopane Art Gallery	EK reduction: >60%—class A >50%—class B >40%—class C
4	Variant 3—Conference and training centre	EK reduction: >60%—class A >50%—class B >40%—class C

Table 3 presents adopted classes for sub-criterion F_1/P_2 dependent upon the proposed function of the 'Stara Polana' building.

Variant 1 (five-star hotel) was adopted as a passive building; therefore, for this variant, energy efficiency is a priority. The variant corresponds to class 'A' for the sub-criterion F1/P2. Variant 2 (Zakopane Art Gallery) due to the need to preserve as much as possible of the natural structure of the building (visible wooden beams, carpentry joints) was assigned to class 'C'. Variant 3 (conference and training centre) should be an energy-efficient building, although this is not the main priority. Variant 3 was assigned to class 'B'.

3.3. Criterion F2/P1-Quality of the Building Envelope; Improving the Tightness of the Building Envelope; Detection of Thermal Bridges through Thermography Tests

3.3.1. Methods

Tightness testing of the buildings is one of the ways to control the quality of construction works. Detection and subsequent removal of unwanted leaks can reduce the energy needed to heat the object. Polish legislation does not impose an obligation to carry out building tightness tests; they are only a recommendation. Suggestions for tightness are contained in [7]. Air tightness is determined for buildings with gravitational ventilation at the level of $n_{50} \leq 3$, 1/h and for buildings with $n_{50} \leq 1.5$, 1/h. Passive buildings should have a coefficient value of $n_{50} \leq 0.6$ [1/h]. Tightness testing is obligatory for passive buildings. The measurement method is included in PN-EN 13829:2002 [24].

Figure 5 presents the results of tests for 48 buildings with mechanical ventilation. According to [7], the n_{50} coefficient should be $n_{50} \leq 1.5$ [1/h].

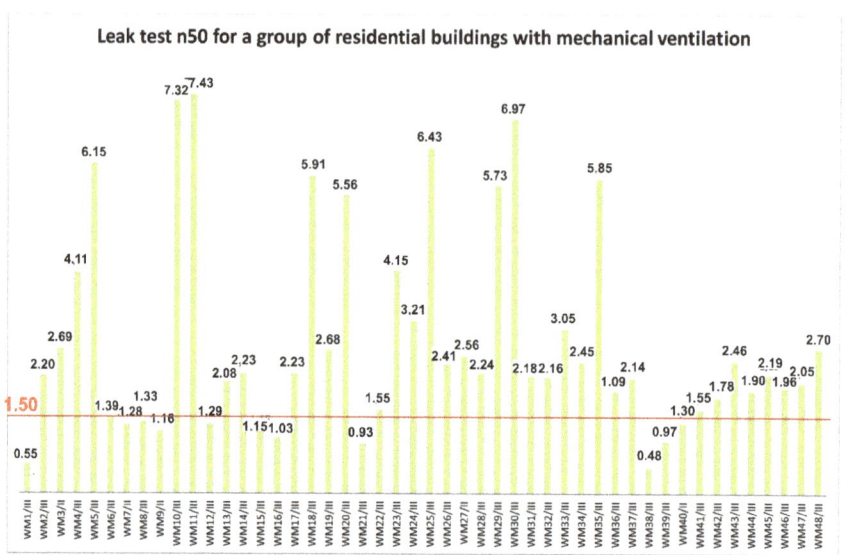

Figure 5. Evaluation of meeting the requirements that ensure air tightness for a group of 48 residential buildings with mechanical ventilation (authors' own image).

The tightness test on the 'Stara Polana' building was performed according to the standard [24] using the pressure measurement method with the use of a fan; it was performed using a system for testing the air tightness of the building envelope by means of the generated Retrotec Q5E pressure system with a capacity of 14,100 m³/h at 50 Pa. The test was carried out at 1:00 p.m. on 8 May 2018 under the following weather conditions: barometric pressure: 91.95 kPa, wind force 3 (light breeze), external temperature 15 °C, internal temperature 19 °C. The building's cubic capacity is 2119.63 m³, Figure 6 shows the method of performing the tightness test in the 'Stara Polana' building.

Figure 6. Tightness test at the 'Stara Polana' hostel (authors' own image).

An additional examination of the construction quality of the 'Stara Polana' building was the implementation of the thermography measurement. Thermography is one of the methods of object diagnostics involving the measurement of radiation in the infrared band. The methodology of thermography tests is described in the PN-EN 13187 [25] standard.

The thermographic test was performed with a FLIR thermal imaging camera with a thermal sensitivity of 0.06 °C and a bolometric matrix resolution of 320 × 240.

3.3.2. Results

For the 'Stara Polana' building, the result of the tightness test for negative pressure n_{50} = 10.09 [1/h] and for overpressure n_{50} = 8.83 (1/h) was achieved. Figure 7 presents a thermal image taken inside the building.

Figure 7. Leak detection in the building envelope using a thermal imaging camera (authors' own image).

The thermographic test showed very large leaks in the structure and enabled locating heat loss sites.

Table 4 presents the adopted classes for sub-criterion F_2/P_1 dependent upon the proposed function of the 'Stara Polana' building.

Table 4. Classes adopted for sub-criterion F_2/P_1 tightness of the building envelope n_{50} (1/h).

No.	Designation of the Building	Criterion F2 F2/P1 n_{50}, 1/h
1	Reference variant—Hostel (existing state)	For negative pressure n_{50} = 10.09 For overpressure n_{50} = 8.83
2	Variant 1—Five-star hotel	0–0.6—class A 0.6–1.5—class B $n_{50} \geq 1.5$—class C
3	Variant 2—Zakopane Art Gallery	0–0.6—class A 0.6–1.5—class B $n_{50} \geq 1.5$—class C
4	Variant 3—Conference and training centre	0–0.6—class A 0.6–1.5—class B $n_{50} \geq 1.5$—class C

The result of the tightness test is significantly different from the value of the proposed classes; this is due to the unsealing of wooden walls and connections. After well-performed insulation, the values proposed in the classes can be achieved. Obtaining the tightness of the building envelope is associated with the minimisation of energy consumption for heating purposes. An example of how to properly insulate a historic building from the inside is presented in Figure 8. The Figure 8 shows the correct insulation of the walls of historic buildings. The graph shows the pressure diagram of saturated steam and the water vapour pressure diagram. These are pressure graphs, therefore, the unit is Pa. The lines do not intersect. The wall will not condense water vapor. The thermal insulation is done correctly.

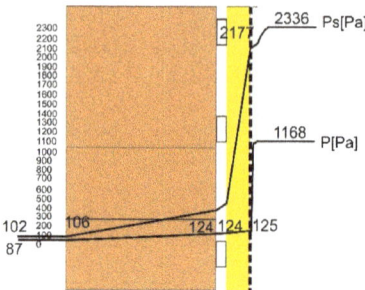

Figure 8. An example of a solution of how to insulate a historic building from the inside (authors' own calculations and image).

3.4. Criterion F_3/P_1-Comfort of Using the Rooms; Thermal Comfort

3.4.1. Methods

Providing the appropriate thermal comfort in NZEB buildings as well as those subjected to thermo-modernisation is one of the most important elements in designing and constructing buildings. Both room overheating and cooling are subjects of research and analysis performed in low-energy and passive buildings [37–39]. Thermal comfort is also affected by design errors, such as leaks in the building envelope, thermal bridges, and unevenly heated surfaces. The PN-EN ISO 7730 [27] standard introduces a division into room categories on the basis of the achieved PMV factor. The classes are presented in Table 5.

Table 5. Room categories depending on the PMV indicator.

Room Category	Coefficients:	
	PMV (–)	PPD (%)
A	−0.2 < PMV < +0.2	<6
B	−0.5 < PMV < +0.5	<10
C	−0.7 < PMV < +0.7	<15

The methodology for determining thermal comfort is based on PN-EN ISO 7730 [27] and the measurement methodology is based on PN ISO 7726 [30]. The tests were performed using measuring equipment that meets standard [30]. The measuring device was a microclimate meter (Figure 9). The tests were conducted in the period 22 May 2018 to 31 May 2018. The measuring device was located in the guest room of the 'Stara Polana' hostel. Thermal insulation of clothing was determined based on the standard PN-EN ISO 9920:2009 [40]. Insulation of clothing was determined as the value for the transitional season of clothing worn at home I_{clo} = 0.7 (clo).

Figure 9. Test device for measuring thermal comfort.

The measured parameters were:

- t_a—air temperature measurement;
- t_g—temperature of blackened sphere (heat radiation meter)—the black sphere, in agreement with the norms, should be 15 cm in diameter;
- t_{nw}—natural wet-bulb temperature measurement;
- RH—measurement of relative air humidity; and
- V_a—measurement of air flow speed.

The frequency of data collection was every 1 min.
The data from the sensors is provided in Table 6.

Table 6. Sensor data.

Type of Sensor	Measurement Range	Scale	Accuracy
Temperature sensors	−20 °C + 50 °C (wet thermometer 0 °C + 5 °C)	0.01 °C	± 0.4 °C
Humidity sensors	0–100%	0.1 RH (relative humidity)	± 2% RH (relative humidity)
Air velocity sensors	0–5 m/s	0.01 m/s	for 0–1 m/s: ± 0.05 + 0.05 × Va m/s for 1–5 m/s: ± 5 %

On the basis of measurements, thermal comfort parameters were calculated from Equation (2). The designated parameters are:

- PMV—predicted average thermal comfort rating [27];
- PPD—predicted percentage of dissatisfied people [27]; and

$$\begin{aligned} PMV &= [0.303 \times \exp(-0.306 \times M) + 0.028] \times ((M - W) - 3.05 \times 10^{-3} \times [x5733 - 6.99 \times (M - W) - p_a] \\ &\quad -0.42 \times [(M - W) - 58.15] - 1.7 \times 10^{-5} \times M \times (5867 - p_a) - 0.0014 \times M \times (34 - t_a) \\ &\quad -3.96 \times 10^{-8} \times f_{cl} \times [(t_{cl} + 273)^4 - (t^-{}_r + 273)^4] - f_{cl} \times h_c \times (t_{cl} - t_a)) \\ t_{cl} &= 35.7 - 0.028 \times (M - W) - I_{cl}\{3.96 \times 10^{-8} \times f_{cl} \times [(t_{cl} + 273)^4 - (t^-{}_r + 273)^4] + f_{cl} \times h_c \times (t_{cl} - t_a)\} \end{aligned} \quad (2)$$

where:

M—the amount of metabolism (W/m^2);

W—the density of energy loss in the form of mechanical work (W/m²);
I_{cl}—clothing insulation (m²K/W);
f_{cl}—surface of clothes (m²);
t_a—air temperature (°C);
t'_r—average radiation temperature (°C); and
t_{cl}—temperature of the clothes surface (°C).

3.4.2. Results

The results of the performed tests are presented in Figures 10–12. Figure 10 displays the temperature recorded on the microclimate gauge. Figure 11 presents the thermal comfort index in the analysed period. Figure 12 displays the dependence of PMV on temperature.

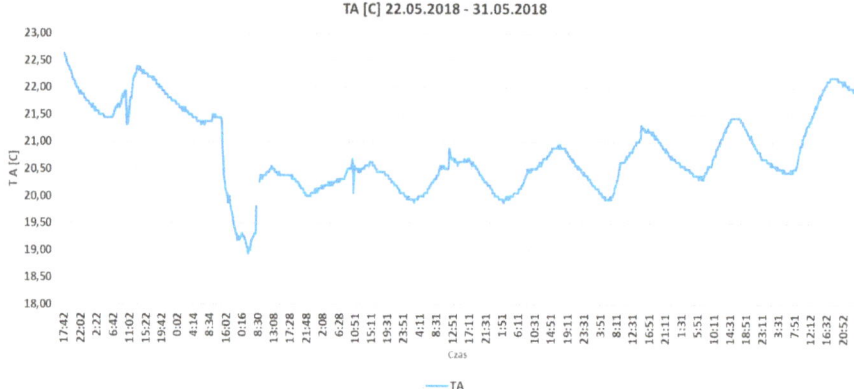

Figure 10. Internal temperature T_A (°C) recorded on the microclimate gauge.

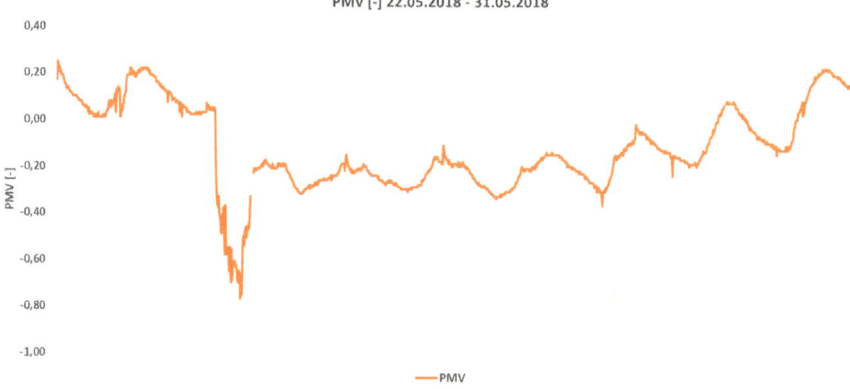

Figure 11. Calculated comfort factor PMV (–) based on the conducted tests.

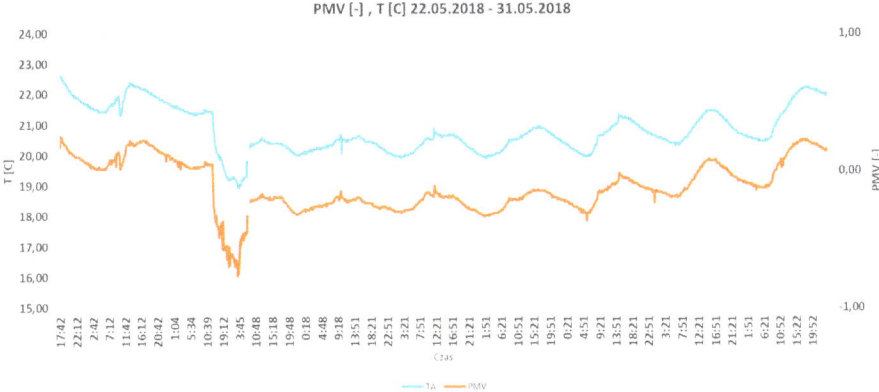

Figure 12. Dependence of the PMV (–) comfort indicator on temperature T_A (°C).

The results presented in Figure 10 show a stable room temperature. Maximum temperatures in the research process were over 22.5 °C and the lowest was nearly 19 °C. The thermal comfort coefficient, expressed by the PMV value, ranged from −0.7 to approx. 0.25. In Figure 12, a clear relationship between PMV and internal temperature can be observed. Thermal comfort is ensured by large expenditures incurred for heating the building. Table 7 presents adopted classes for the sub-criterion F_3/P_1 dependent upon the proposed function of the 'Stara Polana' building.

Table 7. Classes adopted for sub-criterion F_3/P_1 thermal comfort PMV (–).

No.	Designation of the Building	Criterion F_3 F_3/P_1(PMV (–))
1	Reference variant—Hostel (existing state)	−0.7—0.25
2	Variant 1—Five-star hotel	−0.2–0.2—class A −0.5–0.5—class B −0.5 > PMV > 0.5—class C
3	Variant 2—Zakopane Art Gallery	−0.2–0.2—class A −0.5–0.5—class B −0.5 > PMV > 0.5—class C
4	Variant 3—Conference and training centre	−0.2–0.2—class A −0.5–0.5—class B −0.5 > PMV > 0.5—class C

In five-star hotels, in addition to low energy consumption, priority is given to the comfort of staying hotel guests. For this variant, grade A was assigned to the gallery and the training and conference centre was assigned to class B.

3.5. Criterion F_3/P_2-Comfort of Using the Rooms; Vibration Comfort

Discussion about providing vibroacoustic comfort is recently present in [41,42]. The building which was chosen for analysis is located in Zakopane close to Nowotarska Street.

The external source of vibrations, which is Nowotarska Street, is located 20.6 m from the building. The building is located in the zone of dynamic influences [43] and vibrational comfort requires assessment.

3.5.1. Methods

Dynamic measurements were made on 8 May 2018. The measurements were made using accelerometers which properties related to dynamic error measurements were described in [44,45]. Thirty-seven dynamic events, mostly heavy-truck-passing events, were recorded, but only 24 recorded signals were free from internal excitations. Measurement points were located in the hall on the ground floor and in the guest room on the first floor (see Figure 1b). PCB accelerometers were placed in the middle of the floor in accordance with [31] and measured vibrations in three orthogonal directions: two horizontal 'x' and 'y' and in vertical 'z' (Figure 13). Accelerometers were placed on a special disc in accordance with [31] (see Figure 13).

Figure 13. Measurement discs located in (**a**) the hall, and (**b**) the guest room.

An example of a vibration record obtained during measurements is presented in Figure 14.

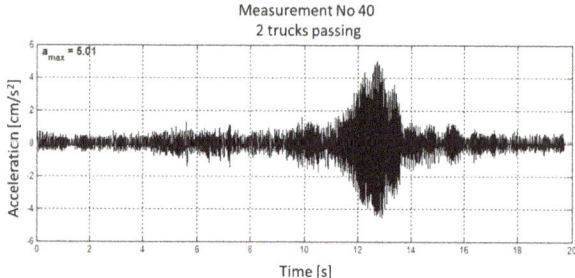

Figure 14. Vertical z component of acceleration vibrations recorded in the guest room.

Vibration records obtained from monitoring were used for human perception evaluation according to the RMS procedure available in [31,46].

3.5.2. Results of Human Perception of Vibrations

For all analysed signals, the human perception threshold was not exceeded. An example of the RMS results for measurement no. 40 is presented in Figure 15.

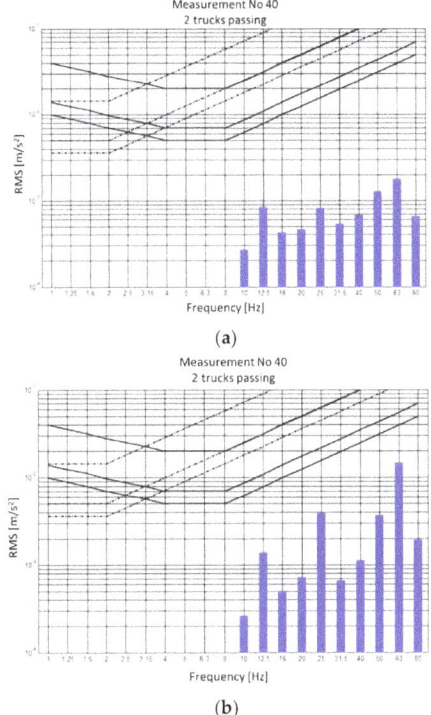

Figure 15. RMS analysis of measurement no. 40: (**a**) in the hall, and (**b**) in the guest room.

HVPR (the human vibration perceptivity ratio) described in [47] never reaches a value of 1, which means that vibrations are not perceptible according to [31]. In this paper, due to the proposed modifications of the utility function, new values of HVPR are proposed (see Table 8). The proposed values of HVPR result from the experience of the authors gained from many years of monitoring the Warsaw Metro [48]. Measurements of the Warsaw Metro were the basis for changes in the requirements concerning human vibrational comfort in buildings in the vicinity of the Metro [48]. Requirements included in the Japan standard [49,50] and described in [51] were also analysed before the proposal of HPVR values.

Twenty-four recorded signals were investigated and an evaluation of the human perception of vibrations was made using the RMS method. In all recorded dynamic events, the human perception threshold of vibrations is not currently exceeded in this building. There is a strong probability that after all three modernisation variants—gallery, conference centre and five-star hotel—vibrations from Nowotarska Street remain non-perceivable. However, internal excitation sources could be annoying for residents in the future. This is especially true for clients the five-star hotel and clients of the conference centre in the hotel part who may complain about human-induced floor vibrations. One of the considered solutions could be a floating floor.

Table 8. Vibrational requirements for different types of room F_3/P_2.

No.	Designation of the Building	Criterion F_3	F_3/P_2
1	Reference variant—Hostel (existing state)		
2	Variant 1—Five-star hotel	Vibration not perceptible	0–0.79—class A
		Vibration perceptible but not harmful	0.8–1.19—class B
		Harmful vibration	>1.2—class C
3	Variant 2—Zakopane Art Gallery	Vibration not perceptible	0–1.19—class A
		Vibration perceptible but not harmful	1.2–3.99—class B
		Harmful vibration	>4.0—class C
4	Variant 3—Conference and training centre-conference rooms	Vibration not perceptible	0–1.09—class A
		Vibration perceptible but not harmful	1.1–1.99—class B
		Harmful vibration	>2.0—class C
5	Variant 3—Conference and training centre—hotel rooms	Vibration not perceptible	0–0.89—class A
		Vibration perceptible but not harmful	0.9–1.29—class B
		Harmful vibration	>1.3—class C

3.6. Criterion F_3/P_4-Comfort of Using the Rooms; Acoustic Comfort

3.6.1. Methodology

The measurement process consisted of obtaining the sound level in room. A procedure based on [52–58], [59] is also acceptable for a requirement check in accordance with European standards [29] and Polish standards [32]. There were three positions of sound levels located at least 1 m from the internal walls and 1.5 m from external partitions with a window. The height of microphone placement was 1.2 ± 0.1 m. The noise level measurement for each position was 4 min long; thus, the total measurement time for each room was 12 min. In addition to the noise level in the room, the traffic noise level was obtained during measurements.

3.6.2. Requirements for the Internal Noise Level

The requirements presented in Table 9 taken from standards [29] and [32] are given for the building equipment. For the purposes of this article and the evaluation of acoustical comfort in the building, it was assumed that these requirements also concern traffic noise. Requirements for the sound level may vary depending on the standard used. Requirements for sound levels in the designed rooms for different variants of the building are given in Table 9. The main difference between these two requirements is the parameter for evaluation. If room is furnished, quantities are equal to each other without any corrections. In the opposite case quantities should be calculated accordingly to Equation (3) taken from [32]:

$$L_{Aeq,nT} = L_{Aeq} - 10\log_{10} T/T_0 \quad (3)$$

where:

T—reverberation time in unfurnished room (s); and
T_0—reference value of reverberation time (s).

Table 9. Requirements for sound levels for different room types for all variants of modernisation of the considered building.

Room Type	Maximal Value of Equivalent Sound Level [29] L_{Aeq}, dB	Maximal Value of Standardized Equivalent Sound Level [32] $L_{Aeq,nT}$, dB
Hotel room	30 *	25
Conference room	35	35
Restaurant kitchen	55	-
Restaurant/bar	45	45
Toilets	45	40
Reception	40	40
Office	35	35
Spa	35	-
Swimming pool	45	50
Cloakroom	45	-

Note: * value for daytime, for night time value decreases by 5 dB.

3.6.3. Results of Measurement

In the measurement process, 28 rooms were tested for equivalent sound levels in the rooms. Tests were performed, in general, for three zones. The first zone is located in the old part of the building and is affected by traffic noise from the nearby street due to the rooms having an external wall. The second zone has no contact with the external partition. The third zone is in a newer part of the building and not directly affected by traffic as its located is in back of the building. All rooms were furnished, so there was no need to measure reverberation time. Inside the building there were no other noise sources, such as mechanical ventilation, air conditioning, pumps and pipes. Measurements were conducted at 12:00 and 18:30.

The positioning of the control point is presented in Figure 16. Table 10 presents the result of the performed measurement.

Figure 16. Location of measurement point in front of the building (2 m from the façade and 4 m above the ground).

Table 10. Results of equivalent sound level in tested rooms in relation to requirements given in [29] and [32].

Room #	Zone	Room Type	Measured Equivalent Sound Level L_{Aeq}, dB	Measured Equivalent Sound Level in Control Point during Room Measurement $L_{Aeq,ext}$, dB	Maximum Permitted Sound Level (EU), dB	Maximum Permitted Sound Level (PL), dB	Maximum Noise Level with a Fast Time Constant L_{AFmax}, dB
1.1	1	Kitchen	31.4	58.9	55 (met)	- (met)	40.6
1.2	1	Dining room	41.0	58.2	45 (met)	45 (met)	52.2
1.3	1	Wardrobe	34.2	58.3	- (met)	- (met)	46.0
1.4	1	Room	30.7	58.1	30 (not met)	25 (not met)	40.5
1.5	1	Room	25.1	57.5	30 (met)	25 (not met)	33.3
2.3	1	Room	27.9	59.3	30 (met)	25 (not met)	37.2
2.4	1	Room	28.2	59.1	30 (met)	25 (not met)	39.2
2.6	1	Room	21.5	60	30 (met)	25 (met)	30.8
2.7	1	Room	22.6	59.1	30 (met)	25 (met)	34.3
3.11	1	Bathroom	33.8	59.9	45 (met)	40 (met)	43.5
3.4	1	Bathroom	32.9	60.3	45 (met)	40 (met)	43.9
3.5	1	Room	32.4	61.1	30 (not met)	25 (not met)	43.7
3.6	1	Room	38.5	62	30 (not met)	25 (not met)	46.6
3.7	1	Room	36.8	60.6	30 (not met)	25 (not met)	48.3
3.8	1	Room	40.5	60.3	30 (not met)	25 (not met)	50.3
3.9	1	Room	33.5	59.6	30 (not met)	25 (not met)	42.4
2.2	2	Reception	23.7	58.4	40 (met)	40 (met)	35.2
2.5	2	Corridor	22.4	59.5	- (met)	- (met)	31.3
3.1	2	Corridor	23.2	61.5	- (met)	- (met)	31.4
1.13	3	Wardrobe	22.3	56.7	- (met)	- (met)	34.0
1.14	3	Laundry	24.6	57.8	- (met)	- (met)	35.8
2.12	3	Room	21.0	59.2	30 (met)	25 (met)	31.4
2.17	3	Room	25.1	60	30 (met)	25 (not met)	34.8
3.14	3	Room	26.4	60.5	30 (met)	25 (not met)	38.3
3.15	3	Room	24.1	60.6	30 (met)	25 (met)	32.3
3.17	3	Room	25.3	59	30 (met)	25 (not met)	37.0
4.4	3	Room	26.9	59.4	30 (met)	25 (not met)	38.0
4.8	3	Room	30.6	59.6	30 (not met)	25 (not met)	38.8

To summarise Table 10, according to [29], 21 rooms met the sound requirements and seven rooms did not; it states that 67% of rooms tested met the requirements. With regard to [32], 14 rooms met the sound requirements and 14 did not; thus, 50% of the rooms fulfilled the given conditions. Lack of requirements means fulfilling requirements by definition. The main observation is that, without any internal noise sources, the only noise relates to external sources infiltrating through external partitions and windows. The main problem of windows installed in the room was the technical condition of the window frames. The degree of tightness of the window frames varied from room to room.

In order to evaluate the given criteria in the context of the percentage of people annoyed in some level by the noise, proper limit levels have to be given. Based on literature concerning low-frequency structural noise [60] and noise exposure at night [61], limits for noise levels can be given. Describing the situation in the more demanding Polish standard [32], around 20% people were dissatisfied by traffic noise [61] in bedrooms. This situation will be used as the reference variant for setting values for 10% and 30% of dissatisfaction. Furthermore, it was assumed that 20% of people would find conference room and exhibition hall noise levels unacceptable when they are at the maximum permitted with the standard requirements [32]. The results are presented in Table 11.

Table 11. Acoustic requirements based on the percentage of dissatisfaction [60,61] and standards [29,32].

Building Type		$L_{A,eq}$, dB	L_{AFmax}, dB	Percentage of Dissatisfied People	Class
museum, exhibition hall		30	37	10%	A
		35	42	20%	B
		40	46	30%	C
five-star hotel rooms		20	27	10%	A
		25	32	20%	B
		30	36	30%	C
conference centre	conference rooms	30	37	10%	A
		35	42	20%	B
		40	46	30%	C
	hotel rooms	20	27	10%	A
		25	32	20%	B
		30	36	30%	C

Based on results obtained from measurements, the following conclusion can be made:

- The main problem of this hotel building is the tightness of windows resulting in low airborne sound insulation.

In order to provide sufficient acoustic parameters for rooms which do not meet requirements, the following actions can be performed:

- Installation of proper windows with a sufficiently high parameter of airborne sound insulation;
- The possibility to increase the percentage of rooms meeting the requirements if proper seals in existing windows are provided; and
- modernisation of the building to take into account the acoustic climate in the building and solve the problem especially relating to noise traffic in bedrooms.

3.7. Criterion F4/P1-Impact on the Environment; Coefficient EP (kWh/(m²y))

3.7.1. Methods

The energy performance of a building can be expressed by an EP index specifying the amount of annual primary energy demand necessary to meet the needs connected with the use of a building, a dwelling or a part of a building being an independent technical and utilitarian whole, expressed in (kWh/(m²year)) and related to 1 m² of rooms with adjustable temperature. The quantitative assessment of energy consumption suggests that the lower the EP value, the higher the efficiency of energy use that protects the resources of raw materials and the natural environment. Energy consumption could refer to more than one parameter here so it is, therefore, a determinant of the environmental impact of buildings. The qualitative assessment of energy consumption leads to a comparison of the EP indicator value for the building being assessed with the calculated EP reference value for new or rebuilt buildings determined according to the requirements of the applicable technical and construction regulations (Table 12). The methodology for calculating energy performance for buildings, dwellings, or parts of buildings constituting an independent technical and utilitarian whole not equipped with a cooling system is specified in the Ordinance of the Minister of Infrastructure and Development of 27 February 2015. This document refers to the methodology for the determination the energy performance of a building or part of a building and energy performance certificate. The EP calculations for the 'Stara Polana' building were made in accordance with [23].

Table 12. Minimum requirements in [7] for EP_{H+W} in Poland.

No.	Type of Building	EP $_{H+W}$ Indicator for Heating, Ventilation and Domestic Hot Water [kWh/(m²rok)]	
		Current Requirements	For NZEB Buildings in Poland
1	Single-family building	95	70
2	Multi-family building	85	65
3	Healthcare building	290	190
4	Public building	60	45
5	Commercial building, warehouse	90	70

3.7.2. Results

It is indicated that the annual primary energy demand for the 'Stara Polana' building necessary to satisfy the needs connected with using a building amounts to 86.24 (kWh/(m²year)).

The 'Stara Polana' building with 604.59 m² of the total heated building area requires 86.24, kWh/(m²year), of the annual primary energy demand. Improving the energy efficiency of buildings by reducing the EP indicator is mainly related to the change of non-renewable sources for renewable energy sources. In the case of the analysed 'Stara Polana' building, the energy supply for heating comes entirely from RES. The main problem of the exceeded limit value stated in [7] (Table 13) is due to the consumption of electricity supplied to the lighting system. To improve the EP index, this article recommends replacing lighting in the 'Stara Polana' building with LED lighting.

Table 13. Classes adopted for the sub-criterion F_4 /P_1 EP_{H+W} index.

No.	Designation of the Building	Criterion F_4 F_4/P_1 EP_{H+W}, kWh/m²rok
1	Reference variant—Hostel (existing state)	86.24
2	Variant 1—Five-star hotel	0–20—class A 21–59—class B $EP \geq 60$—class C
3	varIant 2—Zakopane Art Gallery	0–20—class A 21–59—class B $EP \geq 60$—class C
4	Variant 3—Conference and training centre—hotel rooms	0 20 class A 21–59—class B $EP \geq 60$—class C

Variant 1 has been assigned to class 'A'; variants 2 and 3, to class 'C'.

3.8. Financial Criterion F_5P_1

The financial criterion determines the cost-effectiveness of adapting the object to a given utility function from the investor's point of view. The evaluation of this criterion consists of examining whether the project is financially effective and therefore whether the financial benefits for the investor in the specified operation time of the adapted facility will be greater than the expenditures incurred by it.

3.8.1. Assessment Method

The PI method (profitability index) was proposed for the financial assessment, which in practice is used to select the most effective of several investment projects [62]. This ratio is expressed by dividing the sum of discounted positive cash flows to the sum of discounted negative cash flows:

$$PI = \frac{\sum_{i=0}^{n} \frac{P_i}{(1+d)^i}}{\sum_{i=0}^{n} \frac{N_i}{(1+d)^i}}$$

If the value of utility function is greater than 1 ($PI > 1$) the adaptation of the object is profitable for the considered variant. The higher the value of the indicator, the more profitable the new variant option is.

3.8.2. Results

As a result of the analysis, the value of the profitability ratio for the assumed investment lifetime of n = 15 years and an interest rate of d = 4% for the considered variants of the utility functions is presented in Table 14.

Table 14. Value of the profitability index for the considered variants of the utility functions.

No.	Designation of the Building	Criterion F_5 F_5/P_1 PI (Profitability Index)
1	Reference variant—Hostel (existing state)	1.03
2	Variant 1—Five-star hotel	1.06
3	Variant 2—Zakopane Art Gallery	0.05
4	Variant 3—Conference and training centre—hotel rooms	0.56

Only two variants of utility functions are profitable, of which the most profitable usable function is the five-star passive hotel function. The other two options in terms of the financial criterion are not viable.

3.9. Criteria F6-Social Benefits and F7 Benefits from Preserving Cultural Heritage

Social benefits are achieved as a result of strengthening the sense of identity and national integration (emotional ties of the society with the historic object as a testimony of a bygone epoch). Designating buildings for useful social purposes ensures a sense of security (Table 15) [63,64].

Table 15. Factors describing the criterion of social benefits.

	The Criterion for Social Benefits
1	Sense of security
2	Integration opportunities
3	Strengthening the sense of local identity
4	Social participation in managing heritage resources
5	Solving the pressing needs of the local community

Source: own study based on [63,64].

Benefits from the protection of cultural heritage preserving and restoring the historic cultural features of the historic object and its popularisation. Additional beneficial factors for cultural heritage are the cognitive values accompanying the process of revalorising historic buildings, which translates into gaining a broader knowledge of the object and increasing the experience of the conservation environment (Table 16) [63,64].

Table 16. Factors describing the criterion of benefits from cultural heritage protection.

The Criterion for Benefits from the Protection of Cultural Heritage	
1	Increase in heritage resources
2	Promoting the value of heritage
3	Use of heritage resources
4	Popularisation of local heritage resources
5	Benefits of a professional environment of conservators

Source: own study based on [63,64].

3.9.1. Assessment Method

When analysing the definitions of the above criteria, it can be easily seen that there is some degree of overlap which, in the course of the analysis, justifies the need to take interdependencies into account, including the so-called feedback between these factors, leading to the adoption of a network rather than the standard hierarchical nature of links between them. The adopted network structure of interdependent links between the factors is supplemented with variants of the historic building adaptation that influence the mentioned factors. The impact of decision-making variants on the factors of a given criterion is a measure of the degree of fulfilling these goals. A schematic diagram of the proposed network structure of connections between the factors of a given criterion and variants of new utility functions for an adapted historic building are shown in Figures 17 and 18. In Figures 17 and 18, network nodes symbolize a given factor and the potential dependencies between the factors and a set of variants of new utility functions of a historic object are determined by arrows (arcs of the network). The size (diameter) of nodes symbolizes the significance (weight) of a given factor in the system and the thickness of the arrows determines the intensity of the influence of factors on each other and the impact of variants on these factors.

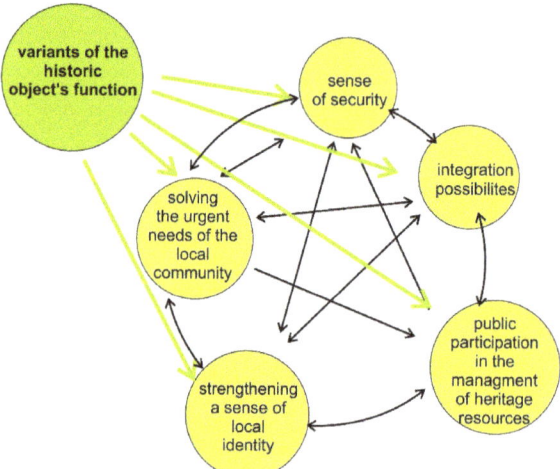

Figure 17. Schematic diagram of the proposed network structure of connections for the analysed problem for the assessment of the social benefit criterion.

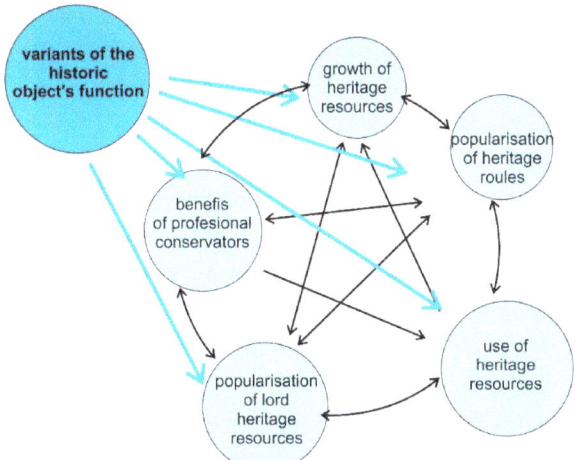

Figure 18. Schematic diagram of the proposed network structure of connections for the analysed problem for the assessment of the criterion of benefits arising from cultural heritage protection.

The assessment of each variant of the historic building's adaptation was determined separately for each criterion of benefits. The assessment of the significance of the factors of a given criterion requires gathering the opinions of a small group of specialists in the specific field of the given criterion. The evaluation of experts provided a group assessment which allowed taking into account differences in the preferences of these opinions. A weighted average was used to aggregate expert opinions. In order to synthetically describe and analyse the above decision problem, it is necessary to choose the proper tool that will enable correct modelling and analysis of the considered relationships between the factors of a given criterion and decision options. At the basis of many methods of analysis lies the concept of the system as an object composed of various elements between which there are some relationships (dependencies). One of the effective strategies for mapping such a system is structural modelling and, thus, a set of various techniques enabling understanding of the properties of complex systems and decision problems [65]. In the literature on the subject, many methods of modelling and the structural analysis of a number of decision problems can be found, the most well-known and effective methods being ANP (fuzzy analytic network process) [66], DEMATEL (decision making trial and evaluation laboratory) [67] and a method recently developed by the WINGS (weighted influence non-linear gauge system) [68].

In these methods, the tool for modelling dependencies between system elements is a directed graph, the vertices of which symbolise system elements and arcs determine the relationships (interactions) between one element and another. The procedure of modelling the structure of the system and its analysis in all the aforementioned methods is based on similar algebraic mechanisms. The input values of ratings are introduced into the matrix, the sum of all powers in the limit sense returns the output values in the analysed model.

3.9.2. Results

Structural analysis results performed using the WINGS [68] determined the ranking of the proposed utility functions based on a normalised percentage of the impact on the given criterion objective fulfilment.

For the criterion of social benefits, the ranking of functional feature variants is as follows:

Variant 3—Zakopane Art Gallery (percentage indicator of the impact on meeting the criterion objective is: 0.42)

Variant 4—Conference and training centre (0.28)

Variant 2—Five-star hotel (0.18)

Variant 1—Reference variant–hostel (existing state) (0.13)

For the criterion of benefits from the cultural heritage protection, the ranking of functional feature variants is as follows:

Variant 3—Zakopane Art Gallery (percentage indicator of the impact on the fulfillment of the objective set by the criterion is: 0.38)

Variant 4—Conference and training centre (0.23)

Variant 2—Five-star hotel (0.22)

Variant 1—Reference variant–hostel (existing state) (0.16)

4. Conclusions and Discussion

In this article, the authors proposed methods to evaluate the criteria proposed in [20] and presented them from the example of the historic 'Stara Polana' building located in Zakopane. The starting point for the analysis was to examine the present condition of the 'Stara Polana' building, now used as a hostel. A series of interdisciplinary studies has determined the potential of the new utility functions considered for the object, defining the evaluation values of the proposed criteria. Table 17 presents a summary of developed criteria and subcriteria for each variant.

Table 17. Summary table.

Criteria/ Sub-criterion No	Variant No.			
	Reference Variant—Hostel (Existing State)	Variant 1—Five-star Hotel	Variant 2—Zakopane Art Gallery	Variant 3—Conference and Training Centre
Criterion F1 F1/P1 (coefficient U (W/m²rok))	0.55	0–0.15—class A 0.16–0.22—class B $U \geq 0.23$—class C	0–0.15—class A 0.16–0.22—class B $U \geq 0.23$—class C	0–0.15—class A 0.16–0.22—class B $U \geq 0.23$—class C
Criterion F1 F1/P2 (EK, kWh/(m²rok))	244.79	EK reduction: >60%—class A >50%—class B >40%—class C	EK reduction: >60%—class A >50%—class B >40%—class C	EK reduction: >60%—class A >50%—class B >40%—class C
Criterion F2 F2/P1 n_{50}, (1/h)	For negative pressure $n_{50} = 10.09$ For overpressure $n_{50} = 8.83$	0–0.6—class A 0.6–1.5—class B $n_{50} \geq 1.5$—class C	0–0.6—class A 0.6–1.5—class B $n_{50} \geq 1.5$—class C	0–0.6—class A 0.6–1.5—class B $n_{50} \geq 1.5$—class C
Criterion F3 F3/P1 (PMV (-))	−0.7/0.25	−0.2–0.2—class A −0.5–0.5—class B −0.5>PMV> 0.5—class C	−0.2–0.2—class A −0.5–0.5—class B −0.5 > PMV > 0.5—class C	−0.2–0.2—class A −0.5–0.5—class B −0.5 > PMV > 0.5—class C
Criterion F3 F3/P2 (Frequency (Hz))		0–0.79—class A 0.8–1.19—class B >1.2—class C	0–1.19—class A 1.2–3.99—class B >4.0—class C	0–1.09—class A * 1.1–1.99—class B * >2.0—class C *
Criterion F3 F3/P3 $L_{A,eq}/L_{AF,max}$ (dB)	40.5/50.3	$\leq 20/27$—class A $\leq 25/32$—class B $\leq 30/36$—class C	$\leq 30/37$—class A $\leq 35/42$—class B $\leq 40/46$—class C	$\leq 20/27$—class A * $\leq 25/32$—class B * $\leq 30/36$—class C *
Criterion F4 F4/P1 EP_{H+W} (kWh/m²rok)	86.24	0–20—class A 21–59—class B $EP \geq 60$—class C	0–20—class A 21–59—class B $EP \geq 60$—class C	0–20—class A 21–59—class B $EP \geq 60$—class C
Criterion F5 F5/P1 PI (Profitability Index)	1.03	1.06	0.05	0.56
Criterion F6 F6/P1 (%)	0.13	0.18	0.42	0.28
Criterion F7 F7/P1 (%)	0.16	0.22	0.38	0.23

* Conference rooms.

The evaluations of individual criteria developed in this article will be the basis for the multi-criteria analysis performed in the future and are based on the hybrid model of the utility function proposed in [20] on the adaptation of the building in question.

The process of adapting the historic building to new functions is more complicated than in the case of other existing buildings. As part of planning such a process, there is a need to thoroughly recognise the material features of the historic building. This is achieved through performing a series of diagnostic tests on the condition of the building with regard to architectural, construction, building physics and conservation aspects. An additional aspect is the recognition of intangible features of the building, such as the history of the building, its significance, symbolism and the utility functions that it used to have. An important element is the analysis of the value of such a building with regard to parameters such as: the value of authenticity, integrity, uniqueness, artistic value, historical value and social identity [63]. It is not insignificant to determine the socio-economic potential of the building in terms of the benefits of its future adaptation, i.e., prospective values. The effect of all these tests is to determine the possibilities and limitations of the building with regard to its adaptation to new utility functions.

Objects of regional architecture in Poland are erected using traditional masonry and wooden technology. They constitute a specific type of historic buildings whose potential to adapt to new functional functions is difficult due to the problem of providing the expected requirements (e.g., energy efficiency, comfort of use) for contemporary functions. Due to the multidimensional character of the adaptation problem, it is necessary to develop a multi-criteria approach to selecting the best variant of the considered options for the new function for the building in the context of the adopted selection criteria. At the initial stage of the multi-criteria analysis, after defining a set of variants and decision criteria, it is necessary to develop an appropriate approach to the assessment of individual criteria (measurable and difficult to quantify) in relation to the considered variants of the utility functions.

Author Contributions: Conceptualization: M.F.-C., A.K.-K., and T.T.; methodology: M.F.-C., A.K.-K., K.N., F.P., E.R.-Z., G.Ś., and T.T.; software: M.F.-C., A.K.-K., K.N., F.P., and G.Ś.; validation: M.F.-C., A.K.-K., F.P., and G.Ś.; formal analysis: M.F.-C., A.K.-K., F.P., and G.Ś.; investigation: M.F.-C., A.K.-K., K.N., F.P., G.Ś.; resources: M.F.-C., A.K.-K., K.N., F.P., and G.Ś.; data curation: M.F.-C., A.K.-K., K.N., B.Z., F.P., and G.Ś.; writing—original draft preparation: M.F.-C., A.K.-K., F.P., and G.Ś.; writing—review and editing: M.F.-C., A.K.-K., F.P., K.N., G.Ś., and T.T.; visualization: M.F.-C., A.K.-K., F.P., and G.Ś.; supervision: M.F.-C., A.K.-K., F.P., and G.Ś.; project administration: M.F.-C., A.K.-K., F.P., and G.Ś.

Funding: This research received no external funding.

Conflicts of Interest: The authors declare no conflicts of interest.

Nomenclature

U	(W/(m^{2}K))—Heat transfer coefficient
EK	(kWh/(m^{2}year))—The final energy value
n$_{50}$	Number of air changes per hour, as a result of the leak test of the building envelope
clo	Clothing unit, 1 clo = 0.155 (m$^2 \cdot$K/W)
I$_{cl}$	Clothing insulation (m^2 K/W)
MET	Metabolic rate (W/m^2), 1 unit = 1 met = 58.2 W/m
PMV	Predicted mean vote—Thermal Sensation Index (ISO 7730)
PPD	Percentage of persons dissatisfied (percentage dissatisfied)
RH	Relative humidity (%)
T$_a$	Measured air temperature (°C)
TMR	Mean radiant temperature (°C)

References

1. Terlikowski, W. The role of rehabilitation, modernization and adaptation of historic buildings in the revitalization process. *J. Civ. Eng. Environ. Arch.* **2015**, *62*, 519–832.
2. Nowogońska, B. The Life Cycle of a Building as a Technical Object. *Periodica Polytech. Civ. Eng.* **2016**, *60*, 331–335. [CrossRef]
3. Nowogońska, B. Proposal for determining the scale of renovation needs of residential buildings. *Civ. Environ. Eng. Rep.* **2016**, *22*, 137–144. [CrossRef]
4. *Collective Work, Antique Wooden Construction in Poland*; Szczecin University of Technology: Szczecin, Poland, 2008; Volume 5.1, ISBN 978-83-7457-052-7.
5. Dz, U. 1994 Nr 89 poz. 414 The Act of 7 July 1994 Construction Law. Available online: http://prawo.sejm.gov.pl/isap.nsf/DocDetails.xsp?id=wdu19940890414 (accessed on 6 February 2019).
6. Dz, U. 2003 nr 162 poz. 1568 The Act of 23 July 2003 on the Protection of Monuments. Available online: http://prawo.sejm.gov.pl/isap.nsf/DocDetails.xsp?id=WDU20031621568 (accessed on 6 February 2019).
7. Regulation of the Minister of Infrastructure on the Technical Conditions to Be Met by Buildings and Their Location (Journal of Laws No. 75, Item 690), Including Changes Introduced. Available online: http://prawo.sejm.gov.pl/isap.nsf/download.xsp/WDU20150001422/O/D20151422.pdf (accessed on 6 February 2019).
8. Radziszewska-Zielina, E.; Śladowski, G. Fuzzy inference system assisting the choice of a variant of adaptation of a historical building. *Inter. J. Contemp. Manag.* **2015**, *14*, 131–148.
9. Radziszewska-Zielina, E.; Śladowski, G.; Sibielak, M. Planning the reconstruction of a historic building by using a fuzzy stochastic network. *Autom. Constr.* **2017**, *84*, 242–257. [CrossRef]
10. Radziszewska-Zielina, E.; Śladowski, G. Proposal of the Use of a Fuzzy Stochastic Network for the Preliminary Evaluation of the Feasibility of the Process of the Adaptation of a Historical Building to a Particular Form of Use OP Conference Series. *Mater. Sci. Eng.* **2017**, *245*, 072029. [CrossRef]
11. Ustinovicius, L.; Jakucionis, S. Application of multicriteria decision methods in restoration of buildings in the old Town. *J. Civ. Eng. Manag.* **2000**, *6*, 227–236. [CrossRef]
12. Zavadskas, E.; Anucheviciene, J. Development of an Indicator Model and Ranking of Sustainable Revitalization Alternatives of Derelict Property: A Lithuanian Case Study. *Sustain. Dev.* **2006**, *14*, 287–299. [CrossRef]
13. Zavadskas, E.; Anucheviciene, J. Multiple criteria evaluation of rural building's regeneration alternatives. *Build. Environ.* **2007**, *42*, 436–451. [CrossRef]
14. Fuentes, J.M. Methodological bases for documenting and reusing vernacularfarm architecture. *J. Cult. Herit.* **2010**, *11*, 119–129. [CrossRef]
15. Wang, H.; Zeng, Z. A Multi-objective decision-making process for reuse selection of historic buildings. *Exp. Syst. Appl.* **2010**, *37*, 1241–1249. [CrossRef]
16. Breil, M.; Giove, S.; Rosato, P. *A Multicriteria Approach for the Evaluation of the Sustainability of Re-Use of Historic Buildings in Venice*; SSRN: Milan, Italy, 2008.
17. Giove, S.; Rosato, P.; Breil, M. An application of multicriteria decision making to built heritage. The redevelopment of Venice Arsenale. *J. Multi Criteria Dec. Anal.* **2010**, *17*, 85–99. [CrossRef]
18. Ferretti, V.; Bottero, M.; Mondini, G. Decision making and cultural heritage: An application of the Multi-Attribute Value Theory for the reuse of historical buildings. *J. Cult. Herit.* **2014**, *15*, 644–655. [CrossRef]
19. Radziszewska-Zielina, E.; Śladowski, G. Supporting the selection of a variant of the adaptation of a historical building with the use of fuzzy modelling and structural analysis. *J. Cult. Herit.* **2017**, *26*, 53–63. [CrossRef]
20. Fedorczak-Cisak, M.; Kowalska, A.; Radziszewska-Zielina, E.; Śladowski, G.; Pachla, F.; Tatara, T. A multicriteria approach for selecting the utility function of the historical building "Stara Polana" located in Zakopane. *MATEC Web Conf.* **2019**, *262*, 07002. [CrossRef]
21. PN-EN ISO 6946: 2017-10. *Building Components and Building Elements—Thermal Resistance and Heat Transfer Coefficient—Calculation Method*; Polish Standardization Committee: Warsaw, Poland, 2017.
22. PN-EN ISO 13370: 2017-09. *Thermal Performance of Buildings—Heat Transfer via the Ground—Calculation Methods*; Polish Standardization Committee: Warsaw, Poland, 2017.

23. Regulation of the Minister of Infrastructure and Development of 27 February 2015 on the Methodology of Determining the Energy Performance of a Building or Part of a Building and Energy Performance Certificates. Available online: http://prawo.sejm.gov.pl/isap.nsf/DocDetails.xsp?id=WDU20150000376 (accessed on 6 February 2019).
24. PN-EN ISO 9972: 2015-10. *Thermal Properties of Buildings—Determination of Air Permeability Of Buildings—Pressure Measurement Method with the Use of a Fan*; Polish Standardization Committee: Warsaw, Poland, 2015.
25. PN-EN 13187: 2001. *Thermal Properties of Buildings—Qualitative Detection of Thermal Defects in the Building Envelope—Infrared Method*; Polish Standardization Committee: Warsaw, Poland, 2001.
26. Fanger, P.O. Assessment of man's thermal comfort in practice. *Occup. Environ. Med.* **1973**, *30*, 313–324. [CrossRef]
27. PN-EN ISO 7730: 2006. *Ergonomics of The thermal Environment—Analytical Determination and Interpretation of Thermal Comfort Using the Calculation of PMV and PPD Indicators and Criteria of Local Thermal Comfort*; Polish Standardization Committee: Warsaw, Poland, 2006.
28. Draft EN 16798-1. *Energy Performance of Buildings—Ventilation of Buildings—Part 1: Indoor Environmental Input Parameters for Design and Assessment of Energy Performance of Buildings Addressing Indoor Air Quality, Thermal Environment, Lighting and Acoustics (Module M1–6. 2018)*; European Committee for Standardization: Brussels, Belgium, 2018.
29. EN 15251: 2007. *Indoor Environmental Input Parameters for Design and Assessment of Energy Performance of Buildings Addressing Indoor Air Quality, Thermal Environment, Lighting and Acoustics*; European Committee for Standardization: Brussels, Belgium, 2017.
30. PN ISO 7726: 2001. *Ergonomics of the Thermal Environment. Instruments for Measuring Physical Quantities*; Polish Standardization Committee: Warsaw, Poland, 2001.
31. PN-B-02171: 2017-06. *Evaluation of Human Exposure to Vibration in Buildings*; Polish Standardization Committee: Warsaw, Poland, 2017.
32. PN-B-02151-2: 2018-01. *Building Acoustics—Noise Protection in Buildings—Part 2: Requirements for Acceptable Sound Level in Rooms*; Polish Standardization Committee: Warsaw, Poland, 2018.
33. Dudzik, M.; Trębacz, P.; Hudym, V. Modeling of contact wire's de-iceing phenomena using artificial neural networks. *Tech. Trans.* **2018**, *115*, 111118. [CrossRef]
34. Dudzik, M. *Współczesne Metody Projektowania, Weryfikacji Poprawności i Modelowania Zjawisk Trakcji Elektrycznej*; Monografie Politechniki Krakowskiej. Inżynieria Elektryczna i Komputerowa; Monografia, Politechnika Krakowska im. Tadeusza Kościuszki: Kraków, Poland, 2018; p. 187s. ISBN 978-83-65991-28-7.
35. Energieeinsparverordnung—EnEV (Verordnung Über Energiesparenden Wärmeschutz und Energiesparende Anlagentechnik bei Gebäuden). Available online: www.enev-online.com (accessed on 6 February 2019).
36. NEEAP. *Erster Nationaler Energieeffizienzaktionsplan der Republik Österreich 2014 Gemäß Energieeffizienzrichtlinie 2012/27/EU*; Bundesministerium für Bildung: Wissenschaft und Forschung Vienna, Austria, 2014.
37. Kisilewicz, T. The influence of thermal insulation of walls on the microclimate in buildings in the summer. *Build. Mater.* **2015**, *5*. [CrossRef]
38. Firlag, S.; Piasecki, M. NZEB Renovation Definition in a Heating Dominated Climate. Case Study of Poland. *Appl. Sci. Basel* **2018**, *8*, 1605. [CrossRef]
39. Piasecki, M.; Kostyrko, K.; Pykacz, S. Indoor environmental quality assessment: Part 1: Choice of the indoor environmental quality sub-component models. *J. Build. Phys.* **2017**, *41*, 264–289. [CrossRef]
40. PN-EN ISO 9920:2009. *Ergonomics of the Thermal Environment—Estimation of Thermal Insulation and Water Vapor Resistance of Clothing Sets*; Polish Standardization Committee: Warsaw, Poland, 2009.
41. Sun, K.; Zhang, W. Combined Annoyance Assessment of Subway Train-Induced Structural Vibration and Ambient Noise. *Shock Vib.* **2016**, *2016*, 3028037. [CrossRef]
42. Ögren, M.; Gidlöf-Gunnarsson, A.; Smith, M.; Gustavsson, S.; Persson Waye, K. Comparison of Annoyance from Railway Noise and Railway Vibration. *Int. J. Environ. Res. Public Health* **2017**, *14*, 805. [CrossRef] [PubMed]
43. Gierke, M.E.; Coerman, R.R. The biodynamics of human response to vibration and impact. *Ind. Med. Surg.* **1963**, *32*, 30–32.
44. Dudzik, M.; Tomczyk, K.; Sieja, M. Optimal dynamic error formula for charge output accelerometer obtained by the neural network. In Proceedings of the 2018 International Symposium on Electrical Machines (SME): SME 2018, Andrychów, Poland, 10–13 June 2018; ISBN 978-153865210-7. [CrossRef]

45. Dudzik, M.; Tomczyk, K.; Jagiełło, A.S. Analysis of the error generated by the voltage output accelerometer using the optimal structure of an artificial neural network. In Proceedings of the 2018 19th International Conference on Research and Education in Mechatronics (REM 2018), Delft, The Netherlands, 7–8 June 2018; pp. 7–11, ISBN 978-1-5386-5413-2. [CrossRef]
46. Marioka, M.; Griffin, M.J. Difference thresholds for intensity perception of whole-body vertical vibration: Effect of frequency and magnitude. *J. Acoust. Soc. Am.* **2000**, *107*, 620–624. [CrossRef]
47. ISO 2631-2: 2003. *Guide to the Evaluation of Human Exposure to Whole Body Vibration. Part 2—Vibration in Buildings*; International Organization for Standardization: Geneva, Switzerland, 2003.
48. Kowalska-Koczwara, A.; Pachla, F.; Stecz, P.; Stypuła, K.; Tatara, T.; Lejk, J.; Sokołowski, M. Vibration-based damage identification and condition monitoring of metro trains: Warsaw Metro case study. *Shock Vib.* **2018**, *2018*, 8475684. [CrossRef]
49. Tamura, Y.; Kawana, S.; Nakamura, O.; Kanda, J.; Nakatà, S. Evaluation perception of wind-induced vibration in buildings. *Struct. Build.* **2006**, *159*, 283–293. [CrossRef]
50. Kwok, K.C.S.; Hitchcock, P.A.; Burton, M.D. Perception of vibration and occupant comfort in wind-excited tall buildings. *J. Wind Eng. Ind. Aerodyn.* **2009**, *97*, 368–380. [CrossRef]
51. Waddington, D.C.; Woodcock, J.; Peris, E.; Condie, J.; Sica, G.; Moorhouse, A.T.; Steele, A. Human response to vibration in residential environments. *J. Acoust. Soc. Am.* **2014**, *135*, 182–193. [CrossRef] [PubMed]
52. Okokon, E.O.; Yli-Tuom, T.; Tiittanen, A.W.; Tiittanen, P.; Juutilainen, J.; Lanki, T. Traffic noise, noise annoyance and psychotropic medication use. *Environ. Int.* **2018**, *119*, 287–294. [CrossRef]
53. Beranek, L.L. *Acoustic Measurements*; American Institute of Physics: New York, NY, USA, 1949; ISBN 088-318590-3.
54. Bruel & Kjaer. *Environmental Noise Measurement*; Bruel & Kjaer: Nærum, Denmark, 2001.
55. Makarewicz, R.; Gołębiewski, R. Estimation of the long term average sound level from hourly average. *Appl. Acoust.* **2016**, *111*, 116–120. [CrossRef]
56. Malchaire, J. *Sound Measuring Instruments*; WHO: Brussels, Belgium, 1994.
57. Costa, J.J.L.; Nascimento, E.O.D.; Oliveira, L.N.D.; Caldas, L.V.E. Pressure sound level measurements at an educational environment in Goiânia, Goiás, Brazil. *J. Phys. Conf. Ser.* **2017**, *975*, 012055. [CrossRef]
58. Park, T.; Kim, M.; Jang, C.; Choung, T.; Sim, K.-A.; Seo, D.; Chang, S.I. The Public Health Impact of Road-Traffic Noise in a Highly-Populated City, Republic of Korea: Annoyance and Sleep Disturbance. *Sustainability* **2018**, *10*, 2947. [CrossRef]
59. Sirin, O. State-of-the-Art Review on Sustainable Design and Construction of Quieter Pavements—Part 2: Factors Affecting Tire-Pavement Noise and Prediction Models. *Sustainability* **2016**, *8*, 692. [CrossRef]
60. Aasvang, G.M.; Engdahl, B.; Rothschild, K. Annoyance and self-reported sleep disturbances due to structurally radiated noise from railway tunnels. *Appl. Acoust.* **2007**, *68*, 970–981. [CrossRef]
61. Frei, P.; Mohler, E.; Roosli, M. Effect of nocturnal road traffic noise exposure and annoyance on objective and subjective sleep quality. *Int. J. Hyg. Environ. Health* **2014**, *217*, 188–195. [CrossRef] [PubMed]
62. Bogucki, D. *Feasibility Study—Guide*, PRESSCOM Sp. z o.o.: Wrocław, Poland, 2016.
63. Affelt, W. *Technical Heritage as a Part of Culture, Towards a Sustainable Heritage (Part 2), Protection of Monuments*; National Heritage Board of Poland: Warsaw, Poland, 2009; pp. 53–82.
64. Radziszewska-Zielina, E.; Śladowski, G. Evaluation of historic building conversion options in the context of sustainable development. *Tech. Trans.* **2014**, *1B*, 153–164. [CrossRef]
65. Roberts, F.S. Applications of the theory of meaningfulness to psychology. *J. Math. Psychol.* **1985**, *29*, 311–332. [CrossRef]
66. Saaty, T.L. *Decision Making with Dependence and Feedback: The Analytic Network Process*; University of Pittsburgh: Pittsburgh, PA, USA; RWS Publications: Pittsburgh, PA, USA, 1996; ISBN 0-9620317-9-8.
67. Gabus, A.; Fontela, E. *World Problems an Invitation to Further Thought within the Framework of DEMATEL*; Battelle Geneva Research Centre: Geneva, Switzerland, 1972.
68. Michnik, J. Weighted Influence Non-linear Gauge System (WINGS)—An analysis method for the systems of interrelated components. *Eur. J. Oper. Res.* **2013**, *228*, 536–544. [CrossRef]

© 2019 by the authors. Licensee MDPI, Basel, Switzerland. This article is an open access article distributed under the terms and conditions of the Creative Commons Attribution (CC BY) license (http://creativecommons.org/licenses/by/4.0/).

Article

The Application of the Multiple Criteria Decision Aid to Assess Transport Policy Measures Focusing on Innovation

Katarzyna Nosal Hoy, Katarzyna Solecka and Andrzej Szarata *

Faculty of Civil Engineering, Cracow University of Technology, Warszawska 24, 31-155 Krakow, Poland; knosal@pk.edu.pl (K.N.H.); ksolecka@pk.edu.pl (K.S.)

* Correspondence: aszarata@pk.edu.pl

Received: 5 February 2019; Accepted: 6 March 2019; Published: 10 March 2019

Abstract: The sustainable development of transport is fostered by innovations. To implement innovations, the European Commission issues different regulations, programs and initiatives and the European Transport Policy has a significant impact on transport policy in the member states. At the same time, transport policy is dynamic and requires new solutions that will allow the planned goals to be achieved. In this context, it is important to analyze the effectiveness of the current innovation policies, and to create recommendations for future actions that bring innovations to the market. This article concerns the subject of innovation policy in the transport sector. It illustrates the possibility of applying one of the methods of the multiple criteria decision aid, i.e., the simple additive weighting (SAW) method to assess the European Union (EU) and national policy measures in surface transport in terms of their influence on the market take-up of innovations. The use of this method allows for the analyzed policy measures to be contemplated in terms of various criteria and to identify those that best meet the adopted criteria, and thus those that could contribute the most to the stimulation of innovation. The article focuses on the method itself, indicating its flexibility and ease of use, while the analyzed collection of policy measures constitutes only the background of the deliberations.

Keywords: surface transport; innovation in transport; policy measures; sustainable transport policy; multiple criteria decision aid

1. Introduction

Transport is one of the strategic sectors of the economy [1] which covers several areas, including: economic, political or tourist in the international, national and regional dimensions [2]. Helping to connect markets plays an important role in the development of international economic relations [3] and is one of the determinants of the competitiveness of the European market [4]. As one of the sectors of the European economy that is subject to legal Community regulations [2], the implementation of the concept of the sustainable development of transport constitutes one of the greatest challenges of the European Union's (EU) transport policy [5–7]. The aim of this concept is to create conditions for the efficient, safe, economically effective, and at the same time socially, economically and spatially justified transport of persons and goods within the limits set by the natural resources available for this purpose and the possibility of releasing pollution resulting from this into the environment [8,9]. The sustainable development of transport is fostered by innovations.

The word innovation, which comes from the Latin language (*innovatio*—renewal; *innovare*—to renew), is subject to constant change and is constantly being expanded with the emergence of new concepts [10]. As a result, there is no uniform, universally accepted definition of innovation in literature. For instance, according to Twiss and Goodridge [11] innovation is a process that combines science, technology, economics and management and allows it to achieve novelty and extends from the emergence of the idea to its commercialization in the form of production, exchange and composition. According to Rogers [12], in turn, it involves both knowledge creation and diffusion of existing knowledge. Chlad and Strzelczyk [13] present two ways of defining innovation, while in the first one, they focus on the process, the sequence of activities and in the second on the outcome, e.g., a new solution. The authors point out that innovations may be introduced as forms of new activities, services, products, devices, processes, strategies or systems not commonly used so far. However, the most frequently quoted definition is that introduced by Joseph Schumpeter [14], who treated innovation as a factor of economic development, and his approach is considered a classic one. According to Schumpeter, innovation concerns one of the following five situations [14]:

- the introduction of a new product that consumers have not yet experienced, or the introduction of new product characteristics;
- the introduction of a new production method not yet tested in a given field;
- opening up a new market, i.e., one in which the industry in question had not previously been active;
- the acquisition of a new source of raw materials or semi-finished products;
- the new organization of economic processes.

In transport, innovation is understood as actions to improve existing or introduce new solutions or processes concerning all aspects of change and contributing to the economic, financial, technical and technological efficiency, environment of transport systems in order to maximize social effects and results of public and private sector management [15]. Innovations concern both infrastructure and means of transport as well as the organization of transport processes [6,16–18]. Examples of innovation would be means of transport greening technologies, for instance alternative, eco-friendly drives or new designs of engines [19–21], ICT-related innovations, concerning, e.g., advanced technologies for the collection and analysis of vehicle traffic data [13], passenger information [19] or autonomous vehicles [22].

The development of innovations results from the need to counteract the low efficiency and functionality of transport systems as well as to reduce external costs in the form of pollution, accidents and noise [19,21–27]. Innovative solutions and tools not only have been changing the way people consume transport and mobility services [28,29], but also are regarded as one of the main sources of competitive advantage in the market [30].

Supporting innovation is an obvious direction of the development of the EU [17,31,32]. The Europe 2020 Strategy published in 2010 [33] is the basis for innovation growth programs within the EU. The strategy indicated the need to develop a knowledge and innovation-based economy, to support a more resource-efficient, more environmentally-friendly and more competitive economy, and to support a high-employment economy that ensures social and territorial cohesion [33]. To implement innovations in the transport market, the European Commission funds different research programs and initiatives [7,17], for example, in the sector of transport and energy, research for SMEs (small- and medium-sized enterprises), and technological or application-oriented programs. Political decisions made by the European Commission towards the environmental and climate protection also form a basis for such calls for proposals. At the same time, the European Transport Policy has a significant impact on the shape and direction of the national transport policy [2], subject to the rules set by the EU. The national transport policy is the influence that the state and public authorities, organizations and institutions, acting on its behalf, have on the transport process and its efficient operation as well as the development of transport in order to achieve all the planned goals [34].

Of note, with the beginning of 2019 the €120bn, the Horizon Europe, a new EU Framework Program for Research and Innovation, passed the initial stage at the EU Parliament (it was approved by the Parliament's Industry, Research and Energy Committee), and if this program is approved by the EU Parliament and the governments of European member states it will constitute a new basis for the innovation projects growth within the EU [35]. The main aims of the program are to strengthen

EU science and technology, to foster industrial competitiveness, and to implement the sustainable development goals. The program would have some new features, such as the European Innovation Council (a new platform supporting high-risk, market-creating innovation projects), EU-wide missions to promote research and innovation outcomes (e.g., for clean transport), and new forms of partnerships, open to all types of stakeholders.

At the same time, it is important to remember that in the near future the EU and the member states will have to face the great challenge of Brexit. It is to be expected that the UK's exit from the EU will not be without an impact on strategic sectors of the economy and it will also affect the transport industry [36]. Kerridge [37], referring to various future scenarios of Brexit, says: 'In each case new agreements will be needed to avoid serious disruption in the event of a "no-deal" Brexit that removes the UK from the single market and customs union, with the UK then being regarded as a third country for trade and transport links' [37]. It will also pose a serious changes for the policy measures and innovations, mentioned in this document, since Britain has been a leader in developing the EU policies of openness, competition, and the single market [37]. On the other hand, as Lyons and Davidson claim [38], who in their paper wanted to examine transport planning and policymaking in the face of an uncertain future, uncertainty is a big challenge, but can also become 'an opportunity for decision-makers with the realization that they are shaping the future rather than (only) responding to a predicted future' [38].

Undoubtedly, transport policy is a dynamic field that requires new solutions, programs and legal regulations that will enable it to meet the challenges and achieve the planned goals [2]. In this context, it is, on the one hand important to analyze the effectiveness of the current EU innovation policy and national policies, and on the other hand, to create recommendations for the future policy actions that help to stimulate the development processes and bring innovative technologies, services, solutions and know-how that support sustainable transport development to the market [19].

The subject of stimulating the innovation policy in transport has been taken up in the EU project entitled 'POlicy measures for innovation in TRANSport sector with special focus on Small- and Medium sized Enterprises-factors and recommendations for success and sustainability' (acronym: POSMETRANS (see Supplementary Materials)), implemented in 2010–2011, under the 7th EU Framework Program [39]. The POSMETRANS project explored the efficiency of the European and national policy measures for innovation in the surface transport sector. Particular emphasis was placed on the analysis of the impact of these policies on small and medium enterprises. The project focused on innovative processes in two areas: (1) public transport and (2) freight transport and logistics. In each of these areas, the analysis of innovative solutions for the means and infrastructure of road, rail and water transport were carried out. Innovations were included in the following five thematic areas: green technologies, new materials, information and communication technologies, safety and security and co-modality. Research on the extension of transport innovations throughout the market was also conducted. Trends which foster the innovation process and key players in innovation were identified and analyzed. The conducted research and analyses enabled a comprehensive assessment of the tools being used by the EU to support innovation in transport, and elaborate recommendations for the future European policy in order to accelerate the market take-up of innovative technologies and processes in surface transport related to SMEs [40].

This article presents a method developed on the basis of the authors' own experience from the POSMETRANS project, where the main tool was the multiple criteria decision aid (MCDA) used for the assessment of the EU and national policy measures in surface transport in terms of their influence on the market take-up of innovation technologies and processes. As the final result of the assessment, rankings of policy measures from best to worst were obtained (rankings indicating the measures that can stimulate innovation in the greatest and in the smallest extent). Information on the MCDA method, that was used to assess policy measures, is presented in Section 2, while the procedure of the assessment, along with the selected final rankings of policy measures—in Section 3.

2. Method

This section provides general information about MCDA and presents one of its methods, i.e., the simple additive weighting (SAW) method, which was used to assess policy measures in terms of their influence on the market take-up of innovations.

2.1. General Information about the Multiple Criteria Decision Aid (MCDA)

MCDA is a methodology derived from operational research, alternatively called multiple criteria analysis or multiple criteria decision aid process [41–43]. In the study of Zeleny [43], MCDA is defined as making decisions in the presence of many criteria/objectives, whereas in the work of Vincke [42], as solving complex decision problems where many, often opposing points of view, must be considered. MCDA is a methodology that has been dynamically developing in recent years [44,45].

According to Roy, the basic attributes of MCDA problems are [46]: a set A of solutions and a coherent family F of assessment criteria. The set A of solutions is a set of decision objects, variants, actions or activities to be analyzed and assessed during the decision-making process. The set A of solutions may be defined: directly by listing all its elements (a sufficiently small set, a definite number of objects) and indirectly, by defining properties that characterize all the elements of set A or conditions limiting set A. The set A may be defined in advance and not subject to changes during the decision-making process or evolving (varying), i.e., subject to modifications during the decision-making process.

A cohesive family F of criteria [46] is a set of criteria that meet the following requirements: exhaustiveness of the assessment (contemplating all possible aspects of the problem under consideration), consistency of assessment (based on proper determination of global decision preferences by the criterion) and the uniqueness of the criteria ranges. Each criterion present in the set F is a function f defined on the set A to assess the set A and representing the preferences of the decision maker in relation to a particular decision problem.

A multi-criteria decision problem is a situation in which, having a defined set A of solutions (actions, variants) and a coherent family F of criteria, the decision maker (DM) seeks to [24]:

- determine the subset of solutions (actions, variants) considered to be the best for the family of criteria under consideration (choice problem);
- divide the set of solutions (actions, variants) into subsets according to certain standards (problem of classification or sorting);
- rank the set of solutions (actions, variants) from best to worst (problem of positioning or ranking).

The MCDA methodology identifies the main participants in the decision-making process, i.e., the decision maker, analyst and other entities interested in solving a given decision problem. The decision maker (individual or collective) determines the objectives of the decision-making process, expresses preferences and ultimately assesses the solutions obtained. The analyst is an external entity in relation to the considered decision problem. S/he is responsible for supporting the decision aid process (including the construction of a decision model, selection of methods and tools to solve the problem, etc.). S/he explains the consequences of making a given decision to the decision-maker and ultimately recommends a solution. As Zmuda-Trzebiatowski claims, those who intervene in the decision-making process are, for example, principals-clients, local community, employees, etc. [47].

In the available literature there are many classifications of MCDA methods. The most popular is the classification presented by Vincke [42], who divided the methods of multi-criteria decision aid into three groups: methods of multi-attribute usability theory, methods based on surpassing relations, interactive methods (Figure 1).

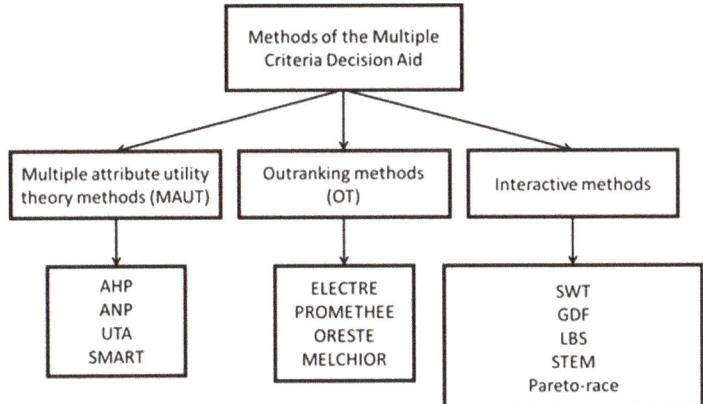

Figure 1. Classification of multi-criteria decision aid (MCDA) methods according to P. Vincke [42].

Methods of multi-attribute usability theory or synthesis to a single criterion derive from the so-called American school and consist in aggregation of different criteria (points of view) to a single optimized, additive usability function. As a result, the multi-criteria function of the goal is reduced to one global criterion, i.e., the usability function. The most popular methods that belong to this group include: the Analytic Hierarchy Process (AHP) [48], Analytic Network Process (ANP) [49], UTility Additive (UTA) [50] and many others.

Surpassing methods belong to the so-called European school. In these methods, the preference of the decision-maker is aggregated by means of a surpassing relation, which allows for incomparability between the considered options (solutions, actions), i.e., a situation in which the decision-maker is not able to identify a better one with two options, the decision-maker does not see discrepancies and fundamental differences between the options [46]. Therefore, they are neither able to consider them equivalent nor to identify the better of the two options. In this group, the most popular methods are: ELimination and Choice Expressing REality (Electre) [47], Preference Ranking Organization METHod for Enrichment of Evaluations (Promethee) [51,52] and Organization, Rangement Et Synthese De Donnes Relationnelles (Oreste) [53].

Interactive (dialogue) methods are a group of methods in which preferences are set in dialogue mode. The interweaving of the computing phase and the decision-making phase are specific, i.e., the dialogue with the decision-maker. In the first stage, the decision-maker obtains a set of compromise solutions. In the second stage, it evaluates the set, introducing additional preferential information. In this group of methods, the most popular methods are Surrogate Worth Trade–Off (SWT) [54] Geoffrion-Dyer-Feinberg (GDF) [55], Light Beam Search (LBS) [56], Step Method (STEM) [57], Pareto-Race [58]. The majority of the interactive methods are used in multi-criteria mathematical programming. Moreover, it is worth mentioning that interactive (dialog) methods can be classified as follows [59]:

- search-oriented methods, i.e., methods building a local approximation of the usability function with an indirect or direct formula of its construction, e.g., the GDF method [55] and methods narrowing the reviewed area of the non-dominated set, where the decision-maker limits the reviewed area by selecting the best variant from a representative sample or defining additional limitations. This group includes, e.g., methods by Steuer [41], Choo and Atkins [60].
- learning-oriented methods, e.g., reference point method, reference direction method (Wierzbicki [61], Pareto-Race [58]).

Due to the nature of the decision-making problem (more precisely the purpose of the decision-making process), the method of multi-criteria decision aid can be divided into [59]:

- multi-criteria selection (optimization) methods;
- multi-criteria ordering methods (ranking, ranking);
- multi-criteria grading (sorting) methods.

Of note, this division corresponds to the general categorization of multi-criteria decision-making problems (described above in the article). The above division of methods together with exemplary methods that belong to particular groups is presented in Figure 2.

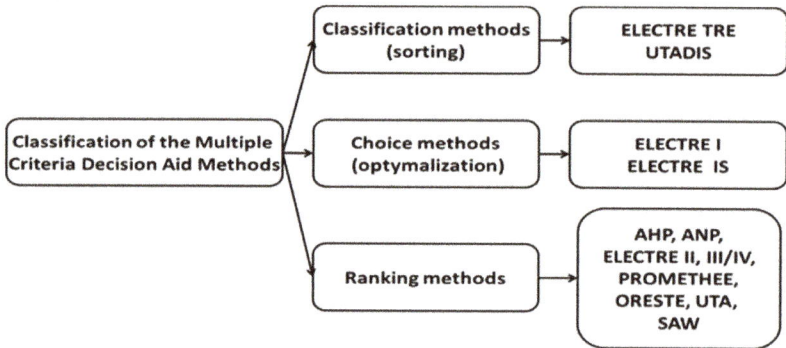

Figure 2. Classification of methods according to the purpose of the decision-making process.

The most popular include methods for positioning solutions (actions, variants), such as: AHP [48], ANP [49], UTA [50], SAW [62], Electre [29], Promethee [51,52] and Oreste [53]. Of note, speaking of the above MCDA methods, some of them belong to the group of methods based on the principle of multiple attribute utility theory (MAUT) called synthesis methods for a single criterion, that do not contemplate the incomparability between the considered solutions (actions, variants) (methods: UTA, AHP, ANP, SAW), and some of them are methods based on the exceedance relation (OT), called methods of synthesis outweighing the incomparability between the considered solutions (actions, variants) (Electre, Promethee, Oreste). There are also methods that are a combination of the two previous MAUT and OT approaches, e.g., the Mappac method (multicriterion analysis of preferences by means of pairwise action and criterion comparisons) [63]. The above-mentioned methods are often used to solve complex decision problems in various areas of life, including transport problems. For example, Kijewska et al. applied the AHP for choosing and analyzing the measures for the distribution of goods [64]), while Hemalatha et al. to evaluate the service quality and obtain the ranking of container terminal operators [65]. Lon et al. as well as Al-Atawi et al. used the same method for the evaluation of the public transport policy design [66] and sustainable transport strategies [67], while Lopez-Iglesias et al. used it to access mobility innovations for sustainability and cohesion of rural areas [68]. In research conducted by de Luca [69] and Chowdhury et al. [70] the AHP was used in order to understand and quantify public preferences in a process of transportation planning. Nosal and Solecka applied the AHP to assess different variants of integration of urban public transport in Krakow [71]. Taleai and Yameqani [72] not only used the AHP method but also integrated it with a geographic information system (GIS) and remote sensing tools in order to search for the healthy walking paths. The results show that the simultaneous use of the above-mentioned methods can help provide both, urban planners and the public with the data and tools needed to take into account different criteria, when choosing to travel within a city. Kiciński et al. [73] presented the example of the application of ELECTRE III in choosing the variant of travel made by public and private transport modes, while Popiolek and Thais [74] implemented the same method to select the best policies in favor of solar mobility in France. These and other types of MCDA, such as ANP and PROMETHEE, were presented in Solecka's research in the multiple criteria assessment of variants of the integrated urban transport system [75]. Nassereddine and Eskandari applied the PROMETHEE method to evaluate public transportation systems in Tehran [76]. Rudnicki recommends the SAW method for the comparison of solutions related to the quality of public transport service [77]. Ivanović et al. presented the multicriteria analysis model to analyze three alternatives of street reconstruction into a pedestrian area [78]. The results of the review made by Mardani et al. who analyzed 89 cases of the MCDA application in transportation system problems, showed that AHP and fuzzy-AHP methods in the individual methods and hybrid MCDM and fuzzy MCDM in the integrated methods were ranked as the first and second methods in use, respectively [79]. Macharis and Bernardini, [80] in their paper, giving an overview of the use of the MCDA for transport project appraisal, highlighted the importance of integrating stakeholders in the decision process, which is not yet very common in the transport projects. The multi-actor multi-criteria analysis (MAMCA) approach suggested by them allows the stakeholders to be involved explicitly in the decision-making process.

2.2. Simple Additive Weighting (SAW) Method

The SAW method [62] expresses the principle of 'something for something'. Failing at meeting one criterion can be compensated by a higher fulfilment of another criterion. The method includes the following elements of the assessment procedure:

- formulation of a list of criteria in a one-stage or multi-stage system;
- determination of the weights of the criteria;
- determination of threshold criteria;
- assessment of the degree of fulfilment of individual criteria by the solutions in question and the determination of the required minimum fulfilment for the threshold criteria;
- elimination of solutions that do not meet the threshold criteria;
- aggregation of partial assessments, obtaining a global assessment;
- ordering solutions by values due to the global rating indicator.

The global assessment S_j of the j-solution is determined by the following formula:

$$S_j = \sum_{i=1}^{n} w_i \cdot s_{ij} \qquad (1)$$

where:

s_{ij}—degree of fulfilment of the i-criterion in the j-solution (in percent on a scale from 0%–100%, where 0% means no compliance with the criterion, and 100% means complete compliance with the criterion or on a 10-point scale, where 1 means that the criterion is not met and 10 means complete fulfillment of the criterion),

n—the number of criteria considered,

w_i—weight of the i-criterion (non-rendered number, normalized), $w_i > 0$.

$$\sum_{i=1}^{n} w_i = 1 \qquad (2)$$

To determine the weights of the criteria and the degree of fulfillment of a given criterion, data from expert opinions are usually used. Based on the formula (1), the values of S_j are obtained on a scale of 1 to 10 points. The calculated values of S_j for particular considered solutions allow their global (aggregated) quality to be assessed. The higher the S_j value, the solution (action, variant) is considered to be better.

3. Application and Results of the SAW Method in Assessing Policy Measures Focusing on Innovation

In the analyses presented in this article, the SAW method was used to assess policy measures focusing on innovation. The analyzed decision problem was defined as a multi-criteria problem of categorizing the EU/regional and national policy measures. For the purposes of the calculation, 62 policy measures were adopted, and they were divided into the following six categories for structuring the analysis:

- EU/regional level measures: funding program (14 measures), law/regulation (42 measures), action plan/guidelines (32 measures);
- national level measures: funding program (25 measures), law/regulation (17 measures), action plan/ guidelines (32 measures). The policy measures adopted for the analysis were provided by 10 experts (in an expert survey) working in the following areas: research institutions, industry and technology transfer and SME intermediaries. They represented 5 European countries and the following units:
- Steinbeis-Europa-Zentrum (DE), responsible for the support of the European research projects and trans-national co-operation in Europe;
- ACCIONA (ES)—a Spanish conglomerate with leadership in, among others, energy, logistic and transport, water and urban services;
- EGE University Scientific and Technology Centre (TR), providing an institutional structure for the industry–academia partnerships and acting as a regional contact point for universities, research centers, SMEs, industrial associations, regional authorities and non-governmental organizations (NGOs);
- Institut fur Verkehrs und Tourismus Forschung (DE), specializing in research and consultancy in the field of mobility, transport, traffic and tourism;
- Cracow University of Technology (PL), represented by the Technology Transfer Center (the unit responsible for technology transfer, facilitating contacts between academia, industry and regional stakeholders and the promotion of entrepreneurship) and the Institute of Road and Railway Engineering operating, among others, in the field of transport planning and transport policy;
- the Unioncamere Piemonte (IT), supporting the Piedmont Chambers of Commerce with regards to innovation and technology transfer matters and services.

The choice of policy measures was dictated by consultations with experts, the availability of full versions of the materials and the possibility of proper interpretation of documents, taking their sectorial importance into account. The consultations with experts familiar with the local conditions having a strong impact on the shape and scope of the analyzed documents and played a very important role. As a result, a consistent set of input data was obtained, ensuring the representativeness of the thematic areas and issues. This article focuses on the method itself, indicating its flexibility and ease of use, while the analyzed collection of documents constitutes only the background of the deliberations.

3.1. Definition of the Criteria

Considering the requirements of defining a cohesive set of criteria (exhaustiveness of assessment, consistency of the assessment and uniqueness of the criteria ranges of meaning [46]) to assess the analyzed policy measures in terms of their impact on the development of innovation, the criteria for the following four groups were proposed by experts: functional, economic, social and environmental. Initially, a total of 15 criteria were adopted, and then—to reduce their number—weights from 1 to 5 were assigned to each criterion, where 1 meant the lowest weight (unimportant criterion), and 5 meant the highest weight (very important criterion). The weights were assigned by experts. In the further assessment procedure, only those criteria that obtained the highest average weight values were taken into consideration, according to the following rules:

- criteria with the weight: $\leq 5,4 \geq$ are accepted;
- criteria with the weight: $<4,3\geq$ are in question;
- criteria with the weight: $<3,0\geq$ are rejected.

In the case of criteria in question, only one criterion, concerning the environmental aspect, was adopted (in order to include this aspect as well). The rest of them were rejected. One of the criteria which obtained the highest values—the "Total allocated budget" criterion, related to the height of the total allocated budget—was rejected, since it was only applicable to the funding programs. Finally, 7 criteria assigned to 4 groups were taken for the analysis. The adopted criteria are summarized in Table 1.

Table 1. Criteria adopted to the assessment of the policy measures on the European Union (EU) and at national level.

No.	Group of Criteria	Name of Criterion	Definition of Criterion
C1	Functional	Ease of enforcement/bureaucracy burden	This criterion indicates the level of complexity in implementing a policy measure/accessing a funding program. It answers the questions if the process is easy to understand and follow, transparent, time-consuming or not, requires taking many non-technical aspects such as social and environmental aspects into account, requires specifically trained personnel.
C2	Functional	Mandatory level	Level of the mandatory nature of the policy measures. For example: recommendations, opinions, communications are low level; regulations, decisions or directives are high level.
C3	Functional	Level of support to research and development (R&D) activities	The criterion means the policy measure (both the EU funding programs and regulations) supports R&D activities (the largest forms of support are, for example, grants allocated to R&D activities, the higher the rank is) in different ways.
C4	Social	Consumer oriented	This criterion indicates to which extent the interest of consumers/end-users of a technology is taken into account (high policy directly intended at improving consumer well-being; low: consumer well-being not considered or only indirectly).
C5	Economic	Small- and medium-sized enterprises (SME) participation	Percentage of funding allocated to SME partners
C6	Economic	Incentive taxes system	This criterion indicates if the use of tax incentives is planned either to penalize those who do not follow a policy measure (e.g., CO_2 tax) or to help/simplify/encourage investments/the implementation of policy measures.
C7	Environmental	Environmental commitment	This criterion indicates the degree of commitment with the environmental sustainability of the policy measure.

3.2. Calculation Experiment and Final Rankings of the Policy Measures

In the next stage, a multiple criteria assessment of the adopted policy measures was conducted. For this purpose, weights for each group of criteria (functional, economic, social and environmental) were determined, and then for individual criteria in these groups. Weights on a scale from 1 to 5 were assigned, where 1 meant the lowest weight (unimportant criterion) and 5—the highest weight (very important criterion). The weights assigned by experts have been averaged and normalized in accordance with the SAW method procedure (Table 2).

Table 2. Weights of the criteria.

No.	Group of Criteria	Weight of Group of Criteria	Normalized Weight of Group of Criteria		Criteria	Weight of Criterion	Normalized Weight of Criterion	Weight of Criterion in Full Collection
1	Functional	3.8	0.25	C1	Ease of enforcement/bureaucracy burden	4.3	0.35	0.09
				C2	Mandatory level	3.8	0.30	0.07
				C3	Level of support to R&D activities	4.3	0.35	0.09
					total	-	1	0.25
2	Social	3.6	0.24	C4	Consumer oriented	3.7	1	0.24
					total	-	1	0.24
3	Economic	4.4	0.29	C5	SME participation	4.8	0.55	0.16
				C6	Taxes incentives system	3.9	0.45	0.13
					total	-	1	0.29
4	Environmental	3.4	0.22	C7	Environmental commitment	4	1	0.22
					total	-	1	0.22
	total		1			-	-	1

Subsequently, the degree s_{ij} of meeting the criteria by each policy measures was determined. The assessments of the fulfilment level of criteria by the policy measures are of a subjective nature and were provided by the experts. The global assessment value S_j of the j-policy measure is calculated as the sum of the products of the weights w_i of the criterion in the full collection and the assessments s_{ij} of the fulfilment degrees of the criterion by the policy measure (according to Equation (1)). After calculating the global values for individual measures, their final ranking (from the best to the worst policy measure according to the considered assessment criteria, i.e., from the measure, that stimulates innovation to the greatest extent, to the measure that influences this development to the smallest extent) was carried out. The rankings were created for all six categories of policy measures under consideration, i.e., the EU funding program, law/regulation and action plan/guidelines as well as national funding program, law/regulation and action plan/guidelines. Table 3 presents an example of the results obtained from the computational experiments for the policy measures at the EU/regional level in terms of the action plan/guidelines. The table lists only the first positions in the ranking, i.e., measures, which achieved the global assessment value S_j above 60%. In the presented ranking the EU/regional action plans/guidelines, which largely stimulate innovation are the 'Alpine convention: Transport and Mobility on the Alps', 'Cooperation on Alpine Railway Corridors' and 'EU Strategy for Bio fuels'. They obtained the highest global assessment values S_j. The global assessment value S_j for 'Transport and Mobility on the Alps' equals 86.77%, for 'Cooperation on Alpine Railway Corridors' equals 78.32%

and for 'EU Strategy for Bio fuels'—74.41%. The first score in the policy measure ranking exceeds the remaining two policy measures by 8.45 and 12.36 percentage points, respectively. The difference between the second and third in the policy measure ranking is small and amounts to 3.91 percentage points. The policy measure, which is the first in the ranking, is the only one to meet 100% four of the seven adopted criteria (C2, C4, C6 and C7), including criteria characterized by high weights (C4, C6, C7), and belonging to the group of criteria of the highest importance (C6—economic criterion), which has an impact on such a high position in the ranking. When compared to other policy measures, it also has a fairly high degree of compliance with criteria C1 and C3. A policy measure ranked second in the ranking meets three out of seven criteria (C4, C6 and C7) in 100% and two out of seven criteria (C4 and C7) in third place. Although there are several other policy measures in the ranking with 100% compliance with the highest weighting criteria, i.e., C4 and C7, the relatively high compliance with criterion C6 provides a third policy measure in the ranking with an advantage over them.

Table 3. The final ranking for the policy measures at the EU/regional level—action plan/guidelines (chosen results).

Positioning the Rank	Level	Name of the Policy Measure	Assessment of the Degree of Fulfillment [%]							Global Assessment S_j (%)
			C1	C2	C3	C4	C5	C6	C7	
1	Other (Regional)	Alpine Convention on Transport and Mobility on the Alps (Alpine Countries)	60	100	80	100	50	100	100	86.77
		Global assessment for each criterion	5.27	7.60	6.89	23.68	7.99	12.96	22.37	
2	Other (Regional)	Cooperation on Alpine Railway Corridors (Alpine Countries)	40	80	20	100	50	100	100	78.32
		Global assessment for each criterion	3.51	6.08	1.72	23.68	7.99	12.96	22.37	
3	EU	EU Strategy for Bio fuels	40	40	60	100	50	67	100	74.41
		Global assessment for each criterion	3.51	3.04	5.17	23.68	7.99	8.64	22.37	
4	EU	Assessment and Management of Report from the EC to the EP and the Council concerning sources of environmental noise—COM (2004) 160	40	20	100	100	50	33	100	72.02
		Global assessment for each criterion	3.51	1.52	8.61	23.68	7.99	4.32	22.37	
5	EU	Towards a European Road Safety Area: Policy Orientations on Road Safety 2011-2020	60	60	40	100	50	33	100	71.64
		Global assessment for each criterion	5.27	4.56	3.45	23.68	7.99	4.32	22.37	
	EU	European Strategy on Clean and Energy Efficient Vehicles	60	60	40	100	50	33	100	71.64
		Global assessment for each criterion	5.27	4.56	3.45	23.68	7.99	4.32	22.37	
6	Other (Regional)	Abkommen zwischen der Schweizerischen Eidgenossenschaftund der Europäischen Gemeinschaft über denGüter- und Personenverkehr auf Schiene und Strasse (Switzerland/EU)	60	100	20	100	50	33	80	68.49
		Global assessment for each criterion	5.27	7.60	1.72	23.68	7.99	4.32	17.89	
7	EU	Thematic Strategy on Air Pollution—COM (2005) 446	60	40	20	100	50	33	100	68.40
		Global assessment for each criterion	5.27	3.04	1.72	23.68	7.99	4.32	22.37	

Table 3. Cont.

Positioning the Rank	Level	Name of the Policy Measure	Assessment of the Degree of Fulfillment [%]							Global Assessment S_j (%)
			C1	C2	C3	C4	C5	C6	C7	
8	EU	A Sustainable Future for Transport: Towards an Integrated, Technology-Led and User-Friendly System	60	40	60	100	17	33	100	66.52
		Global assessment for each criterion	5.27	3.04	5.17	23.68	2.66	4.32	22.37	
9	EU	Commission recommendation on the development of a legal and business framework for participation of the private sector in deploying telematics-based traffic and travel information services in Europe	40	40	20	80	50	100	80	66.07
		Global assessment for each criterion	3.51	3.04	1.72	18.95	7.99	12.96	17.89	
10	EU	Program for the Promotion of Short Sea Shipping, COM (2003) 155	60	40	40	60	50	100	80	64.81
		Global assessment for each criterion	5.27	3.04	3.45	14.21	7.99	12.96	17.89	
11	EU	Trans-European Networks: Toward an Integrated Approach, COM (2007) 135	60	20	100	60	50	33	100	64.30
		Global assessment for each criterion	5.27	1.52	8.61	14.21	7.99	4.32	22.37	
12	EU	Biomass Action Plan—COM (2005) 628	40	20	60	100	50	0	100	64.25
		Global assessment for each criterion	3.51	1.52	5.17	23.68	7.99	0.00	22.37	
13	EU	Position Paper on the European Strategies and Priorities for Railway Noise Abatement	60	20	20	100	50	33	80	62.41
		Global assessment for each criterion	5.27	1.52	1.72	23.68	7.99	4.32	17.89	
14	EU	COM (2007) 96. Brussels, 15 March 2007. Radio Frequency Identification (RFID) in Europe: Steps Towards a Policy Framework	60	20	20	80	50	100	60	61.83
		Global assessment for each criterion	5.27	1.52	1.72	18.95	7.99	12.96	13.42	
15	EU	GREEN PAPER. TEN-T: A policy review. COM(2009) 44	60	80	40	100	33	67	40	61.40
		Global assessment for each criterion	5.27	6.08	3.45	23.68	5.33	8.64	8.95	

Table 3. Cont.

Positioning the Rank	Level	Name of the Policy Measure	Assessment of the Degree of Fulfillment [%]							Global Assessment S_j (%)
			C1	C2	C3	C4	C5	C6	C7	
16	EU	Rail Noise Abatement Measures Addressing the Existing Fleet—COM (2008) 432	60	20	20	80	50	100	60	61.38
		Global assessment for each criterion	5.27	1.52	1.72	18.95	7.99	12.96	13.42	
17	EU	COM (2003) 123 final, Brussels, 19 March 2003. Integration of the EGNOS Program in the Galileo Program	60	20	60	80	50	100	40	60.81
		Global assessment for each criterion	5.27	1.52	5.17	18.95	7.99	12.96	8.95	

3.3. Sensitivity Analysis

An important aspect in the presented approach of the multiple criterion assessment of the policy measures is the sensitivity analysis of the results. It consists in determining the impact of changing the meaning of individual elements on the results obtained (on the final ranking of the policy measures) and shows the stability of the rankings obtained as a result of the changes introduced. The sensitivity analysis was conducted in two ways:

- by changing the weight values of the main groups of criteria (functional, social, economic, environmental). The starting point was to change the weight values of the main groups of criteria and observe how it affected other groups of criteria, and thus the final result. When conducting the sensitivity analysis, the values of individual weights of the main criteria groups were subsequently changed to the following thresholds: 1, 3, 5. The obtained results are presented in Figures 3 and 5–7. When analyzing the results from the figures, it can be noticed that the final ranking is clearly marked by w1 and w2 ('Alpine convention Transport and Mobility on the Alps'; 'Cooperation on Alpine Railway Corridors'). In the majority of rankings, positions 1 to 4 are immutable except for the economic criteria (when changing the weight to 1). For all groups of criteria, the largest differences in global assessment values result in a change in weights up to 1 (Figures 3 and 5–7). This is particularly noticeable in the group of economic criteria (Figure 6), for which the global assessment values for most policy measures increase with this change. This is particularly noticeable for policy measures v4 and v5, whose global scores, with a change in weighting to 1, increased by nearly 10 percentage points, placing them 3rd and 4th in the ranking (Figure 6), thus placing the policy measure w3 in position 5. In the group of functional criteria, the changes in the final ranking (Figure 3) in the case of a change in weights are visible from position 6, where the policy measure w6 decreases to position 8 when the weight changes to 1, while the policy measure w8 moves to position 7 when the weight changes to 3. In this case also, the policy measure w8 moves to a further position, i.e., tenth in the final ranking. The policy measure w11 also falls to item 14. When weights are changed to 5 for a group of functional criteria, the policy measure w14 loses most of its position, occupying the last place in the ranking, i.e., position 17. On the other hand, the policy measure w15 is moved up two places. In the case of the social criterion group (Figure 5), when the weights of the criterion change, the changes are already noticeable on the 5th position in the ranking. Changing the weight to 1 results in a significant strengthening of the policy measure w10, which moves to position 5 in the final ranking. The policy measure w11, which moves to position 7 in the final ranking, is also strengthened. In the case of the environmental criterion group, changes in ranking positions are observed in position 5 in the case of a change in weighting to 1 (Figure 7). The policy measure w15 and w17 significantly strengthen their positions, occupying positions 7 and 8 respectively in the final ranking. The position of the policy measure w8, which ranks 14th in the ranking, is significantly weakened.
- by changing the weight values of criteria (C1 ... C7). The starting point was to change the value of the criteria weights and observe how it affected other criteria, and thus the final result. When conducting the sensitivity analysis, the values of individual criteria weights were subsequently changed to the following thresholds: 1, 3, 5. The analysis results showed that the most sensitive criteria for changing the weights are C2—Mandatory level and C3—Level of support to R&D activities. The selected results of this analysis for criterion C3 are presented in Figure 4. When analyzing the results presented in Figure 4 it can be noticed that the final ranking is clearly marked by: w1, w2, w3 so, respectively, 'Alpine convention Transport and Mobility on the Alps', 'Cooperation on Alpine Railway Corridors', 'EU Strategy for Bio Fuels'.

	Sensitivity of the group of criteria for weight changes - functional						
Initial ranking		Weight change to 1		Weight change to 3		Weight change to 5	
Ranking	S_j [%]	Ranking	S_j [%]	Ranking	S_j [%]	Ranking	S_j [%]
w1	86,77	w1	88,51	w1	87,20	w1	86,20
w2	78,32	w2	85,79	w2	80,16	w2	75,90
w3	74,41	w3	80,62	w3	75,94	w3	72,40
w4	72,02	w4	75,95	w4	72,98	w4	70,74
w5	71,64	w5	75,83	w5	72,67	w5	70,29
w6	68,49	w7	74,78	w7	69,97	w6	67,75
w7	68,40	w9	73,51	w6	69,05	w7	66,33
w8	66,52	w6	70,77	w9	67,90	w8	65,59
w9	66,07	w12	69,54	w8	67,22	w11	64,10
w10	64,81	w8	69,36	w10	65,80	w9	63,66
w11	64,30	w10	68,83	w12	65,55	w10	63,51
w12	64,25	w13	68,81	w11	64,45	w12	62,54
w13	62,41	w14	68,11	w13	63,98	w15	61,24
w14	61,83	w11	64,90	w14	63,38	w16	60,39
w15	61,40	w16	64,44	w16	62,13	w13	60,33
w16	61,38	w17	63,74	w17	61,53	w17	59,86
w17	60,81	w15	61,90	w15	61,52	w14	59,80

Figure 3. The sensitivity analysis—the change in the weight values of the functional groups of criteria (symbols w1 ... w17 correspond to the policy measures in Table 3, the numbers are in line with the obtained ranking in Table 3).

	Criterion C3 - Level of support to R&D activities						
Initial ranking		Weight change to 1		Weight change to 3		Weight change to 5	
Ranking	S_j [%]	Ranking	S_j [%]	Ranking	S_j [%]	Ranking	S_j [%]
w1	86.77	w1	86.68	w1	86.74	w1	86.78
w2	78.32	w2	80.58	w2	79.04	w2	77.96
w3	74.41	w3	73.24	w3	74.04	w3	74.60
w4	72.02	w5	72.82	w5	72.01	w4	72.67
w5	71.64	w6	71.92	w4	70.74	w5	71.46
w6	68.49	w7	70.20	w6	69.57	w7	68.11
w7	68.40	w4	67.95	w7	68.97	w6	67.94
w8	66.52	w9	67.24	w9	66.44	w8	66.60
w9	66.07	w8	65.97	w8	66.35	w9	65.88
w10	64.81	w10	65.44	w10	65.01	w11	64.85
w11	64.30	w13	63.66	w12	63.71	w10	64.71
w12	64.25	w15	63.11	w11	63.22	w12	64.53
w13	62.41	w14	63.09	w13	62.80	w13	62.21
w14	61.83	w12	62.53	w14	62.23	w14	61.63
w15	61.40	w11	60.87	w15	61.94	w16	61.55
w16	61.38	w16	60.29	w16	61.04	w15	61.12
w17	60.81	w17	59.72	w17	60.46	w17	60.98

Figure 4. The sensitivity analysis—the change in the weight value of criterion C3 (w1–w17 refers to the policy measures presented in Table 3).

Sustainability 2019, 11, 1472

Initial ranking		Sensitivity of the group of criteria for weight changes - Social						
		Weight change to 1		Weight change to 3		Weight change to 5		
Ranking	S_j [%]	Ranking	S_j [%]	Ranking	S_j [%]	Ranking	S_j [%]	
w1	86,77	w1	84,04	w1	86,22	w1	87,88	
w2	78,32	w2	73,85	w2	77,43	w2	80,15	
w3	74,41	w3	69,13	w3	73,36	w3	76,57	
w4	72,02	w4	66,24	w4	70,87	w4	74,38	
w5	71,64	w10	65,81	w5	70,48	w5	74,04	
w6	68,49	w5	65,79	w6	67,19	w6	71,15	
w7	68,40	w11	65,19	w7	67,10	w7	71,07	
w8	66,52	w9	63,20	w9	65,50	w8	69,34	
w9	66,07	w6	61,99	w8	65,14	w12	67,27	
w10	64,81	w7	61,88	w10	65,01	w9	67,25	
w11	64,30	w8	59,61	w11	64,48	w13	65,58	
w12	64,25	w14	58,09	w12	62,78	w15	64,65	
w13	62,41	w12	56,87	w14	61,09	w16	64,64	
w14	61,83	w17	56,85	w13	60,86	w10	64,41	
w15	61,40	w13	54,65	w17	60,02	w11	63,94	
w16	61,38	w15	53,43	w15	59,81	w14	63,37	
w17	60,81	w16	53,41	w16	59,79	w17	62,43	

Figure 5. The sensitivity analysis—the change in the weight values of the social groups of criteria (symbols w1 ... w17 correspond to the policy measures in Table 3, the numbers are in line with the ranking obtained in Table 3).

Initial ranking		Sensitivity of the group of criteria for weight changes - Economic						
		Weight change to 1		Weight change to 3		Weight change to 5		
Ranking	S_j [%]	Ranking	S_j [%]	Ranking	S_j [%]	Ranking	S_j [%]	
w1	86,77	w1	90,91	w1	88,23	w1	86,22	
w2	78,32	w2	80,03	w2	78,93	w2	78,10	
w3	74,41	w3	79,29	w3	76,13	w3	73,77	
w4	72,02	w4	80,51	w4	75,01	w4	70,90	
w5	71,64	w5	80,03	w5	74,60	w5	70,54	
w6	68,49	w6	75,96	w6	71,12	w6	67,50	
w7	68,40	w7	75,85	w7	71,02	w7	67,42	
w8	66,52	w8	78,73	w8	70,82	w8	64,91	
w9	66,07	w9	64,25	w9	65,43	w9	66,31	
w10	64,81	w10	62,63	w10	64,05	w10	65,10	
w11	64,30	w11	70,57	w11	66,51	w11	63,47	
w12	64,25	w12	74,81	w12	67,97	w12	62,86	
w13	62,41	w13	68,13	w13	64,42	w13	61,65	
w14	61,83	w14	58,80	w14	60,76	w14	62,23	
w15	61,40	w15	65,18	w15	62,73	w15	60,90	
w16	61,38	w16	66,81	w16	63,29	w16	60,66	
w17	60,81	w17	57,47	w17	59,63	w17	61,25	

Figure 6. The sensitivity analysis—the change in the weight values of the economic groups of criteria (symbols w1 ... w17 correspond to the policy measures in Table 3, the numbers are in line with the ranking obtained in Table 3).

Initial ranking		Sensitivity of the group of criteria for weight changes - Environmental					
		Weight change to 1		Weight change to 3		Weight change to 5	
Ranking	S_j [%]	Ranking	S_j [%]	Ranking	S_j [%]	Ranking	S_j [%]
w1	86,77	w1	84,29	w1	86,41	w1	88,03
w2	78,32	w2	74,26	w2	77,74	w2	80,39
w3	74,41	w3	69,61	w3	73,72	w3	76,85
w4	72,02	w4	66,77	w4	71,26	w4	74,68
w5	71,64	w6	66,33	w5	70,88	w5	74,34
w6	68,49	w5	66,33	w6	68,18	w7	71,41
w7	68,40	w15	65,41	w7	67,55	w8	69,71
w8	66,52	w17	64,71	w9	65,70	w6	69,58
w9	66,07	w9	63,46	w8	65,61	w11	67,70
w10	64,81	w7	62,48	w10	64,40	w12	67,66
w11	64,30	w14	62,18	w11	63,33	w9	67,40
w12	64,25	w10	61,97	w12	63,28	w10	66,26
w13	62,41	w16	61,64	w15	61,98	w13	64,08
w14	61,83	w8	60,24	w13	61,93	w14	61,66
w15	61,40	w13	59,11	w14	61,88	w16	61,25
w16	61,38	w11	57,60	w16	61,42	w15	59,36
w17	60,81	w12	57,55	w17	61,37	w17	58,82

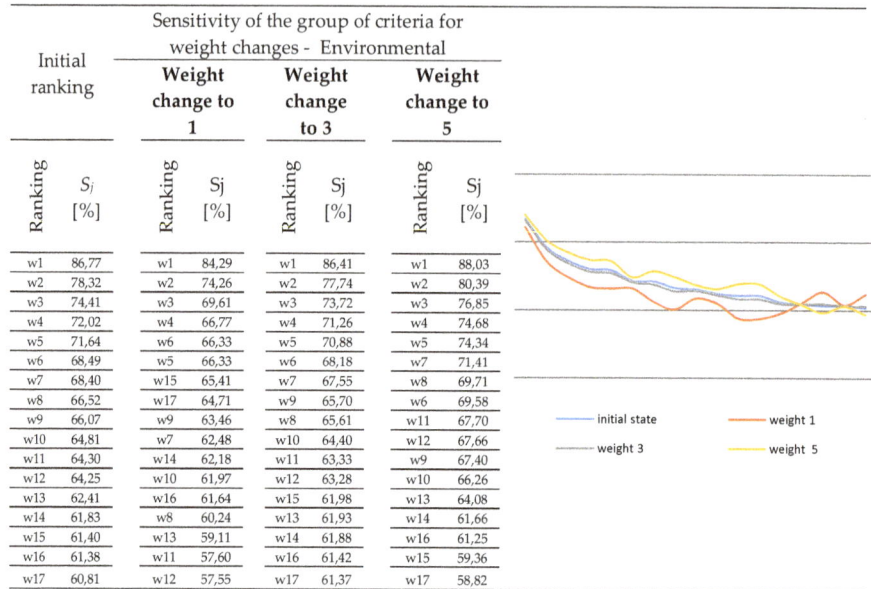

Figure 7. The sensitivity analysis—the change in the weight values of the environmental groups of criteria (symbols w1 ... w17 correspond to the policy measures in Table 3, the numbers are in line with the ranking obtained in Table 3).

4. Discussion

A comparison of transport policies or strategic documents seems to be an impossible task. It is prone to a very high subjectivity and strong characterization of the individual structure of relatively narrow and hermetic issues. When attempting to create a ranking of this type of documents, one can always fall into a schematic approach, taking one feature into account and the comparison of documents will refer to this feature, leaving other threads and issues aside. The whole difficulty of the comparative analysis is intensified by a highly qualitative approach to the issues, which hinders, or, in principle, prevents the separation of numerical features that could be ranked. Therefore, it seems that it is advisable to use the multiple criteria method supported by an expert approach. In this case, the assessment of the documents is reliable (guaranteed by the evaluator's experience), enhanced by the introduction of a uniform group of criteria used by each member of the expert team. The division into groups of criteria, together with the attribution of appropriate weights, results in a great tool, unified in its structure and creating a coherent and transparent form.

The presented method was applied to the process of identification of the level of innovation in transport and, as a result, to emphasize the importance of policy measures for its development with respect to both infrastructure and means of transport as well as the organization of transport processes. The article presents selected research results in the field of the assessment of the EU and national policy measures. It illustrates the possibility of applying one of the MCDA methods, i.e., the SAW method.

The use of this method allows to contemplate the analysed decision problems in terms of various criteria, including technical, economic, social or environmental, and to develop—on this basis—the final rankings of the examined measures, and comparison of obtained results. In the SAW method, in accordance with the principle 'something for something', a failure to meet one criterion can be compensated for by a high degree of fulfilment of another. The use of this method allowed a comprehensive and exhaustive assessment of the policies under consideration to be conducted and the identification of those that best meet the adopted assessment criteria, and thus those that could contribute the most to the stimulation of innovation in surface transport.

The presented example of the results obtained from computational experiments for the policy measures at the EU/regional level for the action plans/guidelines, shows that policy measures largely stimulating innovation are those that are characterized by the highest level of fulfilment of many criteria, including the criteria of greatest significance from the point of view of the entities interested in the final results of the research, proving that the policy measure directly intends to improve the consumer well-being and has the highest degree of commitment with environmental sustainability.

Both the change in the value of the weights for the main groups of criteria as well as for individual criteria in the group in the sensitivity analysis mainly impacted the order in the ranking of solutions placed in the further positions, i.e., from position 4—the first three measures remained in the rankings at the same positions. The various positions of solutions in the rankings means that the results are not stable.

The considered problem of the prioritization of EU/regional and national policy measures under consideration can also be solved by the other methods mentioned in point 2 for solving ranking problems, but it is important to remember that some methods have certain limitations. These limitations may relate to the number of variants/solutions/actions (size of the set), the type of information (i.e., what type of information is allowed by the method: whether the criteria are expressed in quantitative, qualitative or mixed form), the nature of the information (some methods allow deterministic information and others non-deterministic information—stochastic, fuzzy), the distance between variants measured quantitatively (some of the methods give the possibility of reading the distance between variants, which allows to determine precisely, if the option is better than the other option under consideration) etc. It is intuitively convincing and transparent, allowing for splitting the global assessment into a number of partial assessments taking into account factors of different significance and co-creating the synthetic assessment. This method makes allows to determine the distance between variants, which makes it possible to determine the difference between them.

Analyses such as those referred to in this, may constitute one of the elements of the research enabling conclusions about the impact of actions taken by the EU and by the governments of individual member states on the development of transport innovation, which give rise to the development of innovative technologies and processes.

Supplementary Materials: The following are available online at http://www.mdpi.com/2071-1050/11/5/1472/s1, Document S1: POSMETRANS list of policy measures, Document S2: POSMETRANS methodology for analysis.

Author Contributions: The research was designed and theoretically framed by all researchers. The data was gathered and analysed by K.S. and K.N.H, under the supervision of A.S., K.S. and K.N.H. prepared the original draft of the paper, and A.S. undertook the review. All researchers contributed to the final version of the manuscript with results and concluding remarks.

Funding: The study was conducted under POSMETRANS (POlicy measures for innovation in TRANSport sector with special focus on Small- and Medium sized Enterprises—factors and recommendations for success and sustainability)—a European project implemented between 2010–2011, funded from the 7th Framework Program of the European Commission. No funding was obtained in the project to cover the costs of Open Access publication.

Conflicts of Interest: The authors declare no conflict of interest.

References

1. Limani, Y. Applied Relationship between Transport and Economy. *IFAC-PapersOnLine* **2016**, *49*, 123–128. [CrossRef]
2. Sidor, J. Realizacja Polityki Transportowej na Szczeblu Międzynarodowym, Krajowym i Lokalnym (Implementation of Transport Policy at International, National and Local Level). *Eksploat. Niezawodn.* **2006**, *4*, 61–66.
3. Kempa, E. Wybrane Problemy Polityki Transportowej w Przewozach Ładunków (Selected Problems of Transport Policy in Freight Transportation). *Autobusy Technika, Eksploatacja Systemy Transportowe (Buses Technol. Oper. Transp. Syst.)* **2018**, *6*, 1059–1062. [CrossRef]

4. Purwanto, A.J.; Heyndrickx, C.; Kiel, J.; Betancor, O.; Socorro, M.P.; Hernandez, A.; Eugenio-Martin, J.L.; Pawlowska, B.; Borkowski, P.; Fiedler, R. Impact of Transport Infrastructure on International Competitiveness of Europe. *Transp. Res. Proc.* **2017**, *25*, 2877–2888. [CrossRef]
5. The Council of the European Union. *Renewed EU Sustainable Development Strategy*; The Council of the European Union: Brussels, Belgium, 2006.
6. Kadłubek, M. Examples of Sustainable Development in the Area of Transport. *Proc. Econ. Financ.* **2015**, *27*, 494–500. [CrossRef]
7. Schwedes, O.; Riedel, V.; Dziekan, K. Project Planning vs. Strategic Planning: Promoting a Different Perspective for Sustainable Transport policy in European R&D Projects. *Case Stud. Transp. Policy* **2017**, *5*, 31–37.
8. ECMT. *Assessment and Decision Making for Sustainable Transport*; OECD Publishing: Paris, France, 2004.
9. Noy, K.; Givoni, M. Is 'Smart Mobility' Sustainable? Examining the Views and Beliefs of Transport's Technological Entrepreneurs. *Sustainability* **2018**, *10*, 422. [CrossRef]
10. Gorka, M. Wybrane poglądy na temat innowacji jako czynnika konkurencyjności podmiotów gospodarczych (Selected views on innovation as a factor in the competitiveness of economic operators). In *Efektywność Zarządzania Zasobami Organizacyjnymi. Prace Naukowo-Dydaktyczne (Efficiency in the Management of Organizational Resources. Scientific and Didactic Works)*; Lenik, P., Ed.; Państwowa Wyższa Szkoła Zawodowa w Krośnie (Higher Vocational School): Krosno, Poland, 2015.
11. Twiss, B.; Goodridge, M. *Managing Technology for Competitive Advantage: Integrating Technological and Organisational Development: From Strategy to Action*; Trans-Atlantic Pubns: Philadelphia, PA, USA, 1989.
12. Rogers, M. *Diffusion of Innovations*, 4th ed.; The Free Press: New York, NY, USA, 1995.
13. Chlad, M.; Strzelczyk, M. Innowacyjne Rozwiązania w Transporcie (Innovative Transport Solutions). *Problemy Transportu i Logistyki (Transp. Logist. Probl.)* **2017**, *3*, 9–18.
14. Schumpeter, J.A. *Teoria Rozwoju Gospodarczego (Theory of Economic Development)*; Wydawnictwo PWE: Warszawa, Poland, 1960.
15. Centrum Analiz Transportowych i Infrastrukturalnych (Centre for Transport and Infrastructure Analyses). *Innowacyjność w Transporcie do 2020 roku—Podstawowe Pojęcia i Tezy (Innovation in Transport by 2020—Basic Concepts and Theses)*; CATI: Warszawa, Poland, 2012.
16. Sierpinski, G. Model of Incentives for Changes of the Modal Split of Traffic Towards Electric Personal Cars. In *Transport Systems Telematics 2014. Telematics—Support for Transport, CCIS*; Mikulski, J., Ed.; Springer: Heidelberg, Germany, 2014; pp. 450–460.
17. Wiesenthal, T.; Condeço-Melhorado, A.; Leduc, G. Innovation in the European Transport Sector: A Review. *Transp. Policy* **2015**, *42*, 86–93. [CrossRef]
18. Holden, E.; Gilpin, G. Biofuels and Sustainable Transport: A Conceptual Discussion. *Sustainability* **2013**, *5*, 3129–3149. [CrossRef]
19. Thorpe, N.; Namdeo, A. Innovations in Technologies for Sustainable Transport. *Res. Transp. Bus. Manag.* **2016**, *18*, 1–3. [CrossRef]
20. Noel, L.; de Rubens, G.Z.; Sovacool, B.K. Optimizing innovation, carbon and health in transport: Assessing socially optimal electric mobility and vehicle-to-grid pathways in Denmark. *Energy* **2018**, *153*, 628–637. [CrossRef]
21. Wu, S.; Wee, H.M.; Lee, S.B. Technical innovation vs. sustainability—A case study from the Taiwanese automobile industry. *Transp. Res. Part D Transp. Environ.* **2016**, *48*, 20–30. [CrossRef]
22. Skeete, J.P. Level 5 autonomy: The new face of disruption in road transport. *Technol. Forecast. Soc.* **2018**, *134*, 22–34. [CrossRef]
23. Bak, M.; Pawlowska, B.; Borkowski, P. Cases Studies in Improving Interconnectivity between Passenger Transport Modes-the Context of the EU Transport Policy Objectives. *Procedia Soc. Behv.* **2012**, *48*, 2738–2747. [CrossRef]
24. Andrés, L.; Padilla, E. Driving factors of GHG emissions in the EU transport activity. *Transp. Policy* **2018**, *61*, 60–74. [CrossRef]
25. Stephenson, J.; Spector, S.; Hopkins, D.; McCarthy, A. Deep Interventions for a Sustainable Transport Future. *Transport. Res. Part D Transp. Environ.* **2017**, *61*, 356–372. [CrossRef]
26. Lah, O. Continuity and Change: Dealing with Political Volatility to Advance Climate Change Mitigation Strategies—Examples from the Transport Sector. *Sustainability* **2017**, *9*, 959. [CrossRef]

27. Gossling, S. Police Perspectives on Road Safety and Transport Politics in Germany. *Sustainability* **2017**, *9*, 1771. [CrossRef]
28. Tsafarakis, S.; Gkorezis, P.; Nalmpantis, D.; Genitsaris, E.; Andronikidis, A. Investigating the preferences of individuals on public transport innovations using the Maximum Difference Scaling method. *Eur. Transp. Res. Rev.* **2019**, *11*, 3. [CrossRef]
29. Abella, A.; Ortiz-de-Urbina-Criado, M.; De-Pablos-Heredero, C. A model for the analysis of data-driven innovation and value generation in smart cities' ecosystems. *Cities* **2017**, *64*, 47–53. [CrossRef]
30. Przybylska, E. The Role of Clusters in The Development of Innovation in the TSL Industry. *Res. Logist. Prod.* **2018**, *8*, 103–111. [CrossRef]
31. Hyard, A. Non-technological Innovations for Sustainable Transport. *Technol. Forecast. Soc.* **2013**, *80*, 1375–1386. [CrossRef]
32. Goldman, T.; Gorhamb, R. Sustainable urban transport: Four innovative directions. *Technol. Soc.* **2006**, *28*, 261–273. [CrossRef]
33. European Commission. *EUROPE 2020. A Strategy for Smart, Sustainable and Inclusive Growth*; European Commission: Brussels, Belgium, 2010.
34. Hull, A. Policy Integration: What Will it Take to Achieve More Sustainable Transport Solutions in Cities? *Transp. Policy* **2008**, *15*, 94–103. [CrossRef]
35. European Parliament. Horizon Europe—Specific Programme: Implementing the Framework Programme. Available online: http://www.europarl.europa.eu/RegData/etudes/BRIE/2018/628297/EPRS_BRI(2018) 628297_EN.pdf (accessed on 22 February 2019).
36. Gelhausen, M.C.; Berster, P.; Wilken, D. A new direct demand model of long-term forecasting air passengers and air transport movements at German airports. *J. Air Transp. Manag.* **2018**, *71*, 140–152. [CrossRef]
37. Kerridge, M. The Impact of Brexit on the Transport Industry. *Logist. Transp.* **2018**, *40*, 35–42.
38. Lyons, G.; Davidson, C. Guidance for transport planning and policymaking in the face of an uncertain future. *Transp. Res. A-Pol.* **2016**, *88*, 104–116. [CrossRef]
39. POSMETRANS. Available online: http://www.posmetrans.eu/ (accessed on 9 January 2019).
40. Gohla, R.; Roth, J.J. *POSMETRANS. Policy Measures for Innovation in TRANSport Sector with Special Focus on Small and Medium Sized Enterprises—Factors and Recommendations for Success and Sustainability*; Steinbeis-Edition: Stuttgart, Germany, 2012; Available online: http://www.posmetrans.eu/downloads/POSMETRANS_Handbook_final.pdf (accessed on 9 January 2019).
41. Steuer, R. *Multiple Criteria Optimization: Theory, Computation and Application*; John Wiley: New York, NY, USA, 1986.
42. Vincke, P. *Multicriteria Decision-Aid*; John Wiley & Sons: Chichester, UK, 1992.
43. Zeleny, M. *Multiple Criteria Decision Making*; McGraw Hill: New York, NY, USA, 1982.
44. Salo, A.; Hämäläinen, R.P. Multicriteria Decision Analysis in Group Decision Processes. In *Handbook of Group Decision and Negotiation*; Kilgour, D.M., Eden, C., Eds.; Springer: Dordrecht, The Netherlands, 2012; pp. 269–284.
45. Koksalan, M.; Wallenius, J.; Zionts, S. *Multiple Criteria Decision Making. From Early History to the 21st Century*; World Scientific Publishing Co. Ltd.: Singapore, 2011.
46. Roy, B. *Multiple Criteria Decision Aid*; Wydawnictwo Naukowo—Techniczne: Warszawa, Poland, 1990.
47. Zmuda-Trzebiatowski, P. *Partycypacyjna Ocena Miejskich Projektów Transportowych (Participatory Evaluation of Urban Transport Projects)*; Poznan University of Technology Publishing House: Poznań, Poland, 2016.
48. Saaty, T. *The Analytic Hierarchy Process: Planning, Priority Setting, Resource Allocation*; McGraw-Hill: New York, NY, USA, 1980.
49. Saaty, T. Decision Making—The Analytic Hierarchy and Network Processes (AHP/ANP). *J. Syst. Sci. Syst. Eng.* **2004**, *13*, 1–34. [CrossRef]
50. Jacquet-Lagreze, E.; Siskos, J. Assessing a Set of Additive Utility Functions for Multicriteria Decision Making: The UTA Method. *Eur. J. Oper. Res.* **1982**, *10*, 151–164. [CrossRef]
51. Brans, J.P.; Mareschal, B.; Vincke, P. PROMETHEE: A new Family of Outranking Methods in MCDM. *Oper. Res.-Ger.* **1984**, *3*, 477–490.
52. Greco, S.; Ehrgott, M.; Figueira, J. (Eds.) *Multiple Criteria Decision Analysis: State of the Art Surveys*; Springer: New York, NY, USA, 2016.

53. Roubens, M. Preference Relations on Actions and Criteria in Multiple Decision Making. *Eur. J. Oper. Res.* **1982**, *10*, 51–55. [CrossRef]
54. Shimizu, K.; Kawabe, H.; Aiyoshi, E. A Theory for Interactive P-reference Optimization and its Algorithm-Generalized SWT method. *Trans. Inst. Electron. Commun. Eng. Jpn.* **1978**, *61*, 1075–1082.
55. Geoffrion, A.; Dyer, J.; Feinberg, A. An Interactive Approach for Multi-Criterion Optimization, with an Application to the Operation of an Academic Department. *Manag. Sci.* **1972**, *19*, 357–368. [CrossRef]
56. Jaszkiewicz, A.; Słowiński, R. The Light Beam Search Approach—An Overview of Methodology and Applications. *Eur. J. Oper. Res.* **1999**, *113*, 300–314. [CrossRef]
57. Benayoun, R.; De Montgolfier, J.; Tergny, J. Linear Programming with Multiple Objective Functions: Step Method (Stem). *Math. Program.* **1971**, *1*, 366–375. [CrossRef]
58. Korhonen, P.; Wallenius, J. *A Modification of the Zionts-Wallenius Multiple Criteria Methods for Nonlinear Utility Functions*; Helsinki School of Economics Press: Helsinki, Finland, 1985.
59. Żak, J. Multiple Criteria Decision Aiding in Road Transportation. Habilitation Thesis, Poznan University of Technology Publishing House, Poznań, Poland, 2005.
60. Choo, E.U.; Atkins, D.R. An Interactive Algorithm for Multicriteria Programming. *Comput. Oper. Res.* **1980**, *7*, 81–87. [CrossRef]
61. Wierzbicki, A. The Use of Reference Objectives in Multi-objective Optimization. In *MCDM Theory and Application*; Fandel, G., Gal, T., Eds.; Springer: Berlin, Germany, 1980; pp. 468–486.
62. MacCrimon, K.R. *Decision Making among Multiple Attribute Alternatives: A Survey and Consolidated Approach*; The Rand Corporation: Santa Monica, CA, USA, 1968.
63. Matarazzo, B. Mappac as a Compromise Between Outranking Methods and MAUT. *Eur. J. Oper. Res.* **1991**, *54*, 48–65. [CrossRef]
64. Kijewska, K.; Torbacki, W.; Iwan, S. Application of AHP and DEMATEL Methods in Choosing and Analysing the Measures for the Distribution of Goods in Szczecin Region. *Sustainability* **2018**, *10*, 2365. [CrossRef]
65. Hemalatha, S.; Dumpala, L.; Balakrishna, B. Service quality evaluation and ranking of container terminal operators through hybrid multi-criteria decision-making methods. *Asian J. Ship. Logist.* **2018**, *34*, 137–144. [CrossRef]
66. Lon, V.; Higashi, O.; Pheng, P. Analytic Hierarchy Process for Evaluation of Public Transport Policy Design in Phnom Penh City. Proceedings of the Eastern Asia Society for Transportation Studies 2013. Volume 9. Available online: https://www.researchgate.net/publication/301771384_Analytic_Hierarchy_Process_for_Evaluation_of_Public_Transport_Policy_Design_in_Phnom_Penh_City (accessed on 4 September 2018).
67. Al-Atawi, A.M.; Kumar, R.; Saleh, W. Transportation Sustainability Index for Tabuk City in Saudi Arabia: An Analytic Hierarchy Process. *Transport* **2016**, *31*, 47–55. [CrossRef]
68. López-Iglesias, E.; Peón, D.; Rodríguez-Álvarez, J. Mobility innovations for sustainability and cohesion of rural areas: A transport model and public investment analysis for Valdeorras (Galicia, Spain). *J. Clean. Prod.* **2018**, *172*, 3520–3534. [CrossRef]
69. De Luca, S. Public Engagement in Strategic Transportation Planning: An Analytic Hierarchy Process Based Approach. *Transp. Policy* **2014**, *33*, 110–124. [CrossRef]
70. Chowdhury, S.; Hadas, Y.; Gonzalez, V.A.; Schot, B. Public Transport Users' and Policy Makers' Perceptions of Integrated Public Transport Systems. *Transp. Policy* **2018**, *61*, 75–83. [CrossRef]
71. Nosal, K.; Solecka, K. Application of AHP Method for Multi-criteria Evaluation of Variants of the Integration of Urban Public Transport. *Transp. Res. Proc.* **2014**, *3*, 269–278. [CrossRef]
72. Taleai, M.; Yameqani, A.S. Integration of GIS, Remote Sensing and Multi-Criteria Evaluation Tools in the Search for Healthy Walking Paths. *KSCE J. Civ. Eng.* **2018**, *22*, 279–291. [CrossRef]
73. Kiciński, M.; Judt, W.; Kłosowiak, R. Wielokryterialna Ocena Wariantów Dojazdu Mieszkańców Aglomeracji Poznańskiej do Poznania. (Multiple criteria Assessment of Access Options for the Poznań Agglomeration residents). *Autobusy-Technika, Eksploatacja, Systemy Transportowe (Buses Technol. Oper. Transp. Syst.)* **2017**, *12*, 560–563.
74. Popiolek, N.; Thais, F. Multi-criteria analysis of innovation policies in favor of solar mobility in France by 2030. *Energy Policy* **2016**, *97*, 202–219. [CrossRef]
75. Solecka, K. Wielokryterialna Ocena Wariantów Zintegrowanego Miejskiego Transportu Publicznego w Krakowie (Multi-Criteria Assessment of the Options within the Integrated Urban Public Transport in Krakow). Ph.D. Thesis, Cracow University of Technology, Krakow, Poland, 2013.

76. Nassereddine, M.; Eskandari, H. An integrated MCDM approach to evaluate public transportation systems in Tehran. *Transp. Res. A-Pol.* **2017**, *106*, 427–439. [CrossRef]
77. Rudnicki, A. *Jakość Komunikacji Miejskiej (Quality of urban transport)*; Stowarzyszenie Inżynierów i Techników Komunikacji (Association of Engineers and Technicians of Communication, Cracow): Krakow, Poland, 1999.
78. Ivanović, I.; Grujičić, D.; Macura, D.; Jović, J.; Bojović, N. One Approach for Road Transport Project Selection. *Transp. Policy* **2013**, *25*, 22–29. [CrossRef]
79. Mardani, A.; Zavadskas, E.K.; Khalifah, Z.; Jusoh, A.; Nor, K. Multiple Criteria Decision-Making Techniques in Transportation Systems: A Systematic Review of the State of the Art Literature. *Transport* **2016**, *31*, 359–385. [CrossRef]
80. Macharis, C.; Bernardini, A. Reviewing the use of Multi-Criteria Decision Analysis for the Evaluation of Transport Projects: Time for a Multi-Actor Approach. *Transp. Policy* **2015**, *37*, 177–186. [CrossRef]

© 2019 by the authors. Licensee MDPI, Basel, Switzerland. This article is an open access article distributed under the terms and conditions of the Creative Commons Attribution (CC BY) license (http://creativecommons.org/licenses/by/4.0/).

Article

A Novel Hybrid Evolutionary Data-Intelligence Algorithm for Irrigation and Power Production Management: Application to Multi-Purpose Reservoir Systems

Zaher Mundher Yaseen [1], Mohammad Ehteram [2], Md. Shabbir Hossain [3], Chow Ming Fai [4], Suhana Binti Koting [5], Nuruol Syuhadaa Mohd [5], Wan Zurina Binti Jaafar [5], Haitham Abdulmohsin Afan [5,*], Lai Sai Hin [5], Nuratiah Zaini [6], Ali Najah Ahmed [4] and Ahmed El-Shafie [5]

1. Faculty of Civil Engineering, Ton Duc Thang University, Ho Chi Minh City, Vietnam; yaseen@tdtu.edu.vn
2. Department of Water Engineering and Hydraulic Structures, Faculty of Civil Engineering, Semnan University, Semnan 35131-19111, Iran; mohammdehteram@semnan.ac.ir
3. School of Energy, Geoscience, Infrastructure and Society, Department of Civil Engineering, Heriot-Watt University, Putrajaya 62200, Malaysia; m.hossain@hw.ac.uk or realism007@gmail.com
4. Institute of Energy Infrastructure (IEI), Civil Engineering Department, Universiti Tenaga Nasional, Kajang 43000, Selangor, Malaysia; chowmf@uniten.edu.my (C.M.F.); mahfoodh@uniten.edu.my (A.N.A.)
5. Civil Engineering Department, Faculty of Engineering, University of Malaya, Kuala Lumpur 50603, Malaysia; suhana_koting@um.edu.my (S.B.K.); n_syuhadaa@um.edu.my (N.S.M.); wzurina@um.edu.my (W.Z.B.J.); laish@um.edu.my (L.S.H.); elshafie@um.edu.my (A.E.-S.)
6. Department of Civil Engineering, College of Engineering, Universiti Tenaga Nasional, Kajang 43000, Selangor, Malaysia; Nur_Atiah@uniten.edu.my
* Correspondence: haitham.afan@gmail.com

Received: 25 December 2018; Accepted: 19 February 2019; Published: 2 April 2019

Abstract: Multi-purpose advanced systems are considered a complex problem in water resource management, and the use of data-intelligence methodologies in operating such systems provides major advantages for decision-makers. The current research is devoted to the implementation of hybrid novel meta-heuristic algorithms (e.g., the bat algorithm (BA) and particle swarm optimization (PSO) algorithm) to formulate multi-purpose systems for power production and irrigation supply. The proposed hybrid modelling method was applied for the multi-purpose reservoir system of Bhadra Dam, which is located in the state of Karnataka, India. The average monthly demand for irrigation is 142.14 (10^6 m^3), and the amount of released water based on the new hybrid algorithm (NHA) is 141.25 (10^6 m^3). Compared with the shark algorithm (SA), BA, weed algorithm (WA), PSO algorithm, and genetic algorithm (GA), the NHA decreased the computation time by 28%, 36%, 39%, 82%, and 88%, respectively, which represents an excellent enhancement result. The amount of released water based on the proposed hybrid method attains a more reliable index for the volumetric percentage and provides a more effective operation rule for supplying the irrigation demand. Additionally, the average demand for power production is 18.90 (10^6 kwh), whereas the NHA produces 18.09 (10^6 kwh) of power. Power production utilizing the NHA's operation rule achieved a sufficient magnitude relative to that of stand-alone models, such as the BA, PSO, WA, SA, and GA. The excellent proficiency of the developed intelligence expert system is the result of the hybrid structure of the BA and PSO algorithm and the substitution of weaker solutions in each algorithm with better solutions from other algorithms. The main advantage of the proposed NHA is its ability to increase the diversity of solutions and hence avoid the worst possible solutions obtained using BA, that is, preventing a decrease in local optima. In addition, the NHA enhances the convergence rate obtained using the PSO algorithm. Hence, the proposed NHA as an intelligence model could contribute to providing reliable solutions for complex multi-purpose reservoir systems to optimize the operation rule for similar reservoir systems worldwide.

Keywords: hybrid expert system; bat algorithm; particle swarm optimization algorithm; multi-purpose system; water resource management

1. Introduction

Water resource management attempts to control water scarcity during successive drought periods [1]. Climate change phenomena and increasing population demands cause serious natural dilemmas that necessitate the operation of an optimal and reliable system for managing water resources [2–4]. The optimal operation of stored water resources in the form of reservoirs behind dams is an important and complicated issue for decision-makers and designers worldwide, because optimal operations can decrease the expenditure of constructing large dams for policymakers in the water resource management field [5]. Thus, several studies have investigated the optimal operation of reservoirs to satisfy downstream consumer demands and supply water based on high certainty [6–8]. Recently, mathematical models and evolutionary algorithms have been used in the management and planning of water resources [9–12]. The problem with optimal operations related to water reservoirs can be defined within the framework of an optimization problem [13–15]. Thus, meta-heuristic algorithms, which are powerful tools, are used for solving such problems [16]. The water supply problem includes several factors, such as environmental, municipal, and agricultural supply demands [10,17]. Consequently, solving these real-life problems can promote comprehensive visions and plans for the improved management of water resource applications. Various challenges are observed in solving the reservoir operation problem, including the stochasticity in the system input and the uncertainties in the computation of non-linear factors, such as water loss from the reservoir. In addition, the needs of the stakeholders influence the allocation of the reservoir water, and accommodating these needs in the operation of the reservoir is a complex task for decision-makers [18–22]. Furthermore, climate change is one of the most influential variables that might negatively affect the pattern of the water supply, and addressing these problems is critical for decision-makers. Therefore, defining an appropriate optimization algorithm with effective mathematical models is essential to providing effective operation guidance and informing comprehensive planning for current and future periods. The successful determination of optimal operation procedures for reservoir water systems could provide decision-makers with effective tools to optimize the allocation and distribution of these resources [23–25]. In fact, most mathematical models, such as nonlinear programming, cannot be accurately adapted with multi-objective problems and perform the optimization procedure in a reasonable time period. In addition, these models should be able to consider effective parameters that influence the optimization process, such as climate change conditions or uncertain inflow to reservoirs [10]. Furthermore, in a few cases, the proper identification of dam and reservoir water system features (complex problems) requires the application of optimization tools as well as water allocation tools, such as game theory methods, to effectively operate the system [23–25]. Therefore, optimization algorithms capable of receiving and handling large data (non-stationary and stochastic in nature) under different climate change conditions could be used as effective tools for planning and managing water resources. Notably, models that are not limited to one specific problem or one particular boundary condition might not suitable for dam and reservoir water systems, because reservoir operation problems usually present different boundary conditions and are influenced by climate change conditions [25]. The water released for irrigation demands is very important because the development of agriculture in a basin is dependent on the fair allocation to the downstream consumers [17]. Therefore, supplying enough water to meet irrigation water demands requires accurate planning to avoid the risk of serious irrigation deficiencies, which will negatively affect crop production. In addition, water released from the reservoir is dependent on the physical characteristics of the dam and reservoir system, and these characteristics can be highly non-linear, such as the interrelationship among the elevation, surface area, and storage in the reservoir [18]. In this context, generating optimal operation rules for water release based on nonlinear or linear objective functions with different constraints is considered an important problem for policymakers [20].

1.1. Background

Many research efforts have been developed to investigate the potential of using meta-heuristic algorithms to generate optimal operation rules for dams and reservoir water systems. The honey bee optimization algorithm (HBOA) with a mutation operator has been utilized to minimize hydropower deficits [25]. This algorithm has been applied in multiple reservoirs, such as the Karun and Dez reservoirs located in southern Iran. The minimum and maximum operational storage for Dez and Karun are set to (453 and 2813) and (1518 and 2802) MCM (million of cubic metres), respectively. The researchers performed a comprehensive sensitivity analysis and compared the results with those of the genetic algorithm (GA) to verify the outstanding performance of this method. The results indicated that the improved HBOA could be a global solution based on less iteration than that of the GA and the particle swarm optimization (PSO) algorithm.

Genetic programming (GP) is one of the most effective optimization algorithms and has been applied for several optimization problems in the hydrology field. GP was used as an optimization tool to optimize the operation rules of a reservoir to meet the irrigation demands [26], where the released water was considered a decision variable. The methodology was applied to the Karaj reservoir as a case study. This reservoir is located on the Karaj River and has an active volume of 176×10^6 m^3 and an annual average inflow of 415.23×10^6 m^3. The released water based on the GA could meet downstream demand patterns effectively, and the annual average irrigation deficits based on the GA were 12% and 22% less than those achieved using the PSO algorithm and GA, respectively.

The PSO algorithm is a heuristic search tool used by Ostadrahimi et al. [27] to extract rule curves for optimizing the hydropower generation of multi-reservoir operations. The case study used to examine the PSO algorithm was a relatively small section of the Columbia River basin, which includes the Mica, Libby, and Grand Coulee reservoirs. The released water was considered the decision variable, and reservoir storage was considered the state variable. The results indicated that hydropower generation could be increased by approximately 12% and 15% using the PSO algorithm compared with the HBOA and GA, respectively. Additionally, the convergence rate experienced using the PSO algorithm was relatively faster than that of GA and HBOA.

Nonlinear order rule curves have been used with GAs for the operation of water systems with the aim of decreasing irrigation deficiencies, and the results have shown that released water based on the third-order rule curve could supply downstream demands well [28]. Another study conducted reservoir operations of a three-reservoir system (Karoon4, Khersan1, and Karoon3) via GP [29]. The capacities of those reservoirs are 2190, 332.55, and 2522×10^6 m^3, respectively. The aim of these studies was to minimize irrigation deficiencies. Downstream demands were supplied based on a volumetric reliability index of approximately 90%, while the supply for the downstream irrigation demand based on the GA was accompanied by high deficiencies during the operation period of the reservoir. Another study focused on the Karoon4 reservoir and utilized the water cycle algorithm (WCA) to increase the benefit of hydropower generation based on the released water, and the results showed that compared with the PSO algorithm and the GA, the WCA increased the annual benefit of hydropower generation by approximately 30% and 40%, respectively [30]. For the same reservoir, Haddad et al. [31] tested the biography-based optimization (BBO) algorithm for increasing hydropower generation. The results showed the high ability of the BBO algorithm based on a fast convergence speed and highly accurate computations.

An adaptive PSO algorithm was considered in another study [32]. This algorithm was modified based on the correction of the inertia coefficient. Additionally, the new method was used for multi-reservoir operations in a large-scale basin. The proposed method was implemented in the Three Gorges Project, with 42.23 bkW hydropower generation, and the XiLuoDo Project (XLDP), with 30.10 bkW. The new method had faster convergence and could yield solutions that were close to the global solution [32].

For the Karoon4 reservoir, Haddad et al. [31] tested the BBO algorithm for increasing hydropower generation. The results showed the high ability of the BBO algorithm based on a fast convergence speed and highly accurate computations.

The imperialist competitive algorithm (ICA) optimized ten system reservoirs with the aim of increasing power generation. The results showed that the ICA could increase annual power generation and yield the best solution based on fewer iterations during the convergence process [33].

A comparative study has been carried out by Azizipour et al. [8] to optimize the performance of a multi-reservoir system based on the weed algorithm (WA), GA, and PSO algorithm with the aim of decreasing irrigation deficiencies. This study focused on single and multi-reservoir operations of Dez reservoir, which has an average annual inflow to the reservoir of approximately 5950 million cubic meter per year. The results showed that the method could decrease the vulnerability index by approximately 12%, which reduced the deficiency of the operation based on the applied algorithm.

Another comparative study by Ehteram et al. [34] utilized the shark algorithm (SA) to optimize the performance of a multi-reservoir system for increasing hydropower generation in China. The maximum capacity of the hydropower plant was 600 MW. This algorithm is based on the rotational movement of sharks for escaping local optima. The SA could increase the convergence speed compared with the GA and PSO algorithms, and the annual power production was increased by approximately 20% and 40% compared with that of the PSO algorithm and GA, respectively.

The krill algorithm (KA) based on the swarm behaviors of krill is an advanced method used to increase the benefits of hydropower generation for multi-reservoir operations of the Timah reservoir located in Perlis, Malaysia [35]. This reservoir has a storage capacity between 28.74×106 and 40×106 m^3. The results indicated that compared with the PSO algorithm and the GA, the KA could increase the annual benefits of power generation by 12% and 15%, respectively. Additionally, the convergence velocity for the KA was considerable.

The spider monkey algorithm (SMA) has been applied to the Karun reservoir by Ehteram et al. [35] for increasing hydropower generation, where the algorithm is based on the personal and swarm efforts of monkeys to find the best position for acquiring food. The results indicated that the algorithm performed better than the bat algorithm (BA), PSO algorithm, and GA, because it seeks to realize global solutions and convergence velocities.

However, the previous algorithms have key problems. For example, the GA traps local optima for certain multi-reservoir systems or exhibits slow convergence for certain problems [35]. The PSO algorithm encounters immature solutions with early convergence, which is a problem for this algorithm [35]. The BA requires the accurate determination of random parameters, such as maximum frequency, loudness, and pulsation rate, and may also trap local optima for complex engineering problems [3]. Studies have attempted to solve the different weaknesses of the various algorithms. For example, one study used the hybrid gravitational search algorithm (GSA) with GA, where GSA was used to provide a basic solution domain of problems and then genetic operators within the GA were used for upgrading the solutions [36]. A novel PSO algorithm with mutation strategies was introduced to provide solutions, and was then updated by a time-varying acceleration PSO algorithm to achieve the optimal solutions [37]. A hybrid PSO–GA was used to improve the balance between exploration and exploitation ability of the PSO algorithm based on genetic operators [38]. A parameter-free penalty function for the BBO was used to solve reliability redundancy allocation problems [39]. An improved artificial bee colony (ABC) based on the foraging behavior of global and guided best honeybees was used to solve complex optimization tasks [40]. However, these different algorithms have different weaknesses that should be improved. Note that the motivation for exploring a more robust and stable meta-heuristic method for modelling reservoir operation systems is still an ongoing focus for research on water resources by expert system scholars.

1.2. Problem Statement and Novelty

The studied problem is highly complex, and the main motivation behind establishing the current research is to discover the optimal solution for multi-purpose hydropower systems. The complexity arises from the highly stochastic relationship between optimal reservoir releases and various hydrological elements (e.g., water storage, water loss, inflow amount, and actual water demand). The maximized hydropower production constraint is not the only predominant variable for the optimization function, however, irrigation demands and sustainable water storage are tremendously important variables that affect this function. Such conditions of the multi-reservoir water system make the generation of optimal operation rules using a particular optimization algorithm a great challenge for researchers and decision-makers. Therefore, relying on one optimization algorithm to solve such a complex optimization application may be insufficient even when using a highly advanced algorithm. The main concerns in multi-reservoir water systems in terms of optimization include the search for the global optima of the system domain and the time required for convergence. For example, the BA is a well-known meta-heuristic approach that functions as a suitable tool for solving optimization problems [41–43]. Bozorg-Haddad et al. [44] applied the BA for reservoir operations with the aim of increasing power generation, and although power production could be increased, the BA is accompanied by certain weaknesses. One of the main problems is trapped local optima, although the algorithm exhibited a relatively fast convergence rate [44]. Alternatively, the PSO algorithm is known as an effective optimization algorithm in terms of its searching ability to achieve the global optima [5,32,45]. The local and global versions of this algorithm provide direct solutions to attain the optimum solution, while its drawback is the slow convergence rate. Thus, the problems associated with the BA and PSO algorithm, that is, trapping in local optima and slow convergence, respectively, motivated the authors to conduct the current study.

In this study, a new method based on hybridizing two meta-heuristic model structures (BA and PSO algorithm), namely the new hybrid algorithm (NHA), is proposed and developed to generate optimal operation rules for a multi-purpose reservoir water system. Conceptually, the proposed NHA model intends to introduce a hybrid algorithm structure that can replace the weakness of each algorithm with other algorithms. The PSO algorithm is used based on a hybrid framework to improve the BA's ability to search for the global optima, while the BA is used to speed up the convergence rate. In this fashion, the main innovation of this paper is the proposition of an optimization model that can generate optimal operation rules for multi-purpose water operating systems with a high ability to search for global optima with a relatively high convergence rate.

Therefore, the novelty of the current research is focused mainly on two points: (1) introducing a hybrid optimization algorithm that can expand the search domain with sufficient diversity to avoid trapping the local optima and (2) creating an algorithm that is flexible enough to handle multi-purpose systems. To this end, the proposed algorithm should be examined using different benchmark functions to ensure its ability to achieve the global optima. In addition, the algorithm should be applied to a multi-purpose reservoir with different demands, and its results should be examined against the required system's purposes to achieve effective and reliable operations. Furthermore, the current research provides insights on several performance indexes proposed to evaluate the achieved results.

1.3. Research Objectives

The main objective of this study is to propose the NHA to generate optimal operation rules for a multi-purpose reservoir water system, which is of importance for water resource supply and management worldwide. Therefore, a multi-purpose reservoir water system in India, namely the Bhadra reservoir system, which both supplies irrigation demands and produces power, is used in this study to examine the proposed optimization algorithm. In addition, several optimization algorithms and the proposed hybrid algorithm were applied to examine the effectiveness of the proposed NHA over the other algorithms. On the basis of the operations, a comprehensive analysis of the ability of the NHA to achieve the global optima and the convergence rate was carried out.

2. Methodological Overview

2.1. Bat Algorithm (BA)

Bats can produce sounds and receive the echo of the sounds from surrounding objects [41]. Thus, they can identify an obstacle from prey based on the received frequencies. The BA is based on the following assumptions:

- Echolocation is used by all bats, and this ability is helpful for identifying prey from obstacles.
- Bats fly at a random velocity, vl, and at a random location, xl. The frequency of a bat is fl. A0 and λ represent the loudness and wavelength of bats, respectively.
- The loudness of bats varies from A0 (i.e., a large positive number) to Amin.

The velocity, location, and frequency are updated based on the following equations [46]:

$$f_l = f_{min} + (f_{max} - f_{min}) \times \beta, \quad (1)$$

$$v_l(t) = [y_l(t-1) - Y_*] \times f_l, \quad (2)$$

$$y_l(t) = y_l(t-1) + v_l(t) \times t, \quad (3)$$

where f_l is the frequency; f_{min} is the minimum frequency; f_{max} is the maximum frequency; β is the random value between 0 and 1; Y_* is the best position of bats; $v_l(t)$ is the current velocity of bats; $y_l(t)$ is the current position of bats; and t is the time step.

A local search is considered based on the following formula using a random walk algorithm, and this level is referred to as the random fly level [41,42].

$$y(t) = y(t-1) + \varepsilon A(t), \quad (4)$$

where ε is a random value between -1 and 1 and $A(t)$ is the loudness.

The loudness (A_t) and pulsation rate (r_l) are updated in each iteration of the algorithms. The value for loudness decreases and the pulsation rate increases when the bats find their prey. The pulsation rate for the generated sounds is updated based on the following equation [47]:

$$r_l^{t+1} = r_l^0[1 - \exp(-\gamma t)] A_l^{t+1} = \alpha A_l^t, \quad (5)$$

where r_l^{t+1} represents the new pulsation rate and α and γ are constant values. Figure 1 shows the different levels for the BA.

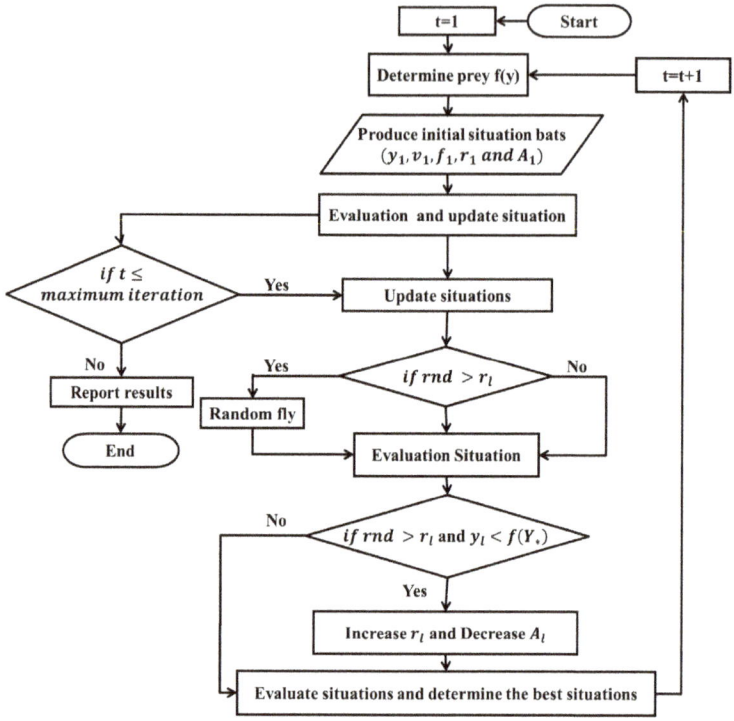

Figure 1. Bat algorithm procedure (rnd: random number).

2.2. Particle Swarm Optimization (PSO) Algorithm

If the search space is considered in the D dimension, the position of the particles is shown by $X_i = (x_{i1}, x_{i2}, \ldots, x_{iD})^T$, whereas the velocity is represented by $V_i = (v_{i1}, v_{i2}, \ldots, v_{iD})^T$. $P_i = (p_{i1}, p_{i2}, \ldots, p_{id})^T$ is considered the best prior calculated position, and the index g in the equations is used to determine the best particle among other particles based on the quality of the objective function. The position and velocity for the PSO algorithm are updated based on the following equations [48]:

$$v_{id}^{n+1} = \chi \left[w v_{id}^n + c_1 r_1^n \frac{(p_{id} - x^n{}_{id})}{\Delta t} + c_2 r_2^n \frac{\left(p_{gd} - x_{id}^n\right)}{\Delta t} \right], \quad (6)$$

$$x_{id}^{n+1} = x_{id}^n + \Delta t v_{id}^{n+1}, \quad (7)$$

where v_{id}^{n+1} is the new velocity for the particles; χ is the constriction coefficient; w is the inertia coefficient; c_1 and c_2 are the acceleration coefficients; Δt is the time step; n is the time index; and x_{id}^{n+1} is the new position of the particles.

First, the random parameters, as well as the initial velocity and position, are considered for the PSO algorithm [49]. The objective function is calculated for each member, and the best particle among the remaining particles is determined; then, the velocity and position are updated based on Equations (6) and (7), respectively [46,49]. Thus, the convergence criteria are stopped, and if the algorithm is satisfied, the algorithm finishes; otherwise, the algorithm returns to the first step. It should be noted here that the used version of the PSO in the current study is the modified one over the standard version. In this version, the one used, the weights are computed based on the following dynamical form equation:

$$w = w_{end} + (w_{start} - w_{end})\left(1 - \frac{T}{G_{max}}\right) \leftarrow if\left(p_{gd} \neq x_{id}\right)$$
$$w = w_{end} \leftarrow if\left(p_{gd}\right) = x_{id} \tag{8}$$

where T is the number of iterations, $T \in [0, G_{max})$; pgd is the global bets position; wstart is the initial weight; and w_{end} is the final value for the weight in the maximum iteration. Thus, the used PSO is an improved PSO that outperforms other versions.

2.3. New Hybrid Algorithm (NHA)

The NHA is considered based on a parallel structure. Each algorithm acts based on an independent process, and then the output population of each algorithm is divided into subgroups (see Figure 2). Subsequently, a communication strategy shares information between the PSO algorithm and BA. The K agent of each algorithm, as the best member, is copied into the other algorithm instead of the worst solutions of the other algorithm. Thus, the worst solution achieved based on the BA is replaced using the one attained using the PSO algorithm. The total size population for the NHA is N, and N/2 represents the size population for the BA and PSO algorithm. R in Figure 2 represents the number of communication steps between the PSO algorithm and the BA, t denotes the current iteration count, and they are at the same level because two algorithms act simultaneously. Both the BA and PSO algorithms are executed concurrently within the same time step, and the achieved solutions at each time step are swapped between them synchronously. Accordingly, the NHA starts from an initial population as decision variables and ends when the convergence criteria are satisfied.

The NHA is based on the following levels:

- The random parameters are initialized for two algorithms, and then the velocity and position vectors are considered for the BA and PSO algorithms;
- The objective function is individually calculated for the two algorithms, and then the best member is determined for the two algorithms;
- The velocity and position are updated for the BA based on Equations (1)–(3), and the velocity and position are updated based on Equations (6) and (7), respectively;
- The K agent, as the best member of each algorithm, is copied to the other algorithms, which are substituted with the worst solutions of the other algorithm;
- The convergence criteria are checked, and if the algorithm is satisfied, the algorithm finishes; otherwise, the algorithm returns to the second step.

Although the proposed NHA procedure is established with a strong linkage between the BA and PSO algorithm, the NHA still faces a challenge during initialization for several random parameters for both algorithms. In addition, there is a need to adapt the random parameters for both the BA and the PSO algorithm within the definition of the NHA communication to enable it to simultaneously update within the mathematical model of the reservoir. This step adds more complexity within the proposed NHA for generating the operation rule to extract the optimal decision variables accurately for both algorithms.

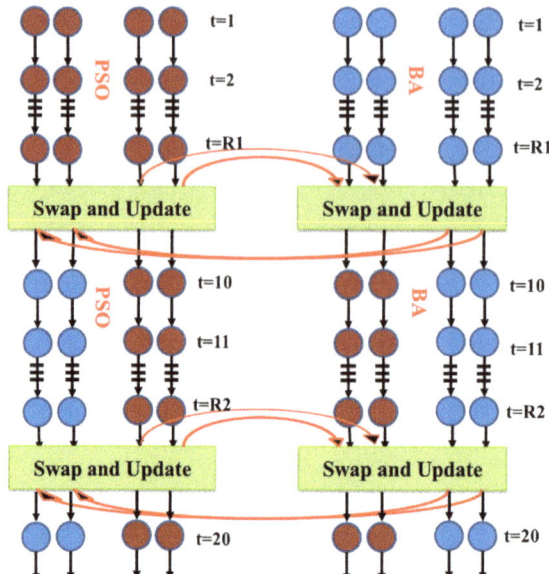

Figure 2. New hybrid algorithm (NHA) diagram of the hybridized particle swarm optimization (PSO)–bat algorithm (BA) with a communication strategy.

2.4. Weed Algorithm (WA)

The WA is based on the characteristics of weeds [50]. Weeds can grow spontaneously and adapt to their surroundings easily. The following assumptions are considered for the WA [34]:

- Weeds are grown based on seeds, which are spread throughout the environment.
- Weeds that grow close to each other are known as a colony, and they can produce seeds based on their equality.
- Each produced seed distributes randomly throughout the environment.
- The algorithm finishes when the number of weeds reaches the maximum number.
- The different levels for the WA are based on the following levels:
- First, the initial population of the algorithm (Pinitial) is considered, and the position of each weed in the environment (i.e., search space) is considered a decision variable.
- The next level is known as the reproduction level. Reproduction causes new seeds to be produced from colonies, and the maximum and minimum numbers of seeds are $(N_0 S_{max})$ and $(N_0 S_{min})$, respectively (see Figure 3). Reproduction is an important level for the WA because there are two group solutions in the evolutionary algorithms. Appropriate solutions have a high chance of reproduction to continue the production of the best member for the next generation, and inappropriate solutions may have a weak chance of reproduction; however, they may have important information for the next levels of the algorithm. Thus, reproduction may be extended to inappropriate solutions that are not removed from the population, and they can continue their life based on suitable reproduction and the improvement in their quality. Some inappropriate solutions have important information, and this information can be used for the next levels of the algorithm.
- The produced seeds are distributed in the search space based on a normal distribution and zero mean.

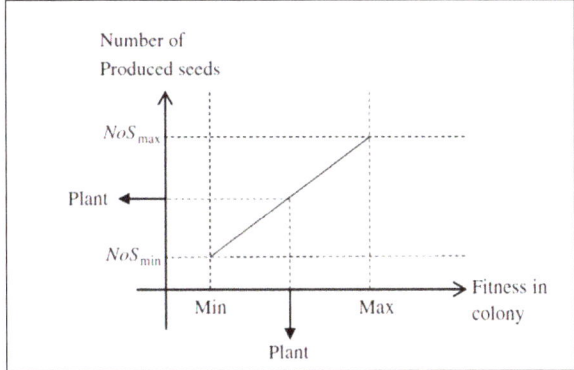

Figure 3. Levels of reproduction for each plant with respect to fitness.

The standard deviation for the distribution of seeds is variable and calculated based on the following equation [34,50]:

$$\sigma_{iter} = \frac{(iter_{max} - iter)}{(iter_{max})^n} \left(\sigma_{initial} - \sigma_{final} \right), \tag{9}$$

where σ_{iter} is the standard deviation; $iter_{max}$ is the maximum iteration number; $iter$ is the current iteration number; $\sigma_{initial}$ is the initial standard deviation; n is the nonlinear modulus; and σ_{final} is the final standard deviation. Equation (9) shows that the distribution of the population is based on the standard deviation.

If weeds cannot produce seeds, they become extinct. Additionally, a number of seeds can be produced based on weeds limited to P_{max}, and there is competition among weeds because weeds of poor quality should be removed for population balance. Figure 4 shows the WA procedure.

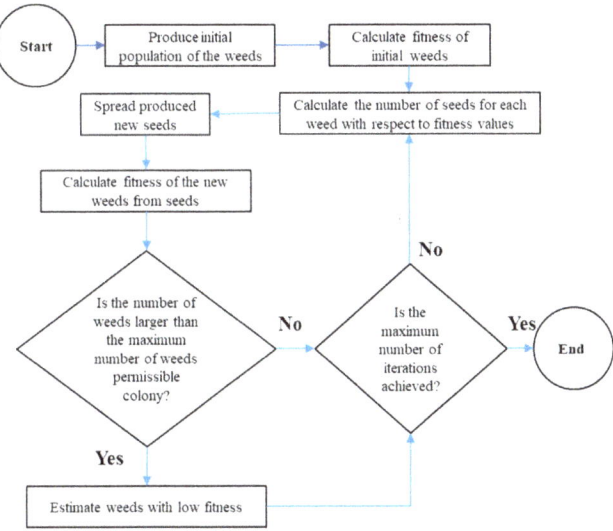

Figure 4. Weed algorithm (WA) procedure.

2.5. Shark Algorithm (SA)

Sharks have powerful olfactory receptors and can find their prey based on these receptors [51]. This algorithm acts based on the following assumptions [35]:

- Injured fish are considered to be prey for sharks, as fish bodies distribute blood throughout the sea. Additionally, injured fish have negligible speeds compared with sharks.
- The blood is distributed into the sea regularly, and the effect of water flow is not considered for blood distribution.
- Each injured fish is considered as one blood production resource for sharks; therefore, the olfactory receptors help sharks find their prey.
- The initial population for sharks is shown by $[X_1^1, X_2^1, \ldots, X_{NP}^1]$, $NP = population(size)$. Each solution candidate or shark position can have the following components based on the following equation:

$$X_i^1 = \left[x_{i,1}^1, x_{i,2}^1, \ldots x_{i,ND}^1\right], \quad (10)$$

where X_i^1 is the initial position vector; $x^1{}_{ij}$ is the jth dimension of the shark position; and ND is the number of decision variables. The initial velocity for sharks is shown by $V_i^1 = \left[v_{i,1}^1, v_{i,2}^1, \ldots, v_{i,ND}^1\right]$. The velocity components are considered based on the following equation:

$$V_i^1 = \left[v_{i,1}^1, v_{i,2}^1, \ldots, v_{i,ND}^1\right], i = 1, \ldots NP, \quad (11)$$

where V_i^1 is the initial velocity vector and $v^1{}_{ij}$ is the jth dimension of the shark velocity. When the shark receives greater odour intensity, it moves faster towards its prey. Thus, if the odour intensity is considered an objective function, the velocity changes with the variation in the objective function based on the following equation:

$$V_i^k = \eta_k . R_1 . \nabla(OF)\Big|_{x_i^k}, \quad (12)$$

where η_k is the number between 0 and 1; R_1 is the random number; and OF is the objective function.

There is inertia in the shark's movement, which should be considered in the shark velocity; thus, Equation (12) is modified based on the following equation:

$$v_{i,j}^k = \eta_k . R_1 . \frac{\partial (OF)}{\partial x_j} + \alpha . R_2 . v_{i,j}^{k-1}, \quad (13)$$

where α is the inertia coefficient and R_2 is the random value between 0 and 1.

Sharks have a specific domain for velocity. Their maximum velocity is 80 km/hr, and their minimum velocity is 20 km/hr. Thus, a velocity limit is considered, and Equation (13) is modified based on the following equation:

$$\left|v_{i,j}^k\right| = \min\left[\left|\eta_k . R_1 . \frac{\partial (OF)}{\partial x_j}\right|_{x_{i,j}^k} + \alpha_k . R_2 . v_{i,j}^{k-1}\right|, \left|\beta_k . v_{i,j}^{k-1}\right|\right], \quad (14)$$

where β_k is the velocity limiter. Then, the shark position is updated based on the following equation:

$$Y_i^{k+1} = X_i^k + V_i^k \Delta t_k, \quad (15)$$

where Δt_k is the time step and Y_i^{k+1} is the new position for the shark. Sharks have a rotational movement operator. This operator indicates which shark can escape from the local optima, and the shark position based on the rotational movement is modified based on the following equation:

$$Z_i^{k+1,m} = Y_i^{k+1} + R_3.Y_i^{k+1}, m = 1,\ldots, M, \tag{16}$$

where $Z_i^{k+1,m}$ is the new shark position and M is the number of local searches for the sharks. Figure 5 shows the SA process.

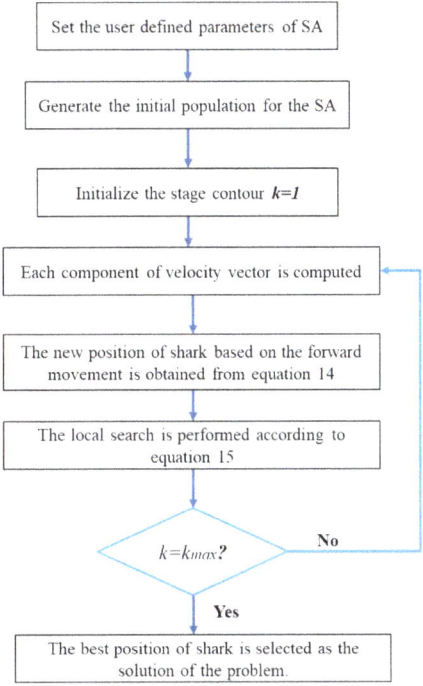

Figure 5. Shark algorithm (SA) procedure.

2.6. Genetic Algorithm (GA)

First, the initial population for the GA consists of chromosomes, and the next population for the next generation is produced based on a repetitive process. The members with the best quality are selected, and the crossover operators and mutation operators are applied to the population to improve the solutions. The crossover is considered based on the following equation [35]:

$$Pop_i^{new} = \alpha Pop_i^{old} + (1-\alpha) Pop_j^{old}, \tag{17}$$

$$Pop_j^{new} = \alpha Pop_j^{old} + (1-\alpha) Pop_i^{old}, \tag{18}$$

where Pop_i^{new} is the i-th child; Pop_i^{old} is the i-th parent; Pop_j^{old} is the j-th parent; α is the random number; and Pop_j^{new} is the j-th child. The mutation is considered based on the following equation:

$$Pop_{j,i}^{new} = Var_{j,i}^{law} + \beta\left(Var_{j,i}^{h_i} - Var_{j,i}^{law}\right), \tag{19}$$

where $Pop_{j,i}^{new}$ is the i-th new gene in the j-th chromosome; $Var_{j,i}^{law}$ is the lower limit of the i-th gene in the j-th chromosome; $Var_{j,i}^{hi}$ is the upper limit of the i-th gene in the j-th chromosome; and β is the random number. This crossover causes a change in the genes between two selected members when producing a new member. The mutation operator changes the chromosomes when producing new members.

3. Case Study and Modelling Procedure

3.1. Benchmark Function

To test the superiority of the NHA, five global optimization problems were selected to compare the new method with the other methods (Table 1). A unimodal function has a single extremum, and multi-modal functions have multiple extrema; thus, if the exploration ability of the algorithm is weak, it cannot search the entire problem space.

Table 1. Details of benchmark functions.

Test Problem	Objective Function	Search Range	Optimum Value	Dimension	Characteristic	Acceptable Error (AE)
Schwefel function [52]	$f_1(x) = \sum_{i=1}^{D} \left(\sum_{j=1}^{i} x_j \right)^2$	$[-100, 100]$	0	30	Unimodal	1.0×10^{-3}
Rastrigin [52]	$f_2(x) = 10D + \sum_{i=1}^{D} |x_i^2 - 10\cos(2\pi x_i)|$	$[-5.12, 5.12]$	0	30	Multimodal	5.0×10^{-1}
Dekkers and Aarts [52]	$f_3(x) = 10^5 x_1^2 + x_2^2 - (x_1^2 + x_2^2) + 10^{-5}(x_1^2 + x_2^2)^4$	$[-20, 20]$	$-24{,}777$	2	Unimodal	1.0×10^{-5}
Step function [52]	$f_4(x) = \sum_{i=1}^{D} (|x_i + 0.5|)^2$	$[-100, 100]$	0	30	Unimodal	1.0×10^{-3}
Axis parallel function [52]	$f_5(x) = \sum_{i=1}^{D} i x_i^2$	$[-5.12, 5.12]$	0	30	Unimodal	1.0×10^{-5}

3.2. Multi-Purpose Reservoir Operation

A multi-purpose reservoir system named Bhadra was considered to evaluate the NHA. The Bhadra Dam is located at 13°42′ N and 75°38′20″ E in the state of Karnataka. The location is characterized by a mean precipitation value of approximately 2320 mm, and 90% of the precipitation occurs during the monsoon period. Bhadra is a multi-purpose system reservoir that supplies water for demand and power production [53]. The active storage capacity for this reservoir is 1784 Mm^3. The irrigation area is 6367 ha, and the total area of the left and right bank canals is 87,512 ha. Figure 6a shows the schematization of the dam and reservoir's basin, and Figure 6b shows the geographical location of the catchment area of the basin. The features of the reservoir can be seen in Table 2. Figure 6a shows the details for the system and Figure 6b shows the location of system on the river section. The command area for the river basin is 162,818 ha.

There are three turbines in this basin. The turbines are located along the right bank canal, left bank canal, and riverbed. The operating head for the right bank canal (Phase1) varies from 38.564 to 54.41 m, that of the left bank canal (Phase2) varies from 36.88 m to 56.69 m, and that of the riverbed varies from 36.88 to 55.12 m. When the water height is within the domain of the defined operation head, it moves in the direction of the turbines; otherwise, it is used for irrigation demands. Figure 7 shows the schematic of the multi-purpose system.

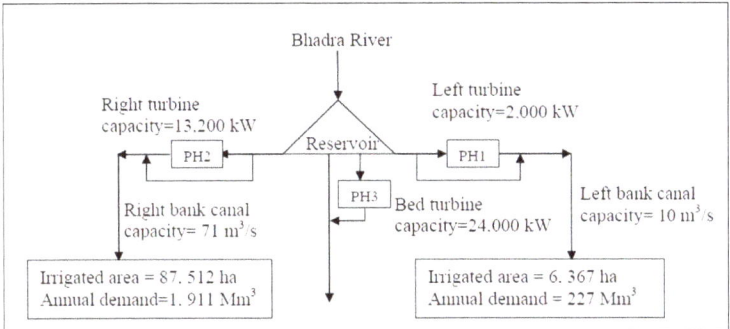

(a) Dam schematic.

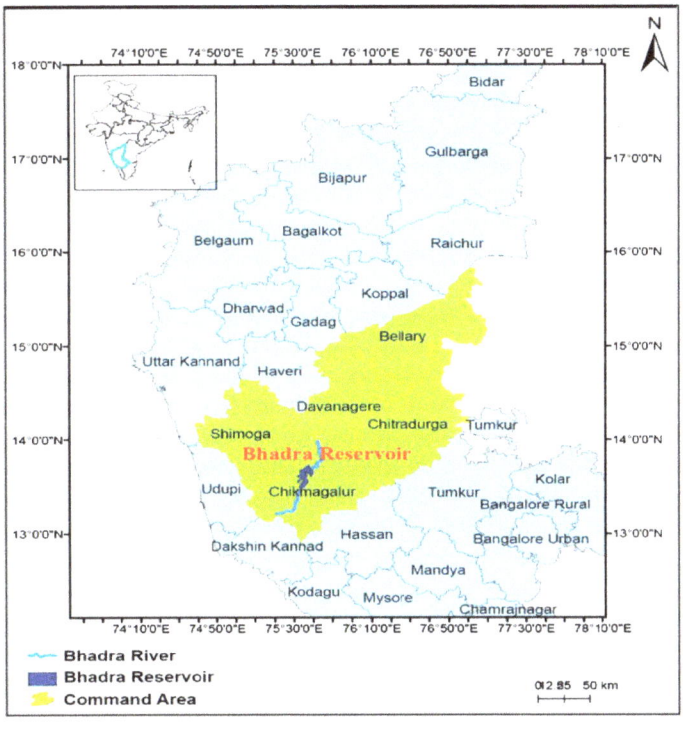

(b) River Basin.

Figure 6. (a) Schematic diagram of the Bhadra reservoir system; (b) location of basin.

The necessary data, such as the monthly inflow, were obtained from the Water Resource Development Organization (Bangalore) and cover 10 years from 1990–1991 to 2000–2001. Semi-dry, garden, and paddy crops are important for this basin. The irrigation demand and power production should be supplied for the downstream region. Thus, the first objective function is to minimize irrigation deficiencies, and the second objective function is related to maximizing power production. Equation (20) is used for minimizing irrigation deficiencies:

$$SQDV = \sum_{t=1}^{12}(D_{l,t} - R_{l,t})^2 + \sum_{t=1}^{12}(D_{r,t} - R_{r,t})^2, \qquad (20)$$

where $SQDV$ is the square deviation in the demand and released water; $D_{l,t}$ is the demand for the left bank canal; $D_{r,t}$ is the demand for the right bank canal; $R_{l,t}$ is the released water for the right bank canal; and $R_{r,t}$ is the released water for the left bank canal.

Table 2. Salient features of the Bhadra system.

Description	Quantity
Gross storage capacity	2025 Mm^3
Live storage capacity	1784 Mm^3
Dead storage capacity	241 Mm^3
Average annual inflow	2845 Mm^3
Left bank canal capacity	10 m^3/s
Right bank canal capacity	71 m^3/s
Left bank turbine capacity	2000 kW
Right bank turbine capacity (Phase2)	13,200 kW
Riverbed turbine capacity (Phase3)	24,000 kW

The second objective function is defined based on the following equation:

$$E = \sum_{t=1}^{12}(k_1 R_{l,t} H_{l,t} + k_2 R_{r,t} H_{r,t} + k_3 R_{b,t} H_{b,t}), \qquad (21)$$

where E is the produced energy; k_1, k_2, and k_3 represent the power coefficients; r is the right side of the bank canal, $R_{l,t}$, $R_{r,t}$, and $R_{b,t}$ represent the released water for the left and right bank canals and the river bed, respectively; and $H_{l,t}$, $H_{r,t}$, and $H_{b,t}$ represent the net head for the left and right canals and the riverbed, respectively. The head values are extracted based on a regression continuity Equation (21) based on storage values. The released water volume is a decision variable to be applied annually for ten years during the period between 1991 and 2000.

The continuity equation is defined based on the following equation:

$$S_{t+1} = S_t + I_t - (R_{lt} + R_{rt} + R_{bt} + EV_t + OVF_t), \qquad (22)$$

where S_{t+1} is the storage at time $t + 1$; I_t is the inflow at time t; EV_t is the evaporation loss; and OVF_t is the overflow.

The constraints are considered based on the following equations:

- The storage constraint is as follows:

$$S_{min} \leq S_t \leq S_{max}, \qquad (23)$$

where S_{max} is the maximum storage and S_{min} is the minimum storage.
- The power production constraints are as follows:

$$k_1 R_{l,t} H_{l,t} \leq E_{1,max}, \qquad (24)$$

$$k_2 R_{r,t} H_{r,t} \leq E_{2,max}, \qquad (25)$$

$$k_3 R_{bt} H_{bt} \leq E_{3,max}, \qquad (26)$$

where $E_{1,\max}$, $E_{2,\max}$, and $E_{3,\max}$ represent the maximum energy for the left canal, right canal, and riverbed, respectively.
- The canal capacity constraints are as follows:

$$R_{l,t} \leq C_{l,\max}, \tag{27}$$

$$R_{r,t} \leq C_{r,\max}, \tag{28}$$

where $C_{l,\max}$ is the maximum capacity for the left canal and $C_{r,\max}$ is the maximum capacity for the right canal.
- The irrigation demands are as follows:

$$D_{l,t}^{\min} \leq R_{l,t} \leq D_{l,r}^{\max}, \tag{29}$$

$$D_{r,t}^{\min} \leq R_{r,t} \leq D_{r,t}^{\max}, \tag{30}$$

where $D_{l,t}^{\min}$ is the minimum demand for the left canal; $D_{l,r}^{\max}$ is the maximum demand for the left canal; $D_{r,t}^{\min}$ is the minimum demand for the right canal; and $D_{r,t}^{\max}$ is the maximum demand for the right canal.
- The steady storage constraint is as follows:

$$S_{13} = S_1. \tag{31}$$

This constraint has been considered to guarantee no change in reservoir storage at the beginning of each cycle of operation in order to avoid the obstacle of reservoir carryover storage.

The above constraint causes the state condition to occur because the storage condition at the end of the year must be equivalent to that at the beginning of the year. There are two objective functions with opposite conditions; one objective function should be maximized, and the other objective function should be minimized. Thus, a weighted method is used to handle these two factors. There are two weight coefficients in Equation (32), and the irrigation demand has greater priority in this case study. When the irrigation demands are supplied, water is used for power production. Thus, Kumar and Reddy [53] suggested values of $wt_1 = 100$ and $wt_2 = -1$ because the irrigation demands have greater importance for policymakers in this basin. The weighted aggregate sum product assessment is used to estimate and obtain accurate values for the weights [53]. Different weights are considered for different terms within the objective function, and their relative indexes are calculated to determine the best values for weights using NHA. Afterward, a ranking process is carried out utilizing the associated indexes for all the allocated weights. Finally, the multi-criteria decision process is used to identify the best allocated weight combination based on the highest rank.

The suggested values for these coefficients were calculated based on a sensitivity analysis by considering the variation in the objective function versus the variation in the value of the weight coefficients. Thus, the following equation is suggested for reservoir operations, and the aim of the problem is to minimize the following objective function:

$$F = wt_1 \sum_{t=1}^{12} \left[\left(\frac{D_{l,t}-R_{l,t}}{D_{l,t}}\right)^2 + \left(\frac{D_{r,t}-R_{r,t}}{D_{r,t}}\right) \right] + wt_2 \sum_{t=1}^{12} \left[\frac{E_{1,\max}-k_1 R_{l,t} H_{l,t}}{E_{1,\max}} + \frac{E_{2,\max}-k_2 R_{r,t} H_{r,t}}{E_{2,\max}} + \frac{E_{3,\max}-k_2 R_{b,t} H_{b,t}}{E_{3,\max}} \right], \tag{32}$$

where wt_1 and wt_2 represent the weight values; $E_{1,\max}$, $E_{2,\max}$, and $E_{3,\max}$ represent the maximum energy for the left canal, right canal, and riverbed, respectively; k_1, k_2, and k_3 represent the power coefficients; $R_{l,t}$, $R_{r,t}$, and $R_{b,t}$ represent the released water for the left and right bank canals and the riverbed, respectively; $H_{l,t}$, $H_{r,t}$, and $H_{b,t}$ represent the net head for the left and right canals and the riverbed, respectively; $D_{l,t}$ is the demand for the left bank canal; $D_{r,t}$ is the demand for the right bank canal; $R_{l,t}$ is the released water for the right bank canal; and $R_{r,t}$ is the released water for the left bank canal.

The decision variable for this problem is released water, the total number of decision variables is 36 for one year (number of time periods = 12), and the number of variables for released water each month is three (left canal, right canal, and riverbed). Thus, there are 360 decision variables in ten years. The hybrid algorithm is considered based on the following levels for reservoir operation:

- The decision variables for the left canal, right canal, and riverbed are initialized based on the initial matrix for the NHA. In fact, the released water for the downstream demands is considered as the initial population.
- The storage reservoir can be calculated based on the continuity equation, and the different constraints should be checked.
- If the constraints are not satisfied, the penalty functions are considered as violations; then, the objective function is calculated based on Equation (31).
- Then, the NHA process is considered for the optimization process based on the independent performances of the BA and PSO algorithm in the NHA.
- The convergence criteria are checked, and if the algorithm is satisfied, it finishes; otherwise, the algorithm returns to the second step.

In fact, the released water for the multi-reservoir system is considered a decision variable, which is inserted into the algorithms based on the initial matrix and population. Then, the reservoir storage should be calculated based on the inflow into the reservoir and the initial values of the decision variables. Subsequently, the storage and released water should be compared with the permissible value so that they are not more or less than the permissible value. Then, the objective function for each member or decision variable is calculated for the total operational period. Then, the operators of the different algorithms are applied to the population and decision variables, and the algorithms continue until the convergence criterion is satisfied.

4. Modelling Evaluation Indexes

It is necessary to evaluate the utilized evolutionary algorithms to investigate their performance for downstream irritation supply. Thus, three important indexes are defined based on the following information.

- Volumetric reliability index. This index is based on the ratio of released water to irrigation demands. Thus, a high percentage of this index represents the high performance of each algorithm.

$$\alpha_V = 1 - \frac{N_{t=1}^T(D_t > R_t)}{T}, \qquad (33)$$

where α_V is the volumetric reliability; R_t is the released water; D_t is the demand; $N_{t=1}^T(D_t > R_t)$ is the number of periods in which demand is not supplied; and T is the total number of operational periods.

- Vulnerability index. This index represents the maximum intensity of the failure that occurred during the operation period of a system. The periods for which irritation demands are not met are known as failure periods or critical periods, and maximum deficiency occurrences during these periods are represented by the vulnerability index; thus, a low percentage for this index is preferable [35].

$$\lambda = Max_{t=1}^T \left(\frac{D_t - R_t}{D_t} \right) \times 100. \qquad (34)$$

- Resiliency index. This index represents the existing speed of a system from failure. Thus, a high percentage for this index is preferable. This index shows the flexibility of different algorithms versus the critical periods when they should manage the system well [35].

$$\gamma_i = \frac{f_{si}}{F_i}, \tag{35}$$

where γ_i is the resiliency index; f_{si} is the number of failure series that occurred; and F_i is the number of failure periods that occurred. These indexes were used to evaluate the percentage of success of the examined optimization algorithms based on their achieved operation rules to minimize the gap between the water release and water demand. Furthermore, to evaluate the performance of each algorithm with respect to the computational time needed for convergence, the time consumption for each algorithm to achieve the operation rule was determined. The best algorithm is the one that could achieve the global optima in less time for convergence.

5. Results, Discussion, and Application Analysis

5.1. Benchmark Functions

The standard deviation (SD), mean error (ME), average number of function evaluations (ANFE), and success rate (SR) are used to compare the results achieved from each algorithm for each benchmark function as shown in Table 3. The ANFE is used as the average of the function evaluations that should be considered to obtain the termination criteria for 100 runs. The main purpose for including several indexes is the possibility of having biased results, which occurs when using a single index. For example, a particular algorithm might achieve the best value using a certain index, suggesting that this algorithm has the best potential to achieve the best results, whereas the same algorithm might fail when examined using another index. The results indicated that the NHA outperforms other methods when examined using all indexes. In addition, the statistical Mann–Whitney rank sum test is applied to evaluate the average function of 100 runs performed by two different methods, and it indicates whether one method is superior to the other. If the NHA is not significantly better than the other methods, the null hypothesis is supported; otherwise, the null hypothesis is rejected and the two methods are compared with each other. The results show that the NHA could outperform other methods based on statistical tests and different indexes. The parameters for the algorithms were obtained by the sensitivity analysis and the methods are in the reference [52].

5.2. Sensitivity Analysis for the NHA

There are two main sources of uncertainty in this application; one is related to the optimization algorithm itself, and the other is related to the nature of the inputs and outputs of the case study. The uncertainty related to the optimization algorithm involves the initial parameters needed to initialize the model. The uncertainty related to the case study is based on the historical reservoir inflow records and water loss calculations from the reservoir due to evaporation and the release of water from the reservoir.

Tables 4–7 show the details of the sensitivity analysis for the proposed and comparable evolutionary algorithms. The sensitivity analysis shows the accuracy values of the random parameters obtained based on the variation in the value of the objective function versus the variation in the values of the random parameters. The size of the population for the NHA is 50 because the objective function has the smallest value (1.98). The maximum frequency for the NHA is 7 Hz, while the minimum frequency is 2 Hz. The acceleration coefficients ($c_1 = c_2$) are equal to 2, and the inertia weight is 0.7. Other accurate values for the other algorithms can be seen in Tables 5–8. The population size for the SA is 30, and the velocity limit for this method is 4. The mutation and crossover probabilities are 0.70 and 0.60, respectively. The size populations for $P_{initial}$ and P_{max} based on the WA are 10 and 30, respectively. Additionally, other parameters can be seen in Tables 5–7.

5.3. Ten Random Results for Evolutionary Algorithms

Table 8 shows the ten random run results for different algorithms for the same year. The average solution attained using the NHA is 1.98, which is the lowest value among the other algorithms. The average solutions for the SA, BA, WA, PSO algorithm, and GA are 2.12, 2.45, 3.12, 3.45, and 4.15, respectively. On the basis of the achieved results, the NHA minimized the objective function better than the other algorithms. The computational time for the NHA is 50 s, whereas it is 70, 79, 83, 91, and 94 s for the SA, WA, BA, PSO algorithm, and GA, respectively. Accordingly, compared with the SA, BA, WA, PSO algorithm, and GA, the NHA decreased the computation time by 28%, 36%, 39%, 82%, and 88%, respectively, which is an excellent enhancement result.

Table 3. Experimental results using benchmark functions. SD—standard deviation; ME—mean error; ANFE—average number of function evaluations; SR—success rate; NHA—new hybrid algorithm.

Function	Algorithms	SD	ME	ANFE	SR
f_1	Differential Evolution Algorithm	1.42×10^{-4} [52]	8.68×10^{-4} [52]	27,378 [52]	100
	Artificial Bee Colony Algorithm	2.02×10^{-4} [52]	7.54×10^{-4} [52]	35,091 [52]	100
	Particle Swarm Optimization	6.72×10^{-5}	9.34×10^{-4}	45,914.5	100
	Bat Algorithm	5.12×10^{-5}	6.12×10^{-4}	231,245	100
	Shark Algorithm	5.01×10^{-5}	5.25×10^{-4}	209,878	100
	Genetic Algorithm	1.34×10^{-5}	9.56×10^{-4}	37,094	100
	Spider Monkey Algorithm	2.12×10^{-6} [52]	5.65×10^{-5}	19,878 [52]	100
	Krill Algorithm	2.22×10^{-6} [52]	7.12×10^{-5}	18,235 [52]	100
	NHA	5.25×10^{-7}	8.12×10^{-6}	14,224	100
f_2	Differential Evolution Algorithm	4.93 [52]	2.09×10^{-3} [53]	200,000 [52]	98
	Artificial Bee Colony Algorithm	3.14×10^{-4} [52]	7.48×10^{-4} [53]	87,039 [52]	98
	Particle Swarm Optimization	$1.35 \times 10^{+1}$	2.98×10^{-3}	200,000	98
	Bat Algorithm	3.24×10^{-5}	3.12×10^{-5}	54,223	98
	Shark Algorithm	4.56×10^{-7}	4.12×10^{-6}	45,221	98
	Genetic Algorithm	8.78	2.12×10^{-3}	205,000	98
	Spider Monkey Algorithm	6.12×10^{-8} [53]	5.12×10^{-7} [53]	32,124 [53]	98
	Krill Algorithm	7.91×10^{-7} [53]	6.12×10^{-7} [53]	35,125 [53]	100
	NHA	9.12×10^{-9}	7.12×10^{-8}	310,191	100
f_3	Differential Evolution Algorithm	1.12×10^{-3}	4.09×10^{-1}	2725.5	100
	Artificial Bee Colony Algorithm	5.25×10^{-3}	4.09×10^{-1}	2567	85
	Particle Swarm Optimization	5.64×10^{-3}	4.02×10^{-1}	4979	85
	Bat Algorithm	4.12×10^{-4}	3.12×10^{-2}	1285	85
	Shark Algorithm	5.12×10^{-5}	3.22×10^{-2}	1100	98
	Genetic Algorithm	1.12×10^{-2}	$4.12 \times 10^{+1}$	1400	98
	Spider Monkey Algorithm	5.78×10^{-5}	2.12×10^{-4}	987	98
	Krill Algorithm	5.45×10^{-3}	3.12×10^{-5}	765	98
	NHA	1.14×10^{-6}	1.12×10^{-6}	654	100
f_4	Differential Evolution Algorithm	$1.12 \times 10^{+2}$	$2.19 \times 10^{+1}$	180,000	84
	Artificial Bee Colony Algorithm	$1.18 \times 10^{+1}$	$1.19 \times 10^{+1}$	170,000	84
	Particle Swarm Optimization	$6.70 \times 10^{+2}$	2.80×10^{-3}	200,000	84
	Bat Algorithm	5.70×10^{-3}	1.12×10^{-4}	180,000	84
	Shark Algorithm	4.71×10^{-3}	5.45×10^{-5}	160,000	84
	Genetic Algorithm	$6.14 \times 10^{+3}$	1.21×10^{-2}	210,000	84
	Spider Monkey Algorithm	1.45×10^{-4}	3.12×10^{-5}	180,000	84
	Krill Algorithm	1.23×10^{-5}	4.21×10^{-5}	165,000	84
	NHA	2.12×10^{-6}	2.12×10^{-7}	140,000	98
f_5	Differential Evolution Algorithm	1.31×10^{-6}	4.90×10^{-1}	2741	100
	Artificial Bee Colony Algorithm	2.00×10^{-6}	4.87×10^{-1}	4811	100
	Particle Swarm Optimization	6.12×10^{-7}	4.75×10^{-1}	4912	100
	Bat Algorithm	2.12×10^{-8}	2.22×10^{-3}	1811	100
	Shark Algorithm	1.11×10^{-8}	2.12×10^{-4}	1712	100
	Genetic Algorithm	1.21×10^{-5}	3.21×10^{-4}	5121	100
	Spider Monkey Algorithm	2.12×10^{-8}	5.12×10^{-3}	1001	100
	Krill Algorithm	1.14×10^{-8}	5.45×10^{-4}	987	100
	NHA	1.41×10^{-9}	6.78×10^{-5}	567	100

Table 4. Details of the sensitivity analysis for the new hybrid algorithm.

Size Population	Objective Function	W (Inertia Coefficient)	Objective Function	$c_1 = c_2$	Objective Function	Maximum Frequency	Objective Function	Minimum Loudness	Objective Function
10	2.45	0.30	2.21	1.6	2.34	1	2.11	0.3	2.23
30	2.24	0.50	2.00	1.8	2.12	2	2.00	0.5	2.05
50	1.98	0.70	1.98	2.0	1.98	3	2.14	0.7	2.0
70	2.01	0.90	2.12	2.2	2.12	4	2.16	0.90	2.1

Table 5. Details of the sensitivity analysis for the shark algorithm.

Size Population	Objective Function	β_k (Velocity Limiter)	Objective Function	α_k	Objective Function
10	2.45	2	2.44	0.20	2.55
30	2.12	4	2.12	0.40	2.12
50	2.24	6	2.34	0.60	2.67
70	2.36	8	2.44	0.80	2.78

Table 6. Details of the sensitivity analysis for the weed algorithm.

Pinitial	Objective Function	Pmax	Objective Function	N0Smax	Objective Function
5	3.69	10	3.55	3	3.78
10	3.12	30	3.12	5	3.34
15	3.24	50	3.28	7	3.12
20	3.36	70	3.32	9	3.44

Table 7. Details of the sensitivity analysis for the genetic algorithm.

Size Population	Objective Function	Mutation Probability	Objective Function	Crossover Probability	Objective Function
10	5.12	0.30	4.88	0.20	4.69
30	4.98	0.50	4.55	0.40	4.34
50	4.15	0.70	4.15	0.60	4.12
70	4.55	0.90	4.24	0.80	4.24

Table 8. Ten random results for the proposed hybrid evolutionary algorithm and the stand-alone algorithms.

Run	NHA	SA	BA	WA	PSO	GA
1	1.99	2.12	2.45	3.16	3.45	4.15
2	1.98	2.12	2.47	3.12	3.51	4.24
3	1.98	2.12	2.49	3.12	3.45	4.26
4	1.98	2.12	2.45	3.12	3.45	4.15
5	1.98	2.14	2.45	3.12	3.45	4.15
6	1.98	2.12	2.45	3.12	3.45	4.15
7	1.98	2.12	2.45	3.12	3.45	4.15
8	1.98	2.12	2.45	3.12	3.45	4.15
9	1.98	2.12	2.45	3.12	3.45	4.15
10	1.98	2.12	2.45	3.12	3.45	4.15
Average solution	1.98	2.12	2.45	3.12	3.45	4.17
Coefficient variation	0.001	0.002	0.005	0.004	0.005	0.006
Time	50	70	79	83	91	94

The variation coefficient for the NHA model is less than that of the commensurate models (i.e., SA, BA, WA, PSO algorithm, and GA). The NHA displayed a reliable outcome based on the average; however, the average results have small variation coefficients, which can be seen in Figure 7, where the average, minimum, and maximum solutions overlap with each other and are well matched. Figure 8 shows the value of the objective function belonging to all data-intelligence models versus the number of function evaluations (NFEs). The NFE for the NHA model is equal to 5000. The other established models have NFE values of 8000, 1000, 12,000, 14,000, and 15,000 (SA, BA, WA, GA, and PSO algorithm, respectively). Thus, the NHA can obtain the best solutions with a smaller NFE, which shows that the NHA can obtain the converged solution faster than other algorithms.

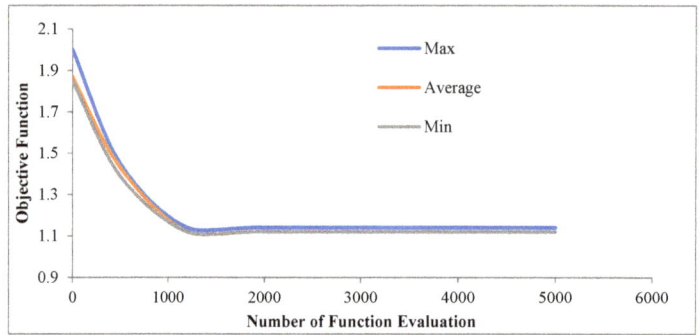

Figure 7. Convergence curve for the maximum, minimum, and average solution.

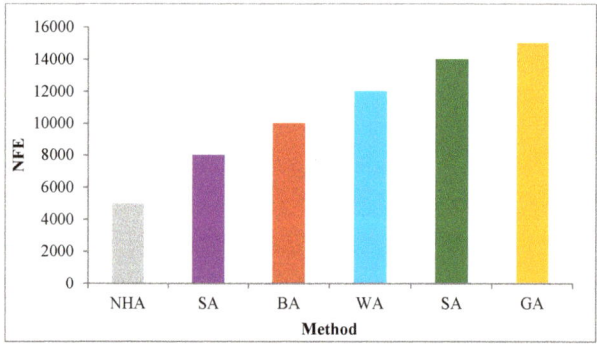

Figure 8. Comparison of the fitness value and number of function evaluation (NFE) for different algorithms. GA—genetic algorithm.

5.4. Computed Irrigation Deficiencies

Different indexes were used to evaluate the irrigation deficiencies tabulated in Table 9. The highest correlation attained for the proposed model had a magnitude of 0.93. Additionally, the absolute error metric values (e.g., the mean absolute error (MAE) and root mean square error (RMSE)) prove that released water can supply the irrigation demand for the left and right canals based on a smaller error index value and greater correlation value. The SA attained an accurate level of modelling after the use of the proposed hybrid model. Figure 9 shows the mode of the irrigation supply for all applied algorithms. The average demand for the total operation period is 142.14 (10^6 m^3), and the average amounts of released water for the NHA, SA, BA, WA, PSO algorithm and GA are 141.25, 140.33, 138.75, 135.43, 134.12 and 133.21 (10^6 m^3), respectively. Thus, the NHA can supply the irrigation demand as a primary priority in this problem. The volumetric reliability, vulnerability and resiliency indexes were used for more detailed information and a deep comparative analysis of all implemented algorithms. The high percentage for the volumetric reliability index found for the NHA showed that irrigation demands can be supplied for more operation periods; therefore, the volume of released water can respond to downstream irrigation demands. In fact, the volumetric reliability index based on the NHA is 5%, 8%, 17%, 18% and 31% greater than that based on the SA, BA, WA, PSO algorithm and GA, respectively.

Table 9. Evaluation of different algorithms for irrigation demands based on different indexes. NHA—new hybrid algorithm; SA—shark algorithm; BA—bat algorithm; WA—weed algorithm; PSO—particle swarm optimization; GA—genetic algorithm; MOGA—multi-objective GA; MOPSO—multi-objective PSO.

Index	Equation	NHA	SA	BA	WA	PSO	GA	MOGA	MOPSO
Correlation Coefficient	$r = \dfrac{\sum_{t=1}^{T}(D_t - \bar{D}_t)\cdot(R_t - \bar{R}_t)}{\sqrt{\sum_{t=1}^{T}(D_t - \bar{D}_t)^2 \cdot \sum_{t=1}^{T}(R_t - \bar{R}_t)^2}}$	0.93	0.91	0.86	0.87	0.75	0.67	0.74	0.83
Root Mean Square Error (RMSE) (10^6 m^3)	$RMSE = \sqrt{\dfrac{\sum_{t=1}^{T}(D_t - R_t)^2}{T}}$	5.1	7.2	8.8	9.3	10.5	11.8	9.6	8.7
Mean absolute Error (10^6 m^3)	$MAE = \dfrac{\sum_{t=1}^{T}|D_t - R_t|}{T}$	4.3	5.59	6.1	7.1	6.9	6.4	6.3	6.1
Volumetric Reliability Index %	$\alpha_V = \dfrac{\sum_{t=1}^{T} R_t}{\sum_{t=1}^{T} D_t} \times 100$	95%	90%	87%	78%	75%	64%	77%	79%
Resiliency Index %	$\gamma_i = \dfrac{f_{si}}{f_i}$	45%	40%	38%	35%	33%	29%	35%	34%
Vulnerability Index	$\lambda = Max_{t=1}^{T}\left(\dfrac{D_t - R_t}{D_t}\right) \times 100$	14%	20%	21%	23%	24%	25%	22%	21%

D_t: demand; $\bar{D}_t$: average demand; R_t: released water; and $\bar{R}_t$: average released water.

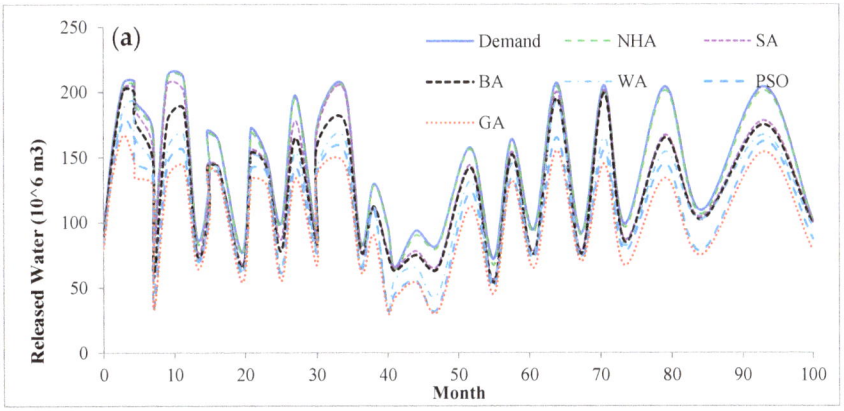

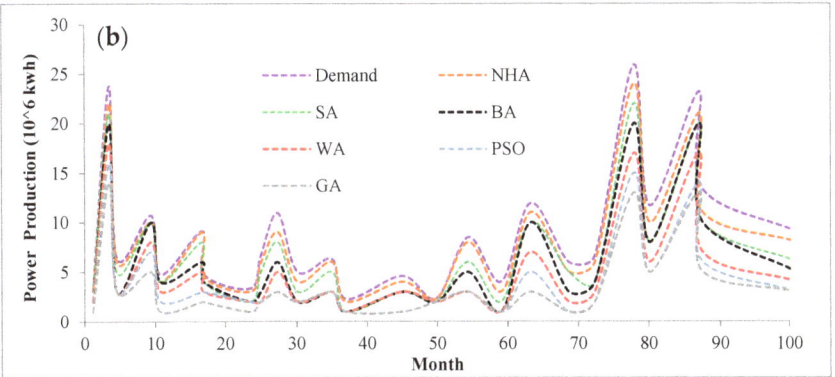

Figure 9. (a) Released water for downstream irrigation and (b) power production for downstream demand.

Additionally, Reddy and Kumar [53] optimized this system based on the multi-objective GA (MOGA) and multi-objective PSO (MOPSO) algorithms. These multi-objective algorithms can be considered substitution strategies instead of weighting methods, and the structure and preparation of such algorithms are complex. The results indicated that the NHA has a better performance than the MOGA and the MOPSO algorithm; therefore, the volumetric reliability index for the NHA is greater than that for the MOGA and the MOPSO algorithms. For example, the Pareto fronts are shown in Figure 10. The marginal rate of substitution strategy [54] is used to select the best solution. The marginal rate of substitution can be calculated based on sacrificing certain terms of the objective function to improve the value of the other terms of the objective function. When one solution has the maximum value of marginal rate of substitution, it is the most suitable solution; in other words, the best solution has the highest slope for two objective functions in the Pareto front. When the MOGA and the MOPSO algorithm are used, a large number of solutions can be observed; thus, the problem must be simplified. Therefore, a simple clustering strategy is used to filter 200 solutions to 20 solutions. First, there are N clusters, and the cluster ranges are calculated for all pairs of clusters; then, each two clusters with the minimum range are combined to generate the large cluster. Finally, the solutions with the minimum average distance from other solutions in the cluster are considered as alternative solutions for clustering (Figure 10). The determined point blue is the optimal solution.

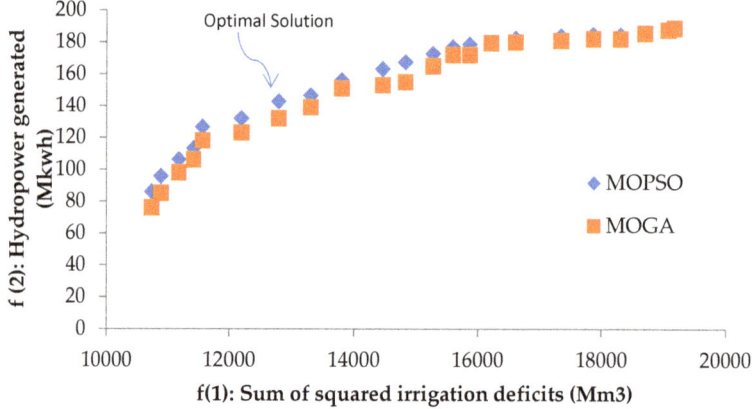

Figure 10. Pareto front for the algorithms. MOGA—multi-objective GA; MOPSO—multi-objective PSO.

The vulnerability index for the NHA was 12%, which was the lowest percentage among the analyzed methods. The maximum intensity of the failure probability occurred with the NHA and was less than that of other evolutionary algorithms. The greatest value of the vulnerability index was related to the GA. Additionally, the NHA had a better performance than the MOGA and the MOPSO algorithms based on the lower value of the vulnerability index.

Finally, the resiliency index of the NHA was 45%, which was the highest percentage among the analysed methods; therefore, the multi-purpose system can escape more quickly from critical periods, such as drought periods.

Figure 11 shows that the NHA has the smallest average annual deficit among the evaluated methods. The average annual deficit for the NHA is 10%, 12%, 15%, 17%, and 18% less than that for the SA, BA, WA, PSO algorithm, and GA, respectively. The historical water demand required for various uses was recorded during an earlier time period, whereas the released water decision pattern was calculated based on the achieved optimal operation rules from each algorithm based on objective functions. Finally, a comparative analysis was carried out to identify the gap between the water demand for the irrigation requirement and power production and the allocated water release. The released water as a decision variable was calculated, and then the power generation was calculated based on released water; the resulting power produced was 106 kWh, which was then compared with the actual power required for downstream demands.

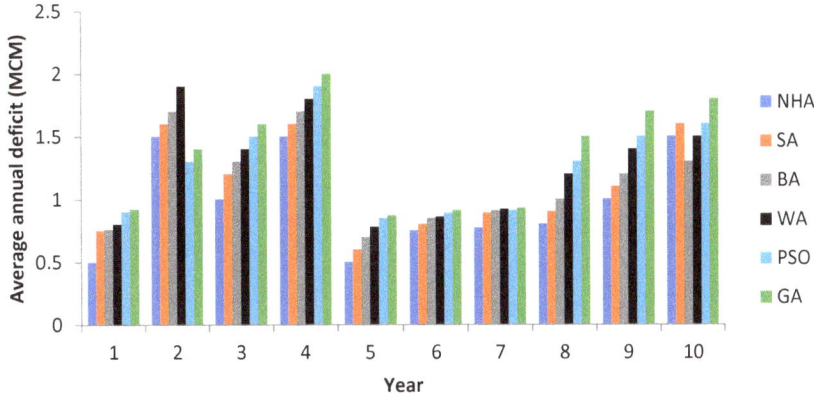

Figure 11. Average annual deficits for different algorithms.

5.5. Computational Power Production

The downstream demand for power is 18.90 (10^6 kwh), and the average amount of produced power based on the NHA is 18.08 (10^6 kwh), while it is 17.99, 17.32, 16.96, 16.32, and 15.34 (10^6 kwh) for the SA, BA, WA, PSO algorithm, and GA, respectively (see Figure 6b). Thus, the NHA can produce more power to supply the demand (Table 10). Additionally, the correlation coefficient for the NHA is greater than that for other algorithms, and the root mean square error (RMSE) and mean absolute error (MAE) have the smallest values in the NHA among the evaluated algorithms based on the difference between demand and power production. Additionally, the NHA has a better performance than the MOGA and the MOPSO algorithms based on the lower values for the error indexes and higher correlation values.

Thus, the NHA can supply the irrigation demand first; then, the power production can be used after the irrigation supply. Additionally, although the release of more water may generate more power, a considerable deficiency in irrigation would result. Thus, more weight is assigned to the irrigation objective function to ensure that the demand for irrigation is met; ensuring the necessary power production is an additional concern for policymakers.

Table 10. Evaluation of different algorithms for irrigation demands based on different indexes.

Index	Equation	NHA	SA	BA	WA	PSO	GA	MOGA (Reddy, 2006)	MOPSO (Reddy, 2006)
Correlation Coefficient	$r = \frac{\sum_{i=1}^{T}(P_{dt}-\overline{P}_{dt})\cdot(P_{st}-\overline{P}_{st})}{\sqrt{\sum_{i=1}^{T}(P_{dt}-\overline{P}_{dt})^2 \cdot \sum_{i=1}^{T}(P_{st}-\overline{P}_{st})^2}}$	93%	90%	87%	75%	69%	65%	73%	75%
Root Mean Square Error (RMSE) (10^6 kwh)	$RMSE = \sqrt{\frac{\sum_{i=1}^{T}(P_{dt}-P_{st})^2}{T}}$	3.1	4.9	4.2	3.8	4.2	3.7	3.5	3.8
Mean Absolute Error (MAE) (10^6 kwh)	$MAE = \frac{\sum_{i=1}^{T}|P_{dt}-P_{st}|}{T}$	3.2	4.1	3.8	3.6	3.4	3.5	3.3	3.4

P_{dt}: power demand; $\overline{P}_{dt}$: average power demand; and P_{st}: simulated produced power by algorithms.

6. Conclusions

The current research is dedicated to the implementation of a new hybrid intelligence model based on integrating two meta-heuristic algorithms for optimizing the operation of a multi-purpose reservoir water system. The optimization problem is solved to satisfy irrigation demands and hydropower production for one case study in India. The capability of the BA is improved by hybridization with the

PSO algorithm based on local and global search strategies and the substitution of weaker solutions in each algorithm with the best solutions of the other algorithms. The main idea behind the procedure of the proposed NHA is to avoid the possible worst solutions using the BA and the resulting decline in local optima; in addition, the NHA enhanced the convergence rate using the PSO algorithm.

After applying the proposed NHA for a multi-purpose reservoir water system, namely the Bhadra Dam in India, it could be concluded that the NHA could provide a satisfactory improvement to decreasing irrigation deficiencies. In quantitative terms, the average irrigation demand was 142.14 (10^6 m^3), and the NHA can release 141.25 (10^6 m^3), which represents a much higher level of accuracy over comparable models. The average demand for power production is 18.08 (10^6 kwh), and the produced power using the NHA is 17.99 (10^6 kwh), which represents the capability of the NHA for applied applications.

It can be concluded that the proposed NHA as an intelligent model could contribute to providing reliable solutions for complex multi-purpose reservoir systems to optimize the operation rule for similar reservoir systems worldwide. In addition, the NHA could be integrated with other forecasting models for additional reservoir hydrological variables to optimize its operation under different climate change scenarios in future periods. Furthermore, the NHA could be used for multi-purpose reservoir systems and other multi-purpose engineering optimization applications.

Although the proposed NHA showed superior performance over the other optimization algorithms, it still experienced a challenge during initialization because several random parameters must be initialized. This step may prolong the computational time for convergence. In addition to the need to initialize the random parameters for the BA and PSO algorithms within the definition of the NHA communication, a simultaneous procedure must also be adopted to update these random parameters within the simulation model of the reservoir, and such requirements should be considered when applying the NHA to other case studies.

Author Contributions: Formal analysis: Z.M.Y., M.E., L.S.H., and A.E.-S.; Methodology: M.E.; Resources: M.S.H.; Supervision: A.E.-S.; Validation: N.Z. and A.N.A.; Visualization: N.S.M., W.Z.B.J., and A.N.A.; Writing—original draft: S.B.K. and H.A.A.; Writing—review & editing: C.M.F.

Acknowledgments: The authors greatly appreciate the financial support received from the Ministry of Education (MOE) research grant Fundamental Research Grant Scheme (FRGS) 20180120FRGS and University of Malaya Research Grant (UMRG) coded RP025A-18SUS, University of Malaya, Malaysia. In addition, this study was partially funded by the TNB Seeding Fund, Institute of Power Energy (IPE) and Institute of Energy Infrastructure (IEI), Universiti Tenaga Nasional, Malaysia, through research grants coded U-TG-CR-18-03 and U-TG-RD-17-06, respectively.

Conflicts of Interest: The authors declare no conflict of interest. The funders had no role in the design of the study; in the collection, analyses, or interpretation of data; in the writing of the manuscript, and in the decision to publish the results.

References

1. Pedro-Monzonís, M.; Solera, A.; Ferrer, J.; Estrela, T.; Paredes-Arquiola, J. A review of water scarcity and drought indexes in water resources planning and management. *J. Hydrol.* **2015**, *527*, 482–493. [CrossRef]
2. You, J.Y.; Cai, X. Hedging rule for reservoir operations: 2. A numerical model. *Water Resour. Res.* **2008**, *44*. [CrossRef]
3. Fang, H.; Hu, T.; Zeng, X.; Wu, F. Simulation-optimization model of reservoir operation based on target storage curves. *Water Sci. Eng.* **2014**, *7*, 433–445. [CrossRef]
4. Srinivasan, K.; Kumar, K. Multi-Objective Simulation-Optimization Model for Long-term Reservoir Operation using Piecewise Linear Hedging Rule. *Water Resour. Manag.* **2018**, *32*, 1901–1911. [CrossRef]
5. Xie, A.; Liu, P.; Guo, S.; Zhang, X.; Jiang, H.; Yang, G. Optimal Design of Seasonal Flood Limited Water Levels by Jointing Operation of the Reservoir and Floodplains. *Water Resour. Manag.* **2017**, *32*, 179–193. [CrossRef]
6. Adeyemo, J.A. Reservoir operation using multi-objective evolutionary algorithms—A review. *Asian J. Sci. Res.* **2011**, *4*, 16–27. [CrossRef]

7. Karamouz, M.; Nazif, S.; Sherafat, M.A.; Zahmatkesh, Z. Development of an Optimal Reservoir Operation Scheme Using Extended Evolutionary Computing Algorithms Based on Conflict Resolution Approach: A Case Study. *Water Resour. Manag.* **2014**, *28*, 3539–3554. [CrossRef]
8. Azizipour, M.; Ghalenoei, V.; Afshar, M.H.; Solis, S.S. Optimal Operation of Hydropower Reservoir Systems Using Weed Optimization Algorithm. *Water Resour. Manag.* **2016**, *30*, 3995–4009. [CrossRef]
9. Han, C.; Zheng, B.; Qin, Y.; Ma, Y.; Yang, C.; Liu, Z.; Cao, W.; Chi, M. Impact of upstream river inputs and reservoir operation on phosphorus fractions in water-particulate phases in the Three Gorges Reservoir. *Sci. Total Environ.* **2018**, *610–611*, 1546–1556. [CrossRef]
10. Wan, W.; Guo, X.; Lei, X.; Jiang, Y.; Wang, H. A Novel Optimization Method for Multi-Reservoir Operation Policy Derivation in Complex Inter-Basin Water Transfer System. *Water Resour. Manag.* **2017**, *32*, 31–51. [CrossRef]
11. Moeini, R.; Babaei, M. Constrained improved particle swarm optimization algorithm for optimal operation of large scale reservoir: Proposing three approaches. *Evol. Syst.* **2017**, *8*, 287–301. [CrossRef]
12. Zyoud, S.H.; Kaufmann, L.G.; Shaheen, H.; Samhan, S.; Fuchs-Hanusch, D. A framework for water loss management in developing countries under fuzzy environment: Integration of Fuzzy AHP with Fuzzy TOPSIS. *Expert Syst. Appl.* **2016**, *61*, 86–105. [CrossRef]
13. Rabiei, M.; Aalami, M.; Talatahari, S. Reservoir Operation Optimization using CBO, ECBO and vps algorithms. *Iran Univ. Sci. Technol.* **2018**, *8*, 489–509.
14. Tayfur, G. Modern Optimization Methods in Water Resources Planning, Engineering and Management. *Water Resour. Manag.* **2017**, *31*, 3205–3233. [CrossRef]
15. Bennett, C.; Stewart, R.A.; Beal, C.D. ANN-based residential water end-use demand forecasting model. *Expert Syst. Appl.* **2013**, *40*, 1014–1023. [CrossRef]
16. Nabaei, A.; Hamian, M.; Parsaei, M.R.; Safdari, R.; Samad-Soltani, T.; Zarrabi, H.; Ghassemi, A. Topologies and performance of intelligent algorithms: A comprehensive review. *Artif. Intell. Rev.* **2016**. [CrossRef]
17. Ehteram, M.; Mousavi, S.F.; Karami, H.; Farzin, S.; Deo, R.; Othman, F.B.; Chau, K.; Sarkamaryan, S.; Singh, V.P.; El-Shafie, A. Bat algorithm for dam–reservoir operation. *Environ. Earth Sci.* **2018**, *77*, 510. [CrossRef]
18. Ehteram, M.; Singh, V.; Karami, H.; Hosseini, K.; Dianatikhah, M.; Hossain, M.; Ming Fai, C.; El-Shafie, A. Irrigation Management Based on Reservoir Operation with an Improved Weed Algorithm. *Water* **2018**, *10*, 1267. [CrossRef]
19. Allawi, M.F.; Jaafar, O.; Mohamad Hamzah, F.; Ehteram, M.; Hossain, M.S.; El-Shafie, A. Operating a reservoir system based on the shark machine learning algorithm. *Environ. Earth Sci.* **2018**, *77*, 366. [CrossRef]
20. Allawi, M.F.; Jaafar, O.; Mohamad Hamzah, F.; Koting, S.B.; Mohd, N.S.B.; El-Shafie, A. Forecasting hydrological parameters for reservoir system utilizing artificial intelligent models and exploring their influence on operation performance. *Knowl.-Based Syst.* **2019**, *163*, 907–926. [CrossRef]
21. Raso, L.; Chiavico, M.; Dorchies, D. Optimal and Centralized Reservoir Management for Drought and Flood Protection on the Upper Seine–Aube River System Using Stochastic Dual Dynamic Programming. *J. Water Resour. Plan. Manag.* **2019**, *145*, 5019002. [CrossRef]
22. Allawi, M.F.; Jaafar, O.; Ehteram, M.; Mohamad Hamzah, F.; El-Shafie, A. Synchronizing Artificial Intelligence Models for Operating the Dam and Reservoir System. *Water Resour. Manag.* **2018**, *32*, 3373–3389. [CrossRef]
23. Ehteram, M.; Karami, H.; Farzin, S. Reservoir Optimization for Energy Production Using a New Evolutionary Algorithm Based on Multi-Criteria Decision-Making Models. *Water Resour. Manag.* **2018**, *32*, 2539–2560. [CrossRef]
24. Ehteram, M.; Mousavi, S.F.; Karami, H.; Farzin, S.; Emami, M.; Binti Othman, F.; Amini, Z.; Kisi, O.; El-Shafie, A. Fast convergence optimization model for single and multi-purposes reservoirs using hybrid algorithm. *Adv. Eng. Inform.* **2017**, *32*, 287–298. [CrossRef]
25. Afshar, A.; Shafii, M.; Haddad, O.B. Optimizing multi-reservoir operation rules: An improved HBMO approach. *J. Hydroinform.* **2010**, *13*, 121. [CrossRef]
26. Fallah-Mehdipour, E.; Bozorg Haddad, O.; Mariño, M.A. Real-Time Operation of Reservoir System by Genetic Programming. *Water Resour. Manag.* **2012**, *26*, 4091–4103. [CrossRef]
27. Ostadrahimi, L.; Mariño, M.A.; Afshar, A. Multi-reservoir Operation Rules: Multi-swarm PSO-based Optimization Approach. *Water Resour. Manag.* **2011**, *26*, 407–427. [CrossRef]

28. Bolouri-Yazdeli, Y.; Bozorg Haddad, O.; Fallah-Mehdipour, E.; Mariño, M.A. Evaluation of real-time operation rules in reservoir systems operation. *Water Resour. Manag.* **2014**, *28*, 715–729. [CrossRef]
29. Akbari-Alashti, H.; Bozorg Haddad, O.; Fallah-Mehdipour, E.; Mariño, M.A. Multi-reservoir real-time operation rules: A new genetic programming approach. *Proc. Inst. Civ. Eng. Water Manag.* **2014**, *167*, 561–576. [CrossRef]
30. Haddad, O.B.; Moravej, M.; Loáiciga, H.A. Application of the Water Cycle Algorithm to the Optimal Operation of Reservoir Systems. *J. Irrig. Drain. Eng.* **2015**, *141*, 04014064. [CrossRef]
31. Haddad, O.B.; Hosseini-Moghari, S.-M.; Loáiciga, H.A. Biogeography-Based Optimization Algorithm for Optimal Operation of Reservoir Systems. *J. Water Resour. Plan. Manag.* **2016**, *142*, 04015034. [CrossRef]
32. Zhang, Z.; Jiang, Y.; Zhang, S.; Geng, S.; Wang, H.; Sang, G. An adaptive particle swarm optimization algorithm for reservoir operation optimization. *Appl. Soft Comput. J.* **2014**, *18*, 167–177. [CrossRef]
33. Hosseini-Moghari, S.-M.; Morovati, R.; Moghadas, M.; Araghinejad, S. Optimum Operation of Reservoir Using Two Evolutionary Algorithms: Imperialist Competitive Algorithm (ICA) and Cuckoo Optimization Algorithm (COA). *Water Resour. Manag.* **2015**, *29*, 3749–3769. [CrossRef]
34. Ehteram, M.; Karami, H.; Mousavi, S.-F.; Farzin, S.; Kisi, O. Evaluation of contemporary evolutionary algorithms for optimization in reservoir operation and water supply. *J. Water Supply Res. Technol.* **2017**, jws2017109. [CrossRef]
35. Ehteram, M.; Karami, H.; Mousavi, S.-F.; Farzin, S.; Kisi, O. Optimization of energy management and conversion in the multi-reservoir systems based on evolutionary algorithms. *J. Clean. Prod.* **2017**, *168*, 1132–1142. [CrossRef]
36. Garg, H. A hybrid GSA-GA algorithm for constrained optimization problems. *Inf. Sci.* **2019**, *478*, 499–523. [CrossRef]
37. Patwal, R.S.; Narang, N.; Garg, H. A novel TVAC-PSO based mutation strategies algorithm for generation scheduling of pumped storage hydrothermal system incorporating solar units. *Energy* **2018**, *142*, 822–837. [CrossRef]
38. Garg, H. A hybrid PSO-GA algorithm for constrained optimization problems. *Appl. Math. Comput.* **2016**, *274*, 292–305. [CrossRef]
39. Garg, H. An efficient biogeography based optimization algorithm for solving reliability optimization problems. *Swarm Evol. Comput.* **2015**, *24*, 1–10. [CrossRef]
40. Shah, H.; Tairan, N.; Garg, H.; Ghazali, R. Global Gbest Guided-Artificial Bee Colony Algorithm for Numerical Function Optimization. *Computers* **2018**, *7*, 69. [CrossRef]
41. Yang, X.S. Bat algorithm for multi-objective optimisation. *Int. J. Bio-Inspired Comput.* **2011**, *3*, 267. [CrossRef]
42. Gandomi, A.H.; Yang, X.S. Chaotic bat algorithm. *J. Comput. Sci.* **2014**, *5*, 224–232. [CrossRef]
43. Yang, X.S. A new metaheuristic Bat-inspired Algorithm. In *Studies in Computational Intelligence*; Springer: Berlin/Heidelberg, Germany, 2010; Volume 284, pp. 65–74.
44. Bozorg-Haddad, O.; Karimirad, I.; Seifollahi-Aghmiuni, S.; Loáiciga, H.A. Development and Application of the Bat Algorithm for Optimizing the Operation of Reservoir Systems. *J. Water Resour. Plan. Manag.* **2015**, *141*, 04014097. [CrossRef]
45. Wang, Y.Y.; Zhou, J.; Zhou, C.; Wang, Y.Y.; Qin, H.; Lu, Y. An improved self-adaptive PSO technique for short-term hydrothermal scheduling. *Expert Syst. Appl.* **2012**, *39*, 2288–2295. [CrossRef]
46. Karami, H.; Mousavi, S.F.; Farzin, S.; Ehteram, M.; Singh, V.P.; Kisi, O. Improved Krill Algorithm for Reservoir Operation. *Water Resour. Manag.* **2018**, *32*, 3353–3372. [CrossRef]
47. Li, L.; Zhou, Y. A novel complex-valued bat algorithm. *Neural Comput. Appl.* **2014**, *25*, 1369–1381. [CrossRef]
48. Kennedy, J.; Eberhart, R. Particle swarm optimization. *Neural Netw.* **1995**, *4*, 1942–1948. [CrossRef]
49. Ehteram, M.; Karami, H.; Farzin, S. Reducing Irrigation Deficiencies Based Optimizing Model for Multi-Reservoir Systems Utilizing Spider Monkey Algorithm. *Water Resour. Manag.* **2018**, *32*, 2315–2334. [CrossRef]
50. Mehrabian, A.R.; Lucas, C. A novel numerical optimization algorithm inspired from weed colonization. *Ecol. Inform.* **2006**, *1*, 355–366. [CrossRef]
51. Hersovici, M.; Jacovi, M.; Maarek, Y.S.; Pelleg, D.; Shtalhaim, M.; Ur, S. The shark-search algorithm. An application: Tailored Web site mapping. *Comput. Netw. ISDN Syst.* **1998**, *30*, 317–326. [CrossRef]
52. Bansal, J.C.; Sharma, H.; Jadon, S.S.; Clerc, M. Spider Monkey Optimization algorithm for numerical optimization. *Memetic Comput.* **2014**, *6*, 31–47. [CrossRef]

53. Reddy, M.J.; Kumar, D.N. Optimal reservoir operation using multi-objective evolutionary algorithm. *Water Resour. Manag.* **2006**, *20*, 861–878. [CrossRef]
54. Deb, K.; Zhu, L.; Kulkarni, S. Multi-scenario, multi-objective optimization using evolutionary algorithms: Initial results. In Proceedings of the 2015 IEEE Congress on Evolutionary Computation, Sendai, Japan, 25–28 May 2015; pp. 1877–1884.

© 2019 by the authors. Licensee MDPI, Basel, Switzerland. This article is an open access article distributed under the terms and conditions of the Creative Commons Attribution (CC BY) license (http://creativecommons.org/licenses/by/4.0/).

Article

A Multi-Criteria Decision-Making Model to Choose the Best Option for Sustainable Construction Management

Seyit Ali Erdogan [1], Jonas Šaparauskas [1],* and Zenonas Turskis [2]

[1] Department of Construction Management and Real Estate, Faculty of Civil Engineering, Vilnius Gediminas Technical University, Saulėtekio al. 11, LT-10223 Vilnius, Lithuania; ali_erdogan1907@hotmail.com
[2] Laboratory of Operational Research, Institute of Sustainable Construction, Faculty of Civil Engineering, Vilnius Gediminas Technical University, Saulėtekio al. 11, LT-10223 Vilnius, Lithuania; zenonas.turskis@vgtu.lt
* Correspondence: jonas.saparauskas@vgtu.lt; Tel.: +370-5-274-52-45

Received: 22 February 2019; Accepted: 10 April 2019; Published: 14 April 2019

Abstract: The article briefly discusses the content and terms of construction project management. It identifies the main problems of construction management and discusses ways to solve those using multi-criteria methods. Well-performed management is one of the critical factors which leads to the success of any significant sustainable project. Construction project management consists of setting goals and defining user requirements, project constraints, and resources needed. This paper aims to create a practically useful model. The paper presents a comprehensive set of criteria, which led to the creation of a decision-making model for construction management, which was applied to a Turkish case study. The Analytic Hierarchy Process (AHP) method and the Expert Choice computer program were used for calculations.

Keywords: project; construction; contractor; multiple-criteria decision-making; AHP; sustainable solution; choice; expert

1. Introduction

Two-thirds of the world's people believe that global warming is the most critical environmental problem in the world. Increasing the impact of construction information has a positive impact on stakeholders' interests and encourages sustainable construction [1]. Given the balanced implementation of ecological, economic, and social needs in the implementation of projects, there is a need to integrate the principle of sustainability into project management practices and the academic community. Creation and management of a healthy artificial environment based on ecological resources and design efficiency is the goal of contemporary construction. Modern construction emphasizes the need to integrate stability into project planning, management, evaluation, and decision-making to improve project quality and value. Planning and the successful implementation of the project directly affect the goals of constant construction. Therefore, continuous project planning reflects project planning methods for economic, social, and environmental sustainability. Systematic approaches, the views of all stakeholders, knowledge, and expertise in implementing a sustainable development project and their ability to apply them properly are critical factors for the success of sustainable construction. Project planning is a well-known theoretical concept in the literature on project management. However, we know little about how much effort is needed to invest in the project planning phase to ensure efficient and systematic project management and to evaluate the planning of the current project. According to existing research, management of permanent projects involves both internal and external perspectives. The essential aspects related to project management are the project life cycle requirements.

The control of external perspectives deals with the life cycle of the product and focuses on planning, implementation, and further support management and processes. The construction project solves stability problems based on ecological, economic, and economic reasons and the life cycle of the project's resources.

There are seven key principles of a building's life cycle in sustainable construction: less resources used, resource reuse, use of recyclable resources, reduction or elimination of negative impacts on the environment, non-use of toxic materials, reduction in the costs of the building's life, and the project's life cycle quality.

Sustainable design is a design philosophy that aims to maximize the artificial environment by reducing or eliminating negative environmental impacts. Building green buildings means improving the efficiency of buildings to use energy, water, and materials efficiently and minimize the negative effects on human health. It means that project managers will be responsible for managing more complex budgets and projects. A green building is carefully designed, built, operated, and reused, or removed from the artificial environment, in an environmentally friendly, energy-efficient, and stable manner. The best location, design, construction, operation, service, and removal (part of the building's life cycle) are the means to achieve this.

The building construction sector is a complex industry. It has a long-lasting impact on the economy, the environment, and society, and requires much investment. Construction management and technology are two critical factors influencing the construction industry. Poor execution of construction projects, taking into account costs and planning, is one of common problems. Over the past three decades, designers and architects have applied dozens of efficient and effective advanced building technologies and engineering innovations to construction projects.

Nevertheless, the overall efficiency of the sector is quite low [2]. Prior practice has shown that digital technology allows flexible and efficient planning, management, and implementation of construction projects [3]. Successful implementation and results of new techniques and technologies depend on the active participation of project management specialists interested in implementing them, the information available to the population concerned about the project, and effective management of the project. Effective project management aims to achieve project goals by applying knowledge, skills, and estimation tools, overall organization, planning and control techniques in such way that the results meet the requirements of acceptable quality, risk, security, and safety levels, and ensures timely implementation of the project with the efficient use of funds [4]. Therefore, sustainability is an essential part of project management.

Sarma [5] described the three main groups of effective management process (Figure 1). Confucius said [6]: "In all things, success depends on previous preparation, and without such previous preparation there is sure to be the failure." The project character changes in each life cycle phase (Project Origination → Project Initiation → Project Planning → Project Execution and Control → Project Closeout → Post-Project Evaluation). In each stage of the project life cycle, new intermediate products are created, with the critical outcome of one phase forming an essential input to the next step. Each project's control system should include costs, planning and scheduling activities, and a change management control. Construction projects of different types of buildings impact the project life cycle and management options. Figure 2 shows a pyramid (hierarchy) of different available approaches, which are applied to select the proper project option.

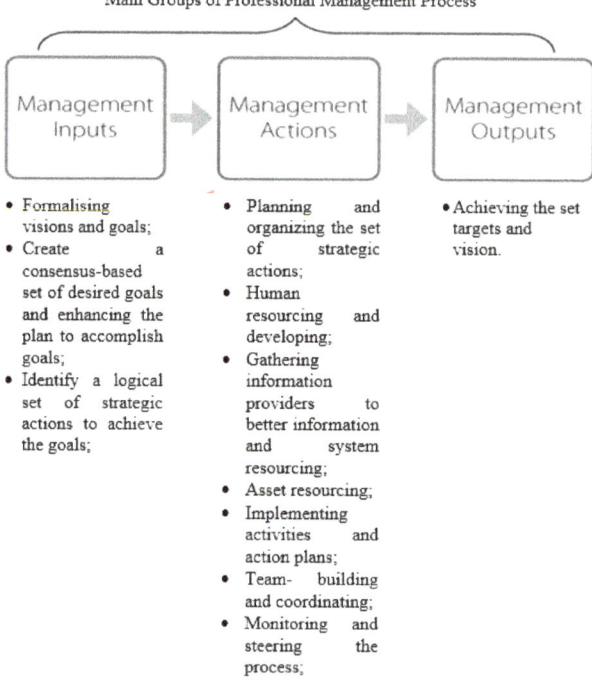

Figure 1. Main groups of professional management processes.

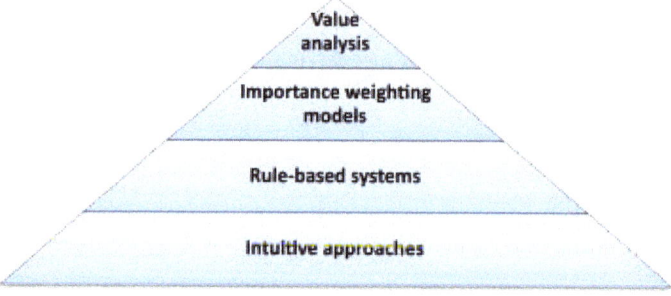

Figure 2. A pyramid of decision approaches [7].

The aim of the article is to identify the main problems in construction management; to develop a model (framework) for decision-making; to present a case study analysis; and to make conclusions.

2. Problems of Construction Management

A successful construction organization does not consider itself to be a producer of goods or services but is looking for ways to buy a customer who wants to do business with it [8,9]. Dickson [10] identified selection criteria, which profoundly influenced later research in this area. The dynamics of the contractor selection studies built on innovation that moved toward the achievements of different fields of sciences. The different motivations of the persons involved were separated into task-related and non-task-related goals [11].

The idea of sustainability was born in the 18th century and applied to forest management issues (von Carlowitz, 1713, in Reference [12]). Options' evaluation and selection of the best contractor are critical issues to reduce financial costs and improve competitiveness in the temporary market. Moreover, environmental requirements and evaluating the potential contractors by incorporating green factors into the selection process are additional concerns. Yazdani et al. [13] presented an approach addressed to the inter-relationships between the customer requirements with the Decision Making Trial and Evaluation Laboratory (DEMATEL) method, while constructing a relationship structure. Finally, the Technique for Order Preference by Similarity to an Ideal Solution (COPRAS) was applied to prioritize and rank the alternatives. Kamali et al. [14] stressed the importance of choosing the right contractor approach between different options. Therefore, it is necessary to evaluate potential contractors according to many criteria, including aspects related to the different stages of the life cycle of a building. The most critical step is to identify and select the right set of criteria and their weightings. Besides, the results have shown that a focus on the social aspect of sustainability is increasing compared to environmental aspects.

In the last thirty years, maintainable progress has extensively expanded its acknowledgement between policy- and decision-makers. Nowadays, this notion objects to delivering a better setting, a more advanced society, and a settled economy in both developed and developing countries. Consequently, in order to reach a sustainable society, you essentially comprehend the basic gauges and espouse suitable sustainable policies in dissimilar parts of society and its subdivisions. As a vibrant element, the construction industry plays a critical role in sustainable growth, which appeals to decision-makers to discover sustainable solutions globally for such an active sector.

Heravi et al. [15] established a two-stage context to ponder uncertainty together with numerous fondness orders and peril attitudes of decision-makers via efficacy functions. The primary step takes advantage of the incorporation of the efficacy function, ELECTRE I (the elimination and choice translating reality), and Grey theory to rank the practicable substitutes. The next step utilizes the ordered weighted averaging (OWA) hand to aggregate the predilections of environmental, public, and economic measurements as three decision-makers, to determine the concluding ranking.

Rashid et al. [16] showed a tentative and analytical inquiry to advance a sustainably castoff concrete by combining ceramic waste as coarse aggregate. Ecological influences were also well thought out regarding the CO_2 footprint and the consumption of raw materials by concrete. They used the analytical hierarchy process (AHP) and Method for Order Preference by Resemblance to the Ideal Solution (TOPSIS).

Infrastructure is the main driver that can accelerate the equilibrium among the financial, public, and ecological features forming the triple bottom line. Diaz-Sarachaga et al. [17] regarded a methodology for the advance of a sustainable infrastructure rating system (SIRSDEC) targeted at encouraging the design, construction, and processing of sustainable infrastructure ventures in these geographical areas. The SIRSDEC was designed into an ordered decision-making tree involving three stages of essentials (requirements, criteria, and indicators) selected to measure infrastructure systems rendering to sustainability principles. The methodology of the SIRSDEC integrates the act of Multiple Criteria Decision Making (MCDM) methods such as the AHP to weight the essentials forming the decision-making tree and the integrated value model for sustainable assessment (MIVES) to value infrastructure projects according to their involvement at the triple bottom line.

The top issue in sustainable projects is the collection of a suitable contractor and construction technique, and they are the conclusive factors for their achievement. Ecological consequences are closely joined with society's built-in uncertainties and perils, and they are uncertain since environmental systems, as well as social systems, will undergo changes in the upcoming years. Therefore, the appointment of an appropriate contractor and a suitable construction method is an MCDM issue vastly important and must operate with fractional knowledge and uncertainty. Bansal et al. [18] implemented a fuzzy synthetic evaluation method using the analytic hierarchy method to deliver an analytical instrument to assess the applicability of prefabricated or on-site construction techniques.

Decision-makers' MCDM model is progressively used to explain sustainable construction matters [19]. Only one out of ten of the reviewed papers are measured comprehensively with limited inadequacies. An MCDM is a decision-making tool applied to an extensive range of ecological supervision difficulties. A thrilling ground of submission of the MCDM model is the assessment and analysis of the diverse features when numerous stakeholders are involved.

Fuzzy and hybrid approaches have been progressively used in construction risk management research. Islam et al. [20] accumulated and analyzed the basic perceptions and methods applied in this area to date. They suggested that the nature of compound projects is such that most risks are symbiotic of each other. Consequently, a fuzzy structured method such as the fuzzy analytical network process (FANP) has commonly been used for unlike compound projects.

Diaz-Balteiro et al. (2017) [21] analyzed and measured 271 papers in the Web of Science database linked to discrete MCDM and sustainability. There were three methods that were most commonly used: AHP, TOPSIS, and Simple Additive Weighting (SAW). A noteworthy part of the MCDM techniques were the hybridized with cluster decision-making techniques, which have been applied to a countless variety of problems, levels, and segments related to sustainability. The purpose of this hybridization procedure entails including in the analysis the likings of the stakeholders concerning the indicators originally recommended. The appearance of new auspicious approaches like the uneven set theory hybridized with MCDM is of interest. The difference between ordinal and fundamental preferences, whole and fractional preferences, or local and universal preferences, leads to different situations that describe precise group decision-making models.

Having the ability to set a winning direction within the sustainable development of the environment and motivating people to follow that direction is the most exciting aspect of the construction industry. Each of the methods for contractor selection has some limitations, depending upon how each is used [22].

Many researchers have highlighted the quality of delivery and products as the primary factor in choosing suppliers [23–25]. One can understand the life cycle of construction projects as a process that involves risks. Contractual risk management is an integral part of effective legal risk management. The contractual risk management objectives do not limit the management of legal risks associated with the conclusion of contracts. Integrated contractual planning and management, as well as contractual risk management approaches, are similar to other risk management measures in the economy [26,27].

There is not one single management mode for managing each different project. The implementation requirements for various projects do not precisely match the needs of other projects.

All construction professionals, such as civil, mechanical, and electrical engineers, financiers, and architects, have a significant impact on the entire construction process. They affect both situations, people's choice and management, goals, efficiency, and quality. The building is classified as a construction project when the planning of the construction is complete. Tenders select contractors through contests from potential and qualified contractors. The contractor is selected using one of three common selection methods: qualification-based selection, selection according to the best-value selection, or low-bid selection. Today's project manager is confronted with many old or new challenges. Many of these challenges directly affect construction performance, while others have an indirect impact on peripheral activities. Implementation of a construction project is an integration of complex interrelated activities for achieving the objectives set, which is the best-organized disorder.

The primary features of the implementation of construction projects:

(a) The work is not carried out under controlled conditions, and therefore is highly dependent on weather conditions and other environmental conditions [28];
(b) The information for a specific building site varies significantly depending on the size and importance of the designed building, its location, and whether the facilities to be provided are in an unmapped area or merely an expansion of the existing facilities [29];
(c) Construction processes depend on the knowledge and abilities of the planners;
(d) Safety: construction by nature is inherently dangerous, with a high degree of hazard and risk;

(e) The threat has to be transferred to those people who best of all can control them. Stakeholders' desires concern all expected risks in the contract. It serves no useful purpose to force an onerous, one-sided contract on contractors and sub-contractors taking all the risk in the contract;

(f) Each project is unique. There is no same road to manage each project. Situations, people, and goals change over time. Never before has a project been available which has had the same circumstances and requirements. Situations, people, and purposes change over time. All new ideas and possible variants of decisions have to be compared by many criteria [30]. The complex nature of decision-making requires practitioners to select investment options by a broader palette of political reasons along with the analysis of a ratio of "expense effect" and purely technical reasons. In the economy and the development of the decision, it is essential that the impacts of cultural, social, moral, legislative, demographic, economic, ecological, state, and technological changes in the business world on the international, national, regional, and local markets are considered. The analysis of multi-criteria is a useful tool for many similar problems [31–33];

(g) The construction business is the industry, which slowly accepts innovations. The choice of more effective technological systems in the building is a complex task with several criteria [34];

(h) A client describes vaguely, continually changing requirements [35];

(i) Clients are slow with communication [36];

(j) Work is frequently seasonal;

(k) The construction process is not defined as predictable;

(l) Temporary restrictions. Time is money for the owner, building customer, and the user of the build facility. The delay in construction causes not only loss of profits, excesses of costs, and sometimes poor quality, but also many significant disputes, even full-time jobs, and many long-term challenges. A delay means the loss of the owner's income, such as production, and other commercial facilities are at disposal not in due time. Baldwin and Manthei [37] described 17 delay factors: weather, labor resources, subcontractors, constructive changes, plans, fund status, material shortage, manufactured items, type approvals, jurisdictional disputes, denial of equipment, contracts, construction mistakes, inspections, finance, solutions, and construction standards and building regulations. Other factors contributing to the construction slowdown are labor-management relations, strikes, poor organization, planning, coordination, deteriorating quality of craft, productivity, lack of craftsmen skills, quality of training, delivery delays, and the high cost of financing. Additionally, Arditi et al. [38], among other things, observed the following reasons for delays in public projects in Turkey: lack of materials, difficulties in receiving payments from agencies, contractors' problems, and the specific characteristics of contractors and state institutions;

(m) Socio-political pressure. Political pressure and society affect public and private sector employees to some extent;

(n) The organization. The level of the structure should establish a formal system of human roles to achieve the goals of the company.

The project team has to solve all identified problems of the leadership in construction as soon as it is possible. Sexton and Senaratne [39] showed that the organization and design theories of management are in connection with problem-solving as an information-processing activity. Members of the project team brought various types of knowledge into the situation of a problem and created, captured, and shared it when solving a problem of management of project involving changes.

3. Model for Multi-Criteria Decision-Making in Construction Management

3.1. Multi-Criteria Methods and Construction Management

Multi-criteria decision-making deals with making decisions where multiple criteria (usually being in contradiction) are present. Different criteria can have different specific qualitative features, units of measurement, and relative weight scales. There is the possibility that some of the criteria can only be described subjectively and others only measured numerically. Scientists developed the foundations of modern MCDM in the 1950s and 1960s. There are dozens of ways to solve MCDM problems. The MCDM methods grant the solutions for a whole series of management issues.

In the 1980s and at the beginning of 1990s, the development of MCDM methods grew rapidly. Koksalan et al. [40] and Kahraman et al. [41] gave a short history of the development of MCDM methods. Zavadskas and Turskis [42] and Zavadskas et al. [43] gave detailed studies about the application of the MCDM methods in different fields of the management and the economy. Jato-Espino et al. [44] reviewed applications of multi-criteria decision-making methods in construction. Mardani et al. [45] looked at the use of some multiple-criteria decision-making techniques. The most popular hybrid MCDM methods demonstrate the advantages over traditional ones to solve complicated problems which involve stakeholder preferences, interconnected or contradictory criteria, and uncertain environments. Decision-makers could use multi-criteria decision-making methods [46] such as analytic hierarchy process [47], fuzzy analytic hierarchy process [48,49], fuzzy Delphi [50], analytic network process under intuitionistic fuzzy set [51], Additive Ratio Assessment (ARAS) [52], simple additive weighting and game theory [53], discrete two persons' zero-sum matrix game theory [54], Evaluation based on Distance from Average Solution (EDAS), COPRAS, TOPSIS [55], as well as developing original models [56].

Saaty [57] published a detailed study on AHP applications. The extension of existing and integration of well-known methods or development of hybrid methods became common practice (primarily by the application of the fuzzy and grey systems theory). Some time ago COPRAS [58,59] and ARAS [33,60] were presented by Lithuanian scientists. Later, MCDM methods such as multi-objective optimization on the basis of ratio analysis (MOORA) and MOORA plus full multiplicative form (MULTIMOORA) [61,62] were developed. Then, Step-Wise Weight Assessment Ratio Analysis (SWARA) [63], Weighted Aggregated Sum Product ASsessment (WASPAS) [64], and KEmeny Median Indicator Rank Accordance (KEMIRA) [65] appeared and were applied to particular real-life cases. Different modifications of the TOPSIS method is the second most widely used group of MCDM methods to solve complicated problems in construction [66]. Table 1 presents the most common problems solved using multi-criteria decision-making methods.

There are several possible consequences of which the owner who chooses a contractor who uses the method of low bidding should be informed of. First, one supposes by the process of the competitive auction that all enterprises (including the material suppliers, the general contractors, and the subcontractors) have submitted a proposal on the work that is as cheap as permitted, as the drawings and the technical specifications of the project have allowed. Secondly, there is the widespread mistake (particularly among the amateurs) that the technical requirements and the drawings will automatically mean that all contractors will provide the same results, and that the results will correspond to the expectations of the owner. Lastly, lacking any contractor input at this stage of project engineering, the total of the final low-bid is still unknown until the contractor actually finishes the project. This means that the architect and owner must wait uneasily until the design and bidding phases are completed before they will know if their plan is on, or under, or (more probably) over budget.

Table 1. Most common problems solved by using multi-criteria decision-making methods (quantitative and qualitative (Q/Q), fuzzy (F)).

Considered Problem	Information Type	Multiple Criteria Method Used	Reference
Construction project selection	Q/Q	COPRAS-G [1]	[59]
	F	TOPSIS	[66]
Choice of operating system	F	TOPSIS, AHP	[67]
Service selection	F	Grey correlation TOPSIS, AHP	[68]
Selection of grippers, Selection for financial investments, Selecting robotic processes, Comparing company performances, Comparing financial ratio performance	F	TOPSIS	[69]
Wastewater treatment process selection	F	TOPSIS, AHP	[70]
Selection of sustainable investment	F	TOPSIS	[71]
Green building material selection	F	ANP [2], DEMATEL	[72]
Determination of strategic priorities by analysis of strengths, weaknesses, opportunities and threats (SWOT)	F	Goal Programming	[73]
Project management critical success factors	F	ANP, DEMATEL	[74]
Material selection and new product development	F	COPRAS	[75]
Choice of the action plan and dynamic supplier selection	F	Mixed integer linear programming	[76]
Sustainable building assessment/certification	Q/Q	ARAS	[77]
Selection of suitable bridge construction method	F	AHP	[78]
Selection of construction site	F	ARAS and AHP	[79]
Design of products	Q/Q	Yin-Yang balance, SWARA	[80]
Supplier selection	F	TOPSIS	[81]
	F	TOPSIS, AHP	[82]
Contractor selection	F	AHP, PERT [3]	[83]
	Q/Q	QBS [4]	[84]
	Q/Q	QBS, Low Bid	[85]
	F	MFPR [5]	[86]
	F	TOPSIS, AHP	[87]
	Q/Q	Best-Value, AHP	[88]

[1] COmplex PRoportional ASsessment of alternatives with grey relations (COPRAS-G); [2] Analytic Network Process (ANP); [3] Program Evaluation and Review Technique (PERT); [4] Qualifications Based Selection (QBS); [5] Multiple-layer Fuzzy Pattern Recognition.

3.2. Model Development for Multi-Criteria Decision-making

The specific steps are essential to solve a multi-criteria decision-making problem. Figure 3 presents the developed approach. First, decision-makers define all feasible alternatives to the problem solution. Second, they should set the alternatives' criteria. Decision-makers identify factors, which have an essential influence on and are important to the contractor's choices. Third, the stakeholder identifies goals and a set of criteria. Fourth, decision-makers define the values of criteria, because each criterion has its value for a different specific choice. As an example, an experience of each contractor given as outstanding (OT) or right, average (AV) or below average (BA), and lastly as unsatisfactory (UN). On the other hand, profitability defined as either high (HG), average (AV) or even low (LW), and others. Fourth, it is necessary to establish criteria weights where one can identify more or less essential criteria. The more critical criteria are given greater weight. Then, decision-makers evaluate alternatives. Lastly, the best option is chosen using calculations aided by computer software.

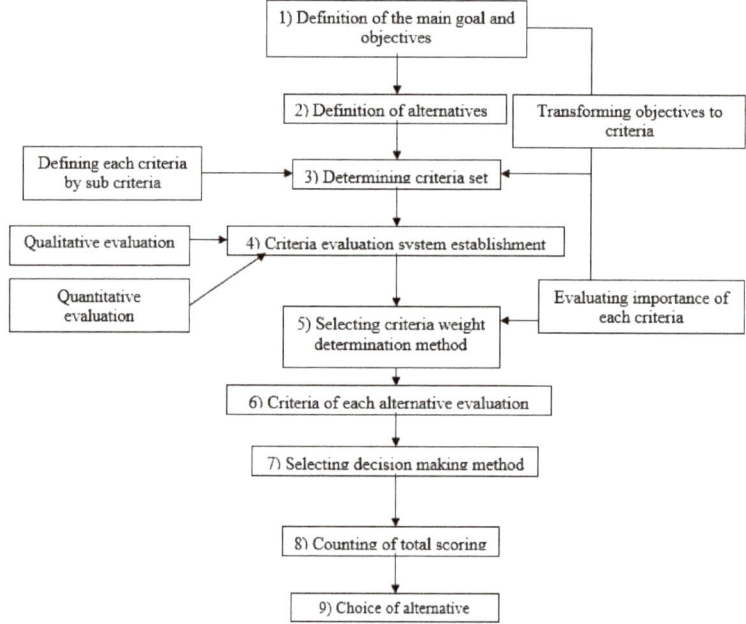

Figure 3. Framework for decision-making in a construction model.

4. Case Study: Turkish Construction Project Management—Sustainable Decision-Making: Finding the Best Contractor

4.1. Project Description and Problem Considered

In construction, one of the most critical tasks is selecting the right contractor. It is a multi-criteria problem including both quantitative and qualitative factors. To choose the right contractor from many applicants available in today's market is a somewhat complicated problem for clients. Selecting of a proper contractor is crucially important to ensure the quality of the constructed building when dealing with long-term assets. To achieve this aim, it will largely depend on the efficiency of the performance of the selected contractor [89]. Studies of contractor selection date back to the early 1960s.

A three-star seven-story hotel is to be built in the south of Turkey, close to Antalya. The hotel stakeholders want to create a swimming pool. The measurements are:

- Oval shape;

- 25-m long;
- 10-m wide;
- 2.2-m deep.

A little amount of work is left to finish the project. The project manager has to select a building contractor. The primary objective is to choose the correct contractor for the pool. Picking the right contractor to build the pool is the primary aim. The main criteria are:

- Good design;
- Good quality;
- Best financial options.

4.2. Making Alternatives

This example shows the selection of the contractor based on analysis using multi-criteria methodologies. The contractor choice is a significant decision for a construction manager, as the success of the whole project will be affected.

Stakeholders will select the contractor from five contractors. The selection of the contractor is based on the use of multi-criteria methods to evaluate and combine objective and subjective criteria with a significant impact on the effective implementation of the construction project. All contractors are well-known companies in Turkey from Ankara, Istanbul, and Izmir.

4.3. Setting the Criteria, Determining Their Values

Contractor choice for the project will be dependent on many different things. Some are more important, for example, technical experience. Others, such as their safety record are not so important.

Thus, when choosing, it is essential to evaluate a contractor's:

(1) technical experience,
(2) record of performance,
(3) financial stability,
(4) the qualifications of the employees and the management,
(5) capacity,
(6) safety record, and
(7) equipment and operation.

These main criteria should be taken into account while choosing, but also secondary criteria must be evaluated, for example, capacity, the number of projects on which the contractor is currently working, etc. The criteria set was determined by questioning experts and stakeholders and based on the literature overview. Figure 4 presents the criteria and sub-criteria sets, which influence the choice of the contractor in this project.

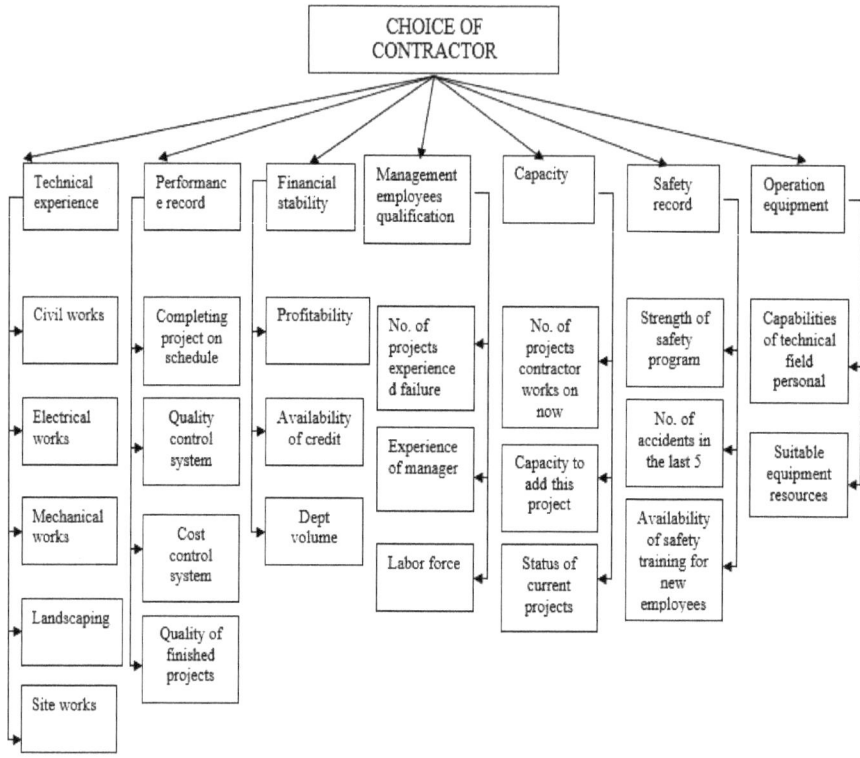

Figure 4. Set of criteria system.

It means that this model has two levels; main criteria and secondary criteria.

- Technical Experience (TE)—this shows the contractor's experience in civil (TE1), electrical (TE2), mechanical (TE3), landscaping (TE4), and site (TE5) works. The project number is considered as an essential criterion. If the contractor has completed >20 projects, the evaluation can be considered as outstanding (OT), 15–10 very good (VG), 10–15 average (AV), 5–10 below average (BA), and fewer than five projects – unsatisfactory (UN).
- Performance Record (PE)—shows if the contractor usually completes projects on time (PE1) (always (AL), sometimes (SM), or rarely (RR)), and will evaluate any quality (PE2) and cost control (PE3) systems, including the finished project quality (PE4). PE2, PE3 and PE4 are assessed as either outstanding (OT) or very good (VG), average (AV) or below average (BA), or unsatisfactory (UN).
- Financial Stability (FS)—evaluates such things as the contractor's profitability (FS1), credit availability (FS2), as well as debt (FS3). Either high (HG), average (AV) or low (LW).
- Qualification of Management Employees (ME)—This evaluates the number of failures in the contractor's projects (ME1) (never (0), 3 or less (≤3), more than 3 (>3), experience of managers (ME2) (less than 5 years (<5), from 5 to 10 years (5–10), more than 10 year (>10) and workers' experience (ME3) (strong (S), moderate (M), poor (P).
- Capacity (CA)—This will evaluate the projects the contractor is working on (CA1) (less than 5 (<5), from 5 to 10 (5–10), more than 10 (>10), and the ability (capacity) to include this project (CA2) strong (S), moderate (M), and weak (W), as well as ongoing project status (CA3). Evaluation of status of current (ongoing) projects: ahead of schedule (SA), as scheduled (SO), behind schedule (SB), and stopped (SS).

- Safety Record (SR)—This is about the strengths of the safety program (SR1) (outstanding (OT) or very good (VG), average (AV) or below average (BA), or unsatisfactory (UN), number of accidents that happened in the last five years (SR2) (less than 5 (<5), from 5 to 10 (5–10), more than 10 (>10), and availability of safety training for new employees (SR3) (available (Yes), not available (No).
- Operation and Equipment (OE)—This shows the expertise of technical field employees (OE1) (outstanding (OT) or very good (VG), average (AV) or below average (BA), or unsatisfactory (UN) and equipment suitability (OE2). The secondary criteria, (e.g., technical field personnel abilities), are evaluated qualitatively, depending on the competencies of employees: very suitable (VS), average (AV), acceptable (AC), unsatisfactory (UN).

Criteria are worked out depending on their origin. Table 2 provides a possible evaluation of criteria and sub-criteria. As it shows, aspects of technical experience can be evaluated on a scale from OT to UN, etc. It means that this model has two levels; main criteria and secondary criteria.

Table 2. Evaluation of criteria.

Criteria	Sub-Criteria	Evaluation				
TE	TE1	OT	VG	AV	BA	UN
	TE2	OT	VG	AV	BA	UN
	TE3	OT	VG	AV	BA	UN
	TE4	OT	VG	AV	BA	UN
	TE5	OT	VG	AV	BA	UN
PE	PE1	AL	SM	RR	-	-
	PE2	OT	VG	AV	BA	UN
	PE3	OT	VG	AV	BA	UN
	PE4	OT	VG	AV	BA	UN
FS	FS1	HG	AV	LW	-	-
	FS2	HG	AV	LW	-	-
	FS3	HG	AV	LW	-	-
ME	ME1	0	≤3	>3	-	-
	ME2	<5	5–10	>10	-	-
	ME3	S	M	P	-	-
CA	CA1	<5	5–10	>10	-	-
	CA2	S	M	W	-	-
	CA3	SA	SO	SB	SS	-
SR	SR1	OT	VG	AV	BA	UN
	SR2	<5	5–10	>10	-	-
	SR3	Yes	No	-	-	-
OE	OE1	OT	VG	AV	BA	UN
	OE2	VS	AV	AC	UN	-

4.4. Calculation According to the Model

The criteria were weighted using "Expert Choice" software (based on the AHP method). From the model, factors (criteria) of level one (Figure 4) were as input, which was calculated using the software. Firstly, the main criteria's weights were worked out. The team of experts discussed the initial matrix for comparing the relative importance of the criteria in pairs. Table 3 provides a comparison matrix.

Table 3. Comparison matrix.

Criteria	TE	PE	FS	ME	CA	SR	OE	Criteria Weights
TE	1	2	5	5	6	6	2	0.33
PE	-	1	6	6	7	6	2	0.29
FS	-	-	1	1	3	3	1	0.09
ME	-	-	-	1	4	3	1/3	0.08
CA	-	-	-	-	1	2	1/5	0.04
SR	-	-	-	-	-	1	1/4	0.03
OE	-	-	-	-	-	-	1	0.15
			Σ:					1
				CR = 0.05				

If CR is less than 0.1, then it is assumed that the expert is consistent in his evaluations.

In a similar way, the weights of the sub-criteria were determined for each of the criteria groups. Table 4 presents the summary of the defined criteria and sub-criteria weights.

Table 4. Weights of the criteria and sub-criteria.

Criteria	Weight	Sub-Criteria	Weight
TE	0.33	TE1	0.19
		TE2	0.02
		TE3	0.07
		TE4	0.02
		TE5	0.03
PE	0.29	PE1	0.07
		PE2	0.07
		PE3	0.07
		PE4	0.07
FS	0.09	FS1	0.02
		FS2	0.05
		FS3	0.02
ME	0.08	ME1	0.06
		ME2	0.01
		ME3	0.01
CA	0.04	CA1	0.01
		CA2	0.01
		CA3	0.02
SR	0.03	SR1	0.01
		SR2	0.02
		SR3	0.00
OE	0.15	OE1	0.15
		OE2	0.00

Therefore, criteria rank according to importance are as follows: TE (the most important); PE; OE; FS; ME; CA; SR (the least important).

Table 5 provides information on the evaluation of each criterion and sub-criterion for each of the five contractors. Criteria evaluated according to their PE and other information.

Table 5. Evaluation of contractors based on the criteria set.

Criteria	Sub-Criteria	Contractor				
		C_1	C_2	C_3	C_4	C_5
TE	TE1	VG	VG	OT	AV	AV
	TE2	VG	VG	OT	BA	AV
	TE3	VG	VG	OT	BA	AV
	TE4	VG	VG	OT	BA	AV
	TE5	VG	VG	OT	AV	AV
PE	PE1	SM	SM	AL	RR	SM
	PE2	VG	AV	VG	UN	AV
	PE3	AV	AV	VG	UN	BA
	PE4	VG	VG	OT	BA	AV
FS	FS1	AV	HG	HG	LW	AV
	FS2	AV	HG	AV	LW	LW
	FS3	LW	LW	LW	LW	AV
ME	ME1	≤3	0	0	>3	0
	ME2	>10	5–10	>10	<5	5–10
	ME3	M	M	M	P	M
CA	CA1	<5	5–10	>10	<5	>10
	CA2	S	M	W	S	W
	CA3	SB	SO	SO	SB	SB
SR	SR1	BA	BA	AV	UN	UN
	SR2	<5	<5	>10	5–10	>10
	SR3	No	No	Yes	No	No
OE	OE1	AV	AV	VG	BA	BA
	OE2	AV	AV	VS	UN	AC

Decision-makers prepared the initial decision-making matrix for problem-solving based on Saaty's [45] scale.

Finally, Table 6 provides the overall scoring of each contractor on different criteria. The "Expert Choice" program scored different criteria values of each contractor.

In Table 6, all optional values are the biggest values:

$$K_j = \sum_{i=1}^{m} \frac{x_{ij} w_i}{\sum_{j=1}^{n} x_{ij}} \tag{1}$$

where: w_i—weight of sub-criteria; x_{ij}—evaluation of i contractor according to the j criterion; $I = 1, m$; $j = 1, n$; m—number of criteria; n—number of contractors.

According to Table 6, the best contractor is C_3 because their score is 0.55, the worst contractor is contractor C_4 because their score is 0.15.

Table 6. Overall scoring of contractors.

Criteria	Sub-Criteria	Contractor				
		C_1	C_2	C_3	C_4	C_5
TE	TE1	0.10	0.10	0.02	0.05	0.05
	TE2	0.01	0.01	0.02	0.00	0.00
	TE3	0.04	0.04	0.03	0.01	0.02
	TE4	0.01	0.01	0.02	0.00	0.00
	TE5	0.02	0.02	0.03	0.01	0.01
PE	PE1	0.02	0.02	0.07	0.01	0.02
	PE2	0.04	0.02	0.04	0.01	0.02
	PE3	0.02	0.02	0.04	0.01	0.01
	PE4	0.04	0.04	0.07	0.01	0.02
FS	FS1	0.00	0.02	0.02	0.00	0.00
	FS2	0.01	0.05	0.01	0.01	0.01
	FS3	0.00	0.00	0.00	0.00	0.00
ME	ME1	0.01	0.06	0.06	0.01	0.06
	ME2	0.01	0.00	0.01	0.00	0.00
	ME3	0.00	0.00	0.00	0.00	0.00
CA	CA1	0.01	0.00	0.00	0.01	0.00
	CA2	0.01	0.00	0.00	0.01	0.00
	CA3	0.01	0.01	0.01	0.01	0.01
SR	SR1	0.00	0.00	0.00	0.00	0.00
	SR2	0.02	0.02	0.00	0.01	0.00
	SR3	0.00	0.00	0.00	0.00	0.00
OE	OE1	0.02	0.02	0.05	0.01	0.01
	OE2	0.02	0.02	0.05	0.00	0.01
Σ		0.40	0.47	0.55	0.15	0.25

5. Conclusions

A large number of problems in construction management are those of MCDM. To counter the complex nature of a problem, one can use four optimization methods. These are multi-criteria, cost-oriented, single-objective, and multi-objective. The case study identified ten groups of significant construction management problems. One of the most important is choosing the right contractor.

Project managers could use optimization, elimination, and probabilistic methods to select and background effective decisions. The multiple-criteria side is significant when decisions deal with construction management.

The research suggested the nine-stage model for decision-making problem-solving. The stages are as follows: (a) definition of the primary goal and objectives; (b) definition of alternatives; (c) determining the criteria set; (d) establishment of a criteria evaluation system; (e) selecting the criteria weight determination method; (f) determining criteria values for each alternative under consideration; (g) selecting a decision-making method; (h) counting of the total performance score; (j) choice of an option to implement.

Based on the overview of the literature, and expert judgement criteria set was worked out as follows: (a) performance; (b) technical experience; (c) stability of finances; (d) management performance/employee qualification; (e) capacity; (f) record of safety; (g) equipment operation.

The model proposed was used to select a sustainable contractor in the construction of the pool at the seven-story hotel near the Mediterranean Sea in Turkey. After analyzing the alternatives, the best contractor was C_3 (with a total score of 0.55).

Author Contributions: Conceptualization, S.A.E. and J.Š.; Methodology, S.A.E. and Z.T.; Formal Analysis, S.A.E. and Z.T.; Investigation, S.A.E.; Data Curation, S.A.E.; Writing—Original Draft Preparation, J.Š.; Writing—Review and Editing, S.A.E. and J.Š.; Visualization, S.A.E.; Supervision, Z.T.

Funding: This research received no external funding.

Conflicts of Interest: The authors declare no conflict of interest.

References

1. Yu, M.; Zhu, F.; Yang, X.; Wang, L.; Sun, X. Integrating Sustainability into Construction Engineering Projects: Perspective of Sustainable Project Planning. *Sustainability* **2018**, *10*, 784. [CrossRef]
2. Aziz, R.F.; Hafez, S.M. Applying lean thinking in construction and performance improvement. *Alex. Eng. J.* **2013**, *52*, 679–695. [CrossRef]
3. Whyte, J.; Stasis, A.; Lindkvist, C. Managing change in the delivery of complex projects: Configuration management, asset information and 'big data'. *Int. J. Proj. Manag.* **2015**, *34*, 339–351. [CrossRef]
4. Hoda, R.; Murugesan, L.K. Multi-level agile project management challenges: A self-organizing team perspective. *J. Syst. Softw.* **2016**, *117*, 245–257. [CrossRef]
5. Sarma, S.P. *Professional Management*; New Age International Pvt Ltd.: Calcuta, India, 1998.
6. Confucius. *The Doctrine of the Mean*; Translated by James Legge; The University of Adelaide: Adelaide, Australia, 2014.
7. Schoemaker, P.J.H.; Russo, J.E. A pyramid of decision approaches. *Calif. Manag. Rev.* **1993**, *36*, 9–31. [CrossRef]
8. Carter, C.F.; Williams, B.R. *Industry and Technical Progress: Factors Governing the Speed of Application of Science*; Oxford University Press: London, UK, 1957.
9. Levitt, T. Marketing Myopia. *Harv. Bus. Rev.* **1960**, *38*, 45–56. [CrossRef]
10. Dickson, G.W. An analysis of vendor selection systems and decisions. *J. Purch.* **1966**, *2*, 5–17. [CrossRef]
11. Strauss, G. Tactics of lateral relationships. *Adm. Sci. Q.* **1962**, *7*, 161–186. [CrossRef]
12. Pretzsch, J. Paradigms of tropical forestry in rural development. In *Forests and Rural Development*; Springer: Berlin/Heidelberg, Germany, 2014; pp. 7–49.
13. Yazdani, M.; Chatterjee, P.; Zavadskas, E.K.; Zolfani, S.H. Integrated QFD-MCDM framework for green supplier selection. *J. Clean. Prod.* **2017**, *142*, 3728–3740. [CrossRef]
14. Kamali, M.; Hewage, K. Development of performance criteria for sustainability evaluation of modular versus conventional construction methods. *J. Clean. Prod.* **2017**, *142*, 3592–3606. [CrossRef]
15. Heravi, G.; Fathi, M.; Faeghi, S. Multi-criteria group decision-making method for optimal selection of sustainable industrial building options focused on petrochemical projects. *J. Clean. Prod.* **2017**, *142*, 2999–3013. [CrossRef]
16. Rashid, K.; Razzaq, A.; Ahmad, M.; Rashid, T.; Tariq, S. Experimental and analytical selection of sustainable recycled concrete with ceramic waste aggregate. *Constr. Build. Mater.* **2017**, *154*, 829–840. [CrossRef]
17. Diaz-Sarachaga, J.M.; Jato-Espino, D.; Castro-Fresno, D. Methodology for the development of a new Sustainable Infrastructure Rating System for Developing Countries (SIRSDEC). *Environ. Sci. Policy* **2017**, *69*, 65–72. [CrossRef]
18. Bansal, S.; Biswas, S.; Singh, S.K. Fuzzy decision approach for selection of most suitable construction method of Green Buildings. *Int. J. Sustain. Built Environ.* **2017**, *6*, 122–132. [CrossRef]
19. Vassoney, E.; Mochet, A.M.; Comoglio, C. Use of multicriteria analysis (MCA) for sustainable hydropower planning and management. *J. Environ. Manag.* **2017**, *196*, 48–55. [CrossRef] [PubMed]
20. Islam, M.S.; Nepal, M.P.; Skitmore, M.; Attarzadeh, M. Current research trends and application areas of fuzzy and hybrid methods to the risk assessment of construction projects. *Adv. Eng. Inform.* **2017**, *33*, 112–131. [CrossRef]
21. Diaz-Balteiro, L.; González-Pachón, J.; Romero, C. Measuring systems sustainability with multi-criteria methods: A critical review. *Eur. J. Oper. Res.* **2017**, *258*, 607–616. [CrossRef]

22. Myers, J.H.; Alpert, M.I. Determinant buying attitudes: Meaning and measurement. *J. Mark.* **1968**, *32*, 13–20. [CrossRef]
23. Luthra, S.; Govindan, K.; Kannan, D.; Mangla, S.K.; Garg, C.P. An integrated framework for sustainable supplier selection and evaluation in supply chains. *J. Clean. Prod.* **2017**, *140*, 1686–1698. [CrossRef]
24. Junior, F.R.L.; Osiro, L.; Carpinetti, L.C.R. A comparison between Fuzzy AHP and Fuzzy TOPSIS methods to supplier selection. *Appl. Soft Comput.* **2014**, *21*, 194–209. [CrossRef]
25. Wu, J. A SD-IITFOWA operator and TOPSIS based approach for MAGDM problems with intuitionistic trapezoidal fuzzy numbers. *Technol. Econ. Dev. Econ.* **2015**, *21*, 28–47. [CrossRef]
26. Zavadskas, E.K.; Vilutienė, T.; Turskis, Z.; Tamošaitienė, J. Contractor selection for construction works by applying SAW-G and TOPSIS grey techniques. *J. Bus. Econ. Manag.* **2010**, *11*, 34–55. [CrossRef]
27. Makovšek, D. Systematic construction risk, cost estimation mechanism and unit price movements. *Transp. Policy* **2014**, *35*, 135–145. [CrossRef]
28. Fouladgar, M.M.; Yazdani-Chamzini, A.; Lashgari, A.; Zavadskas, E.K.; Turskis, Z. Maintenance strategy selection using AHP and COPRAS under fuzzy environment. *Int. J. Strateg. Prop. Manag.* **2012**, *16*, 85–104. [CrossRef]
29. Peldschus, F.; Zavadskas, E.K.; Turskis, Z.; Tamošaitienė, J. Sustainable assessment of construction site by applying game theory. *Inz. Ekon.-Eng. Econ.* **2010**, *21*, 223–237.
30. Turskis, Z.; Zavadskas, E.K.; Peldschus, F. Multi-criteria optimization system for decision making in construction design and management. *Inz. Ekon.-Eng. Econ.* **2009**, *61*, 7–17.
31. Zagorskas, J.; Zavadskas, E.K.; Turskis, Z.; Burinskienė, M.; Blumberga, A.; Blumberga, D. Thermal insulation alternatives of historic brick buildings in Baltic Sea Region. *Energy Build.* **2014**, *78*, 35–42. [CrossRef]
32. Brauers, W.K.M.; Zavadskas, E.K.; Peldschus, F.; Turskis, Z. Multi-objective decision-making for road design. *Transport* **2008**, *23*, 183–193. [CrossRef]
33. Zavadskas, E.K.; Turskis, Z. A new additive ratio assessment (ARAS) method in multicriteria decision-making. *Technol. Econ. Dev. Econ.* **2010**, *16*, 159–172. [CrossRef]
34. Zavadskas, E.K.; Turskis, Z.; Volvačiovas, R.; Kildienė, S. Multi-criteria assessment model of technologies. *Stud. Inform. Control* **2013**, *22*, 249–258. [CrossRef]
35. Sivilevičius, H.; Zavadskas, E.K.; Turskis, Z. Quality attributes and complex assessment methodology of the asphalt mixing plant. *Balt. J. Road Bridge Eng.* **2008**, *3*, 161–166. [CrossRef]
36. Zavadskas, E.K.; Kaklauskas, A.; Turskis, Z.; Kalibatas, D. An approach to multi-attribute assessment of indoor environment before and after refurbishment of dwellings. *J. Environ. Eng. Landsc. Manag.* **2009**, *17*, 5–11. [CrossRef]
37. Baldwin, J.R.; Manthei, J.M. Causes of delays in the construction industry. *ASCE J. Constr. Div.* **1971**, *97*, 177–187.
38. Arditi, R.D.; Akan, G.T.; Gurdamar, S. Reasons for delays in public projects in Turkey. *Constr. Manag. Econ.* **1985**, *3*, 171–181. [CrossRef]
39. Senaratne, S.; Sexton, M. Managing construction project change: A knowledge management perspective. *Constr. Manag. Econ.* **2008**, *26*, 1303–1311. [CrossRef]
40. Köksalan, M.M.; Wallenius, J.; Zionts, S. *Multiple Criteria Decision Making: From Early History to the 21st Century*; World Scientific: Singapore, 2011.
41. Kahraman, C.; Onar, S.C.; Oztaysi, B. Fuzzy multicriteria decision-making: A literature review. *Int. J. Comput. Intell. Syst.* **2015**, *8*, 637–666. [CrossRef]
42. Zavadskas, E.K.; Turskis, Z. Multiple criteria decision making (MCDM) methods in economics: An overview. *Technol. Econ. Dev. Econ.* **2011**, *17*, 397–427. [CrossRef]
43. Zavadskas, E.K.; Turskis, Z.; Kildienė, S. State of art surveys of overviews on MCDM/MADM methods. *Technol. Econ. Dev. Econ.* **2014**, *20*, 165–179. [CrossRef]
44. Jato-Espino, D.; Castillo-Lopez, E.; Rodriguez-Hernandez, J.; Canteras-Jordana, J.C. A review of application of multi-criteria decision making methods in construction. *Autom. Constr.* **2014**, *45*, 151–162. [CrossRef]
45. Mardani, A.; Jusoh, A.; Nor, K.M.D.; Khalifah, Z.; Zakwan, N.; Valipour, A. Multiple criteria decision-making techniques and their applications—A review of the literature from 2000 to 2014. *Econ. Res.-Ekon. Istraz.* **2015**, *28*, 516–571. [CrossRef]
46. Ye, K.; Zeng, D.; Wong, J. Competition rule of the multi-criteria approach: What contractors in China really want? *J. Civ. Eng. Manag.* **2018**, *24*, 155–166. [CrossRef]

47. De la Fuente, A.; Armengou, J.; Pons, O.; Aguado, A. Multi-criteria decision-making model for assessing the sustainability index of wind-turbine support systems: Application to a new precast concrete alternative. *J. Civ. Eng. Manag.* **2017**, *23*, 194–203. [CrossRef]
48. Leśniak, A.; Kubek, D.; Plebankiewicz, E.; Zima, K.; Belniak, S. Fuzzy AHP application for supporting contractors' bidding decision. *Symmetry* **2018**, *10*, 642. [CrossRef]
49. Prascevic, N.; Prascevic, Z. Application of fuzzy AHP for ranking and selection of alternatives in construction project management. *J. Civ. Eng. Manag.* **2017**, *23*, 1123–1135. [CrossRef]
50. Chen, C.J.; Juan, Y.K.; Hsu, Y.H. Developing a systematic approach to evaluate and predict building service life. *J. Civ. Eng. Manag.* **2017**, *23*, 890–901. [CrossRef]
51. Štreimikienė, D.; Šliogerienė, J.; Turskis, Z. Multi-criteria analysis of electricity generation technologies in Lithuania. *Renew. Energy* **2016**, *85*, 148–156. [CrossRef]
52. Shariati, S.; Abedi, M.; Saedi, A.; Yazdani-Chamzini, A.; Tamošaitienė, J.; Šaparauskas, J.; Stupak, S. Critical factors of the application of nanotechnology in construction industry by using ANP technique under fuzzy intuitionistic environment. *J. Civ. Eng. Manag.* **2017**, *23*, 914–925. [CrossRef]
53. Kalibatas, D.; Kovaitis, V. Selecting the most effective alternative of waterproofing membranes for multifunctional inverted flat roofs. *J. Civ. Eng. Manag.* **2017**, *23*, 650–660. [CrossRef]
54. Gardziejczyk, W.; Zabicki, P. Normalization and variant assessment methods in selection of road alignment variants–case study. *J. Civ. Eng. Manag.* **2017**, *23*, 510–523. [CrossRef]
55. Bielinskas, V.; Burinskienė, M.; Podviezko, A. Choice of abandoned territories conversion scenario according to MCDA methods. *J. Civ. Eng. Manag.* **2018**, *24*, 79–92. [CrossRef]
56. Keshavarz Ghorabaee, M.; Zavadskas, E.K.; Olfat, L.; Turskis, Z. Multi-criteria inventory classification using a new method of evaluation based on distance from average solution (EDAS). *Informatica* **2015**, *26*, 435–451. [CrossRef]
57. Saaty, T.L. *The Analytic Hierarchy Process: Planning, Priority Setting, Resources Allocation*; McGraw-Hill: New York, NY, USA, 1980.
58. Zavadskas, E.K.; Kaklauskas, A. Determination of an efficient contractor by using the new method of multicriteria assessment. In *International Symposium for "The Organisation and Management of Construction". Shaping Theory and Practice. Managing the Construction Project and Managing Risk*; Langford, D.A., Retik, A., Eds.; CIBW: London, UK, 1996; Volume 65, pp. 95–104.
59. Zavadskas, E.K.; Turskis, Z.; Tamošaitienė, J.; Marina, V. Multicriteria selection of project managers by applying grey criteria. *Technol. Econ. Dev. Econ.* **2008**, *14*, 462–477. [CrossRef]
60. Turskis, Z.; Zavadskas, E.K.; Kutut, V. A model based on ARAS-G and AHP methods for multiple criteria prioritizing of heritage value. *Int. J. Inf. Technol. Decis. Mak.* **2013**, *12*, 45–73. [CrossRef]
61. Brauers, W.K.M.; Zavadskas, E.K. The MOORA method and its application to privatization in a transition economy. *Control Cybern.* **2006**, *35*, 445–469.
62. Brauers, W.K.M.; Zavadskas, E.K. Project management by MULTIMOORA as an instrument for transition economies. *Technol. Econ. Dev. Econ.* **2010**, *16*, 5–24. [CrossRef]
63. Keršulienė, V.; Zavadskas, E.K.; Turskis, Z. Selection of rational dispute resolution method by applying new Step-Wise Weight Assessment Ratio Analysis (SWARA). *J. Bus. Econ. Manag.* **2010**, *11*, 243–258. [CrossRef]
64. Zavadskas, E.K.; Turskis, Z.; Antuchevičienė, J.; Zakarevičius, A. Optimization of weighted aggregated sum product assessment. *Elektron. Elektrotechnika* **2012**, *122*, 3–6. [CrossRef]
65. Krylovas, A.; Zavadskas, E.K.; Kosareva, N.; Dadelo, S. New KEMIRA method for determining criteria priority and weights in solving MCDM Problem. *Int. J. Inf. Technol. Decis. Mak.* **2014**, *13*, 1119–1133. [CrossRef]
66. Zavadskas, E.K.; Mardani, A.; Turskis, Z.; Jusoh, A.; Nor, K.M. Development of TOPSIS method to solve complicated decision-making problems—An overview on developments from 2000 to 2015. *Int. J. Inf. Technol. Decis. Mak.* **2016**, *15*, 645–682. [CrossRef]
67. Balli, S.; Korukoglu, S. Operating system selection using fuzzy AHP and TOPSIS Methods. *Math. Comput. Appl.* **2009**, *14*, 119–130. [CrossRef]
68. Tian, G.; Zhang, H.; Feng, Y.; Wang, D.; Peng, Y.; Jia, H. Green decoration materials selection under interior environment characteristics: A grey-correlation based hybrid MCDM method. *Renew. Sustain. Energy Rev.* **2018**, *81*, 682–692. [CrossRef]
69. Olson, D.L. Comparison of weights in TOPSIS Models. *Math. Comput. Model.* **2004**, *40*, 721–727. [CrossRef]

70. Karimi, A.P.; Mehrdadi, N.; Hashemian, S.J.; Bidhendi, G.R.; Moghaddam, R.T. Using the fuzzy TOPSIS and fuzzy AHP methods for wastewater treatment process selection. *Int. J. Acad. Res.* **2011**, *3*, 737–745.
71. Escrig-Olmedo, E.; Rivera-Lirio, J.M.; Muñoz-Torres, M.J.; Fernández-Izquierdo, M.Á. Integrating multiple ESG investors' preferences into sustainable investment: A fuzzy multicriteria methodological approach. *J. Clean. Prod.* **2017**, *162*, 1334–1345. [CrossRef]
72. Khoshnava, S.M.; Rostami, R.; Valipour, A.; Ismail, M.; Rahmat, A.R. Rank of green building material criteria based on the three pillars of sustainability using the hybrid multi criteria decision making method. *J. Clean. Prod.* **2018**, *173*, 82–99. [CrossRef]
73. Khan, M.I. Evaluating the strategies of compressed natural gas industry using an integrated SWOT and MCDM approach. *J. Clean. Prod.* **2018**, *172*, 1035–1052. [CrossRef]
74. Mavi, R.K.; Standing, C. Critical success factors of sustainable project management in construction: A fuzzy DEMATEL-ANP approach. *J. Clean. Prod.* **2018**, *194*, 751–765. [CrossRef]
75. Dursun, M.; Arslan, Ö. An Integrated Decision Framework for Material Selection Procedure: A Case Study in a Detergent Manufacturer. *Symmetry* **2018**, *10*, 657. [CrossRef]
76. Jaśkowski, P.; Sobotka, A.; Czarnigowska, A. Decision model for planning material supply channels in construction. *Autom. Constr.* **2018**, *90*, 235–242. [CrossRef]
77. Medineckiene, M.; Zavadskas, E.K.; Björk, F.; Turskis, Z. Multi-criteria decision-making system for sustainable building assessment/certification. *Arch. Civ. Mech. Eng.* **2015**, *15*, 11–18. [CrossRef]
78. Pan, N. Fuzzy AHP approach for selecting the suitable bridge construction method. *J. Autom. Constr.* **2008**, *17*, 958–965. [CrossRef]
79. Zavadskas, E.K.; Turskis, Z.; Bagočius, V. Multi-criteria selection of a deep-water port in the Eastern Baltic Sea. *Appl. Soft Comput.* **2015**, *26*, 180–192. [CrossRef]
80. Hashemkhani Zolfani, S.; Zavadskas, E.K.; Turskis, Z. Design of products with both International and Local perspectives based on Yin-Yang balance theory and SWARA method. *Econ. Res.-Ekon. Istraživanja* **2013**, *26*, 153–166. [CrossRef]
81. Jadidi, O.; Firouzi, F.; Bagliery, E. TOPSIS method for supplier selection problem. *Int. J. Soc. Behav. Educ. Econ. Bus. Ind. Eng.* **2010**, *4*, 2198–2200.
82. Polat, G.; Eray, E.; Bingol, B.N. An integrated fuzzy MCGDM approach for supplier selection problem. *J. Civ. Eng. Manag.* **2017**, *23*, 926–942. [CrossRef]
83. Sonmez, M.; Yang, J.B.; Holt, G.D. Addressing the contractor selection problem using an evidential reasoning approach. *Eng. Constr. Archit. Manag.* **2001**, *8*, 198–210. [CrossRef]
84. AGC of America. *Qualifications Based Selection of Contractors*; AGC of America: Arlington, VA, USA, 2001.
85. Sandquist, R.S. Qualifications-Based vs. Low-Bid Contractor Selection. 2007. Available online: http://www.aia.org/aiaucmp/groups/ek_members/documents/pdf/aiap017687.pdf (accessed on 11 June 2018).
86. Yawei, L.; Shouyu, C.; Xiangtian, N. Fuzzy Pattern Recognition Approach to Construction Contractor Selection. *Fuzzy Optim. Decis. Mak.* **2005**, *4*, 103–118. [CrossRef]
87. Taylan, O.; Kabli, M.R.; Porcel, C.; Herrera-Viedma, E. Contractor Selection for Construction Projects Using Consensus Tools and Big Data. *Int. J. Fuzzy Syst.* **2018**, *20*, 1267–1281. [CrossRef]
88. Turskis, Z.; Zavadskas, E.K.; Antucheviciene, J.; Kosareva, N. A hybrid model based on fuzzy AHP and fuzzy WASPAS for construction site selection. *Int. J. Comput. Commun. Control* **2015**, *10*, 113–128. [CrossRef]
89. Zavadskas, E.K.; Turskis, Z.; Antuchevičienė, J. Selecting a contractor by using a novel method for multiple attribute analysis: Weighted Aggregated Sum Product Assessment with grey values (WASPAS-G). *Stud. Inform. Control* **2015**, *24*, 141–150. [CrossRef]

© 2019 by the authors. Licensee MDPI, Basel, Switzerland. This article is an open access article distributed under the terms and conditions of the Creative Commons Attribution (CC BY) license (http://creativecommons.org/licenses/by/4.0/).

Article

The Evaluation of the Contractor's Risk in Implementing the Investment Projects in Construction by Using the Verbal Analysis Methods

Galina Shevchenko [1], Leonas Ustinovichius [2] and Dariusz Walasek [3,*]

[1] Department of Finance Engineering, Faculty of Business Management, Vilnius Gediminas Technical University, Sauletekio ave.11, LT-10223 Vilnius, Lithuania; galina.sevcenko@vgtu.lt
[2] Department of Construction Management and Real Estate, Faculty of Civil Engineering, Vilnius Gediminas Technical University, Sauletekio ave.11, LT-10223 Vilnius, Lithuania; leonas.ustinovicius@vgtu.lt or leonas959@gmail.com
[3] Institute of Building Engineering, Faculty of Civil Engineering, Warsaw Technical University, Armii Ludowej 16, 00-637 Warsaw, Poland
* Correspondence: dariusz.walasek@pw.edu.pl; Tel.: +48-608-498-979

Received: 5 December 2018; Accepted: 6 May 2019; Published: 9 May 2019

Abstract: The growth of the company's investment potential is closely associated with the evaluation of the attendant risks of the process, various influencing factors, and the expected results. Therefore, the analysis of a number of qualitative and quantitative criteria of the projects and risks, as well as the potential profit-making opportunities in the investment decision making is required. This paper analyzes a decision-making strategy based on qualitative estimates obtained by investigating the risks posed, the management methods used, and the application of the proposed methods for assessing the contractor's risk in construction companies.

Keywords: building investment project; risk; assessment; verbal analysis

1. Introduction

Risk is a relevant part of the life of a business and society. Furthermore, it forms an integral part of a business, as risk is attached to every choice between various alternatives and final decisions. Almost every important economic decision involves some risk and uncertainty [1].

A great number of scientists and practitioners have been analyzing the company's investment objectives from various perspectives [2]. Profitable activities of the company (productive investments) are possible only if they are based on clearly defined investment decisions and the weighed and controlled risk, as well as targeted and supervised investment.

The problems of risk assessment and management have been discussed in the scientific literature [3–21] for a long time, but they are still acute. However, the attitudes towards these problems have been changing over time. It can be argued that the existing theories and the applied methods do not meet the changing requirements.

The need for assessing the importance of the construction investment decision-making and risk assessment under uncertainty particularly increased in the crisis and post-crisis periods in 2007, when the competition for funding a project at all stages of corporate investment project's implementation greatly increased. To gain competitive advantages, companies should continually invest in developing risk assessment methodologies, which could not only help to ensure the expected profit, but would also create capital gains for the investors. There is no doubt that effective risk assessment, as the most important risk management stage, should also become one of the most significant steps in the company's investment decision-making.

Decision–making problems in construction management often involve a complex decision-making process, where multiple requirements and conditions have to be taken into consideration simultaneously [22]. Thus, quantitative and qualitative evaluation is often required to deal with uncertainty, as well as subjective and imprecise data [23].

The construction industry is exposed to higher risks than other industries [24,25]. Construction projects are exposed to various risks. Contractors cope with this problem, while the owners pay for it. The problem of the contractor's selection is very important in developing the construction projects. This process involves the employment of people with different skills and interests. Construction projects are also influenced by a number of uncontrollable external factors.

Risks in developing construction projects have been identified [26–33] and analyzed in References [25,27–38].

The authors show that the process of risk assessment and management in construction projects has many deficiencies which decrease the effectiveness of the project management and its performance [13].

The paper considers the problem of risk assessment in making investment decisions (under risk and uncertainty conditions), whose solution would make a long-term positive effect on the company's capital investment policies in implementing the investment projects in construction and would ensure its development. The paper describes the performed empirical studies and the proposed solutions concerning risk assessment and risk management in making investment decisions (contractor selection) under the uncertainty conditions, using a verbal analysis method.

2. Verbal Analysis and Its Potentialities

Verbal analysis methods (VAM) are based on the principles presented in Figure 1. All the above-mentioned principles state that the methods of verbal analysis have mathematical and psychological backgrounds [30,39–42].

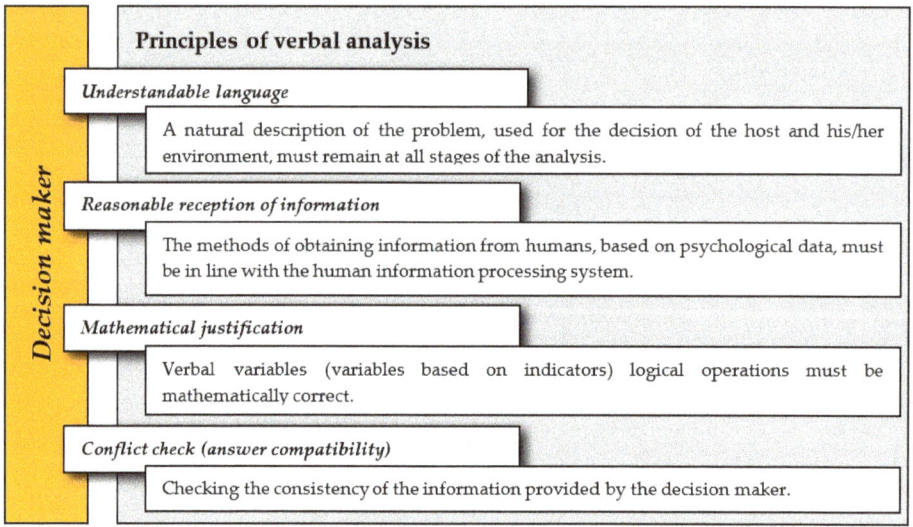

Figure 1. The major principles of verbal analysis methods [37–39,43–46].

These methods (Figure 1) give the possibility to reduce the gap between the demands for the available decision-making methods and human system's abilities to process the data [42–45].

There are three major decision-making problems as follows:

Ranking of alternatives: While solving particular problems, attention is paid to the ranking of alternatives. For example, the investors rank the possible investments, their benefits, etc., according to expedience/profitability. In general, the ranking of alternatives (i.e., their classification/attribution to particular classes) demands the establishment of every alternative's value. There is a method called ZAPROS, which was created for the solution of this problem [46]. While using this method, there is one major rule, according to which there is a possibility to rank the alternatives described by many various criteria by evaluating the decision maker's (DM) needs. The rule's formation requires the selection of the set of criteria, describing the analyzed area, and their scales. The major rule allows for comparing two main alternatives described by the selected criteria.

The alternative's attribution to solution classes. These types of tasks are usually solved in everyday life. For example, people who want to buy a house or to evaluate the available alternatives, divide them into two groups as follows: The ones that interest them and the ones that do not interest them (those, which do not meet their major requirements and those that are not worth their attention and spending of money). The groups are differentiated according to quality. A subcontractor also chooses the best (desirable) clients. The company CEO sets the requirements to the staff, and according to their needs, they do not consider the candidates who do not meet the minimum requirements.

The classification of the alternatives can also be widely used for creating the database for assessing particular areas, for example, in the case of staff selection according to the criterion of adequacy, etc. (the qualification not less than … , having the particular certificates, etc.). It also includes the database of the potential contractors or subcontractors, evaluating their industrial productivity, defining quality criteria, etc., and attributing them to a particular class, such as "reliable", "unreliable" or "not very reliable".

Based on the VAM method, the alternatives can be classified by using various methods (Figure 2). The first method of this type is ORKLASS (Ordinal Classification), allowing for making a complete set of criteria for the alternatives' classification (all the possible alternatives, described by a set of criteria and by their scales' numbers). The other method, which allows for faster solution of the considered task, is CIKL (Catenary Interactive Classification).

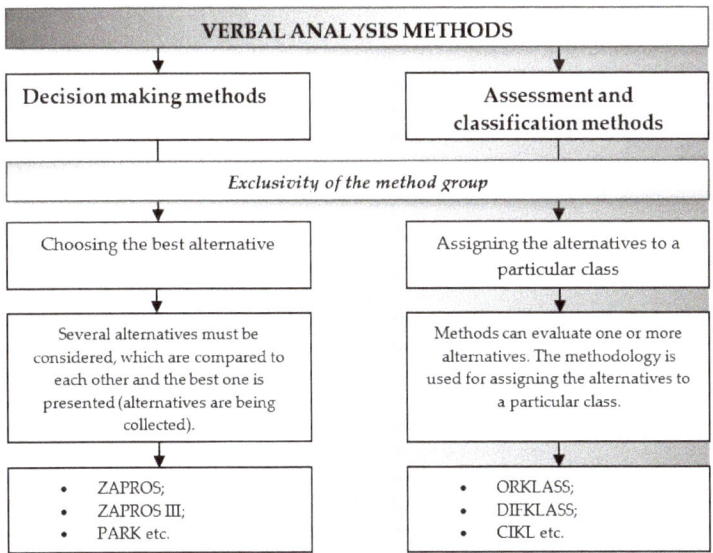

Figure 2. The classification of the verbal analysis methods.

The selection of the best alternative: This task is the main one because the final result depends on its successful solution. This is shown by practical experience. Thus, the right choice of the contractor, the investment project evaluation and selection determine the successful economic, technical, and social development of the company. It should be noted that these tasks are usually solved when important political decisions, where the number of alternatives is not large and which are complicated for evaluation and comparison, are made. For example, it is necessary to determine the best alternative of the currency and land usage reform. It is worth mentioning that one of the conceptual problem's preferential features is the new alternative's generation in the solution-making process. These types of tasks can be solved by using PARK and SHNUR (SNOD) (normalized ranked differences scale) methods [47]. The SNOD method was created later than PARK and gives a possibility to evaluate a larger number of criteria and alternatives. In Figure 2, the considered methods are presented [23,44,46–56].

Another aspect of the expert classification methods is also worth mentioning. The created database can be not only of a consulting type, i.e., the results of these methods can be always interpreted subjectively and are not highly precise, even though they attribute the considered alternative to one or another class of solutions. In the author's opinion, the solution methods of verbal analysis have some advantages when they are used for solving problems with definite characteristics as follows:

1. There are no reliable ways of changing the evaluation of quantitative criteria. The estimate can be obtained only from experts;
2. There are no reliable statistics, based on which the best rule of the alternative's quality evaluation can be chosen objectively. The main rule can only be based on the subjective DM wishes and demands.

3. Verbal Multiple Criteria Evaluation Method CLARA (Classification of Real Alternatives)

The CLARA method (Classification of Real Alternatives) has been created to solve a classification task. By using this method, it is possible to perform the classification of the whole set of objects, as well as the objects of the known part of the set, thereby minimizing the number of experts' queries.

In this method, the priorities of the examined variants and their significance directly and proportionally depend on the system of criteria adequately describing the alternatives, as well as on their significances and values. The values of the criteria and their significances are determined by experts. These data can be adjusted by the interested parties (e.g., clients, consumers, etc.) according to their goals and potential. Therefore, the alternative's evaluation results reflect the initial data provided by the experts and the interested parties.

Several formal definitions are given below:

Definition 1. *The alternatives $x, y \in Y$, are referred to as comparable: $x \sim y$ if $x \geq y$, or $y \geq x$; in the opposite case, they are called incomparable: $x \nsim y$.*

Any other two alternatives, which belong to the same class, are either in a dominating relation, or are incomparable. Thus, in every class, it is possible to determine the subsets of dominating and not dominating alternatives.

Definition 2. *The subset $B^U(C_n)$ of class C_n alternatives is called the upper boundary of this class if $\forall x \in C_n \; \exists \; y \in B^U(C_n)$ is such that $y \geq x$ and $\forall \; x, y \in B^U(C_n), x \neq y \Rightarrow x \nsim y$.*

Definition 3. *The subset $B^L(C_n)$ of class C_n alternatives is called the lower boundary of this class if $\forall x \in C_n \; \exists \; y \in B^L(C_n)$ is such that $x \geq y$ and $\forall \; x, y \in B^L(C_n), x \neq y \Rightarrow x \nsim y$.*

The classification problem can be solved by presenting the alternatives' card (Y^*) to an expert so as to obtain their distribution into classes. Using the dominating relation (1) and consistency condition (2) provides the ability to considerably reduce the provided number of alternatives, as well as the time of the classification procedure. The possibility to minimize the given number of alternatives occurs because of the possibility to use the data about the already classified alternatives for the remaining alternatives' classification.

The numerical functions $C^U(x)$ and $C^L(x)$ are needed, which are specified for the set Y as the largest and the smallest class numbers and the allowable x, i.e., a class, to which the given x would not violate the classification consistency condition (2). Let us assume the vector x to be referred to class C_k if the condition $C^U(x) = C^L(x) = k$ is satisfied. At the beginning, $\forall\, x \in Y^*$ has to be $C^L(x) = 1$, $C^U(x) = M$.

There is an alternative set Y with the given dominating relation P, as well as M solution classes, arranged according to the criterion of quality. The largest and the smallest numbers of the allowable solution classes $C^U(x)$ and $C^L(x)$ are associated with every alternative $x \in Y^*$. Before starting the classification, $\forall\, x \in Y$: $C^L(x) = 1$, $C^U(x) = M$. The classification is considered to be performed when $\forall\, x \in Y^*$: $C^L(x) = C^U(x)$.

Definition 4. *The alternative $x \in Y$ dominates the alternative $y \in Y$, when $x > y$ and $\nexists\, z \in Y: x > z > y$.*

Definition 5. *The alternative $x \in Y$ is dominated by the alternative $y \in Y$, when $x < y$ and $\nexists\, z \in Y: x < z < y$.*

A set of alternatives dominating the alternative x is denoted by $Z^U(x)$, while the set which is dominated by the alternatives is marked as $Z^L(x)$.

Definition 6. *The dominating alternative orgraph $G(Y,E)$ is called the oriented acyclic graph, where the vertex set is the alternatives' set Y, and the set of arches $E \subseteq Y \times Y$ consists of the elements (x, y), where the alternative $x \in Y$ dominates the alternative $y \in Y$.*

Definition 7. *The alternatives' sequence $w = \langle y_1, y_2, \ldots\, y_l \rangle$, where $y_{i+1} \in Z^L(y_i)$, $1 \le i \le (l-1)$, is called a string. The number $L(w) = l$ of the alternatives' string w is called the string's length. A particular alternative is a string of length 1.*

Classification algorithms: The algorithm CLARA (Classification of Real Alternatives) is based on the concept of the dichotomy of the alternatives' strings. It was first applied to the maximum length string, used in the DIFKLASS algorithm [48] and later in the KLANŠ algorithm [50], where it was adapted to the case of the rarefied areas Y. CLARA is also used as a new adaptive dichotomy idea, allowing for finding the boundaries of the solution classes faster and reducing the time of classification.

The major steps of the analysis of the classification algorithm CLARA:

- When the classification is started, the dichotomy ratio d_i of classes C_i and C_{i+1} in searching for the boundary is assumed to be equal to 1/2.
- The alternative's orgraph $G(Y,E)$ can have a number of combination components, therefore, all the available but unclassified alternatives of the set Y^* are analyzed in the consecutive order. The consistency of the alternatives is important. Any selected alternative x_s is called primary.
- In the combination component of the orgraph $G(Y,E)$ (to which x_s belongs) the maximum length alternative's string w_{max}, going through the primary alternative x_s and having the largest number of unclassified alternatives from Y^*, is established.
- Since classes $\{C_n\}$ are arranged according to their quality, the boundaries between the classes in the string are obtained by separating the upper-quality class C_n from the lower quality class C_{n+1}.
- For the expert's evaluation, the element x_d, where $d = d_n \cdot L(w_{max})$, is taken from the string w_{max}, and, if the alternative x_d seems to be unsuitable or has already been classified, the new x_d, the available unclassified string element with the closest index is selected.
- The expert is given the available alternative x_d, of the string w_{max}, and its solution is valid for the maximum possible number of elements, whose belonging to classes C_n and C_{n+1} is not determined.
- If w_{max} still has suitable unclassified elements, the division of the string w_{max} is continued and ends when all the obtained suitable alternatives appear to be directly or indirectly classified with respect to classes C_n and C_{n+1}. In the opposite case, another boundary between the classes is sought (by returning to the 4th step). If the string has been classified with respect to all classes,

there is an index k in the string w_{max} for every class where the change from the class C_n to the class C_{n+1} takes place. This index is $d_{nw} = \frac{k}{L(w_{max})}$. In every further step d_n there is the arithmetic mean of all the above-mentioned calculated d_{nw}.
- The cycle is continued until all possible alternatives of all possible sets Y^* are classified with respect to the pair of these two classes.
- A general schematic view of the CLARA algorithm is given in Figure 3.

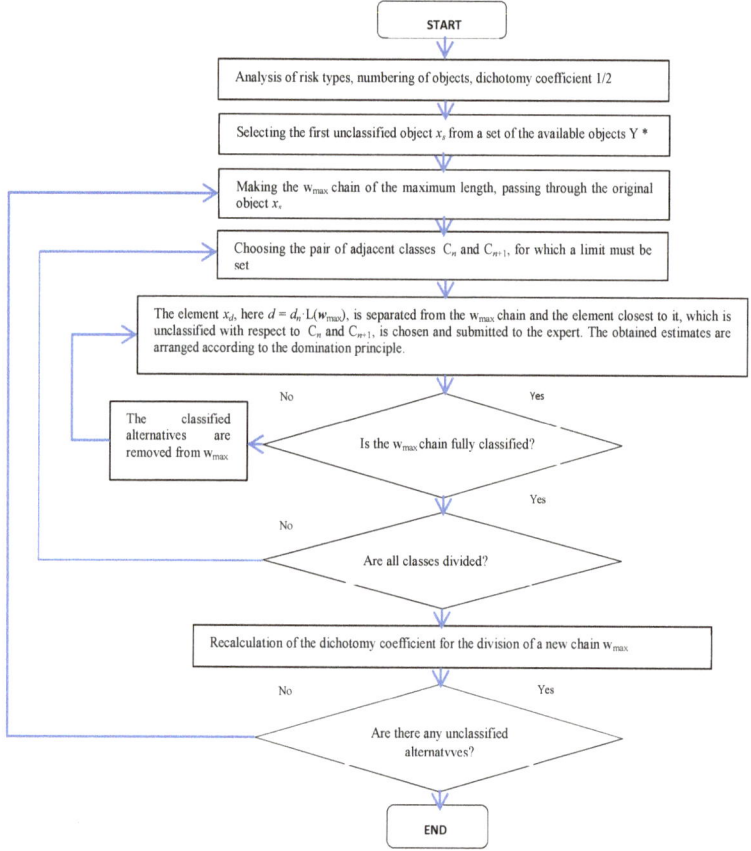

Figure 3. The algorithm of CLARA.

4. Verbal Risk Evaluation of the Companies Performing the Functions of Contractor

The objective is to evaluate the risk level of a building company performing the contractor's functions by using the multi-criteria evaluation method CLARA.

A description of the analyzed object. The considered company is based in Lithuania. The company started its work in 1992 and has the status of JSC. The areas of work: General building tasks; special building tasks; mechanical tasks, etc. To fully satisfy the client's needs, the company pays great attention to the control of the building process quality.

The company's quality principles, goals, and strategy are described. The goal of the JSC "X" quality policies is to justify the client's hopes and trust by performing the tasks on time. To achieve the goals, JSC "X" installed the international quality control software ISO 9001:2000/LST EN ISO 9001:2001. Now, more than 60 people work in this company. The annual turnover in 2007 was 25,000,000 m Eur.

According to the task, verbal risk evaluation of the company "X" performing the contractor's functions was made by using the CLARA method. Only one company was evaluated, and no comparison with any competing companies was made.

Based on the risk analysis of companies performing the contractor's functions (Table 1), as well as the experience of the authors, scientific literature analysis and the data obtained in interviewing managers, the risk types of the hierarchical level 1, which are given below, were determined (the criteria of level 1). The criteria of this risk group refer to hierarchical level 2.

Table 1. The contractor's risks.

No	Types of Risk		
	External (Systemic) Risks		
1.	Environmental (ecological) risk		
2.	Market risk		
3.	Strategical risk		
4.	Legal risk		
5.	Social risk		
6.	Technical-technological risk		
	Internal Risks		
1.	Financial	9.	Resource management
2.	Project	10.	Construction organization
3.	Evaluation	11.	Design
4.	Organizational	12.	Cultural
5.	Contractual	13.	Human resources and work safety
6.	Technological-innovative	14.	Leadership
7.	Investment	15.	Competitiveness
8.	Quality	16.	Operational

The risk types marked in red were determined as most important in analyzing the potential contractors' companies.

The managers of the building companies were interviewed in the regions of Vilnius, Panevezys, and Klaipeda. Based on the obtained data, the risks of the 1st and the 2nd hierarchical levels were combined. When the classification of various risks had been made, the classifier of the incurred risks and the factors causing them was obtained, and when the iterations had been performed, the final evaluation solutions were made (Figure 4). A detailed description of the described groups is given below:

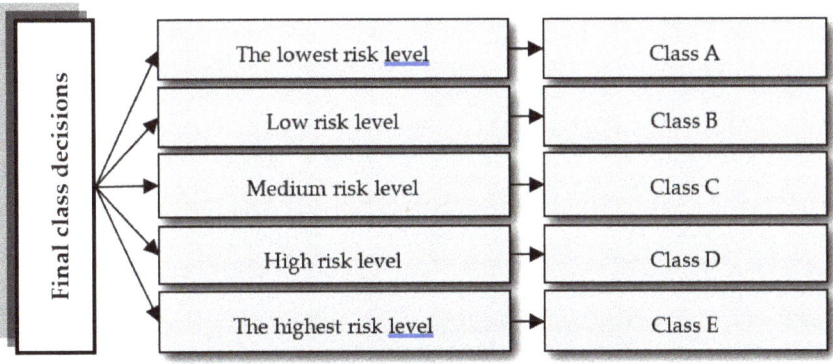

Figure 4. The risk levels.

The "Company's financial risk evaluation" group includes credit evaluation, turnover, liabilities to the bank, interest rate changes, liquidity, profitability, inflation and the evaluation of reserve.

The "Evaluation of the company's technical-technological risk" group includes the experience and qualification of the staff, management skills, innovative technology's adaptation, evaluation/analysis of past factors, optimization of technological processes, quality characteristics/level's standards, project managers' strict responsibility levels, and maintenance of the building and supply processes.

The "Project risk evaluation" group includes the consideration of the projects' types and sizes, designing process coordination, the number of simultaneously performed projects, experience in the field, design solutions, the possibility of failing to finish the project, and the unexpected changes in the project and design faults' analysis.

The "Company's organizational risk evaluation" group includes the company's image and competence, the qualified specialists' team, client's satisfaction, the analysis of failures, claims and lawsuit appearance, the supplier's analysis and the legitimacy of the choices, as well as a set of precise responsibility boundaries in the company, management skills, and the communication processes/policies.

The "Risk evaluation of resources' management" group consists of turnover funds' maintenance, the appropriate use of equipment, the maintenance of the qualified staff number, the maintenance of the appropriate amounts of materials, and the control of the time of the process performance.

The "Quality management risk evaluation" group includes the quality control system, quality management, and risk management policy (company and projects) quality, the environmental requirements' maintenance, and the evaluation of the guaranteed quality.

The "Safety risk evaluation" group includes work safety control, accidents' prevention, work safety requirements, and responsibility assumption.

The "Contractual and legal risk evaluation" group includes uncoordinated agreement conditions, agreement conditions' obscurity, agreement's noncompliance, inaccurate building documentation, uncoordinated laws, law amendments.

The "Company's building risk evaluation" group includes inaccurately planned time of construction, unforeseen problems in transport, problems of transport, supply problems, production quality, and management quality.

The "Ecological risk evaluation" group includes disasters, essential requirements of the environmental laws, the government's attitude to the project's change, etc.

The "Risk evaluation of policies" group—separate criteria.

Then, to determine the risks of the building sector's companies, performing the contractors' functions, a classifier (Figure 5), consisting of the risk evaluation criteria and final classification solutions, was created. Risk evaluation criteria of the contractor's company are given in the description of the hierarchical levels 1 and 2. While evaluating the building contractor's company, the attention was paid to the risk types presented in Figure 4. The first hierarchical level is the main one. Based on the criteria of this level, it is possible to evaluate the risk level of the building contractor's company. All the criteria of the first hierarchical level were evaluated as follows: Low, medium or high. When the evaluation was made, the results were obtained, i.e., risk levels were determined (Figure 4).

The criteria from the first level are not always sufficient (level 1, Figure 6) for determining the risk level of the building contractor. Therefore, all first hierarchical level criteria were divided into subcriteria of a lower level and thus the second hierarchical level was obtained (Figure 7). The criteria of the second hierarchical level were required for performing a thorough analysis of risks (when every type of risk is analyzed).

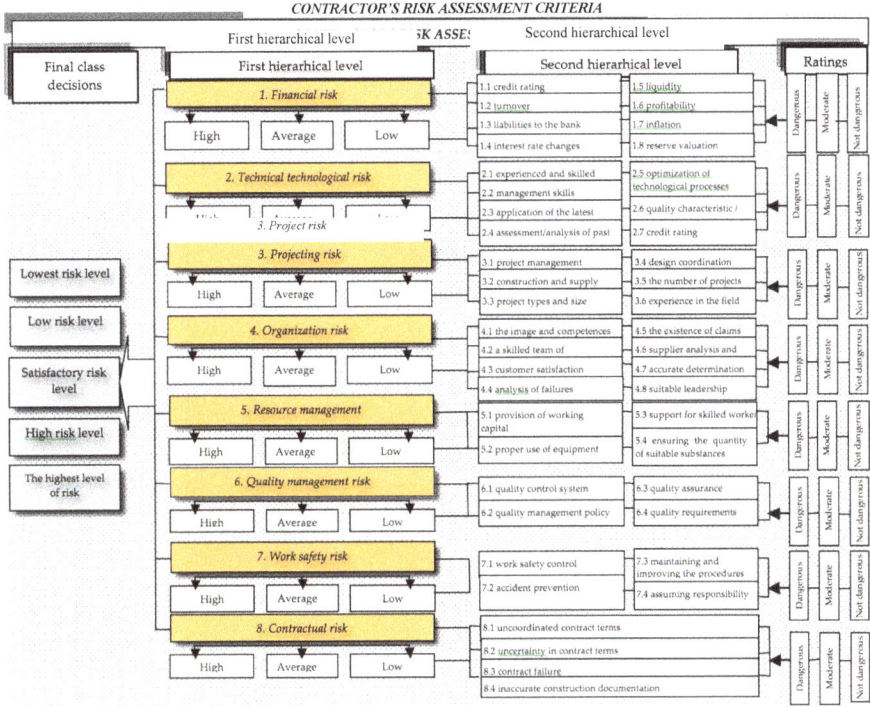

Figure 5. The investment risk evaluation classifier of the contractor.

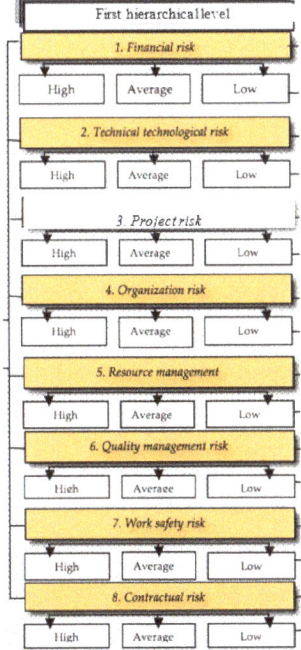

Figure 6. The first hierarchical level.

According to the created scheme (Figure 5), the sequence of risk evaluation procedures is as follows: The evaluation of the second hierarchical level criteria ⇒ the evaluation of the first hierarchical level criteria ⇒ the criteria of the second hierarchical level are given in Table 2.

Table 2. The criteria of the second hierarchical level.

No	Criteria	No	Criteria
1	credit rating	31	supplier analysis and feasibility of choice
2	turnover	32	liabilities of the company
3	liabilities to the bank	33	leadership skills
4	interest rate changes	34	communication processes/policies
5	liquidity	35	provision of working capital
6	profitability	36	use of equipment
7	inflation	37	support of skilled workers
8	the evaluated reserve	38	provision of the required materials
9	experienced and skilled workforce	39	monitoring and ensuring the timelines of ongoing processes
10	management skills	40	quality control system
11	application of the latest and most innovative technologies	41	quality management and risk management policies
12	assessment/analysis of past factors	42	quality and environmental requirements
13	optimization of technological processes	43	quality assurance evaluation
14	quality characteristics/level	44	work safety control
15	credit rating	45	accident prevention
16	project management and the responsibility levels of managers	46	maintaining and improving the procedures ensuring the required work safety level
17	construction and supply processes	47	assumed responsibility
18	project types and sizes	48	uncoordinated contract terms
19	design coordination	49	uncertainty in contract terms
20	the number of simultaneously performed projects	50	contract failure
21	experience in the field of activities	51	inaccurate building documentation
22	design solutions	52	uncoordinated laws
23	possibility of non-completion of design	53	law changes
24	unexpected project changes	54	inaccurately planned and exceeded construction time limit
25	design errors	55	unplanned site conditions
26	the image and competence of the company	56	transport problems
27	a skilled team of professionals	57	supply problems
28	customer satisfaction	58	quality of production
29	the analysis of failures	59	management quality
30	the existence of claims and cases	60	

Therefore, let us determine the risk level of the company "X", performing the contractor's functions. Using the classifier's scheme (Figure 5), the risk level can be determined, but many criteria should be compared. It is a complicated process, which takes much time to perform. Therefore, the use of the SPPS CLARA software, employing verbal classification method (of alternatives) is required.

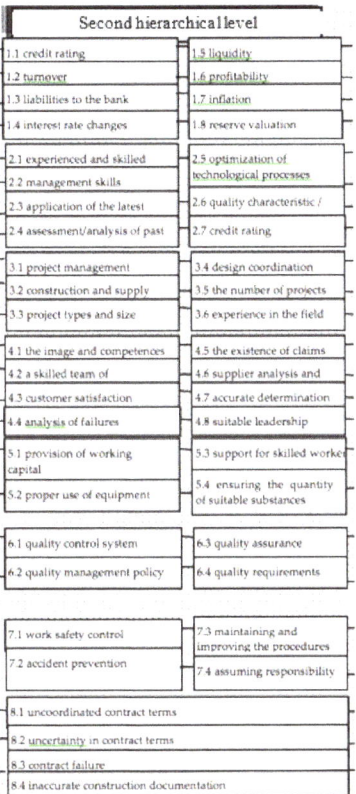

Figure 7. The second hierarchical level.

5. Entering the Data into the Software

Let us demonstrate the operation of SPPS CLARA software by analyzing the evaluation of the risk level of a particular contractor's company at various stages. The provided software screenshots present various stages of the contractor's company's risk level evaluation.

The task is to assess the risk level of the contractor's company at various stages (first hierarchical level: Financial risk; technical technological risk; project risk, etc.) and refer the company to those of the particular risk level (final class decisions: Class A—the lowest risk level; class B—low risk level etc.). For this purpose, a set of evaluation criteria was defined (second hierarchical level). A more detailed company's analysis is given in Section 4.

To perform the task, a classifier was made (Figure 5), including the considered risk levels (final class decisions (Figure 4)), the first hierarchical level (Figure 6), and the second hierarchical level (Figure 7).

According to the classifier (Figure 5), the data of the first and the second hierarchical levels were entered into the program (Figures 8 and 9). In a similar way, the data on the types of risks associated with the project, the company and other types of risks (of the first and the second hierarchical levels) were entered into the program. When all the criteria used in evaluating the contractor's company were entered, the last step, including the comparison, was made. The comparison of the criteria was performed as follows: The program had chosen one estimate of each criterion and made their combinations. An expert assigned the evaluated combination to a particular class. The created database allowed for easy and fast evaluation of the risk level of the considered object (in this case, the contractor's company) by assigning the respective values of the criteria of the first and the second hierarchical levels.

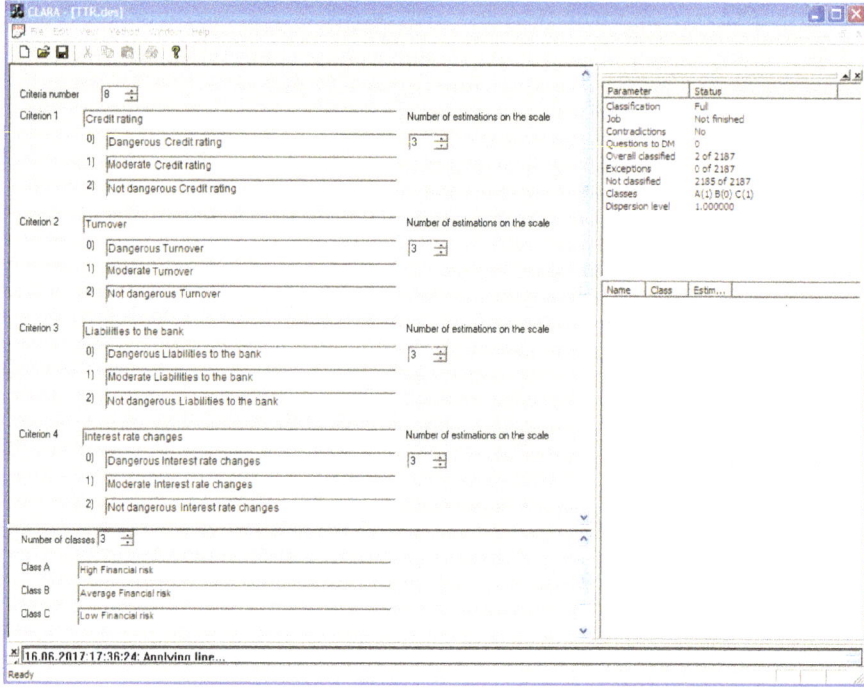

Figure 8. Financial risk evaluation criteria of the contractor's company.

The evaluation of the risk level of the contractor's company was performed with respect to the first hierarchical level (Figure 10), i.e., every risk type could be assessed as high, medium or low. Based on the obtained results, a company could be referred to a particular risk level (final class decision).

If the data allowing for evaluating the criteria (risk types) of the first hierarchical level were insufficient, the criteria of the second hierarchical level were evaluated (Figure 11). In this way, a thorough analysis and evaluation of the company's risk level (taking into account various criteria) were performed.

STAGE 1: Financial risk evaluation of the contractor's company (Figure 8). Eight evaluation criteria of the second hierarchical level were inserted (criterion 1, credit evaluation; criterion 2, turnover; criterion 3, obligations to the bank; criterion 4, interest rate changes; criterion 5, liquidity; criterion 6, profitability; criterion 7, inflation; criterion 8, reserve's evaluation).

Criterion evaluation classes: Class A, high; class B, average; class C, safe. Criteria 1–8 were chosen for the risk evaluation of the contractor's company.

While analyzing the company (alternative 1), the expert determined if the company's credits allow the company to meet the obligations to the bank. Moreover, it was also determined if the turnover complies with the forecasted indicators and if the company's financial indicators ensure the planned company's liquidity and profitability levels. After analyzing the company's financial risk, it was determined if there were any faults or contradictions in the classification.

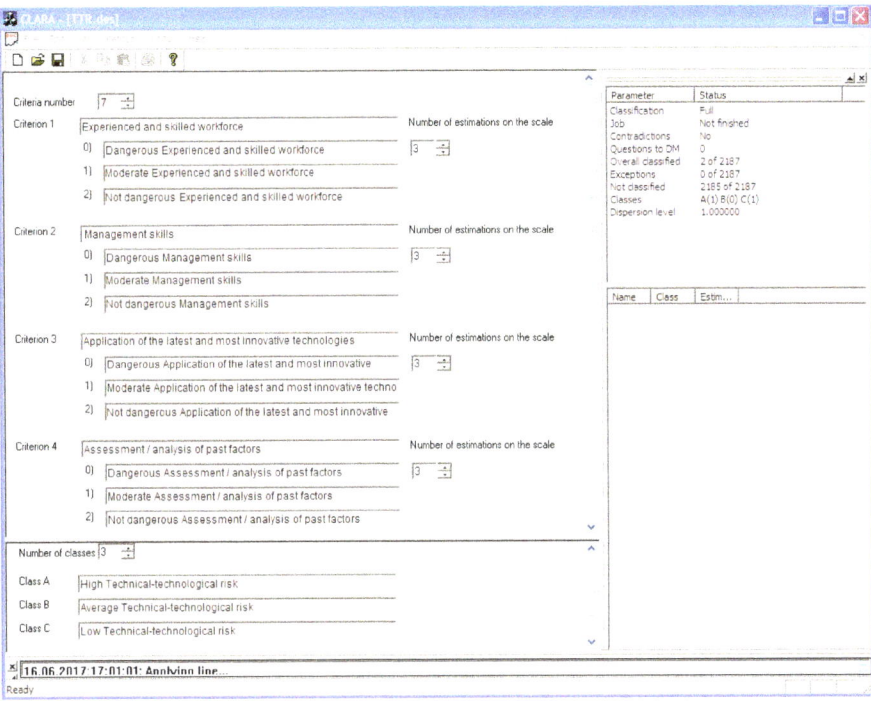

Figure 9. The criteria of technical–technological risk assessment of contractor.

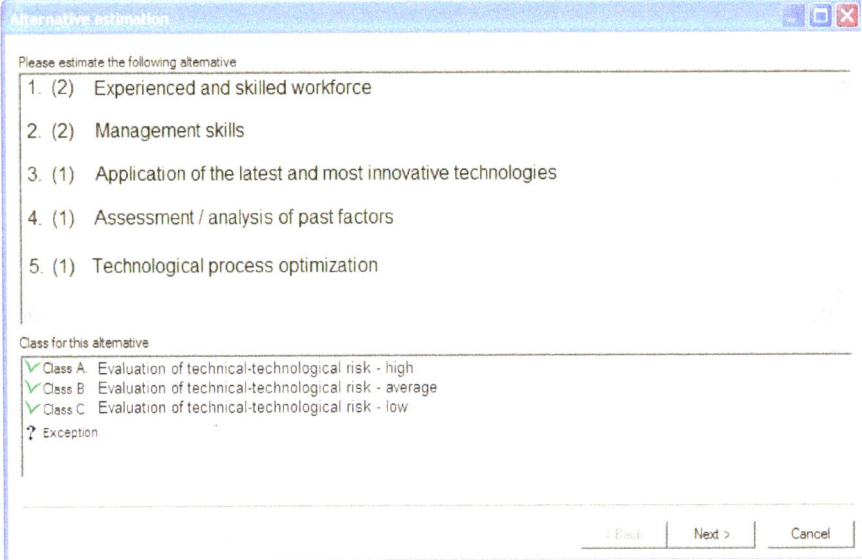

Figure 10. The assessment of alternatives.

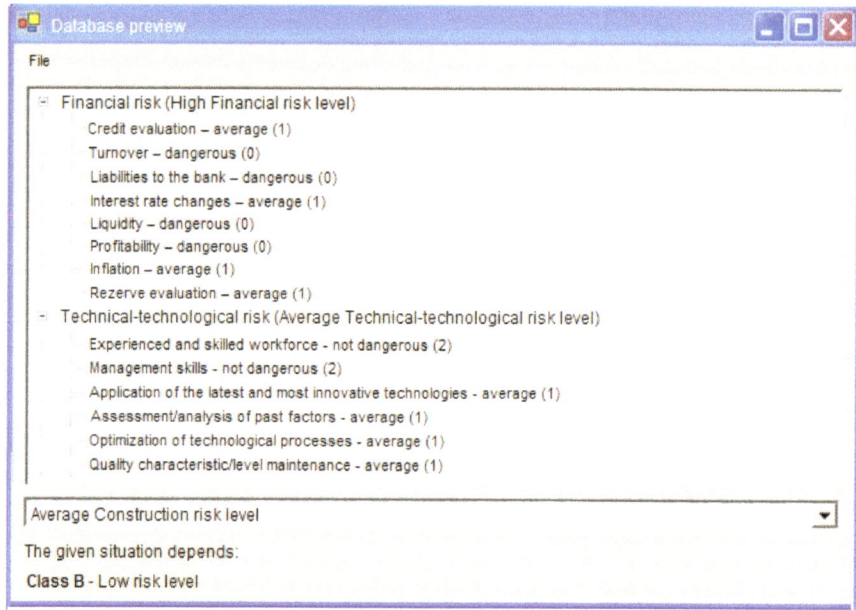

Figure 11. The database with the assessment criteria for the contractor's company.

STAGE 2: The company's technical–technological risk evaluation (Figure 9) includes the analysis of the criteria as follows: Criterion 1, experienced and skilled workforce; criterion 2, management skills; criterion 3, the use of innovative technologies; criterion 4, the assessment/analysis of past factors; criterion 5, technological process optimization; criterion 6, quality characteristics; criterion 7, the boundaries of project managers' responsibility; criterion 8, the processes of building and supply.

The data were inserted in the software in the same way as at the first stage. At this stage, the company's technical–technological potential criteria were evaluated.

All the remaining data were inserted into the software in the same way as at the first and the second stages. After inserting all the data from the hierarchical level 2, the data from hierarchical level 1 were inserted (criterion 1, financial risk; criterion 2, technical-technological risk; criterion 3, project risk; criterion 4, organizational risk; criterion 5, resources management risk; criterion 6, quality management risk; criterion 7, safety management risk; criterion 8, legal–contractual risk; criterion 9, building risk). After inserting the data from the verbal risk evaluation scheme into the software, the classification was started.

The classification process in the software: After inserting all the criteria used in the company's evaluation, the last step of comparing the criteria was made. The comparison (Figure 10) was performed as follows: The software had chosen one of each criterion's estimates and created their combinations. The expert attributed the particular combination of estimates to a particular class. For example, the expert attributed the following combination to class B (the average level): Quality control system—average; quality management and risk management policy—average; quality and environmental requirements—average; quality guarantee's estimate—average.

After performing the attribution, the next step was made (by pressing the button "NEXT"). Another combination of estimates was given. The process was continued until all the combinations were attributed to particular classes. In performing this task, the expert could make mistakes and change his/her judgment, which could result in contradictions in the estimates. In that case, the software could show a warning about the presence of contradictions and ask to confirm the new judgment or change it. By using the CLARA software, all the contradictions were removed.

When the operation was performed, the software saved all the data and performed the analysis, which had shown the number of DM questions, the process of making the combinations and the number of the removed combinations. It also had shown how many evaluated combinations were attributed to classes A, B, and C.

In the same way, the estimates of all the second hierarchical level criteria were determined. In the considered case, ten files were analyzed based on which the contractor's company risk level was determined.

The estimates were inserted into the database of CLARA software (Figure 11):

The financial risk evaluation of the company includes:

- credits' evaluation—(1),
- turnover—(0),
- liabilities to the bank—(0),
- interest rate variation—(1),
- liquidity—(0),
- profitability—(0),
- inflation—(1),
- reserves' evaluation—(1).

The obtained data, which were entered into the software, demonstrated that the company's financial risk was high—class A (risky).

In a similar way, the evaluation of the company's technical-technological risk, designing risk, organizational risk, resources' management risk, quality management risk, safety risk, contractual and legal risk, and the company's building risk was performed. The respective database is given below. It is connected to the criterion classification in the CLARA software. A person who wants to determine the risk level of the building investment project has to enter the estimates of the experts into the database.

Final solution analysis: The final analysis was performed based on the data obtained in the first hierarchical level evaluation (Figure 12). The performed final analysis allows for determining the company's risk level. Five criteria of the first hierarchical level were used. The classes of the evaluation criteria are given in Figure 11.

Result: According to this data, the company was attributed to class B—low risk level.

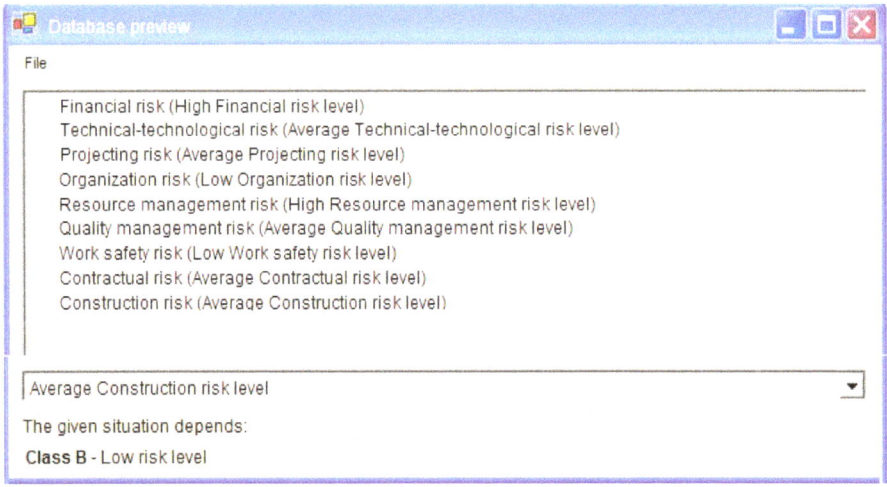

Figure 12. The database (the hierarchical level 1 for the contractor).

6. Conclusions

The analysis of the scientific literature has shown that a number of criteria, describing the activities or projects, should be considered in evaluating social, economic, political, cultural, and other types of risk. New methods allowing for a thorough analysis of the risks to which various activities or projects are exposed should be used and developed.

A great number of decision-making methods and techniques have been created in the world. Some methods were introduced as "universal" methods, allowing for achieving the best (optimal) solutions. However, their application to solving the problems in various areas has revealed some drawbacks of these methods as follows: They are not highly reliable, are difficult to use, and there is a lack of alternatives.

In making investment decisions, risk assessment, and management is one of the main tasks. Risk management is an integral part of project management and investment solutions' assessment.

The effectiveness of applying the verbal analysis methods to solving the problems of the contractor's risk assessment and management was assessed. It has been found that verbal analysis methods could be successfully used in the less structured decision-making areas involving risk assessment problems. The analysis of the global experience has shown that the proposed risk assessment methods could not allow the contractors to assess the risks associated with making companies' investment decisions and to perform multicriteria analysis for evaluating the criteria, expressed not only by discrete but also by lexicographical values. Therefore, the verbal analysis method CLARA was offered for the solution of this problem.

The verbal analysis method CLARA is based on multicriteria classification of the alternatives. The algorithm (CLARA), proposed for the alternatives' classification, helps to create complete and compatible databases allowing the contractors to make the appropriate building investment decisions.

Author Contributions: The individual contribution and responsibilities of the authors were as follows: G.S. designed the research and the methodology used, performed the development of the paper, collected and analyzed the data and the obtained results. L.U. provided the extensive advice throughout the study, assisted with the research design and revised the manuscript. All of the authors have read and approved the final manuscript version.

Funding: This research received no external funding.

Conflicts of Interest: The authors declare no conflict of interest.

References

1. Derecskei, A.K. Relations between risk attitudes, culture and the endowment effect. *Eng. Manag. Prod. Serv.* **2018**, *10*, 7–20. [CrossRef]
2. Damodaran, A. *The Little Book of Valuation: How to Value a Company, Pick a Stock and Profit*; John Wiley & Sons, Inc.: Hoboken, NJ, USA, 2011; ISBN 978-1-118-00477-7.
3. Urbański, M.; Haque, A.U.; Oino, I. The moderating role of risk management in project planning and project success: Evidence from construction businesses of Pakistan and the UK. *Eng. Manag. Prod. Serv.* **2019**, *11*, 23–35. [CrossRef]
4. Arrow, K.J. The Economic Implications of Learning by Doing. *Rev. Econ. Stud.* **1962**, *29*, 155–173. [CrossRef]
5. Knight, F.H. *Risk, Uncertainty and Profit*; Sentry Press: New York, NY, USA, 1964.
6. Arrow, K.J. *Essays in the Theory of Risk-Bearing*; North–Holland Pub. Co.: Amsterdam, The Netherlands, 1971.
7. Kaneman, D.; Tversky, A. Prospect theory: An analysis of decision under risk. *Econometrica* **1979**, *47*, 263–292. [CrossRef]
8. Keynes, J.M. *The General Theory of Employment, Interest and Money*; Stellar Classics; Springer: Cham, Switzerland, 2016; ISBN 978-1987817805.
9. Haimes, Y.Y. *Risk Modeling, Assessment, and Management*, 3rd ed.; John Wiley & Sons, Inc.: Hoboken, NJ, USA, 2009; ISBN 978-0-470-28237-3.
10. Schumpeter, J. *Theory of Economic Development*; Directmedia Publishing: Moscow, Russia, 2008. (In Russian)
11. Holton, G.A. Perspectives: Defining Risk. *Financial Anal. J.* **2004**, *60*, 19–25. [CrossRef]

12. Damodaran, A. *Strategic Risk Taking: A Framework for Risk Management*; Prentice Hall: Upper Saddle River, NJ, USA, 2008; ISBN 978-0-13-199048-7.
13. Zavadskas, E.K.; Ustinovičius, L.; Turskis, Z.; Ševčenko, G. Application of verbal methods to multi-attribute comparative analysis of investments risk alternatives in construction. *Comput. Model. New Technol.* **2008**, *4*, 30–37.
14. Hopkin, P. *Holistic Risk Management in Practice*, 3rd ed.; Withersbys Seamandship International Ltd.: Livingston, UK, 2009; ISBN 978-1856092272.
15. Kaplinski, O. Risk Management of Construction Works by Means of the Utility Theory: A Case Study. *Procedia Eng.* **2013**, *57*, 533–539. [CrossRef]
16. Serpella, A.F.; Ferrada, X.; Howard, R.; Rubio, L. Risk management in construction projects: A knowledge-based approach. *Procedia-Soc. Behav. Sci.* **2014**, *119*, 653–662. [CrossRef]
17. Liaudanskiene, R.; Ustinovičius, L. Review of risk assessment methods and the peculiarities of their application at construction sites. In *Modern Building Materials, Structures and Techniques: Selected Papers of the 10th International Conference, Vilnius, Lithuania, 19–21 May 2010*; Vilnius Gediminas Technical University, Lithuanian Academy of Science, International Association for Bridges: Vilnius, Lithuania, 2010; Volume 1, pp. 446–450, ISBN 9789955285939.
18. Zavadskas, E.K.; Turskis, Z.; Ustinovičius, L.; Shevchenko, G. Attributes weights determining peculiarities in multiple attribute decision making methods. *Inžinerine Ekon. Eng. Econ.* **2010**, *1*, 32–43.
19. Aven, T. Risk assessment and risk management: Review of recent advances on their foundation. *Eur. J. Oper. Res.* **2016**, *253*, 1–13. [CrossRef]
20. Klakegg, O.J. Project Risk Management: Challenge Established Practice. *Adm. Sci.* **2016**, *64*, 21. [CrossRef]
21. Gjerdrum, D.; Peter, M. The new international standard on the practice of risk management—A comparison of ISO 31000:2009 and the COSO ERM framework. *Risk Manag.* **2011**, *31*, 8–13.
22. Kaushalya, F.C.; Reza, H.M.; Zavadskas, E.K.; Perera, B.A.K.S.; Raufdeen, R. Managing the financial risks affecting construction contractors: Implementing hedging in Sri Lanka. *Int. J. Strateg. Prop. Manag.* **2017**, *21*, 212–224.
23. Ustinovičius, L.; Ševčenko, G. Risk level evaluation of construction investments projects. *Comput. Model. New Technol.* **2008**, *12*, 29–37.
24. Peckiene, A.; Komarovska, A.; Ustinovičius, L. Overview of risk allocation between construction parties. *Procedia Eng.* **2013**, *57*, 889–894. [CrossRef]
25. Fouladgar, M.M.; Yazdani-Chamzini, A.; Zavadskas, E.K. Risk evaluation of tunneling projects. *Arch. Civ. Mech. Eng.* **2012**, *12*, 1–12. [CrossRef]
26. Schieg, M. Risk management in construction project management. *J. Bus. Econ. Manag.* **2006**, *7*, 77–83. [CrossRef]
27. Ševčenko, G.; Ustinovičius, L.; Andruškevičius, A. Multi–attribute analysis of investments risk alternatives in construction. *Technol. Econ. Dev. Econ. Balt. J. Sustain.* **2008**, *14*, 428–443. [CrossRef]
28. Schatteman, D.; Herroelen, W.; Van de Vonder, S.; Bone, A. Methodology for integrated risk management and proactive scheduling of construction projects. *J. Constr. Eng. Manag.* **2008**, *134*, 885–893. [CrossRef]
29. Zavadskas, E.K.; Turskis, Z.; Tamošaitiene, J. Risk assessment of construction projects. *J. Civ. Eng. Manag.* **2010**, *16*, 33–46. [CrossRef]
30. Ustinovičius, L.; Shevchenko, G.; Barvidas, A.; Ashikhmin, I.; Kochin, D. Feasibility of verbal analysis application to solving the problems of investment in construction. *Autom. Constr.* **2010**, *19*, 375–384. [CrossRef]
31. Banaitiene, N.; Banaitis, A. Risk Management in Construction Projects. In *Risk Management—Current Issues and Challenges*; Banaitiene, N., Ed.; InTech: Rijeka, Croatia, 2012; pp. 429–448, ISBN 9789535107477.
32. Ševčenko, G.; Ustinovičius, L.; Łoniewski, K. *Risk Assessment Improvement in the Investment Project Management: Verbal Analysis Methods*; Project Planning in Modern Organization: Studia Ekonomiczne. Zeszyty Naukowe Wydziałowe; Wydawnictwo Uniwersytetu Ekonomicznego: Katowice, Poland, 2013; Volume 137, pp. 83–103, ISBN 9788378751021. (In Polish)
33. Tamošaitiene, J.; Zavadskas, E.K.; Turskis, Z. Multi-criteria risk assessment of a construction project. *Procedia Comput. Sci.* **2013**, *17*, 129–133. [CrossRef]
34. Taroun, A. Towards a better modelling and assessment of construction risk: Insights from a literature review. *Int. J. Proj. Manag.* **2014**, *32*, 101–111. [CrossRef]

35. Iqbal, S.; Choudhry Rafiq, M.; Holschemacher, K.; Ali, A.; Tamošaitiene, J. Risk management in construction projects. *Technol. Econ. Dev. Econ.* **2015**, *21*, 65–78. [CrossRef]
36. Burcar Dunovic, I.; Radujkovic, M.; Vukomanovic, M. Internal and external risk based assessment and evaluation for the large infrastructure projects. *J. Civ. Eng. Manag.* **2016**, *22*, 673–682. [CrossRef]
37. Valipour, A.; Yahaya, N.; Md Noor, N.; Antuchevicjene, J.; Tamošaitiene, J. Hybrid SWARA-COPRAS method for risk assessment in deep foundation excavation project: An Iranian case study. *J. Civ. Eng. Manag.* **2017**, *23*, 524–532. [CrossRef]
38. Chatterjee, K.; Zavadskas, E.K.; Tamošaitiene, J.; Adhikary, K.; Kar, S. A hybrid MCDM technique for risk management in construction projects. *Symmetry* **2018**, *10*, 46. [CrossRef]
39. Larichev, O.I.; Brown, R. Numerical and verbal decision analysis: Comparison on practical cases. *J. Multi-Criteria Decis. Anal.* **2000**, *9*, 263–273. [CrossRef]
40. Larichev, O.I.; Olson, D.L.; Moskovich, H.; Mechitov, A. Numerical vs cardinal measurements in multiattribute decision making: How exact is enough? *Organ. Behav. Hum. Decis. Process.* **1995**, *64*, 9–21. [CrossRef]
41. Moshkovich, H.; Autran Monteiro Gomes, L.F.; Mechitov, A.I.; Duncan Rangel, L.A. Infliunce of models and scales on the ranking of multatribute alternatives. *Pescuisa Oper.* **2011**, *32*, 523–542. [CrossRef]
42. Moshkovich, H.M.; Mechitov, A. Verbal Decision Analysis: Foundations and Trends. *Adv. Decis. Sci.* **2013**, *2013*, 697072. [CrossRef]
43. Machado, T.C.S.; Pinheiro, P.R.; Landim, H.F. Aplying Verbal decision analysi in the selecting practices of framework SCRUM. *Comun. Comput. Inf. Sci. (CCIS)* **2013**, *278*, 22–31.
44. Tamanini, I.; Pinheiro, P.R.; Sampaio Machado, T.C.; Albuquergue, A.B. Hybrid approaches of verbal decision analysis in the selection of Project management approaches. *Inf. Technol. Quant. Manag.* **2015**, *55*, 1183–1192. [CrossRef]
45. Larichev, O.I. The structure of expert knowledge in classification problems. *Rep. Acad. Sci.* **1994**, *336*, 750–752. (In Russian)
46. Larichev, O.I. *Verbal Analysis Solutions*; Science: Moscow, Russia, 2006. (In Russian)
47. Ustinovičius, L.; Zavadskas, E.K. *Statybos Investiciju Efektyvumo Sistemotechninis Ivertinimas*; Technika, Lietuva: Vilnius, Lithuania, 2004. (In Lithuanian)
48. Ларичев, О.И.; Ребрик, С.Б. Психологические проблемы принятия решений в задачах многокритериального выбора. Психологический журнал **1988**, *9*, 45–52. (In Russian)
49. Larichev, O.I.; Moshkovich, H.M. *Verbal Decision Analysis for Unstructured Problems*; Kluwer Academic Publishers: Boston, MA, USA, 1997.
50. Larichev, O.I.; Bolotov, A.A. DIFKLASS system: Building complete and consistent expert knowledge bases in the problems of differential diagnostics, Scientific and technical information 2 Inform. *Process. Syst.* **1996**, *9*, 9–15. (In Russian)
51. Korhonen, P.; Larichev, O.I.; Mechitov, A. Moskovich, H.; Wallenius, J. Choice behaviour in a computer–aided multiattribute decision task. *J. Multi-Criteria Decis. Anal.* **1997**, *6*, 233–246. [CrossRef]
52. Naryzhny, E.V. Building Intelligent Learning Systems Based on Expert Knowledge. Doctoral Thesis, ISA RAS, Moscow, Russia, 1998. (In Russian)
53. Larichev, O.I.; Kortnev, A.V.; Kochin, D.Y. Decision support system for classification of a finite set of multicriteria alternatives. *Decis. Support Syst.* **2002**, *33*, 13–21. [CrossRef]
54. Ashikhmin, I.; Furems, E. UniComBOS—Intelligent Decision Support System for Multi-criteria Comparison and Choice. *J. Multi-Criteria Decis. Anal.* **2005**, *13*, 147–157. [CrossRef]
55. Larichev, O.I. *Theory and Methods of Decision Making, as Well as the Chronicle of Events in Magic Countries*, 3rd ed.; Rev. and Add; UNIVERSITY Book: Moscow, Russia, 2008. (In Russian)
56. Górecka, D. On the choice of method in multi–criteria decision aiding process concerning European projects. In *Multiple Criteria Decision Making' 10–11*; Trzaskalik, T., Wachowicz, T., Eds.; The Karol Adamiecki Universityof Economics in Katowice: Katowice, Poland, 2011; pp. 81–103.

© 2019 by the authors. Licensee MDPI, Basel, Switzerland. This article is an open access article distributed under the terms and conditions of the Creative Commons Attribution (CC BY) license (http://creativecommons.org/licenses/by/4.0/).

MDPI
St. Alban-Anlage 66
4052 Basel
Switzerland
Tel. +41 61 683 77 34
Fax +41 61 302 89 18
www.mdpi.com

Sustainability Editorial Office
E-mail: sustainability@mdpi.com
www.mdpi.com/journal/sustainability

www.ingramcontent.com/pod-product-compliance
Lightning Source LLC
LaVergne TN
LVHW071443100526
838202LV00088B/6619